Human Behavior
and the
Social Environment

MICRO LEVEL

Human Behavior and the Social Environment

MICRO LEVEL

Individuals and Families

Second Edition

Katherine van Wormer

OXFORD
UNIVERSITY PRESS
2011

OXFORD
UNIVERSITY PRESS

Oxford University Press, Inc., publishes works that further
Oxford University's objective of excellence
in research, scholarship, and education.

Oxford   New York
Auckland   Cape Town   Dar es Salaam   Hong Kong   Karachi
Kuala Lumpur   Madrid   Melbourne   Mexico City   Nairobi
New Delhi   Shanghai   Taipei   Toronto

With offices in
Argentina   Austria   Brazil   Chile   Czech Republic   France   Greece
Guatemala   Hungary   Italy   Japan   Poland   Portugal   Singapore
South Korea   Switzerland   Thailand   Turkey   Ukraine   Vietnam

Published by Oxford University Press, Inc.
198 Madison Avenue, New York, New York 10016

www.oup.com

Oxford is a registered trademark of Oxford University Press

Library of Congress Cataloging-in-Publication Data
Van Wormer, Katherine S.
Human behavior and the social environment, micro level:
individuals and families / Katherine Van Wormer.—2nd ed.
p. cm.
Includes bibliographical references and index.
ISBN 978-0-19-974007-9
1. Social psychology.   2. Human behavior.   3. Individuality.   4. Families.
5. Developmental psychology.   6. Social service—Problems, exercises, etc.
I. Title.
HM1033.V37 2010
306.87—dc22   2009053940

9 8 7 6 5 4 3 2 1

Printed in the United States of America
on acid-free paper

Because aunts are so special in a child's growing up, I dedicate this book to my mother's younger sisters, Auntie Jane and Auntie Flora—Jane Talmage Burdon (1928–2007) and Flora Talmage Landwehr of New Orleans, Louisiana.

Acknowledgments

A great deal of time and effort went into attending events for the purposes of providing dynamic photographs to capture relevant aspects of human behavior for this book. My gratitude goes to my son, Rupert van Wormer, whose photographs from Seattle and Iowa give one pause to reflect on many aspects of life in the modern world; to my husband, Robert van Wormer, who contributed pictures and typing to this project; and to my sister, Flora Templeton Stuart, and my niece, Natalie Stuart Moorcroft, who contributed family photos depicting the life cycle. Special mention goes to Oxford University Press and to Maura Roessner, social work editor, for her support and diligence. Finally, thanks go to my work-study student, Lynn Rutz, whose expertise in software, proofreading, and diagrams, as well as her warm encouragement, are greatly appreciated.

Contents

Preface to the Second Edition *xi*

Introduction *3*

1 Human Behavior: *Theoretical Concepts* *9*

2 Biological Factors in Human Behavior *52*

3 The Psychology of Human Behavior *105*

4 Birth Through Adolescence *152*

5 Early Adulthood Through Middle Age *202*

6 Late Middle Age Through the
End of Life *243*

7 The Individual in the Family *272*

Epilogue: *An End That Is a Beginning* *308*

Appendix: *Relevant Internet Sites* *310*

Index *313*

Preface

Since the first edition was published in 2007, major changes have taken place in the United States and globally. The changes I am referring to are first of all the collapse of the global economy, secondly, the sweeping political changes in the U.S. Congress and White House, and thirdly, the shifts in demographics. In the interim period between these two text editions, a seemingly new political consciousness has emerged, a paradigm shift of sorts that has the potential of ushering in a more progressive era than the preceding one. Any substantive change is impeded, however, by a palpable and highly vocal right-wing backlash. Nevertheless, common ground is seen in the growing movement toward the creation of a more economically and environmentally sustainable world. Social work education echoes this development. "The good news," according to Nancy Mary (2008), "is that over the past 20 years social workers have begun to see the bigger, long-term picture and to recognize a larger meaning of person-in-environment" (p. 41). In her groundbreaking book, *Social Work in a Sustainable World*, Mary terms this new global ethic for social work "the ecological imperative" (p. 41).

To reflect the recent developments in the economic, demographic, and political realms, this text on human behavior at the micro level and its companion macro-level volume, have been thoroughly updated and expanded. Much of the content and structure of this new edition of *Human Behavior and the Social Environment, Micro Level* will be familiar to readers of the first edition. Yet the differences will be readily apparent as well. New sections have been added to bring greater clarity to a given topic or to enhance the discussion with the benefit of new ideas from the literature. New research findings and recent U.S. Census and global health data are integrated into the text narrative. Consistent with the demographic and economic changes in the United States, for example, the discussions of multiculturalism, Latino identity issues, and late adulthood have been augmented.

The most obvious change to this edition is the addition of a new chapter. In light of feedback and suggestions from readers of the original text, I gladly have expanded the life-span portion of the book into three rather than two chapters. The middle stage of life and the period of late adulthood are now given as much attention as the early life stages. It was my good fortune in the writing of Chapter 6, Late Middle Age Through the End of Life, to have had access to new gerontological research, recent demographic data, and popular writings on the aging baby boom population.

Other substantial additions and revisions of this volume include the following:

- An emphasis on resilience as a theme linking the first and the last stages of the life span
- The addition of even more content on diversity, including material from personal narratives of Latino immigrants and older African American women who grew up under conditions of oppression in the segregated Deep South
- The replacement of a number of photos and boxed readings with new material
- Inclusion of the latest scientific research from the fields of science and medicine
- The addition of exciting new biographical, autobiographical, and literary material
- The rewriting of paragraphs and sections throughout the book in response to feedback from students and social work educators

As before, this new edition is guided by a holistic ecosystems/empowerment theoretical perspective. And as before, the themes of Volume One that are addressed at the individual level are revisited in Volume Two at the level of community and organizational life. The impact of recent global economic trends, for example, is explored in terms of its ramifications for the individual and the family in this book, while the companion volume is more concerned with the structural dimensions. As far as biology is concerned, here within the micro context, we look at aging across the life span, disease, and disability, while at the macro level, the starting point is the physical or natural environment. The emphasis on cultural diversity among humankind in the first instance is paralleled by the stress on biodiversity in nature in the second.

The focus of *Human Behavior and the Social Environment, Micro Level* (second edition) continues to be micro/macro, with the starting point from the inside looking out. The focal point of the companion text, in contrast, is macro/micro, from the perspective of the wider social system, or from the outside looking in. Transcending the micro/macro divide is the focus on the sustainability of human and nonhuman life and the metaphor of the ecosystem for understanding the interconnectedness of all things in nature.

Reference

Mary, N. L. (2008). *Social work in a sustainable world*. Chicago: Lyceum Books.

Human Behavior and the Social Environment

MICRO LEVEL

Introduction

For years, partly inspired by teaching a course in human behavior and the social environment (HBSE), I have dreamed of writing a textbook for the course. My plan was to shape a book that delved into human behavior in all its complexity: the animal drives, the cultural rituals to curb or refine the drives, the influence of the unconscious mind, the genetic factor in how we look and act, the roles we play and are sometimes forced to play, and the amazing resilience people show after catastrophes of the most horrendous sort. How do some people who have endured the "unendurable" survive intact? What is mental health? Aren't we all just a little bit crazy? What is the importance of the spiritual realm to individuals? To families? To nations?

My interest in human behavior began in courses not in the social sciences but in English literature, in probing the motivation of the heroes of novels. We pondered questions such as: Did Hester Prynne of *The Scarlet Letter* (Hawthorne, 1860) really despise her punishment—to forever wear the sign of the scarlet *A* for adultery—or did this symbol (which she embroidered painstakingly on her garments) become for her a mark of identity and pride? And what did the hidden guilt of the love affair do to the young minister? Then, looking to the South, to works such as *Absalom, Absalom!* (Faulkner, 1936), we considered how wounds from the past—historical and personal—continue to shape present-day struggles. "Can there ever be redemption and reparation for harms inflicted?" is a question with much resonance at the present time. Today, as both a sociologist and social worker, I still have the same sense of fascination with universal issues.

To write a book that explores the mysteries of human behavior is the ultimate challenge to any writer or social scientist. Such a book would have to explain as well as record, tackle nature as well as nurture, and explore the sacred as well as the profane. Pursuing such an exciting challenge has always been in the back of my mind, even as I launched into other, narrower projects. I continued, though, to teach in the HBSE foundation sequence and, in collaboration with students, to contemplate the whys and wherefores of human existence. The problem was that my lectures, class discussion, and the book content didn't exactly coincide. So why did I not develop an HBSE text of my own? What held me back? The topic seemed so incredibly vast, for one thing. And weren't there already a dozen or so thick, hardback tomes, all curiously titled "human behavior and the social environment"?

The matter would have rested there if suddenly one day this thought had not struck me: Of all the textbooks on my shelf or that I had ever used, not one was really about human behavior itself. Using these texts as a guide, my students and I learned about developmental approaches and age-appropriate tasks to be accomplished across the life span and wrestled with critiques of the same. We also read about the various models and paradigms relevant to social work practice—for example, role theory, behaviorism, the psychodynamic approach, and postmodernism. But was this, I asked myself, what HBSE, the course designed to equip students with a knowledge base for use in actual client situations, was intended to provide?

I began by rewriting the syllabus. Then, slowly and surely, as often happens in the creative process, the book began to take shape. *The end product, Human Behavior and the Social Environment, Micro Level,* is written in the belief that we social work educators have somehow lost sight of the human behavior component in the HBSE curriculum. This textbook, accordingly, explores the biology, psychology, and sociology of human phenomena (e.g., sex-role behavior, adolescent bullying) to study the ways that people behave in certain situations. The spiritual dimension of human and nonhuman life is stressed as well. In this volume, theory serves a dual function: first to provide an organizational framework, such as that provided by the life-span model, and second to present an explanation so that we can make sense of things (e.g., of resilience in a life of trauma or sorrow, of bonding with one's captor, of hurting the ones we love).

Conceptual Overview

Central to the core curriculum of social work is a course (often two courses) commonly called "Human Behavior and the Social Environment" and usually abbreviated as HBSE (and pronounced variously as "hubsy" or "hibsy"). This subject matter is potentially the most intriguing part of the social work curriculum: The study of human behavior is fascinating because it is about what makes people tick. The knowledge base acquired in such coursework, furthermore, can serve as a bridge between thinking and doing and between social work theory and direct practice.

Of all the courses that comprise the typical social work curriculum, an essentially standardized curriculum, the study of human behavior is potentially the deepest and most abstract. Policy focuses on key historical events and activities to influence such events, while practice is concerned more with interviewing and counseling techniques. The study of human behavior, in contrast, gets into social psychology in its search for the roots of human motivation. Whereas policy can be considered *the what* and practice *the how,* the study of human behavior is concerned with *why.* Thus, HBSE is the bedrock of social work knowledge. The Council on Social Work Education (CSWE, 2008), our accrediting body, lists the application of knowledge of human behavior and the social environment as a major core competency that is to be taught in the educational curriculum. This educational goal is as follows:

> Educational Policy 2.1.7—Apply knowledge of human behavior and the social environment.
>
> Social workers are knowledgeable about human behavior across the life course; the range of social systems in which people live; and the ways social systems promote or deter people in maintaining or achieving health and well-being. Social workers apply theories and knowledge from the liberal arts to understand biological, social, cultural,

psychological, and spiritual development. Social workers utilize conceptual frameworks to guide the processes of assessment, intervention, and evaluation; and critique and apply knowledge to understand person and environment. (p. 6)

In virtually everything we do in the profession, whether this is the quest for an understanding of society's treatment of marginalized groups, for knowledge about strategies for policy making, or the search for evidence-based treatment interventions, we draw on research findings about human behavior. Predictions about what people will do in given circumstances are vital to our work, and before we can make accurate predictions, we must have understanding. Knowledge of a wide range of human behaviors within a given cultural context, including our own, is paramount to the change effort.

Uniquely, social work's mission, in contrast to that of other helping professions, as defined by the Council on Social Work Education (CSWE), is to eliminate poverty, discrimination, and oppression and, guided by a person-in-environment perspective and respect for human diversity, to effect social and economic justice worldwide (CSWE, p. 29). Accordingly, even as we focus our attention on individuals in the social system, we must also heed the sociopolitical side of many personal struggles, the personal and the political in interaction.

The companion to this text has as its central focus the structural components of poverty, discrimination, and oppression. Whereas the concern of the one book is with the person in the environment, the second volume in the series addresses the environmental side of the equation. More specifically, my purpose in writing a human behavior textbook series is *(1)* to produce a work that follows the CSWE guidelines for a holistic approach to human nature and behavior, *(2)* to expand the person-in-environment formulation to include the physical as well as the social environment, and *(3)* to integrate theory and facts pertinent to direct generalist practice. Whether this effort is successful in providing a sound knowledge base while at the same time fostering a sense of excitement about the mystery of human behavior, the following pages will show.

The writing of this book was a personal journey that I embarked on in the spirit of discovery. The destination was uncertain. For the reader, the journey begins with an introduction into the biopsychosocial/spiritual realm of life, or the study of the interconnectedness of body, mind, and soul. To fulfill students' need for familiarity with this type of knowledge, this text draws on qualitative and as well as quantitative research and on truths that are empirical as well as anecdotal in origin. The plan is to go where other books in the field have not ventured, from both an artistic (e.g., in references to literary and personal stories) and a scientific (attention to evidence-based research) standpoint. The underlying assumption is that there is no single way of knowing. This assumption is consistent with social work theory and with the CSWE (2008) expectation that social work education be grounded in liberal arts. Speaking of learning/teaching about the dynamics of human behavior, Dennis Saleebey stated: "We do this, more or less successfully, with the inventiveness of the novelist, the transforming eye of the painter, the cozy mutuality of the conspirator, and the circumspection of the critic" (1993, p. 198).

The liberal arts and humanities have long played an important role in social work education, according to Furman, Langer, and Anderson (2006). In the search for the truth, gaining insights into the human experience, and promoting healing, the poet and social worker share a common ground. In their words:

> The importance of sensitivity, a concern with the relationship between the individual and the social world, a need to comprehend the psyche and the soul, and a belief in the inherent beauty and goodness of people, are some of the attributes that social workers and poets have in common. (p. 34)

Progressive psychologists such as Carol Gilligan (2009) have also looked to the arts for insights:

When I ask myself, why artists are often the best psychologists—why, as Freud noted, poets are often light years ahead—it's because of their use of associative methods. This allows them to break through dissociation, to see the cultural framework, which why artists often are the ones who speak the unspoken and reveal what is hidden. (p. 13)

Organization of the Book

The CSWE directive that the HBSE curriculum include knowledge of one's biopsychosocial/spiritual development across the life course is an ambitious agenda. A major issue facing every social work program is, How should we structure coursework on a topic as broad as the dynamics of human behavior? A myriad of courses would barely do the subject justice.

A comprehensive survey of HBSE programs conducted by Farley et al. (2002) found that, to accomplish CSWE's educational objectives, the majority of schools of social work offer two separate courses. The first and predominant sequencing pattern, which we can label the micro/macro division, focuses on individuals and families in the first semester and on small groups, organizations, and communities the next semester. The second approach provides for a study of normal human development across the life cycle the first semester and a look at abnormal development and social problems in the second semester.

The artificiality of the normal/abnormal division is a major drawback of this second approach. Most human phenomena such as personality characteristics (e.g., emotional stability), as we know, exist along a continuum and cannot be neatly separated out in this way. My preference therefore is for a division in terms of population size. As a dividing point, population size is tangible enough to be readily grasped yet not so rigid as to preclude linkages across the division. This micro/macro emphasis, moreover, is congruent with the ecosystems framework that guides this project, a structure that stresses the interconnectedness of systems and of their biological, psychosocial, and spiritual components.

The path I have chosen for the presentation of the human behavior sequence, then, is an integrative approach in two parts. This design encompasses two comprehensive volumes, of which this text covers the micro portion—individual behavior related to biology and psychology and in interaction with peers and family members. The second volume is devoted to groups, families, organizations, communities, and the natural and spiritual realms of being. The inclusion of extensive sections on the physical environment and human rights is a unique feature of the macro HBSE text. Global concerns are also included throughout the two volumes. Both texts address the biological portion of the biopsychosocial/social configuration—at the micro level with an in-the-body focus and at the macro level with a focus on the physical environment. Similarly, spirituality is discussed at the various system levels—as a source of individual empowerment that parallels development across the life cycle and, at the macro level, as a source of cultural empowerment. Joining the two volumes in the series is an empowerment perspective. Empowerment provides a useful organizing framework for the text in terms of both its versatility in addressing various population sizes and its person centeredness. The empowerment framework looks at power differentials interpersonally and organizationally.

The presentation of material begins with an introduction to the theoretical framework and then more closely examines the biological dimension of human behavior. The central portion of the book explores psychosocial development of people across the life span. The book's integrative, person-in-environment approach is congruent with the profession's long-standing focus on the reciprocal relationship between human behavior and social environments.

I hope that readers of this book will come to see that acquiring knowledge concerning the psychosocial development of the human organism is a necessary but not sufficient condition for mastery of HBSE content. Mastery also involves a grounding in social work ethics and values in preparation for the plethora of challenges that accrue to the helping professions—challenges that require attention at both the individual and the systemic levels.

The Chapters

The aim of Chapter 1 is largely definitional: to introduce the basic terms and concepts that are widely used in the social work literature pertaining to human behavior. Most such concepts are components of the wider theoretical frameworks and models (for example, ecosystems theory and feminist approaches). Implications for social work practice are provided in this and in all succeeding chapters. Similarly, here as elsewhere, the reader will find lively case studies to highlight the more abstract text (e.g., excerpts from narratives describing turning points).

The inclusion of a specialized biology chapter (Chapter 2) is somewhat unique in the HBSE literature. Drawing heavily on empirical research, this portion of the text explores gender differences, genetic studies, aggression in primates, and recent discoveries about the brain. The biological role in the development of mental disorders such as schizophrenia, depression, and addiction problems is highlighted.

In Chapter 3 we turn our attention to the psychological aspects of human behavior. This chapter provides a conceptualization of common human phenomena such as loss and grief, abuse and oppression, victimization and trauma, and, on the positive side, motivation for change and factors conducive to a health-giving therapeutic relationship. Relationships are a major theme of this discussion.

Birth through adolescence is the topic of the first of the life-span chapters. Following a description of Erikson's early stages of development, Chapter 4 reviews significant research findings about earlier and later childhood development and considers what we know about resilience. Issues associated with adolescence (e.g., bullying, homophobia) are addressed in terms of their implications for social work practice.

Chapter 5 brings us into the realm of early adulthood through middle age. Courtship,

marriage, and personality traits are among the topics covered. Erikson's formulation is expanded in light of the contributions of Gilligan and others. Chapter 6, new to this edition, applies risk and resilience theory as introduced in Chapter 4 to persons in the final stages of life.

Family roles and relationships are the major topics of the final chapter of *Human Behavior and the Social Environment, Micro Level* and include the mother–son, father–daughter, and brother–sister relationships. The contribution of grandparents and aunts and uncles is also discussed. This chapter provides a logical stopping point for this book, as well as a stepping stone to volume 2 in the micro/macro human behavior set.

Human Behavior and the Social Environment, Micro Level is informed by the belief that HBSE coursework should have human beings as its starting point and that they should be viewed as thinking, acting creatures within their given social context. By writing this book, I hope that my fascination in exploring the patterns and paradoxes of human behavior will become infectious. By studying some of the intangibles that shape our lives and the contradictions between how we mean to be and how others view us, we can become aware of the crucial importance of learning not just to hear but also to listen.

Note to the Instructor: Because knowledge about human behavior is not linear but circular, the starting point in the HBSE curriculum can be with either the micro or the macro perspective. Each volume of the set comes with access to a companion website, an instructor's manual that includes essay and multiple-choice questions as well as creative class exercises, and a chapter-by-chapter PowerPoint presentation.

References

Council on Social Work Education (CSWE). (2008). *Educational policy and accreditation standards.* Alexandria, VA: Author.

Farley, O., Smith, L., Boyle, S., & Ronnau, J. (2002). A review of foundation MSW human behavior courses. *Journal of Human Behavior in the Social Environment, 6*(2), 1–12.

Faulkner, W. (1936). *Absalom, Absalom!* New York: Random House.

Furman, R., Langer, C., & Anderson, D. (2006). The poet/practitioner: A paradigm for the profession. *Journal of Sociology and Social Welfare, 33*(3), 29–41.

Gilligan, C. (2008). Making oneself vulnerable to discovery: Carol Gilligan in conversation with Mechthild Kiegelmann. *Forum: Qualitative Social Research, 10*(2), 1–19.

Hawthorne, N. (1860/1968). *The scarlet letter, a romance.* San Francisco: Chandler.

Saleebey, D. (1993). Notes on interpreting the human condition: A "constructed" HBSE curriculum. *Journal of Teaching in Social Work, 8*(1/2), 197–217.

Human Behavior

Theoretical Concepts

To see the world in a grain of sand.
And heaven in a wild flower.
Hold infinity in the palm of your hand
And eternity in an hour.

—WILLIAM BLAKE

Auguries of Innocence, 1789

I am part of all I have met.

—TENNYSON

Ulysses, 1842

Thanks to the power of magnetic resonance imaging, scientific researchers can now photograph and study the inner recesses of the brain. While a subject is exposed to selected stimuli, scientists can observe the brain not as a static entity but as an active organ at work. But how do these visual images help us predict human behavior? What do they tell us about the human spirit, character, the mind? Depending on whom you ask and what you are looking for, the answers range from "a lot" to "almost nothing."

In navigating the maze of human behavior, biology alone is insufficient, but so is psychology, not to mention sociology. For a full understanding, a multidimensional and interactionist perspective is required. To chart that difficult maze, we must follow four essential paths—biology, psychology, sociology, and the spiritual realm. Picture these paths as sometimes parallel but more often as overlapping and interlocking. Each depends on the others to make the journey complete. Be prepared for some rough terrain ahead: Much of the trail is not clearly marked, and so much of the territory is unknown.

Unlike other chapters in this book, Chapter 1 is largely theoretical. Its purpose is to lay the building blocks for the more factual material—the evidence-based and narrative-based discussions—to follow. To this end, this chapter:

> ⟩ Introduces concepts relevant to social work theory and the study of micro-level human behavior (e.g., it shows that critical thinking is essential to a holistic conceptualization of human behavior)
> ⟩ Provides an overview of four major theoretical perspectives—psychodynamic, cognitive-behavioral, ecosystems, and empowerment approaches
> ⟩ Presents a critical analysis of each theoretical framework
> ⟩ Shows implications for social work practice

Social work is both a profession and a body of knowledge. In both capacities, social work views people holistically and contextually. People and their environment are seen not in isolation but in constant and dynamic interaction. This interactionist perspective, which is the one taken by this book, is consistent with that of social psychologist Charles Horton Cooley (1909/1983). "Self and society," wrote Cooley, are not separate entities but "are twin-born" (p. 5). We can regard this focus as micro-macro in that the starting point is the individual, and the progression is from the specific (e.g., brain chemistry) to the general (the impact on individuals and their social world). In contrast, the approach of the second volume of this series is macro-micro—from the general to the specific—and the starting point is the environment, both social and physical, and its effect on the people therein. In both approaches, the subject is human behavior.

The Study of Human Behavior

Social workers must have a solid grounding in the science of human behavior and understand the biological, psychological, social, and spiritual needs of people at various stages of development. They also need to know how aspects of the external environment, aspects that are reflected in the social welfare system, give rise to desirable and undesirable patterns of behavior. As social workers and students of human behavior, we are thus obligated to understand, as best we can, those forces that shape and drive human experience in order to help people achieve their highest potential.

Skilled social workers possess a knowledge of people that is born out of personal experience, professional training, familiarity with the literature in the field, and their personal attributes such as resourcefulness and intelligence. Coursework in human behavior and the social environment (HBSE) can enhance this knowledge by providing instruction in the reciprocal relationships between human behavior and the social environment. The Council on Social Work Education (CSWE) (2008) accreditation standards mandate that the HBSE curriculum present conceptual frameworks relevant to our understanding of the person and the social environment. The CSWE additionally stresses the importance of critical

thinking and empirically based research to guide practice.

This emphasis entails a recognition that, for the profession to adequately prepare students for practice in real-life situations, solid theory must be fortified by studies with some degree of validity. Perhaps more importantly, the effectiveness of interventions spawned by such theory must be validated as well. Does the intervention work? This is the question increasingly asked by third-party payers, legislators, and clients who want some assurance that what practitioners do is supported by solid evidence of effectiveness. The credibility of the profession itself rests on such data-gathering efforts. At the policy level as well, presentation of the results of empirical research can be a deciding factor in advocacy for the funding of a particular program.

Thus, HBSE content provides knowledge for use in everyday social work practice. Social workers need to know not only how people behave in certain situations but also how they can work with representative authorities to effect change on behalf of their clients.

From the social work perspective, the individual is a biological, economic, social, and spiritual being. Because human behavior is shaped by multiple forces, a multidimensional assessment of why people do the things they do is essential. A suicidal client, for example, can be helped by recognizing biological aspects of depression (if relevant), the role of medications and cognitive work in improving one's mood, and the need for healthy support systems. Knowledge of the spiritual component of health and healing is an integral part of empowering social work as well.

Assessment of the problem is the first step. Evaluation may be formal (e.g., in administering a standard substance-abuse questionnaire) and/or informal (e.g., in appraising the communication patterns of a large, extended family). The beauty of social work is its ability to frame human behavior holistically, attending to both structural and personal factors in helping people meet their needs.

In contrast to the "how to" content of a skills-based practice course, HBSE course material is highly theoretical and more concerned with *why* than with *what*. This component of the curriculum accordingly builds on knowledge from other disciplines, including biology and social psychology. The knowledge that is grounded in research provides a foundation for the handling of situations such as the following:

> A suicidal adolescent caught in a tug-of-war with his father over his gender identity
> A newly arrived immigrant family in need of social services
> A battered woman who feels that keeping her family together is the best option
> An elderly couple desiring help in reaching a decision before they die concerning care for a daughter who has Down syndrome

As evidenced in these real-life examples, social workers are *generalists* (as opposed to specialists) and accordingly require a wide range of knowledge and skills to help people with an extensive array of problems and issues (Zastrow & Kirst-Ashman, 2010). Social workers, in short, need to be prepared for versatility in practice throughout their career and within culturally diverse situations. An understanding of the ways in which the social systems of various states assist or hinder people in achieving optimal health is also essential.

Social workers adapt a holistic, multidisciplinary approach in their work with individuals, groups, and families. The knowledge base of social work education is grounded in the study of biological, psychological, sociological, and spiritual aspects of human behavior. This biopsychosocial/spiritual approach allows the social worker to view a person holistically, as both an individual with inner biological drives and as a social and cultural being who may or may not have a sense of the sublime. Each component in the system—whether biological, psychological, or social—is intertwined with every other component.

The study of human behavior can be conceived as a quest for understanding about life and ultimately a search for truth about the nature of human existence. This quest is echoed at the personal level when we search for meaning and purpose in life. It is the eternal attempt to answer the question as asked in *David Copperfield*, "whether I should turn out to be the hero of my own life or whether that station will be held by anybody else" (Dickens, 1869/1996, p. 11). We could make this more meaningful to social work by paraphrasing and saying "whether I should turn out to be the hero of my own life or its victim." Like social work, the study of human behavior is both a science and an art; the knowledge base is derived from empirically based findings drawn from mass survey data, as well as from first-hand accounts in the form of personal narratives. One must see the part in the whole and the whole in the part—"the world in a grain of sand" (Blake, 1789).

Learning From the Microcosm

What to do with the profusion of information available in the Internet age is one of the great challenges of our time. One solution is to seek the universals in the particular and to study one element or individual case study in depth instead of trying to survey the ever-expanding field of knowledge. Renowned educator Parker Palmer's (2007) notion of teaching and learning from the microcosm is relevant here. One key passage from a novel, one culminating event from history, one pivotal idea from philosophy—all are examples of learning from the microcosm about the patterns of connectedness. Thus, in studying the causes of one war, one is exploring the reasons for all wars; in examining the intricacies of one closely bonded family, one is uncovering secrets that can be generalized to all families; and in mastering the language and the ways of a foreign culture, we develop insights into our own society.

This principle is implemented every day in social work practice courses. Think of a class role play from which students discover the facts about a client and draw up a case history and treatment plan. This is an example of learning from the microcosm. By delving into the complexity of one case and then another, we learn to think like social workers. Similarly, in policy class a probing examination of one piece of proposed legislation can be excellent training ground for policy analysis of future legislative proposals.

Figure 1.2. This plaque appears beneath the holon statue and explains its significance. Photo by Rupert van Wormer.

Figure 1.1. The holon was carved in 1978 in memory of Gordon Hearn, social worker, general systems theorist, and founder of the School of Social Work at Portland State University, Oregon. It can be seen on the Portland State University campus. Photo by Rupert van Wormer.

Each body of knowledge, Palmer suggests, has an inner logic so profound that every critical piece of it contains the information necessary to reconstruct the whole. Every discipline is thus like a holon from physics; holons are three dimensional and composed of parts, each of which contains all of the information possessed by the whole. The part is not only contained within the whole; the whole is contained in every part, only in lower resolution (Miller & Miller, 2003). For example, the fertilized egg cell contains all the information

necessary to create a complete human being. Each part is a system in itself and composed of smaller systems. Keep in mind Palmer's metaphor as we move on. In this volume—for pedagogical as well as practical reasons—the focus is on depth rather than breadth and, in terms of the size of phenomena studied, small over large. Sometimes, in a very real sense, less is more. The sculpture shown in Figure 1.1 (as in Figure 1.2) was dedicated to systems theorist and founding dean of the Portland State University School of Social Work, Gordon Hearn.

Learning From the Study of Paradox

The essence of human behavior is often revealed in the study of opposites of the subject of investigation. Sometimes, in fact, the only way to fully understand a problem is to study its opposite—to learn about appetite and satiety, for example, to study compulsive overeating and anorexia, to learn about heterosexuality to study homosexuality, and to learn about relationships that work to study relationships that don't. To learn about the normal functioning of the brain, scientists study the brains of persons who have experienced brain damage through strokes and injury. In Western culture, the tendency is to dichotomize and think in "either-or's": You're either an introvert or an extravert; you're either with us or against us; either you're an alcoholic or you're not.

In reality, personal traits tend to exist along a continuum, and most of us lie somewhere in between. Social scientists and other observers of human behavior should therefore seek the truth in "both-and's" rather than in either-or's.

Parker Palmer (2008) has also considered the concept of paradox. In *The Promise of Paradox*, Palmer defines paradox as "a state that seems self-contradictory, but on investigation may prove to be essentially true" (p. 6). It is, in simple terms, a twist or a contradiction. For example, we can turn to a "12-Step philosophy," which states that by acknowledging our powerlessness over alcohol, we are gaining control over our lives. In certain circumstances, Palmer argues, truth is a paradoxical joining of apparent opposites, so if we seek the truth, we must learn to embrace opposites as one. Education should therefore dissolve the partitions between head and heart, thinking and feeling, personal and professional. We can use paradox, Palmer further asserts, to transform a litany of failings into a deeper understanding of reality.

The notion of paradox is extremely useful in social work, where the challenge to somehow transfer a litany of failings (of the self and of the system) into successful practice is a constant. Ideally, therapists will tax their imaginations to help even the most downtrodden clients find a way to "muddle through" and find hope under the most trying of circumstances. The alternative for both social worker and client so often is disenchantment and despair. Paradox occurs when the client says, "This [my alcoholic relapse] happened for a reason."

In his autobiography, *My Losing Season*, Pat Conroy (2003) writes poignantly of the paradox of loss and defeat:

> The great secret of athletics is that you can learn more from losing than winning. No coach can afford to preach such a doctrine, but our losing season served as both model and template of how a life can go wrong and fall apart in even the most inconceivable places.
>
> Losing prepares you for the heartbreak, setback and tragedy that you will encounter in the world more than winning ever can. By licking your wounds you

learn how to avoid getting wounded the next time. . . . Loss invites reflection and reformulating and a change of strategies. Loss hurts and bleeds and aches. Loss is always ready to call out your name in the night. Loss follows you home and taunts you at the breakfast table, follows you to work in the morning. . . . The word "loser" follows you, bird-dogs you, sniffs you out of whatever fields you hide in because you have to face things clearly and you cannot turn away from what is true. My team won eight games and lost seventeen . . . losers by any measure.

> Then we went out and led our lives, and our losing season inspired every one of us to strive for complete and successful lives. All twelve of us graduated from college and many of us with honors. (p. 254)

Before we continue, let us pause for a real-life—albeit highly abbreviated—story of a peak educational experience of another sort—a tale of victory against an entrenched power structure.

Mrs. Anné, 1949

I pushed the stroller with my baby down the street; from house to house I went day after day, then to adjacent blocks.

"You must come," I told the nervous wives. "You simply have to go to the court and speak up." Behind screen doors the murmured excuses, "I do not like to interfere in other people's business." Or "I've never been to court."

"You saw the mother and child; every day she passed: Mrs. Anné walking that little girl to school holding hands, and the child was neat and clean. She could lose her if we don't all appear. We are her only defense."

I had heard the story from Mrs. Silverstein, who lived between our homes; saw the husband, an important physician, never seen in our neighborhood, had arrived at night and thrown his wife out of the house and kept their little girl. Mrs. Silverstein had heard the screaming. The doctor remained in the home, and soon a replacement appeared, an overdressed bleached blonde with a feathered hat parading back and forth while the despondent wife huddled in a cheap motel where we found her while the neighborhood wives continued to peer at the other woman.

Dr. Anné was claiming the discarded wife was an unfit mother and had colleagues who would testify that Mrs. Anné was mentally unstable. He demanded custody.

My husband then was both working and attending law school and had a friend who agreed to take the case while I lined up the defense.

And they showed up, every one of them, all the wives in the neighborhood, and we lined the court from one side to the other.

Unfortunately, I wasn't as much help as I planned to be, as I was young and too nervous and even had trouble finding my right hand, but the others were great. One by one the housewives testified to save the woman's child.

Later on the verdict came based entirely on the "straightforward testimony of the women," and the housewives on State Street Drive won over the experts in the case.

Year after year the card came until the child was grown, just a brief note of thanks and news of mother and child, written by Mrs. Anné, now a schoolteacher in a small town.

(Unpublished story written in 2003, printed with permission of Elise Talmage, aged 87, who lives on a farm near Bowling Green, Kentucky)

There are many different ways of interpreting the story of Mrs. Anné. One can say that this story illustrates the power of grassroots organizing by some unlikely housewives in the late 1940s, or one can interpret this as a tale of personal courage. Finally, the account can be seen as a growth experience, a point of reckoning and consciousness-raising for one woman and possibly for all of the housewives who so bravely took a stand.

Turning Points in People's Lives

A starting point in the science of human behavior is to take a look at the moments in people's lives, usually revealed after the passage of time, that have special meaning for them and that, when viewed retrospectively, can be seen as defining moments. Literature is full of such key events or revelations, sometimes called dramatic climaxes, beyond which life neither could nor would be the same. Many such experiences, of course, are negative.

Consider this account of Hurricane Katrina survivor Toni Miller, who stepped on an airplane, not knowing where she was going and wound up in Des Moines, Iowa. Speaking of her daughter, she said, "If we ever see each other again . . . she'll have to come up here because I'm not going back. These feet will never touch Louisiana soil again. They left us there to die" (Hansen, 2005, p. B1).

Only time will tell whether Miller's fate will ultimately be positive or negative. Palmer (2007) maintains that we learn of the human spirit's potential in the midst of cruel circumstance and of human growth in the face of hardship. In their research on resilience among older African Americans, Becker and Newsom (2005) found that the emotional strength these elders demonstrated had its roots in overcoming challenges early in life. But, as Palmer cautions us, the self is not infinitely elastic. The hardship can be too extreme, and personal growth can be stultified as a consequence.

Think of the traumatized child and the brain-damaged war hero; social workers are apt to encounter both circumstances. The social work profession is built on the results of experience; social workers have experientially learned specific strategies to help people overcome adversity. Researchers in several different fields have recently emphasized the phenomenon that people who have experienced a seriously adverse event frequently report that they were positively changed by the experience (McMillen, 1999). This view is congruent with the shift in focus in recent years from a diagnosis of pathology to an empowerment perspective. The challenge now is not to come up with the right label so much as it is to locate people's own inner power, which they perhaps did not know they had, and to focus more on solutions rather than on problems. Bolstered by a belief in human resilience, we can help clients tap into their own resources (Saleebey, 2006). The strengths perspective does not deny the dark side of the human condition and personal vulnerability within toxic environments. However, while in crisis, an individual may be helped to perceive opportunity and, when in defeat, one may experience a turning point.

Barack Obama (1995) recalls in his autobiography, *Dreams of My Father*, a time in college when his confidence was low and a conversation with a woman named Regina pushed him forward on the road to become the speaker he was later to be:

> Strange how a single conversation can change you. Or maybe it only seems that way in retrospect. A year passes and you know you feel differently, but you're not sure what or why or how, so your mind casts back for something that might give that difference shape: a word, a glance, a touch. I know that after what seemed like a long absence, I had felt my voice returning to me that afternoon with Regina. It remained shaky afterward, subject to distortion. But entering sophomore year I could feel it growing stronger, sturdier, that constant, honest portion of myself, a bridge between my future and my past. (p. 105)

The title of theologian Karen Armstrong's (2004) *The Spiral Staircase: My Climb out of Darkness* captures in understated but gripping language the inner turmoil attached to her decision to leave the cloistered convent in which she lived. Taking this step meant the loss of not only her vocation and livelihood but also her whole identity. Accordingly, Armstrong faced the awesome task of defining anew both herself and her concept of God. Interestingly, *The Spiral Staircase* covers the same period of time as her previous autobiography, written almost 20 years before. "We should probably all pause to confront our past from time to time," the author writes, "because it changes its meaning as our circumstances alter" (p. xix). While the original autobiography (the second in a series) was written too early and lacked perspective, *The Spiral Staircase* provides a far more genuine and mature account of the same

events, in this way achieving a breakthrough to a new level of consciousness. This new understanding, Armstrong states, is symbolized in the metaphor of the spiral staircase.

Armstrong suffered a crisis in her religious faith that changed her life. Many others have experienced a life-changing religious conversion. Sometimes the conversion is immediate such as when an individual, for example, the prophet Paul, receives what seems to be a summons from God. Or the conversion may be more gradual, as we hear from another Paul—Paul Gatewood:

> The indisputable turning point in my life was my incarceration. Although this has been a horrific ordeal, some very positive changes have transpired that reinforce my will to lead a better life, a Christian life. For the first time in my life I have been clean and sober for more than 5 years. I have not even had a cigarette, though many substances are accessible. Second, the loss of my freedom and the grief it has brought me have served to unite my family and rally them together in support of my cause and my future. Third, having reestablished my relationship with the Lord, I have reclaimed yet another family—the Father, the Son, and the Holy Ghost. And lastly, this "minor setback to a major comeback" has made me appreciate virtually everything and everyone. In the past I was notorious for taking people and things for granted, hurting the ones who loved me the most commonplace as I walked through life in a chemically induced state. These bars, razor wire, and fences have made manifest what is truly important and what is not.
>
> In conclusion, the penitentiary has proven to be a practical point of transition for me. A culmination of the aforementioned personal changes derived from it will function as the tools and life skills necessary to guide me down the straight and narrow path of life. They must be utilized daily in order to preserve my freedom and regain my status

as a valued asset to my family and society. (Personal communication, May 14, 2009)

Paul Gatewood wrote of this turning point as a correspondence student in my HBSE course, and he was pleased at the opportunity to share his story with others. The following narratives were shared by Master's of Social Work (MSW) students of the human behavior course on the campus of the University of Northern Iowa. In reading their papers, I recognized the truth of the saying "everyone has a story to tell." When we hear people's narratives, we can identify moments that were decisive for them. In response to an assignment to identify a key turning point, a young woman in her 20s related the following:

> When I was 12 years old, my brother-in-law violated my body, convictions, and esteem by sexually victimizing me. That one moment changed my life course despite my constant struggle to deny its effects upon me. I struggled throughout adolescence in an attempt to create normalcy through silence and a severe lack of validation that has blessed me with finding myself today. I have found strength by validating myself and confronting those who forced me to cope in silence, and this has empowered me to heal.

A young single woman told this story:

> One of the most major turning points in my life would have to be the birth of my son Alec 6 years ago. I became pregnant when I was 21 years old, single, living in a two-bedroom apartment with my sister. And working at what I considered to be a dead-end job. . . . When I had my son, it gave me the initiative and the means to go back to college.

Next, from a mother in her 30s, who lives in a lesbian partnership:

> Going through with the divorce was one of the hardest acts of my life. In order to proceed, it was an experience of putting on blinders to all the people who would be angry, disappointed, hurt, and shocked by my decision. Up to that point, I had spent much of my life making too many decisions based on whether or not it would upset people. Mustering up the courage to proceed was an important turning point, as I learned that achieving integrity and living authentically does not come easily or simply but requires fortitude of conviction and faith. I am fortunate that a strong community of women supported me along the way. This decision has moved my life forward in ways I could not have foreseen. Ultimately it has been an experience of becoming a stronger woman and living with greater integrity.

A middle-aged man remembered this incident:

> The very thought of school frightened me to death, remembering back 18 years to when I had been in high school and how poorly that had gone. However, I quietly told myself that that was then, and this is now. . . . Suddenly, there on the 505 as I was blazing along on a hot August day in 1989, I experienced a major turning point in my life. Within minutes, my life's mission and work were laid out for me. I would attend community college for 2 years, transfer to a 4-year college, and then get my master's degree. My major would be social work. Perhaps I would be a counselor, who knows? . . . The exhilarating feeling I felt immediately upon receiving this epiphany was wondrous to behold. A big smile crossed my face, and I spontaneously broke out into a song. The future was looking *great*, and I was about to embark upon another road trip.

Although people rarely write about them (save for novelists and playwrights), negative turning points—experiences that crush the spirit, grief that is too heavy to bear—are probably as common as positive ones. Their presence is revealed in literature in statements such as "from then on his life was never the same" or "she never looked at a man again." Oscar Wilde (1892/1968), who himself had endured much personal pain and sorrow, summed up life as follows: "In this world there are only two tragedies. One is not getting what one wants, and the other is getting it" (p. 839).

In their review of the literature on turning-point experiences, Finnish social scientists Rönkä, Oravala, and Pulkkinen (2002) summarized the following characteristics of turning points. They:

- Involve both positive and negative effects
- Include both events over which an individual has no control and those subject to individual choice
- Can lead to changes in people's lifestyles, self-concepts, and roles
- Can lead to changes in outlook and one's view of the world
- Are generally recognized as such only after time has passed
- When negative, are often related to a loss, personal failures, and poor health
- May relate to personal adversities and unstable relationships, which, in turn, may accentuate maladaptive patterns that were already there.

Because of a new path that is taken when the individual comes to a crossroads, the rest of one's life may be subsequently altered. American poet Robert Frost (1916/1969) famously noted this in the lines:

Two roads diverged in the wood, and I,
I took the one less traveled by.
And that has made all the difference.
   (p. 105)

Gerontologists Cappeliez, Beaupré, and Robitaille (2008) studied turning points in the personal narratives of 53 older adults. Most of the pivotal events the respondents identified occurred at midlife and most related to the family. Compared to men who identified work as the major domain of impact, women reported more turning points related to health.

We can learn much about individual personality and motivation for change from an analysis of the pivotal moments in people's lives. *Philosophically*, we can analyze the decision making that took place in terms of the existence of free will versus determinism and pursue an analysis of the influence of spiritual factors. *Biologically*, we can explore aspects of mental and physical health that played into the choice that was made. From a *psychological* standpoint we would want to probe the original crisis that led to the need for a change in life's course to begin with and how the immediate decision, in other words, stemmed from earlier decisions, some of which had perhaps gone awry. The *sociological* realm would lead us into an analysis of issues such as social class and perceived opportunity, the presence of support systems, and the influence of societal norms. For a full understanding, of course, a multidimensional perspective is necessary. Keep in mind the preceding personal vignettes and this analysis as we explore the theoretical concepts, both traditional and nontraditional, that comprise the study of human behavior and the social environment. To allow for a little levity before delving into the complexity of theory and theoretical constructs, view Figure 1.3 which reveals a fascinating example of human behavior in the form of an annual parade. Then it's a return to textbook conventionality in Figure 1.4. This diagram illustrates the dynamic interactions among the four major domains of life, the biopsychosocial/spiritual dimensions of human behavior.

Theory, Concepts, and Models

The science of human behavior is so complex as to defy our ability to do it justice and so vast as to challenge our imaginations to even try. Fortunately, our scope is limited here, in this chapter and book, to those aspects of human behavior that are the most relevant to social work practice and policy. The theoretical perspectives that form the heart of this chapter are thus selected because of their goodness of fit with the realities of generalist social work practice.

Generalist practice is informed by theory. According to the *Shorter Oxford English Dictionary* (2007), a *generalist* is "a person competent in several different fields or activities." (The opposite is a specialist.) The holistic, biopsychosocial, and spiritual focus of the

Figure 1.3. World Naked Bike Ride. What must these children be thinking at this nude heterosexual parade in Seattle? This annual event is part celebration of the summer solstice and part a recognition that the world needs to focus on reducing oil dependency. Photo by Rupert van Wormer.

study of human behavior helps prepare social workers for the wide variety of personal situations with which they deal on an almost daily basis. The generalist is a change agent who must be prepared to intervene at multiple levels—from individual to family to society. Social workers require a breadth and range of skills, as well as a theoretical framework to guide the interventions, in order to effect change (where change is needed). Without a grounding in solid theory, practitioners are at the mercy of their own personal biases and contemporary fads, which may not serve the client well.

It is sometimes said that theory is what you learn in the classroom and practice is what is done in agencies. In truth, theory and practice are intertwined; theory informs practice, and practice furnishes the facts and observations that help us develop theory. The framework provided by any given theory or combination of theories provides a lens that shapes what we think and what we say to our clients. By delving deeply into one theory (e.g., the systems theory) and embracing the insight it offers, we can come to develop a greater sense of the whole. From this understanding other theories and insights emerge. Theories help us organize the vast amount of information at our disposal, providing a kind of "mental map to save energy" (Polansky, 1986, p. 4). This mental map helps us both to make predictions about human phenomena and to explain the reasons the patterns of behavior occur in the first place.

Theory is defined in *The Social Work Dictionary* (Barker, 2003) as "a group of related hypotheses, concepts, and constructs, based on facts and observations, which attempt to explain a particular phenomenon" (p. 434). Note the use of the word *attempt*. Because theory is socially constructed and the product of the lens through which we see the world, there are no absolutes. Theories are thus modified and

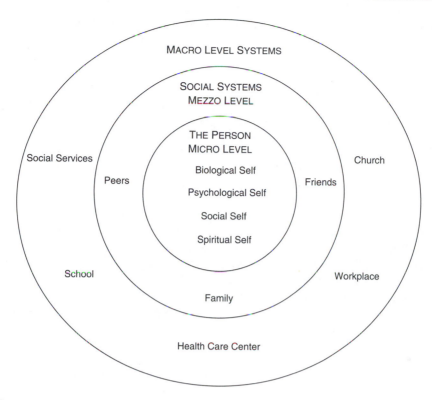

Figure 1.4. Biopsychosocial and spiritual dimensions.

refined over time and within different cultural milieus.

The word *concept* is of significance here as well. Concepts are words that signify ideas. They illuminate theory and theoretical perspectives and provide a sense of consistency. When we hear social workers using certain concepts, we can infer a certain theoretical orientation. Social workers who analyze client problems in terms of drives, attachment difficulties, and transference, for example, likely subscribe to a psychodynamic orientation. Social workers who speak of interaction, feedback, and roles have probably been trained in a systems approach. To social workers, knowledge of the concepts of human behavior is not just a matter of learning the nomenclature; it is also the foundation on which their assessments and change efforts rest. Solutions to problems often depend on how they are defined and which concepts are used.

Good social work is more about understanding than about technique. It is about good theory. Polansky (1986) listed these qualities of

good theory: "Theory should be dynamic if it is to be used in mastering the world, and parsimonious so as to be kept at one's fingertips. It must be capable of resolving seeming paradoxes, and realistic enough to fit our level of experiencing the world. It should of course cover a larger realm of ideas than we use in direct work on any given case, and be capable of inciting us to extend it" (p. 14).

A theory may be *small range* (what Merton [1967] called *middle range*) and explain only certain aspects of human life. Take labeling theory, for example, which says that behavior that is so labeled by society tends to become reinforced in the individual—call certain children bad and they might show you how bad they can be. As explanation, this theory explains both bad (e.g., delinquent) and good behavior; both forms of conduct are explained in terms of socialization; the mother's faith in the child's innate goodness may become a self-fulfilling prophecy. Labeling theory can be applied at the macro or societal level. For example, if the government labels poor single mothers as responsible for their poverty, public sympathy will decline, and their impoverishment will likely increase. The theory is still small range, however, because it explains only one aspect of human behavior.

The advantage of theory at the small range is that it is testable; one can gather data in various ways to test the hypothesis that children's self-concept, for instance, predicts the way they behave and even insulates them from gang delinquency behavior.

Grand theory is theory that is all encompassing—or attempts to be. Psychoanalytical personality or *psychodynamic theory* is one example. Psychodynamic ideas constituted the first strong explanatory theory in social work and so have set the stage for all later theory development, whether in agreement or disagreement with the notions that Freud originally set forth. Psychoanalytical theory had its strongest influence on social work theory during the 1920s, when the field was seeking status as a profession and a uniting theoretical framework. It was prominent again during the 1950s, when the focus was on the individual rather than society as the cause of social problems. Payne (2005) lists the following contributions of psychodynamic ideas: the emphasis on feelings and unconscious factors in behavior; the focus on insight, aggression, conflict, and the importance of both maternal love and maternal deprivation in shaping personality. I would add to that list the understanding of early childhood trauma as a force in later development.

The best-known example of grand theory is *structural functionalism.* Functional theory consistently addresses the following question about any social system or custom: "How is it functional for society?" The focus is on integration as opposed to conflict. *Conflict theory,* which was influenced by Karl Marx, can also be classified as grand theory because of its expansiveness. Both of these models are macro or society level and are discussed in some depth in the companion book to this edition.

The definition of theory that we have been using is the formal, scientific one. Darwin's theory of evolution and Max Weber's narrower theory of the association of the growth of capitalism with the Protestant ethic are examples. More commonly, in social work the word *theory* is used to refer to organizing frameworks or models. Thus, one hears of cognitive theory, behavioral theory, and systems theory. These conceptualizations are more accurately viewed as therapeutic treatment models than as theories in the formal sense of the term. Other appropriate descriptive terms are models, paradigms, and perspectives.

A *theoretical perspective* is often broader than a theory but lacks the explanatory and predictive power. A perspective, after all, is simply a viewpoint that is heavily influenced by one's cultural and political orientations. As a lens through which one observes human behavior and the human condition, a theoretical perspective can direct our assessment of client issues and record treatment progress. Consider the strengths perspective, for example. An evaluation based on strengths might ask the client and/or family members about their strong rather than their weak points. The emphasis is on finding and pointing to resilience and, in doing so, hoping to reinforce it. Such an approach can serve as a conceptual bridge that links the abstract with the practical.

In this book I use the word *theory* for the more highly developed conceptual schemes. At times, however, I use it in its popular form, for example, in discussing theoretical contributions or theorists. This broader usage is in recognition of the fact that, in common usage, theory has a far more casual meaning. One of the definitions of *theory* in the *Shorter Oxford English Dictionary* is simply that it is "a speculative view," as in "one of my pet theories." I hope that the readers of this book will excuse some of the confusion in terminology and recognize that it stems from a confusion in language: There is everyday theory, and there is also theory in the academic sense, as the word is used here.

Due to the complexity of human behavior and of the diverse situations in which it is played out, a variety of theories and concepts is necessary—different theories for different situations. Moreover, as Payne (2005) indicates, value and cultural bases of different societies may be incompatible with presumptions and prescriptions from U.S. social work. In China, for example, and within Chinese American culture, independence and the importance of individual rights are not emphasized. Different societies face different problems and issues as well. In the discussion of theory that is threaded throughout this book, I take into account the cultural relativity attached to the way we see the world. This brings us to a consideration of the importance of critical analysis and the way in which we can apply it to theory criticism and construction.

▮ Critical Thinking

Reviewing one's life in terms of turning points and the analysis of paradox are two forms of critical thinking, discussed earlier, that pertain to the search for meaning in one's personal experience and "the roads taken." Now we come to a discussion of knowledge about the world we live in and about our critical analysis of that knowledge and of how it is acquired. The critical acquisition of knowledge entails not only the accumulation of a series of facts but also the ability to discover patterns in the information and to analyze these patterns in new and exciting ways. There are many ways of knowing, of course, and many kinds of knowers, as Ann Hartman (1990) has wisely suggested. There are, according to Hartman, researchers, practitioners, and clients: "Some seekers of truth may take a path that demands distance and objectivity, whereas others rely on deeply personal and empathetic knowing. . . . Some truth seekers strive to predict, whereas others turn to the past for an enhanced understanding of the present" (p. 4).

Critical thinking is the ability to see without from within—and within from without. It involves perspective. "When you get a long way from home, you can see where you've been," reflected Mary Rose O'Reilley (2000) upon her arrival home from a Buddhist monastery in France. Inasmuch as viewing the world from the perspective of our own cultural beliefs is as inevitable as is thinking in the language we have learned to speak, we need to recognize our own tendency toward ethnocentrism. Self-awareness is a crucial aspect of thinking critically; it both enables such thought to take place and is its product. Individuals must be aware of their own belief systems and biases, which lead them to believe that the cultural norms to which they ascribe are the only way. They must also be cognizant of their natural tendency, when judging the behavior of others, to assume that the opportunities that have come their way have also been available to others. To see in perspective is to see the parts that comprise the whole. Thus, practitioners urge clients to partialize problems (to break them down into manageable parts) and also to recognize the whole in the parts. Critical thinking takes people beyond the surface to grasp what is "really going on," not taking a "fact" that you read or hear about at face value.

One key question for the social worker to ask at either the familial or societal level is, "Who benefits?" For example, within the family, who benefits by the lopsided division of labor? And who benefits by not allowing openly gay and lesbian individuals to teach in the school system? Who benefits by locking up so many persons with drug problems? The "Who benefits?" question helps us be aware of any vested interests by individuals or social institutions in pursuing a certain line of behavior. In searching for the answers, we come face to face with intransigent forces in the power structure and with behavior that is, at least in part, economically motivated. Such questioning is at the heart of critical thinking and critical consciousness. The ability to view contemporary social policy in both a historical and a cultural context and to analyze national policy from a global perspective is a key component of critical analysis.

Critical consciousness involves an understanding of the encompassing social-structural context of human problems. This term has its roots in the form of collective field activities developed in Latin America under the leadership of Paulo Freire. Chilean social work education was revolutionized as a result of the pedagogical instruction of Freire, an exiled Brazilian educator who lived in Chile for several years. From 1965 to 1973, when a military dictatorship intervened to suppress the program and persecute the social workers who were organizing the countryside, a real participatory democracy characterized social work education. Freire's (1973) description of his emancipatory pedagogy is still valid today:

> The critically transitive consciousness is characterized by depth in the interpenetration of problems; by the substitution of causal principles for magical explanations; by the testing of one's findings and by openness to revision; by the attempt to avoid distortion when perceiving problems and to avoid preconceived notions when analyzing them; by refusing to transfer responsibility; by rejecting passive positions; by soundness of argumentation; by the practice of dialogue rather than polemics; by receptivity to the new for reasons beyond mere novelty and by the good sense not to reject the old just because it its old; by accepting what is valid in both the old and new. (p. 17)

Feminist educator bell hooks (1994) articulates Freierian premises in terms of "teaching/learning to transgress" and critical thinking as "the primary element allowing the possibility of change" (p. 202). Within social work, similarly, feminist therapy stresses worker and client collaboration at every stage of the therapy process and the linking of political and personal issues (see Bricker-Jenkins and Netting [2009] and van Wormer [2004]). A related aspect of critical thinking is, of course, cultural competence, an indispensable ingredient for working in a multiculturally diverse and complex environment.

Critical Thinking and Theoretical Analysis

Critical-thinking skills include the synthesizing and application of appropriate theories to the situations that social workers encounter. This text, accordingly, seeks to emphasize critical-thinking skills so that practitioners may be able to make the connections among the biological, psychological, and cultural factors affecting individual development throughout the life cycle. A holistic approach is essential to the treatment task. To counsel clients from a holistic perspective within the traditional agency setting, which is characterized by internal hierarchical constraints and external managed-care directives, is a challenge that requires a high level of intellectual awareness and resourcefulness. The HBSE portion of the social work curriculum alone cannot prepare students for a practice that promotes social justice and empowerment. As a part of a wider, client-centered curriculum, however, the HBSE knowledge base, which is focused on how people shape and are shaped by their worlds, can be pivotal to the making of a social worker.

Most relevant to generalist practice is the ability to discern the underlying, latent purpose in social policies that give it form and structure (e.g., of so-called welfare reform). Critical thinking can help people identify propaganda in the way new government spending policies such as military buildup and changes in the tax law are presented to the public and discussed in the mass media. A comparison of national and international news accounts often reveals alternative perspectives on the same piece of information. The same kind of critical analysis that we apply to politics is also essential to the adoption of treatment practices that have been found to serve the clients well or ill.

Avoiding Practice Fallacies

Critical thinking, notes Gibbs (2009), is vital to effective social work practice. Drawing on the work of Eileen Gambrill, Gibbs provides a list of common errors in reasoning that lead to fallacies in social work practice:

- Relying on a small number of case examples and testimonials
- Vagueness in identifying client problems
- Putting too much faith in newness and trends
- Relying on authorities rather than research to guide practice
- Basing strategies on initial research success without appropriate follow-up

To this I would add becoming "true believers" of a particular theoretical model to the extent that it impedes one's judgment. Even if research is conducted, the bias overwhelms the assessment of results. Fallacious beliefs about the nature of an individual's problem in social work, as in medicine, can lead to incalculable harm. The well-being of clients is at stake if the nature of their problems is not clearly understood. Consider, for example, all of the families that must have been falsely blamed for causing their children's schizophrenia or autism when it was believed, before the new brain technologies revealed otherwise, that dysfunctional communication in the family was responsible (Virginia Satir voiced this belief as late as the 1970s; interviewed by Chase-Marshall, 1976). This view that the roots of mental disorders could be found in unhealthy communication patterns in the family was a boon to family therapy.

Classic family systems theory similarly viewed alcoholism not as the problem but as the solution to the problem. Nevertheless, some critics, including many substance abuse counselors, although they drew on notions of the family as a system, did not view the family as responsible for the addiction problems. Family members were most often seen as reacting to the situation of addiction rather than its cause. The fact that simply helping families improve their communication skills did not eliminate the presenting problem bolstered their skepticism of knowledge that was not based on evidence (see van Wormer & Davis, 2008). The conclusions of these practitioners were based on personal observation, the teachings of the disease model, practice experience, and critical thinking.

Critical Analysis of Theoretical Models

Kirst-Ashman (2009) delineates two dimensions that are integral to critical thinking: *(1)* the questioning of beliefs, statements, and assumptions and the seeking of relevant information about the veracity of a claim, and *(2)* the formulating of an informed opinion or conclusion based on evidence. The criteria for critically

evaluating a theory must be multidimensional and consistent with social work values and ethics. The criteria need to be relevant to the person as a political, gendered, economic, and cultural being.

Creativity plays an important role in this process, and what I term "the social work imagination." Gibbs and Gambrill (2009) differentiate rationalizing from reasoning. Rationalizing is a selective search for evidence in support of a belief or action; this process is often automatic. Reasoning, in contrast, involves reviewing both the evidence against and in favor of a position. Through a creative examination of a practice or policy, we can discover the basic assumptions and latent biases, as well as alternative explanations.

I have selected four theoretical perspectives—psychodynamic, cognitive, ecosystems, and empowerment—because of their influence on social work practice at the individual level. These categories are broad and encompass numerous variations. For example, subsumed under empowerment perspectives are the empowerment strengths, the anti-oppressive approach, and feminist formulations. Consistent with Gibbs' observation that critical thinkers have a predisposition to question what they are doing and why they are doing it, I have chosen to apply a questioning strategy to guide the discussion of comparative treatment models. The criteria included are roughly comparable to those used by Elizabeth Hutchison (2008). Hutchison explored relevant theoretical models on the basis of coherence, testability, comprehensiveness, emphasis on diversity and power, and usefulness for practice. The questions to be directed to each theory or model are as follows:

- To what extent is the model consistent with empirically based research? What does the evidence show?
- What can we learn about human behavior from this model?
- Does the model take into account both risks and resiliencies?
- Does the model account for cultural and gender variations in human behavior?
- Does the model reflect social work ethics and values?

One risk to social workers who so often work at the individual level, doing assessments, treatment, and so on, is the tendency to seek the root of a problem (such as unemployment) in individual pathology while overlooking structural and interactionist factors. Keep in mind this tendency to err on the side of individual determinism as we consider some of the more influential theories and theoretical perspectives that have shaped social work practice. Moreover, because the models selected for analysis have all made major contributions to our understanding of human behavior, I prefer to approach these theoretical perspectives with a view toward appreciation rather than depreciation and evaluation rather than devaluation. In addition, we need some allowance for the historical context within which the model or theory was developed. Remember that no one theoretical approach can do everything and still maintain its distinct character. In appreciating what each contribution has to offer, while being cognizant of blind spots and shortcomings, we expand our consciousness and perceptions to gain a deeper understanding of the human experience. In the interests of critical thinking and equity, we summarize the basic tenets of each model or theory and ask the same questions of each perspective.

Psychodynamic Perspective

Psychoanalytical Theory

We begin with the oldest major scientific theory of human behavior—psychoanalytical theory. Mainly associated with the pioneering work of Sigmund Freud, psychoanalytical theory ultimately had a significant impact on the burgeoning field of social work in the United States by shifting the dominant paradigm from environmental concerns to a pathology perspective of individuals. An Austrian by birth, Freud lived from 1856 to 1939. Trained as a neurologist, he opened a private practice in Vienna, which was initially quite successful. His analysis of patients with brain disorders and neuroses took him into the realm of the unconscious. Through the use of hypnosis, Freud was able to uncover early traumas that were manifesting themselves as phobias and hysteria. It was his discovery of the role that sexuality can play in the development of neurosis and his teachings that the basis of neurosis is sexual conflict, however, that caused his reputation to suffer. Freud's venturing into the taboo area of sexuality shocked Viennese society and inevitably lost him the esteem of his colleagues (Prochaska & Norcross, 2010). Nevertheless, his theoretical development did not falter; his theory of personality, which was developed and refined over his lifetime, was the most comprehensive ever developed.

Psychoanalytic theory is considered scientific because it was built on personal observation and experimentation. Freud's fascination with the problem of hysterical paralysis, for example, eventually led to the development of his whole psychoanalytical model. The impact of his exhaustive and imaginative conceptualizations has been incalculable, both on the professions of social work and psychology and on Western society as a whole.

There is no need to exaggerate Freud's contributions to social thought. He is often credited with the discovery of the unconscious, dream interpretation, and the technique of free association. In fact, as Robbins, Chatterjee, and Canda (2006) inform us, these ideas date back to the ancient Greeks and had been expanded on by French and German philosophers before Freud. What Freud did, however, was to organize principles of human behavior into a cohesive, coherent form and to write volumes on his case histories and theoretical observations.

Freud's theory initially focused on the powerful instinctual forces (e.g., love, hate, sex, aggression) that drive development and behavior and bring us into conflict with social rules. These instincts are seen as biologically based and expressed in fantasies and desires. The individual is therefore forced to develop defense mechanisms to restrain these impulses and keep feelings of guilt (the province of the superego) in check. The following defense mechanisms identified by Freud (1936/1966) are commonly seen in social work practice and, in some cases, can be a normal response to an abnormal situation, such as long-term domestic violence. Among the defenses identified by Freud are as follows:

- Regression—returning to a younger stage of development, feeling like a child
- Repression—inability to remember a disturbing event (not related to alcohol use); sometimes the memory can be retrieved through hypnosis
- Reaction formation—overreaction to one's unwelcome impulses by behaving in the opposite direction (e.g., latent homosexuals attacking gay people)
- Projection—seeing in others what we dislike in ourselves
- Sublimation—channeling drives such as sexual drives into acceptable directions such as sports

These defenses work because the individual is largely unaware of them (Prochaska & Norcross, 2010). They have the effect of controlling undesirable impulses in all of us. Neurotic symptoms emerge when these unconscious sexual and aggressive conflicts become too intense to handle and the resultant defense mechanisms too restrictive (Prochaska & Norcross, 2010).

Freud's theory of the meaning of dreams had a huge cultural impact on treatment circles in the twentieth century even as it attracted intense criticism (Bower, 2001). The key to the unconscious mind, according to Freud (1900/1999), could be found in symbols the mind uses in the form of dreams. The purpose of dreams, he wrote, was wish fulfillment—to express primitive sexual and aggressive wishes. The words spoken in dreams derived from something that was said in waking life but were wrenched from their original context.

In his probing of the mysteries of the human mind, Freud's theories are singularly exciting. In her autobiography, Bertha Reynolds (1963) best expressed the thrill of her own education in this regard:

> We learned about the working of the unconscious, and many things in everyday life became clear to us. We saw fears displaced from childhood, jealousy

> displaced from other persons, hostility disguised as solicitude, desire as fear, and wish as certainty. We watched each other's slips of the tongue with glee and lived in a world where nothing was quite as it seemed and was frequently the opposite. We learned that the normal could best be understood through study of the abnormal, just because, in states of disease, inhibitions are lost and the workings of the mental mechanism can be seen, as are the works of a clock when its back is removed. No wonder we felt that we had been fooled by appearances all our lives and that we now had the key to wisdom in human relations. (pp. 58–59)

Freud's model of psychosexual development included the oral, anal, phallic, oedipal, latency, and genital stages. Fixation, Freud contended, occurred when an individual's development arrested at a certain stage. Regression may occur as well when a person returns to an earlier, more primitive stage. The id (where one's basic drives and instincts originate), the ego (the controlling self), and the superego (conscience) were the three basic parts of the psyche. Freud believed that the id, present at birth, was primarily a sexual drive. Therein lies the controversy that so shocked Austrian society and much of the rest of the Western world as his theories became known. In contrast to the preferred belief that children and infants are asexual, Freud believed that sexuality begins at birth. Furthermore, much that an adult feels and does is determined by resolution of the conflicts that arise related to the psychosexual drives of early childhood (Greene & Uebel 2009). Freud believed that women are inherently inferior to men and that little girls suffer from penis envy. The natural role for them was the domestic role; women who diverted from this path were viewed as "castrating women," a term that was commonly used against assertive women in the 1950s.

Contemporary Psychodynamic Perspectives

Freud's theories have spawned many generations of neo-Freudian scholars. Robbins et al. (2006) divide this work into two branches: mainstream or conservative, and radical reformulations. In common with Freudian theory, these are developmentally based theories that explain individual problems as symptoms of underlying issues, most of which stem from early childhood experiences. Collectively, their focus is on the inner psyche rather than on structural events.

Most noteworthy among the early mainstream Freudians were Alfred Adler and Carl Jung, who were pioneers with Freud at the Vienna Psychoanalytical Society but who later broke with Freud due to theoretical differences (Robbins et al., 2006). Adler, unlike Freud, was not a biological determinist, and Jung disagreed over the sexuality emphasis. Later theorists such as Karen Horney (1939) attributed greater importance to the role of the social and cultural environment in shaping human behavior. She refuted Freud's penis envy theory.

The Smith College School of Social Work, famed for its guiding psychodynamic perspective, infuses its curriculum with what it calls the *four psychologies*—namely, drive psychology, object relations, ego psychology, and self-psychology. I will focus on the two most prominent of these—object relations and ego psychology. According to the *object relations theory*, people have an internal world of representations that are unconscious but are reflected in their interactions with others. Human objects were the focus of much of this theory (Basham and Miehls, 2004). A major contribution of this orientation is the focus on the self in relation to others. (The important work of John Bowlby and René Spitz on the mother–child attachment is discussed in Chapter 4.)

Ego psychology regards the ego as primary in adapting over time in response to personal experiences. Drives toward competence and mastery were added to as key elements of Freud's developmental stages, a much more positive formulation. Erik Erikson (1950/1963) broadened Freud's psychosexual stages to psychosocial stages from birth until old age. Turning to the Freudian left, Robbins et al. (2006) examine the writings of theorists such as Wihelm Reich, Herbert Marcuse, and Erich Fromm, who sought to find a connection, odd as it seems, between the works of Freud and Marx. The link

between them was conflict—the psychic conflict of Freud and the social (class) conflict of Marx. Reich accepted Freud's notion of sexual energy, and Marcuse believed the unconscious could be viewed as basic to societal conflict. Both writers attempted to explain the psychological dynamics of oppression in capitalist societies. The Marxists picked up on Freud's criticism of bourgeois society and social conditioning as repressive, a viewpoint that was compatible with their worldview about social forces.

Erich Fromm (1955, 1968) was a psychoanalyst and humanist who wrote prolifically during the 1960s and had a strong following among protesting youth during that period. It was not the individual, Fromm contended, who was sick but society. *The Sane Society* and *The Revolution of Hope* are among his latest works.

Critical Analysis of the Psychodynamic Perspective

What Evidence-Based Research Shows

Greene and Uebel (2009) include in their chapter on psychodynamic theory a glossary of the terms used in classical psychoanalytic thought. Many of these terms are highly familiar because they are in common use (e.g., the unconscious, id, superego, oral stage of infancy, defense mechanism, regression, transference). In the belief that the existence of these psychological phenomena was self-evident, Freud and his followers did not see the need to gather controlled data for validation.

As a global unidimensional theory of human behavior, psychoanalytical theory is not verifiable, in any case, due to its high level of abstraction. And many of its underlying assumptions (e.g., that the libido, or sexual impulse, is the primary moving force in human development, that women are inferior to men, that women's claims of childhood victimization are mere fantasies or wish fulfillments) have been discounted by psychologists (and feminist theorists) today. There is no scientific basis, moreover, for Freud's belief that dreams are always wish fulfillments or for his concept of castrating women or for his belief that homosexuality is abnormal behavior.

In one area, however, dream research, brain scientists support many of Freud's (1900/1999) ideas as postulated in his book *The Interpretation of Dreams.* Freud's theory was that the purpose of dreams is to express primitive, sexual, and aggressive ideas. This dream theory was largely rejected until recently. Thanks to the new brain-scanning techniques, including functional magnetic resonance imaging (fMRI), the brain can be studied during the REM, or dreaming, stage of sleep. What is now known, reports neuroscientist Allen Braun (quoted by Bower, 2001), is that REM sleep activates the same primitive areas of the brain responsible for instinctual drives, emotions such as fear and anxiety, and sensory responses. Significantly, the prefrontal cortex, the thinking and judgment area of the brain, is shut down during this time. This explains why dreams are highly visual and, we might say, primitive. Thus, we must at least acknowledge that Freud was on to something and that some of his insights anticipated discoveries made about a century later. Clinicians can help clients learn more about their underlying feelings by having them write down their dreams and, in collaboration with the clinician, analyze them. Still, at the present time, dream imagery is a great untapped resource; modern culture and clinicians seem far less interested in dreams than are the brain researchers (Bower, 2001). More recent research by Wierzynski, Lubenov, Gu, and Siapas (2009) further clarifies findings on regions of the brain involved in dreaming and in storing the memories of the dreams.

In its focus on the formative period of personality development and on innate drives such as sex and aggression, the psychodynamic perspective pays some heed to biological processes. Freud's notions of the battle between the desire for life and the death instinct, the libido, and "man's natural aggressive instinct" are decidedly biological (1929/1961, p. 69) but not provable. Although the psychological dimension is primary, the biological impulse is its basis. The main theme of one of Freud's last books, *Civilization and Its Discontents,* is the antagonism between the demands of instinct and the restrictions and prohibitions of civilization.

A major contribution of the psychoanalytical school is trauma theory, which teaches that early childhood trauma can have a detrimental effect on later development. Trauma theory has gained increasing acceptability today. Posttraumatic stress disorder is included as a mental disorder in the *Diagnostic and Statistical Manual of Mental Disorders IV* (*DSM-IV*; APA, 2000). The lasting impact of trauma is empirically verifiable in both survey-generated data and neurological observation (Basham & Miehls, 2004).

The therapy derived from psychoanalytical theory—long-term treatment in which the therapist plays a largely nondirective role while the patient recalls memories—has not been adequately tested under empirically controlled conditions (Prochaska & Norcross, 2010). As analysis is the lengthiest and most expensive of any form of therapy, treatment according to the classical model is not considered cost effective. The treatment objectives—to get patients in touch with unconscious desires and motives and help them resolve transference neuroses, for example—are difficult to quantify.

Later psychodynamic theorists translated Freudian concepts into more measurable terms. Some concepts, such as the importance of mastery and competence, have wide empirical support from developmental psychology (Hutchison, 2008). In addition, longitudinal studies confirm the importance of early childhood experiences. Notable among modern psychodynamic researchers is John Bowlby (1958), who described the ill effects of hospital and institutional care on infants and young children. His attachment theory was derived from his observational data. Later researchers confirmed in comparative designs the disturbed behavior (defensive posture) of infants deprived of healthy caretaker–child bonding experiences (Basham & Miehls, 2004). Adult studies based on reports of early childhood experiences provide additional support for attachment theory.

What This Theory Teaches Us About Human Behavior

The Freudian stress on the psychology of human behavior is evidenced in the attention devoted to probing the unconscious and con-scious mechanisms in human behavior and the impact of earlier experiences in determining who we are and how we behave in certain situations. The social aspect of life tends to be downplayed in the mainstream formulations of psychoanalytical thought apart from family influences. Yet in his book on civilization, Freud himself extended his theories of instinct into the cultural realm. Writers of the Marxist psychoanalytical school such as Erich Fromm (1955, 1968) incorporated social, economic, and political aspects of human development into their theories and wrote biting critiques of modern society.

Except for the work of Jung, whose theory of personality includes physical, mental, and spiritual selves, spirituality was not a concern of the leading theorists of this school. Jung pro-posed that the evolution of consciousness and the struggle to find a spiritual outlook on life were the primary developmental tasks in midlife (Hutchison, 2008). Because of his atten-tion to this spiritual dimension, Jung's work has been influential in the field of alcoholism treat-ment. Freud himself had dismissed religion as delusional. In his discussion of "remolding of reality," he states that "the religions of mankind must be placed among the mass delusions of this kind" (Freud, 1929/1961, p. 28).

Viewed as a whole, we can learn much about the body–mind connection, the impor-tance of early childhood as the formative years, and the role of sexuality in human life from these psychoanalytic perspectives. Addition-ally, we become aware of some of the work-ings of people's unconscious drives, including trauma reactions, which indicate that a part of the past remains in our present life and that crises in relationships are apt to be repeated throughout the life cycle. As most therapists are aware, we relate to each other according to early blueprints, often seeking in a new rela-tionship the correction of an old one. Viewed historically, the psychodynamic framework paved the way for psychotherapy to be built on a special therapist–client relationship, the posi-tive use of transference in treatment, and encouragement of client narrative and expres-sion of past experience. This model laid the foundation for much of our present under-standing of human behavior.

Inclusion of Risks and Resiliencies

Most of the members of the psychodynamic school were more concerned with risks such as relationship problems and the development of neuroses than with health and resilience. Strikingly, most of the best known of the concepts (e.g., trauma, fixation, repression, regression) are decidedly negative. This prob-lem-oriented focus is reflected in the applied aspect of this theory—psychotherapy—as well. Erik Erikson's life span model, which I discuss later (in Chapter 4), however, did introduce a more positive conceptual scheme. Erikson's (1950/1963) work contributed to resilience theory in his focus on the importance of the social development of children.

Attention to Cultural and Gender Variations

In terms of ethnic and gender inclusion, most critics agree that psychodynamic theorists have been remiss. The emphasis has been almost solely on intrapsychic processes; when culture has been mentioned, it has tended to be Euro-American culture. Laws thought to be universal laws of nature, Hutchison (2008) argues, tend to refer only to the mainstream class and cul-ture of the day. Karen Horney's (1939) focus on structural equality and her reversal of penis envy theory into pregnancy-motherhood envy was a notable exception to the rule. And although Erikson's work has been widely criti-cized for its male-centered orientation, his research on childhood upbringing in two American Indian tribes—the Sioux and the Yurok fishermen—is noteworthy.

Consistency in Social Work Values and Ethics

The core social work values as spelled out in the 1996 Code of Ethics of the National Association of Social Workers (NASW) are ser-vice; social justice; dignity and worth of the person; importance of human relationships; integrity; and competence. On the whole, sub-scribers to the psychodynamic perspective are not out of sync with these values apart from advocacy for social justice. Robbins et al. (2006) correctly point to the Freudian and neo-Freudian focus on pathology and deficiency rather than on strengths and the general authoritarianism as areas that are worrisome in terms of the profession's values.

Freud clearly violated two (if not all) of the social work core values—social justice and integrity—in one regard. I am referring to his infamous backtracking on the issue of childhood sexual abuse. When, through hypnosis, he discovered incest in the backgrounds of some of his female patients, he at first revealed the shocking truth to the medical community. However, apparently under political pressure, he later backed down from his stance and voiced a more socially palatable view that the women's memories were mere fantasies (Robbins et al., 2006). This shift in interpretation was to have devastating effects on the treatment of female sexual assault victims for at least the next half century.

Cognitive Approaches

Behaviorism

Classical behaviorism, like many early treatment models, was deterministic and simplistic in its origins. Classical behaviorism views behavior as a conditioned response. One thinks of pigeons that experimentally learned to associate pecking on a certain item with access to food, or a dog conditioned to salivate at the sound of a bell (due to an association with feeding). Cognitive learning theory evolved from these experiments and explained human behavior as learned responses to stimuli. To the stimulus–response conceptualization, cognitive theorists focused on an additional dimension: cognition. The word *cognition* is derived from the Latin *cognoscere* (to learn, to know).

Developed as a reaction to psychodynamic models, the cognitive approach is concerned with the conscious reasoning process and the behavior itself as affected by the individual's own cognitive approach. Also in strong reaction to the psychodynamic approach, cognitive theorists rely on empirical testing to validate their ideas. Cognitive theorists argue that behavior is affected by perception or interpretation of the environment during the process of learning (Payne, 2005). This approach was highly influenced by developments in psychology, especially concerning the cognitive development of children and the search for therapeutic developments of a pragmatic kind, to help people overcome feelings of depression (Payne, 2005). Vourlekis (2008) notes the parallel influence of computer technology, which furnished widely used metaphors such as input, output, and feedback loops. Processing of computer data equates to analyzing speech content. In cognitive therapy the basic premise is that disturbances arise from faulty information processing. In contrast to the medical model, the treatment goal of cognitive-behavioral therapy is not to cure an illness but to prepare people to deal with future situations.

Cognitive-Behavioral Therapy

Behavior modification uses learning theory principles to change behavior (Haight & Taylor, 2007). It is widely used with clients who are developmentally disabled as well as in juvenile institutions. According to the cognitive perspective, troubling thoughts such as anxiety-provoking beliefs are processed through faulty interpretations of stimuli (Dulmus, 2002). The stimuli can be actual or imagined. People suffering from cognitive distortions often develop problematic symptoms, but these can be alleviated through cognitive-behavioral therapy (CBT). In short, the cognitive treatment process involves an evaluation of cognitive distortions unique to an individual and helps in restructuring a person's other thoughts (Dulmus, 2002).

Albert Ellis (1962) and Aaron Beck (1976) are the most prominent writers in this field. In fact, according to the American Psychological Association, Ellis is considered the second-most-influential psychotherapist of the twentieth century (Green, 2003) (Carl Rogers is in first place, while Freud is in third). Ellis is the founder of Rational Emotive Behavior Therapy (REBT; previously called RET). Starting out as a psychoanalyst, he was struck by the fact that his clients were benefiting from therapy but that their gains were not attributable to their reliving of past events, getting in touch with their unconscious, or working through the transference relationship. "Rather, clients' disturbed feelings and behaviors changed largely because of their newly acquired thinking" (Ellis, McInerney, DiGiuseppe, & Yeager, 1988, p. 1). Thus, Ellis's cognitive-behavioral therapy (CBT) was born. By the mid-50s Ellis had worked out its basic principles.

Like CBT, of which it is a part, REBT concentrates on people's current beliefs, attitudes, and statements. As a treatment modality, REBT starts with a formal assessment of the individual's thought processes, often through the use of a standardized questionnaire. Homework assignments are then given to promote client awareness. The core determinant of a person's behavior, according to this approach, is the individual's thinking.

Ellis explains human behavior in terms of the ABC model: A is the activating or antecedent event; B, the resulting behavior; and C, the behavioral consequence. For example, a relationship breaks up; one of the individuals involved is deeply depressed and attempts suicide. Another person might suffer such a loss, grieve for a while, and then develop new interests. It is not the event itself but the way we perceive it that is important (Ellis et al., 1988).

Translated into therapy, Ellis favored short-term treatment, with the therapist taking a very directive, didactic role in exposing the client's irrational thoughts, the "musts" and "shoulds," and the tendency to catastrophize in a crisis. Clients are trained to learn the ABC model, identify self-defeating thoughts, and replace them with healthy ones.

Aaron Beck's (1976) recognition came in the area of clinical depression and anxiety disorders. As Ellis does, Beck sees problems as arising from errors in thinking. Although the roles of genes and brain chemistry are not ignored, the focus is on thinking errors that contribute to dysfunctional moods and psychiatric symptoms. Beck's Inventory of Depression is widely used to gauge the level of a patient's depression. Common thinking errors are all-or-nothing thinking, overgeneralization, minimizing, magnifying, personalizing, and perfectionism. In treatment, clients learn to identify and monitor their automatic dysfunctional thoughts. Like Ellis, Beck sees cognitive growth and change occurring across the life span, thoughts and feelings as interrelated, and a person's construction of life events as more important than the events themselves.

It would be hard to overestimate the influence of cognitive theory. So influential has this intellectual development been in shaping our views about human behavior and efforts to change it that Vourlekis refers to it as the "cognitive revolution" (2008, p. 133). Cognitive principles are pervasive throughout virtually all forms of treatment, including 12-Step approaches that direct attention to an addict's cognitive impairments such as the all-or-nothing pattern of thinking as a factor in relapse. Recovering alcoholics call this "stinking thinking."

Motivational Interviewing

Motivational interviewing (MI), formulated by William Miller (1996) and Miller and Rollnick (2002) combines aspects of a laid-back, client-centered approach (inspired by the teachings of Carl Rogers) with a focus on reinforcement of positive (self-motivational) statements. Unlike REBT, MI is nonadversarial and nonauthoritative in tone. Collaboration and choice are guiding precepts. "Rolling with resistance" is its hallmark. This means basically agreeing as much as possible with the client and avoiding argumentation. Progress is promoted through a technique known as the "developing discrepancy" in the client's thinking. Helping clients to recognize the contradictions in their thinking about substance use can assist them in becoming motivated to change. In a nutshell, the basic principles of MI are as follows:

> Motivation is a state, not a personality trait.
> Resistance is not a force to be overcome, but a cue that we need to change strategies.
> The client is seen as an ally.
> Use discrepancy to explore the importance of change.

> Understand that the goal is to have the client—not the counselor—present reasons for change.

> Support the client's self-efficacy.

Whereas Miller and probably most of his contemporaries draw on the positive aspects of cognitive theory, Stanton Samenow (1984, 2007) has focused on the negative aspects in his understanding of the criminal personality. His theory and techniques, which are geared to criminal thinking and manipulation, are commonly used in correctional addictions programming with both male and female offenders. In such programming, offenders are required to focus on their wrongdoings, with the goal of instilling self-disgust and a desire to reform their errant ways (van Wormer & Davis, 2008). Samenow, whose observations about criminals are based on his work with male psychopaths, recommends an approach that is clearly at odds with the teachings of social workers who generally favor a strengths approach. As articulated in *Inside the Criminal Mind*, Samenow sees criminals as victimizers of their parents and all significant others in their lives. To criminals, people are viewed as their puppets and pawns. Samenow's (2007) more recent book, *The Myth of the Out of Character Criminal*, again dichotomizes criminals from noncriminals with little allowance for individual circumstances or the power of redemption. The terms "rehabilitation" and "strengths" are not contained in the book, and the case examples are almost exclusively male.

I mention Samesow's approach because many social workers in corrections and substance abuse counselors attend workshops that teach this approach. The criminal personality model is totally at variance with social work's predominant strengths perspective model. In social work, as observed by Payne (2005), a humanistic element has been incorporated in the formulations used (Payne, 2005). Social workers do draw on principles from the cognitive approach, which forms the basis for a number of helpful strategies to help clients develop self-efficacy or the confidence in their own ability to overcome difficulty, and techniques of "self-talk" to subdue feelings of depression and low self-worth. Interestingly, a model that can be used to put people down can also serve to lift people up. The next section and Chapter 2 discuss the scientific basis for the effectiveness of an approach aimed at the thinking level.

Critical Analysis of the Cognitive Approach

What Evidence-Based Research Shows

After more than two decades of research, a sound empirical basis clearly exists for cognitive-behavioral therapy. In her review of the literature, Dulmus (2002) has found widespread support for the use of this modality for a variety of mental health difficulties such as anxiety, aggression, depression, attention deficits, pain, and learning disorders. Because cognitively based interventions are short term, they are the treatment of choice in the U.S. mental health care system. In addictions treatment, motivational interviewing has come into its own and follows the widely circulated results of the National Institute on Alcohol Abuse and Alcoholism's multisite study, Project MATCH (1997). Although no control group was provided in the study, the three treatment designs—cognitive strategies, 12-Step facilitation, and motivational enhancement therapy—were found to be more or less equally effective in reducing alcohol abuse. Because MI involves the fewest sessions, it has been promoted by insurance companies (van Wormer & Davis, 2008).

There has been a proliferation of evidence-based research utilizing cognitive interventions, all with promising results. Relapse prevention strategies have been found to have a high rate of success; clients learn the early detection of relapse cues while they are boosted in their perception of self-efficacy (Dulmus, 2002). In suicide prevention, Weishaar (2004) reports, comparison studies of treatment-as-usual and cognitive-based treatment consistently show a significant reduction in suicidal ideation following treatment. Beck (2002) has reported positive results with a large sample of urban minority clients who had attempted suicide.

In the area of mental disorders such as posttraumatic stress disorder (Vonk, Bordnick, & Graap, 2004), obsessive-compulsive disorder

(Begley, 2007), and children's emotional disorders (Payne, 2005), cognitive approaches are of proven effectiveness. The methods are easy to learn and highly structured, and standardized assessment forms are widely available. In short, CBT has been applied with a high degree of efficacy across the diagnostic mental health spectrum (Dulmus, 2002). It has wide applicability in the development of psychoeducational materials as well.

What This Theory Teaches Us About Human Behavior

Cognitive theorists have made a major contribution in defining the role that our thinking plays in our feelings and actions. This theory illuminates a significant aspect of how humans function and the important role that our perception of a situation can play in developing resilience. Keep in mind the concept of resilience as we pursue the journey of this book, as a focus on resilience is what sets social work apart from other disciplines in the helping field. Social workers who intervene early in a situation of distress can help survivors frame the situation in a way that will help them handle the emotions and self-doubts that may arise later.

Cognitive theory, in sharp contrast to its psychodynamic counterpart, is geared directly toward human behavior. In working with clients with depression, for instance, therapists from this school of thought do not label the whole person as abnormal (as psychodynamic theorists might); instead, they focus only on people's thinking and their actions. Motivational theory, as formulated by William Miller (1996), teaches us basic principles of helping clients to want to change behaviors that are self-destructive; these principles are derived from the science of social psychology.

An understanding of cognition reveals a lot about our moods and our ability to control our feelings. This formulation is generalizable and enables us to study moral and cognitive development across the life span (see Chapter 4). Such understanding also enables us to appreciate the success of 12-Step groups, for example, in helping members control the urge to drink through the use of self-talk and slogans such as "one day at a time" and "easy does it" (for a fuller discussion, see van Wormer and Davis, 2008).

More broadly, as Vourlekis (2008 suggests, it is through cognition, or the mental processing and construction of personal meaning, that the environment is made real. That reality may be distorted by self-deprecating notions and thoughts of helplessness. Familiarity with the basic concepts of cognitive theory can help social workers "meet the client where the client is" by directing attention to the meaning of the situation in the client's, not the social worker's, reality.

The biological component of human behavior is taken for granted by most cognitive theorists; organic aspects of disordered thinking (e.g., brain damage, obsessive-compulsive disorder, depression) are not denied but are not emphasized. "Rational-emotive theory," wrote Ellis et al., "has always postulated that humans are biological organisms and frequently, if not always, our psychopathology is rooted in our biology" (1988, p. 23). Recent information on the role of the brain in addiction is not seen as contradictory to this theory. Begley's (2007) review of the cognitive research literature in her groundbreaking *Change Your Mind, Change Your Brain* describes work in alleviating depression through a trained focus on the thinking process itself and success in treating obsessive-compulsive disorder by replacing obsessive thoughts with realistic ways of thinking. This research reveals how cognitions mediate between events (situations) and feelings about them.

The psychological aspect of human behavior is emphasized far more than the social. Work is directed largely at the individual thought processes. In contrast to psychodynamic formulations, however, the focus is exclusively on the here and now rather than on the past (Ellis et al., 1988). There is no reason, however, that cognitive theory cannot be reconceptualized to include dealing with the past realities. Clients, through cognitive therapy, can be helped to reframe disturbing aspects of past victimization, for example, to come to terms with their lives and to see themselves as survivors rather than victims of their childhood. "Start where the client is" is an axiom in social work that means that, if the client's problems (and low self-esteem) are rooted in the past, this is the place to begin. Keeping in mind that the unconscious knows neither past nor present, the starting point of therapy is sometimes in the dark past. The cognitive techniques of restructuring one's thinking, in short, are ideally suited for work within any time frame.

The social side of treatment—group work and family therapy—are areas in need of further development as far as cognitive theory is concerned. Substance abuse counselors, however, do rely on cognitive strategies in their group sessions (van Wormer & Davis, 2008). Since cognitive approaches, Payne (2005) states, are primarily a Western model of practice in their emphasis on psychological change in individuals, rather than broader social purposes that might be more relevant in nonindustrialized nations, they are not particularly useful on a global scale. Spirituality, like the social dimension, does not receive attention by writers of this school. Cognitive theorists have generally not been known to take into account diverse spiritualities or religious beliefs in their writings. One exception is Ken Wilber's (1995) work on cognitive development within the context of transpersonal theory. Wilber drew on insights from Buddhism in his conceptualization of a higher level of consciousness.

Inclusion of Risks and Resiliencies

Central to cognitive theory is the assumption that people are sufficiently resilient so that that they can do the work needed to overcome their personal difficulties. This approach is not collaborative, however, except as practiced in MI. The risk to clients engaged in cognitive therapy may come from the therapy itself in that they may become overly self-critical. Cognitive theory is problem oriented. Risks in life are located in unhealthy thought patterns and in emotions generated by negative thought processes. Environmental factors (e.g., job loss) are rarely taken into account in defining life's risks.

Attention to Culture and Gender Variations

Cognitive theory is widely criticized for its overriding focus on rational thinking and a scientific orientation that shows a white male European American bias (Prochaska & Norcross, 2010). Diverse ways of knowing are not included, and the very terminology of cognitive therapy—testing, challenging, disputing, and so on—can be considered to represent masculine priorities. In general, problems are located inside one's head rather than in structural forces in the society.

Consistency With Social Work Values and Ethics

The fact that cognitive strategies are of proven effectiveness is congruent with the social work ethics of professionalism and competence. Where the approach falls short is in its failure to take into account the role of social forces in oppression or even the existence of oppression itself. The social work values of social justice and service undeniably receive short shrift with this method. Within the criminal justice system, this approach is often used in counseling to have offenders list and be aware of the errors in their thinking. Such a focus goes against the strengths perspective, is often associated with harsh confrontation, and is detrimental to efforts to boost clients' sense of self-efficacy. When cognitive methods are used to bolster clients' self-esteem, however, through a positive reframing of life's circumstances, they can be an invaluable asset to the change effort. Some cognitive work is essential, in fact. All good social work must necessarily encompass the realm of mental processing. As is true with the psychodynamic model, social workers do not have to import this model in its purest form but can adapt it to their own uses.

Ecosystems Framework

Moving from the micro-micro (the mind of the person) to the micro-macro (person-in-environment) realm, we come to ecosystems theory. Volume 1 of this HBSE set examines forces in systems large and small as they affect individuals, whereas the starting point of volume 2 is the wider system—the environment itself, both physical and social.

Historical Origins

General systems theory, like the cognitive school of thought, emerged as a counterreaction to earlier narrow, reductionist thinking. However, unlike the cognitive approach, systems theory is multidimensional in that it emphasizes the interrelatedness and interdependence of the parts of the whole. One point of information before we continue is that general systems theory cannot properly be considered a theory of human behavior because it does not explain anything. Greene (2009) concurs: What is called systems theory is not theory, he writes, but rather a highly abstract set of assumptions that are universal in their application. There is no body of knowledge here. Technically speaking, it is a model or conceptual theme.

General systems theory emerged in the 1950s and 1960s in the fields of biology and computer science (from cybernetics) (Prochaska & Norcross, 2010). This development was a reaction to the traditional scientific method of reducing phenomena to their simplest elements—electrons, protons, and neutrons. General systems theory, in contrast, advocated studying the biological processes as they lead to increasing structural complexity. Cybernetics advocated studying communication and feedback in computer systems as in human organisms, while biologists advocated the opposite—using machines as a metaphor for human processes.

Systems theory, anthropologist Mary Catherine Bateson (1984) writes, allows us to see the same pattern in the life of a group, a cell, or a coral reef. "To understand a living system, it is necessary to look at the constellation of factors, not in and of themselves, like single moving billiard balls, but in their relationships and contexts" (pp. 232–233).

General systems concepts were widely adopted by social work theorists, who, because of their practice, were at least theoretically attentive to the interplay between elements of the environment and the individuals and families within it. Still, as Saleebey (2006) indicates, social workers in practice have tended to ignore the systemic aspects of personal troubles and to individualize and pathologize social problems. And yet the systems framework, as Farley, Smith, Boyle, and Ronnau (2002) found in their review of HBSE course syllabi, has been among the widest taught and used in the vocabulary of social work.

General systems theory, on the other hand, was seen as too abstract and lacking in passion for justice. And it was not readily amenable to social work intervention. Hilarski, Dziegielewski, and Wodarski (2002) attribute the introduction of the person-in-environment concept by William Gordon (1969) as an ecological construct that enlivened systems theory and increased its relevance to social work practice. Ecology is the study of complex reciprocal and adaptive transactions among organisms and their environments. In a later development, Germain and Gitterman's (1980) life model of social work practice reformulated ecological systems theory, emphasizing the importance of stressful life transitions on people's ability to adapt to circumstances. The life model sees people as constantly adapting in an interchange with many different aspects of their environment (Payne, 2005). From this perspective, the aim of social work is to strengthen people's adaptive capacities. The ecological perspective differs from system theories in its tendency to emphasize interfaces (points of interaction) and small groups (Zastrow & Kirst-Ashman, 2010). The primary metaphor that guides this model is that of the biological organism. Social theorists have joined systems concepts to ecology to form the ecosystems approach. Because the notion of an ecosystem originated in the biological science of ecology "pertaining to the physical and biological environment" (Barker, 2003, p. 137), it serves as a useful way to discuss human behavior in the social environment.

Core Concepts of the Ecosystems Framework

The mutually interdependent relationship among systems of different sizes is expressed in the concept of the holon (Figure 1.1). Using the family as an example, each member of the family is a holon; each individual is both a self-contained system and a part of a larger system. The whole is greater than the individual roles in that the behavior of each member affects all of the others. The notion is that every system is a holon, which means that every system is simultaneously a whole with its own distinctive qualities, a part of a larger system, and a container of smaller systems (Robbins et al., 2006). We can summarize the core ecosystems concepts as follows:

> A social system is composed of members organized into a unit.
> All of the systems are subsystems of other systems.
> Cause and effect are intertwined and inseparable (interactionism).
> The parts of the whole are in constant interaction.
> A social system is separated from other systems by boundaries.
> These boundaries must be both open and closed to some degree.
> The system's environment is outside the boundaries.
> The person and the environment are in constant interaction.
> A social system is adaptive or goal oriented and purposive, striving to maintain equilibrium.
> A change in one member affects the whole system and therefore its equilibrium.

This multidimensional approach of viewing reality points to the interrelatedness of social phenomena in the universe: Cause and effect are viewed as intertwined and inseparable. This concept is termed *interactionism:* The parts of the whole are seen as constantly interacting. Viewed from the perspective of the totality, the whole is said to be more than the sum of its parts. Just as the emotional health of the growing child requires a nurturing environment, so the health of the larger whole is essential to the health of the parts.

Systemic Family Therapy

The ecosystems model at the micro-macro level, which is our concern here, has become the intellectual inspiration for understanding family dynamics. The adoption of systems by the field of family therapy in essence marked a paradigm shift or a clean break with past conceptualizations (Prochaska & Norcross, 2010). Steps on the path to the present conceptualization of clients and their families as constantly involved in transactions with other systems included the contributions of family systems therapists such as Murray Bowen. Whereas family treatment had previously treated people as separate entities within the unit, family systems therapy as formulated by Murray Bowen (1978), treated the family as a single unit. The role of the therapist was to analyze communication patterns within that unit. Bowen introduced the use of the genogram as a means of representing historic themes within a family. From this perspective, the therapist sought the cause of emotional illness in a family member in multigenerational patterns. The focus was on inadequate independence or differentiation of self. Bowen's ideas on the importance of differentiation of self from one's family of origin is derived from psychoanalysis; his search for an autonomous self and his concern with family triangulation give his model a Freudian cast (Johnson, 2004). Bowen (1978) and Bateson (1984) studied schizophrenic hospital patients and believed that their symptoms were caused by bizarre communication patterns in the family. Modern family therapists are far less deterministic, taking into account the impact of unusual behavior in the individual family member and the impact of such on the family as well as the impact of family dynamics on the individual (Robbins et al., 2006). The fallacies of early family systems therapists are not found here or in the works of ecosystems theorists who, while using a systems framework to study the family as a system within a wider system, refute beliefs that are not scientifically viable and build on the results of modern biological research into their formulations.

Critical Analysis of the Ecosystems Model

What Evidence-Based Research Shows

General Systems Theory

General systems theory is too broad to be researchable in any practical way. Payne (2005) enunciates the following reasons that this theory does not lend itself to empirical testing: It is expository rather than explanatory; the assumption that a change in one part affects all of the other parts is not provable or even accurate; and the theory is overly inclusive.

Prochaska and Norcross (2010) reviewed the literature for controlled studies on treatment effectiveness and found no controlled outcome studies on Bowen's family systems therapy. They did find that the outcome literature on marital and family therapies showed results as good as (or better than) those from other outcome research in most areas of psychotherapy. Interestingly, a report on dissertation studies of Virginia Satir's therapies (her work was inspired by Bowen) showed no statistically significant positive effect.

In his review of interventions with families of mentally ill persons, Johnson (2004) criticized Bowen's earlier research on schizophrenia. In the first place, Bowen's observations were based on small samples, according to Johnson, and they failed to take into account the possibility of biological illness, not to mention the impact of the mental hospital context. Bowen's conclusions, Johnson states, were later tested in a research hospital context in the 1960s and found wanting. Unfortunately, Johnson further argues, therapeutic intervention based on these theories was conducted on a regular basis, with the result that much blame was placed on families (Johnson, 2004). Only recently, thanks to magnetic brain imaging and the development of effective antipsychotic medication, has family therapy actually begun to help families to cope with mental illness, and families are now belatedly viewed as support systems rather than as the problem.

Ecosystems Theory

In contast to the classic family systems theorists who virtually ignored the biological roots of human behavior, ecosystems theorists have derived their model from the life sciences. As stated in the *Encyclopedia of Canadian Social Work*, ecosystems theory "rests on basic assumptions for which there is strong empirical support" (Rothery, 2005, p. 112). Note that although the systems framework is too broad to be tested as a model, the concept that the person is a system within larger systems is an observation that can be readily demonstrated; diagrams and photographs can substantiate this fact. The empirical research provided, as with psychodynamic theory, is directed to the basic assumptions that comprise the theory.

Many ecosystems writers today (e.g., Fred Besthorn) are concerned with the interconnectedness of all forms of life on the planet and the reciprocal effects of people's activities on the natural environment and, in turn, of the environment on people's lives. Research is drawn from the latest scientific data and reports from international organizations such as the United Nations in support of the theoretical assumptions. At the micro level, social work researchers such as Haight and Taylor (2007) draw on biological research, such as neurological studies, to address the complex way in which biology and environment interact to affect the course of human development across the life span. In their theoretical approach, Haight and Taylor draw on the biology of the individual organism as well as on attention to physical and social ecology.

What This Theory Teaches Us About Human Behavior

General systems theory talks a lot about the individual, yet the level of abstraction is relatively high, too high to teach us much about individual human behavior. From the sociological standpoint, the lowest common denominator—the unit of analysis—is the role and position rather than the person. A helpful contribution of systems theory is the inclusion of concepts from role theory. Role theory (not theory in any formal sense) offers an important framework for studying human behavior and the way in which it is influenced by the roles we are often socialized into early in family life. Role theory links the psychological to the social. Bowen's focus was placed on the desirability of "differentiation of self" from the family of origin. Much of systemic family therapy is concerned more with family roles and boundaries between roles, however, than with real people as psychologically complex human beings. General systems theory thus provides no guidelines for intervention apart from a focus on viewing the family system as a whole and helping family members strengthen the boundaries between individuals in the family unit for better functioning.

Germain and Gitterman's (1980) life model advanced earlier theory and provided systems approaches with a distinctly social work flavor. Their model is considered ecological because of the focus on person and environment in interaction. Moving into the *psychosocial* realm, the focus of the life model was on stress and individual adaptation to it. A comparison of the demands on the system (stresses) versus the supports to alleviate the stress determined the "goodness of fit" of an individual to the environment.

The *social* component of the biopsychosocial/spiritual model is addressed by ecosystems theorists; this is the environmental part of the person-in-environment configuration. Family systems therapists' attention to the family as a unit was a step forward in treatment history and a part of a paradigm shift in its inclusion of sociological realities. At the societal level, we can say that if each part is a whole and a part of another whole, the well-being of the whole is reflected in each part. The opposite is true as well—strengthen the well-being of each individual member and the whole, the system, is enhanced as a result. The implications for the social welfare state in this logic are worth considering.

The systems conceptualization has tremendously enriched our understanding of human behavior by encouraging us to think in terms of wholes. Its sociological focus has expanded our horizons even as it has broadened our vision. Moving from a person focus to the person-in-environment complexity has helped give social work breadth as well as depth. The person-in-environment focus is another way of stating the basic conceptual framework of social work practice (and of social psychology), which is that people and their environment are in constant interaction. The concept of interactionism has been an invaluable contribution to social work by offering a context within which to frame individual problems, showing how cause and effect are often intertwined, and alerting therapists to examine patterns of behavior and social interconnectedness. The systems approach has enriched social work by providing new insights into family and organizational dynamics and the importance of family support systems.

New systems thinking incorporates all aspects of social work's biopsychosocial framework; this framework itself can in fact be viewed as part and parcel of ecosystems theory. It reminds social workers that even in individual micro-level intervention, a holistic, environmental approach will enhance understanding.

From a biological standpoint we must attend to factors of health, nutrition, the potential for disease, and the state of the *physical* environment. As with cognitive theory the systems framework can be reconceptualized to include biological as well as psychosocial systems. The ecosystems theory is the most amenable to inclusion of the physical environment as a key element in healthy living.

Spirituality was not given much attention by the early systems theorists, although Gregory Bateson did, according to his daughter (Bateson, 1984), approach his understanding of biological systems with a sense of religious awe. Ecosystems theorists have done much more in this regard. Besthorn and McMillen (2002) have expanded social work's ecosystems model to include ecofeminist understandings. Spirituality, which had earlier received almost no attention by proponents of ecosystems, has today received the recognition it deserves as a part of the deep ecology movement. Deep ecology looks to the realm of nature for insight and sees all life—human and nonhuman—as one in the universe (see Volume II, Chapter 8, of this HBSE set for a full description of this concept). Mary (2008) is optimistic that social work with sustainability as its focus will be able to deal with spirituality as well as science, and environmental and economic issues as well as politics.

Inclusion of Risks and Resiliencies

Missing from many of the earlier systems perspectives is a realistic appreciation of power dynamics and the need sometimes to confront rather than adapt to oppressive forces in the environment (Saleebey, 2001). Mullaly (2007) goes further and criticizes all systems perspectives for their ready acceptance of the status quo, their failure to allow for conflict in society, and their failure to challenge class, gender, race, and other forms of inequality and oppression. In Mullaly's words:

> ❯ They are not theories because they are descriptive only and have no explanatory or predictive capacities.
> ❯ All social units (or subsystems) are viewed as interacting in harmony with each other and with the larger system (the society). The whole purpose of a systems approach is to eliminate any conflict that disrupts the system.
> ❯ They do not deal with or explain power relationships.
> ❯ Social problems are believed to be a result of a breakdown between individuals and the subsystems with which they interact.

It is true that ecosystems writers are more about describing society the way it is than in showing the way to substantial systemic change. However, when combined with an empowerment approach as is done in this text and the companion text, analysis of the power structure from a radical standpoint can be applied. Nancy Mary's contribution of a sustainable social work model for the study of social institutions is a welcome addition to social work theory that takes us into new realms of investigation.

As far as risks and resiliencies are concerned, general systems thinkers do incorporate risks in their formulations, whether in terms of family communication dysfunctions or external or internal stress. From this framework, people are generally viewed as resilient creatures at least to the extent that they are capable of change as they work on communication and coping skills. Therapists here assume an expert role, especially in family systems therapy, as they instruct family members in ways to overcome their apparent family dysfunction. Ecological theorists are more holistic. At the macro level, they are concerned with risks to the environment through overpopulation and overuse of harmful chemicals in agriculture, transportation, and warfare. At the family level, modern systems theorists integrate a wide range of methods and techniques and look for a fit between the demands on a family and available resources. This approach parallels the risk and resiliency model that similarly stresses the importance of a balance between negative and positive forces (see Chapters 4 and 6).

Attention to Culture and Gender Variation

General systems theory, Roberta Greene (2009) claims, offers a useful framework within which to incorporate cultural differences. She praises the work of modern social theorists who have used the concept of *ethnosystem* to address the issue of empowerment in marginalized communities. From a critical humanistic standpoint, however, ecosystems perspectives are criticized because the emphasis on equilibrium (or homeostasis) as opposed to recognition of the need for institutional change is inherently conservative (Kondrat, 2002). Feminists are rightly displeased with the mother-blaming tendency that emerged in much of family systems therapy in the past. Similarly, Prochastra and Norcross (2010) observe that Bowen's theory is valued for those qualities for which men are socialized—autonomy and "being-for-self"—while traits related to "seeking love and approval," for which women are socialized, are devalued. The fault may be in the theorists' exaggerated use of the theory rather than in the theory itself, however. The neglect of empirical evidence for many of the claims, such as mother neglect, which was reputed to be the cause of autism, was undoubtedly responsible for conclusions that are currently disregarded by modern science (see Chapter 2). There is no reason that the ecosystems' person-in-environment focus cannot be revised for empowerment purposes (as I am doing in this book). The concept of power can be incorporated as a core concept as well (Kondrat, 2002).

Consistency With Social Work Values and Ethics

Ecosystems perspectives are consistent with social work values and ethics and accordingly serve as the organizing framework for a number of human behavior textbooks in the field as previously mentioned. Although the social justice aspect has been lacking, especially in the formulation and practice of classic family systems therapy, family therapy has advanced with the times to be a viable treatment modality. The ecosystems model is moving in new directions as well; the person-in-environment concept is being expanded to include ecofeminist principles and to call for social change. The emphasis on global and economic sustainability today is highly ethical. Nancy Mary (2008) reflects this principle in her groundbreaking *Social Work in a Sustainable World*. Mary outlines four dimensions of sustainability that must be attained to ensure the continuation of all life on the planet: human survival, biodiversity, equity, and life quality. These sustainable values, Mary suggests, are at the root of all major religions and found in our code of ethics. At the personal level, ecosystems theory advocates social justice and looks toward a match between human needs and available resources. Person and environmental aspects of clients' lives are addressed simultaneously (Rothery, 2005).

Empowerment Perspectives

The empowerment framework is a composite group of theoretical perspectives, some of which do not use the term "empowerment." They include, according to my classification, what I call empowerment strengths and anti-oppressive, feminist, and postmodernist approaches. Central to all of these theoretical approaches is the objective of social justice and a reduction in social inequality and oppression. Empowerment perspectives address the dynamics of power and discrimination. They propose that empowerment requires linking a sense of self-efficacy with critical consciousness and effective action (Robbins et al., 2006).

Social Work Empowerment Concepts

In her rigorously documented history of the empowerment tradition in social work, Barbara Simon (1994) traces empowerment thought and practice from the Progressive era, from the common stock of cultural themes and ideals of human potential and the role of social institutions in enhancing it. In the 1980s and 1990s empowerment concepts were widely touted by social work theorists, and, in combination with the strengths perspective, the empowerment model became the predominant theoretical approach in social work.

Gutiérrez and Lewis (1999b) identify three themes of empowerment as a model for practice—concern with power, critical consciousness, and connection. Dominant groups use power to protect their position and control decision-making processes. Being a member of a disempowered group has personal, as well as political, costs. An understanding of power dynamics in society is crucial for empowering social work practice, Gutiérrez and Lewis suggest. *Critical consciousness* is a crucial means of gaining power through a collective solidarity that arises through awareness of the root of power disparities and the need to change the system. *Connection* with others enhances personal transformation and the development of social support networks.

Barbara Solomon's (1976) focus was black empowerment, and her work is widely cited in the literature. Powerlessness by individuals or social groups involves the inability to manage emotions in a way that will lead to personal gratification. Translated into practice, social workers need to help clients see themselves as causal agents in finding solutions to their problems and to see social workers as peers and partners in solving problems.

The Anti-Oppressive Approach

Dalrymple and Burke's (1995) definition of anti-oppressive practice recognizes power imbalances and works toward the promotion of change to redress the balance of power. Central to this formulation is the imperative to challenge "institutional practices that oppress and so systematically disempower those with whom we work" (p. 15). In her groundbreaking work, *Anti-Oppressive Social Work Theory and Practice*, Lena Dominelli (2002) states that anti-oppressive measures "aim to deconstruct and demystify oppressive relations as stepping stones on the road to creating non-oppressive ones" (p. 13). The ultimate goal of social work practice from this perspective is the creation of nonoppressive relations rooted in equality.

Anti-oppressive practice, Dalrymple and Burke inform us, is built on the model of empowerment. Following their logic, the overlap between empowerment practice and anti-oppressive practice is considerable. Inasmuch as empowerment practice addresses power imbalance as a form of oppression and anti-oppressive practice is geared toward the empowerment of oppressed people, the difference may be one of syntax rather than meaning. Payne (2005), however, maintains that empowerment offers a less radical approach to social work than the more ideological anti-oppressive approach, which focuses on the need for transformational change. To anti-oppressive and empowerment theorists, social work practice requires far more than listening skills; the worker becomes a change agent in the political meaning of that term (Boylan & Dalrymple, 2009).

Dalrymple and Burke's (1995) and Boylan and Dalrymple's (2009) formulation advocates change at the personal, cultural, and institutional levels. Their model, accordingly, is three pronged. Empowerment practice takes place on the levels of feeling, ideas, and action.

The *feeling* level begins with the personal reality of people's lives and their emotional response to it. Children who are oppressed are encouraged by their advocates to tell their stories. The advocates help the child feel valued by listening to the child's story; then they share ideas about the situation. Dominelli's (2002) description of the personal dimension of women's consciousness raising is relevant here. Consciousness raising begins with the identification of feelings and perceptions from the vantage point of one's own experiences and the expression of these feelings in one's own words. For women oppressed by cruel circumstances (e.g., sexual victimization), the power to name their experience has often been denied them.

The *idea level* that Dalrymple and Burke discuss is closely, almost seamlessly, bound to the feeling level of empowerment practice. The idea level involves a new evaluation of self and situation through the acquisition of new insight. Sometimes the acquisition of knowledge is gradual; sometimes there is an "aha" moment of realization that what had seemed to be the case is not. Examples of such light-bulb experiences are the battered woman who learns of the power games that were played to put her down, the rape victim who realizes the assault was not her fault, and the boy who acknowledges himself as gay. The counseling relationship can serve as a powerful tool in helping these clients chart a new course toward recognition of self, societal awareness, and self-love.

At the *action* level, the individual moves into the political realm. The advances may be manifested at the interpersonal level, such as by joining a self-help or advocacy group to support and advocate for others in the same situation. We should never underestimate the efficacy of self-help groups. British social work theorist Robert Adams (2008) contends that self-help groups are some of the most effective options available to consumers. Empowerment to Adams is a transformational activity that links to self-help groups. In such groups individuals grow more critical of their own conditions and take control of their circumstances. Typical examples are groups that meet to cope with shared family problems such as debilitating and addictive diseases, single parenting, and bereavement. At the broader level, social action can take the form of organizing to work for new legislation in hopes of having a wider impact. This social action stage involves working with others to change social institutions. See Figure 1.5 for a workshop on health care as a human right that took place in Louisville, Kentucky. The persons attending the workshop, including social workers, had come to Louisville to organize for further campaigns for economic human rights.

In their book on anti-oppressive social work with children, Boylan and Dalrymple

Figure 1.5. Consciousness-raising session. Sponsored by the Women's Economic Agenda Project, this workshop prepared participants to advocate for universal health care. Photo by Candace Marie Bickett.

(2009) examine adult–child power relations and the oppression of children and young people by adults and by social systems. Child advocates, they suggest, can help youths by giving "power to" rather than having "power over" them as together they share ideas and agree on a course of action. Adams (2003) points to a paradox in all empowering social work which is that the very methods that are used with marginalized individuals to reduce their risks of self-destruction may disempower them through the removal of choice. Yet letting them fail can be disempowering in another way, as we all know.

Social action as a theoretical perspective draws on several strands of thought, including those found in the women's movement and the disability movement. More recently, social action has drawn from the writings of black activists such as bell hooks (1994), who was inspired by the radical pedagogy of Freire (1973), who preached education of the masses

for critical consciousness. The radical empowerment pedagogy of Freire is an underpinning of empowerment practice in social work (Lee, 2001). The use of dialogue is central to both social work and Freire's liberation teachings.

The Strengths Perspective

Strengths-based social work is largely associated with the work of Dennis Saleebey, who produced the first edition of *The Strengths Perspective in Social Work Practice* in 1992, and Charles Rapp (1998; Rapp & Goscha, 2006), who spelled out interventions from this model for case management with persons with mental illness. Saleebey (2001, 2006) often speaks of empowerment as a goal of social work, while proponents of the empowerment approach almost always advocate a reinforcing of client strengths. Thus, the overlap is considerable.

My personal impression, based on a familiarity with the literature, is that proponents of empowerment theory tend to emphasize the political realities of coping, while proponents of the strengths perspective focus more on helping clients build on their own resources. Strengths-based therapists, however, are often politicized in their encounters with bureaucratic constraints, both from the government and their own agencies, which limit their client-centered proclivities. My approach in this book is to consider the notion of strengths as an essential component of empowerment theory and practice. This conceptualization is consistent with that of three popular social work textbooks in the United States and United Kingdom: *Social Work: An Empowering Profession* (DuBois & Miley, 2007), *Empowerment in Social Work Practice: A Sourcebook* (Gutiérrez, Parsons, & Cox, 2003), and *Social Work and Empowerment* (Adams, 2003). These texts show us how to effectively incorporate empowering strategies for work with diverse populations.

Within the social work practice literature, a focus on client strengths has received increasing attention in recent years. Unlike related fields, moreover, social work has come to use the term "the strengths perspective" or "the strengths approach" as standard rhetorical practice. In his comprehensive overview of social work theory, Francis Turner (1996) has identified two common threads unifying contemporary theory. These are the person-in-the-situation conceptualization and the holistic understanding of clients in terms of their strengths and available resources. The strengths perspective has been applied to a wide variety of client populations: mentally ill persons and their families; coming-out gays and lesbians and their families; child welfare clients; homeless women in emergency rooms; the isolated elderly; addicted drug users; and troubled African American families (Saleebey, 2006; van Wormer & Davis, 2008). The concept of strength is also part and parcel of the growing literature on family-centered practice, narrative therapy, the person-centered approach, ethnic-sensitive programming, and gender-specified counseling. The strengths perspective, as Ligon (2009) suggests, assumes that power resides in people and that the client rather than the social worker is the expert on his or her own life.

Their relationship, therefore, is collaborative and nonhierarchical. From this perspective, social workers should do their best to promote power by refusing to label clients, avoiding paternalistic treatment, and trusting clients to make appropriate decisions. A presumption of health over pathology and an emphasis on self-actualization and personal growth are key tenets of the strengths approach.

A basic point that strengths theorists emphasize is that assigning labels to clients is fraught with negativism. The problem is often not in the diagnosis itself but in the manner in which the label is applied. Rapp and Goscha (2006) warn us about the process of naming, which belongs to the professional, not the client, and a problems-deficit orientation that can develop a life of its own. A person with schizophrenia, for example, *becomes* a schizophrenic (Saleebey, 2006). Once a client has been labeled, other facts about that person's character and accomplishments, Saleebey suggests, recede into the background. The difference between "I am illness" and "I am a person who has an illness" is profound. Hope is engendered in the latter but not the former.

Although the literature consistently articulates the importance of stressing clients' strengths and abilities, practitioners must be cognizant of the reality of standard clinical practice built on a problem/deficit orientation in treatment, a reality shaped by agency accountability and the dictates of managed care. Third-party payment schemes mandate a diagnosis based on relatively serious disturbances in a person's functioning (e.g., organic depression or suicide attempts) and short-term therapy to correct the presenting problem. Furthermore, the legal and political mandates of the many agencies that shape the professional ethos may strike a further blow to the possibility of partnership and collaboration between client and helper (Saleebey, 2006).

Feminist Empowerment Approach

Theories of gender oppression address the basic structure of patriarchal dominance and social control of the latent sexism in society. While having a realistic awareness of the barriers facing women who are disadvantaged in our society, social workers of the feminist school seek to uncover coping strategies that can be used even in the most difficult of circumstances.

Just as empowerment practice has enriched feminist theory, so has feminist theory enriched empowerment practice theory, especially insofar as women's issues are concerned. These twin perspectives both view power and powerlessness related to race, gender, and class as central to the experiences of women who live in poverty and women of color.

Bricker-Jenkins and Netting (2009) define the major conceptual components of feminist frameworks that distinguish them from general social work models. Their category *human behavior and the social environment* includes the following:

- Strengths and health, which involves mobilizing the individual and the collective capacities for healing, growth, and personal, as well as political, transformation
- Diversity, which creates choices for everyone and thus is a source of strength, growth, and health
- Interdependence
- Constructionism, which views reality as an unfolding, multidimensional, politically shaped process

A pro-woman stance and an understanding of personal oppression as political are other key themes. Many of the ideas of the feminist approaches are subsumed under the anti-oppressive perspective, which sees all forms of oppression as stemming from common psychological and structural causes.

British social work theorist Malcolm Payne (2005) differentiates five types of feminism: liberal, radical, socialist, black, and postmodern. Liberal feminism seeks to reduce inequality and provide equal opportunities through legislation; radical feminism focuses on combating patriarchy and celebrating women's uniqueness within their separate social structures. Socialist feminism emphasizes women's oppression as part of structured inequality within a class-based social system. Black feminism starts from racism and points to the many kinds of oppression to which black women are subject as compared to white women. Postmodern feminism emphasizes the way that language is used to place people in certain categories. To this list I would add Latina feminism (see Lorraine Gutiérrez and Edith Lewis's edited volume *Empowering Women of Color* [1999a], which provides the foundation for a model of empowering practice with Latina women, and Gutiérrez, Zuñiga, & Lum's *Educating Students for Multicultural Practice* [2004]).

Postmodernism

In the 1980s postmodernism emerged in response to the elevation of hard science (positivism) as the way to truth. Inspired by French philosopher Michel Foucault, who was especially critical of the way that scientific knowledge is used to exert control over people, postmodern thought is relevant to social work practice in that it can be regarded as a controlling force (Robbins et al., 2006). Social workers from the postmodern perspective eschew bureaucratic control functions and focus instead on the client's definition of a particular situation. Seeking to appreciate the client's unique understanding of events, social workers of this school ask questions that lead to a collaborative view of solutions. The therapist does not engage in intervention but in therapeutic conversation with the client; the path is one of mutual discovery.

In common with the feminist perspective, postmodernism entails a resistance to knowledge that is dichotomized, when in reality most aspects of human behavior exist along a continuum. Many feminist practitioners have acquired a postmodern stance as a result of the feminist commitment to diversity (i.e., to validating multiple truths) and the appealing focus on the shaping of meaning and criticism of positivism in social science research (Bricker-Jenkins & Netting, 2009). But postmodernism, Schriver (2010) states, claims to be apolitical while failing to recognize that, by definition, feminist and social work are clearly political. While providing useful tools such as narrative therapy and an emphasis on strengths, feminists of this school may give lip service to the role of structural forces in oppression, but these forces may not be actively dealt with under this conceptualization.

Critical Analysis of the Empowerment Perspectives

What Evidence-Based Research Shows

Because empowerment concepts are abstract, they may be difficult to operationalize for the purpose of empirical testing. As Robbins et al. (2006) indicate, in an era when social work is increasingly outcome driven, empowerment theories are subject to criticism for their emphasis on process rather than result. The insights gained from these perspectives, however, can be used to conduct rigorous research framed from the experience of the oppressed people themselves. Empowerment-oriented research, Robbins et al. further suggest, focuses on issues that are deemed important by oppressed groups. Use of personal narratives, which is favored by all of these theorists, can be highly informative in ways that statistical evidence may not be.

Generally speaking, the activist nature of much of empowering social work and attention to inadequacies in social welfare services do not provide the kind of testable data that are attractive to national funding sources. The research goal here may be more to enhance people's empowerment than to test a certain kind of intervention. Dominelli (2002) suggests that social workers collect information that exposes the harsh realities in which people live in order to highlight the structural nature of their problems. Having such knowledge is a form of power in itself.

Regarding direct treatment practice, empirically based studies can be conducted to compare progressive strategies with the more traditional ones. Because strengths-based case management follows a fairly specific set of standards, we can examine research that compares this approach with conventional case management. In the most comprehensive study to date with regard to clients with mental illness, Rapp and Goscha (2006) compared the structural ingredients that made strengths-based interventions more effective than standard practices. In their examination of the nine experimental and quasi-experimental designed reports available, they found that the effectiveness stemmed from professional case management and from helping people tap into their community resources. Although not all of the studies were truly experimental and many used small samples, the results were consistently positive. Concerning the research findings, Rapp and Goscha conclude that application of the strengths model reduces the use of psychiatric hospitalization, increases client retention in the program, and increases client achievement and sense of well-being. Ethnographic interviews, not surprisingly, reveal that client perceptions of work with strengths-based case managers were highly positive and helped them achieve their personal goals.

The research on the effectiveness of a strengths approach, although very preliminary, notes Saleebey (2006), suggests that this is an effective and economically viable framework. Related research on solution-focused therapy (i.e., therapy that assists clients in focusing on solutions rather than problems) has also provided support for the elements of a strengths perspective that make a difference. Empowerment-based interventions are especially relevant for social workers who work with minority groups and older adults. More research to document the effectiveness of these interventions is in order, especially of the less mainstream approaches.

What This Theory Teaches About Human Behavior

The more we learn about the nature of oppression, discrimination, and the roots of powerlessness, the more we will be able to understand and predict human behavior. Empowering clients by helping them tap into their strengths is a key ingredient of the helping process. It is also vital for a healthy family life. These perspectives help us learn about power imbalances in the family and how power can be used to control people by making them feel helpless. In reading the strengths-based literature, we learn how pathology focused the treatment industry is and how intimidating the worker–client relationship can be when negative labels are applied. At the societal level, anti-oppressive theory and practice have facilitated an analysis of the ways that systems of oppression are both interconnected and used to undermine solidarity among groups (Bricker-Jenkins & Joseph, 2008).

Empowerment perspectives largely ignore the importance of biological factors in human development (Robbins et al., 2006). Saleebey (2001), in his book on human behavior, however, which takes a strengths approach, devotes a great deal of attention to the biological components of human behavior, especially the relationship of the brain to mind and consciousness. He also considers resilience in the face of serious adversity.

Biological factors in human behavior tend to be ignored by most feminist theorists. There is one exception, however: One branch of feminism that Van Voorhis (2009) refers to as "cultural feminism" posits that innate personality differences exist between men and women; proponents of this branch of feminism see women as more nurturing by nature and men as more aggressive because of biological differences in the brain and hormones. Gilligan's (1982)'s theoretical scheme of female moral development is representative of this line of thought. Her work has inspired the gender-specific treatment designs that are now the predominant model used in girls' residential institutions. Radical feminism similarly places a major emphasis on biological differences related to gender and on woman-centered values (Mullaly, 2007).

As far as the psychology of human behavior is concerned, many empowerment theorists believe that psychological difficulties are related to structural conditions that promote oppression. At the same time, they have a great deal of faith in people's inner ability to find their way out of oppressive situations. Above all, they treat clients as the experts on their own lives.

Empowerment approaches emphasize the social components of human behavior; to anti-oppressive theorists, the environment (and this includes social services agencies) is often viewed as oppressive—sexist, classist, racist. Clients are viewed in constant interaction with representatives of their community. The immediate social environment is seen in terms of potential resources and strengths. These theorists are very aware of the negative effect of the use of labels, whether by society or by mental health professionals. The concern with power by writers of the empowerment school (apart from proponents of the strengths perspective) necessarily leads into the socioeconomic and political arenas. Consciousness raising for political awareness is a strategy that is associated with this model.

Spirituality is also receiving more attention today than formerly. Canda (2006), for example, provides qualitative research to demonstrate the important role of spirituality in sustaining people who are confronting chronic illness.

Inclusion of Risks and Resiliencies

Of the various perspectives discussed in this section, the strengths perspective is the most concerned with resilience and the least concerned with risks or problems. However, social work and anti-oppressive empowerment theorists do focus a good deal of attention on power differentials, whereas the feminist formulations are concerned with gender discrimination; both of these forms of discrimination create conditions of risk, psychologically and socially. Other risks at the societal level that are recognized by progressive theorists of the empowerment school include the impact on families of the massive employment layoffs that can be attributed to the new labor-reducing technologies and to the outsourcing of work (Bricker-Jenkins & Joseph, 2008). Collectively, the perspectives discussed in this section place faith in what Saleebey (2006) refers to as "the power of the people" or the people's ability to change the way in which they understand their problems so as to better be able to overcome them.

Attention to Cultural and Gender Variations

Feminist theorists of course pay close attention to issues of gender, liberal feminists focusing on equality of opportunity and minimizing differences between men and women and radical feminists emphasizing these differences (Mullaly, 2007). Empowerment perspectives, in general, lend themselves very nicely to a focus on disempowered groups and to a sensitivity to cultural-gender issues. Black empowerment, strengths in minority extended families, Native American ceremonies, gay and lesbian empowerment, and feminist consciousness raising are among these issues. Connecting the personal with the political is a key attribute of these models.

Consistency With Social Work Values and Ethics

Empowerment clearly is what social work is all about. The primary mission of social work, according to the NASW Code of Ethics, is "to enhance human well-being and help meet the basic human needs of all people, with particular attention to the needs and empowerment of people who are vulnerable, oppressed, and living in poverty" (1996, p. 1). Social work helps people to help themselves; one of the major responsibilities of social workers, according to the code, is to recognize the right of the client to self-determination. Of all the theoretical perspectives, empowerment is the most closely aligned with social work values and practice.

Social justice is most clearly represented by the anti-oppressive, empowerment approaches. With regard to the service component of social work values, social workers do a great deal of volunteer work in their power-enhancing capacities. The stress on relationships that are built on trust is especially strong with the strengths approach but is primary with all of these perspectives.

Practice Implications

There is no one correct theory for every client, family, or situation. Social workers, therefore, need to be familiar with the truths that accrue from various theoretical orientations.

Through critical examination of each theory and perspective, we can appreciate the usefulness or irrelevance of each for a particular instance. In helping an individual deal with trauma experienced many years ago, for example, the social worker would do well to draw upon the psychoanalytic perspective to understand how memories are stored in the unconscious and how the mind copes with overwhelming material. In sharing this knowledge, a strengths approach would be invaluable: Through a collaborative process, therapist and client can work together to discover inner resources and enhance coping skills.

Family therapy with an anorexic teen or a child who is acting out might effectively rely on systems constructs to help the family understand the roles of individual members and the way in which their communications are interactive. Cognitive interventions fit well within the context of all therapeutic situations, wherever people can benefit by reframing their perceptions of events. As we listen to a client's personal narrative, for example, we strive to grasp that person's reality and cognitive patterns and at the same time attend to signs of initiative, hope, and frustration with past counterproductive behavior that can help lead the client to a healthier outlook on life.

Social workers who are committed to working with socially marginalized groups in our society (e.g., the frail elderly, homeless people, battered women, gays and lesbians, people of color) can help members of these groups by using strategies of empowerment. Instead of focusing on the individual, family, or community as the problem, the empowerment perspective teaches us to replace the language of pathology with a language of strength. To help clients develop a sense of self-efficacy, practitioners can assess their cognitions of self-defeating patterns as a starting point. Hearing personal narratives is helpful because, as clients tell their own story, elements of the past that are still issues in the present (trauma, insecurities, mental disorders) will reveal themselves. The narrative disclosures can be seen from an ecosystems, interactionist perspective, where action and reaction are intertwined.

In other words, there are truths in the four major perspectives examined in this chapter, truths that inform social work practice for work in a variety of situations. We will delve into other theoretical frameworks (e.g., role theory and life span models in Chapter 3) of the psychology of human behavior. As we have seen in this chapter, theory and practice are clearly intertwined.

Summary and Conclusion

People direct the course of their lives through the choices they make. This choice making is a part of the human behavior with which this social work textbook is concerned. Accordingly, turning-point stories seemed an appropriate way to begin since these provide not only a glimpse into people's lives but also a view of how they interpret them. Such stories are both part of the whole and also encapsulate the whole. The photograph of the holon illustrates this concept—the system within a wider system. For volume 1 of this HBSE series, micro level, the metaphor of the holon is especially appropriate because in this text we are dealing with the smaller entities, the person in the social environment. Yet from the standpoint of the person we must never lose sight of the whole because that is there, too, embodied in the person. Following Parker Palmer's (2007) vision of teaching and learning from the microcosm, we focus on theories and concepts that are smaller but no less complex than the larger, societal-level realities. We can construct a biology and a psychology of human behavior without losing sight of the social aspects.

Courses in HBSE provide a groundwork for vital practice decisions about how social workers can reach their often hard-to-reach clients and about which model or theoretical orientation works best for both themselves and their clients. Successful practice, as we have seen in this chapter, depends on solid theory. Without a firm theoretical base, social workers are unable to critically evaluate their clients' circumstances and thus are unable to comprehend human behavior as, in part, a product of both structural arrangements in the family (at the micro level) and the power disparities in the wider social realm. The same critical-thinking skills that are necessary to understand human behavior can be applied to the study of theories of human behavior, theories that I hope will guide rather than divide us on this journey of discovery about the human species.

This chapter was shaped in the spirit of the NASW Code of Ethics stipulation: "Social workers should critically examine and keep current with emerging knowledge relevant to social work and fully use evaluation and research evidence in their professional policies" (1996, section 5.02c). Thus, we have critically examined the most formidable and enduring of human behavior theories: psychodynamic theory, which showed us the intransigence of the past; the cognitive approach, which put us in touch with idiosyncratic thinking in the here and now; the ecosystems perspective, which broadened our horizons and taught us about spatial relationships and the meaning of wholeness; and last but not least, the empowerment perspectives, which moved us in the direction of *how*. The next chapter will focus on the *why*.

Thought Questions

1. How would you relate the phrase "to see the world in a grain of sand" to understanding human behavior?
2. What is meant by micro/macro and macro/micro approaches to human behavior?
3. Can you give some examples of either/or and both/and concepts?
4. How would you relate the notion of paradox to human behavior?
5. What does the reading about Mrs. Anné say about life?
6. Which of the turning-point narratives relates most closely to your personal experience?
7. How would you describe the metaphor of the spiral staircase?
8. Can you list some common characteristics of turning points?

9. How would you describe the four major domains of life in the biopsychosocial and spiritual dimensions as represented in Figure 1.4?

10. How can theory, concepts, and models be differentiated?

11. "There is nothing so practical as a good theory." How would you explain this statement?

12. Why is critical thinking important to social workers?

13. How did politics affect the development of psychoanalytical theory? What were the long-term consequences?

14. How did Marxism combine with psychoanalytical theory?

15. What do psychoanalytic theories teach us about human behavior?

16. What do cognitive theories teach us about human behavior?

17. What do ecosystems perspectives teach us about human behavior?

18. What do empowerment perspectives teach us about human behavior?

19. Which approach of the four critiqued theoretical perspectives—psychodynamic, cognitive-behavioral, ecosystems, empowerment—is the most consistently evidence based? Discuss the research findings on effectiveness.

20. Which approach of the four perspectives is the most culturally sensitive? How?

21. Which one of the perspectives is the most appealing to you? Why?

References

Adams, R. (2003). *Social work and empowerment* (3rd ed.). Hampshire, UK: Palgrave.

Adams, R. (2008). *Empowerment participation and social work*. Hampshire, UK: Palgrave.

American Psychiatric Association (APA). (2000). *Diagnostic and statistical manual of mental disorders* (4th ed.). Washington, DC: Author.

Armstrong, K. (2004). *The spiral staircase: My climb out of darkness*. New York: Knopf.

Barker, R. (2003). *The social work dictionary* (5th ed.). Washington, DC: NASW Press.

Basham, K., & Miehls, D. (2004). *Transforming the legacy: Couple therapy with survivors of childhood trauma*. New York: Columbia University Press.

Bateson, M. C. (1984). *With a daughter's eye: A memoir of Margaret Mead and Gregory Bateson*. New York: Pocket Books.

Beck, A. (1976). *Cognitive theory and emotional disorders*. New York: International Universities Press.

Beck, A. (2002, December). An early cognitive intervention for suicide attempters. Paper presented at the first annual conference of Treatment and Research Advancements Association for Personality Disorders, Bethesda, MD.

Becker, G., & Newsom, E. (2005). Resilience in the face of serious illness among chronically ill African Americans in later life. *Journal of Gerontology, 60B*(4), S214–S223.

Begley, S. (2007). *Train your mind, change your brain*. New York: Ballantine Books.

Besthorn, F., & McMillen, D. P. (2002). The oppression of women and nature: Ecofeminism as a framework for an expanded ecological social work. *Families in Society, 83*(3), 221–233.

Blake, W. (1789). *Auguries of innocence*. Retrieved, from: http://www.online-literature.com/blake.

Bowen, M. (1978). *Family therapy in clinical practice*. New York: Jason Aronson.

Bower, B. (2001, August 11). Brains in dreamland. *Science News*. Retrieved, from http://www.thefreelibrary.com/Brains in Dreamland Scientists hope to raise the neural curtain on...-a077557195

Bowlby, J. (1958). The nature of the child's tie to his mother. *International Journal of Psychoanalysis, 33*, 350–373.

Boylan, J., & Dalrymple, J., (2009). *Understanding advocacy for children and young people*. Berkshire, England: Open University Press.

Bricker-Jenkins, M., & Joseph, B. (2008). Progressive social work. In T. Mizrahi & L. E. Davis (Eds.), *Encyclopedia of social work* (20th ed.)., (pp. 434–443). New York: Oxford University Press.

Bricker-Jenkins, M. & Netting, F. (2009). Feminist issues and practices in social work. In A. Roberts (Ed.), *Social worker's desk reference* (2nd ed., pp. 277–283). New York: Oxford University Press.

Canda, E. R. (2006). The significance of spirituality for resilient response to chronic illness: A qualitative study of adults with cystic fibrosis. In D. Saleebey (Ed.), *The strengths perspective in social work practice* (4th ed.) (pp. 61–76). Boston: Allyn and Bacon.

Cappeliez, P., Beaupré, M., & Robitaille, A. (2008). Characteristics and impact of life turning points for older adults. *Ageing International, 32,* 54–64.

Chase-Marshall, J. (1976). Virginia Satir: Everybody's family therapist. *Human Behavior* (September), 25–31.

Conroy, P. (2003). *My losing season.* New York: Doubleday.

Cooley, C. (1983). *Social organization: A study of the larger mind.* New Brunswick, NJ: Transaction. Original work published in 1909.

Council on Social Work Education (CSWE). (2008). *Educational policy and accreditation standards.* Alexandria, VA: Author.

Dalrymple, J., & Burke, B. (1995). *Anti-oppressive practice: Social care and the law.* Buckingham, UK: Open University Press.

Dickens, C. (1996). *David Copperfield.* London: Penguin Classics. Original work published in 1869.

Dominelli, L. (2002). *Anti-oppressive social work theory and practice.* Hampshire, UK: Palgrave.

DuBois, B., & Miley, K. K. (2007). *Social work: An empowering profession* (6th ed.). Boston: Allyn and Bacon.

Dulmus, C. (2002). Cognitive variables as factors in human growth and development. In J. Wodarski & S. F. Dziegielewski (Eds.), *Human behavior and the social environment: Integrating theory and evidence-based practice* (pp. 64–83). New York: Springer.

Ellis, A. (1962). *Reason and emotion in psychotherapy.* Secaucus, NJ: Lyle Stuart.

Ellis, A., McInerney, J., DiGiuseppe, R., & Yeager, R. (1988). *Rational-emotive therapy with alcohol and substance abusers.* New York: Pergamon.

Erikson, E. (1950/1963). *Childhood and society* (2nd ed.). New York: Norton.

Farley, O. W., Smith, L., Boyle, S., & Ronnau, J. (2002). A review of foundation MSW human behavior courses. *Journal of Human Behavior in the Social Environment, 6*(2), 1–12.

Freire, P. (1973). *Education for critical consciousness.* New York: Seabury Press.

Freud, S. (1961) *Civilization and its discontents.* (J. Strachey, Trans.). New York: Norton. Original work published in 1929.

Freud, S. (1966). *The ego and the mechanisms of defense.* New York: International Universities Press. Original work published in 1936.

Freud, S. (1999). *The interpretation of dreams* (J. Crick, Trans.). New York: Oxford University Press. Original work published in 1900.

Fromm, E. (1955). *The sane society.* Greenwich, CT: Fawcett.

Fromm, E. (1968). *The revolution of hope.* New York: Harper and Row.

Frost, R. (1969). The road not taken. In E. Lathem (Ed.), *The poetry of Robert Frost: The collected poems, complete and unabridged* (p. 105). New York: Henry Holt and Co. Original work published in 1916.

Germain, C., & Gitterman, A. (1980). *Life model of social work practice.* New York: Columbia University Press.

Gibbs, L. (2009). How social workers can do more good than harm. In A. R. Roberts (Ed.), *Social workers' desk reference* (2nd ed., pp. 168–173). New York: Oxford University Press.

Gibbs, L., & Gambrill, E. (2009). *Critical thinking for helping professionals: A skills-based workbook.* New York: Oxford University Press.

Gilligan, C. (1982). *In a different voice: Psychological theory and women's development.* Cambridge, MA: Harvard University Press.

Gordon, W. E. (1969). Basic constructs for an integrative and generative conception of social work. In G. Hearn (Ed.), *The general systems approach: Contributions toward the holistic conception of social work.* New York: Council on Social Education.

Green, A. (2003, October 13). The human condition: Ageless, guiltless. *New Yorker,* 42–43.

Greene, R. (2009). General systems theory. In R. Greene (Ed.), *Human behavior theory and social work practice* (3rd ed., pp. 165–197). New Brunswick, NJ: Aldine Transaction.

Greene, R.& Uebel, M. (2009). Classical psychoanalytic thought, contemporary developments, and clinical social work. In R. Greene (Ed.), *Human behavior theory and social work practice* (2nd ed., pp. 57–84). New Brunswick, NJ: Aldine Transaction.

Gutiérrez, L. M., & Lewis, E. A. C. (1999a). Empowering women of color. New York: Columbia University Press.

Gutiérrez, L. M., & Lewis, E. A. C. (1999b). Empowerment: A model for practice. In L. M. Gutiérrez & E. A. Lewis (Eds.), *Empowering women of color* (pp. 3–23). New York: Columbia University Press.

Gutiérrez, L. M., Parsons, R., & Cox, E. (2003). *Empowerment in social work practice: A sourcebook* (2nd ed.). Belmont, CA: Wadsworth.

Gutiérrez, L., Zuñiga, M., & Lum, D. (2004). *Educating students for multicultural practice.* Alexandria VA: CSWE Press.

Haight, W., & Taylor, E. H. (2007). *Human behavior for social work practice: A developmental-ecological framework*. Chicago: Lyceum.

Hansen, M. (2005, September 15). Ready to make home in Des Moines after leaving high-water hell. *Des Moines Register*, B1.

Hartman, A. (1990). Many ways of knowing. *Social Work, 35*(1), 3–4.

Hilarski, C., Dziegielewski, S. F., & Wodarski, J. (2002). Mezzo and macro perspectives: Group variables in human growth and development. In J. Wodarski & S. F. Dziegielewski (Eds.), *Human behavior and the social environment: Integrating theory and evidence-based practice* (pp. 141–156). New York: Springer.

hooks, b. (1994). *Teaching to transgress: Education as the practice of freedom*. New York: Routledge.

Horney, K. (1939). *New ways in psychoanalysis*. New York: Norton.

Hutchison, E. (2008). *Dimensions of human behavior: Person and environment* (3rd ed.). Thousand Oaks, CA: Sage.

Johnson, E. (2004). The role of families in buffering stress in persons with mental illness: A correlation study. In A. Roberts & K. Yeager (Eds.), *Evidence-based practice manual: Research and outcome measures in health and human services* (pp. 844–857). New York: Oxford University Press.

Kirst-Ashman, K. K. (2009). *Introduction to social work and social welfare: Critical thinking perspectives*. (3rd ed.). Belmont, CA: Brooks/Cole.

Kondrat, M. E. (2002). Actor-centered social work: Re-visioning "person-in-environment" through a critical theory lens. *Social Work, 47*(4), 435–446.

Lee, J. (2001). *The empowerment approach to social work practice: Building the beloved community* (2nd ed.). New York: Columbia University Press.

Ligon, J. (2009). Fundamentals of brief treatment. In A. R. Roberts (Ed.), *Social workers' desk reference* (2nd ed., pp. 215–225). New York: Oxford University Press.

Mary, N. L. (2008). *Social work in a sustainable world*. Chicago: Lyceum.

McMillen, J. C. (1999). Better for it: How people benefit from adversity. *Social Work, 44*(5), 455–468.

Merton, R. K. (1967). On sociological theories of the middle range. In R. K. Merton (Ed.), *On theoretical sociology: Five essays old and new* (pp. 39–72). New York: Free Press.

Miller, I., & Miller, R. A. (2003, August/September). From helix to hologram: An ode on the human genome. *Nexus Magazine,* pp. 1–7.

Miller, W. R. (1996). Motivational interviewing: Research, practice, and puzzles. *Addictive Behaviors, 21*(6), 835–842.

Miller, W. R., & Rollnick, S. (2002). *Motivational interviewing: Preparing people to change addictive behavior*. The Guilford Press: New York.

Mullaly, B. (2007). *The new structural social work* (3rd ed.). New York: Oxford University Press.

National Association of Social Workers (NASW). (1996). *Code of ethics*. Washington, DC: Author.

Obama, B. (1995). *Dreams of my father: A story of race and inheritance*. New York: Three Rivers Press.

O'Reilley, M. R. (2000). *The barn at the end of the world*. Minneapolis, MN: Milkweed Editions.

Palmer, P. J. (2007). *The courage to teach: Exploring the inner landscape of a teacher's life: The 10th anniversary edition*. San Francisco: Jossey-Boss.

Palmer, P. J. (2008). *The promise of paradox: A celebration of contradiction in the Christian life*. Hoboken, NJ: Wiley and Sons.

Payne, M. (2005). *Modern social work theory* (3rd ed.). Chicago: Lyceum.

Polansky, N. (1986). There is nothing so practical as a good theory. *Child Welfare, 65*(1), 3–15.

Prochaska, J., & Norcross, J. (2010). *Systems of psychotherapy: A transtheoretical analysis* (7th ed.). Belmont, CA: Brooks/Cole.

Project MATCH Research Group. (1997). Matching alcoholism treatment to client heterogeneity. *Journal of Studies on Alcohol, 58*, 7–28.

Rapp, C. A. (1998). *The strengths model: Case management with people suffering from severe and persistent mental illness*. New York: Oxford University Press.

Rapp, C. A., & Goscha, R. (2006). *The strengths model: Case management with people with psychiatric disabilities* (2nd ed.) New York: Oxford University Press.

Reynolds, B. (1963). *An uncharted journey*. New York: Citadel.

Robbins, S., Chatterjee, P., & Canda, E. (2006). *Contemporary human behavior theory: A critical perspective for social work* (2nd ed.) Boston: Allyn and Bacon.

Rönkä, A., Oravala, S., & Pulkkinen, L. (2002). "I met this wife of mine and things got onto a better track": Turning points in risk development. *Journal of Adolescence, 25*, 47–63.

Rothery, M. (2005). Ecological theory. In F. Turner (Ed.), *Encyclopedia of Canadian social work* (pp. 111–112). Waterloo, Ontario: Wilfred Laurier University Press.

Saleebey, D. (Ed.). (1992). *The strengths perspective in social work practice*. Boston: Allyn and Bacon.

Saleebey, D. (2001). *Human behavior and social environments: A biopsychosocial approach*. New York: Columbia University Press.

Saleebey, D. (2006). Introduction: Power to the people. In D. Saleebey (Ed.), *The strengths perspective in social work practice* (4th ed., pp. 1–24). Boston: Allyn and Bacon.

Samenow, S. (1984). *Inside the criminal mind*. New York: Times Books.

Samenow, S. (2007). *The myth of the out of character criminal*. Westport, CT: Praeger.

Schriver, J. (2010). *Human behavior and the social environment: Shifting paradigms in essential knowledge for social work practice* (5th ed.). Boston: Prentice Hall.

Shorter Oxford English Dictionary. (2007). New York: Oxford University Press.

Simon, B. (1994). *The empowerment tradition in American social work: A history*. New York: Columbia University Press.

Solomon, B. (1976). *Black empowerment: Social work in oppressed communities*. New York: Columbia University Press.

Turner, F. (1996). An interlocking perspective for treatment. In F. Turner (Ed.), *Social work treatment: Interlocking theoretical perspectives* (pp. 699–706). New York: Free Press.

Van Voorhis, R. M. (2009). Feminist theories and social work practice. In R. Greene (Ed.), *Human behavior theory and social work practice* (3rd ed., pp. 265–290). New Brunswick, NJ: Aldine Transaction.

van Wormer, K. (2004). Confronting oppression, restoring justice: From policy analysis to social action. Alexandria, VA: Council on Social Work Education.

van Wormer, K., & Davis, D. R. (2008). *Addiction treatment: A strengths perspective* (2nd ed.). Belmont, CA: Wadsworth.

Vonk, E., Bordnick, P., & Graap, K. (2004). Cognitive-behavioral therapy with posttraumatic stress disorder: An evidence-based approach. In A. R. Roberts & K. R. Yeager (Eds.), *Evidence-based practice manual* (pp. 303–312). New York: Oxford University Press.

Vourlekis, B. (2008). Cognitive theory for social work practice. In R. Greene (Ed.), *Human behavior theory and social work practice* (3rd ed., pp. 133–163). New Brunswick, NJ: Aldine Transaction.

Weishaar, M. E. (2004). A cognitive-behavioral approach to suicide risk reduction in crisis intervention. In A. R. Roberts & K. R. Yeager (Eds.), *Evidence-based practice manual* (pp. 749–757). New York: Oxford University Press.

Wierzynski, C., Lubenov, E., Gu, M., & Siapas, A. (2009). State-dependent spike-timing relationships between hippocampal and prefrontal circuits during sleep. *Neuron, 61*(4), 587–596.

Wilber, K. (1995). *Sex, biology, spirituality: The spirit of evolution*. Boston: Shambala.

Wilde, O. (1968). *Lady Windermere's fan*. Lines from act 3, cited in J. Bartlett (1968), *Familiar quotations* (14th ed.). Boston: Little, Brown. Original work published in 1892.

Zastrow, C., & Kirst-Ashman, K. K. (2010). *Understanding human behavior and the social environment* (8th ed.). Belmont, CA: Wadsworth.

Biological Factors in Human Behavior

Nobody doubts that genes can shape anatomy. The idea that they also shape behavior takes a lot more swallowing.

—MATT RIDLEY

Genome

A crucial component in much that is human is biology. Many departments of social work require a course in human biology consistent with the recommendation of the Council on Social Work Education (CSWE, 2008) that the curriculum provide "knowledge from the liberal arts to understand biological, social, cultural, psychological, and spiritual development" (p. 6). Such course material is rarely linked to human behavior, however, much less to social work practice. So, although the "bio" portion of the biopsychosocial/spiritual configuration is included in theory, it is often omitted from the actual person-in-environment transaction. Rosemary Farmer (2009), in her new book, *Neuroscience and Social Work Practice*, refers to the knowledge that is emerging from neuroscience as "a missing link for social work" (p. 1). Yet such insights about the workings of the brain in interaction with forces from the environment can be of direct benefit in improving our understanding of human behavior.

An ecosystems perspective, with its focus on interactionism among systems of all sizes and the guiding concept of adaptation by biological species, sensitizes social workers to the effects of genes, both normal and abnormal, on human behavior. The exposure of parents to environmental hazards, including radiation, alcohol, and other chemicals, on the developing fetus is a natural concern of social workers as well (Riley, 2009).

The intent of this chapter is to bring biology and the biological system into the equation and to explore the link between mind and body. A basic assumption is that human behavior is the result of both cause and effect of certain biological conditions that exist or develop. A second basic assumption is that nature and nurture are intertwined. (A parallel chapter of the companion volume in this series discusses the impact of the *physical* environment—clean air and water, as well as uncontaminated and abundant plant and marine life—on human populations.)

Although the professional concerns of social workers lie generally in the areas of psychosocial situations, biology greatly affects the way people handle those situations. The situations themselves may stem from biological origins, such as physiological attributes. Saleebey (2001) explains this best: "We are, after all, animals—members of a species—and we bring into the world, encoded in our bodies, not only the history of our species, but the history of our family. We carry, remarkably, in each of our cells, our history, and our future unfolding. Environment and experience play a powerful part in this drama, but sometimes we fail to give the body—our biology—its due" (p. 18).

Medical research is discovering that conditions once believed to be entirely environmental in origin actually have genetic roots and vice versa. This chapter begins with a look at genetic factors in our personalities, our capabilities, and our very humanness. Then we turn to a related issue, the study of brain chemistry (especially neurotransmitters) and the role it plays in much of human behavior. Since all human behavior is viewed here as operating along a continuum, both normal and abnormal behaviors are discussed. An overview of recent findings about the workings of the brain with regard to causes and effects of chemical addiction is provided. Since the topic of addiction is a major research area in terms of both neurology and treatment intervention, a major focus of this chapter is addictions research.

The final sections are devoted to a discussion of the biology of gender, constitutional temperament, and the mental conditions of schizophrenia and bipolar disorder. The chapter concludes with a consideration of ethical issues related to biological and especially biogenetic knowledge. Even more so than the other chapters of this book, the material for this discourse is drawn from recent scientific, medical, and other empirical research. This material is highlighted by excerpts from personal narratives and published memoirs.

The Genetic Factor

Genetics is the study of hereditary characteristics carried from one generation to the next. Human development, physical functioning, and behavior result from the interaction of genes and the environment (Riley, 2009). The etiology of mental disorders, general health problems, aggressive and shy behavior, risk taking and addictive behaviors, and the aging process itself is largely genetic. The exact nature of the relationship between genetics and human biology is not known, but the great adventure of the Human Genome Project to map the genes of the human body began in 1990 and was completed in 2003. The results of this groundbreaking project, which is funded by the National Institutes of Health, have contributed to our understanding of the specific roles that genes play in the biological functioning of human beings (Ginsberg, Nackerud, & Larrison, 2004; for the latest findings on this ongoing research, see http://www.genome.gov).

The term *genome* is a combination of the words *gene* and *chromosome* and refers to all of the genes in an organism taken together (Riley, 2009). The research goal of the Human Genome Project was to identify and sequence all of the genes in human DNA. Genes are tiny units of inheritance located in every cell of our body and contain our DNA (Weiss, 2004). Each cell in the body has the same constellation of genes. This project, which produced a human DNA blueprint and mapped the entire genetic material of human beings, estimates that each of us has approximately 24,000 genes. This number is far below the original estimate. Since the mapping of the genes has been completed, rapid advances in gene scanning technology have identified genes linked to cancer, arthritis, diabetes, Alzheimer's disease, and many other diseases. Once the genetic links are identified, researchers can work on strategies for disease prevention and developing effective treatments. As an example of some of the exciting research that is being done, Uhl, Drgon et al. (2008) used a powerful new technique for identifying genes that are associated with diseases, to link at least 89 genes to drug abuse and dependence. Most of the 89 genes were located in the brain and associated with substance dependence among both European Americans and African Americans, although some appeared to affect risk in only one ethnic group. Many of the genes identified in the study were associated with addiction to several different drugs.

These findings help explain why some individuals are highly susceptible to a number of addictions, while others seemingly have more control over their use of addictive products.

The ability to understand the role of genetics in human health and disease is a tremendous leap forward toward prevention, treatment, and potential cures. According to Greco (2003), the leap takes us from the "old genetics" to the "new genetics." In the past, the focus was on hereditary disorders such as cystic fibrosis or sickle cell anemia, which result from the mutation of a single gene. More and more, common maladies such as heart disease, diabetes, cancer, Alzheimer's disease, depression, schizophrenia, and autism have been found to have a genetic component (Weiss, 2004). The social work conceptualization of person-in-environment—the person and environment in constant interaction—is borne out beautifully in the findings of the Human Genome Project because researchers, Greco (2003) states, are now studying the interrelated effects of biological and environmental factors. It is often difficult, in fact, to tell which influences the other. Take cigarette smoking, for example. In families that are genetically predisposed to certain types of cancer, Greco reports that children and siblings who smoked were at very high risk when compared to individuals with the same genotype who did not smoke. So the cancer is a result both of genetic predisposition and personal behavior. We are learning more all the time about such interconnections.

Similarly, genetic variations in people determine the effectiveness or risks involved in taking prescribed drugs. We can consider height as an example. The range of possible heights for an individual is genetically determined, but diet and health influence the actual height achieved. The situation with intelligence is similar. One's potential to achieve high intelligence is determined by one's genetic predisposition in combination with personal experience. Consider also the damage done to genes by high-level radiation and poisonous chemicals such as depleted uranium, dioxin, and Agent Orange. What new genetic understandings mean for the future is a revolution in health care—a new focus on minimizing risk

once relevant genetic information has been obtained (Badzek, Turner, & Jenins, 2008; Greco, 2003). Since individual genes are only a piece of the puzzle in health and illness, current research is focused on looking at the entire genome to identify contributors to common diseases (Badzek et al., 2008). The Social and Behavioral Research Branch of the National Human Genome Project (2009) reveals the social implications of the research that is currently underway:

> The Social and Behavioral Research Branch (SBRB) has the overarching and broad objective to investigate social and behavioral factors that facilitate the translation of genomic discoveries for health promotion, disease prevention, and health care improvements. This research encompasses four conceptual domains: (1) testing the effectiveness of strategies for communicating information about genetic risks; (2) developing and evaluating behavioral interventions; (3) using genomic discoveries in clinical practice; and (4) understanding the social, ethical, and policy implications of genomic research.

The study of hereditary factors goes back to plant and animal studies of the nineteenth century. Darwin's great insight into certain aspects of human behavior dealt with genetic variability, which refers to the variation in heritable traits of a species and leads to natural selection of the fittest. This means that the members of a species who develop traits that are best adapted to the environment live and produce offspring with those traits (Saleebey, 2001). In the popularized and popular book *Genome: The Autobiography of a Species in 23 Chapters*, Ridley (2006) provides a striking example of genetic adaptability to the environment by ethnic groups isolated for long periods. The ability to regularly drink alcohol without developing dependency, which most people acquired in countries where water was unsanitary, resulted from thousands of years of selection of people who could do so. Nomadic peoples in Australia and North America, however, who lived where water was safe, did not require alcohol and developed no resistance to its effects. Such changes have developed through a long evolutionary process (Ginsberg, Nackerud, & Larrison, 2004).

In addition to hereditary factors, the role of intrauterine factors, including hormones, can have profound consequences. Intrauterine exposure to testosterone can masculinize a child and affect the development of sexual orientation and even aspects of learning such as spatial abilities. Rahman and Wilson (2003) tested 60 heterosexual women, 60 lesbians, 60 heterosexual men, and 60 gay men. Results showed that gay men and women performed less well than heterosexual men on cognitive tests of special skill but superior on language tests. More obviously, intrauterine exposure to high levels of alcohol, which is the leading known cause of mental retardation, can cause irreversible brain damage.

Drinking during pregnancy can lead to a range of physical, learning, and behavioral effects in the developing brain, the most serious of which is a collection of symptoms known as fetal alcohol syndrome (FAS). Children with FAS may have distinct facial features (see Figure 2.1). FAS infants have a low birth weight, a small head, a small brain, and characteristic facial features such as wide-set eyes and flattened noses (Andreasen, 2001). Their brains

may have less volume, and they may have fewer brain cells (i.e., neurons) or fewer neurons that are able to function correctly, leading to long-term problems in learning and behavior.

Much of what we are and look like is, of course, determined by the genes we inherit. Temperament, including timidity or tendency toward aggression, is highly hereditary as well (Begley, 2007; Harris, 2009). Genes are implicated in predispositions to certain diseases (e.g., alcoholism, asthma, breast cancer, hypertension, schizophrenia). But nature and nurture, Saleebey (2001) suggests, go hand in hand. How we react to our inborn characteristics determines to a large degree their significance and meaning.

Nature Versus Nurture

Harriette Johnson (2004) traces the paradigm shifts in professional beliefs about mental disorders over time. In the early 1900s most psychiatrists in Europe and the United States saw these disorders as illnesses of the brain. Freud's work led to a focus on childhood experience such as trauma and repression by the mother as key causative factors in psychological problems. From the 1970s to the 1980s, family systems theorists saw the "ill" family member

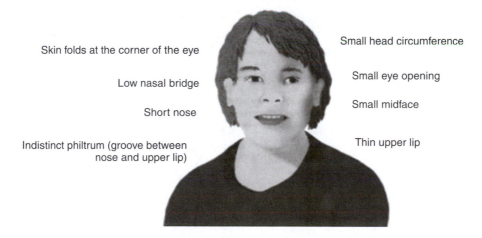

Figure 2.1. Craniofacial features associated with fetal alcohol syndrome. From Warren, K. R., and Foudin, L. L. (2001). Alcohol related birth defects—The past, present, and future. *Alcohol Research & Health*, 25(3): 153–158. Courtesy of the NIAAA website (http://www.niaaa.nih.gov/Resources/GraphicsGallery/FetalAlcoholSyndrome/FetalAlcohol.htm).

as a "symptom carrier" for the dysfunctional family. This view was widely accepted by mental health practitioners to the extent that most treatment focused on the "contribution" the mother made to the child's symptoms.

A shift in emphasis from nurture (the focus was on lack of parental nurturing) to nature accompanied the discovery of antipsychotic medication, which revolutionized treatment. Then the development of brain-scanning techniques brought the history of theories about mental disorders full circle to the beliefs of the pre-Freudians. Equipped with a mass of scientific data, neuroscientists could now show that psychiatric disorders were rooted in biological diseases of the brain, not in toxic family relations. However, as Johnson points out, mental health practitioners are just now beginning to incorporate this new knowledge into the biopsychosocial and systems perspectives.

Today, stories in both the popular media and scientific journals proclaim that every form of human behavior—from criminality to addictive disorders to sexual orientation—is less a matter of choice than of genetic destiny. In his analysis of the genome, Ridley (2006) errs on the side of biological determinism. In a chapter ironically titled "Free Will," he summarizes studies of criminal records of adoptees in Denmark that show a high correlation with the unlawful behavior of adoptees whose biological parent also committed illegal acts and a low correlation with such behavior by the adopting parent. He further refers to research on battered children who grew up to emulate abusive biological parents but not abusive stepparents. "The assumption that parents shape the personality and culture of their children," he concludes, "is mere dogma" (p. 305).

Yet in all of these developmental phenomena the effects of life experience cannot be overlooked. This ongoing research is assessing not only the genome structure but also the influence of other variables, such as environmental factors, on genetically based diseases (Badzek et al., 2008). Even the development of various forms of mental illness, which is generally conceded to have strong biological and genetic components, is related to environmental elements as well. This includes exposure to

harmful substances and/or traumatic experiences. Family and twin studies provide evidence not only of genetic contributions to a wide range of behaviors and personality traits but also of the role of factors external to the self. Thus, the nature-nurture controversy cannot easily be resolved.

To differentiate the impact of genes and environment, researchers have turned to studies of identical twins who were separated at birth. The ongoing University of Minnesota research on twins who were raised apart, often in different countries, reveals uncanny similarities, as well as significant differences in character and behavior (Markon, Krueger, Bouchard, & Gottesman, 2002). Harris (2009) refers to some of the case histories that have emerged from this research as "spooky." Research on twins from around the world (fraternal twins reared together, compared to identical twins) reveal strong likenesses among identical twins in the amount of body fat, attention-deficit disorder, political attitudes, pessimism, and religiosity (Harris, 2009; Newman & Newman, 2006). In the Minnesota study of 74 identical twins separated at birth, Markon and colleagues (2002) found high correlations on a number of abnormal personality traits as measured on the Minnesota Multiphasic Personality Inventory (MMPI). Another University of Minnesota study of personality traits in 180 twins who were reared separately reveals the salience of personality factors in such twins, factors evidenced in how their upbringing was recalled (Krueger, Markon, & Bouchard, 2003). The authors explain these findings by positing that the twins' personality traits (e.g., an easy-going, positive outlook) helped shape their childhood environments. Personality genes, according to these researchers, influence the way people mold and recall their family environments. Even when there were differences in some aspects of the environments, these dissimilarities were not reflected in personality measures. Heredity, rather than family rearing, was thus seen by the authors as the primary factor in the determination of personality.

Some researchers familiar with the same twin study, however, stress the nurturance side of the equation. Ginsberg, Nackerud, and Larrison

(2004), for example, correctly point out that attempts to find single-gene inheritance for schizophrenia, bipolar disorder, and depression have been futile. They hypothesize that the underlying genetic disposition for these disorders may actually consist of a number of genes that are triggered by certain environmental cues such as trauma. The Human Genome Project bears this out. With regard to twins, in about half of all cases of conditions such as schizophrenia, only one of the siblings develops the disease. And in animal research described by Begley (2007), rats that are licked and groomed a lot can handle stress better later than rats that are not licked as much. These findings are indicative of the truism that it is a case not of either/or—either nature or nurture—but a case of both/and. (Nurture can also include the environment in the womb and prenatal nourishment, as we will see later.) Greg Gibson (2009), takes an interactionist perspective, as well, in his small, easy-to-read volume, *It Takes a Genome*. Compared to Ridley's formulation, this one is more in tune with social work's holistic perspective. As Gibson suggests, the genetic tendency toward introversion and other personality traits is grounded in complex interactions between natural predispositions and the social environment. Relevant to diseases, Gibson indicates that genes fashioned for living in the Stone Age are not well suited to modern living and modern diets of processed food. Our genome, he argues, is out of equilibrium with our carcinogenic-inducing environment.

Genes and Addiction

In testimony before the House Subcommittee on Labor, Health and Human Services, and Education, T. R. Insel (2005), director of the National Institute of Mental Health, submitted the following information: "Mental and substance abuse disorders are inherently intertwined with co-occurring diagnoses of substance abuse and mental disorders. . . . Substance use disorders are especially prevalent in individuals with schizophrenia (47%), bipolar disorder (45%), anxiety (25%), and major depression (24%)" (p. 2). An earlier study of

more than 20,000 people in mental hospitals, nursing homes, and prisons found that 53 percent of those who used chemical substances had a mental disorder such as schizophrenia, anxiety, or major depression (Holloway, 1991).

In their review of the literature, Brady and Sinha (2005) similarly found that 45–86 percent of men and women with substance use disorders also had at least one co-occurring psychiatric disorder and that the risk relationship appeared to be reciprocal. These findings of dual disorders in the same person suggest an underlying biological vulnerability for a number of disabilities. This susceptibility is interactive in that it involves a biological predisposition to overreact to stress in combination with a high-risk, nonprotective, stressful environment (Brady & Sinha, 2005; Johnson, 2004). Brady and Sinha's model is based in part on animal studies showing that early life stresses and chronic crisis result in long-term changes in stress responses. Such changes can alter the dopamine system's response to stress and can increase susceptibility to self-administration of mood-altering substances.

The usual inquiry into whether the mental disorder or the addiction came first may thus be futile. Similarly, the specific vulnerability may not be to alcohol dependence but rather to problems with a number of substances. A brain susceptibility to addiction itself may prevail. Several genes, for example, have been implicated in recent genetic research on the susceptibility of alcoholics and other addicts to both schizophrenia and depression (Insel, 2005).

Although the *Diagnostic and Statistical Manual of Mental Disorders* (*DSM-IV-TR;* American Psychiatric Association [APA], 2000) dichotomizes substance dependence and substance abuse for purposes of classification, the most recent genetics research indicates that the tendency toward addiction, like varieties of mental illness, exists along a continuum (Helmuth, 2003). A gene that relates to risk taking and impulsiveness, for example, is found to vary along a continuum from healthy behavior to high risk taking to extremes, with heroin addicts having the gene for extreme novelty-seeking behavior. The new research gives scientific support to long-standing claims that alcoholism and other addictions are intergenerational.

Diane Rae Davis (2009) summarizes the new research on biological factors relevant to compulsive gambling. Brain studies of persons who are addicted to gambling point to deficits in the brain's ability to shift attention and a diminished capacity to weigh in negative consequences. Impulsivity is common to both substance abusers and compulsive gamblers. A few big wins accelerate the gambling addiction because of the surge of dopamine that ensues from winning against considerable odds. It is the seeking of this high that is the basis of the addiction and of the seemingly irrational behavior of sitting for hours at a slot machine or dealing a hand of cards. As one woman, quoted by Davis, said of her gambling, "It became my sex, it became my lover, it became my mother" (p. 45). Compulsive gambling is highly correlated with problems with alcohol, heavy smoking, depression, bipolar disorder, and a history of problem gambling among family members.

Why does alcoholism seem to run in families? Is alcoholic behavior learned or inherited? Why is it that one person can drink and use drugs moderately over a lifetime while another person gets hooked after a short period of time? Why does the alcoholic tend to smoke and have a high tolerance for many of the depressant drugs? The search for genetic links began in earnest in the early 1970s with adoption studies in Scandinavia. The aim of these studies was to distinguish environmental from hereditary determinants. Goodwin (1976) sought an answer by interviewing 133 Danish men who had been adopted as small children and raised by nonalcoholics. Health records were used to substantiate the interviews. The findings are striking: The biological sons of alcoholics were four times as likely to have alcohol problems as the children of nonalcoholics. That result helped put to rest the popular assumption that alcoholics take up drinking simply because they learned it at home or turned to it because of abuse suffered at the hands of an alcoholic parent.

In Sweden, the research undertaken by Cloninger, Sigvardsson, Gilligan, and colleagues (1989) has helped clarify the role of both environment and heredity in the development of alcoholism. In the early 1980s, Cloninger joined a team of Swedish researchers and began gathering extensive data on a large group of adopted-away sons of alcoholics. Sweden was chosen, as Denmark before, because of the availability of thorough government records on every citizen. In their study of 259 male adoptees with alcoholic biological fathers (out of a total of 862 male adoptees), it was found that a significantly larger proportion of the adoptees with alcoholic fathers were registered with Swedish authorities for alcohol-related problems than were adoptees with nonalcoholic fathers.

The Swedish study also made a comparison of children raised in the homes of alcoholic fathers with children of alcoholic fathers raised in other adoptive homes. In both instances approximately one-third of the children were identified as having developed alcoholism. Alcohol misuse in the adoptive parents, however, was not a determinant of alcohol misuse in the sons. The adopted men were also subdivided according to the frequency and severity of their registered misuse. Herein lies the major significance of the study: The findings indicate that there is more than one kind of alcoholism and that one form, which developed quickly in middle childhood with the first drink, was highly hereditary—father to son. However, the results also seemed to show that even with an alcoholic biological father, environmental factors came into play in preventing the onset of this disease.

In conclusion, there is no one genetic marker that predicts who will become alcohol dependent. As with other genetic disorders, Schuckit (2000) cautions, it is likely that a variety of genetic characteristics, in combination with key environmental factors, contributes to the risk of addiction.

Brain Research and Human Behavior

The truth of interactionism is shown most strikingly in studies of the impact of sensory input in changing the brain. Among musicians and blind Braille readers, for example, years of tactile movements of a certain sort are reflected in brain functioning, a difference that can be viewed via the new technologies. The implications of Schwartz and Begley's (2003) book, *The Mind and the Brain: Neuroplasticity and the Power of Mental Force*, are profound: The brain has the ability to rewire itself. This phenomenon is revealed in experimentation with stroke victims, people with dyslexia, and even thinking exercises as described by Schwartz and Begley in their groundbreaking research.

Such new insights, Schwartz and Begley (2003) inform us, herald a revolution in the treatment of depression, addictions, obsessive-compulsive disorders, and even psychological trauma. What we are learning from recent research explains why certain therapies are effective—for example, work with stroke victims in redirecting activities to undamaged regions of the brain, as well as cognitive therapy for alcoholics and persons suffering from obsessive-compulsive disorders to help them replace irrational thoughts and obsessions with healthy thoughts. Self-help groups such as Alcoholics Anonymous (AA) have relied on this approach for years in teaching slogans such as "easy does it" and "one day at a time" to curb addicts' tendency to take their thinking to extremes. We knew these methods worked but did not know why. Now we know more about the impact of cognitive mechanisms. These discoveries from brain studies further reinforce our awareness of the interconnectedness of the biological and psychological dimensions of human behavior. This interconnectedness is most obvious in the effect of psychotropic medications on mental disorders such as psychosis. If we can unravel the secrets of the brain, we can understand the forces that drive humans into paths of destructiveness, as well as their cravings, passions, and dreams.

Today we may not know all of the answers, but for the first time neuroscientists, using magnetic resonance imaging (MRI), have learned that the brains of people with schizophrenia are smaller than those of people without the disease and that they have smaller frontal lobes, the part of the brain responsible for planning and decision making (Kolb & Whishaw, 2008).

Moreover, scientists have captured images of the brain of addicts in the throes of craving a drug. It is this craving that is the root of addiction itself, the craving that sends people back into the abyss of the gambling den, the bar, and the crack house again and again.

The Brain and Addictive Behavior

Substance abuse counselors today are increasingly aware of the *bio* component of the addiction equation. Knowledge of the biology of addiction is crucial for an understanding of the hold that certain chemicals or behaviors have on people, the cravings that grip them, and the health problems associated with substance misuse. Thanks to advances in technology, namely, the development of positron emission tomography (PET) and functional magnetic resonance imaging (fMRI), scientists can capture chemical images of the brain at work; moreover, they can observe not only structures but also actual functions or processes of the living brain.

Low levels of the neurotransmitter serotonin are linked to both addiction and aggression (Science Daily, 2007). When individuals self-medicate with cocaine, for example, the brain adapts to the artificially induced highs, and an unbearable craving for the drug results. Thus, the biochemistry of the brain is a factor in addiction with regard to both its etiology and its continuation.

The actions of alcohol and cocaine that cause intoxication, dependency, and relentless craving during abstinence occur primarily in the brain. Two aspects of brain research are crucial for our understanding of addiction: First is the adaptation factor—how the brain adapts to and compensates for the abnormal signals generated by a drug. The second aspect, one we know far less about, concerns uniqueness in the brains of potentially addicted persons. Before coming to the innate differences in the way the brains of addicts respond to drugs—the genetic component—let us summarize what scientists know about the workings of the brain itself with regard to addiction.

The brain and the spinal cord together make up the central nervous system. Both are

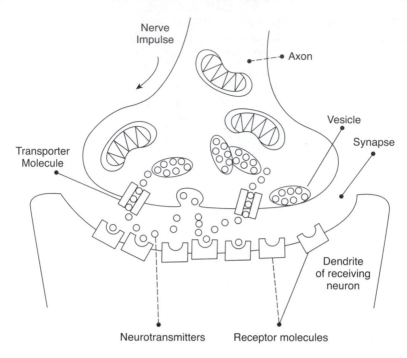

Figure 2.2. The nerve cell. Drawing courtesy of the NIDA website (http://www.nida.nih.gov/MOM/TG/momtg-introbg.html).

hollow structures filled with cerebral-spinal fluid. Each nerve cell of the brain is separated from its neighbor by a narrow gap called a *synapse*. Nerve cells communicate with one another via chemical messengers called *neurotransmitters*. Knowledge of the role of these natural opiates in the brain is important because neurotransmitters are the molecular precursors of behavior and response (Saleebey, 2001). Neurotransmitters underlie every thought and emotion, as well as memory and learning. A good half dozen out of some 50 of these transmitters are known to play a role in addiction (Figure 2.2).

Illicit drugs are popular because they "hijack" the brain. They are able to disrupt neurotransmitter functions because they resemble the chemical structure of the brain's own neurotransmitters (Lambert, 2000). Through the use of MRI technology, scientists can observe the dynamic changes that occur in the brain as an individual takes a drug. Researchers are now recording the brain changes that occur as

a person experiences the rush, or high, and later the craving for cocaine (National Institute on Drug Abuse [NIDA], 2008a). They can even identify parts of the brain—the pleasure circuits that become active when a cocaine addict sees stimuli such as drug paraphernalia—that trigger a craving for the drug. The memories of drug use are so enduring and powerful that even seeing a bare arm beneath a rolled-up sleeve reawakens the cue-induced craving. Biochemical abnormalities associated with chemical abuse trigger mechanisms that demand more of the harmful substances; this is the phenomenon known as addictive craving.

The addicted brain, we now realize, is significantly different from the normally functioning brain. Through long-term drug misuse, the depletion of the brain's natural opiates creates a condition ripe for the kind of relentless craving that is known to all "who have been there." Compounding the problem of molecular alterations in the brain (experienced as a general malaise) is the fact that each time a neurotransmitter such as dopamine floods a synapse through the introduction of a powerful drug like crack or methamphetamine ("meth") into the body, circuits that trigger pleasure are indelibly imprinted in the brain. Thus, when the smells, sights, and sounds associated with the memory are experienced, these "feeling memories" are aroused as well (Whitten, 2005). So palpable, in fact, are they that researchers can now distinguish the brain of an addict in a state of craving (elicited by these behavior feelings) from the brain of an addict in a stationary state (van Wormer & Davis, 2008). The situation is similar to Pavlov's dog salivating when it heard the bell ring, a bell associated with food. Relapse occurs, as every AA member knows, from visiting the old haunts of their drinking days ("slips occur in slippery places"). Now there is scientific proof for this folk wisdom about the importance of avoiding people, places, and things associated with past drug use.

NIDA InfoFacts: Methamphetamine

How Is Methamphetamine Abused?

Methamphetamine is a white, odorless, bitter-tasting crystalline powder that easily dissolves in water or alcohol and is taken orally, intranasally (snorting the powder), by needle injection, or by smoking.

How Does Methamphetamine Affect the Brain?

Methamphetamine increases the release and blocks the reuptake of the brain chemical (or neurotransmitter) dopamine, leading to high levels of the chemical in the brain, a common mechanism of action for most drugs of abuse. Dopamine is involved in reward, motivation, the experience of pleasure, and motor function. Methamphetamine's ability to rapidly release dopamine in reward regions of the brain produces the intense euphoria, or "rush," that many users feel after snorting, smoking, or injecting the drug.

Chronic methamphetamine abuse significantly changes how the brain functions. Noninvasive human brain imaging studies have shown alterations in the activity of the dopamine system that are associated with reduced motor skills and impaired verbal learning. Recent studies of chronic methamphetamine abusers have also revealed severe structural and functional changes in areas of the brain associated with emotion and memory, which may account for many of the emotional and cognitive problems observed in chronic methamphetamine abusers.

Repeated methamphetamine abuse can also lead to addiction—a chronic, relapsing disease, characterized by compulsive drug seeking and use, which is accompanied by chemical and molecular changes in the brain. Some of these changes persist long after methamphetamine abuse is stopped. Reversal of some of the changes, however, may be observed after sustained periods of abstinence (e.g., more than 1 year).

What Other Adverse Effects Does Methamphetamine Have on Health?

Taking even small amounts of methamphetamine can result in many of the same physical effects of other stimulants, such as cocaine or amphetamines, including increased wakefulness, increased physical activity, decreased appetite, increased respiration, rapid heart rate, irregular heartbeat, increased blood pressure, and hyperthermia. Long-term methamphetamine abuse has many negative health consequences, including extreme weight loss, severe dental problems ("meth mouth"), anxiety, confusion, insomnia, mood disturbances, and violent behavior. Chronic methamphetamine abusers can also display a number of psychotic features, including paranoia, visual and auditory hallucinations, and delusions (for example, the sensation of insects crawling under the skin).

Transmission of human immunodeficiency virus (HIV) and hepatitis B and C can be consequences of methamphetamine abuse. The intoxicating effects of methamphetamine, regardless of how it is taken, can also alter judgment and inhibition and lead people to engage in unsafe behaviors, including risky sexual behavior. Among abusers who inject the drug, HIV and other infectious diseases can be spread through contaminated needles, syringes, and other injection equipment that is used by more than one person. Methamphetamine abuse may also worsen the progression of HIV and its consequences. Studies of methamphetamine abusers who are HIV positive indicate that HIV causes greater neuronal injury and cognitive impairment for individuals in this group compared with HIV-positive people who do not use the drug

What Treatment Options Exist?

Currently, the most effective treatments for methamphetamine addiction are comprehensive cognitive-behavioral interventions. For example, the Matrix Model—a behavioral treatment approach that combines behavioral therapy, family education, individual counseling, 12-Step support, drug testing, and encouragement for non–drug-related activities—has been shown to be effective in reducing methamphetamine abuse. Contingency management interventions, which provide tangible incentives in exchange for engaging in treatment and maintaining abstinence, have also been shown to be effective. There are no medications at this time approved to treat methamphetamine addiction; however, this is an active area of research for NIDA.

(From NIDA, 2009.)

Alcohol, as a drug affecting the central nervous system, belongs in a class with barbiturates, minor tranquilizers, and general anesthetics—all depressants. Whereas at low levels of alcohol ingestion, an excitement phase may set in, including emotional expression that is uninhibited and erratic, later a gradual dullness and stupor may occur. The effect of the alcohol on motor activity is reflected in slurred speech, unsteady gait, and clumsiness. Functioning at a higher level—thinking, remembering, making judgments—is tangibly impaired by alcohol. Alcohol affects the brain at the cellular and biochemical levels, where the emotions are directly affected; the neurological consequences of long-term heavy alcohol and other drug abuse can be devastating, especially with regard to short-term memory loss.

Alcohol's Damaging Effects on the Brain

Up to 80 percent of alcoholics have a deficiency in thiamine, and some of these people will develop serious brain disorders such as Wernicke-Korsakoff syndrome (WKS). This is a disease that consists of two separate syndromes, a short-lived, severe condition called Wernicke's encephalopathy and a long-lasting, debilitating condition known as Korsakoff's psychosis.

The symptoms of Wernicke's encephalopathy include mental confusion, paralysis of the nerves that move the eyes (i.e., oculomotor disturbances), and impaired muscle coordination. For example, patients with Wernicke's encephalopathy may be too confused to find their way out of a room or may not even be able to walk. Many people with Wernicke's encephalopathy, however, do not exhibit all three of these signs and symptoms.

Of alcoholics with Wernicke's encephalopathy, 80–90 percent also develop Korsakoff's psychosis, a chronic and debilitating syndrome characterized by persistent learning and memory problems. Patients with Korsakoff's psychosis are forgetful and easily frustrated and have difficulty with walking and coordination. Although these patients have problems remembering old information (i.e., retrograde amnesia), it is their difficulty in holding on to new information (i.e., anterograde amnesia) that is striking. For example, these patients can discuss in detail an event in their lives but an hour later might not remember having done so.

The cerebellum, an area of the brain that coordinates movement and perhaps even some forms of learning, appears to be particularly sensitive to the effects of thiamine deficiency and is the region most frequently damaged in association with chronic alcohol consumption. Administering thiamine helps to improve brain function, especially in patients in the early stages of WKS. When damage to the brain is more severe, the course of care shifts from treatment to the provision of support to patients and their family. Custodial care may be necessary for the 25 percent of patients who have permanent brain damage and significant loss of cognitive skills.

Scientists believe that a genetic variation may explain why only some alcoholics with thiamine deficiency develop severe conditions such as WKS, but additional studies are necessary to clarify the way in which genetic variants might cause some people to be more vulnerable to WKS than others.

Liver Disease

Most people realize that heavy, long-term drinking can damage the liver, the organ chiefly responsible for breaking down alcohol into harmless byproducts

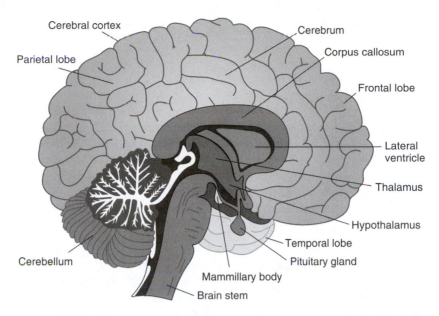

Cerebral cortex

Parietal lobe

Cerebrum

Corpus callosum

Frontal lobe

Lateral ventricle

Thalamus

Hypothalamus

Temporal lobe

Pituitary gland

Cerebellum

Mammillary body

Brain stem

Figure 2.3. Schematic drawing of the length-wise cross-section of the human brain. Drawing courtesy of the NIAAA website (http://www.niaaa.nih.gov/Resources/GraphicsGallery/Neuroscience/211p67.htm).

and removing it from the body. However, they may not be aware that prolonged liver dysfunction, such as liver cirrhosis, which results from excessive alcohol consumption, can harm the brain and lead to a serious and potentially fatal brain disorder known as hepatic encephalopathy.

Hepatic encephalopathy can cause changes in sleep patterns, mood, and personality; psychiatric conditions such as anxiety and depression; severe cognitive effects such as shortened attention span; and problems with coordination such as a flapping or shaking of the hands (called asterixis). In the most serious cases, patients may slip into a coma (i.e., hepatic coma), which can be fatal.

New imaging techniques have enabled researchers to study specific brain regions in patients with alcoholic liver disease, giving them a better understanding of how hepatic encephalopathy develops. These studies have confirmed that at least two toxic substances, ammonia and manganese, have a role in the development of hepatic encephalopathy. Alcohol-damaged liver cells allow excessive amounts of these harmful byproducts to enter the brain, thus harming brain cells.

Physicians typically use the following strategies to prevent or treat the development of hepatic encephalopathy:

- Treatment (e.g., administering L-ornithine-L-aspartate) that lowers concentrations of blood ammonia
- Techniques (e.g., liver-assist devices, or "artificial livers") that remove harmful toxins from the blood (in initial studies, patients using these devices showed lower amounts of ammonia circulating in their blood, and their encephalopathy became less severe)
- Liver transplantation, an approach that is widely used in alcoholic cirrhotic patients with severe (i.e., end-stage) chronic liver failure. In general, implantation of a new liver results in significant improvements in cognitive function in these patients and lowers their levels of ammonia and manganese.

(From National Institute on Alcohol Abuse and Alcoholism [NIAAA], 2004.)

The gateway theory of drug use states that young people who experiment with one drug will likely progress to the use of more harmful substances, similar to descriptions of the progression from the use of alcohol or tobacco to marijuana and later to hard drugs (Tullis, DuPont, Frost-Pineda, & Gold, 2003). Because nicotine is a stimulant and alcohol a depressant, recent speculation is that smoking may increase the risk of the later development of alcoholism by reducing sensitivity to alcohol (NIAAA, 2000). Research findings that show a strong correlation between smoking and alcoholism in twins give some credence to this hypothesis. We might also want to reconsider the truth of the largely discounted gateway theory, which states that the use of one drug promotes the use of another.

In reducing the potency of alcohol, the effect of smoking may well be to increase the tolerance for drinking, and tolerance, as we know, is associated with alcohol dependence. Tolerance, moreover, means one is getting less of a high from the same quantity of substance and would logically increase the likelihood of trying stronger substances. This is the reason prevention should be stressed rather than treatment. For those who wish to curb their own drinking or that of others, smoking cessation might be the place to start rather than end one's battle with addiction (van Wormer & Davis, 2008). The fact that drug use causes alterations in the brain probably increases susceptibility to other drug addiction.

Cocaine, like meth and alcohol, brings about marked changes in brain chemistry. Accumulated evidence indicates that cocaine's chief biological activity is preventing the reuptake (reabsorption) of the neurochemical transmitter dopamine. This drug-generated surge in dopamine is what produces a drug user's high. Drug-addicted laboratory rats will ignore food and sex and tolerate electric shocks for the opportunity to ingest cocaine. A depletion of dopamine following cocaine use probably accounts for cocaine binges, tolerance, craving, and the obsessive behavior of cocaine users. The body cuts back on the oversupply, which is why increasing doses of cocaine are needed to keep the user feeling normal (Ginsberg, Nackerud, & Larrison, 2004). Furthermore, as researchers and the general public are increasingly aware, nicotine behaves remarkably like cocaine, causing a surge of dopamine in addicts' brains. Dopamine is one of the "feel good" neurotransmitters; too little dopamine is implicated in the tremors of Parkinson's disease, while too much causes the bizarre thoughts of schizophrenia (Johnson, 2004). Indeed, some of the antipsychotic drugs, in blocking the powers of dopamine, can lead to Parkinson-like symptoms (e.g., shaking) (Saleebey, 2001).

Methamphetamine is a powerful drug that produces a surge in brain chemicals. It is a high-energy drug that reduces the need for sleep (van Wormer & Davis, 2008). The connection between meth and the work ethic concerns the use of meth to stay awake on the job (Substance Abuse and Mental Health Services Administration, 2001). It is highly popular in the Midwest, partly because of the tradition of hard work and the long hours worked at one or even two jobs. Read the following case study to learn of a young social work student's experience with this drug.

Hooked on Meth

After I began doing meth, it did not take long for me to become completely addicted to the drug. I was meeting my friends before school to "do a line," going and then ditching class, and doing more meth instead of going to school. I had been working at a restaurant as a waitress and hostess and saving money, but that money was gone in no time. I began stealing from my parents and my brother. They still did not know that I did. I returned the money once I got clean and began making money again. I was smoking up to five packs of cigarettes a day and drinking Dr. Pepper constantly. I did not eat much of anything. I went from a muscular, slim 130 pounds to an emaciated 100 pounds or less. I looked like a ghost but did not notice this until after the fact. I was always pale and had bags under my eyes all the time. I did not care much about my appearance—all I cared about was scoring my next quarter or half of meth. When I look at pictures from that time, it still makes me feel sick.

I began sneaking out of the house at night and running a few blocks to where my friends would be waiting, and we would cruise around all night, and they would drop me off to sneak back in before morning. If they did not do that, I would lie awake all night, picking at any bump or blemish I could find on my skin—out of boredom. If my brother was away at school, I would sleep in his room in our basement and play solitaire all night and smoke cigarettes, which was totally forbidden in my parents' house. Honestly, I just did not care about anyone or anything. At one point, I did not sleep for 15 days. I began hallucinating and once again became aggressive toward my parents. I told my dad that I hated him and pounded on his chest when he would not let me leave the house. Then I gave up and crashed. Otherwise, I partied. My friends and I were always the "designated drivers" at parties because we were not drinking; we were "just" on meth.

My parents knew something was wrong, but I was never around long enough for them to talk to me. I would leave for days at a time, and then I think they were so happy I was alive they would wait to talk to me, and I would leave again before they could. Finally, my mom confronted me after finding a quarter of meth in my purse. I got out of there and drove around, trying to score some more because she had thrown out what I had. This is when I feel that fate stepped in. I could not find anyone with meth anywhere. I drove around for a few hours and cried. I knew that I did not want to live like I had been anymore.

A few days before, I had been at a drug party, and a guy was handing out speedballs (cocaine and meth together). He was older and missing most of his teeth. He asked my name, I told him, and he said that he had graduated from high school with my dad. I thought about that as I drove around, and it truly scared me. I did not want to be that way. I realized I still had plans for my life. So I went home and asked my parents for help. They were so wonderful and supportive. They never yelled at me, they just hugged me and let me crash. I slept for 36 hours, and when I woke up, my parents took me to a treatment center. There I did individual counseling sessions and family sessions. I found out so much about myself, and I struggled to stay clean. Going to treatment was a great experience for me. I still keep in touch with my counselors, who helped me find myself again, and I even did a summer internship at that agency. During that time, I was also treated for depression. I now know I was suffering from anhedonia, which is an inability to

feel pleasure normally. I was on antidepressants for a while; I am not sure how long, and I am happy to say that I am now without medications, and I am happy almost every day!

(Printed with permission of Alyssa Prohaski Pate, MSW.)

In his study of the genome, Ridley (2006) refers to dopamine as "the brain's motivation chemical" (p. 163). If people have too little, they are listless and lack motivation. Rodent experiments show that when the genes for making dopamine are knocked out, mice will starve to death from sheer immobility. "Here perhaps," speculates Ridley, "lies the root of a difference in personality" (p. 163). Ridley is referring to a difference in people who seek thrills (related to low levels of dopamine and serotonin) and those who are happy with routine and stability—the former is attracted to experimentation with drugs, and the latter is not.

Serotonin is another neurotransmitter that is highly influenced by alcohol and other drug use. Serotonin is involved in sleep and sensory experiences. It has received a great deal of attention from researchers and the popular press through the interest in antidepressant drugs such as fluoxetine (Prozac) and sertraline (Zoloft), described by their function as "selective serotonin reuptake inhibitors" (SSRIs). Decreased levels of this neurotransmitter have been linked to behaviors associated with intoxicated states, depression, anxiety, poor impulse control, aggressiveness, and suicidal behavior (Johnson, 2004).

Figures 2.4, 2.5, and 2.6 are drawings made from positron emission tomography (PET) scans that show the inner workings of the brain and the brain on drugs. Certain parts of the brain govern specific functions. For example, the cerebellum is involved with coordination; the hippocampus, with memory. Neurons are the basic unit of communication in the brain. Information is relayed from one area of the brain to other parts through complex circuits of interconnected neurons. The conduction of information via electrical impulses transmitted from one neuron to many others is called "neurotransmission." One important pathway to understanding the effects of drugs on the brain

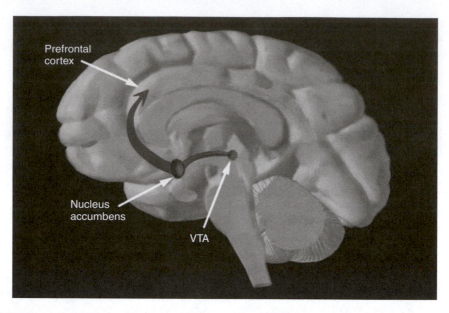

Figure 2.4. The reward pathway. Courtesy of the NIDA website (http://www.drugabuse.gov/pubs/teaching/Teaching2.html).

is the reward pathway (Figure 2.4), which consists of several parts of the brain highlighted in this diagram: the ventral tegmental area (VTA), the nucleus accumbens, and the prefrontal cortex. The reward system is a collection of neurons that release dopamine. When these neurons release dopamine, a person feels pleasure. When the brain is activated by a rewarding stimulus (e.g., food, water, sex), information travels from the VTA to the nucleus accumbens and then up to the prefrontal cortex.

As Figures 2.5 and 2.6 show, cocaine blocks the reuptake of certain chemicals by neurons in the brain. It is these nerve cells that release the neurotransmitters. Not only dopamine but other neurotransmitters such as serotonin may be involved as well. Further research is needed to reveal the exact effect of the multiple neurotransmitters.

In the normal communication process, dopamine is released by a neuron into the synapse, where it can bind with dopamine receptors on neighboring neurons. Normally dopamine is then recycled back into the transmitting neuron by a specialized protein called the dopamine transporter. If cocaine is present, it attaches to the dopamine transporter and blocks the normal recycling process, resulting in a buildup of dopamine in the synapse that contributes to the pleasurable effects of cocaine.

Current theories of addiction rely heavily on neurobiological evidence showing connections between addiction-related behaviors and neural structures and functions. Addiction is a brain disease, as Nora Volkow (2009), director of the NIDA, suggests. Even though the initial drug taking is a voluntary act, once neurochemical changes have occurred with prolonged use, the compulsion to return to drug taking or drinking is no longer voluntary. An addict's brain is different from a nonaddict's brain and the addicted individual must be dealt with as if he or she is in a different brain state. These alterations in the brain are neural adaptations to brain functioning under the influence of the drug (Whitten, 2005). When the use is discontinued, the system experiences a breakdown of sorts. Almost all drugs of abuse are believed to induce two kinds of changes in brain structure and function. These are the loss of motivation—to achieve, engage in fun activities, and so on—and the storing of emotional memories of the high (Johnson, 2004). Memories of the intense pleasure may last a lifetime.

Figure 2.5. Dopamine binding to receptors and uptake pumps in the nucleus accumbens. Cocaine concentrates in areas of the brain that are rich in dopamine synapses. The stars represent dopamine in the synapse and dopamine bound to dopamine receptors and to uptake pumps on the terminal.

Cues related to the drug evoke the memories and pose a dangerous risk of relapse.

Relapse might also reflect the brain changes. To produce a high, a drug such as cocaine keeps the dopamine transporters from clearing the synapse of this natural opiate following its release (U.S. Department of Health and Human Services, 2000). The blocking of the removal of dopamine from the synapse results in an accumulation of dopamine and feelings of euphoria. The way this happens is as follows: When all of the "seats" on this transporter molecule are occupied by cocaine, there is no room for dopamine, which therefore hangs around and keeps the pleasure circuit firing. This firing releases dopamine into the synapse. The neurotransmitter in turn must attach itself to receptors on the next cell in order to fire some more. Repeated activation enhances the high for a while but also leads to cell adaptation over time. With the same dosage, drug users are unable to achieve that original high because their brain has changed. This is called "tolerance" (see NIDA, 2008a).

As some researchers indicate, however, the notion of brain injury is more accurate than the notion of brain disease in describing the course of events involving changes in the brain brought about by substance use. As with other injuries, healing can occur when the source of the injury has been eliminated. Particular regions of the brain, especially the nuclear accumbens, are associated with levels of feeling because cocaine-addicted volunteers now, with the new technology, can rate their rush experiences and their cravings associated with cues (NIDA, 2008a). This memory is triggered by cues such as the smell of marijuana or cigarette smoke or even pictures of drugs such as meth or cocaine. The fact that memory sites are involved in connection with the cues is consistent with drug users' reports of strong feelings associated with drug use and their intense response to their feeling memories.

Figure 2.6. Cocaine binding to uptake pumps: inhibition of dopamine uptake. Cocaine (stars in the upper right) prevents pumps from removing dopamine from the synapse. This leads to a sense of euphoria. Drawings courtesy of the NIDA website (http://www.drugabuse.gov/pubs/teaching/Teaching2.html).

The craving that can preoccupy an addict's mind and very being involves the irresistible urge to get another rush. The memory of past euphoria, coupled with dopamine deficit related to long-term use, means the addict seeks out drugs in order not to feel low. Due to neuronal damage caused by extensive drug use, the individual can no longer feel pleasure normally. Cocaine produces no physical withdrawal symptoms yet is recognizably more addictive than heroin. The drive to return to drug use must therefore be associated with memory, as well as with the changes in brain chemistry. Even the mere anticipation of receiving cocaine has been shown, in rat studies, to lead to a surge in dopamine in the brain (Farmer, 2009; van Wormer & Davis, 2008). How about the craving for alcohol? Viewing pictures of alcoholic beverages does activate specific areas of the brain, including the prefrontal cortex, according to research from the Medical University of South Carolina (George et al., 2001). The significant finding in this research is that heightened brain activity shows up only in problem drinkers and not in moderate drinkers. The same brain activation does not occur when alcoholics view neutral pictures. This result suggests biological differences between persons inclined toward addiction and those not so inclined. Researchers can diminish the euphoric effects of alcohol and other drugs in addicts by giving them drugs that increase the availability of serotonin. Since the addiction is to the feeling of euphoria, not to the substance itself, such medications reduce the craving. Following a year or two of recovery, the brain regains its normal state, even for persons who were heavy users of methamphetamine (NIDA, 2008b). Because the effects of repeated exposure to cocaine and methamphetamine can last for years, long-term treatment may be essential.

Pharmaceutical Interventions

If drug dependency is considered less a matter of will than of brain chemistry, then the development of medications to prevent the lows or block the highs is inevitable. The growing awareness of serotonin's central role in mood and compulsive behavior has been paralleled by a boom in the introduction of drugs that target serotonin levels.

Through brain imaging and genetics, the discovery of the role that serotonin plays in addiction and mental disorders, in conjunction with simultaneous discoveries of drugs that reduce drug cravings in rats and monkeys, has opened up a whole world of medical possibilities. We also now know that nicotine, for example, sends a rush to the brain's "pleasure center," where cocaine and amphetamines do their work (Farmer, 2009). Continued smoking, like other drug use, causes physical changes in the brain. For those with brain receptor types that are more prone to addiction, breaking the smoking habit is reportedly as difficult as ending heroin addiction. These people could be helped with intensive prevention efforts. One antidepressant, Zyban, is widely used as an aid in breaking the smoking habit. Other serotonin reuptake inhibitors such as Prozac, Zoloft, and Paxil are prescribed to treat a wide range of disorders such as binge drinking and eating, obsessive-compulsive disorder, autism, panic attacks, schizophrenia, and uncontrolled aggression (Kolb & Whishaw, 2008). While health care providers, in a time of tight-fiscal constraints, are in search of effective but brief interventions, pharmaceutical companies have a strong economic stake in producing and marketing products to meet the growing medical demand.

The U.S. government is interested in pharmaceutical treatment, too. The findings from brain research have laid the groundwork for a series of clinical trials of various prescription drugs to be funded by the two major research funding organizations—NIAAA and NIDA (information at http://www.nida.nih.gov/Funding/Budget05.html). Even many of the leading treatment centers, such as the Hazelden Treatment Center in Minnesota, are conducting studies on the effectiveness of medications that act on the brain as an aid in recovery—for alcoholics, smokers, cocaine and methamphetamine users, persons with eating disorders, compulsive shoppers, and pathological gamblers. The discovery that different parts of the human brain are activated during cocaine *rush* versus cocaine *craving* should be useful in the development of medications that reduce the craving that makes relapse almost a matter of course (Farmer, 2009; van Wormer & Davis, 2008). For alcoholism and other drug addictions, the pharmaceutical effectiveness in curbing craving has been especially promising.

The Brain and Adolescent Behavior

Although science is solving many mysteries of the neurobiology of addiction, one question left unanswered is why some youths are highly susceptible to the effects of addictive substances while many others can just "take it or leave it." These differences probably have something to do with genetic makeup, the genes involved in human growth and development. Certain features of the adolescent brain may predispose youngsters to behave in ways that place them at particular risk for trying alcohol or other drugs. Many teenagers engage in foolish, high-risk behavior that seems incongruous with their values or intelligence level. Current findings from nonhuman primate research in pediatric neuroscience offer a viable explanation: The prefrontal cortex of the brain does not reach full maturity until later than previously thought. This research demonstrates that changes in brain cell chemicals that make one more susceptible to emotional responses occur during adolescence (Begley, 2007; Spear, 2000). This part of the brain is linked to judgment, novelty seeking, and self-awareness. Most teens lack the skills to resist peer pressure probably for this reason. When hormone changes, peer pressure, smoking (which heightens teenagers' drug susceptibility), and plain old adolescent rebellion are added to the equation, the result can be quite volatile.

Evidence of brain immaturity in humans comes from MRI scans of children's brains as the same children matured (Giedd, 2008. It was found that the prefrontal cortex, or the judgment and common sense center of the brain, matures last, usually as late as age 25. The MRI scans also revealed facts about the learning phenomenon of pruning neurons that were not used. Overall, gray matter volume increases throughout childhood, then is thinned down starting around puberty, which correlates with advancing cognitive abilities. Scientists think this process reflects greater organization of the brain as it prunes redundant connections, as well as increases in myelin, which enhance transmission of brain messages.

This pruning process has important learning implications in that connections that are not used are discarded. This is why learning a foreign language or how to play a musical instrument is so much easier for children and teens. "If you fail to nurture before age twenty or so circuits that support sight-reading music, it will be difficult to recruit them later on," notes Begley (2007, p. 113). Only in early childhood are people as receptive to new information as they are in adolescence. One's alertness to new experience is heightened during this period as well, and emotions run strong. These processes have a bearing on teen susceptibility to substance use, anorexia, and addiction (van Wormer & Davis, 2008). Research on the adolescent brain helps us understand why schizophrenia develops during this period. Scientists believe that the natural teenage process of pruning may be accelerated or otherwise altered in schizophrenia, bipolar disorder, and other neurodevelopmental disorders (Society for Neuroscience). (See the section on schizophrenia later in this chapter.)

The Brain and Attention-Deficit/ Hyperactivity Disorder

Attention-deficit/hyperactivity disorder (ADHD) is a psychiatric diagnosis that is based largely on behavioral characteristics. The most commonly recognized behaviors associated with this diagnosis are early childhood onset, impulsivity, extreme risk taking, short attention span, and excessive physical movement (APA, 2000). The excessive physical movement (fidgeting),

however, is not a requirement for a diagnosis of ADHD. Attention-deficit disorder (ADD) is the older term still used for the same phenomenon minus the hyperactivity. This term is no longer used in the *DSM-IV-TR*. The most common psychiatric diagnosis for children is ADHD, affecting nearly 7 percent of all children. Many adults have the same symptoms since children do not necessarily outgrow these characteristics. Its existence has only recently been diagnosed in adults, however.

The most recent physiological explanation for ADHD is that it involves deficiencies in dopamine activity. Volkow, Wang et al. (2009) collected detailed images of almost 100 participants' brains with PET scans after injecting them with a radioactive chemical that binds to dopamine receptors. Over half were diagnosed with ADHD; the others were the control group. The imaging showed that people with ADHD have fewer of the receptors and transporters than do other people in the mid-brain structures that make up the pleasure circuit of the brain. This research, which was recently published in the *Journal of the Medical Association* is consistent with earlier scientific investigations that posited that children with ADHD have deficiencies in dopamine and in another neurotransmitter, norepinephrine, along the pathways near the prefrontal cortex, the region that controls attention and short-term memory (Comings, 2001). Stimulant medications such as Ritalin may slow down the so-called vacuuming (reabsorption) of the dopamine, which makes more of the neurotransmitter available and improves concentration. The finding of the dopamine deficiencies helps explain why persons with ADHD get bored easily, are highly distractible, impulsive, and lack the discipline to pursue projects that are unexciting. This research also helps explain why persons with ADHD end up in high-stimulus jobs such as in sales or the media, are so susceptible to gambling and drug abuse. ADHD is highly hereditary, according to researchers (Volkow, Wang et al., 2009).

Thom Hartmann's (2005) hypothesis regarding genetic traits that have been carried over from hunter and farmer societies gives some credence to the notion that societies that evolved from an agricultural tradition tend to be more stationary and less adventure seeking than societies (or tribes) of hunters. Farmers, according to Hartmann, are cautious, not easily bored, and patient. Hunters are more impulsive and multifocused on the environment. School-children who are descendants of hunters find it hard to concentrate and are easily distracted, highly energetic, and restless. They are liable to be diagnosed as having ADHD. In fact, Hartmann's book is entitled *The Edison Gene: ADHD and the Gift of the Hunter Child.* So-called ADHD children and adults are inclined to excel in many ways outside the classroom, especially in sales and other competitive fields. Attention-deficit/hyperactivity disorder is prevalent in the United States but rare in Japan. Hartmann states that the ancestors of Japanese people today lived in a purely agricultural society for at least 6,000 years. Recent empirically based research on the worldwide prevalence of ADHD is consistent with Hartmann's hypothesis in terms of hereditary factors—twin studies show this trait is 75–91 percent hereditary—and with regard to Asia in that the prevalence rate is quite low in that part of the world (Xiang, Luk, & Lai, 2008).

Europeans view Americans and Australians as "brash and risk-taking," Hartmann further suggests. Consider the types of people who would have fled the "old world" to take a dangerous journey across the Atlantic. These adventurers would presumably have carried with them the genetic material that might have caused their descendants to crave mobility over a more routine lifestyle and competition over cooperation. Eisenberg, Campbell, Gray, & Sorenson (2008) tested the hunter-farmer hypothesis among groups of pastoral nomads and hunter-gatherers in Kenya. About one-fifth of the population in both groups had a gene that is associated with ADHD. Interestingly, among the nomads who move around quite a bit, persons with the genetic variant were better nourished than those without it. In the more sedentary hunter-gatherers, the opposite was true. The researchers conclude that hyperactivity might be an advantage for the nomads in rewarding the more adventurous types but a disadvantage in modern society when the tendency to take risks can lead to getting into trouble.

Two other books published in 2005, *Delivered from Distraction* by Hallowell and Ratey (2005) and *The Gift of ADHD* by Honos-Webb (2005), similarly stress situations in which the characteristics such as distractibility, poor impulse control, and emotional sensitivity can be regarded as strengths. Many successful artists and CEOs have these same traits. Whether people with these personality traits turn them into a gift or a curse depends largely on the environment in which they find themselves.

Rapport, Bolden, et al. (2009) studied 23 preteen boys—12 with ADHD and 11 without—and watched how the boys tackled problems that taxed their "working memory," the short-term memory that most of us use unconsciously each day. What they found was that the boys augmented their concentrations by moving around. Rather than preventing learning, their fidgeting most likely promotes it, concluded the researchers. Drugs such as Ritalin or Adderall are often prescribed for what is considered a neurological disorder but may, in my opinion, be a personality trait of someone who is not disabled but differently abled. In any case, the prescribed drugs help learners concentrate on their tasks and be more like other people. Moreover, it is hard for children with ADHD to sit still all day at school and learn under those conditions. What these children need is a specialized learning environment; let the school conform to their needs rather than forcing the children to be medicated to meet the school's needs. Kuo and Taylor (2004) report that, of 406 children diagnosed with ADHD, those who were involved in outdoor activities in natural settings, compared with those who spent time indoors or surrounded by pavement, experienced a significant reduction in learning problems, according to parents' reports.

Biological Aspects of Aggression

At first glance, a consideration of biological factors in aggression may seem surprising. However, biology is a crucial component in much that is human. Increasingly, brain studies clarify differences in male and female thought processes relating to factors such as communication and aggression (Gur, Gunning-Dixon, Bilker, & Gur, 2002; Science Daily, 2007). Other research that is relevant to aggression toward the weak by the strong are testosterone studies and observational reports of primate behavior (Howell, Chavanne et al., 2007).

Using MRI technology, scientists are on the threshold of discoveries concerning biochemical processes associated with the exploitative attitudes, blaming of victims, and impulsive, forceful activities that are characteristic of antisocial personality. In general, eight times as many men as women receive this label. Aggressive behavior of a pathological nature, the kind evidenced in male-on-female battering, has been found to be linked to low levels of the neurotransmitter serotonin (Science Daily, 2007). In a comparison of school performance and head injury histories of violent and nonviolent male prisoners, León-Carrión and Ramos (2003) found that what differentiated the two groups was a history of an untreated head injury.

Brain scans of male teenagers with and without a history of uncontrolled aggression revealed that the aggressive teens exhibited greater activity in the amygdala and lesser activity in the frontal lobe in response to fear-inducing images (Science Daily, 2007). Other studies on aggression look at male-female differences. The fact that men have a lower volume of gray matter (the bodies of nerve cells) in the prefrontal cortex than women do may account for the fact that antisocial behavior is far more common among men than among women (Miller, 2008). Still, in a study of over 200 African American females who had a genetic structure that is closely associated with the risk of antisocial behavior plus fathers with criminal records were significantly at risk for serious delinquent behavior (Delisi, Beaver et al., 2009). The effect is considered to be an interactive one between a certain genetic makeup and exposure to a high-risk social environment.

Hormones, too, have been implicated in criminal behavior. Research on prison inmates reveals that males and females with abnormally high levels of testosterone tend to have been convicted of violent crimes and to show high dominance and aggression toward other inmates (Dabbs & Dabbs, 2000). Evolutionists such as Wrangham and Peterson (1996), authors of *Demonic Males: Apes and the Origins of Human Violence*, look to biology to explain patterns of dominance. Emphasizing male domination, these authors have studied predatory violence, including rape and murder among chimpanzees and other apes, our closest living relatives. We need to study such violence, they suggest, as biological phenomena and to examine its reality in the lives of all members of the animal kingdom. Their findings have important implications for the study of oppression in human society in revealing the degree to which aggressive behavior, if goal oriented and calculated, can be rewarding in terms of the possession of power.

Kurzban and Leary (2001) argue from an evolutionary perspective as well. They focus on the social exclusion of individuals and groups whom society devalues or stigmatizes in one way or another. In strong contrast to writers such as Gil (2001), who refutes the innateness of drives for dominance, Kurzban and Leary draw on primate studies to make a case for the evolutionary basis of between-group competition and the stigmatizing and rejecting of undesirable group members. From this perspective, the attacking of "out groups" involves a set of distinct psychological systems designed by natural selection to enhance group survival. Human beings reflect similar mechanisms in their avoidance of people who are undesirable in some way and who seemingly have little to offer the group as a whole. Experiments to gauge unconscious racism in whites showed a correlation between scores on implicit association tests and brain activity registering fear and anger in response to photos of black faces (Cunningham et al., 2004). Perhaps we are hardwired, suggests Begley (2004), to view the world in terms of "us" versus "them." The dividing category may not be race, however, but sex, age, or religion.

Whether or not we accept the hypothesis that there is a biological force driving interpersonal violence and aggression, we can certainly appreciate the role of biology in certain aspects of social life such as territorial conquest for access to vital resources—food, water, and, yes, oil. We can also appreciate the relevance of theories of the "survival of the fittest" in coming to see how particular groups of people, including whole nations and classes, are able to acquire and maintain power over others. This brings us to a consideration of violence in the animal kingdom.

Infanticide among chimpanzees in Tanzania was studied by Murray, Wroblewski, and Pusey (2007), who found that when males kill infants they tend to kill male infants. The most likely reason for the attacks is the elimination of male competition. Battering may be conceived of in terms of cultural, psychological, or, as is our concern here, biological causation. The biological aspect is pursued by Wrangham and Peterson (1996) in their fascinating exploration of ape male-on-female battering in the wilderness. Battering, according to these authors, is rare in nonhuman animals and occurs only in species where females have few allies or where males have each other. The key predictive factor in primate battering is vulnerability. Significantly, even in the animal kingdom, the authors suggest, "The underlying issue looks to be domination or control" (Wrangham & Peterson, p. 146). Human battering is about the coercion and intimidation that men impose on women in order to control them (van Wormer & Roberts, 2009). Biological factors that play a role in human male aggression and violence are the male hormone testosterone and low levels of the neurotransmitter serotonin, which is also associated with aggression and addiction.

Not only does testosterone affect behavior, but apparently behavior can affect testosterone as well. This was a surprising finding of a new study by Alvergne, Faurie, and Raymond (2009) of rural villagers from Senegal where polygamy is common. Under age 50, men with multiple wives had high levels of testosterone compared to monogamous men. However, once the high-testosterone men had children, if they spent time with their children, their levels of testosterone declined. So once again, culture and biology are intertwined.

Rape and Biological Theory

In *A Natural History of Rape: Biological Bases of Sexual Coercion*, Thornhill and Palmer (2000) argue from a decidedly antifeminist approach that rape exists in the evolutionary scheme of things and is inherently a sexual, not a violent, act. The existence of rape can be accounted for in the biological imperative to impregnate as many females as possible. And how, according to these authors, can rape be prevented? Women must not dress provocatively, and they should not venture out alone; boys must be taught how to resist their natural impulses to rape, and the effectiveness of "chemical castration" should be used experimentally for men who cannot control their instincts. The evidence that Thornhill and Palmer present for the evolutionary nature of rape is that rape victims are women of child-bearing age and that rape occurs in a variety of animal species. The fact of child molestation is not explained in this work.

Citing Thornhill and Palmer's hypothesis of the evolution of rape, Gottschall (2008) in *The Rape of Troy* suggests that the aggressive drive to rape is simply a by-product "of adaptations for consensual sexuality" (p. 77) but not as an essential aspect of reproduction. The reproductive advantage to men in evolutionary terms, Gottschall sees occurs due to the achievement of power and wealth rather than in use of force; men with material possessions and status would be rewarded with expanded access to women and therefore would father more children. This then, in evolutionary terms, is an explanation for aggression and ambition in men, as the more aggressive men would have had more offspring and carried the trait down the generations. But it is not an explanation for rape.

The Sexual Coercion in Primates and Humans, an edited volume by evolutionary biologists Muller and Wrangham (2009), offers an intriguing discussion of rape among human and nonhuman primates. Contributors present extensive field research and analysis to evaluate the existence of sexual coercion in a range of species and to clarify its role in shaping social relationships among males and females. Together the chapters in this book describe how some species such as orangutans, chimpanzees, and baboons rape and batter females and gorillas kill infant offspring, while other primates such as bonobos inhabit a peaceful kingdom. Female bonding among the bonobos is seen to have an inhibiting effect on male violence. Evolutionists must consider that much of rape among humans is for nonreproductive purposes, for example, for bonding with fellow gang members or to teach certain women a lesson. If there is an evolutionary aspect to rape, as Wrangham and Peterson (1996) speculate, it may be that "rape is an evolved male mechanism whose primary aim is not fertilization in the present but control—for the ultimate purpose of fertilization in the future" (p. 141). Out of fear, the female may later accept the male. However, this is only an hypothesis, as the authors are quick to point out. They emphasize that patriarchy is more than a solely cultural invention and, although not inevitable, that it is grounded in biology. Their point that nature and nurture are not dichotomous but are in constant interaction is well taken.

Criminality and Character

Brain research is the province of psychologists, psychiatrists, and neurobiologists, who today are on the threshold of discoveries related to biologically based disorders such as antisocial personality, addiction, and compulsive risk taking. Antisocial personality, which used to be called psychopathy, is a controversial mental disorder listed in the *DSM-IV-TR* (APA, 2000). People who qualify for this diagnosis are impulsive, blaming of others, and seemingly unable to feel empathy or guilt. Traditionally, mothers have been blamed for causing this disorder through abuse. Research is increasingly looking toward biological explanations. In her review of recent scientific research on antisocial personality, Farmer (2009) states that a strong genetic component has been shown to be a factor in the development of this disorder. Prefrontal lobe abnormalities are among other biological factors implicated.

Dutch neurobiologist Dick Swaab (2009b), who has studied men who have committed murder, notes that as well as having deficiencies in the prefrontal cortex, these men tend to have an aberrantly functioning amygdala. This defect also explains why psychopathic individuals fail to respond normally to facial expressions like sadness and fear. Patients with damage to the prefrontal cortex have been shown to make judgments differently from other people in hypothetical situations of moral dilemmas. In one such dilemma presented to a group of patients with different types of brain damage that concerned whether or not to throw someone overboard on a ship to save others, the patients with damage to the prefrontal cortex quickly arrived at the pragmatic decision to do what needed to be done. Because of their lack of empathy, they did not experience a moral dilemma, unlike the other patients. Also according to Swaab, patients with frontotemporal dementia, a brain disorder that starts in the prefrontal cortex, can display antisocial, criminal behavior, such as unwanted sexual advances, driving away after committing traffic violations, and physical violence; no remorse is felt for these acts.

Damage to the prefrontal cortex impairs concern for other people, as reflected in the dysfunctional real-life social behavior of patients with such damage, as well as their abnormal performances on tasks ranging from moral judgment to economic games. Krajbich, Adolphs, Tranel, Denburg, & Camerer (2009) demonstrated this phenomenon in setting up economic games that allowed for winning through taking advantage of other players. Players who had experienced brain damage to the prefrontal cortex were totally uninhibited in their strategies and showed a lack of the ability to feel guilt. Earlier research from the University of Iowa has identified rare cases in which injuries to the brain in infancy prevented people from learning normal moral behavior and from feeling guilt or remorse about bad behavior (Blakeslee, 1999). Significantly, while still an infant, one young woman was run over by a car and sustained injuries to the prefrontal cortex. By age 3 she was ignoring all scolding and punishment and later compulsively lied, stole from the family, and had no friends. As we saw earlier, the orbital frontal cortex is the region of the brain that plays a big part in judgment and impulse control. Damage done to one side of the brain is generally compensated by growth on the other side. If both areas are damaged, however, the individual may lack self-control altogether. This research may be of special relevance to male and female offenders because it reveals that early brain injury prevents people from learning the difference between right and wrong and inhibits the development of conscience as an internal control (Black, 1999).

A rare, empirically based study of 26 psychopathic offenders (13 male, 13 female) incarcerated for alcohol-related crimes, measured the existence psychopathy based on scores on the Psychopathy Checklist Revised (Walsh, 1999). This device, developed by R. D. Hare, determines the presence of psychopathy in terms of attitudes that are exploitative and blaming of others, as well as a lack of empathy, affect, and remorse. Interviews with female psychopathic offenders revealed a tendency to react violently to seemingly trivial personal insults. One 43-year-old female offender, for example, reacted to her neighbor's racial slur in this way: She pulled out her knife and slashed the offending woman's face several times, which required the woman to have more than 100 stitches. In addition, a 26-year-old offender who was serving time for assaulting a police officer described feeling "psyched" when engaging in violence. Several of the women, moreover, reported feelings of power and excitement while "beating the defenseless," such as dogs and children. The recommended treatment for such individuals is a behavioral cognitive approach to enable these clients to plan, rehearse, and practice alternative ways of reacting to slights other than resorting to violence. A significant finding is that many women labeled as antisocial because of their alcohol-induced criminal behavior were misdiagnosed; they did not possess the underlying character pathology that their alcoholic behavior seemed to indicate.

The influence of testosterone as a link to criminal behavior in both males and females resurfaces from time to time. Dabbs and Dabbs (2000) measured the testosterone levels via saliva samples taken from 87 female inmates of all ages. In the prison context, women who had the highest levels of testosterone (not unlike male inmates) tended to have been convicted of violent crimes and to evidence domineering, aggressive behavior in prison. Keep in mind that men have on average 10 times as much testosterone as do women. Testosterone is also linked to appetite to risk. Since women have lower testosterone levels than men, one would expect them to be more cautious in making business decisions and in other areas. Research widely reported in the business media concerned research that showed women who had higher ratios of their index fingers to their ring fingers (evidence of high testosterone exposure prenatally) and high levels of testosterone in their saliva were equally willing to gamble for higher winnings in an experimental situation as were men (*The Economist*, 2009).

Studies of female offenders shows that antisocial personality occurs far less frequently than among male offenders. Caspi, Moffitt et al. (2006) examined the relationship between personality variables and delinquency in large population samples from the United States and New Zealand. Negative emotionality and lack of impulse control were found to be highly correlated with juvenile delinquency across race, ethnicity, and gender.

A mental disorder that does occur frequently in female offenders and especially adolescent girls is organic depression. Because of their reputation for high levels of activity, one would not ordinarily expect delinquents to be depressed. Depression, however, has been found to be a key factor in juvenile delinquency and to be closely linked to early childhood victimization (Manasse & Ganem, 2009). Research from the National Institute of Justice (Bureau of Justice Statistics, 1999), in summarizing the work of Dawn Obeidallah and Felton Earls, helps explain this relationship. Whereas during childhood, the rates of depression among males and females are similar and relatively low, the rates clearly diverge in early adolescence, with girls showing a pronounced increase. Difficulty in concentrating, loss of interest in previously enjoyed activities, and feelings of hopelessness and low self-worth may all contribute to self-destructive acts and alliances. To document a relationship between depression and antisocial behavior in an ethnically diverse population, interviewers gathered self-reported data on 754 girls in urban Chicago. Comparing the antisocial behavior of girls who were depressed with those who were not, Obeidallah and Earls found that 40 percent of nondepressed girls engaged in property crimes, compared to 68 percent of girls with depression. Fifty-seven percent of depressed girls engaged in seriously aggressive behavior, compared to only 13 percent of those who were not depressed. Overall, these findings suggest that depression in girls may put them at high risk for antisocial behavior. Future research will examine potential intervening links between depressive symptoms and troubled behavior such as substance use and association with troubled peers.

Addictions researchers, as discussed earlier, are devoting more and more attention to brain chemistry. Furthermore, substance abuse, as we have seen, can cause severe and often irreversible damage to brain cells and to the nervous system in general. In women's lives, the connection between addiction and crime is both direct and indirect, direct through involvement in uninhibited lawbreaking behavior (not to mention perhaps careless use of the illegal drug itself) and indirectly through involvement in destructive relationships, perhaps with people who are involved in the criminal underworld.

Other personality factors related to criminal behavior in myriad and curious ways are traits such as hyperactivity and a tendency toward risk-taking behavior. Unless their energy is channeled elsewhere, hyperactive, extreme risk-taking girls and women can be predicted to "take a walk on the wild side" every now and then and perhaps pay the consequences. Since males are far more prone to manifest each of these traits than females, traits which are almost synonymous with getting into trouble, one would expect males to have a comparably higher crime rate, and they do.

The Biology of Gender

In our quest for knowledge, sometimes it is best to disregard the political ramifications. From this perspective, we cannot reject all of the biological theories of sex differences simply because they might seem repugnant to us in light of our ideas of equality. A biological approach posits that there are fundamental differences between male and female and that these differences interact with cultural norms to influence disparities in male/female criminality. Traditional feminists disparage biological research, Rosin (2008) suggests, because the theories hark back to the days when women were told they must fulfill their natural role as wives and mothers. The whole notion of gender was seen and still often is seen as a social construction.

In sociology, anthropology, and even in the medical sciences from the 1950s through the late 1980s, similarly, sex-role behavior and gender identity were viewed as primarily a product of socialization. Accordingly, in those rare cases in which infants were intersexed or born with ambiguous genitalia, the response was to assign sex at birth so the child could develop a normal gender identity. The belief that sexual identity was purely cultural was most widely propagated by researcher John Money of Johns Hopkins Gender Identity Clinic (Martin, 2002). The process that was followed was that doctors would test the individual genetically, physically, and a team (geneticists, pediatric endocrinologists, urologists, and psychologists) would then assign a sex at birth, performing surgery and follow-up hormonal therapy to reinforce the sexual assignment. Since surgically it was easier to construct a female vagina than a penis, most of the infants were surgically turned into girls. Their parents were instructed to raise them as girls. The results, in many cases, were disastrous. The suicide of a Canadian man, David Reimer (one of a set of identical twins) who had suffered a botched circumcision in infancy in the 1960s brought public attention to the biological aspect of gender identity. Following "corrective" surgery at Johns Hopkins, the boy was raised as Brenda, and not told the circumstances of his birth. Still he fought against being dressed as a girl and always identified as a boy. Dr. Money falsely proclaimed his story as a success story and proof that gender is a result of socialization. Later when his tragic life story was told in books and film documentaries, voice was given to others who had also had surgeries of the same nature—intersexed people, or those who were born with ambiguous genitalia. A strong advocacy group, The Intersex Society of North America (ISNA), was formed. The founders who had had similar experiences denounced the mutilations they had suffered at the hands of modern medicine and described the pain of being forced to grow up as girls when they were really boys. Today the ISNA strongly recommends against sex reassignment surgery until the child is old enough to know his or her true gender.

As a result of the work of the ISNA in getting their stories out, the major specialties involved in treatment of intersexed children at Johns Hopkins and elsewhere throughout the world are questioning their earlier presumptions about sexual assignment. Long-term studies are being initiated to add to the new body of research. Basic assumptions about human gender, sexual identity, and sexual reassignment, and what makes a person male or female, or man or woman, are being reevaluated in light of David Reimer's experience and subsequent revelations from intersexed individuals in conjunction with new understandings about the nature of gender identity (Martin, 2002). The stories of the intersexed children who were genetically male yet surgically made to appear female reveal the indominable power of gender in our lives.

Feminists are divided over the issue of nature versus nurture as it relates to gender. While liberal feminists stress the nurture side of gender and are highly skeptical of recent claims of innate gender differences, radical feminists, as we saw in Chapter 1, often have been appreciative of the new research findings, which they view as favoring the female of the species. Yet the fear in other feminist circles is that an emphasis on genetic differences between male and female will have political consequences that will hinder women's bid for sexual equality. In any case, today there is a new, scientifically based imperative to explore sexual differences that manifest themselves in every system of body and brain (Brizendine, 2006). Brain research provides us with evidence that is nonideological, evidence that a sizeable portion of human behavior is neurological.

What the new research shows us based on the new technologies is that although women's brains are smaller than men's, they have a higher processing quality. The region at the base of the brain, which includes the amygdala, is involved in emotional arousal and excitement and is about the same size in men and women. Another region, the hippocampus, manages our memories. It may become active as we associate sights and smells with past highly moving experiences. However, women have a significantly higher volume in the orbital frontal cortex than men do. When emotionally charged information is introduced, a woman's amygdala response is stronger that a man's, according to neuropsychiatrist Louann Brizendine (2006), author of *The Female Brain*. The gender difference is significant when it comes to memory of milestone events such as a wedding or a graduation. Years later, women typically will remember more of the details of the event than men will. Regarding aggression, however, men quickly respond and remember related incidents. In women's brains, the aggression-control center or the prefrontal cortex is relatively larger than in men (Gur, Gunning-Dixon, et al., 2002). This suggests, according to Gur et al. (2002) and Brizendine (2006), that when anger is aroused, women are better equipped than men to exercise self-control. So how did these rather significant differences come about? Until the first eight weeks every fetal brain looks female, notes Brizendine. In males a huge testosterone surge takes place at the time "killing some cells in the communication centers and growing more cells in the sex and aggression centers" (p. 14). Brizendine discusses advances in neuroimaging that supply exciting new insights into how women and men use their brains differently because, as she suggests, they have different brains to use. Women have 11 percent more neurons in the area of the brain devoted to emotions and memory, she notes. Hormone differences affect the emotions as well. Different levels of estrogen, cortisol, and dopamine can cause strong emotional responses in a woman to events that a man may be able to shrug off.

Some gender biologists are looking to research on transgendered people for evidence of a biological basis for gender identity (see, for example, Hines, 2004, and the next section). The fact that some children show a gender orientation early in life that is at variance with their bodies and that some small-scale studies show that certain regions of their brains are closer in size to those of typical females than males, points in the direction of nature over nurture (Rosin, 2008).

Evolutionary biologists look to the animal kingdom to discover facts about characteristics that may be genetic. Evolutionists such as Muller and Wrangham (2009) report on observations of primates in the wild and at primate centers. Such ape studies reveal that male chimpanzees compete aggressively for rank and dominance (i.e., to be the alpha male). Reports show occasions in which male chimpanzee predators attack the weak male members of a group and gain access to females, who often bond with the predators.

Is the frequency of male violence a mere artifact of physical strength? Wrangham and Peterson (1996) ask. For answers, they look to human society. Examining data drawn from global crime statistics on same-sex murder (to eliminate the factor of male strength), Wrangham and Peterson (1996) found the statistics to be amazingly consistent. In all societies except for Denmark, the probability that a same-sex murder has been committed by a man, not a woman, ranges from 92 to 100 percent. (In Denmark, all of the female same-sex murders were cases of infanticide.) We need to remove our inhibitions based on feminist politics, these researchers argue, and study violent acts such as murder and rape as biological phenomena. The origins of male violence, Wrangham and Peterson conclude, are reflected in the social lives of chimpanzees and other apes, our closest living nonhuman relatives.

Arguing against innate male-female differences in brain structure, Lise Eliot (2009), a neuroscientist and author of *Pink Brain, Blue Brain: How Small Differences Grow into Troublesome Gaps—And What We Can Do About It*, indicates that there is little solid evidence for sex differences in children's brains. Such differences that develop emerge in male and female adult brains, she suggests, and are a product of the interaction between parents and other caretakers and girls. The caretakers reinforce the small differences that are present to the extent that infants and children settle into sex-based play preferences, and changes in the brain reinforce the differences. Eliot's arguments are intriguing—yes, there are brain differences in adults, but these are the result of the way little girls and little boys are brought up. We do know that learning experiences in childhood strengthen certain neural connections based on usage, while disuse leads to a pruning of the brain. More research is needed cross-culturally on male and female neurological development.

Right Brain/Left Brain

Our brain consists of two separate structures—a right brain and a left brain—that are linked by a row of fibers. In most people, the left side specializes in speech, language, and logical reasoning (a fact that has been known for years due to the impact of strokes on this or the other side of the brain). The right hemisphere specializes in reading emotional cues (Cabeza, 2002). Much has been made of the differences in the kind of consciousness and in the functioning of the right and left hemispheres of the brain (Saleebey, 2001). The left brain is equated with reasoning, while the right brain has been presumed, almost contemptuously, to be more primitive than the left—feminine as opposed to masculine.

Studies analyzing brain flow data to locate active regions associated with particular kinds of reasoning reveal new insights. Using PET scans, Parsons and Osherson (2001), for example, learned that deductive logic activates areas of the right brain; simple recall of knowledge, on the other hand, is associated with the left side. These findings are consistent with Saleebey's stress upon the "remarkable division of labor" between the two hemispheres of the brain: The left "supplements the opaque, holistic comprehension of the right to function with detail, focus, and analysis" (p. 127). The left side checks out the syntax, grammar, and literal meanings of words, but the right side works to understand nuances of meaning. Interestingly, the left hemisphere is dominant for speech in about 90 percent of right-handed people and 60 percent of left-handed people.

As scientists have discovered through PET and fMRI scans, the pattern of right-brain, left-brain specialization changes to some extent in middle age and beyond. Neuroscientist Robert Cabeza (2002) has labeled this phenomenon "hemispheres asymmetry reduction in older adults," or HAROLD, which relates to the use of both hemispheres for greater flexibility. Not all older people are capable of such flexibility, however. Cabeza has found that high-functioning elders (as measured through memory testing) use both hemispheres of the brain, perhaps as a means of compensating for the decline. Sometimes the high-functioning older adults that he observed integrated the hemispheres so efficiently that their thought and reasoning processes were in all likelihood better than they were before. In any case, the result of this evolving flexibility in thought and feeling in many aging persons may be what psychological maturity is all about.

Neuroscientist Nancy Andreason (2001) indicates that the right hemisphere can be considered a companion language region, as we know from direct functional imaging observations. She cautions us, therefore, against too much simplification in breaking the brain into component parts. We almost never do only one mental activity at a time. Advances in neuroscience have shown us to what extent the brain is a system; no single region can perform any mental or physical function without coactivation and cooperation from multiple other regions. "The human brain," notes Andreasen, "is like a large orchestra playing a great symphony" (p. 85).

The advent of imaging techniques that can be used to explore the structure and function of the living brain has led to an explosion of research findings on sex differences. We now know, for example, that the male brain is more asymmetrical during fetal development than the female brain (Hines, 2004).Women, Saleebey contends, seem to be more hemispherically egalitarian than men. We see this in the impact of strokes, which are more clearly identifiable— right and left—in men. In normal aging in healthy adults, as we learn from fMRI research,

more brain atrophy occurs with aging in males than in females (Xu et al., 2000). Brizendine (2006) summarizes research based on experiments comparing the thinking patterns of men and women. In the experiments women were found to use both sides of the brain, while men relied more on one side. Several independent studies suggest that, for gay men, cognitive performance on measures that typically elicit sex differences is shifted in a "female-like" direction (Rahman & Wilson, 2003). Klar (2004), in his investigation of brain hemispheres in male homosexuals, found differences that relate to left- and right-handedness and suggest a biological/genetic factor in sexual orientation.

Sexual Orientation

Gender nonconformity is measured in terms of boys who hate rough-and-tumble play and like to play house or play with dolls and girls who play exclusively with trucks and GI Joe action figures rather than Barbie dolls. Research on homosexuality reveals a link between early gender nonconformity and later homosexuality (Bem, 2000). Studies of lesbians indicate that "butch lesbians" recall more gender nonconformity, have higher waist-to-hip ratios, higher testosterone levels, and less desire to give birth than "femme lesbians" (Rahman & Wilson, 2003). Even feminine lesbians were shown to be more gender nonconforming than heterosexual women. This research indicates that sexual orientation develops early in life and is not solely a matter of choice (Zastrow & Kirst-Ashman, 2010). Taken as a whole, the research literature indicates that sexual orientation includes a wide range of behaviors only indirectly related to sexuality but stemming, at least in part, from a biological predisposition.

Some psychologists have been offering treatments to gay and lesbian clients who were hoping to change their sexual orientation to heterosexual. Following a close examination of all the research literature on the subject, the Council of Representatives of the American Psychological Association (APA) took a strong stand, passing a near-unanimous resolution urging mental health professionals not to tell clients that they can change their sexual orientation through therapy or any other methods (Lafsky, 2009). The conclusion of the APA's statement is that there is no evidence that "reparative therapy" or any other attempt to change sexual orientation is effective. Counselors who make such attempts were reproached for playing into the hands of a reactionary morality. The APA maintains that homosexuality is natural and cannot be changed. In reaching this decision, the APA was, in effect, favoring the biological position on sexual orientation as the National Association of Social Workers did previously.

The biological school holds that there is something fundamental, unchanging, and biologically wired in lesbians, gay males, and straight people that causes their differences. The psychosocial or learning school, on the other hand, holds that variation in human sexuality is largely a product of cultural forces operating at crucial moments in one's life. Interactionist theory considers both nature and nurture as key ingredients in sexual orientation and thus combines the biological and psychosocial positions into a holistic approach.

Biological theories of homosexuality can be clustered under three kinds of research; these pertain to the brain, genes, and hormones.

Brain Research

One of the first brain studies commonly cited in the literature on homosexuality is LeVay's (1991) research on the brains of 19 gay men who died of AIDS, 16 heterosexual men, and 6 heterosexual women. His findings revealed that the anterior hypothalamus in gay men was approximately half the size of that in the other men. Since these men had died of AIDS, however, the research was largely invalidated.

Allen and Gorski (1992) examined brains obtained from autopsies from 90 homosexual and heterosexual men and heterosexual women. They found that an important structure connecting the right and left sides of the brain, known to be larger in women than men, is larger still in gay men. Due to the obvious sample bias related to death by AIDS, as in the foregoing study, their results are by no means generalizable to male homosexuals as a whole.

Nevertheless, one could theorize from the findings that something unusual happens when the brain is being formed in the fetus, something with enduring consequences for one's later sexuality. Future research should help confirm or refute these preliminary results and help unravel mysteries pertaining to lesbians, a population largely ignored in empirical research. What we do know is that when asked, gay males tend to attribute their homosexuality more to biology and lesbians more to situational factors (Mondimore, 1996). Several of the genetic studies of sexual orientation in men examined by Mondimore indicate that men tend to be more exclusively gay or straight, whereas women are more fluid in their orientations.

From the Stockholm Brain Institute comes brain research that graphically shows brain differences among the sample of 90 subjects, divided into heterosexual and homosexual males and females, in the expected direction (Savic & Lindström, 2008). Magnetic resonance imaging was performed on all 90 and PET measurements of cerebral brain flow to study functional connections from the right and left amygdalae. The heterosexual men and homosexual women showed a rightward cerebral asymmetry, whereas volumes of the cerebral hemispheres were symmetrical in homosexual males and heterosexual females. This, as we saw in the gender studies, is indicative of more flexible thinking patterns from both sides of the brain as characteristic of women. Homosexual subjects also showed sex-atypical amygdala connections. This would be indicative of a certain emotional sensitivity. The authors concluded that these results show differences in brain structure and function within the same sex when the sexual orientation is diverse.

Genetic Studies

The best means of studying the role of hereditary factors is to examine differences between identical and fraternal twins. Identical (unlike fraternal) twins develop from a single fertilized egg, yet both types of twins, when raised together, inhabit similar environments. Comparisons of characteristics among the more genetically similar sets of twins can provide evidence of a genetic link. Through advertisements in gay publications, Bailey and Pillard (1991) recruited gays or bisexuals who had twin siblings. Results showed that, when one brother was gay, 52 percent of the time the identical twin was also gay. This compared to 22 percent of fraternal twins. In a later study involving sisters, the concordance rate was 48 percent in identical twins and 16 percent for nonidentical twins (Bailey, Neale, & Agyei, 1993). These results support the theory of a genetic link in homosexuality, but they also indicate that environmental factors play a role as well. Otherwise the concordance rate would be 100 percent for identical twins. An alternative explanation would be to speculate that if one twin is gay or lesbian, the other twin might have tendencies in that direction as well. Kirk, Bailey, Dunne, and Martin (2000) investigated a sample of almost 5,000 Australian twins. Based on the participants' answers to a questionnaire, the authors concluded that homosexuality ranged between 50 and 60 percent if one twin was lesbian but was only 30 percent among male twins. These results are intriguing, and more research on this point would be helpful.

In their analysis of extensive research findings on homosexuality, neuroscientists Puts, Jordan, and Breedlove (2006) accept the fact of a possible genetic link to homosexuality but look at another factor that apparently has an impact in other cases. These researchers take as their starting point the well-documented correlation of birth order and homosexuality, the finding that a man with one or more elder brothers is more likely to be gay than a man without older brothers. Their explanation is that a set of genes that produces an immune reaction in the mother upon delivery is likely to get stronger in successive male pregnancies; the effect is to prevent the masculinization of the brain but not of the genitals. This theory is grounded in Bogaert's (2006) empirically based study of four large samples of males in which the fraternal birth-order effect was found in males who had the same mother, even if reared in an adoptive home and not found among male step-siblings. Earlier studies of

fetal development showed that the expression of sex is determined by genes first before hormones are ever released (Foreman, 2003). Ponder this finding for a better understanding of those whose outward appearance is unmistakably of one gender but whose brain tells them they are of another gender—transgenderism.

In summary, behavioral genetic studies have provided the strongest evidence of the role of biology in influencing human sexual behavior (Ginsberg, Nackerud, & Larrison, 2004). Most of the studies concern men, however; for women, hormones (and experience) may well play a more active role. Sexuality experts caution that no specific gene linked to homosexuality has been identified (Zastrow & Kirst-Ashman, 2010).

Hormonal Factors

In humans, the study of rare medical conditions (e.g., pregnant women who were exposed to a synthetic hormone) indicates that prenatal hormonal events can influence human behaviors. Animal studies likewise reveal the potency of prenatal influences. Testosterone-treated female rats, for example, are shown to have better navigational ability than untreated rats (Mondimore, 1996).

In general, the findings of hormonal studies involving humans are extremely contradictory (Zastrow & Kirst-Ashman, 2010). The greatest likelihood is that such effects occur prenatally rather than later in life. Hormonal therapies for medical conditions unrelated to sexuality have proven ineffective in altering sexual orientation or behavior. According to Puts et al. (2006), lesbianism develops prenatally as a result of exposure to testosterone in the womb. Rat experiments demonstrate that fetal exposure to testosterone masculinizes the brain. Brown, Finn, and Breedlove (2002 surveyed individuals from a gay pride street fair and found that lesbians who identified as "butch" had hands that resembled a typical man's in that the index finger was smaller than the ring finger. This trait is associated with exposure to testosterone in utero.

Many feminist lesbians are troubled by the implications of the biological explanation of homosexuality. Because women tend to be more flexible in their sexual orientation (some women favor the term *preference*) than men, the notion of homosexuality as an inborn trait may be less relevant to their personal experience (Foreman, 2003). A close reading of the biological reports gives credence to the nature *and* the nurture arguments. Whether or not it is politically acceptable to say so, it appears that same-sex experiences during a crucial stage in one's life can alter one's sexual identity. The process of being or becoming a heterosexual is surely a combination of both innate predisposition and socialization history. For both social and physical scientists, the debate should no longer center on nature versus nurture but on the contributions that each makes and ways in which they interact.

Transgenderism

As many as 3 million American adults are "gender variant" according to an article in *Time* magazine (Fitzpatrick, 2007). Transgendered people are those whose gender identity does not conform to their physical manifestations. Autobiographies of male-to-female transgenders reveal that from their earliest memories they saw themselves as little girls rather than as little boys. Until recently the decision to live as the gender of one's choice and to get a sex change was not made until middle age. Today there is a new openness about transgenderism that allows people to come out sooner and be who they want to be. As a consequence, there is now a growing population of transgender students on college campuses. According to a *Boston Globe* article, transmale students, or female-to-male transgenders, sometimes gravitate toward women's colleges where they can be themselves and where gender nonconformity is more tolerated than it as in coeducational institutions (Brune, 2007).

The transition from female to male, or, more commonly, from male to female, is now taking place even in childhood. Some parents of children who identify with the opposite sex are being advised by therapists who specialize in gender nonconformity to enable the child to dress as he or she wishes and not to force the child to identify as the sex to which he or she was born. The reason for the urgency is the high rate of suicide among adolescents who believe they are "in the wrong body." Around half of all transgendered children attempt suicide before the age of 20 (Fitzpatrick, 2007). Puberty is an especially difficult time. In some cases, puberty is being artificially delayed with hormone blockers, such as that provided at Children's Hospital, Boston, which specializes in treatment for gender-variant children. The Boston team of specialists is engaging in clinical trials to gauge the long-term effects of blocking the maturation hormones.

The following case study involves a situation in which nature and nurture do not come together but are in conflict. Read about a social worker and former male police officer named Barbara Cole (Figure 2.7), whose being crosses genders and whose personal narrative illustrates that, even with gender, there is no clear-cut dichotomy of male and female.

Transgendered: A Self-Portrait: Nature or Nurture?

Am I a man or a woman? The answer is not that simple, for I am neither a male nor a female. I am I.

I was raised as a male and had a successful career in law enforcement. I was given all of the privileges of a white male in our society. Yet inside I knew it was all a lie; I had wanted to be a girl for as long as I can remember. I was arrested for wearing a dress in the sixties. I had a doctor tell my family since "he" has testes, he is a man. So I was treated as a man. No more dolls, only football for this girl. Since the word was out, I was labeled a faggot. I faced hatred and was the target of abuse both physical and mental. I figured out quickly that I needed to hide what I felt inside or I would be killed. So began many years of self-loathing but great acting; I should have won an Oscar. It almost ended one night 15 years ago, with pills, alcohol, and my gun, but I failed to kill myself. I couldn't even get that right.

I started the long process of coming out, first to myself, and then to my family. I talk to everyone about being transgendered. I write about it. I pray that no one else will try to commit suicide because

Figure 2.7. Barbara Cole videotapes speakers at an open house for a supportive housing project in Seattle. Photo by Rupert van Wormer.

of his or her gender identity. I had a friend try to castrate herself, only to almost bleed to death and then have the ER doctors sew her testes back on because she was born with them so she should keep them. I know people that are no longer with us because they could not stand up to our "civilized" society.

Being in law enforcement was an accident. I had joined the army on my seventeenth birthday, and they put me in the military police. So I found that being an officer was a safe place for me to hide. Who would guess that I sometimes wore panty hose under my state police uniform?

Early in 1992, I was working as a parole officer in north Idaho. My boss was homophobic and proud of it. In several conversations he had said he would fire any officer that had a sex change. We had a transgendered client, which even I had to make fun of for fear of being ridiculed by my peers. I had found that I really enjoyed working with people and somehow carrying a gun and a badge did not seem too helpful. So since I needed a new career

I decided to go into social work. So off to college I went at 45.

The first few years I was still very closeted. I would dress as a woman and go to group meetings over a hundred miles away. My hair was long, but I kept it pulled back. When it came time for my field placement, I told my advisor that I wanted to work with gay people. I never really said why, but he was happy to try and set it up. As it had never been done and our campus did not even have a GLBT (gay/lesbian/bisexual/transgendered) student group, he had to put some work into it. I was placed as a GLBT organizer with the local YWCA, and I was off and running.

After the first semester I was traveling all over Idaho and to Chicago, meeting with people, talking about what it means to be a transgendered person. I even met briefly with Elizabeth Birch, the director of the Human Rights Campaign. At that time HRC did not want to include transgendered people in the Employment Nondiscrimination Act. At the same time I was getting confused. Sometimes I had to change clothes three times a day, a meeting in the morning as a female, back to school as a man, then to meetings in the evening as a female. My makeup bill was outrageous. So I decided to transition while still in college, in a small town in north Idaho. I was attending a college with around 3,000 students.

I personally spoke with each of my professors and told them that I would like to transition midway through the semester. I wrote articles in the student newspaper and spoke in my classes. When the big day came, everyone was mostly supportive. The dean of students did call me in and voice some concerns about the "bathroom" issue. I was assigned to two bathrooms on campus. In the process of all of this, my supporters and I formed a GLBT student organization on campus. I spoke in classes at five different colleges and universities during that year. I was trying to expose new social workers and counselors to transgendered people.

When it came time to look for work, I decided to move to Seattle since it was a very "transfriendly" city. I started looking for work, and I was hired at the first place I applied. I spent the next 2 years working with the developmentally disabled adults. Though I really liked working there, I was really concerned about the homeless folks I was seeing everywhere.

I went to work 6 years ago for an agency that specializes in housing homeless adults. Our clients have to be homeless, plus two of the three categories of HIV affected—chemically dependent and mentally ill. A large number of our clients are from all three categories and basically unhouseable without assistance. We use the harm-reduction model. Our goals are directed toward keeping them safe, meeting their needs, and being available as counselors. We meet them where they are and facilitate change when they are ready.

As a social worker, I have finally relaxed as a person. I am mostly no longer ashamed of myself. When I was in law enforcement, I was always terrified that someone would discover my real secret. I felt like an imposter. I knew I was a pervert so I overcompensated and was way too macho. Years later, a few people that I knew during that time said they always thought I was a gay man. I used to think that being gay would be better than wanting to pretend to be a woman. I have been lucky. I have always been able to find work. I know that many of my brothers and sisters are not so lucky.

I might look like a man in a dress, but I feel like I am a woman. I do not claim to be a woman in every sense of what that means [because] I cannot have children. I was not raised a female with all of the meaning of the word. I cannot have "the operation" since I have a heart condition, so I can never have a vagina.

Genitals according to the social norm define one's sex. However, I have incorrect genitals for my mind's view of myself. My sexual identity is female, yet if I were arrested I would be jailed with the men. When I am in the hospital, people call me sir because they see those things, even though my legal name is Barbara—a simple matter in Washington—go to court and pay a fee. I know in my lifetime people like me will always face abuse and discrimination. Each day I hope that a few more people will come to understand what it means to be transgendered.

When I walk down the street and some people turn and stare it hurts. When people point and laugh, it hurts. I have been verbally assaulted to the point the police were called. Each day I get up [and] I say a prayer that I have the strength to go forward today. To deny my feelings would result in my killing myself sooner or later. My feelings of needing to be a female are that strong. People like me are killed all of the time. For a memorial to our dead, explore the website at http://www.gender.org/remember. Even with the risk of death, I cannot go back to what I was before.

If they could invent a pill tomorrow to cure gender identity disorder, would I take it? Though at first thought, I would jump at it, after some soul searching I would refuse it. Since I have grown as a person in the last few years and have a greater understanding of myself, I now like who I am. I would not like to go back to being my prior phony hateful self.

I do regret that it took me so long to figure out that it was all right to be myself. I married twice, with the hopes that it would make me a real man. I never really succeeded in doing anything but bringing misery into other people's lives. I do have a wonderful accepting daughter, but I feel bad about using other people to hide behind. After all, I was married; who would guess my secret?

In our society it is currently okay to discriminate against gay or transgendered people. I have been denied housing because I was a boy in a dress. I have been assaulted because I wear a dress. As a social worker, I would like to think that we are agents of change.

I have survived the jungles of Viet Nam to the sale rack at J.C. Penney's. Life is a journey—enjoy. And when asked what sex I am, I reply "I am I."

(Printed by permission of Barbara Cole.)

The Biology of Temperament

A dimension of human behavior and development that is heavily influenced by genes has been called temperament (Johnson, 2004). Many aspects of temperament—moodiness, risk taking, shyness, extraversion—have biological roots (see Zuckerman & Kuhlman, 2000). Mood-related behavior—irritability, the tendency to go to extremes, and to use mood-altering substances for self-medication—is associated with levels of neurotransmitters in the brain, as we discussed earlier. Kolb and Whishaw (2008), in their textbook on the fundamentals of neuropsychology, provide numerous example of the impact of brain injury in various parts of the brain on human personality, even on the inability to appreciate humor or respond to facial expressions when damage is done to the right frontal lobe. These researchers also review studies showing the relationship between lack of environmental stimulation to the young child and poor brain development leading to learning problems later. Related aspects of personality—aggression, character and criminality, and behavior related to mental disorders—are covered in later sections. The complex subject of love and attachment is taken up in Chapter 4.

Shyness Versus Extraversion

Although most people would be somewhere in the center of the introversion-extraversion continuum, let us look at the extreme ends of this continuum for the sake of comparison. In focusing on individual differences, such as the fact that some people are inclined to be anxious and high strung, others more confident and laid back, we are venturing into the area of what is called personality. Ridley (2009), author

of *Genome*, discusses these personality differences in terms of the chemicals of the brain. For example, serotonin largely determines how one responds to external stimuli such as social signals; some people are more sensitive to these than others are.

Ridley explains personality differences in novelty-seeking behavior (a trait related to extraversion) in terms of one genetic trait—possession of a long D4DR gene on the eleventh chromosome. People with these long genes have low responsiveness to dopamine, the argument goes, so they need to take a more adventurous approach to life to get the same dopamine "buzz" that short-gened people get from simple things. Thus, they are inclined to seek out more sexual partners and engage in greater risk-taking behavior than their short-gened counterparts, who are more satisfied with less diversity and stimulation. "This is the reality of genes for behavior," Ridley concludes.

Can the social environment influence such innate predispositions? Ridley refers to experimental studies of naturally shy infant monkeys who, when placed in the care of confident monkey mothers, quickly outgrew their shyness. Thus, the right kind of parenting is probably a factor in helping human infants who are shy by nature feel more secure, Ridley speculates.

In her review of the literature on child development, Johnson (2004) cites a study by McManis, Kagan, Snidman, and Woodward (2002), who conducted observations of children at 4 months and again at 11 years of age. There was a congruence between infant neurochemical profiles for high reactivity to stress at early and later ages. A powerful implication that Johnson draws from this longitudinal evidence is that children's temperaments can actually shape their environments by eliciting reactions that reinforce their fearfulness or confidence regarding the world.

Following an earlier version of a study that identified unusually inhibited types as early as 4 months of age, Kagan (1994) compared Nordic Europeans with darker, Southern Europeans. The Nordic types—blue eyed, tall, thin, with faster heartbeats and more heat-generating activity in the brain—were better able to withstand the cold, harsh climate of the Ice Age than were other people. However, they were also more likely than others to suffer from high anxiety. And behaviorally, they found it much harder to adapt to new situations, unfamiliar people, and to stress in general.

Stress and Health

Anxiety and depression are physiological states that affect health as clearly as environmental factors such as nutrition, clean air, and water. Scientists today are mapping the pathways that link emotion to health; mind–body research, such as the Integrative Neural Immune Program, is investing millions to link mental states to health (Benson, Corliss, & Cowley, 2004). Two factors that are being studied are the impact of stress on the body and individual differences. Prolonged stress wears the body down. Under conditions of fear-provoking stress (e.g., a loud noise, a confrontation with a wild animal), the adrenal glands release cortisol. This hormone helps keep up blood sugar, giving the body extra energy to act. The heart and breathing rates increase; blood pressure rises (Johnson, 2004).

However, in extreme situations the stress response—preparing the human animal for fight or flight—can kill. Chronic stress, though not always fatal, can disrupt the digestive system (stomach vessels constrict to force blood elsewhere), interfere with sleep, and lead to age-related diseases. The stress hormones (norepinephrine and cortisol) also act on the brain, creating a state of heightened alertness and supercharging the circuitry involved in memory formation (Johnson, 2004; Kolb & Whishaw, 2008). To learn more about what happens to molecules when people live under conditions of continuous stress, Epel et al. (2004) measured telomere lengths (telomeres protect the ends of chromosomes) in the immune cells of 39 mothers who cared for chronically ill children. They found that many of the highly stressed women had cells that resembled those of the low-stressed mothers who were 10 years older. It stands to reason that people who are acutely sensitive to stimuli would have more health problems and weaker immune systems.

While studying the replication of the AIDS virus in 54 men in the early stages of the disease, researchers found that introverted men responded more poorly to medication than did those who were more outgoing (Treisman, 2005). It had earlier been observed that socially inhibited, sensitive people became ill and died several years earlier than other people. Health researchers are experimenting with pet therapy, exercise programs, religious experience, relaxation exercises, and herbal medicine to help these people ward off infectious diseases and reduce stress (Johnson, 2004). Environmental stress plays a role in the etiology of addiction and even in the development and exacerbation of mental disorders. An important study on prison inmates compared a group that performed aerobic exercise on a regular basis with a control group that did not do so (Buckaloo, Krug, & Nelson, 2009). The exercise group scored lower on the Beck Depression Inventory than did the sedentary group.

Mental Disorders

There has been a slow but perceptible shift in our understanding of the basis of mental health problems from a family-centered orientation (focus on mother–child interactions) to a medical model. Accordingly, interventions today are largely medical. Evidence of a physical basis for mental disorders such as schizophrenia comes from neuroimaging of the brain, which reveals structural abnormalities in the brains of persons with schizophrenia and the fact that drugs that block certain dopamine receptors reduce the symptoms of the disease (Andreasen, 2001; Ginsberg, Nackerud, & Larrison, 2004).

Not only does schizophrenia (which is thought to result from an excessive amount of the neurotransmitter dopamine) have a physiological basis, but posttraumatic stress disorder (PTSD), which is caused by external experiences, also has biological underpinnings. Whereas with schizophrenia, brain abnormality precedes the development of the disease, with PTSD, the mental disorder itself is associated with the changes in the brain's chemistry (Pittman & Delahanty, 2005). In the latter situation, extreme and horrific stress occurring in one or more events is continuously repeated in the memory, to the extent that immediate and long-term alterations to brain chemistry take place. Ginsberg, Nackerud, and Larrison (2004) cite MRI studies that indicate that the size of the hippocampus (region of learning and memory) is reduced in trauma victims when compared to that of nontraumatized individuals. For more information on PTSD, read Chapter 3 (section on war trauma) and Chapter 4 (section on childhood trauma).

Schizophrenia

Schizophrenia is the most serious and personally destructive of all of the major mental illnesses. It can wreak havoc on the lives of individuals and their families. According to the *DSM-IV-TR* (APA, 2000), schizophrenia is a form of psychosis characterized by symptoms of disordered thoughts, hallucinations, delusions, and social withdrawal. Most specialists believe schizophrenia is a developmental disorder that originates before birth and involves circuits in several regions of the brain (Harvard Medical School, 2005). The developmental pattern of the illness is consistent across cultures, with the onset usually occurring when the individual is making the transition to adulthood.

People with schizophrenia have a deficiency in gray matter in the frontal cortex and in the hippocampus, which controls memory and emotion. In children who show signs of schizophrenia, there is a progressive loss of gray matter that is correlated with the severity of the disease (Kolb & Whishaw, 2008). One of the abnormalities found with this disease is the decreased size of various parts of the brain (Ginsberg, Nackerud, & Larrison, 2004). In schizophrenia, the size of the ventricles (cavities with spinal fluid that cushions the brain's delicate tissue) increases; this puts pressure on the prefrontal cortex. Because there is only so much room in the skull, the reasoning region of the brain is likely to be damaged (since it must get smaller). Perhaps this is why schizophrenia

so often manifests itself during the late teens and early twenties, when a burst of growth occurs and the connections in the prefrontal cortex of the teenage brain grow stronger (see Reig, Moreno, Burdalo et al., 2009)

The Public Broadcasting System (2002) aired a program titled "The Secret Life of the Brain," in which two young people and their families were interviewed. What emerged was the story of the teenagers' descent from normalcy into madness as erratic thoughts and an overwhelming sense of emptiness took over the young people's minds. Hope was provided in the form of intensive treatment and antipsychotic medication.

Schizophrenia is an illness that can be difficult to explain or define because patients have so many different kinds of symptoms. Loss of pleasure and inability to complete tasks are often the first signs of the disease to appear. Hallucinations and delusions, which occur later, are the hallmark signs and often lead to a diagnosis of mental illness (Andreasen, 2001; Saleebey, 2001). Hallucinations are sensory experiences—seeing, hearing, feeling—with no grounding in reality. Delusions are beliefs also with no grounding in reality. Persons with mental illness often claim that they hear voices; later they realize the voices were not real. "The voice comes to me over the TV set" is a typical comment. Delusions, I have found, are much more tenaciously believed. Trying to talk these people out of them is often futile. The 2001 Academy Award-winning movie *A Beautiful Mind* provides a gripping portrayal of the life of Nobel Prize-winning economist John Nash. For long periods of time, Nash was completely at the mercy of his fantasy world. One of Nash's sons, who like his father was a mathematical genius, developed schizophrenia as well, as a CBS *60 Minutes* interview with Nash revealed about the movie of his life.

Although schizophrenia usually manifests itself in young adulthood, some research suggests that the disorder can be detected in childhood and even traced to the womb. In one study, observers of old home movies could distinguish 2-year-olds destined to develop schizophrenia by their clumsiness, lack of emotional warmth, and avoidance of eye contact

(Harvard Medical School, 2005). In another important study, Cannon and colleagues (1999) tracked down the elementary school files of 400 Finnish residents diagnosed with schizophrenia. Compared to the files of stable adults, the children who later developed the disorder performed well in academic subjects but performed poorly in sports and handicrafts. A second study by Brown and Susser (2002) suggests that in utero infection may disrupt the development of the fetal forebrain during the first trimester of pregnancy. Schiffman and his colleagues (2009) conducted a longitudinal study that included a standardized neurological examination and tests of physical coordination on 265 Danish children, over one-third of whom had parents with schizophrenia. They found that both coordination scale scores and genetic risk significantly predicted an adult diagnosis of schizophrenia. Animal studies such as those of Rehn and Rees (2005) provide further evidence that an adverse prenatal event disrupts normal brain development and creates a vulnerability that predisposes an at-risk individual to develop the disorder later in life. This research bolsters the predominant belief today that schizophrenia reflects aberrations in development rather than a degenerative process that begins in maturity.

Can early intervention help prevent the development of schizophrenia? Although more extensive research is required, there is some encouraging preliminary evidence from a small-scale study from Australia that fish oil supplements may prevent or at least delay the onset of psychotic illness (Amminger et al., 2010). This randomized, placebo-controlled study, monitored 81 youths who already suffered from early symptoms of mental disease for one year. At the end of the study, five percent of those taking fish oil supplements developed full-blown psychosis compared to 28 percent of the control group. If these results can be replicated, the advantages will be enormous for teenagers at high risk of developing schizophrenia who can avoid taking antipsychotic medications which come with a range of problems from weight gain to sexual dysfunction and are expensive as well.

As far as treatment is concerned, there are a number of antipsychotic medications to target the chemical imbalance in the brain. Previous studies have demonstrated that taking such medications is effective in the management of the disease, side effects notwithstanding. It was commonly believed that the new, more expensive pharmaceutical products had significant advantages over the older drugs in eliminating side effects. However, a large study funded by the National Institute of Mental Health (NIMH, 2005) compared the effectiveness and side effects of five medications. Contrary to expectations, the newer medications brought about no real improvement on the whole in terms of the development of tremors and restlessness; substantial weight gain was a major problem with the newer medications. Keep this in mind as you read the following case study.

Adam's Story: Journals, Paintings Trace Young Man's Journey Into Schizophrenia

Adam Samec was a creative, sensitive, and gentle child. As a young man, he loved to paint and write music, songs, and poetry. He taught himself to play guitar and dreamed of becoming an anthropologist.

He was 20 when he killed himself.

Adam left behind a devastated family, along with more than 30 journals, [as well as] songs, drawings, and paintings that reveal the inner turmoil, struggle, and pain of his illness, offering insight into the thought processes of a young man diagnosed with schizophrenic affective disorder/depressed type.

"Looking at all of it, I think he left behind something very special that could help professionals in the mental health field and help parents who find themselves dealing with a child's mental illness," says Adam's mother, Vicky Reicks of Cresco. "I can't pack them all away. It's a gift he left behind, and within his writings, he left behind messages to me. He knew his mom would read these journals."

Adam shot himself on April 11, 2001.

Vicky couldn't bear to look at the journals until last winter, and what she read on page after tightly written page were not ramblings, but a kind of poetry, vivid word portraits tracing the chronology of her son's illness, the medications, the voices he heard in his head, the angels and demons who sat on the edge of his bed or hovered near the ceiling regaling him with tales, his intense loneliness and isolation, and eventually, his flirtation with suicide.

I had grown ill over time, though I took my pills as a good boy should. I was fretting now terribly, unable to think, rest, my moody temperament coming forth. More pills, more days, it would all be better. Found little rest in my routine, knowing that my purpose was also to the point of breaking. . . . Dosage after dosage of medication would not be allowed to take hold, for I was on the outside, severely incapable of change. . . . The doctors had seen nothing but my dismal face and thus subscribed me to a long list of takers of a specific drug meant to target symptoms which I had, though the disease was all around a different story.

The notebooks, computer print-outs, and loose-leaf binders are scattered across the dinner table. Passages are marked with yellow Post-it notes, where Vicky has made notations. This passage, she points out, is about practicing suicide, and this entry was written when Adam was hospitalized, and here is a direct appeal to his mother to forgive him.

"He was so lonely. Everyone went their own way in the end. He lost his friends, he lost himself, and he didn't know what to do," Vicky says. "There is so much here, I think there's enough material for a book. I'd like to tell Adam's story in some way, to help other people because there is so much stigma attached to mental illness."

Adam was first hospitalized in 1999. The high school student had become increasingly withdrawn, and his personality changed. With a mother's instinct, Vicky knew something was wrong. Although she respected his privacy, she sneaked a peek at his writings and was disturbed by what she read. A crisis was brewing; she felt it in her bones.

Vicky sought advice and intervention from doctors and guidance counselors. Adam's behavior was dismissed as a teenage phase. He was going to school, had a girlfriend, held down a part-time job. She worried too much and perhaps should seek counseling herself. Adam refused to see a doctor despite his mother's entreaties. Then she received a phone call from his girlfriend's parents. Adam was having an anxiety attack and needed medical help.

"He was committed to Allen Hospital on Aug. 28, 1999, and that was the beginning of a long, painful, and rough journey," says Vicky. He was hospitalized for 19 days and received electroshock therapy treatments for depression. In late 1999,

he was finally diagnosed with schizophrenic affective disorder/depressed type.

"It makes you feel desperate as a parent. I hoped it would be psychotic depression. Isn't that something for a mother to hope for? Something that could be successfully treated? The diagnosis was difficult to accept because schizophrenia was something that wasn't going to go away," she recalls.

In the United States, three-quarters of people with schizophrenia are diagnosed between the ages of 17 and 25. Approximately 2.2 million American adults ages 18 and older are affected by the brain disorder, according to the National Alliance for the Mentally Ill.

The disorder interferes with a person's ability to think clearly, manage emotions, make decisions, and relate to others. Symptoms can include hallucinations, such as hearing internal voices; delusions; confused thoughts; poor eye contact; reduced body language; anxiety and terror; bizarre or rigid postures; decreased emotional expression; loss of motivation; and social isolation. Medication is used to control the disorder. Statistically, most persons with schizophrenia commit suicide within the first 10 years of their illness.

Vicky accompanied her son to every doctor's appointment. "He was hurting. Thoughts flowed out of him, and he wrote constantly. I found out he was cutting himself on his chest, arms, and legs. He showed me, and I was horrified. He said it was the only way he could feel anything," Vicky says, "and his inner voices told him he deserved to suffer."

Adam wrote about the cutting episodes, swallowing countless pills in rainbow hues, and alternating feelings of hopelessness and acceptance. He also described episodes of hospitalization and interactions with doctors, including "faking them out" while recognizing he knew they were aware he was faking.

"Eaten up by pills and pimples and Prozac, I simmer down from my cues, shifting down, someone always there. . . . I alter my views as I alter my face. . . . Help me not to fall down."

Medication improved Adam's condition, and he continued to write, draw in ink and charcoal, and paint watercolors. He presented a self-portrait to his mother for Mother's Day and drew numerous other self-portraits at various stages of his illness. He also painted demons and angels and other images, mingling bright and dark colors into startling, affecting images.

Adam was hospitalized off and on for a total of 135 days in a 1½-year period. His medication changed numerous times, often causing other medical problems, such as stomach ailments. He enrolled in a research program at the University of Iowa in Iowa City before deciding not to go through with it. He was hospitalized in Fall 2000 for nearly a month. While he was gone, someone broke into his apartment and stole his guitars and amplifiers.

In February 2001, Adam attempted suicide by taking a medication overdose. His stomach was pumped, and he was hospitalized.

Her son's suicidal thoughts never stopped, Vicky believes. "It was a way to end the pain. His mind was never at rest. He was never at peace. The illness brought him to his knees. My ex-husband, Adam's father, still can't read the journals because it's too sad and painful for him."

Adam shot himself on April 11 in his father's home. His brother discovered his body. The final entry in Adam's last journal reads: "I hope that they will find my body cool, warmed only by the remaining heat under the blanket. Breathless, I lie upon the pillow drooling no more, cotton-mouthed from all of the drugs. My body no longer functions and my heart is dead now; never had room for anyone else anyway. Don't let them find me all insecure like this, but instead, let them find me secure with death."

Vicky says, "All of the doctors, all the pills, all of the treatments. I'm left with the thought that, in spite of it all, we somehow let him down. I have a lot of bitterness about a society that still treats mental illness as something that should be hidden away in the dark. When you have someone in your family who is mentally ill, people walk the other way. If he'd had cancer or some other disease, they would be more sympathetic and understanding."

Figuring out what to do with his writings and artwork is something tangible that keeps mother connected to son.

"All of this," she says, gesturing at the journals, "multiplies my pain. I think about my child suffering through this, and it just about kills me. I just want him back, to hug him and tell him how sorry I am that this happened to him."

(From Parker, 2004; reprinted with permission of the *Waterloo–Cedar Falls Courier*.)

Bipolar Disorders and Other Mood Disorders

Approximately 8 million American adults may be affected by bipolar disorder, a serious psychiatric condition also known as manic depressive illness. Bipolar disorder consists of recurring episodes of mania and depression (APA, 2000). Bipolar I disorder is characterized by one or more manic or mixed episodes, often with one or more episodes of major depression, whereas bipolar II disorder is distinguished by one or more major depressive episodes accompanied by at least one hypomanic episode (Medical News Today, 2009). Throughout their lives, patients with bipolar I disorder experience depressive symptoms approximately three times longer than manic symptoms, while those with bipolar II rarely experience hypomania. Suicide is a high risk in both instances. Up to 50 percent of patients with bipolar disorder attempt suicide, and approximately 15 to 20 percent complete suicide (Oquendo, Chaudhury, & Mann, 2005).

In *Madness: A Bipolar Life*, a haunting book that takes us into the world of the madness of what used to be called manic depression (the term *bipolar disorder* was first introduced in 1980), Marya Hornbacher (2008), provides basic facts on this disorder:

> ❯ Average age of onset: 23
> ❯ Average age of correct diagnosis: 40
> ❯ Bipolar patients who go off their medications because of side effects, the desire for manic energy, or impaired insight: 50 percent
> ❯ Rate of alcoholism in bipolar women: seven times higher than in the general population. (p. 282)

Kay Redfield Jamison (1995), a psychologist and professor of psychiatry at the Johns Hopkins University School of Medicine, shares with us in her compelling memoir, *An Unquiet Mind*, her personal struggle with bipolar disorder (manic depression):

> People go mad in idiosyncratic ways. Perhaps it was not surprising that, as a meteorologist's daughter, I found myself, in that glorious illusion of high summer

days, gliding, flying, now and again lurching through cloud bands and ethers, past stars, and across fields of ice crystals. Even now, I can see in my mind's rather peculiar eye an extraordinary shattering and shifting of light; inconstant but ravishing colors laid out across miles of circling rings; and the almost imperceptible, somehow surprisingly pallid, moon of this Catherine wheel of a planet. (p. 90)

Until the dosage was finally reduced to a tolerable amount, Jamison struggled with not only the vicissitudes of the mood disorder itself but also the side effects of the drug lithium— blurred vision, nausea, impaired concentration, and memory problems. Lithium is a mood stabilizer that has been used for the treatment of bipolar disorder for years. It works by penetrating cells in such a way as to block the particular neurotransmitter and hormones associated with mood (Ginsberg, Nackerud, & Larrison, 2004). Then we must understand the allure of the high-energy manic state, which provides a rush as powerful as any drug. When in the manic phase, people with this disorder are disinclined to take medication to bring themselves down from this high. "It was difficult," Jamison explains, "to give up the high flight of the mind and mood, even though the depressions that eventually followed nearly cost me my life" (p. 91).

Hornbacher (2008) describes manic or mixed episodes as times when both the despair of depression and the agitation and impulsivity of mania are present at the same time. This results in "a state of rapid, uncontrollable energy coupled with racing, horrible thoughts— people are sometimes led to kill themselves just to still the thoughts" (p. 6). The irony, notes Hornbacher, is that when people appear to improve, they are at the highest risk for suicide, because they now have the energy to do it. Biological factors clearly play a role in mood disorders, including salient ones such as neurological and neuroendocrine influences (Lawrence & Zittel-Palamara, 2002). The alteration of chemicals in the brain, of course, has a strong impact on human behavior. Not much is yet known about the etiology of mood disorders,

although studies of identical twins show a 70 percent concordance rate for the development of mood disorders. Similarly, adoption studies show an increased presence of the disorder in biological parents of adoptees (Lawrence & Zittel-Palamara, 2002).

Easier to understand and more common are the general depressive states that stem from low or irregular levels of neurotransmitters (e.g., serotonin and dopamine) in the brain. Over the course of their lives, 13.2 percent of men and women experience at least one bout of major depression, and women are twice as likely as men to experience this disorder (National Institutes of Health [NIH], 2005). The racial/ethnic breakdown ranges from around 19 percent Native American, 14.6 percent white, and about 9 percent black, Hispanic, and Asian.

Currently available antidepressants act primarily by blocking the reuptake or absorption of the neurotransmitters, which makes them available to improve mood. In 1988 the introduction of SSRIs in the United States revolutionized pharmacological therapy for a number of depressive, anxiety, and eating disorders (Ginsberg, Nackerud, & Larrison, 2004). Moreover, obsessive-compulsive disorder is a mental condition that can be controlled by SSRIs to some extent.

Family generational studies reveal that certain forms of severe depressive illness have a strong genetic component (Hammen, 2009). Moreover, research shows that people who are related to seriously depressed individuals are twice as likely as relatives of nondepressed people to develop either a depression or substance abuse disorder. Research reported by Hammen (2009) on children of depressed parents consistently showed tendencies in the children when compared to a control group to think in a more negative direction. Brain studies as well show similar patterns in depressed mothers and their daughters. Jamison (1995) captures the essence of the dark moods she experienced:

Depression is awful beyond words or sounds or images; I would not go through an extended one again. It bleeds relationships through suspicion, lack of confidence and self-respect, the inability to enjoy life, to walk or talk or think normally, the exhaustion, the night terrors, the day terrors. There is nothing good to be said for it except that it gives you the experience of how it must be to be old, to be old and sick, to be dying; to be slow of mind; to be lacking in grace, polish, and coordination; to be ugly; to have no belief in the possibilities of life, the pleasures of sex, the exquisiteness of music, or the ability to make yourself and others laugh. . . . People cannot abide being around you when you are depressed. (pp. 218–219)

Obsessive-Compulsive Disorder and Anorexia

Obsessive-compulsive disorder (OCD) is marked by intrusive, reoccurring thoughts. Let us examine the psychiatric criteria provided by the American Psychiatric Association (2000). Under the heading OCD, obsessions and compulsions are defined separately; a person with OCD may have one or the other or both conditions. *Obsessions* are defined as recurrent and persistent thoughts or impulses that are experienced as intrusive and cause marked anxiety or distress. *Compulsions* are the repetitive behaviors (compulsive hand washing, checking, etc.) often associated in the public mind with OCD. These rituals may be unrealistically associated with some dreaded event. According to the NIMH (2001a), scientists have found biochemical similarities between people with eating disorders and OCD. The parallels relate to abnormal serotonin levels (Kaye, Fudge, & Paulus, 2009). NIMH researchers have found that many patients with bulimia have OCD as severe as patients actually diagnosed with OCD. A genetic trait is likely a key factor in the development of eating disorders, according to recent observational research based on fMRI technology (Murphy, Nutzinger, Paul, & Leplow, 2004). Similar metabolic abnormalities in the prefrontal cortex and caudate nucleus in both anorexic and OCD patients suggest a considerable overlap in these diagnoses.

The fact that anorexia occurs primarily in cultures or subcultures that value thinness and present media images of Barbie doll–shaped bodies attests to a cultural element. The usual explanation is that mothers, concerned about their own weight, transmit the cultural prescription to their daughters. Davison and Birch (2001), however, have reported that girls who were constantly dieting said it was the impact of their father's opinion that was driving them to this behavior. For men, homosexuality is a risk factor, owing to an emphasis on slimness in the gay community. Lesbians, on the other hand, rarely have this disorder (Payne, 2006).

OCD, like anorexia, often begins in adolescence. Schwartz and Begley (2003) state that OCD can be described in terms of "brain lock" because, simply put, messages from the front part of the brain get stuck there. This leads to the maddening repetition of unwanted thoughts. The form of the process—the relentless intrusiveness—is universal in those with OCD, but the content varies with the person and the culture. Depending on the culture, the source of the obsession may be germs or body fat or religious rituals. Persons who feel compelled to perform certain rituals over and over would do anything if these compulsions would stop. There is treatment for them in the form of training the mind. As the title of Begley's book—*Train Your Mind, Change Your Brain*—suggests.

We now know that that psychological counseling can actually alter the brain's chemistry and lead to more normal functioning. So how does this happen? Begley (2007) describes an experiment conducted by neuropsychiatrist Jeffrey Schwartz in which clients who were suffering from OCD were guided to substitute healthy for unhealthy thoughts every time an obsessive urge came over them. After 10 weeks of behavioral instruction, neuroimaging revealed observable chemical changes in the part of the brain thought to be affected by this disorder. This experiment demonstrated the phenomenon of neuroplasticity, or how the mind can shape the fundamental biology of the brain.

Studies of the impact of psychological trauma on the brain lend further support to the notion that brain structure and function can be altered by cognitions. Particular hormones secreted in times of severe stress can alter neurochemistry sufficiently to effect long-term changes in neurons and brain systems. Harriette Johnson (2004) states that PET scans of eight children reared in Romanian orphanages until their adoption showed just such abnormalities. Begley (2007) describes the situation in the Romanian orphanages of infants lying in their cribs all day deprived of sensory stimulation and having little contact with caregivers. Upon adoption, most of the children made rapid progress in learning but many failed to play with other children or to become emotionally attached to their adoptive parents. The impact of the early deprivation was long lasting. And levels of social bonding hormones that rise in normal children as they engage in close interaction can be forever stunted in children deprived of nurturance in the first years of life.

The technological revolution in neuroresearch is providing documentation for theories about brain changes and development that were previously based only on behavioral observation. Although much has been learned in the past few years, we are just on the brink of understanding addiction and its roots in the brain.

Dementia

Dementia, an organic brain syndrome largely associated with old age, affects an estimated 30–50 percent of those aged 85–100 (Newman & Newman, 2006). The most common and best-known form of dementia in people aged 65 and older is Alzheimer's disease. Symptoms of the gradual failure of the brain associated with this disease include severe problems in cognitive functioning, especially increased memory and verbal impairment, confusion, problems with self-care, and extreme mood swings often accompanied by hostility (Alzheimer's Association, 2009). Early in the illness, plaques and tangles form in the temporal lobes, particularly in the hippocampus, or the memory region (Andreasen, 2001). As the disease progresses, the plaques and tangles become more widely dispersed throughout the brain. According to research from Medical

News Today (Paddock, 2008), a vaccine was developed in the United Kingdom that can clear the brain of the plaques. This was exciting news. The problem was that the Alzheimer's patients did not benefit in any way. This has caused medical scientists to look beyond the plaques to understand the nature of this disease.

Relevant to diagnosis, two tools that hold promise for diagnosis are a cognitive test called the Mini-Mental State Examination, which assesses short-term recall and spatial reasoning, and a PET scan, which allows for active areas of the brain to "light up" the scan. A PET scan can detect the accumulation of a certain protein, the buildup of which has been found to be evident in Alzheimer's patients (Selkoe, 2005).

A study of mental declines associated with aging shows that, while younger adults turn off certain regions of the brain associated with daydreaming when required to concentrate on a task, people with Alzheimer's lack the flexibility to turn off those areas (Lustig, Snyder, Bhakta, et al., 2003). Perhaps this is why many elderly people seem to operate on automatic pilot and do things, going through the motions, without remembering what they did later.

Vascular dementia is the second most common form of dementia; its symptoms are associated with a series of small or major strokes. During a stroke, the blood vessels supplying the brain become clogged by clots, which shut down the blood supply in a specific brain region. A major stroke produces symptoms such as paralysis, which occurs on the opposite side from the brain region injured by the stroke (Kolb & Whisham, 2008). Aphasia, or impairment of the ability to speak clearly, is especially common in people who have had left hemisphere strokes. Damage on this side of the brain is also associated with depression because connections with emotional centers are often disrupted. For vascular dementia, the onset and course are different from Alzheimer's. Stroke victims may show symptoms very suddenly but recover with little impairment. Immediate treatment is a must. Because it used to be thought brain cells could not grow back and new neural connections could not be reestablished, little was done for elderly people who had strokes (Farmer, 2009). Today, equipped with knowledge of brain plasticity, aggressive therapies are performed from the earliest possible moment.

For people who are caring for family members debilitated by strokes or Alzheimer's, the issues are relatively similar. As dementia advances, the changes in personality and emotional responsiveness become more severe, and, Andreasen (2001) states, the person no longer seems to be "the same." Ethical issues arise for the grown children of people with dementia in terms of the care that is needed and that family members are willing or able to provide.

These forms of dementia discussed above have been widely known for decades. Dementia caused by direct blows of the head or *dementia pugilistica* ("punch drunk" syndrome) has received less attention than it deserves. Until recently, the majority of cases of this disease were identified in boxers. But today, the diagnosis is most often associated with America's most popular sport, football. Commonly referred to now as chronic traumatic encephalopathy or CTE, this condition has been identified by neurologists at Boston University School of Medicine in autopsies of brains of former football players (Schwartz, 2009). Out of six brains of National Football League (NFL) veterans that were donated for examination for suspected brain damage, all six showed evidence of CTE. This condition, which is extremely rare in the general population, is a major risk to football players because of the concussions they receive on a regular basis. The cumulative effects of brain trauma is associated with dementia in former football players who sometimes manifest the symptoms while in their forties or fifties. Symptoms include lethargy, memory loss, impulsiveness, and inability to pay attention.

Music and the Brain

Music appreciation is a uniquely human function that remains intact in the memory for a very long time. In *Musicophilia: Tales of Music and the Brain*, neurologist Oliver Sacks (2008) writes of "the remarkable tenacity of musical memory" (p. xii). In his words:

> The imagining of music, even in relatively nonmusical people, tends to be remarkably faithful not only to the tune and feeling of the original but to its pitch and tempo. . . . Our auditory systems, our nervous systems, are indeed exquisitely tuned for music. (p. xii)
>
> Music is a part of being human, and there is no human culture in which it is not highly developed and esteemed. (p. 385)

The effects of music on human behavior are noted throughout life, from the prenatal period through the latest stage of life. As noted by neurobiologist Dick Swaab (2009a), premature babies are calmer, have better oxygen levels, and leave the incubator sooner if music is played. Newborn babies pay much more attention to their mother's singing than when she speaks, and they are sensitive to musical rhythms.

The effects of music on brain functions can be studied in patients with Alzheimer's disease (Swaab, 2009a). Language and music are stored in a part of the memory that is affected late in the disease. Speech does not disappear until very late-stage Alzheimer's, and musical skills can persist for a long time after that. Swaab describes a patient who had once been a professional pianist. She could not recall any spoken or written text or music notation. But she was still able to remember new, unfamiliar music that she had just heard and to reproduce it with an excellent musical feeling. In a later stage she still played her favorite melodies with great pleasure. Another case of lasting musical talent involved a violinist who still retained his response to music long after other brain faculties were gone.

In *Musicophilia*, Sacks recalls many cases from his personal life and medical practice involving experiences with music. Among the situations he describes are these: a surgeon who is struck by lightning and suddenly develops an obsession with Chopin; blind children who have the gift of perfect pitch; people who suffer from amusia, or the inabllity to hear music as anything other than noise; people who hear musical themes so loudly in their heads continuously to the point they can attend to little else; patients with epilepsy who have seizures brought on by music; and people with serious brain diseases who can only move when music beckons them. Sacks's chapter on music therapy describes examples of psychological breakthroughs when people were reached through music who could not respond otherwise. Following a stroke, patients who cannot speak can be taught through singing to communicate. This observation by Sacks has recently been confirmed by further research presented at the annual meeting of the American Association for the Advancement of Science (Wang, 2010). The theory behind the treatment, which is called melodic intonation therapy, is that if a brain damaged on the left side can recruit the fibers from the right side, which are more engaged with music, then the system can adapt.

I remember a personal experience at a nursing home, surrounded by patients with Alzheimer's who could no longer speak. As my daughter began to play "Amazing Grace" on the cello, one woman's moans and groans almost miraculously turned into humming to the beat of the song. Later the social worker, who seemed moved by the experience, said that the woman had once been a church choir director. Another incident reveals how learning and memorizing are enhanced through setting the words and phrases to music. When my son was working at a half-way house for persons with severe brain damage, he found that a man who could not remember how to read could be reached through singing the ABC's. The song brought back the letters, and that brought back the written words.

Ethical Issues

Dramatic scientific breakthroughs provide a new source of understanding, but they also pose perplexing moral quandaries. There are many ethical issues related to health and biology, ranging from when life begins to when it ends (euthanasia). Others involve who should get organ transplants and how far cloning should be allowed to go. Relevant to this chapter are the issues of genetic testing and forced treatment for those with mental disorders and substance abuse problems.

The starting point in making wise ethical judgments is the acquisition of knowledge. Every day social workers see clients who have genetic illnesses or who are at risk for developing them. These clients might have to make difficult decisions about the future, especially about whether to have children or whether to have an abortion based on the results of ultrasound. Social workers therefore need to be prepared to help people decide whether to engage in genetic testing and to adjust to a genetic diagnosis that is unfavorable.

Medical genetic testing is not always necessary to determine one's susceptibility to disease. Estimates of one's chances of developing alcoholism, an eating disorder, or even schizophrenia, for example, can be made based on the number of close relatives that have the problem. Harm reduction—"first do no harm"—is the guiding theme for health and mental health professionals. Moral principles such as those inscribed in the social work code of ethics can help us decide what we ought to do on a contextual basis and how we can help individuals and families reach the decision that is best for them. Often with new technology, our knowledge exceeds our grasp; ethical dilemmas abound. Consider the new developments in neuroscience, for example: implants can be inserted in the brain to treat mental disorders, in effect, altering control of brain functioning in various ways. Consider also the issue of mandatory medication and the effect this has on the patient's right to self-determination. As scientists use the new technologies to conduct research on matters such as sexual attraction, unconscious racism, religious feeling, truth telling, and even the appeal of commercial products, the risks of human rights abuses in the absence of strict guidelines is considerable. An organization called MindFreedom International is a coalition of more than 100 groups that advocates limits to the role of the state and medical community (see http://www.mindfreedom.org). Members of Mad Pride, a branch of MindFreedom, raise the ethical issue concerning whether or not persons with mental disorders who are a danger to themselves and others should be forced to take medication. As described on their website, Mad Pride activists believe in embracing their mental disorders as a gift and in seeking alternative remedies to control them. The National Alliance on Mental Illness (see http://www.nami.org/) takes a more moderate stand. The NAMI website has detailed descriptions of the basic mental disorders, of the medications used to treat them, and of the common side effects. This advocacy group has worked for years for adequate insurance reimbursement for the treatment of mental illness.

Kurtz (2004) states that ethical values should be available for inquiry and critical examination of the use of science, and that people have a right (and duty) to object to practices that we think are based on punitive drives or crass economics. He further asserts that "We might live in a better world if *inquiry* were to replace faith; *deliberation*, passionate commitment; and *education and persuasion*, force and war. We should be aware of the powers of intelligent behavior, but also of the limitations of the human animal and the need to integrate the cold, indifferent intellect with the compassionate and empathic heart" (p. 12).

Practice Implications

Clients can benefit from direct social work interventions to help them make informed decisions about genetic testing and to cope, both as individuals and family members, with the results. In the field of substance abuse, for years counselors have been advising clients about the risks of drinking and using other mood-altering substances when they come from so-called alcoholic families. In the mental health field, the issue is usually compliance with medical orders to take antipsychotic medication. The social worker can help the client communicate any problems with certain

medications so that alternative medications or dosages may be administered.

Moreover, clients in the throes of mental illness and their families can benefit greatly from educationally based therapy to help them understand the biological etiology of the disease and reduce any sense of self-blame. Therapy is also indicated in a prevention capacity—to assist vulnerable people in reducing stress and crises in their lives as a means of preventing episodes of illness. In conjunction with medical treatment of mood disorders, the social worker can assist clients in the development of personal responsibility for health and lifestyle changes. Stress management techniques such as relaxation, exercise, and a strengthening of interpersonal relationships can serve as a buffer in times of crisis (Lawrence & Zittel-Palamara, 2002). Referral to appropriate self-help groups can also be of great value in relapse prevention.

Treatment follow-up studies with former clients have shown that education is one of the key benefits of the therapy experience. Now that we know so much more about the brain and the role of various parts of the brain in mood disorders and the like, some therapists are discovering the power of neuroscience in their everyday counseling work (Johnson, 2004). New research findings that link heart and brain health can be shared with clients to help them fend off Alzheimer's. As studies on laboratory animals have shown, regular exercise seems to stimulate the body's production of molecules that help maintain a healthy cardiovascular system (Marx, 2005). By enhancing the flow of blood to the brain, a healthy heart can compensate for tiny cerebral defects associated with dementia. The family therapist in the role of educator can draw on such research and use a physical model of the brain to illustrate problems in an objective and positive way. This approach allows both therapist and client to engage in the manageable task of learning to live with one's biological predispositions and to understand one's problems in a more compassionate and less blaming way.

The social work profession has a long history of working to shape public policy that protects the interests of consumers of health care services. There is a continuing need to advocate for universal health care and parity for mental health and addictions treatment. Regarding the criminal justice system, advocacy for sentence reform is in order so that people with mental disorders and substance abuse problems can receive the treatment they need within the community insofar as possible. Treatment from a harm reduction model has been shown to be more attractive to persons in trouble with their consumption of alcohol and other drugs (see Marlatt & Donovan, 2005; van Wormer & Davis, 2008). Advocates for drug and mental health courts can present data to legislators and other policymakers proving the cost-effectiveness of such initiatives.

Summary and Conclusion

An understanding of the biological aspects of human behavior and of relevant interventions promoting good health can inform the field of social work for optimal treatment effectiveness. For social work practice as it is carried out in most professional settings—child welfare, schools, mental health centers, and nursing homes, for example—the practitioner must have knowledge of psychopathology, substance abuse, mental illness, health problems, and disease in general. The ecosystems perspective, which is gaining in popularity among social workers, is biological in its origins, interdisciplinary in its teachings, and is a model that aids in our acceptance of the new knowledge coming from genetic research and studies of the brain. The notion of interactionism, for example, a basic construct of ecosystems, guides our understanding of the interconnectedness of nature and nurture influences in human growth and development. We can expect that most children raised in mentally enriched and healthy environments will benefit neurologically as well as socially and be better equipped to cope with later challenges in life. For a discipline such as social work, which is grounded in the study of human behavior, insights from neuroscience on the intricacies of the brain can have profound

implications for the development of effective interventions.

A basic awareness of the effects of drugs such as alcohol and cocaine on the mechanisms underlying brain function is essential to an understanding of addictive behavior, which on the surface appears self-destructive and incomprehensible. New research on the brain and behavior is forthcoming all the time; these studies help clarify the mysteries of addiction. The research is bidirectional—focused on the impact of drugs on the brain and the risk factors of addiction susceptibility.

The impact of the sequencing of the human genome cannot be underestimated. Whereas in the past, researchers studied one gene or a few at a time, they are now taking an entirely new approach to biological research by looking at how thousands of genes work together. This unraveling of the secrets of our genes reinforces our understanding of the body as a system within itself and also in constant interaction with the environment. Genes determine much of what makes up human behavior, and one's behavior has a reciprocal effect upon the genes. As the avalanche of genome data grows daily, new ethical and social challenges arise.

This chapter has highlighted the biological basis of human behavior in the following selected areas: addiction, ADHD, adolescent development, aggression (including battering and rape), antisocial personality, the shyness-extraversion continuum, stress, schizophrenia, OCD, and bipolar disorder. Matters of gender, including sexual orientation and transgenderism, were considered as well. Despite the plethora of topics considered in these pages, there is no way to do justice to the wealth of biological research now available to enhance social work practice in a single chapter or in a single book, for that matter. But I hope that this chapter has provided an overview of recent research in genetics and neurology with the most direct bearing on human behavior, both normal and abnormal.

Due to neuroimaging technology, we know things today that in previous decades we could only guess at or infer from behavior. The ability to directly observe the effects of neurological damage caused by long-term substance abuse is a significant accomplishment in itself; being able to demonstrate the impact of craving on the pleasure circuits of the brain is even more remarkable. To see, as we can today, a slide of a serotonin-depleted brain is to see, in a very real sense, the face and the insanity of addiction. In providing this glimpse into the inner workings of the mind, modern technology is truly revolutionary. The new insights, Schwartz and Begley (2003) contend, herald a revolution in treatment for stroke, depression, addiction, obsessive-compulsive disorders, and even psychological trauma. Such advanced knowledge about the genetic and biochemical links to individual problems and exciting discoveries about the dynamics of the brain provide an awareness of the link between the inner workings of the mind and outward behavior.

Biology and psychology are intimately linked; so are mind and body. Studies have established connections between the incidence of psychological attitudes and several other diseases, including cancer, Parkinson's disease, epilepsy, stroke, and Alzheimer's disease (Lemonick, 2003). However strong the biological component of human behavior is, the nature versus nurture controversy is fallacious. There is no either/or in the real world. People and their environment are in constant and dynamic interaction. Nature *and* nurture, as well as biology *and* culture, are intertwined. Interceding between biology and culture is the human psyche. With recognition of this fact we move to a consideration of psychological factors in human behavior, that aspect of being that includes our dreams, visions, and determination to keep going against all odds or, conversely, to give up at the first sign of defeat.

Thought Questions

1. What can we learn from the Human Genome Project? How do the findings relate to the person-in-environment conceptualization?
2. What do studies of twins tell us?
3. How are nature and nurture both important in the development of disorders?
4. What did Cloninger's study of male adoptees reveal about alcoholism?
5. How is new knowledge about the brain advancing social work treatment today?
6. How is the addicted brain a changed brain?
7. What are "feeling memories"?
8. How would you explain the process of cocaine addiction?
9. How would you describe Hartmann's hypothesis about the frequency of ADHD in the United States?
10. Can changes in thinking change the brain chemistry, as Schwartz claims? What is the evidence?
11. What are some biological factors in aggression? What do studies of apes tell us?
12. What is the evidence for biologically based behavioral differences in males and females? Relate this to crime data.
13. How would you explain the structure of the brain in terms of right brain and left brain?
14. What is the biological evidence relative to homosexuality?
15. Based on the case study of Barbara Cole, what is your understanding of transgenderism? Relate this to scientific brain studies mentioned earlier in the chapter.
16. Do you think shyness is biologically based? Why or why not? Does the social environment play a role?
17. How would you explain the interaction between stress and health problems?
18. How would you describe the schizophrenic brain?
19. How does the drug lithium help people with bipolar disorder? What are the side effects?
20. What can SSRIs do for OCD? What are the criteria for diagnosing OCD?
21. What would you say are some of the health issues related to ethics?
22. For social workers, what are the implications of genetic information?

References

Allen, L. S., & Gorski, R. A. (1992). Sexual orientation and the size of the anterior commissure in the human brain. *Proceedings of the National Academy of Science, 89*(15), 7199–7202.

Alvergne, A., Faurie, C., Raymond, M., (2009). Variation in testosterone levels and male reproductive effort: insight from a polygynous human population. *Hormones and Behavior, 56,* 494–497.

Alzheimer's Association. (2009). *2009 Alzheimer's disease facts and figures.* Retrieved from http://www.alz.org/national/documents/report_alzfactsfigures2009.pdf

American Psychiatric Association (APA). (2000). *Diagnostic and statistical manual of mental disorders* (4th ed.). Arlington, VA: Author.

Amminger, G., Schafer, M., Papageorgiou, K., Klier, C., Cotton, S., Harrigan, S.and Berger, G. (2010). Long-chain w-3 fatty acids for indicated prevention of psychotic disorder. *Archives of General Psychiatry, 67* (2), 109.

Andreasen, N. (2001). *Brave new brain: Conquering mental illness in the era of the genome.* New York: Oxford University Press.

Badzek, L., Turner, M., & Jenkins, J. (2008). Genomics and nursing practice: Advancing the nursing profession. *Online Journal of Issues in Nursing, 13* (1). Retrieved from: http://www.nursingworld.org/MainMenuCategories/ANAMarketplace/ANAPeriodicals/OJIN/TableofContents/vol132008/No1Jan08/GenomicsandAdvancingNursing.aspx

Bailey, J. M., & Pillard, R. C. (1991). A genetic study of male sexual orientation. *Archives of General Psychiatry, 48,* 1089–1096.

Bailey, J. M., Neale, M. C., & Agyei, Y. (1993). Heritable factors influence sexual orientation in women. *Archives of General Psychiatry, 50,* 217–223.

Begley, S. (2004, May–June). The roots of hatred. *AARP* [magazine], 49–51.

Begley, S. (2007). *Train your mind, change your brain.* New York: Ballantine Books.

Bem, D. (2000). Exotic becomes erotic: Interpreting the biological correlates of sexual orientation. *Archives of Sexual Behavior, 29*(6), 531–548.

Benson, H., Corliss, J., & Cowley, G. (2004, September 27). Brain check. *Newsweek,* 45–47.

Black, D. W. (1999). *Bad boys, bad men: Confronting personality disorder.* New York: Oxford University Press.

Blakeslee, S. (1999, October 19). Study links antisocial behavior to early brain injury that bars learning. *New York Times,* p. A15.

Bogaert, A. (2006). Biological versus nonbiological brothers and men's sexual orientation. *Proceedings of the National Academy of Sciences in the USA, 103* (28), 10771–10774.

Brady, K., & Sinha, R. (2005). Co-occurring mental and substance use disorders: The effects of chronic stress. *American Journal of Psychiatry, 162,* 1483–1493.

Brizendine, L. (2006). *The female brain.* New York: Broadway Books.

Brown, A. S., & Susser, E. (2002). In utero infection and adult schizophrenia. *Mental Retardation and Developmental Disabilities Research Reviews, 8*(1), 51–57.

Brown, W. M., Finn, C. J., & Breedlove, S. (2002). Differences in finger length ratios between self-identified "butch" and "femme" lesbians. *Archives of Sexual Behavior, 31*(1), 123–127.

Brune, A. (2007, April 8). When she graduates as he. *Boston Globe,* Retrieved from http://www.boston.com/news/globe/magazine/articles/2007/04/08/when_she_graduates_as_he/?page=2

Buckaloo, B., Krug, K., & Nelson, K. (2009). Exercise and the low-security inmate. *The Prison Journal, 89,* 328–343.

Bureau of Justice Statistics. (1999). *Adolescent girls: The role of depression in the development of delinquency.* Washington, DC: Department of Justice.

Cabeza, R. (2002). Hemispheric asymmetry reduction in older adults: The HAROLD model. *Psychology and Aging, 17,* 85–100.

Cannon, M., Jones, P., Huttunen, M., Tanskanen, A., Huttunen, T., Rabe-Hesketh, S., & Murray, R. (1999). School performance in Finnish children and later development of schizophrenia: A population-based longitudinal study. *Archives of General Psychiatry, 56*(5), 457–463.

Caspi, A., Moffitt, T., Silva, Ph., Stouthamer-Loeber, M., Krueger, R., & Schmutte, P. (2006). Are some people crime-prone? Replications of the personality-crime relationship across countries, genders, races, and methods. *Criminology, 32*(2), 163–196.

Cloninger, C. R., Sigvardsson, S., Gilligan, S., van Knorring, A., Reich, T., & Bohman, M. (1989). Genetic heterogeneity and the classification of alcoholism. *Advances in Alcohol and Substance Abuse, 7,* 3–16.

Comings, D. E. (2001). Clinical and molecular genetics of ADHD and Tourette syndrome. *Annals of the New York Academy of Sciences, 931*, 50–83.

Council on Social Work Education (CSWE). (2008). *Educational policy and accreditation standards.* Alexandria, VA: Author.

Cunningham, W., Johnson, M., Raye, C., Gatenby, J. C., Gore, J. C., & Banaji, M. (2004). Separable neural components in the processing of black and white faces. *Psychological Science, 15*(12), 806–813.

Dabbs, J. M., & Dabbs, M. G. (2000). *Heroes, rogues, and lovers: Testosterone and behavior.* New York: McGraw-Hill.

Davis, D. R. (2009). *Taking back your life: Women and problem gambling.* Center City, MN: Hazelden.

Davison, K. K., & Birch, L. L. (2001). Weight status, parent reaction, and self-concept. *Pediatrics, 107*(1), 46–53.

Delisi, M., Beaver, K., Vaughn, M., & Wright, J.P. (2009). Gene x environment interaction between DRD2 and criminal father is associated with five antisocial phenotypes. *Criminal Justice and Behavior, 36* (11), 1187–1197.

Economist (2009, August). Risky business. *The Economist,* 71.

Eisenberg, D. T, Campbell, B., Gray, P. B., & Sorenson, M. D. (2008). Dopamine receptor genetic polymorphisms and body composition in undernourished pastoralists: An exploration of nutrition indices among nomadic and recently settled Ariaal men of northern Kenya. *BioMed Central Evolutionary Biology, 8,* 173.

Eliot, L. (2009). *Pink brain, blue brain: How small differences grow into troublesome gaps—And what we can do about it.* New York: Houghton Mifflin Harcourt.

Epel, E., Blackburn, E., Lin, J., Dhabhar, F., Adler, N., Morrow, J., & Crawthon, R. (2004). Accelerated telomere shortening in response to life stress. *Proceedings of the National Academy of Sciences, 101*(49), 17312–17315.

Farmer, R. (2009). *Neuroscience and the social work practice: The missing link.* Thousand Oaks, CA: Sage.

Fitzpatrick, L. (2007, November 19). The gender conundrum. *Time,* p. 59.

Foreman, J. (2003, December 2). The biological basis of homosexuality. *Boston Globe.* Retrieved from http://www.boston.com/yourlife/health

George, M. S., Anton, R., Bloomer, C., Teneback, C., Drobes, D., Lorberbaum, J., Nahas, A., & Vincent, D. (2001). Activation of prefrontal cortex and anterior thalamus in alcoholic subjects on exposure to alcohol-specific cues. *Archives of General Psychiatry, 58,* 345–352.

Gibson, G. (2009). *It takes a genome: How a clash between our genes and modern life is making us sick.* Upper Saddle River, NJ: Pearson.

Giedd, J. (2008). The teen brain: Insights from neuroimaging. *Journal of Adolescent Health, 42*(4), 335–343.

Gil, D. (2001). Challenging injustice and oppression. In M. O'Melia & K. K. Miley (Eds.), *Pathways to power: Readings in contextual social work practice* (pp. 35–44). Boston: Allyn & Bacon.

Ginsberg, L., Nackerud, L., & Larrison, C. (2004). *Human biology for social workers: Development, ecology, genetics, and health.* Boston: Allyn & Bacon.

Goodwin, D. (1976). *Is alcoholism hereditary?* New York: Oxford University Press.

Gottschall, J. (2008). *The rape of Troy: Evolution, violence, and the world of Homer.* Cambridge, England: Cambridge University Press.

Greco, K. E. (2003). Nursing in the genomic era: Nurturing our genetic nature. *MedSurg Nursing, 12*(5), 307–313.

Gur, R. C., Gunning-Dixon, F., Bilker, W., & Gur, R. E. (2002). Sex differences in tempero-limbic and frontal brain volumes of healthy adults. *Journal of Cerebral Cortex, 12*(9), 998–1003.

Hallowell, E., & Ratey, J. (2005). *Delivered from distraction.* New York: Random House.

Hammen, C. (2009). Children of depressed parents. In I. Gotlib & C. Hammen (Eds.), *Handbook of depression* (2nd ed.), (pp. 275–297). New York: Guilford.

Harris, J. R. (2009). *The nurture assumption: Why children turn out the way they do, Revised and updated.* New York: The Free Press.

Hartmann, T. (2005). *The Edison gene: ADHD and the gift of the hunter child.* Rochester, VT: Park Street Press.

Harvard Medical School. (2005, March). On the trail of schizophrenia. *Harvard Mental Health Letter.* Retrieved from: http://www.schizophrenia.com/sznews/archives/001638.html

Helmuth, L. (2003). In sickness or in health? *Science, 302,* 808–10.

Hines, M. (2004). *Brain gender.* New York: Oxford University Press.

Holloway, M. (1991, March). Treatment for addiction. *Scientific American, 264*(3), 95–103.

Honos-Webb, L. (2005). *Gift of ADHD: How to transform your child's problems into strengths.* Oakland, CA: New Harbinger Publications.

Hornbacher, M. (2008). *Madness: A bipolar life.* New York: Houghton Mifflin.

Howell, S., Chavanne, T., Shoaf, S., Cleveland, A., Snoy, P., Westergaard, G., Hoos, B., Suomi, S., & Higley, J. (2007). Serotonergic influences on life-history outcomes in free-ranging male Rhesus Macaques. *American Journal of Primatology, 69*(8), 851–865.

Insel, T. R. (2005, April 27). Testimony before the House Subcommittee on Labor-HHS-Education Appropriations. Congressional Session information.

Jamison, K. R. (1995). *An unquiet mind: A memoir of moods and madness.* New York: Vintage Books.

Johnson, H. C. (2004). *Psyche, synapse, and substance: The role of neurobiology in emotions, behavior, thinking, and addiction for nonscientists* (2nd ed.) Greenfield, MA: Deerfield Valley.

Kagan, J. (1994). *Galen's prophecy: Temperament in human nature.* New York: Basic Books.

Kaye, W., Fudge, J., & Paulus, M. (2009). New insights into symptoms and neurocircuit function of anorexia nervosa. *Nature Reviews Neuroscience, 10*, 573–584.

Kirk, K., Bailey, J., Dunne, M., & Martin, N. (2000). Measurement models for sexual orientation in a community twin sample. *Behavior Genetics, 30*(4), 345–356.

Klar, A. (2004). Excess of counterclockwise scalp hair-whorl rotation in homosexual men. *Indian Academy of Sciences Journal of Genetics, 83*(3), 251–255.

Kolb, B., & Whishaw, I. (2008). *Fundamentals of human neuropsychology* (6th ed.). New York: Worth Publishing.

Krajbich, I., Adolphs, R., Tranel, D., Denburg, N., & Camerer, C. (2009). Economic games quantify diminished sense of guilt in patients with damage to the prefrontal cortex. *Journal of Neuroscience, 29*(7), 2188–2224.

Krueger, R., Markon, K., & Bouchard, T. (2003). The extended genotype: The heritability of personality accounts for the heritability of recalled family environments in twins reared apart. *Journal of Personality, 7*(5), 809–833.

Kuo, F., & Taylor, A. (2004). A potential natural treatment for attention-deficit/hyperactivity disorder: Evidence from a national study. *American Public Health Association, 94*(9), 1580–1586.

Kurtz, P. (2004, September). Can the sciences help to make wise ethical judgments? *Skeptical Inquirer.* Retrieved from http://www.csicop.org/si/show/can_the_sciences_help_us_to_make_wise_ethical_judgments

Kurzban, R., & Leary, M. R. (2001). Evolutionary origins of stigmatization: The functions of social exclusion. *Psychological Bulletin, 127*(2), 187–209.

Lafsky, M. (2009, September 9). Is it possible to systematically turn gay people straight? *Discover.* Retrieved from http://discovermagazine.com

Lambert, C. (2000, March–April). Deep cravings: New research on the brain and behavior clarifies the mysteries of addiction. *Harvard Magazine,* 60–68.

Lawrence, S. A., & Zittel-Palamara, K. (2002). The interplay between biology, genetics, and human behavior. In J. S. Wodarski & S. F. Dziegielewski (Eds.), *Human behavior and the social environment: Integrating theory and evidence-based practice* (pp. 39–63). New York: Springer.

Lemonick, M. D. (2003, January 20). The power of mood. *Time,* 67–72.

León-Carrión, J., & Ramos, F. (2003). Blows to the head during development can predispose to violent criminal behavior: Rehabilitation consequences of head injury is a measure for crime prevention. *Brain Injury, 17*(3), 207–216.

LeVay, S. (1991). A difference in hypothalamic structure between heterosexual and homosexual men. *Science, 253*, 1034–1037.

Lustig C, Snyder, A.Z., Bhakta, M., O'Brien, K.C., McAvoy, M., Raichle, M.E., Morris, J.C., Buckner, R.L. (2003) Functional deactivations: change with age and dementia of the Alzheimer type. *Proceedings of the National Academies of Science, 100*, 14504-14509.

Manasse, M., & Ganem, N. (2009). Victimization as a cause of delinquency: The role of depression and gender. *Journal of Criminal Justice, 37*(4), 371–378.

Markon, K., Krueger, R., Bouchard, T., & Gottesman, I. (2002). Normal and abnormal personality traits: Evidence for genetic and environmental relationships. In the Minnesota Study of Twins Reared Apart. *Journal of Personality, 70*(5), 661–693.

Marlatt, G. A., & Donovan, D. (Eds.). (2005). *Relapse prevention maintenance strategies in the treatment of addictive behaviors.* New York: Guilford Press.

Martin, P. L. (2002, Summer). Moving toward an international standard in informed consent: The impact of intersexuality and the Internet on the standard of care. *Duke Journal of Gender, Law and Policy, 9*(4), 135–170.

Marx, J. (2005). Preventing Alzheimer's: A lifelong commitment? *Science, 309*(5736), 864–866.

McManis, M., Kagan, J., Snidman, N., & Woodward, S. (2002). EEG asymmetry, power, and temperament in children. *Developmental Psychobiology, 41*(2), 169–177.

Medical News Today (2009, August 28). AstraZeneca traveling exhibit helps Americans understand and manage bipolar depression. Retrieved from http://www.medicalnewstoday.com/articles/162164.php

Miller, M.C. (2008, September 22). Sad brain, happy brain. *Newsweek*, 51–53.

Mondimore, F. (1996). *A natural history of homosexuality*. Baltimore: Johns Hopkins University Press.

Muller, M., & Wrangham, R. (2009). *The sexual coercion in primates and humans: An evolutionary perspective*. Cambridge, MA: Harvard University Press.

Murphy, R., Nutzinger, D. O., Paul, T., & Leplow, B. (2004). Conditional-associative learning in eating disorders: A comparison with OCD. *Journal of Clinical and Experimental Neuropsychology, 26*(2), 190–199.

Murray, C. M., Wroblewski, E., & Pusey, A. (2007). New case of intragroup infanticide in the chimpanzees of Gombe National Park. *International Journal of Primatology, 28*(1), 23–38.

National Human Genome Research Institute (2009, September 18). *The social and behavioral research branch*. Retrieved from http://www.genome.gov/11508935

National Institute on Alcohol Abuse and Alcoholism (NIAAA). (2000). Why do some people drink too much? *Alcohol Research and Health, 24*(1), 17–26.

National Institute on Alcohol Abuse and Alcoholism (NIAAA). (2004, October). Alcohol's damaging effect on the brain. *Alcohol Alert, 63*, 3–5.

National Institute on Drug Abuse (NIDA) (2008a, September 17). *Drugs and the the brain*. Retrieved from http://www.drugabuse.gov/ScienceofAddiction/brain.html

National institute on Drug Abuse (NIDA) (2008b, September 17). *Treatment and recovery*. Retrieved from http://www.drugabuse.gov/ScienceofAddiction/treatment.html

National Institute on Drug Abuse (NIDA) (2009, July). *NIDA: Info facts: Methamphetamine*. Retrieved from http://www.drugabuse.gov/Infofacts/methamphetamine.html

National Institutes of Health (NIH). (2005, October 3). *National survey sharpens picture of major depression among U.S. adults*. Retrieved from http://www.niaaa.nih.gov/NewsEvents/NewsReleases/Sept2005.htm

National Institute of Mental Health (NIMH). (2005, September 19). *NIMH study to guide treatment choices for schizophrenia* [Press release]. Retrieved from http://www.nimh.nih.gov/science-news/2005/nimh-study-to-guide-treatment-choices-for-schizophrenia-phase-1-results.shtml

Newman, B., & Newman, P. (2006). *Development through life: A psychosocial approach* (9th ed.). Belmont, CA: Thomson.

Oquendo, M., Chaudhury, S., Mann, J. (2005). Pharmacotherapy of suicidal behavior in bipolar disorder. *Archives of Suicide Research, 9*(3), 237–250.

Paddock, C. (2008, July 21). Alzheimer's vaccine cleared plaques but did not slow the disease. *Medical News Today*. Retrieved from http://www.medicalnewstoday.com/articles/115683.php

Parker, M. (2004, January 4). Adam's story: Journals, paintings trace young man's journey into schizophrenia. *Waterloo–Cedar Falls (Iowa) Courier*, Sunday Lifestyles section, p.1.

Parsons, L., & Osherson, D. (2001). New evidence for distinct right and left brain systems for deductive versus probabilistic reasoning. *Cerebral Cortex, 11*(10), 954–965.

Payne, S. (2006). *The health of men and women*. Cambridge, England: Polity Press.

Pittman, R., & Delahanty, D. (2005, February). Conceptually driven pharmacologic approaches to acute trauma. *CNS Spectrums, 10*(2), 99–106.

Puts, D., Jordan, C., & Breedlove, S. M. (2006). O brother, where art thou? The fraternal birth-order effect on male sexual orientation. *Proceedings of the National Academy of Sciences in the USA, 103*(28), 10531–10532.

Rahman, Q., & Wilson, G. D. (2003). Large sexual-orientation differences in performance on mental notation and judgment of line orientation tasks. *Neuropsychology, 17*(1), 25–31.

Rapport, M. D., Bolden, J., Kofler, M. J., Sarver, D. E., Raiker, J. S., & Alderson, R. M. (2009). Hyperactivity in boys with attention-deficit/hyperactivity disorder (ADHD): A ubiquitous core symptom or manifestation of working memory deficits? *Journal of Abnormal Child Psychology, 37*, 521–534.

Rehn, A., & Rees, S. (2005, September). Investigating the neurodevelopmental hypothesis of schizophrenia. *Clinical and Experimental Pharmacology and Physiology, 32*(9), 687–697.

Reig, S., Moreno, C., Moreno, D., Burdalo, M., Janssen, J., Parellada, M. . . . and Arango, C. (2009). Progression of brain volume changes in adolescent-onset psychosis. *Schizophrenia Bulletin, 35* (1), 233–243.

Ridley, M. (2006). *Genome: The autobiography of a species in 23 chapters*. New York: Perennial.

Riley, J. G. (2009). Human behavior theory and social work practice: Genetics, environment, and development. In R. Greene (Ed.), *Human behavior theory and social work practice* (3rd ed.). (pp. 291–314). New Brunswick, NJ: Aldine Transaction.

Rosin, H. (2008, November). A boy's life. *The Atlantic*. Retrieved from http://www.theatlantic.com/doc/200811/transgender-children

Sacks, O. (2008). *Musicophilia: Tales of music and the brain*. New York: Vintage Books.

Saleebey, D. (2001). *Human behavior and social environments: A biopsychosocial approach*. New York: Columbia University Press.

Savic, I., & Lindström, P. (2008). PET and MRI show differences in cerebral asymmetry and functional connectivity between homo- and heterosexual subjects. *Proceedings of the National Academy of Sciences USA*, *105*(27), 9403–9408.

Schiffman, J., Sorensen, H., Maeda, J., Mortensen, E., Victoroff, J., Hayashi, K., et al. (2009). Childhood motor coordination and adult schizophrenia spectrum disorders. *American Journal of Psychiatry*, *166*, 1041–1047.

Schuckit, M. A. (2000). Genetics of the risk for alcoholism. *American Journal on Addictions*, *9*, 103–112.

Schwartz, A. (2009, January 28). New signs of brain damage in N.F.L. *New York Times*, p. B11.

Schwartz, J. M., & Begley, S. (2003). *The mind and the brain: Neuroplasticity and the power of mental force*. New York: Regan Books.

Science Daily. (2007, November 7). Brain chemicals involved in aggression identified: May lead to new treatments. Retrieved from http://www.sciencedaily.com/releases/2007/11/071106122309.htm

Selkoe, D. (2005, October). By the way, doctor. Is there a brain scan that can specifically diagnose Alzheimer's disease? *Harvard Health Letter*, *30*(12), 8.

Spear, L. (2000). Modeling adolescent development and alcohol use in animals. *Alcohol Research and Health*, *24*(2), 115–123.

Swaab, D. (2009a, March 13). Alzheimer's deterioration process. *NRC Handelsblad*. Retrieved from http://weblogs.nrc.nl/swaab/2009/03/13/alzheimers-deterioration-process-2/

Swaab, D. (2009b, February 27). Damage to the moral brain network. *NRC Handelsblad*. Retrieved from http://weblogs.nrc.nl/swaab/2009/02/27/damage-to-the-moral-brain-network/

Thornhill, R., & Palmer, C. (2000). *A natural history of rape: Biological bases of sexual coercion*. Boston: MIT Press.

Treisman, G. (2005). Treating mental illness in the HIV patient. *Audio Digest Psychiatry*, *34*(24). Retrieved from http://www.audio-digest/org/ (accessed May 2006).

Tullis, L. M., DuPont, R., Frost-Pineda, K., & Gold, M. S. (2003). Marijuana and tobacco: A major connection? *Journal of Addictive Diseases*, *22*(3), 51–62.

Uhl, G., Drgon, T., Johnson, C., Fatusin, O., Liu, Q-R., Contoreggi, C., Li, C. Y., Buck, K., & Crabbe, J. (2008). "Higher order" addiction molecular genetics: Convergent data from genome-wide association in humans and mice. *Biochemical Pharmacology*, *75*(1), 98–111.

U.S. Department of Health and Human Services. (2000). *Special report to the U.S. Congress: Alcohol and health*. Washington, DC: Government Printing Office.

van Wormer, K., & Davis, D. R. (2008). *Addiction treatment: A strengths perspective* (2nd ed.). Belmont, CA: Brooks/Cole.

van Wormer, K. & Roberts, A. R. (2009). *Death by domestic violence: Preventing the murders and the murder-suicides*. Westport, CT: Praeger.

Volkow, N. (2009, February 19). Addiction: Drugs, brains and behavior: The science of addiction. National Institute on Drug Abuse (NIDA). Retrieved from http://www.drugabuse.gov/ScienceofAddiction/

Volkow, N., Wang, G-J., Kollins, S., Wigal, T., Newcorn, Telang, F., et al. (2009). Evaluating dopamine reward pathway in ADHD: Clinical implications. *Journal of the American Medical Association*, *302*, 1084–1091.

Walsh, T. C. (1999). Psychopathic and nonpsychopathic violence among alcoholic offenders. *International Journal of Offenders and Comparative Criminality*, *43*(1), 34–48.

Wang, S. (2010, February 22). Music helps stroke victims communicate, study finds. *The Wall Street Journal*. Retrieved from http://online.wsj.com

Weiss, J. O. (2004, October). What social workers need to know about genetics. *Inter-Sections in Practice: NASW Specialty Annual Bulletin*, *3*(1), 17–20.

Whitten, L. (2005). A single *Practice Sections* cocaine "binge" can establish long-term cue-induced drug seeking in rats. *NIDA Notes*, *19*(6). Retrieved from http://www.drugabuse.gov/NIDA_notes/NNVol19N6/Single.html

Wrangham, R., & Peterson, D. (1996). *Demonic males: Apes and the origins of human violence.* Boston: Houghton Mifflin.

Xiang, Y., Luk, S., & Lai, K. (2008). A review of genetic studies on attention deficit hyperactivity disorder in Han Chinese population. *Hong Kong Journal of Psychiatry, 18* (4), 166–173.

Zastrow, C. H., & Ashman, K. K. (2010). *Understanding human behavior and the social environment.* (10th ed.). Belmont, CA: Brooks/Cole.

Zuckerman, M., & Kuhlman, D. M. (2000). Personality and risk taking: Common biosocial factors. *Journal of Personality, 68*(8), 999–1029.

The Psychology of Human Behavior

The rigid righteous is a fool . . .
What is done we partly can compute
But know not what's resisted.

—ROBERT BURNS 1786

Now we come to the will, the mind, and the self. As we saw again and again in the previous chapter, biology alone cannot explain human behavior; it is always the biological attribute in conjunction with the psychosocial—the mind–body dyad. Whereas the preceding chapter looked at human behavior from the standpoint of the body, this chapter reverses the formula and starts with the mind—the thinking processes. As before, theories are supported insofar as possible with scientific research. Also as before, we will consider a number of questions: Why and how do people develop a moral sense? Why do people who were unwilling to change their unhealthy practices at one point in life become willing to alter them at some later point? How does one's identity develop, and what are the pitfalls of negative identities? What do we know about fear, anger, and other emotions? How can we control them? How do feelings sometimes play into victimization? How are male and female expressiveness alike and different? What is psychological trauma? What are its causes and consequences? Is there such a thing as brainwashing or mind control? How much does the experience of being battered affect one's self-concept and subsequent behavior?

We begin with a discussion of the mind–body relationship and then proceed to an examination of relevant life span developmental perspectives. The nature of identity formation is the next topic, and we follow it with a discussion of the psychology of feeling. The dynamics of family violence from the perpetrator's point of view leads to an in-depth study of psychological trauma. The earlier sections on life span development, self-identity, and feelings can be viewed collectively as building blocks for the understanding of trauma and what the experience—whether of war or sexual abuse—does to people. The chapter ends with a discussion of strategies for working with trauma survivors.

Psychology examines human behavior from the viewpoint of the individual. Emphasis is placed on learning, drives, and motivation. Psychological variables interact with innate, biological tendencies to produce personality characteristics. On the school playground, for example, recess is a dreaded time for shy, non-athletic kids. Some children are aggressive and tend to dominate the playground; others retreat to the background. Social variables thus come into play and reinforce psychological predispositions to encompass what we know as personality. How people handle the vicissitudes of life and build up defense mechanisms to cope with adversity and defeat—these are the defining characteristics of personality, the traits we know as character. William Shakespeare (1599/1952), whose genius showed in his knowledge of psychology, grappled with the age-old question of how some rise above their circumstances while others fall. As Cassius says in *Julius Caesar:* "Men at some time are masters of their fates; The fault, dear Brutus, is not in our stars, But in ourselves, that we are underlings" (act 1, scene 2).

Shakespeare also knew about the role that the unconscious mind plays in human behavior. Guilt, a key theme of *Macbeth*, is revealed in the behavior of Lady Macbeth, who, unable to stop washing her hands after murdering Duncan, asks her husband, "Will not all great Neptune's ocean wash this blood clean from my hand?" (Shakespeare, 1605/1952, act 2, scene 1).

Our concern in this section is with psychological aspects of human behavior as exemplified in issues of personal trauma and resilience, as people endure both ordinary and extraordinary crises. We start with the concept of developmental psychology, which concerns human growth and development from childhood to old age. Most human behavior and the social environment (HBSE) courses draw on the theory of psychological development proposed by Erik Erikson (1950), whose contribution is highly compatible with social work theory. Erikson's formulation focuses on the way in which our personalities evolve as a result of the interaction between biologically based maturation and the demands of society (Zastrow & Kirst-Ashman, 2010). At each stage of development, from birth to old age, there are crises to resolve. For the practitioner, knowledge of psychological milestones that are normally achieved, such as when leaving adolescence and entering young adulthood,

is important in individual evaluations. In Erikson's conceptualization, at each juncture of life an individual must resolve the crisis relevant to that developmental stage before moving on to the next phase. Unresolved crises from the past, such as issues from early childhood, can come back to haunt people later in life.

Much of human behavior is irrational and difficult even for the individual actors to explain, as anyone familiar with courtroom testimonials will come to appreciate. Using the courtroom as illustration, offenders, victims, and even witnesses often have a hard time explaining what they did and even what they were doing at the scene of a crime. Sometimes the defendants, their victims, and/or other witnesses for the prosecution were drunk or high on illicit drugs at the time the incident took place. Intoxication, of course, compounds the inexplicability of much of the behavior—people do things when they are drunk that they would never dream of doing while sober—even as it plays havoc with the memory. However, even much of sober behavior defies our ability to understand.

The public's fascination with bizarre and destructive behavior is revealed in newspaper headlines, on the covers of tabloid magazines, and in the popularity of the syndicated newspaper column called "News of the Weird." Much attention is also given to unhealthy, life-threatening behaviors, especially those associated with disease—high blood pressure, alcoholism, and HIV/AIDS.

It is well established that lifestyle choices such as nutrition, exercise habits, smoking cigarettes, and the use of alcohol and/or drugs have an impact on our physical health, our immune system's ability to fight disease, and our mental health (Zittel, Laurence, & Wodarski, 2002). The interplay between one's mental outlook and physical well-being is receiving increasing attention today in conjunction with the heightened interest in general health issues. As more people are living longer and the baby boom population approaches retirement age, chronic illness is much more widespread. The search for psychological variables in controlling such illness has begun. Another major area in health research identified by Zittel et al. (2002) is the role of stress in conjunction with illness and individual differences in the handling of stress. When the perception of control over health increases—the psychological factor—health-promoting activities can occur. When a sense of hopelessness ensues, however, self-medication through smoking, drinking excessively, and failing to eat a healthy diet only exacerbates the symptoms. Part of the evidence for the influence of mind over body comes from placebo-based studies—medical research shows that even sugar pills bring relief due to the psychological effect of believing the supposed drug was real (Saleebey, 2001). Such is the power of suggestion. Another more recent source of evidence of the mind–body link is the opposite experience—stress-related psychosomatic illness that is genuine physical illness related to the physiological response of the body to stress (see, e.g., studies of the impact of workplace bullying by Djurkovic, McCormack, & Casimir, 2006).

Evidence of the power of the mind involves experiments in pain sensation. After women received brief electric shocks to the hand, their magnetic resonance imaging (MRI) results registered that their pain network was activated when they felt the jolts. Curiously, when men were shocked, the emotional regions of suffering in their loved ones were activated as well (Singer et al., 2004). There is a great deal we do not yet know about the mind since many of its processes are unconscious. The thought processes develop throughout one's life span.

Human Growth and Development Theories

In this section, the developmental theorists we discuss (Maslow, Erikson, Levinson, Kohlberg, and Gilligan) have focused on changes in psychological thinking and behavior over time. (Piaget's work is described in Chapter 4 in conjunction with the part of Erikson's developmental scheme most relevant to children.) For an understanding of spiritual development, we review the contributions of Fowler and Wilber. Finally, because of its relevance to contemporary treatment, as well as to the psychology of motivation, Prochaska and DiClemente's developmental, stages-of-change theoretical framework is presented.

Developmental Theories

The following four theorists all view development as a sequential process. For Maslow and Erikson, each basic accomplishment rests on the preceding one. Although Levinson focused on men and Gilligan on women, their theoretical schemes are included here because of their attention to development in a broad sense.

Maslow

Psychologist Abraham Maslow (1950/1971) developed a theoretical model for explaining some aspects of human behavior related to the fulfillment of human needs. The basic assumptions of his framework are that needs may be both conscious and unconscious and that the gratification of needs determines behavior by extinguishing the drive to fulfill them. Conversely, chronic deprivation of needs places them foremost in the mind and stymies our development. Psychologically, Maslow believed that humans strive to reach the highest level of their capabilities.

Maslow's contribution to development theory is represented in his well-known construction of human needs, each one of which has to be fulfilled successively before the next higher level of need can be achieved. As Maslow's *hierarchy of needs* (Figure 3.1) shows, the basic physical needs of human survival must be met first before higher level needs—safety, belongingness, love, esteem, and self-actualization—can be realized. Needs theory demonstrates the importance of biological factors in human behavior (Barsky, 2010). A number of physiological needs that are crucial to human development are sleep, food, water, breathing, physical security, and excretion. Deprived of any of these basic needs, as Barsky asserts, an individual may be motivated to do whatever is necessary to satisfy them. Consider also needs that are induced through unhealthy behavior, for example, the need of another

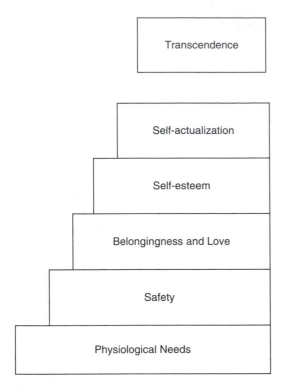

Figure 3.1. Maslow's hierarchy of needs.

"fix" for the drug addict. Many moral lapses are associated in the seeking of satisfaction of this seemingly urgent need.

The road from meeting one's physiological needs and self-actualization is a long one. Self-actualization, in fact, is achieved only rarely. Because each person in Maslow's conceptualization tries to satisfy these needs in ascending order, high self-esteem is not likely to occur in the absence of love, and self-actualization is not apt to be realized without a certain degree of financial security. Moreover, the stage of self-actualization is not permanent. Given life's uncertainties, you could lose your balance at any moment and be reduced to the lower rungs of the ladder, struggling at the level of mere survival. At the end of his life, Maslow (1971) added a sixth level, transcendence, to his hierarchy of needs. He defined transcendence in less egocentric and more spiritual terms. Helping others find self-fulfillment is the defining characteristic of this level. Although other HBSE textbooks use a triangle to illustrate the hierarchy, I have chosen instead to use a step design

to better reflect the notion of movement across the various levels.

The psychological, as opposed to social, nature of this conceptualization is revealed in its emphasis on individual drives and the concepts of self-esteem and self-actualization. Strength comes from one's inner resources, not from rootedness in the community. Dominelli's (2002) critique of Maslow's formulation rightly focuses on his neglect of social-cultural attributes related to race and gender. Dominelli draws our attention to the influence of capitalism in manufacturing artificial needs through the marketing of commercial products that may be downright harmful. Maslow's paradigm, in short, reflects the values of individualism in mainstream culture. Traditional Native American culture, for example, was geared toward group and spiritual satisfaction rather than elevation of self.

Still, because of its relevance to social welfare, Maslow's conceptualization of human needs is commonly cited in the social work literature. With slight modification (such as linking self-actualization to generativity—giving to others and posterity), the hierarchy-of-needs construct can offer a holistic guide to personal and even collective fulfillment. It offers a paradigm that can be adapted, moreover, for viewing a society's level of success in meeting the needs of people or even a particular group in society. At the micro level (which is clearly how Maslow intended for his model to be applied), physical needs may be met, yet other factors such as physical or sexual abuse can diminish one's sense of safety, belongingness, and self-esteem. This framework, because it is not age based (like Kohlberg's and Erikson's) and because it is much simpler, can more readily serve as a model to reflect the impact of life's cruelties and exposure to unfavorable events such as long-term family violence, the horrors of warfare, or more immediate experiences such as rape.

Life-Span Theories

Erikson

Erik Erikson published his influential *Childhood and Society* in 1950. Trained as a psychoanalyst, Erikson (1950/1963) nevertheless offered an optimistic, biopsychosocial view of development. His concern was with the human capacity for healthy growth and the resolution of predictable, age-based crises. In contrast to many other theoretical schemes, Erikson's developmental stages extend across the life span.

From this perspective, each stage of human development presents a characteristic crisis that must be resolved. Failure to resolve a crisis in an earlier stage affects a person's ability to cope well with the later conflicts. The underlying assumptions of the eight major stages that follow are that each stage represents a continuum from positive to negative; each stage presents a crisis that must be resolved; the psychosocial crises are universal and not limited to one culture; and one's personality is revealed in the way one resolves the crises. The stages are as follows:

1. Trust versus mistrust (infancy to 18 months). Infants who receive nurturing care learn to trust, and this prepares them for lifelong intimacy.
2. Autonomy versus shame and doubt (18 months to 3 years). By accomplishing various tasks, children develop confidence and feelings of self-worth.
3. Initiative versus guilt (ages 3–6). Small children learn to take the initiative when they are encouraged to do so; if stymied, they are apt to experience feelings of guilt.
4. Industry versus inferiority (ages 6–12). How children succeed academically and master other activities determines whether they will feel industrious or inferior.
5. Identity versus role confusion (adolescence). This is the time for identity crisis—the trying out of new roles and the shedding of old ones.
6. Intimacy versus isolation (young adulthood). The quest for intimacy—the finding of a soul mate—dominates this period. An ethical sense also emerges at this time.
7. Generativity versus stagnation (middle age). Generativity involves a genuine concern for the future beyond one's own life, a consideration for what one is leaving behind.

8. Ego integrity versus despair (old age). The crisis of old age occurs as people look back over a life of purpose or, conversely, one that seems meaningless and causes feelings of regret.

To Erikson, personality development follows a predictable sequence over time and space punctuated by definable moments during which epigenetic crises must be resolved. Erikson (1982) defines *epigenesis* as "a progression through time of a differentiation of parts. This indicates that each part exists in some form before its decisive and critical time normally arrives and remains systematically related to all others so that the whole ensemble depends on the proper development in the proper sequence of each item. Finally, each part will also be expected to take its place in the integration of the whole ensemble" (p. 29).

Because of its logical and concise organizational structure and inclusion of social and environmental elements, Erikson's framework has stood the test of time and is included in virtually all human behavior textbooks. His focus on normal developmental processes (unlike psychodynamic theory) is also an attractive feature since most courses in human behavior are concerned with normal human growth and development. And yet, as the following chapter points out, this theoretical model can also serve as a springboard for the discussion of extreme and abnormal behavior.

Critics of Erikson point to the theory's preoccupation with the male experience to the neglect of female concerns (Gilligan, 1982); to Erikson's heterosexual bias (Greene, 2009); and to his taken-for-granted assumption that the sequential stages to emotional and social development that he delineates are universal (Greene, 2009).

Levinson

Daniel Levinson's (1979) theory is another sequential or stage theory. This model reflects research that Levinson and his colleagues carried out with 40 men aged 35–45, most of whom had careers in the professions. From data obtained from this sample, Levinson constructed a theory of adult male development. Belatedly, after almost 20 years and following a great deal of criticism for his blatant male centeredness, Levinson, with his wife's help, applied the approach to women.

For Levinson, the central conceptual organizing scheme was life structure. The *life structure*, or underlying pattern of a person's life, incorporates a sequence of seasons, or epochs. In *The Seasons of a Man's Life*, Levinson (1979) explains that the life structure shapes and is shaped by a person's interaction with the environment. Each season has a distinctive character biologically, psychologically, and socially. The adult seasons last almost 5 years each and extend from early adult transition through late adult transition. Levinson's primary focus was on middle-aged men. An interesting inclusion in the early adulthood period is the relationship between young men and a successful older mentor, a relationship that has historically been denied to young women who might have had similar ambition.

A later volume on the seasons of a woman's life (Levinson, 1996) categorizes gender difference in four parts. These are the split between the domestic sphere for women and the public sphere for men; the homemaker and provider; men's work and women's work; and masculine and feminine attributes in the individual psyche.

Moral Development Theories

Moral behavior concerns the should's and should-not's as directed by the norms of society, the way in which humans progress in moral reasoning, and the principles on which they base their ethical thinking. Theories of moral development consider how children and adults are socialized to conform to the norms of their culture.

Kohlberg

Lawrence Kohlberg's (1981) linear stage theory of moral development places primary emphasis on how people think, not what they do, as they move toward progressively higher levels of ethical understanding. Kohlberg's three levels break down into six stages as follows:

Level 1: Preconventional (ages 4–10), behavior related to conditioning
Stage 1: Avoid punishment, obedience to authority
Stage 2: Work toward rewards
Level 2: Conventional (ages 10–13), what is found in society
Stage 3: Please others to gain approval
Stage 4: Obey norms and laws; respond to obligations
Level 3: Postconventional, rarely achieved by most adults
Stage 5: Laws subject to interpretation; genuine interest in others' welfare
Stage 6: Morality completely internalized; respect for universal principles

Kohlberg's contribution was in delineating stages of cognitive development, taking into account the interface between the environment and the person. Building on Piaget's theoretical continuation of childhood mental growth and development, Kohlberg provided details based on his observational research on 50 American males aged 10–28. His focus was on the reasoning behind the answers given to the moral dilemmas provided (Robbins, Chatterjee, & Canda, 2006). His theoretical model was far more interactional (depending on the influence of socialization) and less age based than those that preceded it. Kohlberg believed that most moral development occurs through social interaction. Children learn qualitatively different modes of thinking sequentially. In his research on other cultures such as that found in Israeli kibbutzim, Kohlberg found the that stages of moral development could be applied worldwide. His work helped to lay a foundation of legitimacy for further incorporation of values and spirituality into social work practice. Three major criticisms are the rigid linear sequencing; the cultural bias of stage 6, which fails to take into account communal consciousness; and the male-centeredness in that the behaviors observed were those of boys and men rather than including girls and women (Zastrow & Kirst-Ashman, 2010).

The exclusively male orientation is revealed in the focus on law and order rather than personal caring (Gilligan, 1982).

Gilligan

Carol Gilligan (1982) has articulated what so many women in the social and behavioral sciences who were forced to study these theories must have felt for some time: These theories do nothing for girls and women. Nevertheless, she did not just criticize; she developed her own theoretical construction. In contrast to the dominant theories that emphasized the development of separation and autonomy (typical male, Euro-American values), Gilligan centered her research on the capacity for connectedness and caring in girls and women. Her work pays particular attention to the conditions in families, schools, and communities that support or impede the development and maintenance of girls as they grow from infancy into adulthood (Van Voorhis, 2009).

Moral development in women is very different from moral development in men. Sacrifice is a frequent concomitant of female maturity. This contrasts with the male focus on independent decision making and justice. Gilligan interviewed 29 women who were receiving pregnancy and abortion counseling to discover their concerns and feelings of morality. From her data, she filtered out the following levels of moral development: *(1)* orientation to personal survival—caring for the self in order to promote survival, *(2)* goodness viewed as self-sacrifice and caring for others, and *(3)* the morality of nonviolent responsibility for meeting her own needs as well as those of others. The transition here, the personal growth for the woman, involved accepting the responsibility for making her own decisions. The overriding principle of moral development is the minimization of hurt, both to herself and to others (Zastrow & Kirst-Ashman, 2010).

Although Gilligan is cited in the literature mainly in terms of her criticism and reaction to the life-span theories of others, she is also a noteworthy theorist in her own right and, in my opinion, a better writer—both more literate and literary—than those with whom her work is usually compared. In *The Birth of Pleasure*, Gilligan (2002) uses stories and metaphors from Shakespeare's plays, Freud's case histories, and the novels of Nathaniel Hawthorne, Toni Morrison, and Arundhati Roy, as well as her personal dreams, to write about love in this book that, as she says, "was conceived in love" (p. 30). Of love, which Gilligan likens to rain, she says, "When it rains, when we love, life grows. To say that there are two roads, one leading to life and one to death and therefore choose life, is to say in effect: choose love. We have a map. We know the way" (p. 235). Gilligan's goal, realized in family therapy and one that is threaded throughout her book, was to discover the language of love and pleasure and to see love and pleasure freed from the trappings of a manhood or womanhood that holds them captive. In her couples therapy, she came to "see love as a courageous act and pleasure as its harbinger" (p. 19).

Gilligan's insights on what happens to a 5-year-old boy—suppression—and an adolescent girl—the same—reveal much about detrimental forces in the cultural landscape. Masculinity, she contends, often implies an ability to stand alone and forgo relationships, whereas femininity connotes a willingness to compromise oneself for the sake of relationships. Since the initiation of boys into the codes of masculinity intensifies around the age of 5, while girls are given more leeway to express themselves until adolescence, there is a common ground here that is rarely recognized. The difference is that, when she comes face to face with societal norms, what Gilligan calls "a process of revision," the girl is more likely than the boy to name and openly resist the loss of her freedom.

Gilligan's contribution, as she sees it, has centered on listening for the voice behind the spoken voice, the voice of the psyche. In her work she attends to the silences between men and women, and in her more recent book, *The Birth of Pleasure*, published two decades after *In a Different Voice*, she shows us how a path leading toward tragedy can be turned into a road leading to pleasure.

Theories of Faith Development

Fowler and Wilber

James Fowler's (1995/orig.1981) theory of faith development was based on 359 intensive interviews with residents of Boston, Chicago, and Toronto. Fowler focused on one theme—religious faith—and traced its development across the life cycle. He conceptualized faith development as moving through six discontinuous, sequential, and hierarchical stages (Carroll, 1999). What he found was that people move from intuitive faith in early childhood, to literal faith in middle childhood, to conventional faith in adolescence, and to a more reflective faith in early adulthood. The first stage of faith development—the Intuitive-Projective stage—occurs during the early childhood stage when the child has an active and sometimes overactive imagination. Some religious groups, according to Fowler (1995), subject children to the kind of preaching and teaching that vividly emphasizes "the pervasiveness and power of the devil, the sinfulness of all people without Christ and the hell of fiery torments that await the unrepentant" (p. 132). Other children, however, can get pleasure from the stories, and learn morals from parables that are told. During the second stage—the Mythic-Literal Faith stage—school-aged children make sense of the stories and construct a more orderly, linear world while enjoying the rituals and beliefs that symbolize belonging to the community. The risk at this stage is that some children become rigid and perfectionistic. Conventional beliefs characterize the third stage, or Synthetic-Conventional period of adolescent faith. The capacity for abstract thinking is characteristic of this time of life. Although Fowler does not use the term *rebellion*, he does say that personal clashes may take place as youths critically reflect on what they were taught. This conflict may lead to a transition to the next stage or to leaving the beliefs behind as one leaves home. Fourth is the Individuative-Reflective stage of young through middle adulthood. Most people stop here. One-sixth of the interviewees, however, advanced to what Fowler termed Conjunctive Faith, usually during the middle years. Those who advance to this level embrace paradox and think in both-and rather than either-or terms. Conflict is resolved and one's beliefs are integrated with conventional views. Furthermore, the believer recognizes the limitations in his or her understanding of truth (Carroll, 1999). The highest level of faith development—Universalizing Faith—is achieved by only a tiny minority. Here the self is no longer the primary reference point, but all of humanity.

Karen Armstrong (2009), a former nun, who has become one of the world's leading theologians, refers to her spiraling spiritual development in her new treatise, *The Case for God*. The following passage captures some of the essence of her spiritual climb from the particular to the universal:

> My study of world religion during the last 20 years has compelled me to revise my earlier opinions. Not only has it opened my mind to aspects of religion as practiced in other traditions that qualified the paraochial and dogmatic faith of my childhood, but a careful assessment of the evidence has made me see Christianity differently. One of the things I have learned is that quarreling about religion is counterproductive and not conducive to enlightenment. (p. xvii)

Criticism of Fowler's paradigm focuses on the fact that the sample was more than 97 percent white and 85 percent Christian. Matters of diversity and oppression, moreover, were not taken into account (Zastrow & Kirst-Ashman, 2010). Maria Carroll (1999) who introduced me to Fowler's work, likens Fowler's perspective to that of Maslow. Each is based, as she suggests, on a belief in an inner dynamic force that is responsible for the impulse to grow; spiritual growth as a lifelong process; a core inner self that needs to develop; and the importance of a deep interconnectedness with others.

We can appreciate Fowler's contribution, nevertheless, to moral development stage theory. To see to what extent Fowler's faith development model holds up against more recent data, we can take a look at *Souls in Transition* by Christian Smith (with Patricia Snell, 2009).

Drawing on data from the General Social Survey (GSS) conducted by the National Opinion Research Center, a scientific research center that focuses on American social life, sociologist Christian Smith presents a portrait of the religious and spiritual life of adults across the life course. The focus of Smith's book is on young, college-age adults, whom he calls "emerging adults."

The statistics from GSS, collected from 1990 to 2006, show the following:

- A good 42 percent of emerging young adults pray daily, while 76 percent of persons over age 75 do so.
- Only 27 percent of young adults consider themselves to be very religious compared to 53 percent of the oldest age group.
- Around 80 percent of all age groups believe in life after death.
- Young black adults and young white evangelical Protestants are the most apt to pray daily.

Although religious affiliation varies widely across the life span, Smith believes the young people today are no different than those from the previous generation in this regard. Having children will bring their level of church, synagogue, and mosque attendance back up to the level of their parents. Moving away from religious activities associated with one's upbringing relates to the period in American life when young adults learn to think for themselves and stand on their own two feet, according to Smith. Almost one-fourth of those aged 18 to 23 are not religious. This is an increase from the 13% who were not religious in late childhood. The decline in religious faith was especially apparent among Catholics and Jews.

The period of emerging adulthood—between young people leaving home and their marrying and setting up a home of their own—is growing longer these days, because people marry later and start their families later. The costs could be high, according to Smith, of this prolonged adolescence because the time without steady religious observance is also prolonged. Religious young adults, as Smith indicates, are less likely to binge drink, use drugs, and smoke than are more secular young

people, and they are more likely to actively engage in community life. Smith's presentation of data is roughly compatible with Fowler's stages of religious development, although his focus is more on college-age adults, and especially on those who have drifted away from the beliefs of their upbringing. Smith's bias, as evidenced throughout *Souls in Transition*, is toward membership in organized religion, to the neglect of idealistic young people who see themselves as spiritual beings but who find their spiritual beliefs difficult to define.

Transpersonal theory such as that of Ken Wilber relates to what is known as a higher level of consciousness, a seeking of a source of power that comes from beyond the personal—from a universal spirit. Transpersonal theory makes major contributions to our understanding of spiritual development and of the integration of body, mind, and spirit (Robbins et al., 2006). Such theory is highly relevant to our study of the psychology of behavior in showing, as Robbins et al. suggest, that biology does not necessarily dictate behavior (e.g., prayer or healing rituals) but that behavior can determine biology. The two, in fact, are intertwined. Recall from Chapter 1 Wilber's concept of the holon, which states that, in nature, being a whole in one context is simultaneously being a part in another. The potential is that every conscious individual as a holon can experience the self in union with the ultimate sacred reality.

Wilber's theoretical scheme is ambitious. Drawing on Eastern contemplative traditions, his scheme attempts a universal stage theory of religious development. His primary focus, however, is individual consciousness. In excerpts from his spiritual diary, Wilber (1998) explores the world of dreams, which he examines at various levels of conscious control. In the diary he teaches that the powers of meditation can remove everyday pain and torment and provide an "egoless state" that can "be swallowed by Spirit and awaken to a glory that time forgot to name" (pp. 6 and 9). When one finds such inner peace, even at the center of a cyclone, one can feel safe. The process that leads to this state of peak experience operates in a spiraling (as opposed to a linear) fashion; people will have to make sense of this experience within their current stage of maturity (Sheridan, 2008).

Critics of transpersonal theory maintain that creating universal theories of religious evolution is of dubious value (Robbins et al., 2006). Wilber's theoretical scheme, moreover, is criticized for being highly Eurocentric in his stage theory of religious development and lacking in a cultural anthropological research base. Nevertheless, transpersonal theory has important contributions to make to the expansion of our approaches to research. This formulation expands the repertoire of conventional science by recognizing the usefulness of subjective knowledge. The focus is on the seeking of direct experience of the sacred through deep meditation. If we are to develop a full understanding of the whole person in the environment, it is crucial that we take the insights of transpersonal theories into account (Robbins et al., 2006).

Stages of Change

Prochaska and DiClemente

Moving from the highly abstract to the more concrete, Prochaska and DiClemente (1986) have constructed a model that, like Fowler's, pertains to one aspect of human thought and behavior. In this case, the concern is self-destructive behavior and ways to help people change. The *stages-of-change model*, as it is called, is sometimes referred to as a *transtheoretical* model because it relies on several theories of social psychology. This sequence of stages toward change was first proposed by Prochaska and DiClemente for use in helping smokers break their nicotine habit. Their formulation is included here in the presentation of developmental models for the first time, to my knowledge, in a human behavior textbook. I have chosen to highlight this model because of its relevance to social work practice and because of the insights it affords into human motivation in general.

The underlying theoretical framework of Prochaska and DiClement's model is optimistic—the belief that people are ultimately capable of making informed decisions in their own best interest. The choices they make depend on their readiness to change (i.e., what stage of change they are in at a certain point in time) (van Wormer & Davis, 2008). The model has since been applied and adopted in many addiction treatment and other helping settings around the world. DiClemente and Velasquez (2002) describe the series-of-change model: "In this model change is viewed as a progression from an initial *precontemplation stage*, where the person is not currently considering change; to *contemplation*, where the individual undertakes a serious evaluation of considerations for or against change; and then to *preparation*, where planning and commitment are secured" (p. 201).

Once the tasks of the initial stage are accomplished, DiClemente and Velasquez further inform us, clients can be expected to take *action* toward change; such action steps, in turn, lead to the final and fifth stage of change, *maintenance*, in which the person works to maintain long-term change. If the individual falters, however, a sixth stage—*relapse or recurrence* of the behavior—may occur. Such backtracking is considered a normal part of the behavior change process.

The stages-of-change model is a natural fit with motivational enhancing and harm reduction practices because of its primary focus on client choice and its emphasis on helping people progress through the stages at their own pace. Instead of a dualistic, one-size-fits-all framework, where there is either complete recovery or total failure, this approach incorporates the concept of small steps punctuated by expected setbacks on the road to recovery or, as we might say, maturity. Unlike most linear stage theories, people are seen as progressing in a spiral pattern, regressing at times to an earlier stage for indefinite periods before moving on.

The starting point for the therapist is to determine where the client is, that is, at what level of change. According to Boyle (2000), it is not unusual for involuntary clients to enter treatment at the *precontemplative* stage. When precontemplators present themselves for help, they often do so because of pressure from others (Prochaska & Prochaska, 2009). For the

Table 3.1   An Ambivalent Teen Progresses Through the Stages

Stage of Change	Adolescent Comments
Precontemplation	My parents can't tell me what to do. I still use. So what if I get high now and then?
Contemplation	I'm on top of the world when I'm high, but then, when I come down, life is a drag. It was better before I got started on these things.
Preparation	I'm feeling good about setting a date to quit, but who knows?
Action	Staying clean may be healthy, but it sure makes for a dull life. Maybe I'll check out one of these groups.
Maintenance	It's been a few months. I'm not there yet, but I'm hanging out with some new friends.

purposes of illustration, let us assume the client is a hard-drinking teenager brought to treatment through a court order. Table 3.1 contains typical teenage comments at each level of the stages of progression.

During the initial precontemplation stage of work with the typical teen drug user, the goals for the therapist are to establish rapport, to ask rather than tell, and to build trust. Eliciting the teen's definition of the situation, the counselor can reinforce discrepancies between the client's and others' perceptions of the problem. During the *contemplation* stage, while helping to tip the decision toward reduced drug/alcohol use, the counselor emphasizes the client's freedom of choice. "No one can make this decision for you" is a typical way to phrase this sentiment. Information is presented in a neutral "take-it-or-leave-it" manner. Typical questions include "What do you get out of drinking?" "What is the down side?" Questions to elicit strengths include "What makes your family member believe in your ability to do this?"

At the *preparation* for change and *action* stages, questions like "What do you think will work for you?" help guide the client forward without pushing the youth too far too fast.

The stages-of-change model helps the client progress toward healthy living by boosting his or her sense of self-efficacy and helping the client move from an "I can't do it" to an "I think I can" stance. Even better, if the client connects with a self-help group, the movement is from a position of "alone I can't" to a position of "together we can." One's sense of self-efficacy relates to one's personal identity. Self-efficacy theory concerns the relationship between knowledge and action, with how individuals assess their capabilities and how their self-perceptions of efficacy affect motivation and behavior (van Wormer & Davis, 2008). A strong self-concept is related to a strong sense of self and proud group identity.

Social Identity

The question "Who are you?" addresses the matter of one's identity. Erikson (1950/1963) viewed adolescence as the key time for resolving the "identity versus role confusion" crisis. Identity development is closely associated with the roles that one plays. The purpose of having an identity is to lay the groundwork for a synthesized self—a self that integrates roles, values, and cultural attributes (Saleebey, 2001). As roles change throughout life, personal identities shift as well. The development of personal identity is a lifelong biological, psychological, and social process that is affirmed and reaffirmed through observation, practice, and incorporation of meanings from family, friends, and community. Given the human capability of higher thought, people often rethink and rewrite the past, present, and future on encountering new experiences; as they contemplate their failures and successes, the personal narrative changes accordingly. Personal relationships and work experiences have much to do with our emerging sense of self; we come to see ourselves, at least to some extent, as others see us.

One type of identity emerges within the family as various family members assume roles—provider, caretaker, achiever, placater—so that the family can function as a unit. At the same time, these family members may share a collective or social identity based on ethnicity, race, class, and so on. In her book on anti-oppressive practice, Dominelli (2002) describes identity formation in terms of both individual and cultural dimensions that people draw upon when they say "I am a . . ." Members of the dominant group often take their racial identity for granted until they find themselves in a situation (e.g., in an urban jail setting) where their majority status is called into question. Minority group members, on the other hand, typically develop a strong sense of difference from the dominant group, as well as a strong sense of belonging to their own cultural or religious group.

The Impact of Race

Being of a high socioeconomic status did not help African American Harvard scholar Professor Henry Louis Gates, Jr., who was arrested after the police were called when he was breaking into his own home from which he was locked out. As he was later quoted in *The New York Times*, "I can't wear my Harvard gown everywhere I go. . . .We—all of us in the cross-over generation—have multiple identities, and being black trumps all of those other identities" (Cooper, 2009, p. WK6).

Affirmative action benefits are obvious to students who seek scholarships or to job applicants, especially in areas where lack of diversity is an issue. White privilege is less obvious. Popular college lecturer and white antiracist activist Tim Wise, author of *Between Barack and a Hard Place* (2009), argues that the election of Barack Obama to the presidency did not signal the end of racism in the United States. In housing, employment, the justice system, shopping in a store, and education, the evidence is clear: White privilege and discrimination against people of color are still realities of which most white people are unaware. Except in situations where they are a minority, whites do not have a strong racial identification, but rather an acceptance of themselves and their beliefs as the norm. Members of racial and ethnic minority groups, in contrast, have a strong identity based on race and ethnicity because, as with all of us, they see themselves as others see them, and because they experience aspects of discrimination on a daily basis.

Chestang (1984) delineates three barriers to the healthy development of a black person's psyche: social injustice, society inconsistency, and personal impotence. When all three barriers are raised continuously, trust in society and in the social institutions, including education, break down. Finding themselves in such circumstances, many youths fail to develop a positive sense of self-worth. Resentment is played out at multiple levels and seen most vividly in inner-city school dropout rates. Resistance to mainstream cultural values and mistrust of authority may be early markers of risk status for educational underachievement, according to Irving and Hudley (2008). Their recommendation is for school policies and practices that support positive identity development to help more African American youth cultivate a strong positive cultural identity that is consistent with academic achievement (Irving & Hudley, 2008). Dropping out of school closes the door on success within the social norms, but it does not extinguish the desire to achieve material success. As a result, many youths turn to crime and other forms of antisocial behavior; anger is often displaced onto other African Americans. Membership in a disempowered group has personal as well as political ramifications. As bell hooks says, "Black people are indeed wounded by forces of domination. Irrespective of our access to material privilege we are all wounded by white supremacy, racism, sexism, and a capitalist economic system that dooms us collectively to an underclass position. Such wounds do not manifest themselves only in material ways, they affect our psychological well-being" (1993, p. 11).

Minority group identity is often affirmative, however. Community (including church) affiliation and family support are also protective factors in the African American and Latino American communities. Individual identity is likely to be defined through intergenerational family ties and the tradition of mutual aid. Larkin and Beverly (2007) view Afrocentricity as a transforming power that helps African Americans to achieve a higher consciousness of being and a willingness to join the struggle for their psychological liberation. "One truth is abundantly clear," assert Larkin and Beverly. "There is an intimate connection between acceptance of self and acceptance of others." Only with the development of a positive racial/ethnic consciousness will people of African descent cease to apologize for their existence and "be able to remember their souls and find their unquestionable worth and value in the simple dictim 'we are because we are'" (p. 323).

Robert Hill (2007), drawing on the principles of the Kwanzaa celebration, singles out the following Afrocentric values of black families: respect for parents and parenthood, the centrality of children, flexible family roles, control and discipline of children, education, emphasis on community supports, and kinship networks, including "fictive" kin.

The legacy of past oppression is with us still, and government steps to rectify the situation have resulted in resentment by some in the white community. When race became a heated issue over incendiary sermons preached by Chicago minister Reverend Wright, the minister of then candidate for President Barack Obama, Obama (2008) decided to address the nation. At the Constitution Center in Philadelphia, following a synopsis of U.S. history of constitutional rights, this is what he said:

> For the men and women of Reverend Wright's generation, the memories of humiliation and doubt and fear have not gone away; nor has the anger and the bitterness of those years. That anger may not get expressed in public, in front of white co-workers or white friends. But it does find voice in the barbershop or around the kitchen table. At times, that anger is exploited by politicians, to gin up votes along racial lines, or to make up for a politician's own failings.
>
> And occasionally it finds voice in the church on Sunday morning, in the pulpit and in the pews. . . . In fact, a similar anger

exists within segments of the white community. Most working- and middle-class white Americans don't feel that they have been particularly privileged by their race. Their experience is the immigrant experience—as far as they're concerned, no one's handed them anything, they've built it from scratch. They've worked hard all their lives, many times only to see their jobs shipped overseas or their pension dumped after a lifetime of labor. So when they are told to bus their children to a school across town; when they hear that an African American is getting an advantage in landing a good job or a spot in a good college because of an injustice that they themselves never committed; when they're told that their fears about crime in urban neighborhoods are somehow prejudiced, resentment builds over time.

> Like the anger within the black community, these resentments aren't always expressed in polite company. . . . Just as black anger often proved counterproductive, so have these white resentments distracted attention from the real culprits of the middle-class squeeze—a corporate culture rife with inside dealing, questionable accounting practices, and short-term greed; a Washington dominated by lobbyists and special interests; economic policies that favor the few over the many.

Whites' perceptions of people of color reflect ambivalence and contradiction. This observation by Appleby (2007) was echoed openly and honestly in Obama's speech above. Coupled with the ambivalence, there may be a sense of guilt over the mistreatment of blacks in society and resentment over affirmative action measures. Moreover, admiration for black heroes may exist side by side with a denigration of poor and uneducated black people. Well-meaning whites often make the mistake of denying African Americans their pride of identity by trying to be or pretending to be color blind and arguing that we are all the same. In mixed company, discussion of race can be uncomfortable for both races. Read the following personal narrative, which is written in the style of a consciousness-raising exercise. For this assignment, the participant was asked to write about an experience that involved a revelation, one where the participant had witnessed injustice and decided "enough is enough" and that it was time to take a stand. The italicized words—*heard, saw, smelled,* and so on—are provided to respondents, who are asked to fill in the blanks. Here, an African American social worker describes a turning point in her life that ended her reticence to join an ally to assert her identification with her race.

Consciousness Raising Against Racial Oppression

I *heard:* open air, silence, one voice begging for acceptance, one voice seeking affirmation.

I *saw:* the pleading face of a person rebuked, a wrinkled face, small frail hands then I saw blank faces, heads turning, no speaking, heads down, legs crossed, eyes glaring into space, eyes rotating back and forth.

I *smelled:* stale air.

I *tasted:* sticky saliva.

I *felt:* tension, my heart pounding, my body heating up in expectation, a flood of emotions, nervous, scared, out of control, the need to escape.

This to me was racism: racism disguised as professionalism, unacceptable, especially for a group of well-educated professionals, especially for a profession that embraces differences. But in the midst of this intolerance, there was courage. One woman who looked like these others; she had straight hair like them, and she was privileged like them. What was the difference, what made her not like them? She thought like us; she related to us; she identified with our struggle, she tried to empower us, and on that day I should have taken a risk, to stand up for what I believed in, to challenge the authority, to risk my cloak of protection that my silence was affording me. Never again will I remain silent. I will stand for my beliefs, I will stand for my race, I will stand for all humanity and if all else fails, I will simply stand.

(Printed with permission of Charletta Suddeth, MSW.)

Class Identity

The United States is a nation in which class differences are vast, and yet class identity is generally lacking. Class is seldom talked about in the United States, notes Appleby (2007). Nor, as he continues, do we talk about class privilege, class oppression, or the class structure of society. Persons at both the higher and lower echelons often identify themselves as middle class. Yet bell hooks (2000) contends that "Class matters. Race and gender can be used as screens to deflect attention away from the harsh realities class politics exposes. Clearly, just when we should all be paying attention to class, using race and gender to understand and explain its new dimensions, society, even our government, says let's talk about race and racial injustice. It is impossible to talk meaningfully about ending racism without talking about class" (p. 7).

In *Outliers*, Malcolm Gladwell (2008) does for social class mobility what his earlier book *The Tipping Point* did for social psychology. "Success," he writes, "arises out of the steady accumulation of advantages: when and where you are born, what your parents did for a living and what the circumstances of your upbringing will all make a significant difference in how well you do in the world" (pp. 175–176). This is how privilege counts, Gladwell notes, even in cultural legacies that are transmitted through attitudes about achievement or even the need to get ahead. In his presentation of numerous examples from various ethnic groups, including the people of Appalachia, Gladwell reveals how attitude can hold people back despite their individual gifts. His work effectively challenges the myth that individual merit alone is responsible for achieving the American dream. Still, his focus on social mobility is very American; parents often expect their children to do better than they themselves have done.

Much attention has been devoted in the media to the fact that Latinos (apart from Cubans who are predominantly middle class) have a consistently high school dropout rate. The public perception has been that lack of ambition and/or drug involvement is the reason for the low educational attainment of Latinos.

New research findings, however, dispute this perception. A national survey conducted by the Pew Hispanic Center (2009) found that 9 in 10 Latinos believe a college education is necessary, yet most do not plan to attend college. The reason given by 74 percent of the young people in the survey who were not in school was the need to support their families. Having limited English skills was cited by almost half of the respondents as an additional reason. And because of a reluctance to take on financial debt, Latinos often fail to apply for the student loans that assist others in paying for college tuition.

In England, in contrast to the United States, class identity is salient and reflected in accent, political party loyalty, and even newspaper affiliations. The working-class identity empowers the British to organize politically to assert their rights through unions and the Labour party. In the United States, people of the same class are often divided by race and ethnicity and are subject to manipulation by members of the power elite to vote along racial, rather than class, lines. Similarly, people at the lowest echelons are manipulated by the capitalist right to vote against their economic interests on emotionally charged, abstract issues such as patriotism or preserving traditional values. This phenomenon is well explained in *What's the Matter With Kansas? How Conservatives Won the Heart of America* by Frank Thomas (2004).

At the upper-class level, class identity is strong; here identity is expressed in private education, including elite colleges for the children; careers in business and law; and political behavior consistent with their economic interests. Because of their exclusivity, the doings of this group are little known to the general population. The award-winning film depicting the exclusivity of some of New Orleans old line Mardi Gras organizations such as Proteus and Comus is uniquely revealed in the documentary film, produced by an insider, *By Invitation Only*. Questioning its social and racial exclusivity, filmmaker Rebecca Snedeker (2006) decided to forego the debutante tradition that was a birthright of women in her family—but still she could not ignore its hold on her identity.

In any social setting, for women as well as men, introductions are followed by "What do you do?" In the United States, class has a great deal to do with occupation. In the *Newsweek* column "My Turn," Christie Scotty (2004) contrasts the courteous treatment she received from the public in an earlier office job with the treatment she received in the role of waitress: "As someone paid to serve food to people, I had customers say and do things to me I suspect they'd never say or do to their most casual acquaintances. It seemed that many customers didn't get the difference between *server* and *servant*" (p. 24). Still, would *you* treat a servant that way? In any case, this op-ed piece shows how our perception of class determines attitude, which, in turn, determines behavior.

The Gender Factor

From the earliest age, little boys and girls have a sense of their own gender. This sense is constantly reinforced by family members, what Saleebey (2001) refers to as "that steady hum of voices that tells boys and men to do everything we must to ensure that we are not girls" (p. 381). The masculine ethos, accordingly, is very strong and has a significant impact on behaviors. Among them, Saleebey lists drinking four cans of beer in 30 minutes, picking fights, playing sports, driving recklessly, and making unsuccessful sexual advances. Where the father–son relationship is unhealthy or non-existent, emotional constriction (except for expression of anger) is often the result. (The father–son relationship is explored in greater depth in Chapter 7.) In Latino culture, the code of male honor—machismo—prevails; the man is defined as the provider, protector, and head of the household (Colon, 2007). Yet, as Falicov (2005) indicates, despite the patriarchal view of gender roles that persists among Mexican Americans regarding sexuality, decision making is often shared by the parents, and children are very respectful of both parents.

Women share a common bodily experience of femaleness, as well as the social oppression of sexism, regardless of whether they are consciously aware of the fact. Girls are often socialized to assume subordinate roles and to value sexual attractiveness over academic or career success. Stereotyping of women's roles furthers oppression in three ways, according to Worden (2007): rigid female roles; a lack of recognition of an individual woman's needs; and internalization of stereotypes, which makes it hard to seek validation of her own needs. Gender role socialization in the Latino community is especially pronounced (Alvarez & Ruiz, 2001).

Studies of adolescent girls indicate that, from the seventh to the tenth grade, they regress in self-confidence and intellectual development (Pipher, 1994). Obsessions with body image and efforts to appeal to the opposite sex take center stage. (The subject of teen body image is covered in Chapter 4.) Given the salience of pressures toward role conformity, especially in high school, girls who are gender nonconforming have an especially difficult time.

The Psychology of Homophobia

Related to sexism and the rigid codes of gender conformity is the societal oppression of gays, lesbians, and bisexuals. Cultural attitudes play a significant role in all matters related to sex and sexuality. Discrimination against persons perceived as sexually deviant can be horrendous and in many cases dangerous. Pressures during the latter school years for gender conformity fall especially hard on gay and lesbian teens. Pressures from peers are reflected internally as youths often try to force themselves into a heterosexual mode even if their natural inclination is otherwise. In contrast with other minority groups, sexual minority groups keep their identity largely hidden. In revealing it, gays and lesbians risk the loss of their major support systems—family, church, and peer groups. Thus, their wrestling with the key crisis of Erikson's stage of adolescence—identity versus role confusion—lands them on the confused side of the continuum. The literature on gay and lesbian identity places a strong emphasis on the coming-out process and confirms that many face a disturbing choice in coming out—to live a lie or to risk torment and persecution.

Gays, lesbians, and transgendered people constitute approximately 5 percent of the population ("Gays Comprise 5 Percent of Electorate," 2002). This estimate is actually higher than the 2.8 percent of the male and 1.4 percent of the female population who identify themselves as exclusively gay, lesbian, or bisexual, according to the most recent estimate made by a coalition of leading pro-gay activist groups in a legal brief (Sprigg, 2005). (Keep in mind, however, that many gays and lesbians also have heterosexual experiences.)

Being gay, lesbian, bisexual, or transgendered is not a problem of gender or sexual orientation but a heterosexual problem in a moralistic culture. (Transgender persons are those who identify with the gender different from their biology; they dress as the opposite sex and may or may not take hormones or have surgery.) Because the heterosexism is internalized, often before children realize their own inclinations and attractions, conflict arises. Chapter 4 discusses gay and lesbian identity issues in depth in relation to the adolescent years. Here, in this chapter, since our concern is more with the inner psyche, let us examine the phenomenon of homophobia—the fear of homosexuality, including fear of homosexual tendencies in oneself.

Homophobia is an outgrowth of heterosexism. For sexual minorities, *heterosexism* can be considered the counterpart of sexism for women. Prejudice is involved but in a different way. Because homosexuality is so often hidden, the interests of gays and lesbians, not to mention bisexuals, are often ignored. Homophobia relates to the psychology of heterosexism; it entails a heightened attention to the doings of gays and lesbians and often a scapegoating of people of different sexual orientation.

Is homophobia associated with homosexual arousal? This is the research question that was explored by psychologists Adams, Wright, and Lohr (1996) in a unique, physiologically based experiment. Sixty-four exclusively heterosexual men were given questionnaires to determine their level of homophobia. The men were then exposed to erotic stimuli while changes in their penile circumference were monitored. All of the subjects responded to the female erotic videos, but only the homophobic men showed an increase in penile erection in response to male homosexual stimuli. The results seem to confirm psychoanalytical teachings that attribute homophobia to repressed homosexual urges. Consistent with this research, Zeichner (2008) studied 148 heterosexual men on a measure of masculinity. Those who scored as hypermasculine on a questionnaire, when exposed to homosexual erotica on a videotape, displayed angry responses, in contrast to others in the experimental situation.

Hate crimes against gay males and lesbians have become particularly pronounced in both military and civilian life in recent years. The torture and murder of Matthew Shepard in Wyoming in 1998 has come to symbolize gay bashing in the extreme (see van Wormer et al., 2000). The National Coalition of Anti-Violence Programs Annual Report (2005) recorded 2,131 antigay hate crimes in 2004. Although no national statistics are as yet available, regional studies reveal that violent crimes against transgender persons are common. For example, in her analysis of targeted attacks against transgender people in Los Angeles County, Stotzer (2008) found 49 such cases over the past four years. Sometimes the hate crimes against gays, lesbians, and transgender persons are homicides. Figure 3.2, which shows a group of fundamentalist extremists from Topeka, Kansas, was taken at a memorial church service for Jason Gage, an openly gay youth from Waterloo, Iowa. Gage was murdered in 2005 by a 23-year-old homophobic man who was later sentenced to 50 years in prison (for details of the antigay protest, see Stanton, 2005).

More commonplace are the razzing and innuendoes directed toward youths by others seeking to prove their own heterosexuality and to separate themselves from nonconforming gender behavior.

Disability and Identity

One's self-concept is modified over time as social realities change. When a child has a congenital disability, the youngster internalizes the role of being a person who is deaf or blind or has some other handicap right from the start. The psychological impact of the disability depends on the child's coping ability and the response of the parents and other family members (Michilin & Juarez-Marazzo, 2007). When chronic illness or some other disabling condition strikes later in life, a person's self-image may change from a normal, healthy one to one that perceives the self as tainted or damaged. The sense of loss of the formerly able-bodied self can be overwhelming. Such people can become stigmatized both in their own minds and in the minds of others. Those who are in a state of transition from a healthy to a disabled condition are often distraught by anticipated role changes. In his book *Stigma*, Erving Goffman (1963) argued that such illness involved a process of role reassignment and internalization, which is a special discrepancy in a person's identity. Mental illness, tragically, can become someone's personal and social identity; for example, consider the descriptive statement "he's a schizophrenic" (Rapp & Goscha, 2006). An altered sense of self may thus result. Mental illness disrupts daily life and work, thereby stripping people of their primary status and sense of accomplishment.

Rapp and Goscha describe the stigmatizing myths that often accompany the treatment of persons with mental disorders in our society. Labeling all of the needs of individuals as originating with their illness reinforces the notion that clients are defined by their impairment. People with psychiatric disabilities are seen as unable to make choices about where they will live and as too incompetent for regular housing, work, and social relationships. When programs do not work out, clients typically are viewed as unmotivated; the stigma leads to blaming the victim and the perceived need for highly restrictive programming.

Regarding people with physical disabilities, Evans (2002) suggests, there may be an evolutionary factor in people's natural aversion to those with disfigurement even as there is an evolutionary component in seeking out healthy sex partners for procreation. A possible explanation for the revulsion is that people with disabilities may simply remind the rest of us of our own physical vulnerability and mortality. People who have relatives who have faced such challenges, however, rarely respond with

Figure 3.2. Antigay activists from a small religious sect in Kansas make their feelings known outside a church in Waterloo, Iowa, where a memorial service was held for a gay hate-crime victim. Signs attacked gay supporters and the late pope for his humanism. Photo by Rupert van Wormer.

the same negative emotions as those who do not know anyone with a disability.

Dominelli (2002) writes of the body as socially constructed in terms of an idealized image. Such images are sexualized in accordance with heterosexual norms and standards that do not allow for physical or mental flaws. Consider how photographs of fashion models are airbrushed to present an image of the perfect body and how hard some magazine readers try to emulate what they perceive as real from the advertisements.

Seeing ourselves as others see us is crucial to the formation of a self-identity. When Susan Boyle, who suffered from severe learning problems and ridicule her whole life, walked out on the stage of *Britain's Got Talent*, people in the audience generally looked disgusted at what was later termed her "frumpy" appearance. The show's judges egged her on and promoted

the audience's badgering with sarcastic questions and responses. Then she sang, and most of the readers will know the rest of her story—how her song received a record number of hits on www.youtube.com and how Susan Boyle became an overnight sensation with her beautifully rendered "I Dreamed a Dream" from the musical *Les Misérables* (read *The New York Times* story by Lyall, 2009). When Susan Boyle had a difficult time following her bout with fame and had to be hospitalized after an emotional collapse, there was some acknowledgment of her handicap, including reports that she had suffered brain damage at birth due to oxygen deprivation (Fisher & Ibanga, 2009). The point here is the stereotyping that Boyle endured, a fact reflected in her general lack of self-confidence and a total devaluation until recently of her actual talents and achievements.

The mental health professional who is working with clients who are mentally or physically challenged must be cognizant of societal oppression and the need for these people to develop coping mechanisms to offset the oppression they may encounter. Social workers can help them develop support systems, perhaps through self-help groups or the religious community, to bolster their courage and to establish or reestablish meaningful roles essential for a positive self-identity.

Social workers also need to be aware of the psychological strength that many people display as they wrestle with major challenges, for example, coping with a major disability. Consider facts presented in the previous chapter about the wondrous ability of the brain to prune and strengthen neural connections depending on which ones are used as you ponder the life of rhythm and blues musician Ray Charles. Blind from the age of 7, Charles was not coddled by his strong-willed mother but pushed into independence. That this lesson was learned well is revealed in the 2004 biographical film *Ray*. In an informative scene, Ray Charles explains why he can get around so well without the use of a cane or dog:

> My ears got to be my eyes, man.
> Everything sounds different, you know?
> That's why I wear hard sole shoes so I can hear the echo of my footsteps off the wall. When I pass an open doorway the sound changes. . . .I hear like you see. Like that hummingbird outside the window, for instance.

We also have much to learn of resilience from the Deaf community, a close-knit community in which many of the members see deafness not as a genetic defect, but as a blessing. A serious ethical issue facing this community comes with the invention of the cochlear implant, an electronic device that enables a child or adult with little or no hearing to pick up sounds. The issue as revealed in the provocative documentary film *Sound and Fury* produced in 2000 concerns whether or not a child's parents should have the surgery which will, to some extent, remove her from her family and the Deaf community. Deaf culture is discussed in some detail in the family and community chapters of the companion volume to this book.

The Spiritual Self

Spirituality involves both physical and nonphysical dimensions of being. The mind–body dualism that pervades European American culture is less relevant to other peoples. "The emphasis placed on spirituality and the capacities of the emotional and intellectual realms by indigenous people in both Western countries and other parts of the world," says Dominelli, "challenges this binary division" (2002, p. 19).

Spirituality expands consciousness to a realm beyond the physical. It reflects our struggle to find meaning and purpose in life that extend beyond material and self-centered concerns. Spiritual sensibility might be reflected in visions, peak experiences, and cosmic revelations (Saleebey, 2001). Whereas spirituality refers to a search for purpose, meaning, and connectedness with the universe, religion refers to a specific set of institutionalized beliefs and rituals. Spirituality is often manifested in the form of religion, but it can also be demonstrated in social activism and ministry to the poor and sick. The sense of calling to engage in teaching, nursing, or social work is another example where the motivation may derive from a higher purpose.

It may come as a surprise to many, but Freud's writings contain multiple references to the soul. In *Freud and Man's Soul*, Bettelheim (1983) has done what persons fluent in German should have done years before—read Freud in the original German. Freud's work, as we read it today, Bettelheim argues, is encumbered with medical and Latin terms designed to help it appeal to a medical audience. The word *soul*, for instance, was changed to *mental apparatus*. In fact, Freud wrote extensively of the human soul, its nature and structure, and, like Marx, the way in which it reveals itself in our behavior and dreams. Freud was opposed to organized religion mainly because of the moral strictures it placed on people's drives. Jung, a fellow psychoanalyst, disagreed with Freud on the role of religion in society. His belief in the collective unconscious is one that goes beyond ordinary experience. In his writings on alcoholism, Jung traced the roots of the cravings to a spiritual thirst for wholeness (Bill Wilson/C. G. Jung Letters, 1961/1987).

In my work as an alcoholism counselor in Norway, I found that the people there were not religious in any conventional sense but that they were highly spiritual. They found their higher power in nature, a sense of oneness with the universe. Their sense of the Holy Spirit could best be likened to Wordsworth's (1798/1999) discovery in nature of:

> A presence that disturbs me with the joy
> Of elevated thought, a sense sublime
> Of something far more deeply interfused
> Whose dwelling is the light of setting suns,
> And the round ocean and the living air.
> (lines 94–98)

Social work today is witnessing a resurgence of interest in spirituality to the extent that the Council on Social Work Education (2003) now requires the inclusion of the spiritual aspects of human behavior in the core curriculum. Consistent with this trend, the prestigious social work journal *Social Thought* changed its name (in the fourth issue of 2001) to *Journal of Religion and Spirituality in Social Work: Social Thought*. One key concept that has emerged is *spiritually sensitive social work*. Sheridan (2002) conceptualizes such practice as consisting of knowledge of relevant theory, an appropriately spiritually diverse setting, and assessment of the client's spiritual background and propensity. The spiritual self is not only an important component in personal identity but also a major strength within virtually all ethnic (including rural white) communities.

Many social work theorists err in attempting to draw a tight distinction between religion and spirituality and in failing to acknowledge the extremely rich body of religious scholarship from many disciplines (Praglin, 2004). With solid educational preparation in diverse religious concepts, social workers can help clients draw on the healthy elements of their religious/spiritual backgrounds and on religious support systems consistent with their clients'

beliefs. Additionally, social workers can help put into perspective elements (such as heterosexism) that may be personally troubling or socially divisive within a family or a peer group. Social workers can also help clients get in touch with their feelings and concerns about their personal faith. (For a background in the historic role of religion in the black community, see *Spirituality and the Black Helping Tradition in Social Work* by Martin and Martin [2002]).

Feelings and Human Behavior

A psychology of human behavior would be remiss if it did not examine the feeling dimension. Much of what is noble or repulsive in human behavior is rooted in the thinking/feeling processes. In this section we consider a few of the primary emotions—fear, anxiety, depression, anger, jealousy—and what research reveals about them. (The positive emotion of love is discussed in Chapter 4 in terms of bonding and attachment and in Chapter 5 in connection with intimacy.)

Fear and Anxiety

Emotionally and evolutionally, the brain is attuned to signs of potential danger. Fear is physically experienced as a rush of energy as the body prepares for fight or flight. Physical strength and attentiveness are intensified. Some who have experienced fear can remember hearing and/or feeling a loud heartbeat and/or a stabbing sensation in the stomach. An outpouring of sweat, tightening of the throat, and irregular breathing have also been reported. These responses, revealed in rat studies, are the result of activation of the amygdala, the fear center of the brain; this activation sends warning signals to all parts of the body (Johnson, 2004). When the fear response is generated, as through a shock, the hippocampus portion of the brain stores a memory of the incident. Stress can spark all kinds of fears and phobias. The avoidance, anticipation, or distress when confronted with the feared object or situation interferes with one's functioning and creates anguish (Williams, 2002).

There is a difference between fear and anxiety. With fear, the source of the feeling is clearly identified: a growling dog, deep water, a crashing car. With anxiety, the source of the distress is often not clearly known or defined. Stress may be less acute but more enduring. Anxiety is often chronic.

Stress Management

The perpetual nervousness that plagues some people can be readily reduced through cognitive therapy techniques. Anxiety-provoking self-talk ("I'm going to fail the test, and my parents will kill me") can be replaced with new ways of thinking ("I'll do my best; I can always repeat the course; my parents weren't the greatest students in their day"). Medication such as beta blockers can help people get through upcoming anxiety-producing events such as giving a speech or interviewing for a job. One of the most efficient ways to reduce stress is to focus inwardly on one's breathing. The practice of taking slow, deep breaths, perhaps repeating a word silently as you inhale, has been found to lower blood pressure and produce an overall feeling of calm (American Psychological Association, 2006). When one practices a form of meditative breathing, brain images show an inhibition of the amygdala and increased activity in the left side of the brain.

Some commonly set therapeutic goals pertaining to fear and anxiety are learning to handle fears and to face them calmly, identifying what one is truly afraid of, and being emotionally prepared for likely outcomes. Imagining the worst possible thing that can happen is often helpful. For clients who have phobias (irrational fears), the origins of the phobias should be traced. Behavioral treatment provides for exposure to the feared source (e.g., a snake) in slow steps until the panic response is extinguished.

By cutting down on the use of stimulants such as coffee and tea, clients may find that their physical anxiety is greatly reduced. A glass of warm milk at any time can produce a quieting effect—milk contains tryptophan, an amino acid that acts as a natural sedative (National Institute of Health, 2004). When one's adrenaline level is high, brisk exercise aids in using up the excess energy and enhancing relaxation. One of the most effective sleep aids is melatonin, a synthetic form of the hormone produced by the body that helps us know when it is time to sleep (Wyatt, Derk-Jan, et al., 2006). Melatonin can be purchased inexpensively over the counter and has few if any side effects.

The usefulness of physical exercise as a treatment intervention for reducing both anxiety and depression has been confirmed in numerous studies. In his review of the treatment literature, Smith (2006) found widespread evidence that exercise interventions have beneficial effects on depression and perhaps other psychological disorders. Exercise is also useful in the management of a wide variety of medical disorders that often co-occur with depression and related emotional conditions.

Depression

Depression is a mood disorder as discussed in its organic variety in Chapter 2. Whether biologically or situationally based, feelings of hopelessness, fatalism, and loneliness are characteristic. Depression is often expressed as a negative view of oneself, the world, and the future (Vonk & Early, 2009). It is often accompanied by a visceral sensation of heaviness, overwhelming inertia, and sluggishness. Behavior is clearly affected by this feeling, often by acts of omission rather than commission. Depressed persons have serious relationship problems in that their constant gloominess tends to drive people away. The ensuing isolation of the depressed person compounds the original feelings of loneliness and hopelessness.

Cognitive-behavioral therapy has proven effective (either in conjunction with medication or by itself) in treating depression. People can be taught to monitor their thoughts for negativism and to replace them with positive ones (Vonk & Early, 2009). The sense of feeling good can be enhanced by the natural highs that come with exercise, by being in stimulating company, and by engaging in enjoyable hobbies. Just as thinking controls behavior, so a change in behavior can change the thinking, which ties into the feeling area of the brain. The kind of polarized thinking described next is often at the heart of problematic emotions, and this kind of destructive thought process can easily be controlled through awareness and practice.

All-or-Nothing Thinking

An all-or-nothing mode of thinking causes people to get trapped in their negativism and destructive behavior. "I can't quit until I win the jackpot" is typical of this line of thought. "If I can't be in perfect health, I might as well be dead" is another. And "If this relationship isn't the greatest, I might as well end it right now."

The following examples of illogical thoughts or thought processes can be very effectively used as a checklist in group sessions (van Wormer and Davis, 2008):

> All-or-nothing thinking
> Jumping to negative conclusions
> Overgeneralizing about others
> Making mountains out of molehills
> Putting down members of your own group
> Self-blaming
> Thinking "I can't live without" a certain person
> Thinking "I must be perfect"
> Thinking "Everyone must like me"
> Thinking that if things do not go according to plan, a catastrophe will result
> Thinking that you can never forgive or forget a wrong
> Thinking that people are either all good or all bad
> Thinking that victims of crime have themselves to blame

For clients, sometimes the simple act of realizing that their present thinking is irrational brings about a major improvement in this area. In talking to a counselor who is nonjudgmental and enthusiastic about analyzing the thought processes we all share, clients will begin to question and challenge many of their long-held assumptions and find they can change the way

they feel (depressed, anxious, guilty) by being more accepting of themselves and of others.

Anger

Anger is a stimulus for all kinds of human behavior, much of it impulsive since it can flow from a strong emotional feeling coupled with an adrenalin rush. It is an "I want to do something feeling." Even very young babies display outbursts of anger when their wants are frustrated. (See Figure 3.3 for an amazing representation of this primary emotion that is experienced early in life.) Parents quickly learn the art of distraction. Two facts on which most members of Western societies agree is what anger looks like on the outside and what it feels like on the inside. When asked, children can imitate an angry parent's expression quite readily or draw an angry face. Clients (and students) typically describe the following visceral responses to anger:

> I feel myself turn red all over.
> I'm told I go completely white [indicates readiness to fight].
> I feel hot; I'm boiling over and can hardly breathe.
> My body tightens up.
> I don't know what anger feels like [rarely a male response].
> I cry [typical female response].

Behaviors associated with anger are, for some people, an inward seething, while others externalize their feelings and may shout, hit something or someone, or throw things. Still others sublimate their anger through sports or exercise, such as taking a brisk walk. Anger is often a positive force in motivating people to do something about an intolerable situation— actions range from assertively confronting the source of the anger, to reporting the problem to a higher authority, to organizing others for a collective response, to simply voting for a change in administration. Anger based on a response to sexism, racism, or ageism can promote consciousness raising and organization of others to do something about an intolerable situation.

Because other deeper emotions—for example, hurt and sadness—are often played out as

Figure 3.3. Little angry boy. Anger is an emotion commonly expressed in early childhood as displayed in this famous statue by Gustav Vigeland. The statue is one of many found in Vigeland Sculpture Park, Oslo, Norway. Photo by Robert van Wormer.

anger, especially by men, treatment centers can help clients identify the underlying emotion, one which may be less accessible. (Recall from Chapter 2 the brain studies of Gur, Gunning-Dixon, Bilker, and Gur [2002], for example, that provide evidence that women have a better brain capacity than men for censoring their anger and impulsiveness.) And there are other instances when its expression would be appropriate, as with many female clients who often internalize their anger. Still, anger is a real emotion, and we do it an injustice to deny its existence.

Feeling Work

Substance abuse treatment centers often have clients list their losses in connection with their addictive behaviors. Sometimes clients have to add up the costs in dollars as well. Such exercises, however, only reinforce the negative feelings of loss compounded now with public shame as these consequences are shared in group sessions. Addicted persons such as compulsive gamblers and spenders have enough problems with self-flagellation; there is no need to accentuate these kinds of thoughts. An alternative approach would be to provide information about how slot machine owners bilk their customers or how marketers of products seduce unwitting buyers. Information about the brain and addiction can also help clients, who may be overwhelmed with the consequences of their behavior, make sense of things. Being with others in a supportive group can bring home the awareness that good people can make foolish choices.

Sometimes anger that surfaces is a cover for another, deeper emotion such as a feeling of betrayal or even insecurity. An intriguing question to ask the perpetually angry client is, "If you weren't feeling anger, what would you be feeling?" The answer may be a revelation to the client, as well as to the therapist.

Some women who have difficulty labeling or expressing anger become compulsive house cleaners, energizing themselves in the endless war on dust and dirt. Such people need coaching to help them learn to absorb the angry feeling without fear and to mobilize that energy in a positive direction. Assertiveness training can also help people get their needs met. Those who have difficulty containing their anger should work on the de-escalating techniques of anger management.

Anger Management

Knowledge of one's feelings and the thought processes connected with them ("I hate my mother," "I hate myself") will help clients work toward change. Substance abuse counselors spend a lot of time dealing with clients who are angry—angry about being forced into treatment, angry at themselves for getting into trouble with their drinking or drug use, angry about having to give up the substance that has become their lover, their best friend. These counselors also know that to obtain sobriety, the clients often need to learn to handle their feelings, and that the best way to do this is through becoming aware of their automatic thoughts that lead to the angry feelings. Monti, Kadden, Rohsennow, Cooney, and Adams (2002) in their coping skills training guide offer useful tips for helping clients with alcohol problems to get their feelings under control. The following guidelines are adapted from their book *Treating Alcohol Dependence* (pp. 106–107):

1. Identify what you are feeling and thinking right now.
2. Note the triggers that are bringing out the resentments and anger—direct attack on you or an insult? Insinuations? Sense of being blamed?
3. Replace any extreme thoughts about the trigger with a more objective approach. Listen to your self-talk. Look for extremes in thinking—avoid the use of words such as *never, can't, always*, and *everybody*.
4. Examine objective reality. Once the facts are identified, relax, take a deep breath, and say to yourself a self-soothing statement such as in response to a negative remark about a person's past drug use: "I used drugs to escape from problems. I have now learned solid coping skills, and I have been clean for 2 years. My children are proud of me. My life is not ruined."
5. Try various interpretations of the situation and have empathy for the person who is the source of the anger.
6. If emotions are still strong, say to yourself a preferred slogan such as: Slow down; Easy does it; I can fix this.
7. Consider the consequences of overreacting to the event by blowing up.
8. Call a friend to help you calm down. And practice assertive responses to help rectify the situation if needed.
9. Note how your feelings change.

Sometimes anger at one source (for example, at the judicial system) is displaced onto another (the counselor or correctional officer). Anger-management training explains the origins of anger, triggers that provoke extreme anger, and the concept that there is nothing wrong with having stormy feelings. Learning to calmly express anger verbally, for example, to say, "When you do . . . I feel insulted [or rejected or annoyed]," instead of lashing out physically or cursing, is the kind of training that can be offered in groups. Group members enhance their self-esteem as they take more responsibility for themselves and learn to channel the energy that goes into angry outbursts into more productive and rewarding directions.

One anger-management program with a great deal of promise is an outgrowth of ongoing research at the UCLA Neuropsychiatric Institute on the link between hostility and brain chemistry (see Demaree, Harrison, & Rhodes, 2000). Hostile people, as brain studies from this institute seem to indicate, have deficits in the right side of the cerebrum and an inability to control negative emotions; they are also unaware of physiological changes that occur when they are angry. Teaching people to be more self-aware of bodily cues, such as a racing heart, the program at the institute helps them to protect themselves from chronic anger. More recently, Yilmaz (2009) measured the effects of emotional intelligent skills trainings in 12 sessions that help university students learn to reduce their levels of anger. Emotional intelligence trainings consist of education in managing one's emotional responses, recognizing the feelings and needs of others, and drawing on empathy. Compared to a control group, the students who received the trainings showed lower levels of anger in an experimental situation.

Venting anger inappropriately might not only get people in trouble but also actually increase their level of hostility. This is what psychology research has consistently shown, in fact (American Psychological Association, 2006). Repression is bad, but an unhealthy release of anger (such as beating the dog) is bad as well. To be successful, anger-management programs must be relevant to the treatment population (that is, anger must be the clients' problem) and grounded in evidence-based research about the physiology of anger. Unfortunately, the customary treatment interventions used in these programs are centered on the widespread but untested assumption that suppressed anger is the cause of violence and that the anger must be released to prevent an eventual explosion. These traditional notions are derived from Freud's therapeutic idea of catharsis—when pressure builds, it must be released. People who do not release their anger bottle it up and may sooner or later fly into an aggressive rage.

Bushman (2002) has challenged catharsis theory. His review of the experimental literature shows that when subjects were insulted and then allowed to vent their anger against a substitute target, their aggressive behavior increased. He set up an experiment with a large sample of college students in an anger-inducing situation. The students who punched a bag demonstrated an escalation of aggression compared to a control group who did not vent their anger at all. Bushman's recommendation to de-escalate aggression is to engage in a soothing act such as petting a dog. Carol Tavris (1982), whose well-known book *Anger: The Misunderstood Emotion* also dispelled many of the myths about anger, has now co-authored *Mistakes Were Made (But Not by Me)* (Tavris & Aronson, 2008) that documents many of the less obvious truths about human nature. Decades of experimental research, note Tavris and Aronson, have found that when people vent their feelings aggressively, they often feel worse and even more angry. And if you attack another person, directly or indirectly, a new factor comes into play—you have to justify your initial attack. The resulting anger might even lead to another attack of victimization. These authors describe an experiment in which two groups of students were insulted by the experimenter. The group that was allowed to vent their anger to a "supervisor" were found to have higher blood pressure than the control group.

Healthy ways to deal with anger include the use of time-outs from the disturbing situation; sublimation of hostile feelings into a healthy activity such as sports or walking; use of healthy self-talk to replace provocative thoughts; practice with verbalizing feelings of anger in an assertive way; and seeking to understand the underlying reasons for over-reactions (van Wormer & Davis, 2008).

Anger-management programs, often recommended for batterers, have been notoriously ineffective. In a review of 22 studies of such state programs for partner abusers, a team of psychologists found little positive effect produced by traditional programming (Carcy, 2004). The reason may well be that the underlying problems of these individuals run deeper than such treatment designs (the emphasis is on power balance in relationships) allow for. Second, most participants are court ordered due to violence. Many have problems (e.g., substance abuse, distress from past trauma, depression) other than anger that are not addressed (Carey, 2004). Stosny (2005) achieved a low dropout rate with male batterers enrolled in his program, and, in most cases, their abusive behavior ended. His approach was to focus on helping men in a supportive setting to draw on their own strengths and good intentions and to thereby turn their resentful, angry, or emotionally abusive relationship into a compassionate, loving one.

Jealousy

An emotion that is closely related to anger (and may underlie it) and the motivation for crime and other destructive behavior is jealousy. The biblical stories of Cain and Abel (Genesis 4:1–17) and "the coat of many colors" (Genesis 37:5–11) come to mind. Both involve the favoritism of one brother over the other and dire consequences for the favored one. The feeling of jealousy is obvious in small children, but in adults it is camouflaged by a wide variety of subterfuges. Physiologically, this feeling involves an inner tension and restlessness as obsessive thoughts of the resented person prevail.

Freud (1922/1955) believed that jealousy was universal because it originates in painful childhood experiences that everyone shares. He further regarded jealousy as irrational in that it stems from an unconscious memory of being displaced in love by another person. Feelings of resentment from the family of origin can get redirected in adult relationships, including marriage and work.

Psychologists Meston and Buss (2009), in their bestselling book *Why Women Have Sex* take a different view. Although they concede that this emotion has two sides and can interfere with a relationship, their focus is on the functions as well as the negatives. Jealousy, they say, evolved over millions of years as a primary defense against threats of infidelity and abandonment. Jealousy is activated for protective reasons when one perceives signs of defection. Moreover, jealousy can spark or rekindle sexual passion in a relationship.

In their survey of over 1,000 women, Meston and Buss found that women more than men report flirting with others in front of their partner to evoke jealousy. The more insecure the women in their relationship, the more apt they are to induce jealousy as a means of correcting the imbalance and boosting their self-esteem. Sometimes the jealousy does not involve the partner (or spouse) but the partner's friends, and this reaction may be expressed in selfish possessiveness. Within the family, a parent may resent the children for attention paid to them by the other parent. In battering situations, jealousy, born out of insecurity, is a key emotion to consider on the part of the perpetrator.

Battering Men

Lori Heise (1998) correctly observes that, to understand gender-based abuse, we must be holistic; we must conceptualize violence in multidimensional terms as a biopsychosocial phenomenon. While some researchers err in the direction of attributing all male-on-female violence to individual pathologies such as poor impulse control, others of a feminist persuasion err in the opposite direction. The feminist community, Heise states, has been especially reluctant to acknowledge factors other than patriarchy in the etiology of abuse. Yet this explanation, while a crucial part of the whole, fails to explain why some men beat and rape women and others do not and why partner violence is more often male to female than female to male.

Clinicians who work with battering men must be especially cognizant of the psychology of male abuse and of the thinking/feeling dimension that characterizes the worldview of such men. Intrapsychic attributes, for example, a hypersensitivity to abandonment, seeming inability to control negative emotions, and poor impulse control, combined with the biological predisposition mentioned earlier, including low serotonin levels and brain injury, have been found in the backgrounds of abusive men (Johnson, 2004; Mehlman et al., 1995). Heise (1998) sees a history of child abuse as a risk marker of later relationship violence and the witnessing of parental violence as an even stronger factor in later abuse. Interestingly, she also cites research showing that sexual victimization of boys (by men) emerges as a significant risk factor for future sexual aggression against women.

In one of the most significant studies of its kind, Jacobson and Gottman (2007) monitored 140 couples with electronic sensors while they discussed marital problems. The couples were recruited from public service announcements offering to pay people who were experiencing marital conflict. The researchers were surprised to find that the ones they eventually labeled as "cobras," the most violent men, who sounded and looked aggressive, were actually internally calm. Those labeled "pit bulls," in contrast, became internally aroused, with heart rates that increased with their anger; they never let up. These sensitive individuals are driven, Jacobson and Gottman suggest, by deep, underlying insecurity; they can therefore be helped through therapy. In the study, the wives of the pit bulls showed that they often took the risk of arguing back. The big problem these women face is that, if they ever leave the relationship, their partners tend to stalk them.

The cobras are a different species. So self-centered are they that, once out of the way, they tend to let go of the relationship. With cobras, violence is most likely to occur during the initial separation, whereas pit bulls become more dangerous following separation due to their ambivalent and obsessive feelings of love mixed with hate. The cobras, who constitute about 20 percent of the total of the most violent husbands, are sadistic, prone to make death threats, and, according to these researchers, not amenable to treatment. Because these men have a certain charisma, Jacobson and Gottman maintain, their wives find them hard to resist. Separation is relatively rare because the wives are terrified of leaving.

Sometimes the violence is precipitated by a buildup of rage, which is commonly set off by situations such as a separation, a child custody battle, an affair, or a pregnancy. These men typically exhibit jealousy and possessiveness toward their wives and girlfriends (van Wormer & Roberts, 2009). Abusive men may fly into a rage when their wives go out with friends. Immigrant wives may even be discouraged from learning the language of their adopted country or from learning to drive as a way to control them, especially when living in a country in which women are relatively unrepressed. The power of a man over a woman is thus as much about male insecurity (overcompensation through a show of bravado is typical) as it is about cultural attitudes. For a visual representation of the interplay between power and control, visit http://www.duluth-model.org.

The Power and Control Wheel developed by the nationally recognized Domestic Abuse Intervention Project in Duluth, Minnesota, reflects the system of privilege that perpetuates violence and the dynamics of maintaining that power. The wheel can be used as an effective heuristic device for helping survivors of domestic violence externalize their maltreatment and develop an understanding of their own sense of powerlessness. The spokes of the wheel display the types of strategies one can use to maintain power and control, such as intimidation; emotional abuse; isolation; minimizing and blaming; children; male privilege; economic abuse; coercion; and threats. Women who have been psychologically and physically abused can readily identify with such strategies, and many of their personal stories are horrific.

When used in treatment with male batterers, the same presentation of the Duluth domestic abuse intervention curriculum based on the Power and Control Wheel has not been well received. This fact is in sharp contrast to the presentation of the Equality Wheel, the second part of the Duluth model curriculum, which I

have found to be helpful in describing the qualities of a healthy relationship. Anecdotal reports confirm that male batterers sentenced to treatment often see themselves as victims rather than victimizers (despite the violence they have inflicted). They fail to recognize the power dynamics that they have used as represented in the wheel (see van Wormer & Roberts, 2009). In a research article whose purpose was to determine whether intervention programs served African American and Caucasian batterers equally well, Buttell and Carney (2005) found that the Duluth model curriculum did not work well with either group.

The wheel is immensely popular and has been adapted for gender-neutral treatment through the removal of gender-specific items such as the term *male privilege*. This adaptation, however, is not sanctioned by the Domestic Violence Intervention Project (DVIP) (interview with Michelle Johnson, training coordinator, Duluth, Minnesota, February 21, 2006) because, as explained by Johnson, it is not reflective of the reality of intimate-partner violence in a male-dominated society. Even in the case of lesbian violence, the DVIP does not find this curriculum acceptable because the Power and Control Wheel refers specifically to male-generated violence. For women who have been sentenced to batterer education because they fought back and who are far more victims than victimizers, any attempts to teach them how they used power dynamics to control their partners will be entirely irrelevant (van Wormer & Roberts, 2009).

Although most children who were beaten in childhood do not grow up to be batterers and most soldiers traumatized in war do not return to beat their wives, a background of violence is commonly found in the biographies of abusive men. This includes military service. Prigerson, Maciejewski, and Rosenheck (2001) administered diagnostic interviews to a national sample of 2,583 Vietnam veterans and found that slightly more than one-fifth of current spouse or partner abuse cases were attributed to combat exposure. In rare cases, war trauma is associated with domestic homicide in returning combat veterans. Regarding domestic homicide in general, neurologist Jonathan Pincus

(2002) singles out the following key factors: neurological damage, drug use, or a history of child abuse.

Every now and then along comes a study that is a real eye opener. So it is with a recent study in the *Journal of the American Medical Association*. Bell and Orcutt (2009) report preliminary research findings on a large sample of Vietnam veterans that show a striking correlation between war trauma and domestic partner violence following exposure to combat. The key aspect of posttraumatic stress disorder (PTSD) that emerged as closely correlated with aggression was the hyperarousal or hypervigilence response. Even when early childhood antisocial behavior was controlled, the relationship held. Alcohol problems that were related to the war experience were linked to the aggression as well. These findings have important implications for batterer intervention programming. Given that the trauma exposure leads some men to develop certain information processing and anger regulation deficits that increase the risk for domestic violence perpetration, as Bell and Orcutt suggest, these deficits may be more directly targeted as part of treatment. Meanwhile, social work researchers from Washington University who are experts in veteran mental health report that the increasing prevalence of traumatic brain injury and substance abuse disorders along with PTSD among veterans of recent wars poses unique challenges to treatment providers (Martin, 2008). Research shows that male veterans with PTSD are two to three times more likely than veterans without PTSD to engage in intimate partner violence. These veterans require mental health treatment for the PTSD in addition to specialized domestic violence intervention programs.

Now let us consider domestic violence from the point of view of the victim-survivor.

The Impact of Being Battered

What does it feel like at a visceral level to live with battering? In private correspondence (of November 5, 2007) a social work graduate student contributed for readers of this text the following account from deep inside her feeling memories of the sensory experience of being beaten:

> I lay in bed, not moving a muscle, trying to fake sleep while he fumbles at the back door at 3 a.m., drunk again. Maybe he'll go to bed and pass out. *I smell* a sweet, sickening beer stench pass by. *I feel* the bed move as he crawls in. I hear his heavy breathing, labored, even. *I hear* my heart racing in fear. I lay paralyzed, time suspended. I must have dozed off. I feel a sharp blow to my face, then another. I hear flesh on flesh. I feel heavy hands on my neck, but I slip out of his grasp, out of bed. Oh, no, I'm stuck in the corner of the room. *I see* fists coming down like a meteor shower. Not again, please stop! I hear these words echoed as if from nowhere. I feel the floor as I roll in a ball. I feel my arms around me for protection, but there isn't any. I see sweat dripping down on me, sticky, dirty. I dared to raise my head, I see familiar wild, red eyes, staring. I see more sweat, smells damp, I can't breathe. I crawl to another part of the room, can't get away. I feel blows slowing down, he must be getting tired. I'll play dead.
>
> I hear thick silence. I smell fear all around me, seeping into the cracks in the walls. If walls could talk. . .I trailed off in thought, I see him drop in bed, exhausted, smells sour. I hear snoring, I'm safe. I hope the kids are still asleep.

This was an all too familiar scene. The children and I would never talk about it the next day, they would never ask. I will get up early and check for glass or torn clothes and clean up the mess before anybody sees it. I look in the mirror to assess the damage. The woman staring back knows he probably won't remember if he's in another blackout.

Deeply disturbing and violent events can leave an indelible mark on the human psyche. Typical problems that bring women survivors of long-term violence into treatment are difficulties in new relationships, inability to sleep, depression, and addiction disorders. Survivors' psychological defense mechanisms cause them to repress overwhelming emotions and thoughts related to trauma. The unconscious knows even when the memory does not.

The challenge to feminist theorists is how to explain the often irrational attachment of battered women to their abusers. Most writers of the feminist school (e.g., Frank & Golden, 1992), focus on rational aspects (such as economic considerations and death threats) in a battered woman's decision to stay with her man. Wallace (2008), in contrast, refers to the concept called the Stockholm syndrome (referring to a hostage situation in Sweden in which the captives bonded with their captors to some extent). This psychological phenomenon of bonding with the captor occurs in a situation marked by exposure to intermittent kindness within the context of a life-and-death situation from which there is only limited possibility of escape. It may explain the seemingly strange behavior of the Swedish women who hugged and kissed their captors after their rescue and testified on their behalf in the eventual court proceedings (Fitzgerald, 2009). Montero-Gómez (2001) refers to this phenomenon as "a cognitive bond of protection in battered women" (p. 196). Basically, one's connection with powerful individuals who can exact terrible punishments and withhold the necessities of life can be understood as regression to a dependent, childlike state. Bettelheim (1943) defined this phenomenon in his classic study of concentration camp survivors. Instead of being angry, many prisoners identified with the SS troops and tried to emulate them. This response is not gender specific but human. It is a point worth noting that, in positions of vulnerability (such as old age), men, as well as women, can and clearly do experience battering in relationships. Vulnerability, in short, is the issue here, not gender.

The female may be the dominant victimizing partner; she may use psychological abuse and manipulations that are as harmful in their way as physical violence. In lesbian partnerships, physical violence may well be used for purposes of intimidation and control (Kristen & Sullivan, 2003). Similarly, in gay male relationships, battering by the dominant partner of the subordinate partner is not uncommon. Greenwood, Relf et al. (2002) found in a sample of almost 3,000 men who have sex with men that around 22 percent reported physical victimization, a rate that is roughly the same for heterosexual women and significantly higher than those of homosexual women. The National Coalition of Anti-Violence Programs (NCAVP) (2008) in its annual report on domestic violence in the gay, lesbian, bisexual, transgender community concluded that the rates of domestic abuse are especially high among young people. Out of the over 3,000 cases of same-sex domestic violence reported to domestic violence services in 14 regions across North America, about the same number of callers were women as were men, with around five percent involving transgendered people. Research analyzed by the National Violence Against Women Survey (Tjaden & Thoennes, 2000), however, was consistent with the conclusion of the authors that intimate-partner violence is perpetrated primarily by men, whether against male or female partners. This statement is based on data from lesbian and gay partnerships and also from violence in previous heterosexual partnerships by the gays and lesbians in the survey. The fact that stalking and rape rates were included in the measures of violence, as they should have been, probably accounts for the significant difference in the male-on-male domestic violence and the female-on-female domestic violence. Much more research is needed, nevertheless, on male and female same-sex intimate partner violence before we can make definitive statements about the male-female differences.

The empowerment/strengths approach does not dwell on the reasons people stay in life-threatening situations; it does explain, however, how they manage to leave. Ulrich (1998) perceives leaving as a process that may require many attempts to be successful. Stages in the process of breaking loose involve changes in one's level of self-awareness, combined with a reevaluation of the relationship as dangerous. During this gradual process of recognition, survivors build up their courage to retreat from the dangers. In her study of women who have managed to leave, Ulrich found that women with adequate self-esteem to make the break identified social support as helping them to start a new life.

When the trauma is ongoing and caused by a partner, the likelihood that the victim will cope in maladaptive ways may be especially high. Unlike a single sudden traumatic event, long-term psychological abuse affects a woman's well-being by gradually eroding her taken-for-granted assumptions. Damage to the mind and to one's self concept can cause as much lasting harm as the physical aspect of abuse (see Dowda [2009], *Invisible Scars*). Psychological abuse always accompanies physical abuse, because such abuse has to be justified and will be justified in terms of claims that the victim "had it coming." Also in situations of domestic violence, the verbal assaults often escalate into physical assaults. The feeling that one has no control is key to behavior that may appear unduly submissive and a loyalty that defies reason. Let us now look at the phenomenon of deliberate mind control.

Controlling Behavior Through "Brainwashing"

The fear, helplessness, and social isolation facing the long-term victim of partner violence has much in common with the plight that befalls kidnap victims and interrogated detainees. The term *brainwashing* comes to mind. Brainwashing is not an official psychiatric diagnosis. The term was first coined as a description of the political indoctrination of U.S. soldiers who were captured by the Chinese communists during the Korean War. "Brainwashing" is a translation of Chinese characters meaning "wash heart," or thought reform. Captured soldiers were subjected to prolonged interrogations, removal of group leaders, and a "good-cop, bad-cop" approach. Some Americans became so convinced of the Communist party line that they defected to China (see Lifton, 1961/1989).

With kidnap victims such as Patty Hearst and Elizabeth Smart, both of whom were beaten and raped while held captive for months, the indoctrination may have been less deliberate. In any case, both hostages strangely conformed to the lifestyle of their captors (Browning, 2003). Hearst went so far as to take on the identity of "Tania" and rob banks. The process by which her very identity was transformed is a psychological phenomenon that may take place when people under conditions of extreme helplessness are exposed to intermittent kindness by the captor, kindness that is experienced within the context of a life and death situation, and become emotionally dependent on the captor.

Both Patty and Elizabeth resumed their original identities upon their return to society, as did all but one of the Communist converts. I discuss the psychological process in the section following "Traumatic Bonding."

The U.S. government uses sophisticated techniques to persuade detainees to "crack." According to a report on these methods, the most efficient technique is to break down suspects' defenses through a combination of physical discomfort and psychological deprivation (of light or dark, regular meals, sleep, comfortable sitting positions). The good-cop, bad-cop strategy is used so that the detainees will confide in the supposed ally (Prados, 2002). Once they talk a little, they are told, "You're ruined now with your people, so you might as well tell all and let us help you." Loners take longer to break down. Recently the roles of military psychologists, such as those employed by the CIA to advise interrogators in effective methods of instilling terror and pain in terrorism suspects in order to "break them down," has received much scrutiny (Shane, 2009). Ethicists and the American Psychological Association have condemned participation by its members in torture, but psychologists who have engaged in such practices have not been censured. It is interesting to note that the tactics that have been used on the suspected terrorists to gain psychological control over them are roughly similar to the techniques used by kidnappers to subdue their victims. Let us look more closely at how the victims survive.

Traumatic Bonding and Recovery in the Victims of Kidnapping

Traumatic bonding is a term introduced by Carnes (1997) to explain the seemingly incomprehensible behavior of the victim in becoming attached to his or her captor and even, in some cases, adopting a new identity. This response, which takes place over time, can be conceived as both an emotional reaction to the situation of terror and as a survival mechanism. Think back to the discussion of Bettelheim's concentration camps in which the inmates eventually focused their minds only on living under the present circumstances. This became the only reality and took over their lives. Bearing this in mind, we might make sense of the fact that long-term captivity can be so devastating to the self and to one's ability to take initiative that one does not seek the opportunity to escape even when the chains are removed. The psychological chains are not removed so easily (see van Wormer, 2004).

Animal research shows the impact of extreme stress on behavior. Behavioral scientists have found that, in experiments with mice, for example, if the creatures are provided with an escape route, they learn very quickly how to avoid an electrical shock that occurs right after they hear a bell ring (Anisman & Merali, 2009). However, if the escape route is blocked, the mice eventually quit trying to run away, even after the escape route is cleared. In humans, this phenomenon is referred to as "learned helplessness." Keep this experiment in mind as we examine several high profile cases of kidnap and torture of children by child molesters.

Consider the strange case of Jaycee Dugard, kidnapped at age 11 and discovered 18 years later living as a member of Phillip Garrido's family. She was found when suspicions were aroused about the strange behavior of the children she had borne by her kidnapper and who were now ages 11 and 15. Highlighted in media reports across the world, this was a wonderful, unexpected breakthrough in a case that had baffled the police for almost two decades. Inevitably, the questions began to mount— how long had Jaycee lived in relative freedom? And why didn't she make any effort to escape? (See Associated Press, 2009.)

For many of us, our minds flashed back to 2002. News reports in January of that year were of the search for a missing 13-year-old boy. This search led police to the home of his suspected kidnapper, Michael Devlin. There they found not one, but two kidnap victims. Shawn Hornbeck had been abducted while riding his bicycle 4 years before. The 15-year-old Hornbeck was well known to neighbors and friends. The story, as flashed out over the TV networks, left Americans stunned. Here was a boy who had surfed the Internet, owned a cell phone, ridden a bike, and even called the police to report that an earlier bicycle had been stolen. Here was a boy who had helped in the capture of a second, younger boy. As a kidnap victim himself he had every opportunity of escaping, but he had failed to do so (see Campo-Flores and Thomas, 2007).

Another well-known case is that of Elizabeth Smart, kidnapped in 2002 at age 14 and discovered by an alert police officer as she was sitting on a street corner with her captors. At first, Elizabeth denied who she really was (Associated Press, 2009).

Not only in the United States but also in Austria such strange psychological phenomena as bonding with the captors have been reported. In 2006, much media coverage in Austria was devoted to the case of Natascha Kampusch, who disappeared at the age of 10. Kept in a basement cell and likely sexually abused for 8 years, Natascha managed to escape the man she was forced to call "master" when she was trusted to wash his car. When the police went to arrest her captor, he threw himself in front of a commuter train to his death. Upon hearing of this, Kampusch reportedly wept inconsolably. She had a brief reunion with her family but has chosen not to see them since. Police psychologists speculated that Kampusch may have suffered from the Stockholm syndrome (see Spiegel Online International, 2009).

Interestingly, these survivors of kidnapping shortly resumed their original identities upon their return to their families of society. This fact is indicative of the psychological reality that the mind can help us survive, physically and mentally, by allowing us to identify with someone who holds us in a life-or-death situation, although, as mentioned earlier, there may be a delayed effect in bringing us back to normal before the mind has absorbed the new reality.

So what is the process by which persons in these highly vulnerable situations come to identify so closely with their tormenters and victimizers? Basically, one's identity with powerful individuals who can exact terrible punishments and withhold the necessities of life can be understood as regression to a dependent, childlike state. This response is not gender specific, but human; it derives from a state of powerlessness and regression under situations of extreme stress.

The seemingly irrational behavior of the victim—remaining in an abusive environment, even when means to leave are available—is an emotional reaction to a situation of terror and a functional survival skill in adopting the captor's attitudes and belief system. Unlike a single, sudden, traumatic event, long-term psychological abuse affects a person's well-being by gradually eroding his or her taken-for-granted assumptions. A long-term sexual relationship causes havoc with the emotions as well. Kidnap victims, like battered women, are subject to extensive sexual exploitation and game playing.

So what is the prognosis for a recovery for Jaycee Dugard and her children, age 11 and 15? (Keep in mind that the kidnapper is the children's biological father.) Leading a normal life will of course be difficult for all of them. Still, there are many signs that indicate the three of them will do well. Jaycee knew love and stability for the first 11 years of her life, and she reportedly has shown love for her children. Other kidnapping victims, such as Patty Hearst, have been reunited with their families and reestablished their previous identities. I believe Jaycee will do the same and get the education she missed. Her 11-year-old child is young enough to be successfully socialized into what must seem like a foreign culture to her. She will likely go to school and ultimately will catch up. The 15-year-old child will have more problems because she is older. There is a small risk of mental illness developing later due to the apparent schizophrenia of the father. And Jaycee and her daughters will all have deep emotions to deal with as their kidnappers with whom they bonded for so many years go off to prison and they go off to a happier life.

Just as the psychological impact of being at the mercy of others has serious consequences for the individual psyche, so too does the experience of being exposed to constant danger in war in situations of "kill or be killed." The brutalizing aspects of combat can leave psychological wounds, especially in the minds of impressionable young men and women.

Impact of War Trauma

Social workers are apt to be concerned with three basic kinds of trauma. The first one stems from events in childhood such as sexual abuse, severe physical abuse, and the witnessing of domestic violence. (These forms of trauma are dealt with in Chapter 4 and Chapter 6.) Trauma of the second type is nonwar trauma that occurs in adulthood, for example, men and women who are victimized by rape (male on female or male on male). The third type is trauma related to mass situations such as earthquake or tsunami disasters and the horrors of war. The differences between these lie in the fact that one is natural and that the other is human generated, than in the effects.

In light of the contemporary militarization of U.S. society and the international repercussions of U.S. war crimes, I have chosen to devote much of the remainder of this chapter to the impact of war on the domestic front. I am talking here not about the impact on social services (indirect consequences), which is huge and probably irreversible (refer to Volume 2 of this series), but about the psychological wounds accruing to warfare. We can define war as an endeavor in which governments fight, the strongest wins, and everyone—both winners and losers—pays the price. Since the first casualty of every war is the truth (a saying attributed to the Greek tragic dramatist Aeschylus, fifth century B.C.) and the real price of military engagement is inevitably underplayed, much of the following information is not well known. Figure 3.4 highlights U.S. involvement in war: This photograph is of a protest display of boots that both honors those killed in war and emphasizes the human side of the loss of

Figure 3.4. Each pair of used combat boots symbolizes one U.S. soldier who died in Iraq. The American Friends Service Committee uses these images of worn shoes to symbolize the human cost of war. Photo by Rupert van Wormer.

life in combat; each pair of boots represents one U.S. soldier killed in Iraq. The name of the person sacrificed in this war is provided for each pair of boots.

Bombing Victims

The horrors that were visited upon the Japanese people at Hiroshima and Nagasaki in 1945 are widely known though rarely talked about. Every year in many parts of the world, however, peace groups on August 6 and August 9 light candles in remembrance and pledge "Never again." While the sufferings of British civilians during the German bombings have been immortalized in history books and films, the terrible death and destruction inflicted upon the German civilians by Allied bombing have been buried in the annals of history.

An article in the *Wall Street Journal* (Rhoads, 2003) written in conjunction with the publication in Germany of the book *The Fire* (*Der Brand;* Friedrich, 2002) has momentarily broken

the silence. A sense of guilt over the Holocaust and shame at Germany's failed aggression in World War II have kept most Germans from publicly mourning their losses. Yet over a period of 2½ years, 161 German cities were obliterated by firebombing, and between 350,000 and 650,000 civilians were killed. Many elderly residents of Germany today were small children who survived the death and destruction. Now their stories are being told for the first time: "More than 150 people listened silently in a small church one recent evening to a reading about the bombing of German cities in World War II. They heard about how a boy carried the charred remains of his parents in a wash basin. About how the rush of air from the bomb blasts decapitated people when they peered outside to see what was happening. About the piles of dead" (p. 1).

When the U.S.-led war on Iraq broke out, Germany's opposition was reinforced by an awareness of what bombing from the air does to people on the ground. Many of the elderly survivors had nightmares and flashbacks as they watched the continual replays of the airplane attacks of September 11 on their TV screens and the "shock and awe" campaign that eventually followed with the attack on Iraq.

Vietnam veterans had flashbacks as well. Flashbacks and a preoccupation with combat-related events are examples of war trauma. The dynamics of surviving a natural disaster such as the earthquake-triggered tsunami in Southeast Asia or terrorism in Israel or the Palestinian territories are relatively the same.

The Diagnosis of Posttraumatic Stress Disorder

Although people have been tormented by horrible memories since the beginning of humankind, an actual syndrome related to trauma was not identified until the 1860s, characteristics that Freud (1896) also identified somewhat later. In their book *Transforming the Legacy: Couple Therapy With Survivors of Childhood Trauma*, Basham and Miehls (2004) summarize this history. Freud identified trauma in terms of the hysteria that stems from repressed memories of premature sexual experience from early childhood. Psychological disorders in veterans of World War I and II did not receive much attention from the medical community. The Smith College School of Social Work did, however, respond to these problems. The school was founded, in fact, to assist the shell-shocked veterans of World War I, an expertise that is still unique to their program today.

Then, in the 1970s, in response to the veterans of the Vietnam War and the vibrant antiwar movement, the American Psychiatric Association (APA, 1980), after much consideration and extensive lobbying by interested parties, provided the diagnosis of PTSD. The impact of the feminist movement, which was strong at this time, was evidenced in the inclusion of rape as a precipitating condition.

As spelled out today by the APA (2000) in the *DSM-IV-TR*, a diagnosis of PTSD requires the development of characteristic symptoms following exposure to an extremely traumatic stressor, including rape, natural disasters, threatened death or serious injury, assault, torture, kidnapping, or military combat. For children, inappropriate sexual experiences with or without threats of violence and witnessed events of serious injury are applicable. The disorder is apt to be especially severe or long lasting when the stressor is of human design, such as torture or rape. This diagnosis requires a duration of more than 1 month of symptoms.

Common symptoms delineated by the *DSM-IV-TR* are recurrent and intrusive recollections or dreams of the event and intense psychological distress or physiological reactions when the person is exposed to incidents that are reminders of the traumatic episode. Hyperarousal and a strong startle response, as discussed earlier, are other symptoms. Amnesia for an important aspect of the event may be present; there may also be a markedly reduced ability to feel emotions or express intimacy. The individual may have sleeping difficulties, anxiety, or increased arousal that was not present before the event occurred.

Trauma From the Iraq/Afghanistan Wars

Returning from service in Iraq where he had fought in the U.S. Marine Reserves, Jeffrey Lacey was haunted with memories and images that he could not get out of his head. Speaking in a monotone, he told of a small boy who had been shot in the head by crossfire, elderly people who had been killed as they tried to run from the marines, and two unarmed Iraqi soldiers he had killed on direct orders. Lacey was placed on suicide watch at the Veteran's Administration Hospital. He was wearing the dog tags of the two men he had killed. Then, when released, he took off the dog tags, smoked his last cigarette, and hanged himself with a hose in the basement of his home (Gisick, 2004).

This Iraq veteran was not alone. The number of suicides reported by the Army has risen to the highest level since record keeping began three decades ago, according to a story in *The New York Times* (Goode, 2009). The year 2008 saw 192 suicides of active-duty soldiers and soldiers on inactive reserve status; this was twice as many as in 2003, when the war began.

Homicide too may be an end product of the war. After six soldiers were charged separately in murders in a 12-month period, the commanders of the 4th Brigade Combat Team at Fort Carson, Colorado, commissioned a special report (Roeder, 2009). The report investigated these and other acts of violence by returned combat soldiers and concluded that those who experienced the most combat were the most likely to get into trouble. Singled out in the report as precipitating factors in the violence were drug abuse and mental disorders and lack of treatment for these problems.

A national survey has found that men suffering from lifetime PTSD related to combat have a higher rate of unemployment, divorce, and violent outbursts than men suffering from other traumas (Prigerson et al., 2001). After the war in Vietnam was over, some 30 percent of Vietnam veterans suffered PTSD; flashbacks were common. A 2004 study involving 6,200 soldiers who had served in Iraq for several months was conducted by a team at the Walter Reed Army Institute of Research (Hoge et al., 2004). The results show that one in six of the veterans experienced symptoms of PTSD, depression, or anxiety; 12 percent had symptoms of PTSD alone. (These figures are an underestimate since the study was done before the far more brutal urban combat efforts got underway.) A more recent estimate of PTSD is as high as 35 percent, according to a report by Atkinson, Guetz, and Wein (2009) published in *Management Science*. The researchers used a sophisticated mathematical model that was built on time lag estimates of the development of PTSD to arrive at their conclusions.

For these veterans, the risk of developing PTSD rose in proportion to the number of instances of combat in which they had engaged. These figures need to be seen in comparison to the 5 percent rate of PTSD in a sample of soldiers before deployment. An Israeli psychiatrist with extensive relevant experience was interviewed for an article and recommended immediate intervention with cognitive-behavioral

therapy (CBT) and serotonin-enhancing drugs. Serotonin-enhancing drugs and even tranquilizers (or alcohol) are likely to offset the formation of traumatic memories because they dull the senses and reduce the flow of adrenaline associated with the imprinting of memories. People in Manhattan who experienced the horrors of 9/11 and who were taking psychotropic medications, for example, seemed to cope better in the wake of the attack (Jackson, 2003). An important finding from empirical research by Saxe, Stoddard, Courtney, Cunningham, Chawla, et al. (2001) is that children who had been severely burned suffered significantly less from PTSD when given heavy doses of morphine when compared with an unmedicated control group. Harvard psychiatric researcher Roger Pitman (2009) is working to understand brain changes in the aftermath of trauma. His current major research interest is whether medications administered immediately following traumatic memory reactivation can weaken traumatic memories through reconsolidation blockade. According to the description on the Center for Integration of Medicine and Innovative Technology website, Pitman is working in conjunction with the U.S. Department of Veterans Affairs for the prevention of PTSD in combat veterans. An earlier article in *Time* magazine describes his experiment in the emergency room at Massachusetts General Hospital in which he gave one group of patients who had suffered severe trauma a placebo and another group the drug propranolol, which interferes with adrenaline uptake (Lemonick, 2007). A follow-up 8 months later revealed that most of the placebo patients had developed nervous reactions and symptoms of PTSD, while none of the other patients did so.

Other experts who have researched the efficacy of preventive interventions recommend against the immediate debriefing of trauma survivors but report that cognitive-behavioral treatments delivered several weeks or months after exposure to trauma may reduce the incidence of PTSD (McNally, Bryant, & Ehlers, 2003). Edna Foa's "restore resilience" technique, devised for work with rape survivors, has the survivors repeat the narrative over and over, make a list of "avoidance behaviors" (such as avoiding walking outside), and expose themselves to cues and memories of the trauma until the response is extinguished (Groopman, 2004). When used with Israeli Defense Forces, the results were excellent; 29 of the 30 persons with PTSD who received the treatment showed a marked improvement in their symptoms. The philosophy of debriefing—that a single outpouring of emotion can heal a scarred psyche—is devoid of any scientific merit, Groopman contends, and can actually make things worse. Sadly, the Iraq war veterans with the most symptoms are the ones in the study who expressed the greatest reservation about receiving help.

Zabriskie (2004) describes the psychological toll on men and women who have served in the front lines of Iraq: "They express anger, confusion and guilt about killing, guilt about surviving when a buddy doesn't. They confess to mood swings, depression, indifference to life, hypervigilance, isolation, suicidal tendencies. And all are plagued by images they can't forget, some so disturbing that combat-stress workers in the field have to monitor one another for a state known as 'vicarious traumatization'" (p. 41).

The United States can expect to be paying for the war in Iraq for many years to come. One very worrisome fact is contained in information again supplied by the Walter Reed Army Medical Center (Okie, 2005). This is the fact that more than 60 percent of soldiers injured in the war in Iraq have potentially life-altering brain injuries. Those who survive head injuries often suffer from emotional problems, including difficulty with memory, as well as high rates of depression, alcohol use, and post-traumatic anxieties.

The toll on the Iraqi people can only be speculated on at present. We do know that more than 100,000 civilians and countless soldiers have died—both allies and enemies (Rosenthal, 2004). Whether any good will come from this enormous sacrifice and bloodshed, only the future can tell. In general, however, the conclusion of one war sets the stage for another. Let us now look at the brutalization of women in war.

Rape in War

In the past, victims of rape in general and of the mass rape in war were silenced out of shame. It has been only in the late 1990s that Korean "comfort women" have been able to overcome their shame sufficiently to reveal that they were forced into sexual service by the Japanese invaders. Most people are even unaware that rape is a routine part of the brutality of war and that most military leaders implicitly tolerate it (Farwell, 2004). In her groundbreaking book *Against Our Will: Men, Women, and Rape*, Brownmiller (1975) documented its widespread occurrence. International media and feminist activists have begun to bring attention to this phenomenon—military and insurgency groups using rape as a weapon and the targeting of women in the enemy group to achieve political objectives (e.g., ethnic cleansing, cultural humiliation, destruction).

Responding to the media publicity over the mass rape committed in Bosnian villages, Brownmiller (1993) explains the logic of this behavior and the depth of the inflicted pain: "Rape of a double dehumanized object—as woman, as enemy—carries its own terrible logic. In one act of aggression, the collective spirit of women and of the nation is broken, leaving a reminder long after the troops depart. And if she survives the assault, what does the victim of wartime rape become to her people? . . . A pariah. Damaged property" (p. 37).

Recently, acts of rape committed during military hostilities have been recognized as war crimes, "crimes against humanity," prosecutable under international law. Historic precedents were set by the United Nations at the International Criminal Tribunals in Rwanda, as well as at the tribunal on behalf of the survivors of rape from former Yugoslavia (Farwell, 2004). Although we can expect continued international outcry against the wartime sexual degradation of women, and prosecution under the new International Criminal Court, as long as men are trained to kill and dehumanize the enemy, wartime rape will continue. To read more about the violation of women internationally, see the following case study on the psychological effects of human trafficking.

Human Trafficking: Snaring the Spirit

Lured by promises of lucrative waitressing and child-care jobs in Florida, more than two dozen Mexican women and girls agreed to be smuggled into the United States by the Cadena family in 1996 and 1997. Instead of getting the gainful employment and $400 per week they'd been promised, the women were raped, beaten, and then forced to have sex with 25 to 30 men per day as part of a prostitution ring that ultimately earned the Cadenas millions of dollars.

The story of the Cadenas' victims, which came to light after federal agents coordinated a raid of six of Florida's brothels in 1997, is one of the most high-profile examples of human trafficking in the country. Often referred to as modern-day slavery, human trafficking is defined by U.S. law as the "recruitment, harboring, transportation, provision or obtaining of a person" for the purpose of sexual exploitation or forced labor.

The U.S. government estimates that between 800,000 and 900,000 people are trafficked across international borders every year. And the problem is only getting worse: Next to the drug trade, human trafficking is now tied with illegal arms dealing as the second-largest criminal industry in the world. Of those trafficked annually worldwide, between 18,000 and 20,000 are brought to the United States.

NASW's policy statements on human rights, refugees, child welfare, and cultural competence all speak to the issue of human trafficking. "We are emphatically opposed to human trafficking, and we recognize that this is a topic that needs further attention," said Luisa Lopez, NASW's affirmative action officer and manager of the association's Human Rights and International Affairs Department.

Congress passed the Trafficking Victims Protection Act in 2000. The legislation, which entitles trafficked persons to the same social services and benefits as those with refugee status—including resettlement services, food stamps, refugee medical assistance, and foster care—has sparked interest among social workers and provided more funding and opportunities to get involved. "Social work training related to the person-in-environment perspective is very helpful in being able to navigate these victims' complex and often disparate needs," said Margaret MacDonnell, a social worker and children's services specialist with the Migration and Refugee Services unit of the United States Conference of Catholic Bishops (USCCB).

With the support of grants from the federal government, USCCB and Lutheran Immigration Services help place trafficked children in Unaccompanied Refugee Minor programs, foster care settings with a focus on cultural competence, specialized services, and smaller caseloads.

Lasting Trauma

According to the Department of Health and Human Services, many trafficking victims will have permanent physical damage from being brutally beaten or raped by their traffickers. Those who've been used as prostitutes may have sexually transmitted diseases, while those who've slaved as laborers may have back problems, hearing loss, and respiratory or cardiovascular diseases. A number of victims, especially children, also show signs of malnourishment.

From a mental health perspective, those who have been trafficked suffer from many of the same symptoms as other victims of abuse: feelings of shame, humiliation, helplessness, depression, and anxiety. Aside from these, there are other psychological effects that plague trafficked persons in particular. "All sex-abuse victims suffer emotional and psychological trauma," said Robin Perry, a Florida State University social work professor who co-authored an in-depth report on Florida's human-trafficking problem last year. "For human-trafficking victims, this is augmented by the way in which they've been trafficked."

The deleterious effects of fraud, force, and coercion—the favored tools of traffickers—are undeniable. Many trafficking victims come to the United States voluntarily based on what they later find out are nonexistent jobs or false marriage proposals. Other victims are kidnapped by traffickers or even sold to traffickers by their own families.

Once they arrive in the United States, they are forced to perform sex or hard labor to repay their "debt" for being smuggled into the country. If they disobey their "employers," they've been told, they'll be physically harmed or reported to immigration officials. Others have been told their families back home will suffer the consequences as well.

Experts say rebuilding a sense of trust, however difficult, is essential in helping trafficking victims. "How well a service provider builds trust will be the basis for how well the client can be served," said Katherine Chon, executive director of Polaris Project, one of the largest anti-trafficking organizations in the United States.

Chon said social workers also need to be aware that victims' lack of trust might be magnified if they are disoriented or confused as to their whereabouts—something that recent research has shown to be common among trafficked persons.

Richard Estes, a professor at the University of Pennsylvania School of Social Work, published in 2001 what is regarded as the most comprehensive study of the sexual exploitation of children to date. Enlisting research partners like NASW for his study, he found, among other things, that trafficking routes are highly complex by design. "Prior to passing through the last gateway, typically, children have traveled great distances, across several countries, and have been transported using a wide range of conveyances," Estes wrote in his final report.

Efforts to keep victims disoriented do not end once they enter the States. The Cadenas' victims, for example, were smuggled in via a fairly simple route from Mexico. But once in Florida, the women were rotated between brothels to keep them unaware of their location and to prevent them from building relationships with clients or community members. In his interviews with the Cadenas' victims for his report on trafficking in Florida, Perry found that the psychological effects of such tactics persisted well after the women had been extricated from their situations. "The trauma and emotional wounds that the women carry as a result of their experience were clearly visible, even after the passage of six years," Perry wrote. "Most felt a sense of guilt and shame, and a number spoke of ongoing depression and nightmares."

According to Estes' research, the psychological effects on children are similarly devastating. "The effects of this [abuse] are long lasting," Estes said at a press conference held at the NASW national office in 2001. "This will impair the child for life." Another lasting issue is a need for physical security. "The overwhelming need that all the women shared following their emancipation from sexual servitude was that of physical security,

and that was articulated repeatedly throughout the interviews," Perry wrote of the Cadenas' victims.

"We need to understand that trafficked persons are an extremely useful commodity in the eyes of the criminals who traffic them," said NASW member Mindy Loiselle, a clinical consultant for USCCB. "Therefore, traffickers often are trying to locate their victims. Foster care agencies and foster parents need to be aware of these issues and help these children to stay safe."

Barriers to Identification

Despite the services and programs available to trafficked persons, efforts to identify and reach out to victims in the first place have not been very successful. As of April 2004, only 500 people had been certified by HHS as eligible for benefits available to trafficking victims. "There isn't anyone involved in this program that would consider this a satisfactory rate," said Steven Wagner, director of the Trafficking in Persons program at the agency, in a statement.

After releasing these statistics, HHS launched "Rescue and Restore," a trafficking awareness and outreach program to help identify more victims. But the myriad barriers to identification persist for now. "Many of our members may be helping victims of human trafficking and not even be aware that they are," NASW's Lopez said. "All too often, we don't recognize that perhaps central to some of our clients' problems is their virtual enslavement."

The most obvious roadblock to identification is the extreme isolation to which many of these victims are subjected. Efforts to identify trafficking victims—who arrive from all parts of the world—are also often hindered by linguistic and cultural differences. Many victims, for example, do not speak English. Some also have a fear of public officials because they've been told they'll be deported if they speak to public authorities or because they come from countries where social workers are seen as agents of the government rather than allies. In addition, victims of sex trafficking may fear speaking up because of how their situation might be perceived by their families or stigmatized within their communities. Oftentimes, it is these types of barriers that are the least understood among service providers.

"The biggest problem we come across is lack of cultural sensitivities," said Polaris Project's Chon, whose organization trains social service agency workers and local law enforcement officers in how to identify and reach out to victims of trafficking by better understanding their cultural differences and needs.

A Community Effort

According to Loiselle, social workers, with the proper training, should be uniquely qualified to identify victims of human trafficking. "Social workers' assessment ability already allows us to 'look below the surface,' a critical skill in identifying and helping those whose situations would lead them to be circumspect if not terrified," she said.

According to Perry, teaming up with others in the community can only augment an organization's ability to identify and help trafficked persons. "There's a need for multidisciplinary task forces and also collaborative activity between social service agencies and law enforcement," said Perry. "Without a sense of trust and collaboration among these organizations, many of these cases will fall through the cracks." (For more information, see http://www2.acf.hhs.gov/trafficking/index.html)

(From Fred, 2004, p. 4; reprinted with permission of the National Association of Social Workers.)

Practice Implications

Consistent with the theme of this chapter—the psychology of human behavior—the topics have largely concerned oppression and victimization. The most relevant social work focus would therefore be the prevention of such oppression in the first place. Prevention work with potential perpetrators of oppression is often more important for society than is treatment after the patterns of violence and other harmful practices are established. Treatment of would-be oppressors or victimizers such as violent family members and school ground bullies can help individuals change through the development of self-awareness and empathy skills. Other methods that are useful in the reduction of self-destructive patterns of behavior are motivational interviewing tailored to a person's level of readiness for change, anger management for the redirection of negative energy, and stress management to help reduce irrational fears and anxieties.

However, victims, too, need support, sometimes even years after the violation took place. In counseling oppressed and traumatized people, the social worker can begin by entering the world of their subjugation—hearing the pain, anguish, and confusion and drawing on the client's own language and concepts to become the dominant mode of expression (van Wormer, 2004). An understanding of how sexism, racism, and class oppression affect a client's outlook on life is essential to effective intervention. A history of personal victimization is often evident in the backgrounds of clients seeking treatment for trauma and other problems, like addiction, that might on the surface seem unrelated to ill treatment. Through reflective listening and reinforcing revelations of strength, the social worker can seek pathways to possibility when even the most convoluted life stories are offered. The strengths/empowerment approach is especially effective in helping people reclaim a degree of personal power in their lives—if, indeed, they ever had any—and in helping them gain a sense of it if they did not.

In her book on black women and self-recovery, bell hooks (1993) connects the struggle of people to "recover" from suffering and injury caused by political oppression and exploitation with the effort to break with addictive behavior. "Collectively, black women will lead more life-affirming lives," she writes, "as we break through denial, acknowledge our pain, express our grief, and let the mourning teach us how to rejoice and begin life anew" (p. 111).

"To heal our wounds," hooks tells us, "we must be able to critically examine our behavior and change" (hooks, 1993, p. 39). As clients begin to take responsibility for their lives, the healing process can begin. This involves generally recognizing how past events influence present feelings, thoughts, and behavior. Women's and men's healing may involve a journey back in time to childhood or early adulthood, where trauma has occurred. Healing may require a working through of guilt feelings, which are real regardless of whether there is any actual guilt. Inner change often comes through identifying irrational thoughts, understanding how thoughts and feelings are intertwined, and learning to reframe unhealthy assumptions and beliefs.

Recognition of the ways that people of different ages find meaning in life and wrestle with major challenges can increase empathy and help clients' understanding of the changes they face. In working with women, therapists can aid them to recognize that they themselves are worthy of care, to acquire a more holistic understanding of the ethic of care. All of the developmental or stage models discussed in the earlier pages of this chapter enlighten our understanding of significant issues; the two most relevant to direct practice are knowledge of spiritual development (an important component in grief counseling) and stages of change in behavior.

Patricia Dunn (2000) finds that the stages-of-change model is appropriate for social work because it is an integrative model that is compatible with the mission and concepts of the profession and is grounded in empirical research. By building a close therapeutic relationship, the counselor can help the client develop a commitment to change. The way motivational theory goes is this: If the therapist can get the client to do something—*anything*—to get better, this client will have a chance at success. This is a basic principle of social psychology. Examples of tasks that William Miller (2006) pinpoints as predictors of recovery are attending Alcoholics Anonymous (AA) meetings, coming to therapy sessions, completing homework assignments, and taking prescribed medication. The question, according to Miller, then becomes, How can I help my clients take action on their own behalf? A related principle of social psychology is that, in defending a position aloud, as in a debate, we become committed to it. One would predict, from the motivational enhancement perspective, that if the therapist elicits defensive statements in the client, the client will become more committed to the status quo and less willing to change. For this reason, explains Miller, confrontational approaches have a poor track record. Research

has shown that people are more likely to grow and change in a positive direction on their own than if they get caught up in a battle of wills.

Summary and Conclusion

The passages of life bring with them many challenges. Quoting his mother, poet Langston Hughes (1922/1994) eloquently expressed this notion: "Life . . . ain't been no crystal stair; It's had tacks in it; and splinters, And boards torn up" (p. 52). Identity is a major arena in which group membership is played out in relation to mainstream society. In this chapter we have considered social identity based on race, class, gender, sexual orientation, and disability. The spiritual self was considered as an aspect of personal definition as well.

Age is a social identity dimension; people change the way they see themselves based on interaction factors that include role playing. Stage theorists, including Freud, Erikson, Maslow, Kohlberg, and Fowler, have all viewed development as a series of relatively fixed, linear stages, the accomplishments of each serving as groundwork for the next. Another stage theorist, Gilligan, stresses relationship in female moral development, while Prochaska and DiClemente view development in terms of upward-spiraling steps toward self-improvement. Wilber's concept of spiritual growth is hierarchical, yet spiraling as well.

The focal point of this chapter is that most psychological of human experiences: trauma. In preparation for the discussion on trauma, this chapter presented an analysis of feelings—fear and anxiety, depression, anger, and jealousy. The latter two—anger and jealousy—led in to the topic of abusive men and the emotional impact of being beaten.

Trauma, whether from battering or other adult experiences such as war, has been described in terms of the biological imprinting of one or more deeply disturbing events on the mind and the ensuing personal torment. This chapter has drawn on historical, scholarly, and personal accounts to depict the horror of taking human life and surviving the unspeakable brutality inflicted by soldiers upon the enemy and the enemy's family.

Denial, numbing, flashbacks, intrusive thoughts, edginess (extreme startle response), sleeplessness, and nightmares are among the striking symptoms of PTSD, which is the aftermath of war. The only clear means of prevention is to keep wars from happening. The social work profession has a long tradition of both working for peace and working to pick up the pieces when the peace mission has failed. Social work students need to be prepared for cognitive work with the survivors of war trauma and for understanding the difficulty that many war refugees will face in starting life anew when one's trust in the world has been broken.

In summary, this synthesis of theoretical life stage models and psychological material concerning horrific psychological events—wars, exposure to long-term violence—have the capability of crushing the human spirit. But more often than not, human beings are able to get on with life, managing to control those things that can be controlled, and passing on to the next generation the wisdom born of suffering. As William Faulkner (1950) famously said, they are able to "not only endure but prevail"— individually and collectively. This is the miracle of survival. To prevail in the Faulknerian sense requires inner resilience, a stable self-concept, social support, and a sense of purpose that may include a spiritual or moral sensibility that transcends material concerns.

I shaped this chapter with the thought of delving into some of the mysteries of human nature as befits a book on human behavior. Our journey has taken us beyond an exploration of normative behavior into the realm of the ineffable and the profound. Specifically, our journey has taken us across the human developmental theory, including the spiritual dimension, and into the realm of family violence, the savagery of war, and, most disturbingly perhaps, the susceptibility of the human psyche to indoctrination and brainwashing. All of these phenomena have important implications for social work practice, in helping people live with what they have done and with what has been done to them.

Thought Questions

1. Compare and contrast Erikson's theoretical theory with that of Maslow. How equipped is each to handle international concerns?

2. Which aspects of the stage theories seem specific to males? Refer to Gilligan's criticism.

3. Discuss how religious faith develops and changes throughout life. How would you critique Fowler's theory in terms of positives and limitations?

4. How can social workers from a harm-reduction perspective use the stages-of-change model in their work? In what areas is it relevant?

5. How does racial identity develop, and what are its uses?

6. How can class and race be studied separately and as intertwined?

7. Why does class matter?

8. How does gender identity differ in males and females?

9. What are the unique challenges in assuming a gay and lesbian identity? Is homosexuality a choice? Why or why not?

10. How does society stigmatize people with disabilities? Discuss the various degrees of stigma accorded to individuals with various handicaps.

11. What is the spiritual self? What role does a sensitivity to the spiritual realm play in ordinary life?

12. Describe your visceral response to fear, anxiety, and anger. How can such feelings be controlled?

13. Why do anger-management programs often fail to bring about the desired results?

14. How does jealousy relate to partner abuse?

15. How does the impact of being battered over the long term become internalized for changes in one's behavior?

16. Is brainwashing a reality? Cite examples where this process might or might not apply.

17. How would you describe the phenomenon of PTSD in terms of diagnosis?
18. What is the psychology of war trauma? Provide some historical examples.
19. How would you describe the war in Iraq from the perspective of trauma?
20. How would you describe the universality of rape in war?
21. Refer to the case study on human trafficking. How might social workers help?
22. How can the healing process begin?
23. Which aspect of human behavior discussed in this chapter is the most disturbing to you and why?

References

Adams, H. E., Wright, L. W., & Lohr, B. A. (1996). Is homophobia associated with homosexual arousal? *Journal of Abnormal Psychology*, *105*(3), 440–45.

Alvarez, L., & Ruiz, P. (2001). Substance abuse in the Mexican American population. In L. A. Straussner (Ed.), *Ethnocultural factors in substance abuse treatment* (pp. 111–36). New York: Guilford.

American Psychiatric Association. (1980). *Diagnostic and statistical manual* (3rd ed.). Washington, DC: Author.

American Psychiatric Association. (2000). *Diagnostic and statistical manual of mental disorders* (4th ed.). Washington, DC: Author.

American Psychological Association (APA). (2006). *Controlling anger before it controls you.* Retrieved from http://www.apa.org/pubinfo/anger.html

Anisman, H., & Merali, Z. (2009). Learned helplessness in mice. In T. Gould (Ed.), *Mood and anxiety related phenotypes in mice: Characterization using behavioral tests* (pp. 177–196). New York: Springer.

Appleby, G. A. (2007). Culture, social class, and social identity development. In G. A. Appleby, E. Colon, & J. Hamilton (Eds.), *Diversity, oppression, and social functioning: Person-in-environment assessment and intervention* (2nd ed.)., (pp. 16–36). Boston: Allyn & Bacon.

Armstrong, K. (2009). *The case for God*. New York: Random House.

Associated Press. (2009). Why didn't kidnapped girl escape? *Waterloo/Cedar Falls Courier*, p. A4.

Atkinson, M. P., Guetz, A., & Wein, L. (2009). A dynamic model for post-traumatic stress disorder among U.S. troops in operation Iraqi Freedom. *Management Science, 55*(9), 1454–1468.

Barsky, A. (2010). *Ethics and values in social work: An integrative approach for a comprehensive curriculum.* New York: Oxford University Press.

Basham, K. K., & Miehls, D. (2004). *Transforming the legacy: Couple therapy with survivors of childhood trauma.* New York: Columbia University Press.

Bell, K. M., & Orcutt, H. (2009). Post-traumatic stress disorder and male-perpetrated intimate partner violence. *The Journal of the American Medical Association, 302,* 562–564.

Bettelheim, B. (1943). Individual and mass behavior in extreme situations. *Journal of Abnormal and Social Psychology, 38,* 417–452.

Bettelheim, B. (1983). *Freud and man's soul.* New York: Knopf.

Bill Wilson/C. G. Jung Letters. (1961/1987). The roots of the society of Alcoholics Anonymous. *Parabola, 12*(2), 71.

Boyle, C. (2000). Engagement: An ongoing process. In A. Abbott (Ed.), *Alcohol, tobacco, and other drugs* (pp. 144–58). Washington, DC: NASW Press.

Browning, M. (2003, March 14). Brainwashing agitates victims into submission. *Palm Beach Post.* Retrieved from http://www.rickross.com

Brownmiller, S. (1975). *Against our will: Men, women, and rape.* New York: Penguin.

Brownmiller, S. (1993, January 4). Making female bodies the battlefield. *Newsweek,* 37.

Burns, R. (1786/1905). Address to the unco guid [uncommonly good]: On the rigidly righteous (pp. 52–55). In *Selected poems of Robert Burns.* London: Kegan Paul, Trench, Trubner and Co., Ltd.,

Bushman, B. (2002). Does venting anger feed or extinguish the flame? Catharsis, rumination, distraction, anger, and aggressive responding. *Personality and Social Psychological Bulletin, 28,* 724–731.

Buttell, F., & Carney, M. (2005, January). Do batterer intervention programs serve African American and Caucasian batterers equally well? *Research in Social Work Practice, 15*(1), 19–28.

Campo-Flores, A., & Thomas, E. (2007, January 29). Living with evil. *Newsweek*, pp. 48–55.

Carey, B. (2004, November 24). Anger management may not help at all. *New York Times*. Retrieved from http://www.nytimes.com/2004/11/24/health/24anger.html

Carnes, P. (1997). *The betrayal bond*. Deerfield, FL: Health Communications, Inc.

Carroll, M. (1999). Spirituality and alcoholism: Self-actualization and faith stage. *Journal of Ministry in Addiction and Recovery*, 6(1), 67–84.

Catalano, S., Smith, E., Snyder, H., & Rand, M. (2009, September). *Female victims of violence*. Washington, DC: Bureau of Justice Statistics.

Chestang, L. (1984). Racial and personal identity in the Black experience. In B.W. White (Ed.), Color in a White society (pp.83–94). Washington, DC: National Association of Social Workers (NASW) Press.

Colon, E. (2007). A multidiversity perspective on Latinos: Issues of oppression and social functioning. In G. A. Appleby, E. Colon, & J. Hamilton (Eds.), *Diversity, oppression, and social functioning: Person-in-environment assessment and intervention* (2nd ed.)., (pp. 115–134). Boston: Allyn & Bacon.

Cooper, H. (2009, July 26). Meet the new elite, not like the old. *New York Times*, pp. WK1, 6.

Demaree, H. A., Harrison, D. W., & Rhodes, R. D. (2000). Quantitative electroencephalographic analyses of cardiovascular regulation in low- and high-hostile men. *Psychobiology*, 28(3), 420–431.

DiClemente, C. C., & Velásquez, M. (2002). Motivational interviewing and the stages of change. In W. R. Miller & S. Rollnick (Eds.), *Motivational interviewing: Preparing people for change* (2d ed.) (pp. 201–216). New York: Guilford.

Djurkovis, N., McCormack, D., & Casimir, G. (2006). Neuroticism and the psychosomatic model of workplace bullying. *Journal of Managerial Psychology*, 21(1), 73–89.

Dominelli, L. (2002). *Anti-oppressive social work theory and practice*. New York: Palgrave Macmillan.

Dowda, C. (2009). *Invisible scars: How to stop, change or end psychological abuse*. Far Hills, NJ: New Horizon Press.

Dunn, P. (2000). Dynamics of drug use and abuse. In A. Abbott (Ed.), *Alcohol, tobacco, and other drugs: Challenging myths, assessing theories, individualizing intervention* (pp. 74–110). Washington, DC: NASW Press.

Erikson, E. H. (1950/1963). *Childhood and society* (2nd ed.). New York: Norton.

Erikson, E. H. (1982). *The life cycle completed*. New York: Norton.

Evans, D. (2002). *Emotion: The science of sentiment*. New York: Oxford University Press.

Falicov, C.J. (2005). Mexican families. In M. McGoldrick, J. Giordano, & N. Garcia-Preto (Eds.), *Ethnicity and family therapy* (3rd ed) (pp. 229-241). New York: Guilford Press.

Farwell, N. (2004). War rape: New conceptualizations and responses. *Affilia*, 19(4), 389–403.

Faulkner, W. (1950, December). *Acceptance speech, Nobel prize for literature. Stockholm, Sweden*. Retrieved from the Nobel Prize website http://nobelprize.org/nobel_prizes/literature/laureates/1949/press.html

Fisher, L., & Ibanga, I. (2009, May 29). Why Susan Boyle may not win it all. *ABC News*. Retrieved from http://abcnews.go.com/Entertainment/Television/Story?id=7701849&page=2

Fitzgerald, L. (2009, August 31). Stockholm syndrome. *Time*. Retrieved from http://www.time.com/time/nation/article/0,8599,1919757,00.html

Fowler, J. (1995). *Stages of faith: The psychology of human development and the quest for meaning*. San Francisco: Harper & Row.

Frank, P. B., & Golden, K. (1992). Blaming by naming: Battered women and the epidemic of codependence. *Social Work*, 37(1), 5–6.

Fred, S. (2004, September). Shame, helplessness are effects of "modern-day slavery." *NASW News*, p. 4.

Freud, S. (1896/1959). The aetiology of hysteria. In E. Jones (Ed.), *Sigmund Freud's collected papers* (vol. 1, pp. 189–221) New York: Basic Books.

Freud, S. (1922/1955). Certain neurotic mechanisms in jealousy, paranoia, and homosexuality. In J. Strachey (Ed. & Trans.), *The complete psychological works of Sigmund Freud* (Vol. 18, pp. 221–232). New York: Basic Books.

Friedrich, J. (2002). *Der Brand: Deutschland im Bombenkrieg*. Munich: Propylaen.

"Gays comprise 5 percent of electorate in 2002, new poll finds." (2002, November 21). Human Rights Campaign. Retrieved from http://www.hrc.org

Gilligan, C. (1982). *In a different voice: Psychological theory and women's development*. Cambridge, MA: Harvard University Press.

Gilligan, C. (2002). *The birth of pleasure*. New York: Knopf.

Gisick, M. (2004, August 4). A soldier's downward spiral. *Daily Hampshire Gazette (Northhampton, MA)*, pp. Al, A8.

Gladwell, M. (2008). *The outliers: The story of success*. New York: Little, Brown & Co.

Goffman, E. (1963). *Stigma: Notes on the management of spoiled identity*. Englewood Cliffs, NJ: Prentice-Hall.

Goode, E. (2009, August 2). After combat, victims of an inner war: Suicide's rising toll. *New York Times*, p. A1.

Greene, R. R. (2009). Eriksonian theory: A developmental approach to ego mastery. In R. R. Greene (Ed.), *Human behavior theory and social work practice* (3rd ed.) (pp. 85–111). New York: Aldine Transaction.

Greenwood, G., Relf, M., Huang, B., Pollack, L., Canchola, J., & Catania, J. (2002). Battering victimization among a probability-based sample of men who have sex with men (MSM). *American Journal of Public Health, 92*(12), 1964–1969.

Groopman, J. (2004, January 26). The grief industry. *New Yorker*, p. 30.

Gur, R. E., Gunning-Dixon, F., Bilker, W., & Gur, R. C. (2002). Sex differences in temporal-limbic and frontal brain volumes of healthy adults. *Journal of Cerebral Cortex, 12*(9), 998–1003.

Heise, L. L. (1998). Violence against women: An integrated ecological framework. *Violence Against Women, 4*(3), 262–290.

Hill, R. (2007). Enhancing the resilience of African American families. In L. A. See (Ed.), *Human behavior in the social environment from an African American perspective* (2nd ed.) (pp. 75–90). New York: Haworth.

Hoge, C. W., Castro, C. A., Messer, S., McGurk, D., Cotting, D., & Koffman, R. (2004). Combat duty in Iraq and Afghanistan, mental health problems, and barriers to care. *New England Journal of Medicine, 351*(1), 13–22.

hooks, b. (1993). *Sisters of the yam: Black women and self-recovery*. Boston: South End Press.

hooks, b. (2000). *Where we stand: Class matters*. New York: Routledge.

Hughes, L. (1922/1994). Mother to son. In G. Muller & J. Williams (Eds.), *Bridges:Literature across cultures* (p. 52). New York: McGraw Hill.

Irving, M., & Hudley, C. (2008). Cultural identity and academic achievement among African American males. *Journal of Advanced Academics, 19*(4), 676–699.

Jackson, K. (2003, June). Trauma and the national psyche. *Social Work Today*, 20–23.

Jacobson, N. S., & Gottman, J. M. (2007). *When men batter women*. New York: Simon and Schuster.

Johnson, H. (2004). *Psyche and synapse: Expanding worlds* (2nd ed.). Greenfield, MA: Deerfield Valley Publishing.

Kohlberg, L. (1981). *The philosophy of moral development: Moral stages and the idea of justice*. San Francisco: Harper & Row.

Kristen, K., & Sullivan, A. (2003). Gay and lesbian victimization: Reporting factors in domestic violence and bias incidents. *Criminal Justice and Behavior, 30*(1), 85–97.

Larkin, R., & Beverly, C. C. (2007). Black on black crime: Compensation for idiomatic purposelessness (revisited). In L. A. See (Ed.), *Human behavior in the social environment from an African American perspective* (2nd ed.)., (pp. 309–332). New York: Haworth.

Lemonick, M. (2007, January 29). The flavor of memories. *Time*, pp. 101–104.

Levinson, D. J. (1979). *The seasons of a man's life*. New York: Knopf.

Levinson, D. J. (1996). *The seasons of a woman's life*. New York: Knopf.

Lifton, R. J. (1961/1989). *Thought reform and the psychology of totalism*. Chapel Hill: University of North Carolina Press.

Lyall, S. (2009, April 17). Unlikely singer is Youtube sensation. *New York Times*, p. C1.

Martin, E. P., & Martin, J. M. (2002). *Spirituality and the black helping tradition in social work*. Washington, DC: NASW Press.

Martin, J. (2008, November 6). A growing problem for veterans—Domestic violence. Retrieved from the Washington University News and Information website, http://news-info.wustl.edu/tips/page/normal/12902.html

Maslow, A. (1950/1971). *The farther reaches of human nature*. New York: Viking.

McNally, R. J., Bryant, R. A., & Ehlers, A. (2003, November). Does early psychological intervention promote recovery from posttraumatic stress? *Psychological Science in the Public Interest, 4*(2), 45.

Mehlman, P. T., Higley, J. D., Faucher, I., Lilly, A. A., Taub, D. M., Vickers, J., et al. (1995). Correlation of CSF 5–HHIAA concentration with sociality and the timing of emigration in free-ranging primates. *American Journal of Psychiatry, 152*, 6.

Meston, C., & Buss, D. M. (2009). *Why women have sex: Understanding motivations—from adventure to revenge (and everything in between)*. New York: Times Books.

Michilin, P. M., & Juárez-Marazzo, S. (2007). Ableism: Social work practice with individuals with physical disabilities. In G. A. Appleby, E. Colon, & J. Hamilton (Eds.), *Diversity, oppression, and social functioning: Person-in-environment assessment and intervention* (2nd ed., pp. 205–226). Boston: Allyn & Bacon.

Miller, W. R. (2006). Motivational factors in addictive behaviors. In W. R. Miller & K. M. Carroll (Eds.), *Rethinking substance abuse: What the science shows, and what we should do about it* (pp. 134–152). New York: Guilford Press.

Montero-Gómez, A. (2001). Featuring domestic Stockholm syndrome: A cognitive bond of protection in battered women. *Aggressive Behavior, 27*(3), 196–197.

Monti, P., Kadden, R., Rohsennow, D., Cooney, N., & Adams, D. (2002). *Treating alcohol dependence: A coping skills training guide.* New York: Guilford Press.

National Coalition of Anti-Violence Programs (2005, April 26). Annual report on anti-LGBT hate violence released. *National Coalition of Anti-Violence Programs.* Retrieved from http://www.avp.org/publications/media/20050426NCAVP_hate_violence.htm

National Institute of Health (NIH). (2004). *Aging changes in sleep.* Retrieved from http://www.nlm.nih.gov/medlineplus/ency/article/004018.htm

National Coalition of Anti-Violence Programs (2008). *Annual report on lesbian, gay, bisexual, and transgender domestic violence in the United States in 2007.* Retrieved from http://www.ncavp.org/common/document_files/Reports/2007%20NCAVP%20DV%20REPORT.pdf

Obama, B. (2008, March 18). *A more perfect union. Constitution Center, Philadelphia.* New York Times. Retrieved from http://www.nytimes.com/interactive/2008/03/18/us/politics/20080318_OBAMA_GRAPHIC.html

Okie, S. (2005). Traumatic brain injury in the war zone. *New England Journal of Medicine, 352,* 2043–2047.

Pew Hispanic Center (2009, October 7). *Changing Latino pathways to adulthood: More work, more school—But gaps remain.* Retrieved from http://pewhispanic.org/files/reports/114.pdf

Pincus, J. (2002). *Base instincts: What makes killers kill?* San Francisco: Last Gap.

Pipher, M. (1994). *Reviving Ophelia: Saving the selves of adolescent girls.* New York: Putnam.

Pitman, R. (2009). *Biography listed on the Center for Integration of Medicine and Innovative Technology Website.* Retrieved from http://www.cimit.org/bios/pitman.html

Prados, J. (2002, September 9). Artificial intelligence. *American Prospect.* Retrieved from http://www.prospect.org/cs/articles?article=artificial_intelligence

Praglin, L. J. (2004). Spirituality, religion, and social work: An effort toward interdisciplinary conversation. *Journal of Religion and Spirituality in Social Work: Social Thought, 23*(4), 67–84.

Prigerson, H., Maciejewski, P., & Rosenheck, R. (2001). Population attributable fractions of psychiatric disorders and behavioral outcomes associated with combat exposure among U.S. men. *American Journal of Public Health, 92* (1), 59–63.

Prochaska, J., & DiClemente, C. (1986). The transtheoretical approach. In J. C. Norcross (Ed.), *Handbook of eclectic psychotherapy* (pp. 163–200). New York: Brunner/Mazel.

Prochaska, J. M., & Prochaska, J. O. (2009). Transtheoretical model guidelines for families with child abuse and neglect. In A. R. Roberts (Ed.), *Social workers' desk reference* (2nd ed.)., (pp. 641–647). New York: Oxford University Press.

Rapp, C. A., & Goscha, R. (2006). *The strengths model: Case management with people with psychiatric disabilities* (2nd ed.). New York: Oxfod University Press.

Rhoads, C. (2003, February 25). Behind Iraq stance in Germany: A flood of war memories. *Wall Street Journal,* pp. A1, A8.

Robbins, S. P., Chatterjee, P., & Canda, E. R. (2006). *Contemporary human behavior theory: A critical perspective for social work* (2nd ed.). Boston: Allyn & Bacon.

Roeder, T. (2009, July 15). Fort Carson report: Combat stress contributed to soldiers' crimes back home. *Colorado Springs: The Gazette.* Retrieved from http://www.gazette.com/articles/soldiers-58520-report-army.html

Rosenthal, E. (2004, October 29). Study puts Iraqi deaths of civilians at 100,000. New York Times. Retrieved from http://www.nytimes.com/2004/10/29

Saleebey, D. (2001). *Human behavior and social environments.* New York: Columbia University Press.

Saxe, G., Stoddard, F., Courtney, D., Cunningham, K., Chawla, N., Sheridan, R., King, D., & King L. (2001). Relationship between acute morphine and course of PTSD in children with burns. *Journal of the American Academy of Child and Adolescent Psychiatry, 40*, 915–921.

Scotty, C. (2004, October 18). Can I get you some manners with that? *Newsweek*, 24.

Shakespeare, W. (1599/1952). *Julius Caesar*. In *William Shakespeare: The complete works* (pp. 969–998). New York: Random House.

Shakespeare, W. (1605/1952). *Macbeth*. In P. Alexander (Ed.), *William Shakespeare: The complete works* (pp. 999–1027). London: Spring Books.

Shane, S. (2009, August 11). Two U.S. architects of harsh tactics in 9/11's wake. *New York Times*, p. A1.

Sheridan, M. J. (2002). Spiritual and religious issues in practice. In A. R. Roberts & G. J. Greene (Eds.), *Social workers' desk reference* (pp. 567–571). New York: Oxford University Press.

Sheridan, M. J. (2008). The spiritual person. In E. D. Hutchison (Ed.), *Dimensions of human behavior* (2nd ed.)., (pp. 183–224). Thousand Oaks, CA: Sage.

Singer, T., Seymour, B., O'Doherty, J., Kaube, H., Dolan, R., & Frith, C. (2004). Empathy for pain invokes the affective but not sensory components of pain. *Science, 303*(5661), 1157–1162.

Smith, C., & Snell, P. (2009). *Souls in transition: The religious and spiritual lives of emerging adults*. New York: Oxford University Press.

Smith, T. W. (2006). Blood, sweat, and tears: Exercise in the management of mental and physical health problems. *Clinical Psychology: Science and Practice, 13*(2), 198–203.

Snedeker, R. (2006). *By invitation only*. Documentary film produced with funding from Newcomb College Center for Research on Women and Louisiana Endowment for the Arts. Retrieved from http://www.byinvitationonlythefilm.com/

Spiegel Online International (2009, October 10). *Abducted Austrian girl details ordeal*. Retrieved from http://www.spiegel.de/international/0,1518,435775,00.html

Sprigg, P. (2005). Homosexual groups back off from "10 percent" myth. *Family Research Council*. Retrieved from http://www.frc.org

Stanton, J. (2005, April 10). Community fights back at Gage protesters. *Waterloo–Cedar Falls (Iowa) Courier*. Retrieved from http://www.wcfcourier.com

Stosny, S. (2005). *You don't have to take it anymore: Turn your resentful, angry, or emotionally abusive relationship into a compassionate, loving one*. New York: Free Press.

Stotzer, R. (2008). Gender identity and hate crimes: Violence against transgender people in Los Angeles County. *Sexual research and Social Policy, 5* (1), 43-52.

Thomas, F. (2004). *What's the matter with Kansas? How conservatives won the heart of America*. New York: Metropolitan Books.

Tjaden, P., & Thoennes, N. (2000). *Extent, nature, and consequences of intimate partner violence: Findings from a National Violence against Women Survey*. Washington, DC: U.S. Department of Justice.

Tavris, C. (1982). *Anger: The misunderstood emotion*. New York: Simon & Schuster.

Tavris, C. & Aronson, E. (2008). *Mistakes were made (But not by me): Why we justify foolish beliefs, bad decisions, and hurtful acts*. Orlando, FL: Harcourt.

Ulrich, Y. C. (1998). What helped most in leaving spouse abuse: Implications for interventions. In J. C. Campbell (Ed.), *Empowering survivors of abuse: Health care for battered women and their children* (pp. 70–78). Thousand Oaks, CA: Sage.

Van Voorhis, R. M. (2009). Feminist theories and social work practice. In R. R. Greene (Ed.), *Human behavior theory and social work practice* (3rd ed.)., (pp. 265–290). New York: Aldine Transaction.

van Wormer, K. (2004). *Confronting oppression, restoring justice: From policy analysis to social action*. Alexandria, VA: CSWE.

van Wormer, K., & Davis, D. R. (2008). *Addiction treatment: A strengths perspective* (2nd ed.). Belmont, CA: Brooks/Cole.

van Wormer, K., & Roberts, A.R. (2009). *Death by domestic violence: Preventing the murders and the murder-suicides*. Westport, CT: Praeger.

Vonk, M. E., & Early, T. J. (2009). Cognitive-behavioral therapy. In A. R. Roberts & G. J. Greene (Eds.), *Social workers' desk reference* (2nd ed., pp. 116–120). New York: Oxford University Press.

Wallace, H. (2008). *Family violence: Legal, medical, & social perspectives* (5th ed.). Boston: Allyn and Bacon.

Wilber, K. (1998). Spiritual diary. *Tikkun, 13*(5), 37–45.

Williams, J. B. (2002). Using the *Diagnostic and statistical manual of mental disorders*. In A. R. Roberts & G. J. Greene (Eds.), *Social workers' desk reference* (4th ed., pp. 171–180). New York: Oxford University Press.

Wise, T. (2009). *Between Barack and a hard place: Racism and white denial in the age of Obama.* San Francisco: City Lights Books.

Worden, B. (2007). Women and sexist oppression. In G. A. Appleby, E. Colon, & J. Hamilton (Eds.), *Diversity, oppression, and social functioning: Person-in-environment assessment and intervention* (2nd ed., pp. 93–115). Boston: Allyn & Bacon.

Wordsworth, W. (1798/1904). Lines composed a few miles above Tintern Abbey. In *The complete poetical works by William Wordsworth.* Boston and New York: Houghton Mifflin Co.

Wyatt, J., Derk-Jan, D., De Cecco, A., Ronda, J., & Czeisler, C. (2006). Sleep-facilitating effect of exogenous melatonin in healthy young men and women is circadian-phase dependent. *Sleep, 29* (5), 609-618.

Yilmaz, M. (2009). The effects of an emotional intelligence skills training program on the consistent anger levels of Turkish university students. *Social Behavior and Personality, 37* (4), 565–576.

Zabriskie, P. (2004, November 29). Wounds that don't bleed. *Time*, 40–41.

Zastrow, C. H., & Kirst-Ashman, K. K. (2010). *Understanding human behavior and the social environment* (8th ed.). Belmont, CA: Brooks/ Cole.

Zeichner, P. (2008). Determinants of anger and physical aggression based on sexual orientation: An experimental examination of hypermasculinity and exposure to male gender role violations. *Archives of Sexual Behavior, 37* (6), 891–901.

Zittel, K., Lawrence, S., & Wodarski, J. S. (2002). Biopsychosocial model of health and healing: Implications for health social work practice. *Journal of Human Behavior in the Social Environment, 5*(1), 19–33.

Birth Through Adolescence

Your children are not your children.
They are the sons and daughters of Life's
longing for itself.
They come through you but not from you.
And though they are with you yet they belong
not to you.

—KAHLIL GIBRAN

Often we trace the origins of individual behavior to a person's background and upbringing, to what was taught and not taught, to genes, culture, and class. There is the nature argument (based on studies of the transmission of IQ), the nurture assumption (the old Jesuit saying, "Give me a child to age seven, and he is mine for the rest of his life," cited by Saleebey, 2001), and the nature plus nurture position. Most researchers take the third—the holistic—approach. Peer group socialization theory regards out-of-the-home, same-age peer groups as the primary shapers. Contained in each theory is an important part of the puzzle about the essence of human nature.

Unlike in other human behavior and general social work texts, the focus in this chapter is on key variables in childhood behavior. Social work educator Carlton Munson (interviewed by Jackson, 2004) decries this situation. Even human behavior courses, which are broad and deal with the whole life span, Munson observes, give short shrift to child behavior. Furthermore, they teach little of the long-term importance of early attachment. This educational neglect means that social writers are often ill prepared to participate in child welfare cases regarding custody decisions. They are also poorly prepared to engage in child therapy. Topics presented in this chapter, although they cannot do justice to a field as complex as child therapy, thus ask, "What is the impact of event A or event B on the child's development?" as opposed to "Why do some parents commit child abuse?" or "What is the motivation of child molestation?" The focal point of Chapter 4 is not the parent; rather, it is the child.

This chapter is structured chronologically, addressing behaviors across the life span according to the key accomplishments expected of children from infancy through adolescence. In addition, we look at the life-span theories of Piaget and Erikson.

Childhood resilience, viewed as the counterpart to risk, is a major theme. Both childhood risk (to healthy growth and development) and resilience (in overcoming obstacles to a productive life) are considered. Among the risks discussed are abuse and neglect, disability, school bullying, and gender identity crisis.

A fact sheet from the U.S. Department of Health and Human Services reveals the extent of child mistreatment in the United States.

Readers of this chapter will note the attention to global and cross-cultural aspects of child development. A global view is deemed essential as a means of differentiating universal from culturally specific patterns and distinguishing, where possible, the biological from the cultural in human behavior.

Childhood resilience is a common literary theme. The novels of Charles Dickens exemplify this pattern—the child prevails over dire misfortune and persecution mostly due to love and education from a benefactor who appears at a crucial moment. The success of Dickens's stories probably have something to do with their autobiographical and social context. Even in autobiographical literature, the theme of resilience runs more or less throughout the authors' histories. For example, Benjamin Franklin (1771/1968) relates that he was able to turn to his advantage the early childhood mistreatment he experienced during his apprenticeship to a cruel brother. And even more poignantly, we learn of the trials and tribulations of escaped slave and abolitionist Frederick Douglass (1845/1968). Douglass's narrative describes the horrors of slavery, in which children born of slavemaster fathers and slave mothers were singled out for special cruelty. Teaching himself to read through his play with white kids, Douglass was able to escape his surroundings to become a great orator and leader of his people. A century later Maya Angelou (1969) survived segregation, economic hardship, and psychological trauma related to childhood sexual abuse to also become an orator, as well as dancer, actress, and renowned poet. Other remarkable examples of the resilience of the human spirit are given in *Zami* by Audre Lorde (1982) and the *Autobiography of Malcolm X* (Malcolm X & Haley, 1965). In the 1950s Lorde came of age as a lesbian in Harlem. Malcolm X went from common criminal to Muslim leader, from a rebellious, lawbreaking youth to a renowned world citizen in his final years.

To help us understand children's developmental needs, several theories offer useful conceptual frameworks. First, Piaget's cognitive theory addresses intellectual growth, and Erikson's psychosocial theory explains how development can be conceived as occurring in a series of fixed, predetermined stages. The psychosocial model extends psychoanalytical theory by focusing on the child's emotional development. Finally, attachment theory, which, unlike the other two frameworks, is not stage oriented, provides insights about relationship that cut across the early childhood period. Together these perspectives and relevant facts from the research literature should help us view child behavior patterns holistically.

Birth to Two Years

To Piaget, this earliest period in human life (refer to the infant in Figure 4.1) is the time of *sensorimotor development*, a stage characterized

Figure 4.1. This 3-month-old baby is taking in a lot more information from her surroundings than research has previously indicated. Photo by Cindy Murphy.

by the formation of increasingly complex sensory and motor development. The period begins physiologically with sucking and grasping reflexes. Repetitive use of these reflexes, supported by neurological and physical maturation, forms the beginnings of learned behavior and acquired habits (Samantrai, 2004).

Behaviors that were automatic gradually become deliberate responses to familiar stimuli. Information is assimilated, and the infant repeats operations such as thumb sucking for tension relief. The following months are characterized by imitating gestures, complex movements, and goal-directed behavior. Between 12 and 18 months, the infant learns that objects out of sight still exist (object permanency). Peek-a-boo, for example, is a game that brings much amusement at this time. Progress in cognitive development depends on innate ability and interpersonal interactions.

Erikson's (1950/1963) concern during the same time frame is not with intellectual development but with what he terms the crisis of *trust versus mistrust*. Recall from Chapter 3 that Erikson's psychosocial stages are concerned with crises at key age periods and occur across the life span. His stages are sequential but not hierarchical. This means that each new stage emerges according to the predetermined genetic plan irrespective of how successful the resolution of the previous stage was. The unhealthy resolution of the stage crisis, however, affects the outcome of all subsequent stages. The development of a healthy personality entails a positive resolution at each interval. Erikson's formulation takes into account physical drives such as the pull toward "nipple and breast and the mother's focused attention and care" (p. 248). However, in contrast to Piaget's formulation, Erikson's focus is on matters more directly relevant to personality and therefore to clinical practice. Although written in 1950 and infused with the sexist stereotyping of his day, Erikson's work is far more appealing and profound, in my opinion, than Piaget's. His juxtaposition of infant milestones (or setbacks) and the evolution of social institutions, micro and macro, are major contributions. "The human life cycle and man's institutions have evolved together," he explains (p. 250).

Erikson's description of each stage of development accordingly includes a parallel to some basic elements of social organization. Stage 1, for example, is juxtaposed with the communal side of religion: "Trust born of care is, in fact, the touchstone of the actuality of a given religion. All religions have in common the periodical childlike surrender to a Provider or providers who dispense earthly fortune as well as spiritual health . . . and finally, the insight that individual trust must become a common faith, individual mistrust a commonly formulated evil" (p. 250).

If we accept Erikson's notion of the importance of the early development of trust, we will also see that the first stage of development is all about the relationship between mother (or other caretaker) and child. Trust develops as the "infant, mewling and puking in the nurse's arms" (Shakespeare, 1600/1954, *As You Like It*) learns to coordinate its movements and sounds with those of the mother-provider. Trust begins to develop, Samantrai (2004) states, "when there is a mutual coordination and regulation of rhythms between mother and child" (p. 53). When this coordination of rhythms does not occur, neurological and emotional consequences can result. Before we turn to research on neurological damage caused by prenatal drinking or outright abuse and neglect, let us pursue the concept of trust with an overview of attachment theory.

Attachment Theory

It used to be thought that infants who were born prematurely should remain untouched in an incubator. Mothers who instinctively reached to cuddle their babies were abruptly stopped. The rationale was to protect the infants from germs. Eventually, however, it was discovered that babies who were touched and held were more likely to live than those who were not. We now know that simulating the womb experience by keeping newborns physically close is both medically and psychologically necessary. If the experts had only taken heed of the classic research of Spitz and Bowlby and the experimentation of Harlow, many lives could probably have been saved.

René Spitz (1945) studied the psychological effect on orphans who were removed from their parents and deprived of personal care. Spitz observed that in the nineteenth century a large proportion of infants died in orphanages and hospitals, even where adequate medical care and nutrition had been provided. The key factor was lack of physical contact with parents, nurses, or some other human being. Attachment theory was first introduced by Bowlby (1952, 1969), a British child psychiatrist. In his studies of delinquent boys, Bowlby discovered a pattern of maternal separation. He concluded that, like other animals, human infants must have close, comforting relationships and that their development would be impaired if this were not provided. Attachment behavior, which is demonstrated by the infant moving toward the mother for protection when frightened, is regarded as a biologically based response that enhances one's chances for survival. Through such interactions with the world and the primary caregiver, children learn to make sense of the world and to seek comfort from other people. They will, according to Bowlby, develop trust in the parent as loving and in themselves as worthy of love. The nature of attachment relationships early in life, in short, determines the course of later relationships.

Today, Henry Harlow is credited with bringing about a paradigm shift in our understanding of early growth and development (Harlow & Harlow, 1962). To fully appreciate the impact of his research, we need to understand that conventional wisdom held that youngsters were essentially machines and responded to rewards (food) and punishments (deprivation) (Blum, 2002). Harlow proved that babies would cling to dolls even when food was offered elsewhere, in other words, that touch and love are key ingredients in mental health. Following Harlow's work, psychologists could no longer dismiss the role of physical closeness and cuddling in long-term personality development. As a result of this pioneering research and that of Spitz and Bowlby before him, a change in policy was instituted so that babies would be picked up and nurtured (Zastrow & Kirst-Ashman, 2010). The infant mortality in institutions dropped sharply as a result.

Harris (2009) directs our attention to some other significant findings in Harlow's study. Monkeys raised with mothers but without peers developed serious problems later on when placed with other monkeys. Harris then refers to a historical account of concentration camp children who bonded with each other and became inseparable. When freed, the children (aged 3–4 years) shunned all interaction with adults. Years later, they reportedly led normal lives. "Although a mother cannot substitute for peers, peers can sometimes act as a substitute for a mother," concludes Harris (p. 143).

When things go wrong during the gestation period or soon thereafter, however, the consequences can be permanent. Consider the leading known cause of mental retardation, fetal alcohol syndrome (FAS), the roots of which are found in heavy drinking during the first trimester of pregnancy (Lupton, Burd, & Harwood, 2004). Prenatal exposure to alcohol can disrupt brain development and interfere with cell development crucial to the maturation of the central nervous system. Also consider postnatal abuse and neglect and the implications of such maltreatment for later attachment. The infant's development is adversely affected by both experiences (Newman & Newman, 2006).

Brain Development

Because of its vital role in future human behavior, we return briefly to the topic of Chapter 2: brain development. Unique to the human brain is the development of the frontal lobes, much of which takes place postnatally. Maté (1999) explains this phenomenon in terms of evolution. Were we born with our wiring rigidly fixed by heredity, the frontal lobes would be far more limited in the capacity to learn and adapt to the environment. At the same time, when humans began to stand upright, the pelvis had to narrow; thus, the growth of the fetus inside the womb was limited. The tremendously large brain therefore had to develop after birth. The conditions that are necessary for favorable growth are nutrition, a physically secure environment, and mental stimulation.

The importance of childhood nutrition was revealed in a report by the United Nations

Children's Fund (UNICEF, 2005). The report discusses the influx of refugees from famine-torn North Korea into South Korea by way of China. Whereas the average height of the North Korean males was less than 5 feet and their weight less than 100 pounds, South Korean males were 5 feet, 8 inches on average. (So when the North Korean children were placed in school, they were far behind their South Korean counterparts and were, for many reasons, unable to catch up.)

Physical attachment and human warmth are primary elements in the essential simulation of conditions in the womb. The neurons and connections most useful to the organism's survival are maintained; others wither and die. Hence, active stimulation of an infant is essential and helps it develop in certain directions—linguistically, musically, and visually. An example of the role of mental stimulation in this process occurs when those who are blind in early childhood later have their eyesight restored. They have to learn to see, a process that may never be wholly successful (Fine et al., 2003).

Healthy brain development, Maté states, requires a calm and consistent emotional milieu. Otherwise the wiring of the neurophysiological circuits of self-regulation is disturbed. If the level of endorphins, or "feel good" opiates, is reduced, the child's emotional development can be adversely affected by emotional turmoil such as exposure to domestic violence. Attachment capabilities may be affected by such instability or by psychological withdrawal on the part of the troubled caretaker as well. Thus, environmental influences and biology are intertwined and contribute directly to an imbalance of brain chemicals and indirectly to the thought processes that follow.

Communication between infants and caretakers is often frustrating because, although infants after the age of 9 months or so are beginning to respond to language, they are not always able to communicate their wants or needs. What they are ready to do is respond to visual cues. Sign language, accordingly, is attracting a new group of enthusiastic teachers and parents as part of a national movement to enhance communication with preverbal infants (Owens, 2004). Even before age 1, some babies can sign "hungry" and "thirsty" and know the sign for "bath." Such signing often calms an anxious baby by communicating what is about to take place. Infants who have been taught to sign have actually been found to learn spoken language earlier than other infants. Observations of children born to deaf parents show that they can communicate their needs at a much earlier age than children of parents who can hear.

Does the brain have a gender? Previously it was believed that most of the behavioral differences in males and females were cultural—a difference in socialization. So when, in the 1960s, a botched circumcision in Winnipeg, Canada, left one of a pair of male twins with a badly damaged penis, the doctors decided to amputate and to reassign the injured twin to the female gender. This case, which was discussed in Chapter 2, was described in college textbooks as evidence that sex-role behavior and gender identity were the result of socialization (Harris, 2009). Not until 1997 did another researcher check the facts. The full story then became apparent: At age 14, Joan was desperately unhappy and insisted on mixing with boys and acting like a boy. When his mother told him the truth, he found great relief and resumed life as a male, later getting married and adopting his wife's children (Ridley, 2000). Further facts revealed that the ending was not happy, however, as both twins committed suicide—first, the one who had been reared as Joan, and the other, presumably from either close identification or guilt over having been spared the suffering that Joan had endured (Burkeman & Younge, 2004).

Medical researchers no longer believe that children are sexually and psychologically neutral at birth. A more recent study conducted by John Gearhart of Johns Hopkins Medical Institution followed 16 cases of children with cloacal exstrophy, a condition in which males are born with a little penis or none at all. No matter how they were raised, most of the children behaved like boys; many resisted wearing dresses after age four even when they believed they were female (Emery, 2004).

However, now that adult intersexuals are speaking out against assignment to the wrong sex and the secrecy their families often impose, the American Academy of Pediatrics has begun to reconsider the earlier practice of reconstructive surgery. Similarly, in a remote corner of the Dominican Republic, researchers have investigated cases of genetic males who resemble females at birth due to a regional mutation. Although reared as girls, when their bodies became manlike at puberty, all but one of them chose to switch genders (Harris, 2009).

It is possible that sexual identity and physical attraction are hardwired by the brain. Research at the University of California–Los Angeles on the brains of mice provides evidence on why we feel male and female and why we are physically attracted by males or females. Genetic differences in embryonic male and female mouse brains show anatomical differences that occur before birth (Challender, 2003). The female brains have greater symmetry, which makes it easier for both sides of the brain to communicate, leading to enhanced verbal abilities. These findings with regard to the brain's genes related to sexuality help explain the transgender phenomenon (see Chapter 2) and give us a reason to dismiss the myth that early childhood nonconformity to sex role expectations is simply a choice that can be directed.

Abuse and Neglect in Infancy

Child development is also greatly affected by the treatment accorded infants and children. The most common obstacle in healthy child adjustment, according to Bowlby (1969), is maternal neglect or emotional inaccessibility. Abuse and neglect in infancy can leave physical and psychological scars. Death, brain damage, developmental disability, low IQ, and sensory deficits are among the consequences. Samantrai (2004) summarizes the literature on the differential impact of various kinds of maltreatment. Physically abused infants, according to research, tend to show low frustration tolerance and low attention span and are easily distractible. Verbal abuse in early childhood tends to be associated with anger and avoidant behavior. Neglected children are generally the least flexible and the most clingy and whiny

and have substantial language delays compared to other groups.

Cross-Cultural Perspectives on Infant Care

From sleeping patterns to feeding patterns to responses to infants' numerous needs, there are vast cultural differences around the world and even within a single country. These customs shape the infants' experiences and help define the nature of their future relationships. Parental permissiveness as evidenced in eating and sleeping on demand among indigenous cultures, for example, is associated with development of the kind of individual autonomy encountered among hunting and gathering peoples (Javo, Rønning, & Heyerdahl, 2004). The Norwegian Sami and other indigenous people of the Arctic regions exemplify this child-rearing pattern.

Gardiner and Kosmitzki (2005) have studied sleeping arrangements cross-culturally. Generally, societies that encourage close bonding and dependence sleep with their infants and small children. Examples are found in Mayan (Indian peoples of Latin America) culture and Japan, where children typically sleep in the bed with their parents until the age of five or six. In rural Appalachia, likewise, children either sleep in the same bed or same room with their parents. In these cultures, Gardiner and Kosmitski suggest, social maturation is not associated with increased independence and self-reliance but rather with increased interdependence. Brandell and Rindel (2007) look at research on attachment patterns across various ethnic groups in the United States. Some differences emerge, for example, Puerto Rican mothers are more likely to focus on their desire for their children to be calm and have a close relationship with themselves, in contrast to Anglo mothers who are inclined to stress independence.

An advantage of cross-cultural studies is the transfer of knowledge about successful innovations. The reliance on the so-called kangaroo care for premature infants in Columbia is one such example. The term comes from a kangaroo's pouch, which provides a womblike closeness of mother and baby. Kangaroo care leaped into North American consciousness when a medical team returned from a hospital in Columbia and reported that doctors, lacking incubators, gave a new baby to the mother right after birth. The mother held the covered baby between her breasts, skin to skin. A study from Israel showed that babies under this kind of care improve in breathing and heartbeats much more quickly than premature infants raised in incubators (Feldman, Weller, Sirota, & Eidelman, 2002).

In the United States, researchers from the University of Texas, led by Yolanda Padilla, received a major grant to study the Mexican American "epidemiological paradox" (Neff, 2004). This paradox refers to the fact that Mexican American mothers have healthier birth outcomes than would be expected in view of their low income, inadequate prenatal care, and teenage pregnancies. According to the Centers for Disease Control and Prevention (CDC, 2009), infant mortality rates of infants under 1 year of age are the lowest for Asians, high for Native Americans, and the highest for African Americans. The Hispanic rates are just slightly higher than the white rates and only around half of the rates for blacks. Considering the high level of poverty and lack of health care for Latinos, this relatively low rate of infant deaths requires explanation. Neff (2004) suggests that the closeness of their family ties and family solicitude are the probable reasons for this phenomenon. Nevertheless, despite their healthy start in life, the babies can be expected to experience disproportionately high rates of health and developmental deficiencies later on in childhood, according to the article.

Feeding practices also may shape the early relationship between parent and child. Nursing and bottle feeding necessarily provide close contact. Later feeding customs vary from force feeding in one part of Nigeria to use of the high chair and persistent attempts to entice the child to eat selected foods (as in England, the United States, and Canada) and much more freedom (in the Philippines, northern India, and Sardinia, Italy), where the child gets to decide when, what, and how much to eat (Gardiner & Kosmitzki, 2005).

How do parents of various cultures respond to infant crying? Gardiner and Kosmitzki (2005) describe research from a German sample in which parents seemed relatively unresponsive to an infant's crying, compared to traditional mothers in Japan, who are always available to cater to the needs of their small child. The fact that Japanese children are highly dependent on their mothers (they exhibit separation anxiety when separated from their mothers) and that they are later strikingly susceptible to social pressure may have its origins in these child-rearing patterns. In his research on child development, Bowlby (1969) found that allowing infants to cry unattended is related to later feelings of insecurity.

In societies that devalue women, abandonment and mistreatment of infant girls are commonplace. In China, India, and Pakistan, for example, female fetuses are more often aborted; accordingly, the ratio of girls to boys in the early childhood years is plummeting. In the heavily male-dominated societies of South Asia, women in many families do not work outside the home. Boys are favored, and the incentive is to do away with female offspring (Terzieff, 2004). Both Pakistan and India have instituted changes to improve the status of women and enhance their participation in government.

Use of day care is common in the United States to accommodate the need of parents who work outside the home. Multiple mothering is characteristic of child care in Israeli kibbutzim. In much of Africa, infants and small children remain with their parents all day. Women in parts of Indonesia adjust their work patterns to accommodate their children. Mothers in the Peruvian mountains use a backpack-like device to carry their infants while engaging in their daily work (Gardiner & Kosmitzki, 2005).

Before leaving these cross-cultural perspectives, a return to attachment theory is in order. Writing from the perspective of Canadian aboriginal people, Neckoway, Brownlee, Jourdain, and Miller (2003) address cross-cultural and contextual elements of attachment theory. Aboriginal peoples believe that the child belongs not only to the family grouping (based on blood ties) but also to the community and the nation. This concept, according to Neckoway et al., involves not only an extended family but also an "extended-extended" family that includes others of the same clan. Attachment theory, which focuses on the emotional aspects of the mother–infant relationship, represents only part of the full reality of an aboriginal infant's socialization experience. Still, as Brandell and Rindel (2007) suggest, in their review of the best research available on attachment patterns worldwide, attachment needs and styles have a universal quality that applies across cultures. The methodology used in attachment studies, which is called the Strange Situation Procedure, is based on observation of infants and small children and their caregivers in situations of separation and reunion in unfamiliar surroundings. The researchers observe the behavior of the infant as the caregiver returns, whether he or she responds warmly to the caregiver and calms down. In North America approximately two-thirds of children are classified as secure and the remainder as avoidant or ambivalent. Research in Israel, Uganda, Columbia, China, and Germany using the same methodology has produced more or less the same results. The universality of these relationships thus can be seen as self-evident. Bowlby (1982) believes that the bonding of the infant to the mother serves an evolutionary function in that proximity to the mother assured the infant's odds of being protected and surviving in a threatening world. This early bonding also produces a growing sense of emotional security and self-confidence. Attachment theory, as Page and Norwood (2007) suggest, should be a cornerstone of theories presented in social work human behavior courses "because of its roots in human biology, its theoretical grounding in evolution theory, its explanatory power in addressing fundamental aspects of human experience . . . and the vast empirical literature that supports it" (p. 32).

Two to Seven Years of Age

Piaget's stage of preoperational thought consists of two substages—the preconceptual and the intuitive. Preoperational thought extends from toilet training and rapid language development to social perceptiveness. After age 2, children begin to verbalize their needs. Language can thus be used, Piaget (1952) stated, to contemplate objects even when they are out of sight. Before age 5, language is concrete and superficial, without depth of insight or a sense of connectedness among objects. Concepts such as numbers and time, accordingly, have little meaning. By age four or five, children learn to sort objects by color, shape, and size. Conservation refers to the child's ability to grasp the idea that, while one aspect of a substance (e.g., quantity) can remain the same as the shape changes, the tall thin glass does not necessarily contain more liquid than the shorter, wider one. Children achieve the ability to understand the conservation of substances around age six or seven.

Piaget's theory is one dimensional, concerned only with certain limited aspects of thinking. Nor does he take into account cultural learning differences. Erikson's conceptualization, in contrast, is far more holistic. Piaget's preoperational thought stage covers two of Erikson's psychosocial crises: autonomy versus shame and doubt (ages 2–4) and initiative versus guilt (ages 4–6).

The autonomy versus shame and doubt stage is characterized by holding on to and letting go of objects and emotions. Their environment encourages children to "stand on their own feet." The risk to independence is the sense of shame, which is born out of self-consciousness. Erikson's thoughts on shame say much about the impact of this feeling that is so central in the life of the child who is subject to continual put-downs and humiliation:

> One is visible and not ready to be visible; which is why we dream of shame as a situation in which we are stared at in a condition of incomplete dress, in night attire, "with one's pants down." Shame is early expressed in an impulse to bury one's face, or to sink, right then and there, into the ground. Too much shaming does not lead to genuine propriety but to a secret determination to try to get away with things, unseen—if, indeed, it does not result in defiant shamelessness. (Erikson, 1950/1963, p. 253)

Doubt is defined by Erikson as "the mother of shame." In its adult expression, doubting is played out in paranoid fears concerning hidden persecutors. The opposite of feelings of doubt and shame is the development of autonomy and freedom of self-expression in the child. Erikson locates the parallel to this stage at the societal level to the principle of law and order and the social institution of courts of justice.

Initiative versus guilt is how Erikson characterizes the period from age 4 to 6. Erikson's male bias is glaringly apparent in this section of *Childhood and Society*, not only in the consistent use of the male pronoun (as was the norm in the 1950s) but also in an almost exclusive concern with typically male developmental accomplishments such as "pleasure in attack and conquest," "acts of aggressive manipulation and coercion," "a final contest for a favored position with the mother," and "fantasies of being a giant and a tiger" (pp. 255–256). This, Erikson concludes, is the stage of the "castration complex." Any mention of girls or girl things is limited to their striving to make themselves "attractive and endearing" (p. 255). The female child's development, whether in terms of being "Daddy's little girl" or caring for her doll babies or being a tomboy, is simply passed over.

Nevertheless, Erikson offers insights concerning the guilt side of the initiative-versus-guilt equation with relevance to both genders. Guilt arises in the children's internalization of standards "where they develop an over-obedience more literal than the one the parent has wished to exact; or where they develop deep regressions and lasting resentments because the parents themselves do not seem to live up to the new conscience" (p. 257). Social institutions that are the counterpart to this stage of initiative are economic, work-related ones, and these areas of enterprise are ripe for creative expression as evidenced in early childhood. The moralistic aspect of childhood development is not addressed in Erikson's formulation.

Let us turn to scientific experiments to learn what they tell us about the power of conscience and moral drives during the preschool years. In an experiment conducted by Forman, Aksan, and Kochanska (2004), a mother set her three-year-old child in front of a pile of tempting toys, told the child not to play with them, and left the room. The same children had been studied at age one to see how well they mimicked their mothers. It was discovered that the babies who were the best imitators were the most apt to resist temptation later on. A child's willingness to imitate evidently indicates a general receptiveness to socialization and is related to the development of internal controls.

Can socialization be overdone? Psychiatrist Alvin Rosenfeld and journalist Nicole Wise (2001), coauthors of *The Over-Scheduled Child: Avoiding the Hyper-Parenting Trap*, seem to think so. Their book and those that follow its precepts are reacting to what Rosenfeld calls "hyper-parenting." Preschool tutoring, early high-pressured music and dancing lessons, and engagement in competitive sports can overwhelm children with performance anxiety. Lenore Skenazy, when she sent her nine-year-old son to ride the New York City subway alone, received a Google label of "America's Worst Mom" after she mentioned this fact in a newspaper column. To fight back, she did research on child endangerment in the United States and found a significant reduction in the child death-by-injury rate since 1980 and authored *Free-Range Kids: Giving Our Children the Freedom We Had Without Going Nuts with Worry*. There is no reason, Skenazy (2009) asserts, that a generation of parents who grew up walking alone to school, riding the bus or streetcar, selling Girl Scout cookies and trick-or-treating door to door should be holding their children back from exploring their world. Children today are being closely supervised and monitored.

The marketing of educational products for preschool children is a several-billion-dollar growth industry (Ferguson, 2004). Leap Frog is one of the most successful manufacturers of such products, many of which are electronic. In England, the United States, and Canada, preschool children are expected to demonstrate early numeracy and literacy skills. Children in Scandinavia, in contrast, do not get formal reading lessons until age 6 or 7, and they do not do homework until years later (Ferguson, 2004). The literacy rate in Scandinavia is at least 99 percent, and these countries have the highest per-capita newspaper reading rates in the world.

As families grow smaller (especially in Europe, Japan, and China), many children will be without siblings for playmates and will have to look elsewhere. Yet play in itself is vital in terms of learning survival functions for later life. Parallel play (playing side by side) with little seeming interaction is characteristic of 2-year-olds. Imaginative play peaks when a child is 4 years old, and much of this type of activity is mastery play, which leads to the acquisition of new skills. Since children work out their anxieties and fears through play, play therapy is an excellent strategy for social workers to employ in order to help the troubled child. Too much structured activity (as in the rush to teach 3-year-olds to read and count) can hinder growth in other areas. Too much television viewing, of course, stifles creativity in a different way. According to curriculum and instruction professor Anne Haas Dyson (2009), play and imagination are integral to a child's intellectual and social development. She is concerned about the marketing to parents of the "baby genius" products and other more advanced commercial teaching products used in the schools that may impede a child's natural development of learning.

This is not to say that mental stimulation is not important for later learning accomplishments in children. The small child's brain, it is often said, is like a sponge. How about the so-called Mozart effect? The claims that exposure of infants and small children to the music of Mozart and of intensive musical training would help produce mathematical abilities later received much media coverage. Although as neurologist Oliver Sacks (2007) points out in *Musicophilia*, these claims were greatly exaggerated, magnetic imaging of the brain revealed striking changes in the left hemisphere of children who have had only a single year of violin training compared to children who had no training. According to Sachs, for the vast majority of students, early exposure to music can be every bit as important educationally as reading or writing.

Attachment in Early Childhood

Attachment theory, as we have seen, views personality development in the context of close social relationships. Attachment is not about food but rather about feeling secure enough to explore the world and, whenever danger strikes, pulling more closely to the mother or mother figure for protection. The mother figure—supportive or rejecting—comes to be internalized. Operating outside of consciousness, internal working models of the significant attachment figures and of the self become the templates within which subsequent relationships are interpreted and experienced (Samantrai, 2004).

Kate Jackson (2004) enlightens us on some of the intricacies of attachment and attachment disorder. Attachment, according to Jackson, can be differentiated from bonding in that attachment is about feeling secure—the child with the parent—while bonding refers to the affectional ties between parent and child. *Attachment disorder* refers to a continuum of conditions characterized by difficulty in developing loving and secure attachments throughout life. This process is often misunderstood. A large part of the misunderstanding stems from reliance by mental health professionals on the *DSM-IV-TR*'s criteria for a mental disorder called "reactive attachment disorder." This condition is said to appear in children before the age of five and to be manifested in frequent changes in caregivers and/or a failure to meet the child's basic needs. Missing from this definition, Jackson asserts, is a recognition that attachment disorder may occur in children older than age five and that the source can be found in birth families, as well as in foster care families. Attachment disorders are widespread today due to poor parenting marred by substance abuse, single-person parenting, and lack of extended family supports. Substance abuse in itself often leads to other problems such as domestic violence and child mistreatment, both of which have an impact on the child's emotional, as well as physical, development.

Childhood Abuse and Neglect

Children who are abused in middle childhood are probably almost as dependent on the perpetrators as infants who are abused, but they have much more comprehension of what has taken place. Mistreatment early in life is likely to lead to children's inability to be secure in their attachment; this sets the stage for depression and later relationship problems and criminal behavior (Mignon, Larson, & Holmes, 2002). Children who are regularly exposed to violence may suffer from difficulties with attachment, regressive behavior, anxiety and depression, and aggression and conduct problems. They may be more prone to dating violence, delinquency, further victimization, and involvement with the child welfare and juvenile justice systems (Finkelhor, Turner, Ormrod, Hamby, & Kracke, 2009). One's risk of victimization varies—cases of physical abuse that result in death are most likely to occur under age 2; the risk of sexual abuse jumps sharply between ages six and 10, sibling abuse during middle childhood, and assaults with a weapon and handgun homicides are associated with the teenage years (Finkelhor & Hashima, 2001; Finkelhor et al., 2009). The risk of bullying peaks during middle childhood in a pattern similar to that for sibling assault (Finkelhor et al., 2009).

According to the latest data from the CDC, 3,184 children and teens died from gunfire in the United States in 2006—a 6 percent increase from 2005. This means one young life lost every 2 hours and 45 minutes, almost nine every day, 61 every week. More preschool children were killed by gunfire than law enforcement officers in the line of duty in the year of the report (Children's Defense Fund, 2009). As a result of the recent high death rate of children killed by gunfire, the Children's Defense Fund has issued a Protect Children, Not Guns campaign.

Neigh, Gillespie, and Nemeroff (2009), in their study of the neurobiological toll of child abuse and neglect, indicate that victimization that takes place during puberty is especially harmful. The degree of the damage done relates in part to the level of the stress experienced and to the meaning of the abuse to the individual. Research reviewed by Neigh et al. indicates that women who were sexually abused before age 13 are likely to develop either posttraumatic stress disorder (PTSD) or major depressive disorder. Women who were abused after that time are more likely to develop PTSD than major depressive disorder. The effects are

not only reflected in one generation but are multigenerational. The mental health of subsequent generations is affected because children raised by a traumatized parent do not receive the quality of mothering they would otherwise. We know from studies of Holocaust survivors with PTSD, for example, that the adult children of survivors have a greater lifetime prevalence of PTSD than do comparable children of parents without this disorder.

A little-studied but significant problem facing many children is sibling abuse. Given the large number of families in which parents hold two or even three jobs and leave small children in the care of older brothers and sisters, one could speculate that physical and psychological abuse of younger siblings is commonplace. Wiehe (2002), in his book on sibling abuse, discusses the following likely consequences of psychological mistreatment by siblings: somatic symptoms, nightmares, aggression, withdrawal, and low self-esteem.

There is a direct link between domestic violence and child abuse. Batterers do not always limit their attacks to adult partners. Studies reviewed by Friend and Mills (2002) document that in about half of the families investigated, batterers who had children abused them. Victims of domestic violence are twice as likely as other women to abuse their children. The witnessing of domestic violence is itself a form of child abuse. Friend and Mills contend that children who witness such violence are at risk of the same internalized and externalized behaviors as children who are physically or sexually abused. Internalized behaviors by the child include withdrawal, anxiety, and somatic complaints. Externalized behaviors include aggression and other disruptive acts.

Consistent with the behavioral theme of the book, it is appropriate to consider aspects in the infant's or child's personality or behavior that interact with corresponding attributes in the caretaker to reduce the risk of neglect and abuse. Thomlinson (2004), in her extensive review of child abuse literature, found that children who are more impulsive and quick to anger tend to overwhelm parents and raise the risk of harsh parental responses. Infants and children with health problems, developmental disabilities, and even nonnormative gender behavior are at increased risk of physical abuse. In contrast, children who are socially skilled, appealing, and perceived as cuddly can often dispel violence in a violence-prone parent.

Statistics on childhood victimization are presented in the following fact sheet from the U.S. Department of Health and Human Services. Data are drawn from reports by state child protection agencies. Keep in mind that, as Finkelhor et al. (2009) indicate, although victimization has enormous consequences for children, often affecting personality development, many of the most harmful forms of attacks on children are discounted in the data and by agencies. The physical abuse of children, although technically criminal, is not frequently prosecuted; peer assaults and many forms of family violence—for example, physical punishment—are generally ignored by the criminal justice system. Such acts would clearly be crimes if committed by one adult against another adult. Note the high rate of fatalities revealed in the report. An analysis of the data by the report from the Every Child Matters Education Fund (2009) puts these figures on the fatalities in international perspective. The U.S. death rate is more than double the rate in France, Canada, Japan, Germany, Great Britain, and Italy, countries that have less teen pregnancy, violent crime, and poverty, according to the report. One in five children in the United States is now living below the poverty line, a factor that is highly correlated with child abuse and neglect. To learn the specifics of these children's economic circumstances, see Table 4.1 that follows.

Child Maltreatment 2007: Summary of Key Findings

This fact sheet presents excerpts from Child Maltreatment 2007, a report based on data submissions by the states for federal fiscal year 2007. The National Child Abuse and Neglect Data System was developed by the Children's Bureau of the U.S. Department of Health and Human Services
in partnership with the states to collect annual statistics on child maltreatment from state child protective services (CPS) agencies.

Who Reported Child Maltreatment?

For 2007, more than one-half (57.7 percent) of all reports of alleged child abuse or neglect were made by professionals. The three largest percentages of report sources were from such professionals as teachers (17.0 percent), lawyers or police officers (16.3 percent), and social services staff (10.2 percent).

Who Were the Child Victims?

During 2007, an estimated 794,000 children were determined to be victims of abuse or neglect. The following are among the children confirmed as victims by CPS agencies in 2007:

- Children in the age group of birth to 1 year had the highest rate of victimization at 21.9 per 1,000 children of the same age group in the national population.
- More than one-half of the child victims were girls (51.5 percent) and 48.2 percent were boys.
- Approximately one-half of all victims were white (46.1 percent), 21.7 percent were African American, and 20.8 percent were Hispanic.

What Were the Most Common Types of Maltreatment?

As in prior years, neglect was the most common form of child maltreatment. CPS investigations determined the following:

- Nearly 60 percent (59.0 percent) of victims suffered neglect.
- More than 10 percent (10.8 percent) of the victims suffered physical abuse.
- Less than 10 percent (7.6 percent) of the victims suffered sexual abuse.
- Less than 5 percent (4.2 percent) of the victims suffered from psychological maltreatment.

How Many Children Died From Abuse or Neglect?

Child fatalities are the most tragic consequence of maltreatment. Yet each year children die from abuse and neglect. During 2007 the following occurred:

- An estimated 1,760 children died due to child abuse or neglect.
- The overall rate of child fatalities was 2.35 deaths per 100,000 children.
- More than 30 percent (34.1 percent) of child fatalities were attributed to neglect only; physical abuse also was a major contributor to child fatalities.
- More than three-quarters (75.7 percent) of the children who died due to child abuse and neglect were younger than 4 years old.
- Infant boys (younger than 1 year) had the highest rate of fatalities, at 18.85 deaths per 100,000 boys of the same age in the national population.
- Infant girls had a rate of 15.39 deaths per 100,000 girls of the same age.

Who Abused and Neglected Children?

In 2007, nearly 80 percent of perpetrators of child maltreatment (79.9 percent) were parents, and another 6.6 percent were other relatives of the victim. Women comprised a larger percentage of all perpetrators than men, 56.5 percent compared to 42.4 percent. Nearly 75 percent (74.8 percent) of all perpetrators were younger than age 40.

- Of the perpetrators who were child daycare providers, nearly 24 percent (23.9 percent) committed sexual abuse.
- Of the perpetrators who were parents, nearly 90 percent (87.7 percent) were the biological parent of the victim.

Who Received Services?

During an investigation, CPS agencies provide services to children and their families, both in the home and in foster care.

- More than 60 percent (62.1 percent) of victims and 31.2 percent of nonvictms received post-investigation services.
- More than 20 percent (20.7 percent) of victims and 3.8 percent of nonvictims were placed in foster care.

(From U.S. Department of Health and Human Services. Administration for Children and Families (2008). Summary: Child Maltreatment 2007. Retrieved from http://www.acf.hhs.gov/programs/cb/pubs/cm07/summary.htm)

Cross-Cultural Considerations

Japanese education begins at home, even before preschool. The mother teaches the small children to read, write, and perform simple mathematics (Gardiner & Kosmitzki, 2005). During my visit to Korea, I visited a family who expressed pride in teaching their preschool child English ABCs; their stated goal was to prepare her for the global economy. When riding in the car, they played English educational tapes and nursery rhymes. Asian traditions, which can be understood as an exaggerated form of the pressure placed on U.S. and Canadian children, stand in sharp contrast to the learning in certain African and South American tribal groups. There, small boys learn hunting and fishing skills and methods of navigation through the wilderness, while girls learn cooking, gathering, and child care (Gardiner & Kosmitzki, 2005). This pattern of education through parental modeling of occupational behavior was prevalent in early U.S. history and survives on small farms.

How is aggression in children handled cross-culturally? In their review of recent anthropological literature, Gardiner and Kosmitzki see vast differences in how adults handle childhood aggression. Haitian society, based on hierarchy by age, allows older siblings to hit younger ones in their care. In a study of a village in southern France, adults separate fighting children, and both may be punished. Throughout France, however, physical fighting is said to be rare. In the United States, punishment for fighting generally falls on the child who started the altercation, and there is a strong taboo against bullying smaller kids. Much violence is displayed in video games and TV shows, however. Studies of aggression content show that children in the United States include more aggression in their story content than do children from Sweden, Germany,

Table 4.1   Demographics and Economic Circumstances

Demographic Background

> ▶ In 2008, there were 73.9 million children ages 0–17 in the United States (or 24 percent of the population) down from a peak of 36 percent at the end of the "baby boom" (1964). Children are projected to remain a fairly stable percentage of the total population through 2021, when they are projected to compose 24 percent of the population.
> ▶ Racial and ethnic diversity in the United States continues to increase over time. In 2008, 56 percent of U.S. children were White, non-Hispanic; 22 percent were Hispanic; 15 percent were Black; 4 percent were Asian; and 5 percent were of other races. The percentage of children who are Hispanic has increased faster than that of any other racial or ethnic group, growing from 9 percent of the child population in 1980 to 22 percent in 2008.

Family and Social Environment

> ▶ In 2008, 67 percent of children ages 0–17 lived with two married parents, down from 77 percent in 1980.
> ▶ In 2008, 19 percent of children were native children with at least one foreign-born parent, and 3 percent were foreign-born children with at least one foreign-born parent. Overall, the percentage of all children living in the United States with at least one foreign-born parent rose from 15 percent in 1994 to 22 percent in 2008.
> ▶ In 2007, 21 percent of school-aged children spoke a language other than English at home and 5 percent of school-aged children both spoke a language other than English at home and had difficulty speaking English.

Economic Circumstances

> ▶ In 2007, 18 percent of all children ages 0–17 lived in poverty, an increase from 17 percent in 2006. Among children living in families, the poverty rate was also 18 percent in 2007.
> ▶ The percentage of children who had at least one parent working year round, full time was 77 percent in 2007, down from 78 percent in 2006.
> ▶ The percentage of children living in households with very low food security among children increased from 0.6 percent in 2006 to 0.9 percent in 2007. In these households, eating patterns of one or more children were disrupted and food intake was reduced below a level considered adequate by caregivers.

Source: http://www.ChildStats.gov (2009). *America's Children: Key Indicators of Well-Being, 2009.* Highlights. Retrieved from http://www.childstats.gov/americaschildren/index3.asp

and Indonesia. Among the least aggressive children in the world are the Inuit of North America, the Pygmies of Africa, and the Zuni Indian tribes. At the other end of the aggression continuum are some tribes in the Amazon region of South America. Mexican parents tend to be more punitive regarding displays of aggression against other children than are parents north of the border. The difference is attributed to interdependence within extended Mexican families.

Finland takes the prize for both outstanding and child-friendly education. And why shouldn't all education be both? Students at the Vaajakumpu Primary School put on their snow gear and for 15 minutes after every class they frolic on ice skates, sleds, and skis (Khadaroo, 2009). Thousands of educators from around the world have visited this Nordic nation to see how the students achieve some of the highest scores on reading, math, and science literacy in the world. Apart from the fresh air and exercise, educators are considering the prestige of the teaching profession and the strong social welfare system that supports parental leave for child care, day care, and universal health care. The national teachers' union is very strong, ensuring excellent working conditions for the teachers. Classes for immigrant children are kept to five or ten.

Six to Twelve Years of Age

Piaget (1952) termed this the period of concrete operations because the child thinks logically but still on a concrete level. Mental development of the primary school child is shown in several ways: concepts of numbers, time, space, and speed begin to coalesce, and the child comes to grasp the idea of conservation—this concerns the realization that the taller container may contain less liquid than the wider, shorter one. Young children of this age possess a sense of obligation to abide by the rules of the game. Understanding and empathy are also developed during this period. The focus, however, is on thinking about things rather than ideas.

Erikson's (1950/1963) delineation of the key crisis during this early-to-middle childhood period is termed *industry versus inferiority*. The child now learns to win recognition by making things such as drawings and paper airplanes. The literacy taught in the schools of industrialized societies is matched in other societies by training in the use of tools and weapons. There is a real risk at this stage that children will not measure up and will then feel inadequate or inferior to their peers. The parallel aspect of this stage of development is found at the societal level, when technology takes over and people's horizons are thereby restricted.

When adults recall the middle childhood period, most of their memories center around the school—one's role in the school play, cruel and beloved teachers, failures, and honors won and not won, and perhaps moments of festive togetherness as is illustrated by Figure 4.2.

School brings new information and exposure to a wide variety of individuals from diverse class and racial backgrounds. Children become aware of other parent–child relationships and may see their own home life (and language or religion) as different. So powerful

is the socialization experience at school that children generally grow up with the speech patterns and language of their classmates rather than of their parents (Harris, 2009). School-aged children quickly become aware of how they compare with their classmates and how they are regarded by them. Low status in the peer group, if it continues for very long, can wreck one's childhood and leave permanent scars on personality (see Harris; Newman & Newman, 2006). The main thing kids want is to be normal and to fit in. Intellectually, groups of children who do stand out, although in different ways, are those with cognitive disabilities, such as mental retardation, and intellectually gifted children.

Mental Retardation

The term *mental retardation* is used by the American Psychiatric Association (APA, 2000) to denote subaverage general intellectual functioning that is accompanied by significant limitations in adaptive functioning "in at least two of the following skill areas: communication, self-care, home living, social skills, use of community resources, self-direction, functional academic skills, work, leisure, health and safety" (p. 41). Mental retardation has many different etiologies. The four degrees of severity range from mild (IQ 50–70), moderate (IQ 35–50), severe (IQ 20–40), and profound (IQ below 20). Prenatal damage is the cause of fetal alcohol syndrome as discussed in Chapter 2. About 85 percent of children with a developmental disorder are in the "mild" category. These children can grow up to adapt fairly well to life in the community and can acquire vocational skills for minimum self-support. At the severe retardation level, language skills are very poor, and many will live in group homes. The mental disability known as Down syndrome is caused by chromosomal aberrations and is therefore a congenital disorder. There are no specific personality and behavioral features uniquely associated with mental retardation; children with developmental disabilities run the gamut from passive to aggressive, according to the *DSM-IV-TR* (APA, 2000).

Figure 4.2. Children engaging in spontaneous dance at a Cinco de Mayo celebration in Cedar Falls, Iowa. Photo by Rupert van Wormer.

Learning Disabilities and Giftedness

In England, the term *learning disability* refers to all developmental disabilities; in the United States, the term is used somewhat differently. Children are diagnosed usually by a school psychologist as having a learning disability if there is a distinct discrepancy between the child's IQ test scores and school achievement. Such children process information differently from others and may have difficulty learning to read. The first clue that a child has a learning disability often comes with problems in academic work. It is estimated that approximately 5 percent of school children have such a disability (APA, 2000).

Dyslexia is a form of learning disability that often involves a lack of sense of left and right. The words "dog" and "bog" and "god" may all be confused. Children with dyslexia have an inherent difficulty in deriving meaning from phonemes or sounding out words from the letters. They require intensive training in phonics and vocabulary building for fluency. Of individuals diagnosed with a reading disorder, 60–80 percent are males (APA, 2000). Sally E. Shaywitz (2003), author of *Overcoming Dyslexia*, states, however, that boys are more likely than girls to be noticed because they act out when frustrated. In any case, there is a strong hereditary factor in learning disorders.

Because their brains are wired differently, children with dyslexia are often creative and skilled problem solvers, but their struggle to read and learn can have negative psychological consequences. They are apt to drop out of school early, withdraw from friends, and are overrepresented in prison populations (Shaywitz, 2003). Early intervention is therefore crucial.

Mel Levine (2002), author of *A Mind at a Time*, directs the Clinical Center for the Study of Development and Learning at the University of North Carolina. The cofounder of the nonprofit institute All Kinds of Minds, Levine works with children who have trouble learning to read or do math and who cannot manage time. An inability to pay attention is another characteristic of dyslexia. To both parents and teachers, Levine's message is the same: Everyone is wired differently, and we must provide individualized education to help children with learning differences enhance their innate strengths.

Attention-deficit/hyperactivity disorder (ADHD; discussed in Chapter 2) is perhaps more of a personality trait than a disability but is seen by the schools as a disorder that impedes learning. Children with ADHD vary in their symptoms, but to receive a diagnosis of ADHD, they must display the characteristics of short attention span, distractibility, and/or hyperactivity. To meet the *DSM-IV-TR* (APA, 2000) criteria, the symptoms must be maladaptive and inconsistent with developmental level. Many children who receive an ADHD diagnosis when they reach school age are placed on medication. What these children might need instead is a challenging way to release their energy. An interesting experiment provides evidence for this supposition. Researchers from the University of Illinois recruited 406 children who had been diagnosed with ADHD (Kuo & Taylor, 2004). One part of the group played indoors after school or outside on pavement; the rest of the children spent their after-school time playing in green, natural settings. Results were tabulated from parent responses. The latter group showed a significant reduction in symptoms, but the other group did not. Because getting fresh air is beneficial, walking to and from school might help some children learn better, as well as reduce the rate of obesity in other children. Unfortunately, according to a report from the Centers for Disease Control and Prevention, only one-third of children who live within a mile of school walk today, and this compares to 87 percent in 1969 (Moore, 2004). Another ominous development is the elimination of recess and physical education in many schools.

Zastrow and Kirst-Ashman (2010) discuss the psychological ramifications of growing up with learning disabilities. Learning disabilities affect children in several ways, including fear of failure, withdrawal, a sense of helplessness,

and low self-esteem. Subject to ridicule by their peers and irritated reactions by teachers and parents, these children are likely to develop an abiding sense of inadequacy. The long-term effects can be devastating. On the other hand, because these children can often learn to compensate for their early handicap, eventually reading quite well, and because they often have unique talents, many develop highly successful careers. Sometimes the effort to prove themselves has the later effect of leading children who failed in the early years to phenomenal success.

Since learning disability, according to the standard definition, is unrelated to IQ, a significant number of children so diagnosed are, in fact, gifted. Even more so than for school children with a diagnosable disability, the needs of gifted children are frequently ignored. Possessing abilities beyond their years but not necessarily emotionally mature, gifted children inspire admiration, but they also suffer ridicule, neglect, and misunderstanding (Winner, 1998). Many are unevenly gifted, strong in one area and weak or weaker in another. Such kids are expected to excel on their own, and many fail to reach their full potential.

Autism and Asperger's Syndrome

In these two categories as well, mainstream schools often fail to see the strengths for the differentness. According to *DSM-IV-TR* (APA, 2000), "Individuals with autistic disorder have restricted, repetitive, and stereotyped patterns of behavior, interest, and activities" (p. 71). Inflexibility in following routines, repetitive motor mannerisms, and preoccupation with objects are also common. Minor changes in routine may lead to wild tantrums. The disturbance may be reflected in delayed language and social development. There may or may not be an associated diagnosis of mental retardation.

The rise in autism rates has been a phenomenon without any clear explanation. In California, one of the extreme examples, the numbers increased 273 percent between 1990 and 2000 (Silberman, 2001). A recent analysis of the National Survey of Children's Health that was published in *Pediatrics* (Kogan et al., 2009) revealed that at the time of the survey over one out of 100 children are diagnosed with autism spectrum disorders. The authors conclude that the reason for the increase may be due to increased awareness by the medical community today. The earlier increase was attributed by Silberman to an expanded definition of autism to include Asperger's syndrome, which is at the high-functioning end of the autism spectrum. People with Asperger's syndrome are able to function normally but have difficulty reading the emotions of others or picking up on social cues (Baren-Cohen, 2003; Grandin, 2006). This syndrome has been included in the *DSM* as a disorder since 1994, yet this diagnosis may be dropped from the DSM-V by the American Psychiatric Association. The planned change that is attracting a lot of attention is the move to eliminate Asperger's syndrome from the autism diagnosis and to combine it with another mild form of autism to create a new category (Mercer, 2009).

One reason for the apparent rise in the incidence of this mild variety of autism is offered in a popular computer news source, *Wired News* (Silberman, 2001). Titled "The Geek Syndrome," the article speculates that increased intermarriage among people carrying a gene for the autism trait is responsible. In the Silicon Valley, where most parents are engineers and programmers, the autism rate has skyrocketed; similarly, Rochester, Minnesota, which is home to IBM, has seen an upsurge in cases of Asperger's syndrome among the city's children. Many such children will no doubt have great facility with computers themselves. The most successful people who have mild Asperger's, suggests Grandin (2008), a doctor of animal science, work in places such as Silicon Valley, where superior talent trumps the requirement for social skills.

Temple Grandin (2006), who has written compellingly of her personal experience with autism, discusses geek theory in her autobiography. Many who used to just be called simply geeks or computer nerds, she indicates, are now labeled as having Asperger's syndrome. Much of this labeling now results from referrals for diagnosis by the school system. Grandin confirms that Asperger's syndrome rates are

extremely high in the regions of the country where the computer industries are located, such as Redmond, Washington. Another theory she thinks is deserving of further research is the claim that environmental factors, such as heavy mercury exposure, in conjunction with genetic susceptibility, is responsible for the increase in an especially severe form of autism. Evidence of a genetic factor in autism is evidenced by the increase in the incidence of this characteristic in the children of technological employees (Grandin) and the concordance in the existence of this disorder among identical twins when compared with a control group of fraternal twins (HealthScout, 2002). The genetic factor is revealed in the fact that the concordance in identical twins is 90 percent; in fraternal twins it is 35 percent, but among non-twin siblings it is only four percent (Grandin, 2006). This indicates to Grandin that environmental elements should be considered in our analysis of causes of autism.

The biological aspects of autism have eluded researchers until recently. In the 1980s the convergence of new methods of studying mental disorders and the formation of the National Alliance for the Mentally Ill led to widespread questioning of concepts such as "the schizophrenogenic mother" and, concerning the mothers of children with autism, "the refrigerator mother" (Johnson, 2004, p. 17). Feminist outrage undoubtedly was a factor leading to change as well.

New technologies such as functional magnetic resonance imaging (fMRI) show that persons with autism rely heavily on parts of the brain that specialize in working with the meanings of individual words. In contrast, nonautistic subjects showed greater activity in areas that integrate the words of a sentence into conceptual wholes (Just, Cherkassky, Keller, & Minshew, 2004). Brain scans show that the amygdala, a part of the brain that appears to be the center of emotion, is not activated when people with Asperger's syndrome are judging facial expressions; instead, they rely on the prefrontal cortex to figure out the meaning of the expressions. Sometimes they are unusually sensitive to sounds, smells, and touch (*Harvard Mental Health Letter*, 2005). They have one-track minds that focus narrowly but intensely, sometimes producing long-winded lecturing on subjects of interest only to themselves. Lack of communication among otherwise normal brain areas seems to be responsible for the noted rigidity in autistic behavior. Much more research is needed, however, before the origins of this condition are sufficiently understood.

Males account for more than 80 percent of the million-plus Americans with autistic disorders. Autistic people score very low on tests that involve predicting people's feelings and interpreting their facial expressions. Simon Baron-Cohen (2003), in *The Essential Difference*, asserts that studies show that females have higher levels of empathy and males a stronger knack for systemizing. Therefore, he argues, autism is an exaggerated version of the male profile. (We consider the impact of developmental disability on siblings and other family members in Chapter 7.)

Shonda Schilling (2010) in *The Best Kind of Different: Our Family's Journey with Asperger's Syndrome*, records her struggle in raising a son who was so different from his siblings. Over time the mother developed an appreciation for this difference. Whatever is the causation of this syndrome, these children are benefiting today from a new conceptualization, and from innovative programming that stresses that in difference there is strength. A school program in Boiceville, New York, trains students in self-advocacy; there children recite the positives that autism brings, including the ability to develop uncanny expertise in a certain area of interest (Harmon, 2004). Pro-autistic activists are demanding more tolerance and acceptance from the general public rather than focusing attention on finding a cure for their difference or conditioning the students to "act normal." An encouraging development has taken place in Denmark, where an information technology specialist with an autistic son set out to start a company staffed almost entirely by people with this disorder. Today Specialisterne employs about 40 people and is opening a branch in Scotland (Saran, 2008). The inspiration for this venture came from the realization that the talents of high-functioning autistic people—facility with numbers, concentration, attention to detail, and memory—were in demand among computer software companies.

Gender Differences in the Classroom

During prepuberty, girls mature much faster than boys. More girls than boys have best friends at school; while the quality of their friendships is different, girls' friendships have a higher level of intimacy, an exchange of confidences, and caring (Newman & Newman, 2006). There is no doubt that the physical male and female differences are as pronounced as ever at this stage of development. In the 1990s a great deal of attention was paid to the needs of girls. The publication of works such as the American Association of University Women's (1995) study *How Schools Shortchange Girls* and Mary Pipher's (1994) *Reviving Ophelia* was accompanied by a wave of media accounts and follow-up studies questioning the premise that sexual equality exists in U.S. schools. Evidence was provided in studies such as these to show that boys get the bulk of educational resources and are called on in class by teachers more frequently. Renewed attention was paid to Gilligan's (1982) thesis that the way girls think, interact, and develop is psychologically distinct from the male-based model. A growing awareness of the disparities in the treatment of boys and girls in the coed classroom ensued.

Why, asked Pipher, are more American girls falling prey to depression, eating disorders, addictions, and suicide attempts than ever before? She found the answer in our look-obsessed, media-saturated society, which stifles girls' creative spirit and natural impulses. Girls generally have a free spirit, she argued, until they reach puberty (around age 11 or 12); then their confidence and energy drop precipitously. Today, the media focus has shifted to the neglect of the needs of boys. Whichever gender receives the focus, the stress on different ways of learning has led to some experimentation with sex-segregated education.

In light of those apparent differences, single-sex education became the subject of increasing interest. According to a massive study of over 6,000 graduates of 225 independent girls' schools compared to a much larger number of their peers in coeducational high schools, the girls' school graduates were found to consistently rate their confidence in math and computer abilities high, to consider a career in engineering and to rate their speaking ability high to a greater degree than did graduates of coed schools (National Coalition of Girls' Schools, 2008). They were more politically engaged as well. A review of research from the UK, however, suggests that single-sex classes have the potential to raise the achievement level of both boys and girls, but only if the initiatives are developed within gender-relational contexts (Younger & Warrington, 2006).

To what extent is gender equity achieved in sex-segregated schools? A large-scale observational study conducted by researchers at the University of California found results that are less positive than those cited earlier. Teachers in these schools were found to reinforce traditional gender stereotypes: Boys were expected to be strong, and girls were reinforced in their close attention to physical appearance. In the absence of the opposite sex, girls were "catty" toward one another, and boys taunted other boys (Datnow, Hubbard, & Wood, 2001). At best, we can say the results are mixed.

What we do know, however, is that small schools and small classes have certain advantages over their large-school, large-class counterparts. In an empirically controlled experimental situation conducted by education specialists Finn, Gerber, and Zaharias (2005), 12,000 students from varied backgrounds were assigned to various class sizes. Twelve years later, those who spent the first 4 years in small classes had superior scores on all academic tests compared to the other children. The individualized attention apparently accounted for the differences. Other studies show that small public schools have higher attendance rates and lower dropout rates, benefits that are especially pronounced in lower-income communities (Ark, 2002). Ark describes the results in midtown Manhattan, which has reorganized its school system into a consortium of small schools, each with no more than 300 students: "Metal detectors have been replaced with teachers who know every student's name, and incidents of violence have plummeted" (p. 56).

The Bill and Melinda Gates Foundation has invested millions of dollars in helping to finance the small-school movement nationwide, even at a time when many rural schools are consolidating. Their investment is inspired by research that consistently shows that, in small schools, students are apt to engage in extracurricular activities; there is greater inclusiveness across class lines; graduation rates are higher; and there is less substance abuse and violence than in large schools (Moriarty, 2002. Recent research on the results of the small-school movement in New York City shows that in small schools with close monitoring of students, truancy and dropout rates have lowered and achievement rates have improved, whereas the larger schools continue to have problems (Pytel, 2009).

Let us return to the issue of media attention to gender issues. During the latter part of the twentieth century, as part of the backlash against feminism perhaps, a strange reversal occurred. It was not girls whose needs were being neglected by the school system; it was boys. The title of Christina Sommers's (2000) book sums up the shift in sentiment: *The War Against Boys: How Misguided Feminism Is Harming Our Young Men*. A barrage of newspaper articles cited psychologists and other commentators in an attempt to redefine the crisis in our educational system as a boy—not a girl—crisis (British Broadcasting Company, 2004). And according to an article in *Science Daily* (2009), both boys and girls have issues, but boys seem to be the ones getting the raw deal because their needs have been neglected by policy makers. The statistics seemed to bear out the commentators. Compared with girls, American boys have lower rates of literacy, lower grades and engagement in school, higher dropout rates from school, and dramatically higher rates of suicide, premature death, injuries, and arrests. Autism, ADHD, and dyslexia are far more prevalent among boys than among girls.

Shaywitz (2003) provides an alternative explanation for the contemporary zeroing in on boys' as opposed to girls' problems in growing up. Why are more boys identified by their schools? The answer, she claims, is behavior. Her own research in the schools has found that teachers identify boys as the ones with learning problems. Yet when children were tested individually, comparable numbers of boys and girls were having difficulties. That more boys than girls have problems sitting still in the classroom is obvious. Perhaps instead of forcing children to conform to unnatural demands of the schoolroom (such as by drugging them with Ritalin), it would be more productive to shape schoolwork to the rhythms and interests of the children.

In the meantime, the headlines continue in the same vein: "Girls Get Extra Help While Boys Get Ritalin" (*USA Today*, 2003); "When It Comes to School, Girls Rule" (Hupp, 2005); "We Need to Pay More Attention to Boys" (Winik, 2005); "Pay Closer Attention: Boys Are Struggling Academically" (*USA Today*, 2004). Is some sort of a backlash against feminism evident here? Ransome and Moulton (2004) of the National Coalition of Girls' Schools think so. They responded to the latter (the *USA Today* editorial) as follows: "Too often . . . girls' rising educational fortunes are considered spoils in a 'war,' against boys. We have actually heard girls' achievement indicators described as 'alarming statistics,' as though well-educated girls and women are some sort of threat to homeland security. . . . There's every reason to support comparable work on behalf of boys. What we must not do, however, is think of this as some sort of 'either/or' choice" (p. 14A). *Time* magazine (Von Drehle, 2007) in an article entitled "The Boys Are All Right" examines the statistics on high school and college students and finds that females do seem to be doing better academically, but both genders have improved in terms of achievement and reduced involvement in delinquent behavior. The significant gap as stated in the article is not the gender gap but the gaps for minority and disadvantaged boys.

I, like Ransome and Moulton, would argue for a both/and position, not an either/or stance, sufficient funding for small classes, and small schools designed for active learning experiences for both boys and girls. I also favor some gender-specific programming on an experimental basis to find out what works best for both genders. Special attention to gender identity issues is important during the puberty and early adolescent stages. Now we turn to an issue of concern to children of both genders—corporal punishment and other forms of child abuse.

Abuse Including Physical Punishment

Picture a continuum with mild physical punishment at one end and death by murder at the other. This is the continuum of violence against children. In the belief that physical punishment causes fear and anger and teaches aggression as we have seen, NASW (2009) opposes all forms of violence against children. One of the roles that child welfare workers and counselors at women's shelters play is to teach parents nonviolent forms of discipline.

Describing the widespread use of harsh discipline in many African American households, bell hooks (2001) says:

> Ironically and sadly in many black households where parents are adamantly anti-racist, regimes of discipline and punishment exist that mirror those utilized by white supremacists to subordinate black people. Some of those practice physical abuse, verbal aggression, shaming, and withholding of recognition (which may include refusal to give praise or show affection). Verbal assault is so common in American families of all races as to be considered simply normal. Whether it has been normalized or not, we know it has harmful consequences. (pp. 83–84)

Studies of African American parenting styles bear out hooks's observation on the preference of black parents for physical forms of discipline (see Belgrave & Allison, 2010). This form of discipline is especially pronounced among the lower classes in all racial and ethnic groups, but among African Americans punishment tends to be physical among the middle classes as well. This is generally seen as a legacy of slavery as a survival strategy when obedience had to be learned early. According to research studies summarized by Belgrave and Allison, in a book on African American psychology, the negative consequences associated with spanking as used on European American children such as aggressive acting out at school are not found among the African American children as a result of harsh but not out-of-control discipline. The authors suggest that the meaning of the physical discipline is different in homes where it is viewed as the parent's duty. More research is needed on this point, in my opinion. In any case, physical discipline that is considered abusive, such as that which involves the use of a belt or an extension cord or some other instrument as is sometimes used in black families, is responsible for the overrepresentation of black children along with lower-class whites in foster care.

Not only are children regularly subjected to physical punishment in the home but as revealed in a new report from the American Civil Liberties Union (2008) and Human Rights Watch, more than 200,000 school children are subjected to such punishment, usually by paddling on the buttocks, each year. Disabled students receive a disproportionate share of the punishment. States with the highest levels of corporal punishment are in the South.

According to a national survey by DYG, Inc., (2000) a marketing research firm founded by Daniel Yankelovich, 61 percent of American parents of children under age 7 viewed spanking as an appropriate form of regular discipline (DYG, Inc., 2000). The number that actually do spank is probably much higher. In their review of a number of large-scale, longitudinal studies of children who had been subjected to injury-causing assaults in connection with punishment, Finkelhor and Hashima (2001) concluded that these children develop much higher rates of antisocial behavior than other children. Keep in mind that these studies involved incidents of extreme violence. Still, the psychological impact of violence and crime on children must be taken seriously; the physical wounds generally heal a lot faster than the wounds to the psyche. Social Work Speaks (National Association of Social Workers, 2009) has issued a strong policy statement against corporal punishment of children. According to the NASW website:

> NASW opposes the use of physical punishment in homes, schools, and all other institutions where children are cared for and educated. . . . Research has demonstrated a link between physical punishment and several negative developmental outcomes for children: physical injury, increased aggression, antisocial behavior, poorer adult adjustment, and greater tolerance of violence can easily cross the line into child abuse. (p. 254)

Childhood Trauma

As we learned earlier in the fact sheet on child maltreatment from the U.S. Department of Human Services (2008), approximately 800,000 children were found to be victims of child maltreatment, a figure that represents 10.6 per 1,000 children in the population. In their analysis of a similar report from a previous year, Basham and Miehls (2004) noted the close relationship between class and victimization: Children from families with the lowest income experienced rates of neglect and physical and sexual abuse far out of proportion to their numbers.

Transforming the Legacy by Basham and Miehls (2004) provides a clinical context for grasping the legacy of psychological, sexual, and /or physical abuse. Mostly the emphasis is on childhood trauma and its impact on partner relationships, but the impact of cultural trauma such as that experienced by refugees from armed conflict and the victims of mass persecutions is also considered. Basham and Miehls take a biopsychosocial approach that is designed to "serve as both a compass that directs the course of the work and an anchor that stabilizes the focus" (p. 133).

Posttraumatic stress disorder, as discussed in the previous chapter, involves the following major symptoms: denial of event, numbing, flashbacks, intrusive thoughts, guilt feelings, sleep disturbances, jumpiness, and preoccupation (APA, 2000). Such compulsive reexperiencing of pain may be regarded as an unconscious attempt to integrate and heal the past. The biological aspect of PTSD is seen in alterations in the traumatized person's brain neurophysiology. In contrast to normal everyday memories that are processed in the hippocampus, traumatic memories due to the fight-or-flight stress response are processed in the amygdala and stored permanently in this region of the brain (Lein, 1999). Adults who have been traumatized as children retain their immature responses (fight-or-flight reactions) to stress. This memory is a sensorimotor response, or "body memory," as Basham and Miehls (2004) explain. Years later it may be reactivated by sights, sounds, touch, or smells.

When childhood trauma occurs with the accompanying brain chemistry changes, the stage is set for future psychological problems, especially under conditions of repeated stress (Arehart-Treichel, 2001). When confronted with stress in adult life, the adult brain might then regress to an infantile state. The relationship between childhood trauma and the later use of substances such as alcohol and nicotine by survivors for relief of emotional pain is well known (van Wormer & Davis, 2008).

The link between trauma and the inability to handle stress receives some confirmation in a study on child abuse published in the *Journal of the American Medical Association* (Heim et al., 2000). Touted as the first human study to find persistent changes in stress reactivity in adult survivors of early trauma, the research included both a physiological and an experimental component. A comparative study of 49 healthy women revealed detectable biochemical abnormalities in persons who had been severely abused in childhood. In a laboratory situation, women survivors were four times more likely than other women to develop excess stress responses to mild stimuli. Those who were abused and now have anxiety disorder or depression are six times more likely than other women to suffer an abnormal stress response.

There is a great deal we do not know about the legacy of severe abuse. Take memory, for example. How is it that some survivors replay the horrifying experience over and over while others seem to be unable to recall much of the experience? Even more puzzling, some things that are recorded in the mind are actually false memories that have been placed there by suggestion. Eliot Aronson revealed this fact in the unreliability of courtroom eyewitness testimony and in experimental situations in which memories of childhood experiences that never happened are planted through periodic questioning about certain events (Aronson, 2004).

In recent years there has been a backlash against survivors making claims of past abuse. The reversal in public sentiment is a result of some widely publicized false reports. The net effect is that adults who have recently recovered long-repressed memories of childhood abuse are no longer so readily believed. Lein (1999) states that some contemporary psychologists are even referring to the repression of memories as myth. However, we know from extensive documentation, including hundreds of recovered traumatic combat experiences from World War II, that the mind protects itself at times from sights, sounds, and pain too gruesome to bear. Then, Lien points out, when a person's life is more stable and secure, these memories are apt to surface.

Memories can be planted through suggestion to the extent that the unreal seems real. Eyewitness testimony in trials is notoriously flawed with regard to details. The general thrust of the memory, especially one imprinted on the brain through trauma, is apt to be accurate, however.

There is a great deal of controversy over techniques for recovering repressed memories of painful events. Much of the disagreement centers around widely publicized media reports of "recovered" memories that turned out to be false (Mignon et al., 2002). Few outcome studies prove the value of therapeutic interventions to assist in the retrieval of abuse memories; in fact, recovered memory therapy may lead to deterioration rather than improved functioning, Robbins (2002) argues.

Basham and Miehls (2004) refer to a "freeze response" in traumatized children as a self-protective stance in response to cumulative attacks. Frozen states and speechless terror are often reported by trauma survivors. Individual responses are different, but this pattern seems to fit Maya Angelou's childhood speechlessness following rape by her mother's boyfriend and the even more disturbing murder of the rapist by members of Maya's family. We hear from Angelou (1969) in this excerpt from *I Know Why the Caged Bird Sings*:

> Just my breath, carrying my words out, might poison people and they'd curl up and die like the black fat slugs that only pretended.
>
> I had to stop talking.
>
> I discovered that to achieve perfect personal silence all I had to do was to attach myself leechlike to sound. I began to listen to everything. I probably hoped that after I had heard all the sounds, really heard them and packed them down, deep in my ears, the world would be quiet around me. I walked into rooms where people were laughing, their voices hitting the walls like stones, and I simply stood still in the midst of the riot of sound. After a minute or two, silence would rush into the room from its hiding place because I had eaten up all the sounds.
>
> In the first weeks my family accepted my behavior as a post-rape, post-hospital affliction. (Neither the term nor the experience was mentioned in Grandmother's house where Bailey and I were again staying.) They understood that I could talk to Bailey, but to no one else. (p. 85)

Another type of trauma we can call "soul trauma," or what bell hooks calls "soul murder" (2001, p. 23). The word *trauma* here is not used in the medical sense but as a descriptive term to denote the legacy of psychological woundedness of a people. Referring to African Americans as, in essence, a colonized people, hooks believes that black people should acknowledge the ways in which "living in a white supremacist society and being the constant targets of racist assault and abuse are fundamentally psychologically traumatic" (p. 134). Many black people, argues hooks, are so far from acknowledging the legacy of racial trauma that they feel a desperate need to "prove" to white people that they are not wounded; this is in itself a manifestation of trauma, a counterreaction. "We can claim our triumph and our pain without shame," she concludes (p. 135). We need to connect political injustice with psychological pain.

Cross-Cultural Considerations

The U.S. educational system is lax compared to the very high-pressured approach in Japan, China, and Korea, where math achievement is pronounced. Nevertheless, U.S. schools encourage individual competition, while the Japanese system is built around group work and collective rewards (Gardiner & Kosmitzki, 2005).

In Northern Ireland, where I was once a teacher, the educational experience is high pressured and divisive, based on testing at an early age. An IQ test taken by 11-year-olds has strong implications in terms of the development of self-esteem, as most children are destined to fail; test results largely determine one's eventual career options. The notorious test is slowly being phased out (BBC News, 2004; Paton, 2008). Another matter related to this part of the world and more widely known is the religious divisiveness, based on which branch of Christianity one is brought up to favor. The bonding that takes place among schoolchildren in Northern Ireland is largely along religious lines. In an article titled "In Northern Ireland Hate Begins Early," Cadwallader (2002) quotes Protestant and Catholic children expressing the prejudices they have been taught from early on.

The U.S. system of education is one of mass instruction. Failure at one level can be compensated for later on. Another advantage of this system, claim Gardiner and Kosmitzki (2005), is its attention to diversity and concern for minority rights. De facto segregation persists, however, especially in urban school systems, and property tax money goes to schools in rich neighborhoods while schools in poor communities go begging.

In some impoverished countries, children often do not get to go to school at all. The struggle to survive there takes precedence over the need for education. Heightened competition in the global marketplace, enormous debt burdens by countries and individuals, and bloated military budgets have pushed families to look to their children as a financial resource (UNICEF, 2003). In Southeast Asia the child sex trade is rampant—the result of dire poverty. Street children work as prostitutes or in the porn industries in places as diverse as Brazil, Columbia, and Russia (van Wormer, 2006). They are both victims and victimizers; pushed out of their homes, they survive as leeches on society.

The consequence of such neglect and abuse is irreparable developmental damage. Although poor, Romania is attempting to transform the legacy of one of the cruelest Communist regimes of the past. Birth control was prohibited, and sick and disabled children were left to vegetate or die. Sociologist Ron Roberts (2001) describes a visit to a caring, progressive children's home in that country: "The children were taught Montessori principles, and their rooms were cheerful and immaculate. At least two of the children came from settings where they had been locked in rooms all day and had food shoved under the door. Their fear and ignorance convinced them that contact with the children was too risky. The mommas took wonderful care of these abused and sick children" (p. F2).

In many parts of the world, the problems of abject poverty are compounded by the horrors of war. In parts of war-torn Africa, children are commonly kidnapped to serve as child soldiers (boys) or sex slaves (girls). Some of the children escape; others are so brainwashed and inured to killing that they lose all desire to leave. How does one survive such wartime trauma?

Psychologist Neil Boothby (2006) has studied children who escaped war in Mozambique and ended up in an orphanage. Interventions there were designed to help them heal and become normal kids again, even after having undergone indoctrination into the savagery of guerrilla warfare. Save the Children operated a model therapy program for the former child soldiers. Interventions at the orphanage consisted of playing soccer to relearn the art of play, participating in art therapy, and engaging in psychodramas to act out experiences of trauma.

To gauge the long-term damage, Boothby located the former child soldiers who had been cared for at the orphanage and were now grown. What he found seems to indicate that there is an emotional threshold somewhere between months and years beyond which the psychological damage is impossible to repair. Boothby found that nightmares and flashbacks were common in the survivors; one man who became mute as a result of the trauma drowned himself. However, some success stories emerged from the work of traditional healers who, in rituals of spiritual cleansing, removed from the survivors what they believed were the spirits of the dead victims. The healers intervened immediately to ward off illness by realigning the spirits so that the trauma did not take a toll on the child. These cleansing rituals were reportedly essential to the child's successful return to the home community.

Adolescence

Identity formation is usually viewed as a process that, for young people, requires them to distance themselves from the strong expectations and definitions imposed by their elders. To achieve an individual identity, one must create a vision of the self that is (or seems at the time) authentic (Newman & Newman, 2006). This is the primary task of growing up.

Identity, peer group, and rebellion—these are the key terms associated with adolescence, that time of life often referred to as the period of "Sturm und Drang" (storm and stress). From the cognitive perspective, Piaget (1952) called this the period of *formal operations*. Cognitive changes take place as adolescents begin to think beyond the present to the future; their conceptual world is now full of ideas about how things ought to be and the discrepancy between the ideal and the real. Societal and family values may be questioned. By middle adolescence, they have thus made the progression from the world of objects through the world of social relations to the world of ideas. Piaget's stages of development end here, unlike Erikson's, which encompass the whole span of life.

Many youths look physically mature, and adults treat the more mature-looking youths with greater respect than those who appear more childlike (Harris, 2009; Zastrow & Kirst-Ashman, 2010). Yet the outer appearance can be deceptive. Piaget may have been correct about the advanced cognitive development that takes place in the teenage years. A new-found appreciation of the dynamic nature of the child brain is emerging from magnetic reso-nance imaging (MRI) studies that scan a child's brain every 2 years. Striking growth spurts can be seen from ages 6 to 13 in areas connecting brain regions specialized for language and spa-tial relations. This growth drops off sharply after age 12, coinciding with the end of a criti-cal period for learning language (National Insti-tute of Mental Health, 2001b). The brain continues to mature into the 20s, in fact, espe-cially in the prefrontal cortex, the area respon-sible for sound decisions and judgments (Goldberg, 2001). Some youths may look fully mature, but their emotions may not have caught up to the rest of the mind (cognitive portion of the brain), and the mind may not have caught up to the body (physical level of maturity). How else can we explain some of the wild and erratic behavior of youth? How else can we explain the fact that so many of these kids will settle down as they grow older?

Society has often recognized the immaturity of youth by imposing legal restrictions on young people. Modern developments in neu-roscience can now explain the reason for some of the rash behavior associated with youth. Such developments have even entered the courtroom to provide evidence that teens are less blameworthy for criminal acts than adults are. A coalition of psychiatric and legal organi-zations prepared a legal brief to argue against the death penalty for juvenile crime on this basis (American Bar Association, 2004). Their argument derived from evidence from MRI scanners documenting age-related brain differ-ences in the frontal lobe region. Together with neurological findings showing the behavioral impact of frontal lobe brain damage (e.g., from head injuries), the recent MRI investigations showing late maturation of the frontal lobe are changing the way some legal experts view juvenile culpability for crime. (In fact, in 2005, the U.S. Supreme Court struck down the use of

the death penalty for juveniles, so this scientifi-cally based argument may have carried some weight.)

Erikson (1950/1963) anticipated recent brain research findings in his perception of adolescence as a period in life that involves more dangers to the individual than any other. His focus, however, was not on risks but on identity. Erikson's stage five, the period of ado-lescence (identity versus role confusion), is his most widely cited stage and probably the best defined.

As we discuss the concept of identity for-mation, we need to be cognizant of Dominelli's (2004) cautionary note that we recognize that identity is multifaceted and fluid and that indi-viduals choose which aspects of their identity they wish to emphasize in any particular con-text. Our identity is formed, Dominelli explains, "through dialogical processes that are con-stantly being created and recreated through social interactions" (p. 77). To defend them-selves against identity confusion, Erikson claimed, "young people form cliques and dif-ferentiate themselves from others, in taste and often in petty aspects of dress and gesture as have been temporarily selected as the signs of an in-grouper or out-grouper" (1950/1963, p. 262). In adolescence, peers surpass parents in importance as sources of intimacy and support.

Saleebey (2001) concurs: No matter how good the relationship with parents, he says, peers become the benchmark or beacon for adolescent behavior. Kids do not look to grownups for guidelines on how to behave, speak, or dress because kids and their elders belong to different social categories that have different rules (Harris, 2009). Children emulate the high-status kids at school. And collectively, in modern societies, teens seek ways of signal-ing their group identity and loyalty to other members of their group. They invent new words and novel forms of adornment. One of the ways peers flout convention is to smoke and drink (Saleebey, 2001). Harris describes the process this way: "The big question of ado-lescent life—the unspoken question that teen-agers are constantly answering—is: Are you one of *us* or one of *them?* If you're one of *us*, prove it. Prove it by showing you don't care about *their* rules. Prove it by doing something—a tattoo would be nice, a hole through your nose even better—that will mark you irrevocably [as] one of *us*" (2009, p. 257).

However, as Saleebey is quick to tell us, "Identity is never a done deal" (2001, p. 384). Keeping this caveat in mind and acknowledging, as Dominelli (2004) indicates, that Erikson's delineation of discrete stages of development is greatly oversimplified, let us return to Erikson's stress on identity formation and consider the facts.

Risk-Taking Behavior

Erikson explains the risks attached to the adolescent period in these words:

> The growing and developing youths, faced with this physiological revolution within them, and with tangible adult tasks ahead of them are now primarily concerned with what they appear to be in the eyes of others as compared with what they feel they are, and with the question of how to connect the roles and skills cultivated earlier with the occupational prototypes of the day. In their search for a new sense of continuity and sameness, adolescents have to refight many of the battles of earlier years. (1950/1963, p. 261)

Among the risks Erikson associates with role confusion are overidentification with the heroes of cliques; uncertainty about one's occupational course; "falling in love"; the rapidity of genital maturity; and clannishness and cruelty in the exclusion of those who are different. At the macro level, to Erikson, susceptibility to the mass appeal of totalitarian doctrines is a further risk to the adolescent mind.

The National Survey of Children's Exposure to Violence, which is the most comprehensive national survey of its kind and which questioned children directly, confirms that most children and especially teenagers have been exposed to serious violence (Finkelhor et al., 2009). The study found that nearly one-half of the children and adolescents surveyed were assaulted at least once in the past year, and more than 1 in 10 were injured in an assault;

1 in 4 were victims of robbery, vandalism, or theft; 1 in 10 suffered from child maltreatment (including physical and emotional abuse, neglect, or a family abduction); and 1 in 16 were victimized sexually. Around 6 percent of children have witnessed one parent assaulting the other. The survey showed that as children grow older the incidences of victimization increase. Among 14- to 17-year-old participants, 1 in 10 witnessed a shooting in the past year, 1 in 75 witnessed a murder, and 1 in 20 was sexually assaulted. Girls aged 14 to 17 had the highest rates of sexual victimization: 7.9 percent were victims of sexual assault in the past year and 18.7 percent during their lifetimes.

As confirmed in the national survey of children's exposure to violence, adolescents who have recently been victimized are significantly more likely than others to have suffered from multiple instances of abuse at an earlier stage. Bearing this in mind, we should consider the factors influencing violence within a developmental context. The impact of victimization is cumulative. Brown and Gourdine (2007) report that in focus groups girls from the inner city, having been exposed to both direct and indirect violence, showed that living in a highly stressful environment had serious implications for their psychological and social development. Fear was a constant companion of these girls. Sexual harassment, fighting, and dating violence are the norm. It was clear to the girls that many teen relationships set the stage for adulthood domestic violence. A subgroup of girls described the risky situation of sex with one partner that might lead to coerced sex with multiple partners—"a chain experience."

Substance abuse involvement is one of the leading causes of death for youth. The highest risks come from car crashes, violence, drug overdoses, and so on. Regular abuse of inhalants ("huffing"), for example, is a continuing problem among youths 12–13 years of age, perhaps because of the availability of these chemicals in the home. Even a single session of repeated inhalant abuse can disrupt heart rhythms and cause death from cardiac arrest or suffocation. According to the 2008 annual survey of high school students, which was conducted by researchers from the University of

Michigan, while the use of inhalant and many other illicit drugs has declined, the use of prescription medications for nonmedical purposes continues to rise. Over 15 percent of 12th graders reported use of such drugs over the past year (National Institute on Drug Abuse, 2008). Also cigarette use continues to decline (illegal for those under age 18). The use of OxyContin, a pain reliever prescribed to cancer patients, has stabilized but is still a major problem for some. The addictive potential of this drug is high. Among the findings was that, over the past year, 12th graders used the following:

> Any illicit drug: 36.6 percent
> Marijuana: 32.4 percent (5.4 percent use daily)
> Inhalants: 3.8 percent
> Cocaine: 4.4 percent
> Crack cocaine: 1.6 percent
> Heroin: 0.7 percent
> Other narcotics (OxyContin): 4.7 percent
> Alcohol: 65.5 percent (2.8 percent drink daily)
> Cigarettes: 20.4 percent
> Smokeless tobacco: 6.5 percent
> Steroids: 1.5 percent
> Methamphetamines: 1.2 percent
> LSD: 2.7 percent
> Ecstasy: 6.2 percent
> Vicodin: 9.7 percent
> Tranquilizers: 6.2 percent
> OxyContin: 4.7 percent

While media attention focuses on illicit drugs and the government spends billions on the controversial war on drugs, little attention is directed toward the abuse of teenagers' drug of choice—alcohol (van Wormer & Davis, 2008). The fact that almost one-third of high school seniors report that they have been drunk in the past 30 days is worrisome. During the 1980s, the drinking age was raised to 21. Fewer kids have been drinking since then, but those who do drink today consume huge amounts at one time. Marketing alcohol to youth is big business. For arguments in favor of lowering the drinking age and encouraging moderate drinking in the presence of older family members, see van Wormer and Davis (2008). In 2008, 130 college presidents concerned about the drinking-related crimes, including vandalism and date rape on their campuses, have signed the Amethyst Initiative to study the possibility of changing the underage drinking laws, which only seem to encourage secret and excessive drinking among college students (Sack, 2008).

Rose (1998) presents an overview of longitudinal studies conducted in several countries to ascertain whether behavior assessments made by teachers and classmates could predict which children were likely to abuse alcohol by middle or late adolescence. Findings from Sweden were that evaluations done at ages 10 and 27 showed that high novelty seeking and low harm avoidance—daredevil behavior—predicted early-onset alcoholism. Similar results were obtained in Canadian and Danish research studies. Data from Finland differentiated the pathway to alcoholism in males and females. Aggression at age 8 predicted alcoholism 18–20 years later in males. For females, children who cried easily when teased or who were anxious and shy were most apt to develop problems later. For both genders, poor school success was a predictor of later drinking problems.

Teen dating violence is a risk that is highly associated with a number of risky adolescent behaviors such as binge drinking, illicit drug use, unsafe sex, early pregnancy, and suicide attempts. Intimate partner violence peaks in youth and young adulthood (Noonan & Charles, 2009). The following dating violence statistics are provided by the Centers for Disease Control and Prevention (CDC, 2009):

> One in 11 adolescents reports being a victim of physical dating violence.
> One in 4 adolescents reports verbal, physical, emotional, or sexual violence each year.
> One in 5 adolescents reports being a victim of emotional violence.
> One in 5 high school girls has been physically or sexually abused by a dating partner
> Dating violence occurs more frequently among black students (13.9 percent) than among Hispanic (9.3 percent) or white (7.0 percent) students.

❥ Seventy-two percent of eighth and ninth graders reportedly "date"; by the time they are in high school, 54 percent of students report dating violence among their peers.

❥ Seventy percent of girls and 52 percent of boys who are abused report an injury from a violent relationship.

❥ Eight percent of boys and 9 percent of girls have been to an emergency room for an injury received from a dating partner.

The time to help teach adolescents about the hazards of dating violence coupled with the heavy drinking that is often associated with it is in middle school when dating first begins. To this end, the CDC has begun developing a violence prevention campaign to help change social norms that support victimization. To first learn what the middle school dating norms are, they set up boys' and girls' focus groups (Noonan & Charles, 2009). The common form of female-to-male violence discussed by the teens was slapping. Girls slapped boys as punishment when the boy was "out of line" or in self-defense. Male participants described situations of retaliation or to assert themselves in front of their peers as reasons guys hit their girlfriends. The participants strongly disapproved of sexual violence. Van Wormer and Roberts (2009) have filtered out from the literature on teen domestic violence warning signs that a relationship is abusive and that such violence is likely to escalate. For the warning signs, see Table 4.2.

Identity and Body Image

For boys, the increase in the rate of growth in height starts at about 12.5 years and reaches a peak at age 14. The peak increase in muscle strength, however, usually occurs 12–14 months later. This time lag results in a temporary period, during which a boy may experience body image dissatisfaction (Newman & Newman, 2006).

The extent to which obsessive bodybuilding is a major problem for young males is revealed in the popularity of anabolic steroids, synthetic substances related to male sex hormones. According to the nationwide survey cited earlier, slightly less than 1 percent of seniors used steroids in a 30-day period during the study. Pressure from coaches, parents, and peers to gain muscle weight and strength are named as factors in enticing athletes and weightlifters to take anabolic steroids. Fortunately, the use of these drugs is on the decline.

Girls, barraged by images of extremely thin models that bear little relationship to the reality of changes wrought by pubescence and that create an impossible standard to achieve, allow their appearance to dictate their sense of self (Saleebey, 2001).

Media-generated weight obsession is a major problem among girls of European American ethnicity. Young women with eating disorders share certain personality traits: low self-esteem, clinical depression (which often runs in their families), and an inability to handle stress (National Institute of Mental Health, 2001a). Perfectionism is pronounced among anorexics and is undoubtedly related to brain chemical imbalance—nature as well as nurture, so to speak (Bulik et al., 2003; van Wormer & Davis, 2008). Not only does this kind of obsessive behavior—perfectionism—lead to major problems with eating, such as anorexia and bulimia, but many white females are resorting to another high-risk behavior—cigarette smoking—for the purpose of weight control. New insights from brain-imaging studies indeed reveal an aberration in serotonin pathways in limbic structures related to anxiety and body image distortions in anorexics and bulimics (Kaye et al., 2005). Rat studies too have shown that weakened dopamine systems lead to compensation by overeating as a pleasure-seeking function (Geiger et al., 2008).

Gender Identity: Male

Boys are generally not well prepared by their parents with information on the maturation of their reproductive organs. Mothers often have a closer emotional connection to their sons than fathers do, yet their knowledge of male adolescent anatomy may be limited. What information boys gain about the changes in their bodies often comes from friends and, hopefully, school

Table 4.2   Teen Dating Abuse: Warning Signs

Based on the literature on domestic violence, we have developed the following list of warning signs that a young woman should consider to determine if the relationship is likely to become violent. The warning signs are geared toward heterosexual female teens but can be adjusted to pertain to same-sex or male respondents.

_____1. Does your date or boyfriend brag about beating up or intimidating people?

_____2. Does he ever suggest that he knows how to kill, for example, by playfully putting his hands on your neck, then say he was only joking?

_____3. Does he own or have access to a gun or show a fascination with weapons?

_____4. Has he ever forced you to kiss or have sex? Does he show a lack of awareness of your feelings?

_____5. Does he use illegal drugs, especially amphetamines, speed, meth, or crack?

_____6. Does he get drunk on a regular basis or brag about his high tolerance for alcohol? Does he push you to drink alcoholic beverages or take illicit drugs?

_____7. When you are with him, does he control how you spend your time? Is he always the one to drive or criticize you severely if you take the wheel?

_____8. Is he constantly jealous? Does he control your friendships with other people and seem to want to have you all to himself?

_____9. Is he rapidly becoming emotionally dependent on you; for instance, does he say things like "I can't live without you?" Is his thinking of an all-or-nothing pattern (either you are his best friend or his worst enemy—often about past relationships)?

_____10. Do you have the feeling that only you understand him, that others do not or cannot?

_____11. Note the relationship between his parents. Is his mother very submissive to his father? Is there heavy drinking and/or lots of tension in his family?

_____12. Is there a history of past victimization by his father?

_____13. Is there a history of animal abuse in his background?

_____14. Has he ever struck you? Have you known him to lose control of his anger for certain periods of time?

_____15. Has he ever threatened or tried to commit suicide?

_____16. Does he get out of patience quickly with children or is he verbally abusive toward them?

_____ Total "Yes" answers.

If you have answered yes to two or more of these items, you should talk to a mature person before pursuing this relationship further. Before getting romantically involved with someone, consider what it would be like to break up with this person. Would you be able to cool the relationship and still remain friends or end the relationship if you wanted to? Consider how he would handle this. It is a lot easier to get out of a potentially dangerous relationship in the early stages than to wait and see how things turn out or to see whether or not you can change a person.

Source: *Death by Domestic Violence: Preventing the Murders and the Murder-Suicides* by K. van Wormer and A.R. Roberts, 2009. Westport, CT: Praeger, pp. 154–155.

sex education. The development of facial and body hair has strong psychological meaning for boys; shaving thus becomes a symbol of a boy's transition into adolescence and often continues to be an element of a young man's masculine identity throughout young adulthood (Newman & Newman, 2006).

The Macho Paradox by Jackson Katz (2006) considers the epidemic of violence against women as a male issue and the socialization of boys to discount all aspects of the feminine and to associate power and dominance with manhood. The forging of a firm identity for young males, in the absence of masculine role models who present the range of human expression, is a difficult proposition (Saleebey, 2001). In a society that sends mixed messages about cultural expectations for male sex role behavior, personal confusion abounds. Demands to be tough in one setting (on the streets for urban youth) can be contradicted by demands (from the family or girlfriend) to be gentle and expressive of affection. Faludi (1999), for example, relates that, in her interview with members of a tough California gang, members collected "points" for every female they had sex with. Taken together, the problems for many boys, she believes, are rooted in lack of nurturance from stable male role models, especially their fathers.

In *Killing Rage: Ending Racism*, hooks (1995) offers insights into the risks of patriarchal child rearing. As you read this passage, keep in mind that the word *patriarchy* literally means a hierarchy, a rule of priests. It defines an order of living that elevates fathers (Gilligan, 2003). In hooks' words:

> Within black life, as well as in mainstream society, males prove they are "men" by the exhibition of antisocial behavior, lack of consideration for the needs of others, refusal to communicate, unwillingness to show nurturance and care. Here I am not talking about traits adult males cultivate, I am talking about the traits little boys learn early in life to associate with manhood and act out. . . . Much of the recent emphasis on the need for special schools for black boys invests in a rhetoric of patriarchal thinking that uncritically embraces sexist-defined notions of manhood as the cure for all that ails black males. (pp. 74, 89)

The mass media promote macho images for males. Boys, like girls, Gilligan (2003) observes, "are also silenced by codes of masculinity" (p. 101) but in a different way. Peer group pressure on boys to prove they are not sissies, not girls, is also pressure to assume an exaggerated male identity that may not bode well for future intimate relationships.

Gender Identity: Female

For girls, the pressures for gender conformity mount during the teenage years. "Having become the subjects of their own lives, many girls become the objects of others' lives," Saleebey (2001, p. 385) informs us. Earlier we saw the extent to which unrealistic media-generated body images plague the life of the maturing female.

For girls and women, the sense of self, Gilligan (2003) states, is invested more in maintaining relationships than in establishing hierarchy. The sense of self, Gilligan found in her study of women's voices, starts from a premise of connectedness rather than separateness; when imagining relationships they see them not as hierarchies but as webs. In my own study of inmates in a women's prison, I observed the same phenomenon—deep emotional entanglements and family-style allegiances, a construction of so-called state or prison families by many (van Wormer, 2010).

Bringing girls into the study of adolescence has brought a new dimension to the science of psychology. Research with adolescent girls, Gilligan (2003) maintains, is critical because it illuminates how a process that can otherwise be conceived in purely psychological terms has a political dimension. In her interviews with adolescent girls, Gilligan found that, in adolescence, girls may discover that the abilities they rely on to repair relationships (articulating feelings, being honest) are socially unacceptable. Adolescence for them is an initiation into silence, culturally scripted and enforced. When they express themselves spontaneously, their remarks are often construed as rudeness or insensitivity to people's feelings.

Kiini Salaam (2001) captures this phenomenon in her personal narrative: "As a girl, I was put on notice that the world demanded my acquiescence. When at 13, 14, and 15 years old, my growing hips, legs, and breasts drew stares, leers, and ooh baby's, I'd cross the street to avoid confronting men's sexual aggression. Like my friends I'd lie when pressed for personal information, I'd give out false numbers, claim my phone was broken, create a boyfriend or a husband. What I didn't do was say 'no'" (p. 9).

Yet Gilligan finds hope in resisting an initiation that takes the form of breaking relationships and establishing hierarchy. Resisting patriarchy involves resisting "the subordination of women to men, the division of women into Good and Bad, the sacrifice of love for 'honor,' the splitting of reason from emotion, the dividing of themselves from their relationships" (2003, p. 100).

Gay and Lesbian Identity

The question "who am I?" begins the quest for external confirmation, as well as internal cohesion (Swann & Spivey, 2004). When we talk about gender and racial identity, we usually mean a visible identity; there is a congruence between the inner and outer self. Gay and lesbian youths are in the position of often being assumed to be heterosexual, especially by their parents, unless there is evidence to the contrary. The message sent by society, including one's own community, is that gay or lesbian orientation, unlike racial identity, is something that can and should be concealed.

As early as 4 or 5 years of age, children in school or at home will call another age mate "fag" or "queer." Although children are not cognizant of the meaning of these words, they know that they have powerful and hurtful implications. Children have usually heard homophobic and other prejudicial words used by parents, older siblings, and classmates or through the media early in their development.

No child wants to be called or known as a "fag." Hence, children actively try to assume a persona that the culture values, often covering up or denying who they are. A student from the Midwest provides the following account:

> As a very young child of about 5,
> I couldn't reconcile the differences that
> I felt between my ranging gender
> proclivities and attractions to good-looking
> same-sex individuals with what my
> parents, teachers, and peers were telling
> me. I remember sitting with my mother
> and some of her friends when they were
> talking about the upcoming marriage of
> my older sister. I said that I wanted to
> marry a person like David. My
> embarrassed mother said that that was
> sick. I remember feeling shamed and
> humiliated. It was a few years later that
> I realized she was talking about fags.
> (van Wormer, Wells, & Boes, 2000)

Although unstated, a fundamental and underlying assumption of the bulk of the research literature on childhood adolescence and identity formation is that "normative" development is presumptively heterosexual. The successful transition from childhood to adulthood involves developing an attraction for and an attachment to individuals of the other sex. Although many theorists in the social and behavioral sciences acknowledge that same-sex feelings and attractions are typical among children and adolescents, developmental theorists such as Erikson (1950/1963) assert that this typical phase of development gives way to mature relationships that develop between people of the "opposite" sex. This standard assumption is problematic because it omits a significant segment of the population and assumes that youthful gays and lesbians either do not exist or are so marginal that it is not worth dealing with them.

What if, because of society's negative views about your sexual identity, you do not feel good about yourself at home, in school, or with peers? How does this affect and frame your identity? What if the basic messages you receive do not acknowledge or support you as someone who self-identifies as being a lesbian, gay, or bisexual young person? These questions illustrate the need for reframing social development theory to encompass lesbian, gay, and bisexual identity formation, a process that occurs in a hostile, rather than nurturing, environment.

Much of the hostility is against gender-nonconforming youth, a population that includes many gays and lesbians, kids who fear they might be gay or lesbian, and male heterosexuals who are effeminate. Statistics on verbal, physical, and sexual harassment at school tell the same story worldwide. In May 2001 Human Rights Watch issued its comprehensive report aptly titled "Hatred in the Hallways." This report offers the first comprehensive look at the human rights abuses suffered by lesbian, gay, bisexual, and transgender students at the hands of their peers. When taunting remarks were uttered, teachers and administrators looked the other way. Interviews with 140 youth and 130 teachers nationwide combined with data from state surveys revealed the following:

➤ Youths who identify as sexual minorities reported a rate of alcohol and drug use more than three times that of their peers; the rate for use of injected drugs was nine times as high.

➤ Around one-third of the students reported recent participation in unsafe sex.

➤ Although the exact numbers are unknown, a substantial percentage of homeless youths are gays and lesbians who have been forced out of their homes because of lifestyle issues.

➤ Gay, lesbian, and bisexual youth are more than three times as likely as other young people to report that they attempted suicide; being perceived as gay or lesbian and harassed on that basis appeared to be the key factor.

Kids who survive the cruelties and injustices preserved for those who are "different" rarely forget. Consider the following poignant description contained in the writing of social work educator Mary Bricker-Jenkins (2001):

Kids know when their teachers are talking about them. If they are feeling shame, confusion, or have "secrets," they *really* know. They see their teachers' averted eyes, the glances at other teachers, counselors, and even other kids; they hear the sudden silence when they walk by school administrators or the coach. Fear and self-degradation are likely consequences. Or bravado, risk-taking, and defiance. Or all of these and more, but seldom anything positive.

I am speaking from experience here. I was one of those kids who "knew they knew" and did everything I could to please them. But nothing worked, because they *knew*. When I was denied admission into the "gold leaf" club despite my stellar academic performance, when I did not make the team despite my athleticism, when I was not invited to return to the boarding school I loved, I knew exactly

why. The hurt was magnified to suffering and despair when there was nobody to talk with about what was really going on in my life. Sometimes, when nobody was around to see which stacks I was exploring, I skulked around the library looking for a name for my "condition." I didn't find anything good. I was "circling the drain," sometimes contemplating suicide, when a teacher took me aside and showed me some kindness. She talked to me about the life of the mind, about the theater and music and poetry, about my friendships, about my wild ideas about a just world. She made me her assistant director for the annual school play. She saved my life. (pp. 93–94)

The developmental stages are said to consist of a general sense of feeling different; an awareness of same-sex feelings; an identity crisis; and an eventual acceptance of a gay or lesbian identity. For teenagers who are members of both racial/ethnic minority and sexual minority groups, the social life of the school presents special difficulties. A national survey by the Gay, Lesbian, and Straight Education Network (GLSEN, 1999) provides a grim picture of the experiences of gays, lesbians, and transgender students of color in school. Exposure to derogatory homophobic comments and racial/ethnic slurs is a daily occurrence in most American schools, and especially pronounced in the South. Around one-third of the African American respondents said they had experienced physical violence in school, while over one-half of Native American students did so as well. In their much smaller survey of over 100 sexual minority youths, Rosario, Schrimshaw, and Hunter (2004) found that black youths reported involvement in fewer gay-related social activities, reported less comfort with others knowing their sexual identity and disclosed that identity to fewer people than did white youths. Latino youths disclosed to fewer people than did white youths. White students were more actively involved in school advocacy groups.

Attendance at small religious schools can present special problems related to the influence of religious fundamentalist groups with their "love-the-sinner-hate-the-sin" ideology. Recently in a question-answer column in the Waterloo-Cedar Falls, Iowa newspaper, the following dialogue appeared (note: the respondent was clearly aware of a new non-discrimination law protecting sexual minorities in Iowa):

Q. Does Valley Lutheran School accept gay and lesbian students?

A. "Valley Lutheran Middle and Senior High School will not discriminate against anyone on the basis of sex, race, religion or sexual orientation," responded Principal Nathan Richter. "We will treat every student in a kind, loving manner as we are all children of God. However, we will be upfront and open that our doctrine states that this lifestyle choice is a sin and goes against God's teachings in scripture. For all of our students, if we know they are making sinful choices we will address it with them in a loving manner to help them to grow in their faith. Our motto is that we confront sin while loving the sinner." (*Waterloo-Cedar Falls Courier*, 2009, p. B1)

African American and Latino American gays and lesbians face potential racial prejudice coupled with a lack of full acceptance by their home communities. As Morales, Sheafor, and Scott (2010) suggest, members of minority groups within the United States tend to have close ties to their communities and to maintain a residence nearby. Viewing their racial and ethnic heritage as primary, they frequently live as "heterosexuals" and may identify as bisexuals. Because their communities tend to be religiously and culturally traditional, coming out may not be a practical option.

To assume, as some gay and lesbian commentators do, that you have to come "out of the closet" or that you are in denial of who you are shows a lack of cultural understanding for African Americans, Asian Americans, and Latinos who choose to conceal their homosexuality and for whom their sexual identity may not be their central defining characteristic. Their choice to disclose their orientation to a very small, select group must be viewed within the context of structural forces, Martínez and Sullivan (1998) argue. The cautionary note here for social workers is that they may do harm if they reinforce an ideology of openness in the belief that adopting a gay or lesbian identity is vital to healthy adjustment. The decision to come out is best left up to the person who has to live with that decision. The opposite problem occurs when people who want to "be who they are" are forced by social pressure into silence. The societal pressure as reflected in the military's "don't ask, don't tell" policy, which is "Just keep silent and you'll be all right," is a denial of the gay's or lesbian's selfhood and a refutation of the possibility of gay pride (and activism).

In the United Kingdom, attention is being devoted to the fate of school children who face intimidation (Charles, 2000). In an interview of 190 lesbian and gay young adults who were bullied at school, researchers found that 4 out of 10 who were harassed because of their sexuality attempted suicide or harmed themselves by cutting or burning their skin. Many dropped out of school. More than 1 in 6 suffered PTSD in later life. It was found that bullying started at age 10, before they had even begun to think of their sexual orientation. The researchers concluded that the schools were doing little about the problem and that some of the counselors were even making things worse. A common phenomenon in junior high and high schools in the United States is the bullying of youths whose dress and/or behavior are seen as gender inappropriate or different in some other way. The American Medical Association (2002) has warned that bullying is a public-health issue with long-term mental health consequences for both bullies and their victims. In research conducted by Olweus (2001), boys who were bullies between the ages of 13 and 16 were more likely than other youths to be connected with a crime by age 24.

In parts of the Middle East, all forms of out-of-wedlock sexuality are suppressed with a vengeance: Adulterers and gays are beaten or worse. In a climate of severe oppression of women, lesbians rarely reveal their sexual orientation.

It took the tragedy at Columbine High School in Littleton, Colorado, where unpopular students who did not fit in with the masculinized culture of their school went on a murder and suicide rampage, to finally spark a national debate on the culture of harassment and hatred that can lead to violence. Columbine, in fact, marked the fourth time during the previous 2 years that a student-on-student attack in U.S. public schools involved antigay taunting or harassment of boys who were out of sync with the masculine code (Klein, 2006). In 2005, the second most devastating school shooting spree took place at Red Lake High School on an Ojibwa reservation in Minnesota. Again, a boy who had been teased by his peers went on a rampage, killing students in the hallways before taking his own life (Paulson, 2005). These tragedies expose the need to hire more school counselors, psychologists, and social workers, although at the present time little has been done in this regard.

Ryan, Huebner, Rafael, Diaz, and Sanchez (2009) in a survey of 224 white and Latino lesbian, gay, and bisexual young adults found that family rejection in adolescence was a key factor in self-destructive behavior, then and later. The young people were over eight times more likely to report having attempted suicide than were their peers. Rates of depression, illicit drug use, and unprotected sex were also high. This study is consistent with earlier studies that consistently show a high suicide rate among gay youth. According to a report by the U.S. Department of Health and Human Services (1989), for example, gay and lesbian youth are two to three times more likely to commit suicide than other youth; 30 percent of all completed youth suicides are related to issues of sexual identity. Risk factors for suicide, such as gender nonconformity, appear to be particularly salient with regard to boys and men. Surveys large enough to examine sex differences, such as those done in Massachusetts and Minnesota, have reported finding an association between homosexuality and suicide for males only (Remafedi, 1999), which seems consistent with our knowledge of sex role socialization. Remafedi notes that "tomboys" are more accepted by their peers and parents than are "sissy" boys.

In a Canadian study (King, 1996), young adult males from a cross-section of the population answered questions on portable computers.

(This innovative technique of having respondents answer questions via computer for more privacy lends special credence to the findings.) Results were startling in that gays and bisexuals were found to have nearly 14 times the suicide ideation of heterosexual males. Interestingly, celibate males were found to have the highest rate of attempted suicide. The sample size for celibate males, however, was extremely small.

Eisenberg and Resnick (2006) found that for adolescents of all sexual orientations connectedness to one's family is the primary factor that prevents suicide attempts. The survey was conducted on over 22,000 Minnesota youths which determined that over 2,200 respondents had same-gender sexual experience. Of these, 29 percent of the male gays reported having attempted suicide, over twice as many as heterosexual males, and 52 percent of the females reported suicide attempts compared to less than half as many heterosexuals. Protective factors for all the youth were family ties, adult caring, and school safety.

More recent suicide data were gathered by the Gay Men's Health (2004) in research funded by the National Health Service of Scotland. Researchers from this advocacy organization distributed questionnaires to be completed anonymously by men who were located at gay hangouts in Edinburgh. In the end, 112 questionnaires were completed and returned. The results revealed that substantial numbers had engaged in self-injury acts and that more than half (54 percent) had seriously contemplated suicide (compared to 13 percent from the general population); 27 percent had attempted suicide, some of them four or five times. Most of the suicide attempts were in the 14–17 age group range.

Girls are also somewhat protected by the fact that they recognize their lesbianism at a later age, on average, than do boys. This fact, that many are mature women when they resolve their sexual identity crisis (being lesbian in a straight society), gives them time to develop greater coping skills. Teenage lesbians are not immune to problems, however. The dating period can be especially troublesome.

Swann and Spivey (2004) examined the relationship between identity development and self-esteem in a sample of 205 young women between the ages of 16 and 24. They found that the young women who seemed to understand themselves as lesbian but to have little or no affiliation with a larger peer group emerged as the group with the lowest self-esteem in the study. This finding, the authors maintain, suggests that group membership may act as a protective factor for self-esteem, even when the group with which one is identifying is stigmatized.

Children who are constantly exposed to ridicule or who know they would be if their true sexual attractions became known are vulnerable to internalized homophobia. Bullied children are prone to self-hatred. As such they are apt to engage in health risk behaviors, sexually or otherwise. When gay youth are pushed out of their homes because of having an "unacceptable lifestyle" as their parents claim, they may act in self-destructive ways and even court death. In a real sense, therefore, prejudice kills. The compelling 2009 TV drama, *Prayers for Bobby* (produced by Lifetime TV) tells the true story of a devoutly religious housewife and mother of a gay son whose continuing preaching that God can cure him of his "sin" drives him to suicide. Eventually, the mother resolves her religious crisis and is today a crusader for human rights. The film is unique in containing extensive discussion concerning certain passages in the Bible, some that are adhered to by religious groups and many others that are completely ignored.

Racial and Ethnic Identity

About one-third to one-half of adolescents who live in the United States belong to a minority ethnic group such as African Americans, Latinos, Native Americans, Arab Americans, and Asian Americans. Many are the children of immigrants, so they exist at the interface of two or more cultures. Such children often assume a dual identity due to the pull in two directions. In terms of identity formation there are disadvantages in feeling marginalized and having aspects of the self that are foreign to both the mainstream and the home culture; in addition, there are social and economic disadvantages in

being from a marginalized group. On the other hand, pride in one's ethnic identity has its own compensations—bilingualism in some cases and participation in lifelong support systems.

One of the most challenging aspects of establishing group identity for adolescents in a multicultural society is the formation of a firm ethnic-group identity (Newman & Newman, 2006). Individuals may vary in the degree to which they identify with their respective racial-ethnic groups as a result of the combined influence of personality and ascribed identity (Miehls, 2001). Issues of ethnic-group identity may not become salient until the adolescent period. This new awareness can be attributed to the influence of teenage peer groups. Moreover, there is the dating scene. As members of minority groups join mainstream peer groups or are excluded from them, a conflict between home and the outside world may ensue. Further clashes may arise through cross-cultural and interracial dating. Girls from the majority race or ethnicity who date guys from a minority group may be treated with hostility by other girls from that ethnicity who are resentful. Then the value conflicts, including religious and political differences, may seem overwhelming to immature youth.

For whites (as the dominant group), the pathway of racial identity development is different from that for people of color (Basham & Miehls, 2004). Youths of European American background start from a position of privilege. Based on an extensive review of the literature on ethnic identity development, Cooper (2005) has presented a theoretically integrated scheme for use in teaching. Whites, contends Cooper, start from a place of little racial awareness, accepting the ethnic stereotypes they are taught. Conflict arises as they discover, through interpersonal contact with members of minorities, facts that contradict the stereotypes. Some adopt a strong pro-minority stance, feeling guilt over their previous views and those of their environment. Others, however, resolve the cognitive dissonance by retreating within the safe confines of their own ethnicity. They become defensive and fail to have empathy for people who suffer discrimination.

In her research on ethnic identity in adolescents, Ward and Redd (2007) found that youths from diverse backgrounds, and especially biracial youth, often experience a crisis (what Erikson termed role confusion), whereby they either challenge everything associated with the dominant group or the reverse—they reject their own cultural heritage. But later, as young adults, the crisis is generally resolved with an acceptance of their unique ethnicity and a clearer, more confident sense of self-identity. At the level of consciousness raising, some members of the minority group will become political activists and advocate for the rights for their fellow citizens.

Smokowski, Buchanan, and Bacallao (2009) studied acculturation in a sample of 281 Latino adolescents. The degree to which the parents were actively engaged in U.S. culture had a beneficial effect in reducing social problems in the kids. Adolescent involvement in cultural events was positively related to self-esteem 1 year later. Inability to speak English well is a risk factor for violence and for school dropouts. Those students who do the best, in short, are fluent in both English and Spanish. In the following passages from the autobiography *Being Latino in Christ*, a fair-complexioned Puerto Rican youth, Orlando Crespo (2003) from Springfield, Massachusetts, traces his journey to a healthy ethnic identity:

> To survive such hatred of Puerto Ricans, I learned to live in two worlds even as an adolescent. At home I spoke Spanish, ate Puerto Rican food, danced salsa and merengue with my three sisters, and enjoyed cultural events like parrandas . . . with my extended family. But when I walked out the front door and joined my white friends, I left behind my Puerto Rican identity. (p. 15)

> I was not proud to be Puerto Rican. We were told we were dirty, loud, uneducated, immoral and unable to speak English "good." . . . In all it was the love of *mi familia*, their warmth, nurture and sacrifices, that initially sheltered me from the hard blows of prejudice, racism and alienation. (p. 16)

Orlando's great awakening came at the age of 16, when he traveled alone to stay with his relatives in Puerto Rico: "Cousins, aunts and uncles I had only heard about loved me without knowing me. . . . This was the summer that I fell in love with my people, my culture, my parents and my land—Puerto Rico, la Isla del Encanto [the Island of Enchantment]. This was also the summer I began to love myself and my ethnic identity" (p. 18).

Alternatively, bell hooks (1995) asserts, there will be rage because of a system that does not address the psychological wounds caused by "the madness of forming self and identity in white supremacist capitalist patriarchy" (p. 142). A collective cultural refusal to assume any accountability for the psychological wounding of black people creates a climate of repression and suppression. When this reality is linked to a culture of shame, a breeding ground is created for learned helplessness and powerlessness. This lack of agency, hooks contends, nurtures compulsive behavior and promotes addiction.

The story of 16-year-old Jeff Weise at Red Lake High School, who went on a shooting spree, killing nine people, mostly his classmates, before killing himself, is a tale of twisted self-identity. Weise, a Native American living on a reservation in northern Minnesota, expressed admiration for Adolf Hitler and espoused Nazi beliefs related to racial purity. While high school shooting incidents in Littleton, Colorado, and Jonesboro, Arkansas, demonstrate that school shootings can happen anywhere, sociologists have been concerned for years about violence among some Native American teenagers and their high rates of suicide and substance abuse (Paulson, 2005). Many of the problems go back to the U.S. government's legacy of mistreatment and the resulting disconnection from native land and culture.

Multicultural Identity

To the extent that the models of racial-ethnic identity development assume that youths growing up have just one racial identity, they fail to reflect the reality for biracial, bicultural children. Because society is organized around a tendency to categorize people in either/or categories, there is pressure on children from mixed backgrounds to identify with just one racial-ethnic group. In addition, there may be rejection from one community or family or the other.

In 2000 the U.S. Census Bureau for the first time permitted respondents to select from multiracial categories (U.S. Census Bureau, 2001). The change came about because of the outcry from many U.S. citizens of mixed heritage who resented being forced to choose among two or more categories when more than one applied. The results obtained by the 2000 census were an eye-opener. Slightly fewer than 7 million people, or 2.4 percent of the population, reported they and/or their children were of two or more races. Most of these individuals were young (about 42 percent were under 18). The multiracial population as reported by respondents is about one-third white and some other race; about one-eighth white and Asian; one-sixth white-black; about one-sixth white, Native American, and Alaska Native; and the rest (about half) are mostly of some other race (mainly Latino). Within each population group, 2.5 percent of whites were in the category "two or more races," compared to 4.8 percent of blacks, 13.9 percent of Asians, 39.9 percent of Native American and Alaska Natives, and 6 percent of Latinos. Hawaii and the West had the highest percentages of mixed racial groups. Preliminary reports on the 2010 Census are that the number of people choosing multiple racial categories will show a significant increase (El Nasser, 2010). Mixed race marriages are now eight percent of the total number of marriages. Individuals who were defined as being of one race by their parents in 2000 may now themselves respond differently to the survey.

In a world in which racial identity matters, how do biracial people identify themselves? Historically, mixed-race offspring were expected to identify with the minority group, especially in the case of black-white biracial individuals (Henriksen & Trusty, 2004). The pressure placed on people to identify themselves with just one racial group, a fact that continues in certain social circles today, undermines their development of a healthy racial identity. Ward and Redd (2007) studied the identity development of biracial children and the way they contend with both parts of their heritage. Issues related to skin color variations, according to these authors, have historical linkages to colonial America. She concluded that the identity process begins as children from mixed backgrounds come to the realization that they are different from their single-race friends and hence do not belong exclusively to any one group. Their problems reach a crisis point in adolescence. Resolution of the identity crisis occurs when there is no longer an internal need to compartmentalize the different parts of one's heritage. Ward and Redd recommend an understanding of biracial identity issues from an Afrocentric perspective—one that embodies a worldview of oppressed people and the strengths required for survival, as well as an understanding of the strengths of a family with many shades of color among its members.

Henriksen and Trusty (2004) interviewed six biracial women and one biracial man who were between 18 and 22 years of age. All had a white mother and a black father. The researchers delineated six periods in the movement toward the development of a racial identity. The progression is from the neutrality of early childhood to acceptance of difference (through negative remarks made by others) to awareness of the impact of the difference, especially when dating begins, to experimentation with various types of peer groups to a transition period to a final recognition of "this is who I am." The participants in the study identified themselves variously as black, white, mulatto, biracial, and mixed.

Barack Obama (1995), in his autobiography, *Dreams from My Father: A Story of Race and Inheritance*, dealt with his wrenching adolescent racial identity crises, one rendered more difficult in the almost total lack of contact with his African father and the black community while reared by his white mother and grandparents. The book records conversations the young Barack had with black friends who had a strong African American identity. The difference between Obama and "most of the man-boys around me" who were at the stage of rebellion from their fathers—would-be surfers and rock-and-roll guitarists—as he writes, was "the limited number of options at my disposal" (p. 79). But finally as a young man, in his emotionally charged visit to Africa to the grave of his father, he finds solace. In his words:

> I felt the circle finally close. I realized that who I was, what I cared about, was no longer just a matter of intellect or obligation, no longer a construct of words. I saw that my life in America—the black life, the white life, the sense of abandonment I'd felt as a boy, the frustration and hope I'd witnessed in Chicago, all of it was connected with this small plot of earth an ocean away. (pp. 429–430)

Coming of Age Cross-Culturally

Because the educational process in nonindustrialized societies is much shorter, adolescents there are expected to assume adult responsibilities early on. Still, most cultures have coming-of-age ceremonies and rituals for young people. Most Western societies have social markers such as the earning of privileges to drive, drink, or vote. In Japan, 20-year-olds dress in new kimonos or suits on January 15 to celebrate their entrance into adulthood (Knight Ridder Newspapers, 2004). For 13-year-old Jewish boys and 12-year-old Jewish girls, a bar or bat mitzvah marks the day they start to observe religious commandments. Since this ceremony was restricted to boys until recent years, women of all ages are claiming their right to this community affirmation. As reported in the *New York Times* (Maab, 2009):

> BEACHWOOD, Ohio—Ann Simon is worried she might forget all the Hebrew words she has memorized to become a bat mitzvah, a Jewish girl marking the transition into religious adulthood.
> Ms. Simon is no 12-year-old, though. At 94 she can be forgiven her fear that she might be seized by a senior moment or two as she stands on the bimah on Sunday to recite the section of the Torah that was read in synagogue on the Saturday closest

to her 12th birthday. So can the other nine women who will take part in the bat mitzvah ceremony at the service in the synagogue of the Menorah Park senior residence in this Cleveland suburb. (p. A14)

In the Latino world, the most important day for a girl is her *quinceañera*, the ceremony that takes place when she reaches the age of 15. *Quinceañera* festivities, which have roots in Aztec and Catholic traditions, have been a tradition in Latin America for centuries. In the United States, as the number of Latinos has grown, such celebrations have become more commercial and more mainstream (Miranda, 2004). The ceremony often costs between $10,000 and $15,000 and includes an expensive evening gown; a popular band; lavish dining, drinking, and dancing for a large crowd; and, of course, birthday presents that are opened at the party (Knight Ridder Newspapers, 2004). Despite the commercialism, the *quinceañera* has a religious aspect, beginning with a Mass.

We see quite a contrast in Korean culture, as mentioned previously. The economic burden on parents to ensure a place in society for their children involves supplementary, private education, which is quite expensive. The better students do academically in this highly competitive society, the better their chances of getting into a "good" high school (Sang-Hun, 2007). The ultimate goal is acceptance at the top universities. Most Korean children attend multiple institutes for hours on end following a full school day. Rote memorization is the typical teaching style; many Koreans nowadays believe it is time for a change so that children can grow up at their own pace.

Childhood Resilience

In this chapter we have discussed the trauma of brutalization and the social strain of growing up as a member of a disadvantaged or disaraged minority group. The striking thing about so many personal narratives of people who have survived the most difficult of circumstances is what is tritely referred to as "the strength of human spirit," or resilience. Why do some children bounce back from adversity and others do not? How can extreme circumstances such as the loss of one or both parents, street shootings, natural disasters such as tsunami, and physical disease be overcome psychologically?

Resilience is defined as the ability to cope successfully in the face of significant change, adversity, or risk (Holleran, Young-Mi, & Dixon, 2004). Scientists who have studied this trait have come up with two basic explanations, depending on the angle of their studies. Resilience theory has its origins in developmental psychology in research on children who were exposed to psychological trauma or who lived in situations of severe adversity and stress (Harris, 2008). The most widely reported resiliency study is the longitudinal study of Werner & Smith (1992), which followed children who had endured problems ranging from extreme poverty to violence up to middle age. This longitudinal study of more than 6,000 people looked at social factors. They identified three clusters of protective factors that set the resilient youth apart from their unsuccessful counterparts. These were *cognitive development* or personal temperament; *relationships* with someone older who cared about them, which encouraged trust, autonomy, and initiative; and *external support systems* such as church, school, or youth groups, which rewarded competence and provided them with a sense of belonging.

Rather than focusing on the children who were casualties of negative factors within their high-risk environments, the research concentrated instead on those who had not succumbed. What they found was that a robust relationship with one's parents or with another adult in the community was a buffer against risk factors such as dire poverty and exposure to crime.

Another massive study identified protective factors in high-risk situations. Conducted by Resnick et al. (1997) and reported in the *Journal of the American Medical Association*, this study was based on a randomized sample of 10,000 youths across social classes. Two factors that were correlated with positive outcomes were solid connections with one's parents and positive feelings about school. Relationships were critical in helping youth avoid violence, delinquency, substance abuse, and school dropout. More recently, Marsh, Evans, and Weigel (2009) explored measures of risk and protective factors in over 1,500 high school students. Significantly, they found that exposure to some risk appeared to be a learning experience for students and heightened their resilience, but beyond a certain level of victimization, the outcomes were harmful. The authors recommend the teaching of coping and problem-solving skills to help children avoid risk exposure.

Scientific studies of children at high risk (from maltreatment, poverty, etc.) are looking at brain chemistry to learn more about the nature of resilience. The research shows that the extent to which mistreatment such as neglect and abuse will have long-term consequences involves not only biological factors but also positive relationships.

Research conducted at the Yale University School of Medicine examined the possession of shortened and full-size versions of a gene that makes a protein critical to the normal transmission of serotonin (Kaufman et al., 2004). The research team conducted saliva analyses of 101 children, 57 of whom had recently been removed from the parents' care because of abuse or domestic violence. Children who had not been abused displayed few signs of depression even if they had inherited the version of the gene—the short version—that makes people more vulnerable to depression and other problems. The findings indicate that the maltreated children who suffered from depression tended to have the genetic predisposition in combination with the absence of a supportive adult in their lives. Depression scores were low among violence-exposed kids with at least one copy of the longer version of the gene in question. The findings of their research are consistent with a similar study done with depressed adults who had been abused as children and with research on monkeys raised under stressful conditions (Barr et al., 2004). The monkeys drank alcohol to excess when stressed but only if they possessed two copies of the short serotonin-transporter gene.

These reports confirm the view taken in this text that biological and psychosocial factors, not alone but in interaction with each other, often determine behavioral outcome. Further evidence of this theoretical perspective comes from longitudinal adoption studies of children who were mistreated early in life. Case Western Reserve social work professor Victor Groza has been following more than 300 Romanian adoptees since 1992 (see Dickens & Groza, 2004). All of the children brought out of the dismal Romanian orphanages bore telltale signs of neglect from lack of stimulation—in speech, in relationships with others, and in eating habits. They were horribly underweight and often covered in sores.

Dickens and Groza (2004) found that, after the first year, 20 percent of the adoptees were completely normal while another 60 percent had subtle problems such as poor coordination. Another 20 percent had severe cognitive and emotional problems. This research shows that neglected children who are adopted even after age 2 can make remarkable progress with special nurturance and guidance. The longer the period of neglect, clearly, the more serious the damage.

One irrefutable source of strength is religious faith. Studies on resilience, such as the ones in this section, nevertheless tend to omit religious belief in their studies on protective factors. Similarly, in *Risk and Resilience in Childhood*, Fraser (2004) devotes only one paragraph to religious institutions and no attention to any other aspects of religion or spirituality.

Spiritual Development

Social theorists Fowler (1981) and Wilber (1980, 1996) looked at how children's religious beliefs are modified with maturity. Fowler envisioned seven stages in the development of a mature, universalistic spirituality. During each respective life period, an individual grows closer to a concept of a higher power and is more concerned with the welfare of all people. Small children's view of religious faith is what they do to worship God, for example, going to church and singing hymns. For some believers, God is a being who rewards and punishes. Adolescents expand the capacity for self-reflection but still adhere to conventional beliefs. Adolescents and young adults search for meaning and perceive conflicts between values and beliefs. In short, Fowler's model is reminiscent of Piaget's in that it is cognitively oriented, proceeding across time and advancing from the concrete to more abstract levels.

Like Fowler, Wilber was influenced by Piaget's structured cognitive model, yet he ventured into the realm of levels of consciousness that transcend the personal. Also, like Fowler, Wilber described a general trend of development from an early infancy experience of confusion between self and others to a sense of autonomy. The potential is there for a human to later experience the true self in union with a divine being. Wilber mapped out a progression of spiritual development for the individual that he conceived as an upward spiral of expanding concentric circles. This advancing spiraling sequence at the micro level is replicated at the macro level in terms of movement from one historical period, in which a certain mode of consciousness dominates, to ever-higher levels of mental functioning. Wilber's theoretical scheme blends Eastern and Western philosophical and religious notions.

Religious faith, whatever form it may take, helps provide structure for children and closeness to relatives and people of all ages through participation in rituals, develops an aesthetic appreciation through art and music used in the rituals, and provides for stress reduction and support (as through prayer) in times of trouble. Religious faith helps provide a sense of purpose in life. Children often develop confidence through the roles they play in the religious life of the community and, ideally, learn moral values and altruism through the teachings of their religious community. Two aspects of religious upbringing that breed disturbance in late adolescence are the hypocrisy seen in the discrepancy between what adults preach and their actual behavior and a sense of loss of the simplicity and anthropomorphism of early childhood faith as the young person's horizons are broadened and powers of critical thinking enhanced. The questioning teen may experiment with other religions and finally come up with the mature realization that you can do as they say in Alcoholics Anonymous (AA): "Take what you need and leave the rest."

Practice Implications

Consistent with the acceptance of the strengths and empowerment perspective as the dominant approach in social work, the social work profession has experienced a resurgence of interest in the healing powers of spirituality and an understanding of the role of religious faith in resilience. Religious faith can be viewed as one of the protective factors that promote positive developmental outcomes and help children prevail over adversity.

Practitioners will want to minimize all risk factors for children generally (in society or in their care) and maximize their natural resilience to events in their lives that are beyond any-

one's control. The harm-reduction model, which utilizes public health initiatives, is highly relevant to this discussion. The earlier one starts in the lives of children, the better. Head Start is more comprehensive than most preschool programs. In dozens of studies on health, nutrition, and school readiness, Head Start has been shown to be highly effective (Newman & Newman, 2006). Social workers often work with the children and their families in Head Start programs, which are means tested (see Figure 4.3).

Training parents is one goal of the federally funded Child-Parent Centers, a Head Start–like program in Chicago that operates throughout the city's poorest sections and actively involves parents from the start with preschool programming. Classes are offered in parenting, and parents are encouraged to pursue their own education further. The results are striking (Graue, Clements, Reynolds, & Niles, 2004). For the first two decades of the study, the young people who were enrolled in the program were found to be far less likely to get

Figure 4.3. Head Start social worker interacting with children at lunchtime, Waterloo, Iowa. Photo by Rupert van Wormer.

involved in crime than their peers and far more likely to graduate from school on time. Even their rate of victimization has been shown to be reduced beyond expectations.

Harm reduction works with people in high-risk situations (drug abusers, homeless youths, prostitutes) to help keep them safe and reduce the harm associated with their behavior. The opposite of harm reduction is zero tolerance and "one size fits all" abstinence-based programs. Harm-reduction efforts aimed at gays and lesbians in the schools would involve safe sex education and alcohol prevention, school-based support groups led by an openly gay or lesbian adult, and, above all, the instituting of programs to prevent bullying and verbal abuse of students who are gender nonconforming. Social workers can help initiate such programs through involvement in the self-help group called Parents, Families, and Friends of Lesbians and Gays (PFLAG), which has chapters all across North America. Preventive measures need to be aimed at all school-age youths to help them with sexual identity issues.

Harm-reduction efforts should also be applied to help schoolchildren and other children who have been exposed to violence, whether through schoolyard bullying or at home. A society built on harm reduction or a public health philosophy would start with nationalized health care, extensive prenatal care, and public health nurse visitation to the homes of all infants. In short, children are placed at risk by many family, peer group, and environmental conditions. Evidence-based interventions and public policies that reduce risk and build resilience offer new promise for millions of children and families across the land.

Summary and Conclusion

Risk and resilience in the first part of the life span—this in a nutshell can be considered the topic of this chapter. Many of the risks to healthy development are biological in origin, including malnutrition, sensory deprivation, abuse, neglect, and botched circumcision. The wonder is that, even from the most brutal and dysfunctional of environments, so many individuals manage to emerge relatively unscathed. Rather than concentrating exclusively on the outcomes of children who were casualties of their en vironment, the focus instead has been on those who had somehow not succumbed. The question we pursued was, What enabled some children to rise above their circumstances?

The organizational structure of this chapter was drawn from Piaget's insights on cognitive growth and development, Erikson's psychosocial scheme (which pinpointed key issues to be resolved throughout childhood), and Fowler's and Wilber's conceptualizations of the evolution of spiritual understanding. We considered cross-cultural customs in child rearing and initiatives (e.g., the simulated kangaroo pouch for premature infants in Columbia), as well as trauma-reducing rituals for former child soldiers in Mozambique. We can learn a lot about the correlates of human behavior from both negative and positive examples of child care. Success stories illustrate that resilience is real, but it is not inevitable.

Thought Questions

1. Looking back over this chapter on children, what do you think a global view can teach us?
2. How can failure to resolve Erikson's trust versus mistrust stage lead to problems in later relationships?
3. What can we learn from the research of Spitz and Bowlby?
4. What do studies of intersexuals teach us about gender?
5. How does a male bias extend throughout Erikson's theory?
6. Discuss the theme of *The Overscheduled Child*. How far should kids be pushed?
7. What is attachment disorder?
8. What is the connection between partner violence and child abuse?
9. What are the facts on child fatalities?
10. What are some of the salient points about early childhood education in Asia?

11. How is Piaget's period of concrete operations different from industry versus inferiority?
12. "When adults think back to the middle childhood period, most of their memories center around the school." How would you elaborate on this observation?
13. What are some positive aspects of ADHD?
14. How do gender differences manifest themselves in the classroom?
15. Why is it illegal to assault an adult but not a child?
16. How would you compare personal childhood trauma and soul murder?
17. What can we learn from the children of Romania?
18. "Identity is never a done deal." How would you explain this remark?
19. How would you describe substance abuse among today's teens?
20. "Boys who are like girls are silenced by codes of masculinity." What does this mean?
21. What is the explanation for the taunting of gays and lesbians at school? How did one girl who was gender nonconforming find her teacher a lifesaver?
22. How would you relate the events at Columbine and Red Lake high schools to internal and external factors?
23. How would you describe racial identity differences for people of various races?
24. How would you describe multicultural identity with reference to Census 2000?
25. What does research show us about resilience?
26. How would you describe the importance of religious rituals among U.S. and ethnically diverse populations?
27. How would you describe harm-reduction principles in relation to the school system?

References

American Association of University Women (AAUW). (1995). *How schools shortchange girls: A study of major findings on girls and education*. New York: Marlow.

American Bar Association. (2004, January). Adolescent brain development and legal culpability. Juvenile Justice Center. Retrieved from http://www.abanet.org/crimjust/juvjus/Adolescence.pdf

American Civil Liberties Union (ACLU). (2008, August 19). *A violent education: Corporal punishment of children in U.S. public schools*. Retrieved from http://www.aclu.org/intlhumanrights/gen/36476pub20080819.html

American Medical Association. (2002, May 3). *Proceedings: Educational forum on adolescent health and youth bullying*. Retrieved from http://www.ama-assn.org/ama1/pub/upload/mm/39/youthbullying.pdf

American Psychiatric Association (APA). (2000). *Diagnostic and statistical manual of mental disorders* (4th ed.). Washington, DC: Author.

Angelou, M. (1969). *I know why the caged bird sings*. New York: Random House.

Arehart-Treichel, J. (2001, March 2). Psychological abuse may cause changes in the brain. *Psychiatric News*. Retrieved from http://pn.psychiatryonline.org/content/36/5/36.full

Ark, T. V. (2002, February). The case for small high schools. *Educational Leadership, 59*(5), 55–59.

Aronson, E. (2004). *The social animal* (9th ed.). New York: Worth.

Baron-Cohen, S. (2003). *The essential difference: The truth about the male and female brain*. New York: Basic Books.

Barr, C., Newman, T., Lindell, S., Shannon, C., Champoux, M., Lesch, K., Suomi, S., Goldman, D., & Higley, J. (2004). Interaction between serotonin transporter gene variation and rearing condition in alcohol preference and consumption in female primates. *Archives of General Psychiatry, 61*(11), 1146–1152.

Basham, K., & Miehls, D. (2004). *Transforming the legacy: Couple therapy with survivors of childhood trauma*. New York: Columbia University Press.

Belgrave, F., & Allison, K. (2010). *African American psychology: From Africa to America* (2nd ed.). Thousand Oaks, CA: Sage.

Blum, D. (2002). *Love at goon park: Harry Harlow and the science of affection*. Cambridge, MA: Perseus.

Boothby, N. (2006). What happens to child soldiers when they grow-up?: The Mozambique case study. *International Journal of Mental Health, Psychosocial Work and Counselling in Areas of Armed Conflict, 4* (2), 244-259.

Bowlby, J. (1952). *Maternal care and mental health*. Geneva: World Health Organization.

Bowlby, J. (1969). *Attachment*. New York: Basic Books.

Bowlby, J. (1982). *Attachment and loss, Vol.1: Attachment* (2nd ed.). New York: Basic Books.

Brandell, J., & Rindel, S. (2007). *Attachment and dynamic practice: An integrative guide for social workers and other clinicians*. New York: Columbia University Press.

Bricker-Jenkins, M. (2001). Book review of social work with lesbians, gays, and bisexuals. *Journal of School Social Work, 11*(2), 93–95.

British Broadcasting Company (BBC). (2004, January 26). Eleven-plus to be abolished. *BBC News*. Retrieved from http://news.bbc.co.uk/2/hi/uk_news/northern_ireland/3429541.stm

Brown, A.W., & Gourdine, R. (2007). African-American adolescent girls: Facing the challenges and consequences of violence in the inner city. In L. A. See (Ed.), *Human behavior in the social environment from an African American perspective* (pp. 253–275). New York: Haworth.

Bulik, C., Tozzi, F., Anderson, C., Mazzeo, S., Aggen, S., & Sullivan, P. (2003). The relation between eating disorders and components of perfectionism. *American Journal of Psychiatry, 160*, 366–368.

Burkeman, O., & Younge, G. (2004). Being Brenda. *Guardian*. Retrieved from http://www.guardian.co.uk/books/2004/may/12/scienceandnature.gender

Cadwallader, A. (2002, September 4). In Northern Ireland hate begins early. *Christian Science Monitor*, pp. 7, 12.

Centers for Disease Control and Prevention (CDC). (2009, August 19). *National Vital Statistics Reports, 58*(1), p.22. Retrieved from http://www.cdc.gov/nchs/data/nvsr/nvsr58/nvsr58_01.pdf

Challender, M. (2003, November 25). Why do we feel female or male? Sexual identity rooted in biology. *Des Moines Register*, p. 19W.

Charles, D. (2000, July 18). Victims of gay bullying drop out of school. *London Times*, p. 1.

Children's Defense Fund. (2009). *Protect children, not guns 2009*. Retrieved from http://www.childrensdefense.org/child-research-data-publications/data/protect-children-not-guns-report-2009.html

Cooper, G. (2005). *Models of white identity development*. Retrieved from the University of Oregon, Teaching Effectiveness Program website http://tep.uoregon.edu/workshops

Crespo, O. (2003). *Being Latino in Christ: Finding wholeness in your ethnic identity*. Downers Grove, IL: InterVarsity Press.

Datnow, A., Hubbard, L., & Wood, E. (2001). Is single-gender schooling viable in the public sector? Lessons from California's pilot program. [Research monograph funded by Ford and Spencer foundations].

Dickens, J., & Groza, V. (2004). Empowerment in difficulty: A critical appraisal of inter-national intervention in child welfare in Romania. *International Social Work, 47*(4), 469–87.

Dominelli, L. (2004). *Social work: Theory and practice for a changing profession*. Cambridge, England: Polity Press.

Douglass, F. (1845/1968). *Narrative of the life of Frederick Douglass: An American slave*. New York: Signet.

DYG, Inc. (2000). *What grown-ups understand about child development: A national benchmark survey*. Retrieved from the Zero to Three website http://www.zerotothree.org/parent_poll.html

Dyson, A. H. (2009, February 12). All work and no play makes for troubling trend in early education. *ScienceDaily*. Retrieved from http://www.sciencedaily.com/releases/2009/02/090212125137.htm

Eisenberg, M., & Resnick, M. (2006). Suicidality among gay, lesbian, and bisexual youth: The role of protective factors. *Journal of Adolescent Health, 39*(5), 662–668.

El Nasser, H. (2010, March 2). Multiracial no longer boxed in by the census. *New York Times*, p. 1A.

Emery, G. (2004, January 21). Boys raised as girls find male identity study. *Reuters*. Retrieved from the Mermaids website http://www.mermaidsuk.org.uk/reut002.html

Erikson, E. (1950/1963). *Childhood and society* (2nd ed.). New York: Norton.

Every Child Matters Education Fund. (2009). We can do better: Child abuse and neglect deaths in America. Washington, DC. Retrieved from http://www.everychildmatters.org/images/stories/pdf/wcdb_report.pdf

Faludi, S. (1999). *Stiffed: The betrayal of the American man*. New York: Putnam.

Feldman, R., Weller, A., Sirota, L., & Eidelman, A. (2002). Skin-to-skin contact (kangaroo care promotes self-regulation in premature infants). *Developmental Psychology, 38*(2), 194–207.

Ferguson, S. (2004, November 22). Stressed out! *Maclean's*, 31–38.

Fine, I., Wade, A., Brewer, A., May, M., Boyton, G., Wandell, B., & MacLeod, D. (2003). The effects of long-term deprivation on visual perception and visual cortex. *Nature Neuroscience, 6*(9), 915–916.

Finkelhor, D., & Hashima, P. (2001). The victimization of children and youth: A comprehensive overview. In S. O. White (Ed.), *Law and social science perspectives on youth and justice* (pp. 49–78). New York: Plenum.

Finkelhor, D., Turner,H., Ormrod, R., Hamby, S., & Kracke, K. (2009, October). *National survey of children's exposure to violence.* Retrieved from the National Criminal Justice Reference Statistics website http://www.ncjrs.gov/pdffiles1/ojjdp/227744.pdf

Finn, J., Gerber, S. B., & Zaharias, J. (2005). Small classes in the early grades, academic achievement, and graduating from high school. *Journal of Educational Psychology, 97*(2), 214–223.

Forman, D. R., Aksan, N., & Kochanska, G. (2004). Toddler's responsive imitation predicts preschool age conscience. *Psychological Science, 15*(10), 699–704.

Fowler, J. W. (1981). Stages of faith: *The psychology of human development and the quest for meaning.* San Francisco: Harper.

Franklin, B. (1968/1771). *The autobiography of Benjamin Franklin.* New York: Lancer.

Fraser, M. (2004). *Risk and resilience in childhood: An ecological perspective.* Washington, DC: NASW Press.

Friend, C., & Mills, L. (2002). Domestic violence and child protective services. In A. R. Roberts & G. J. Greene (Eds.), *Social workers' desk reference* (pp. 679–683). New York: Oxford University Press.

Gardiner, H., & Kosmitzki, C. (2005). *Lives across cultures: Cross-cultural human development.* Boston: Allyn & Bacon.

Gay, Lesbian, and Straight Education Network (GLSEN). (1999, September 24). Report on anti-gay school violence. Retrieved from http://www.glsen-la.org

Gay Men's Health. (2004). *Suicide research.* Edinburgh: Gay Men's Health.

Geiger B., Behr, G. Frank, L., Caldera-Siu, A., Beinfeld, M., Kokkotou, E., & Pothos, E. Evidence for defective mesolimbic dopamine exocytosis in obesity-prone rats. *The FASEB Journal, 22*(8), 2740–2746.

Gibran, K. (1923). *The prophet.* New York: Random House.

Gilligan, C. (1982). *In a different voice: Psychological theory and women's development.* Cambridge, MA: Harvard University Press.

Gilligan, C. (2003). Sisterhood is pleasurable: A quiet revolution in psychology. In R. Morgan (Ed.), *Sisterhood is forever: The women's anthology for a new millennium* (pp. 94–102). New York: Washington Square Press.

Goldberg, E. (2001). *The executive brain: Frontal lobes and the civilized mind.* New York: Oxford University Press.

Grandin, T. (2006). *Thinking in pictures, expanded edition: My life with autism.* New York: Vintage.

Grandin, T. (2008). *The way I see it: A personal look at autism and Asperger's.* Arlington, TX: Future Horizons.

Graue, E., Clements, M. A., Reynolds, A. J., & Niles, M. D. (2004). More than teacher directed or child initiated: Preschool curriculum type, parent involvement, and children's outcomes in the Child-Parent Centers. *Education Policy Analysis Archives, 12*(72), 1–38.

Harlow, H., & Harlow, M. (1962). Social deprivation in monkeys. *Scientific American, 207*, 135–146.

Harmon, A. (2004, December 20). How about not "curing" us, some autistics are pleading. *New York Times.* Retrieved from http://www.nytimes.com/2004/12/20/health/20autism.html

Harris, J. R. (2009). *The nurture assumption: Why children turn out the way they do, revised and updated.* New York: Free Press.

Harris, P. (2008). Another wrinkle in the debate about successful aging: The undervalued concept of resilience and the lived experience of dementia. *Aging and human development, 67*(1), 43–61.

Harvard Mental Health Letter. (2005, February). Asperger's syndrome. *Harvard Mental Health Letter, 21* (8), 4-8.

HealthScout. (2002). Autism. *Health Scout Network.* Retrieved from http://www.healthscout.com/ency/1/001526.html

Heim, C., Newport, J., Heit, S., Graham, Y., Wilcox, M., Bonsall, R.and Nemeroff, C. (2000). Pituitary-adrenal and autonomic responses to stress in women after sexual and physical abuse in childhood. *Journal of the American Medical Association, 284*, 592–597.

Henriksen, R., & Trusty, J. (2004). Understanding and assisting black/white biracial women in their identity development. *Women and Therapy, 27*(1/2), 65–83.

Holleran, L., Young-Mi, K., & Dixon, K. (2004). Innovative approaches to risk assessment within alcohol prevention programming. In A. R. Roberts & K. R. Yeager (Eds.), *Evidence-based practice manual: Research outcome measures in health and human services* (pp. 677–684). New York: Oxford University Press.

hooks, b. (1995). *Killing rage: Ending racism.* New York: Henry Holt.

hooks, b. (2001). *Salvation: Black people and love.* New York: HarperCollins.

Human Rights Watch. (2001). *Hatred in the hallways: Violence and discrimination against lesbians, gay, bisexual, and transgender students in the U.S. schools.* Retrieved from http://www.hrw.org/reports/2001/usight

Hupp, S. (2005, January 4). When it comes to school, girls rule. *Indianapolis Star.* Retrieved from http://www.indystar.com

Jackson, K. (2004, September–October). Attachment disorders: The education gap. *Social Work Today*, 20–24.

Javo, C., Rønning, J. A., & Heyerdahl, S. (2004). Child rearing in an indigenous Sami population in Norway: A cross-cultural comparison of parental attitudes and expectations. *Scandinavian Journal of Psychology, 45*, 67–79.

Johnson, H. (2004). *Psyche and synapse expanding worlds: The role of neurobiology in emotions, behavior, thinking, and addiction for non-scientists* (2nd ed.). Greenfield, MA: Deerfield Valley.

Just, M. A., Cherkassky, V. L., Keller, T. A., & Minshew, N. J. (2004). Cortical activation and synchronization during sentence comprehension in high-functioning autism: Evidence of underconnectivity. *Brain, 127*, 1811–1121.

Katz, J. (2006). *The macho paradox: Why some men hurt women and how all men can help.* Naperville, IL: Sourcebooks.

Kaufman, J., Yang, B-A., Douglas-Palumberi, H., Houshyar, S., Lipschitz, D., Krystal, J., & Gelernter, J. (2004). Social supports and serotonin transporter gene moderate depression in maltreated children. *Proceedings of the National Academy of Sciences, 101*(49), 17316–17322.

Kaye, W., Frank, G., Bailler, V., Henry, S., Meltzer, C., Price, J., Mathis, C., & Wagner, A. (2005). Serotonin alteration in anorexia and bulimia nervosa: New insights from imaging studies. *Physiological Behavior, 85*(1), 73–81.

Khadaroo, S. (2009, March 24). Lessons from most successful schools abroad. *Christian Science Monitor*, p.01.

King, M. (1996, November 12). Suicide watch. *Advocate*, 41–44.

Klein, J. (2006). An invisible problem: Everyday violence against girls in school. *Theoretical Criminology, 10*(2): 147–177.

Knight-Ridder Newspapers. (2004, January 26). Quinceañera: Passage to adulthood begins at age 15 for Hispanic girls. *Waterloo–Cedar Falls (Iowa) Courier Journal*, p. B4.

Kogan, M. D., Blumberg, S. J., Schieve, L. A., Boyle, C.A., Perrin, J. M, Ghandour, R. M., et al. (2009). Prevalence of parent-reported diagnosis of autism spectrum disorder among children in the U.S., 2007. *Pediatrics, 124* (4), 1-10.

Kuo, F., & Taylor, A. F. (2004). A potential natural treatment for attention-deficit/hyperactivity disorder: Evidence from a national study. *American Journal of Public Health, 94*(9), 1580–1586.

Lein, J. (1999) Recovered memories: Context and controversy. *Social Work, 44*(5), 481–484.

Levine, M. (2002). *A mind at a time.* New York: Simon & Schuster.

Lorde, A. (1982). *Zami: A new spelling of my name.* Trumansburg, NY: Crossing Press.

Lupton, C., Burd, L., & Harwood, R. (2004). Cost of fetal alcohol spectrum disorders. *American Journal of Medical Genetics, 127C*(1), 42–50.

Maab, C. (2009, March 22). Having a bat mitzvah in their 90's because it's a hoot. *New York Times*, p. A14.

Malcolm X, & Haley, A. (1965). *Autobiography of Malcolm X.* New York: Ballantine.

Marsh, S., Evans, W., & Weigel, D. (2009). Exploring models of resiliency by gender in relation to adolescent victimization. *Victims and Offenders, 4*, 230–248.

Martínez, D. G., & Sullivan, S. C. (1998). African American gay men and lesbians: Examining the complexity of gay identity development. In L. A. See (Ed.), *Human behavior in the social environment from an African American perspective* (pp. 243–264). New York: Haworth.

Maté, G. (1999). *Scattered: How attention deficit disorder originates and what you can do about it.* New York: Plume.

Mercer, J. (2009, November 4). Away with the Asperger's diagnosis: What's it all about? *Psychology Today blog.* Retrieved from http://www.psychologytoday.com/blog/child-myths/200911/away-the-aspergers-diagnosis-whats-it-all-about

Miehls, D. (2001). The interface of racial identity: Development with identity complexity in clinical social work student practitioners. *Clinical Social Work Journal, 29*(3), 229–244.

Mignon, S. I., Larson, C. J., & Holmes, W. M. (2002). *Family abuse: Consequences, theories, and responses.* Boston: Allyn & Bacon.

Miranda, C. (2004, July 19). Fifteen candles. *Time.* Retrieved from http://www.time.com/time/magazine/article/0,9171,994683,00.html

Moore, M. (2004, December 22). For kids, trek to school not like it used to be. *USA Today*, p. 15A.

Morales, A., Sheafor, B., & Scott, M. (2010). *Social work: A profession of many faces* (12th ed.). Boston: Allyn & Bacon.

Moriarty, A. (2002, August 7). Just right: School size. *Washington Post*, p. H9.

National Association of Social Workers (NASW). (2009). *Social work speaks: NASW policy statements 2009-2012*. Washington, DC: Author.

National Coalition of Girls' Schools. (2008). What the research shows. Retrieved from http://www.ncgs.org/researchshowsgirlsschoolgraduates haveanedge/

National Institute of Mental Health (NIMH). (2001a). Eating disorders. National Institutes of Health. Retrieved from http://www.nimh.nih.gov

National Institute of Mental Health (NIMH). (2001b). Teenage brain: A work in progress. National Institutes of Health. Retrieved from http://www.nimh.nih.gov

National Institute on Drug Abuse (NIDA). (2008, December). InfoFacts. High school and youth trends. Retrieved from http://www.nida.nih.gov/pdf/infofacts/HSYouthTrends08.pdf

Neckoway, R., Brownlee, K., Jourdain, L. W., & Miller, L. (2003). Rethinking the role of attachment theory in child welfare practice with aboriginal people. *Canadian Social Work Review, 20*, 105–119.

Neff, N. (2004). Health of Mexican American children is focus of School of Social Work study. *Utopian University of Texas School of Social Work, 6*(1), 7.

Neigh, G., Gillespie, C., & Nemeroff, C. (2009). The neurobiological toll of child abuse and neglect. *Trauma, Violence, & Abuse, 10* (4), 389–410.

Newman, B., & Newman, P. (2006). *Development through life: A psychosocial approach* (9th ed.). Belmont, CA: Wadsworth.

Noonan, R., & Charles, D. (2009). Developing teen dating violence prevention strategies. *Violence Against Women, 15*, 1087–1105.

Obama, B. (1995). *Dreams from my father: A story of race and inheritance*. New York: Three Rivers Press.

Olweus, D. (2001, March). Bullying at school: Tackling the problem. OECD Observer, 24–26.

Owens, R. E. (2004). *Help your baby talk: Introducing the shared communication method to jump-start language and have a smarter and happier baby*. New York: Penguin.

Page, T., & Norwood, R. (2007). Attachment theory and the social work curriculum. *Advances in Social Work, 8* (1), 30–48.

Paton, G. (2008, November 21). 11-plus axed in Northern Ireland *Telegraph*. Retrieved from http://www/telegraph.com

Paulson, A. (2005). School shooting: Familiar echoes, new concerns. Christian Science Monitor, p. 1.

Piaget, J. (1952). *The origins of intelligence in children*. New York: International Universities Press.

Pipher, M. (1994). *Reviving Ophelia: Saving the selves of adolescent girls*. New York: Ballantine.

Pytel, B. (2009, June 19). Small school success causes problems. *Suite101.com—educational issues*.

Ransome, W., & Moulton, M. (2004, December 17). It's not boys vs. girls for educational gains. *USA Today*, p. 14A.

Remafedi, G. (1999). Sexual orientation and youth suicide. *Journal of the American Medical Association, 282*(13), 1291.

Resnick, M. D., Bearman, P. S., Blum, R. W., Bauman, K. E., Harris, K. M., Jones, J., et al. (1997). Protecting adolescents from harm. *Journal of the American Medical Association, 278*(10), 823–832.

Ridley, M. (2000). *Genome: The autobiography of a species in 23 chapters*. New York: Harper Collins.

Robbins, S. (2002). Working with clients who have recovered memories. In A. R. Roberts & G. J. Greene (Eds.), *Social workers' desk reference* (pp. 604–609). New York: Oxford University Press.

Roberts, R. (2001, June 10). Romanian children endure inhumane existence. *Waterloo–Cedar Falls (Iowa) Courier*, p. F2.

Rosario, M., Schrimshaw, E., & Hunter, J. (2004). Ethnic/racial differences in the coming-out process of lesbian, gay, and bisexual youths: A comparison of sexual identity development over time. *Cultural Diversity and Ethnic Minority Psychology, 10*(3), 215–228.

Rose, R. (1998). A developmental behavior-genetic perspective on alcoholism risk. *Alcohol Health and Research World, 22*(2), 131–143.

Rosenfeld, A., & Wise, N. (2001). *The over-scheduled child: Avoiding the hyper-parenting trap*. New York: St. Martin's Griffin.

Ryan, C., Huebner, D., Rafael, M., Diaz,R., & Sanchez, J. (2009). Family rejection as a predictor of negative health outcomes in white and Latino lesbian, gay, and bisexual young adults. *Pediatrics, 123*, 346–352.

Sack, K. (2008, October 29). At the legal limit. *New York Times*, EdLife p. 20.

Sacks, O. (2007). *Musicophilia: Tales of music and the brain.* New York: Vintage Books.

Salaam, K. (2001, June–July). No: Its power is distinct and uncompromising. *Ms.*, p. 9.

Saleebey, D. (2001). *Human behavior and social environments: A biopsychosocial approach.* New York: Columbia University Press.

Samantrai, K. (2004). *Culturally competent public child welfare practice.* Belmont, CA: Wadsworth.

Sang-Hun, C. (2007, May 23). Tracking an online trend, and route to suicide. *New York Times.* Retrieved from http://www.nytimes.com/2007/05/23/world/asia/23korea.html

Saran, C. (2008, February 8). Specialisterne finds a place in workforce for people with autism. *Computer Weekly.* Retrieved from http://www.computerweekly.com/Articles/2008/02/08/229318/specialisterne-finds-a-place-in-workforce-for-people-with.htm

Schilling, S. (2010). *The best kind of different: Our family's journey with Asperger's syndrome.* New York: William Morrow.

ScienceDaily. (2009, June 8). What about the boys? Boys face serious issues which are being ignored, experts argue. Retrieved from http://www.sciencedaily.com/releases/2009/06/090608125114.htm

Shakespeare, W. (1600/1954). *As you like it.* In *William Shakespeare: Complete works* (pp. 254–283). New York: Random House.

Shaywitz, S. (2003). *Overcoming dyslexia.* New York: Knopf.

Silberman, S. (2001, December). The geek syndrome. *Wired News.* Retrieved from http://www.wired.com/wired/archive/9.12/aspergers_pr.html

Skenazy, L. (2009). *Free-range kids: Giving our children the freedom we had without going nuts with worry.* San Francisco: Jossey-Bass.

Smokowski, P., Buchanan, R., & Bacallao, M. (2009). Acculturation and adjustment in Latino adolescents: How cultural risk factors and assets influence multiple domains of adolescent mental health. *Journal of Primary Prevention, 30*, 371–393.

Sommers, C. H. (2000). *The war against boys: How misguided feminism is harming our young men.* New York: Simon & Schuster.

Spitz, R. (1945). Hospitalism: An inquiry into the genesis of psychiatric conditions in early childhood. *Psychoanalytic Study of the Child, 1*, 53–74.

Swann, S., & Spivey, C. (2004). The relationship between self-esteem and lesbian identity during adolescence. *Adolescence, 21*(6), 629–646.

Terzieff, J. (2004, October 22). *Baby girls fill Pakistan's public cradles.* Retrieved from the Feminist.com website http://www.feminist.com/news/vaw33.html

Thomlinson, B. (2004). Child maltreatment: A risk and protective factor perspective. In M. Fraser (Ed.), *Risk and resilience in childhood: An ecological perspective* (pp. 89–131). Washington, DC: NASW Press.

United Nations Children's Fund (UNICEF). (2003). *The state of the world's children.* New York: Author.

United Nations Children's Fund (UNICEF). (2005). *At a glance: Korea, Democratic People's Republic of.* Retrieved from http://www.unicef.org/infobycountry

U.S. Census Bureau. (2001, March). Overview of race and Hispanic origin. *Census 2000 Brief.* Retrieved from http://www.census.gov/prod/2001pubs/cenbr01-1.pdf

U.S. Department of Health and Human Services. (1989). *Report of the Secretary's Task Force on Youth Suicide.* Vol. 3: *Prevention and interventions in youth suicide.* Rockville, MD: Author.

U.S. Department of Health and Human Services. (2008). Summary: Child Maltreatment 2007. Retrieved from http://www.acf.hhs.gov/programs/cb/pubs/cm07/summary.htm

USA Today. (2003, August 28). *Girls get extra help while boys get Ritalin.* Retrieved from http://www.usatoday.com/news/opinion/editorials/2003-08-28-our-view_x.htm

USA Today. (2004, December 2). *Pay closer attention: Boys are struggling* [Editorial]. Retrieved from http://www.usatoday.com/news/opinion/2004-12-02-boys-girls-academics_x.htm

van Wormer, K. (2006). *Introduction to social welfare and social work: The U.S. in global perspective.* Belmont, CA: Brooks/Cole.

van Wormer, K. (2010). *Working with female offenders: A gender sensitive approach.* Hoboken, NJ: Wiley & Sons.

van Wormer, K., & Davis, D. R. (2008). *Addiction treatment: A strengths perspective*. Belmont, CA: Brooks/Cole.

van Wormer, K. & Roberts, A.R. (2009). *Death by domestic violence: Preventing the murders and the murder-suicides*. Westport, CT: Praeger.

van Wormer, K., Wells, J., & Boes, M. (2000). *Social work with lesbians, gays, and bisexuals: A strengths approach*. Boston: Allyn & Bacon.

Von Drehle, C. (2007, August 6). The boys are all right. *Time*, pp.38–47.

Ward, N. & Redd, A. (2007). An examination of the self-esteem and self-identity of biracial children in the United States. In L. See (Ed.), *Human behavior in the social environment from an African American perspective* (pp. 183–206). New York: Haworth.

Waterloo-Cedar Falls Courier (2009, April 26). Call the Courier, p. B1.

Werner, E.E. & Smith, R.S. (1992). *Overcoming the odds: High-risk children form birth to adulthood*. Ithaca, NY: Cornell University Press.

Wiehe, V. (2002). *What parents need to know about sibling abuse: Breaking the cycle*. Bel Air, CA: Bonneville Books.

Wilber, K. (1980). *The Atman project: A transparent view of human development*. Wheaton, IL: Quest.

Wilber, K. (1996). *A brief history of everything*. Boston: Shambala.

Winik, L. W. (2005, January 16). "We need to pay more attention to boys." Interview with Laura Bush. *Parade*, pp. 4–6.

Winner, E. (1998). Uncommon talents: Gifted children, prodigies, and savants. *Scientific American*, 9(4), 32–37.

Younger, M., & Warrington, M. (2006). Would Harry and Hermione have done better in single-sex classes? A review of single-sex teaching in coeducational secondary schools in the United Kingdom. *American Educational Research Journal*, 43,(4), 579–620.

Zastrow, C., & Kirst-Ashman, K. K. (2010). *Understanding human behavior and the social environment* (8th ed.). Belmont, CA: Brooks/Cole.

Early Adulthood Through Middle Age

When I was a child, I spake as a child,
I understood as a child, I thought as a child,
but when I became a man I put away
childish things.

—1 CORINTHIANS 13:11

5

The key developmental stages are not limited to those that take place during childhood and adolescence. Throughout adult life, too, change rather than stability is characteristic. And even beyond the key moments defined by classic life-span theory, many crucial passages occur as turning points in our lives.

Change can often be startling, sending our lives into a tailspin until reality sets in. With transition frequently comes a new identity, as in realizations such as "I am married," "I am a mother," "My kids have grown up," and "We are middle aged." With time, people come to adjust their self-image to match life's passages. Change may come early or late and be sudden and catastrophic or slow and drawn out, but it is one's awareness of a fundamental change that is the important factor (Greer, 1993). Speaking of a woman's life, Germaine Greer, author of *The Change: Women, Aging, and the Menopause*, states that these changes (from child to woman to lover to wife to mother to grandmother) are signaled by contrasting body status (from skinny to curvaceous or pregnant or obese and back again). Greer singles out three stages of womanhood: defloration, childbirth, and menopause. The last one, she argues, is exceeded in importance only by the grand climacteric of dying. But, of course, menopause is the subject of her book.

Erikson (1950/1963) identifies the major achievements of adult life in terms of intimacy in young adulthood, generativity during the middle years, and ego integrity during the final stage of life. Because of their descriptive power, I have chosen these three major themes for the structural divisions of this chapter. Erikson calls these achievements the psychosocial strengths of the adult life portion of the life cycle. Each strength is related to the others, and each exists in some form before its critical time normally arrives. Erikson actually says little about these adult stages inasmuch as the focus of *Childhood and Society* is childhood. His life-span framework is useful nevertheless.

Beginning with young adulthood, that period of experimentation and self-discovery, our discussion takes us into the world of career preparation and romance. We will address questions such as how is youth being prolonged today?

Why do people fall in love? What personality characteristics relate to intimacy or to its opposite, isolation?

Middle age is the next passage, one for which we often are not very well prepared. A discrepancy between people's self-image and their role expectations may occur. Successful navigation of this stage results in what Erikson calls *generativity*, the finding of meaning in life through our contributions to the lives of others. Failure to do so, on the other hand, leads to what Erikson sees as stagnation in feeling and purpose, which can lead to an old age of despair. This chapter, in short, has as its goal a delineation of the major tasks and risk factors of the Eriksonian stages of the adult life span excepting the final stage. The case study on life "in the middle of a middle" provides moving narratives to supplement the text.

Intimacy Versus Isolation

College is traditionally a time of transition and questioning of the beliefs of one's upbringing. Education, which means a "leading out," broadens students' horizons and encourages critical thinking about practically everything. That is the academic side of college; on the social side, there is exposure to unchaperoned parties, binge drinking, and unbridled sexuality, for which the student may not be prepared. For devoutly religious youth of whatever spiritual faith, the task of fitting in and resisting temptation on a secular campus can be formidable. Faith tends to lapse. A national study conducted by the University of California–Los Angeles found that, of more than 100,000 first-year students surveyed, 79 percent professed a belief in God, 69 percent said they pray, 57 percent have questioned their faith, and 26 percent called themselves born-again Christians (Astin, 2004).

During the college period and later is a time when many young people question their particular religious affiliation and, especially if they are dating someone of another faith, consider switching denominations or religions. Loveland (2003) studied the phenomenon of what he terms *religious mobility*. He found in his analysis of extensive religious survey data that people who were brought up in a religious faith that was distinctively different from the mainstream were apt to maintain their faith, and that geographical mobility was a significant factor in switching, as was the absence of close ties with one's relatives. Moving from one mainline denomination was common, although Catholics and Episcopalians were less likely than others to switch. To African Americans, cultural solidarity and community ties were key factors cited in the literature for stability in their affiliations, while for whites status seeking and political concerns were factors in leading them to consider a change.

Compared to previous generations of college students, there is now both more binge drinking, coupled with more unplanned sexual activity in some circles, and a higher degree of religiosity in others. An earlier study on a smaller sample of third-year college students found that the undergraduates' sense of well-being declined during the college years, with 40 percent of students reporting that they felt overwhelmed by the junior year, while more than half frequently felt depressed (Astin, 2004). Students who do not participate in religious activities are more than twice as likely to report poor mental health or depression as those who do participate, according to the survey results. For all students, especially those who reside on campus, the challenge of dealing with the new freedoms can be enormous (Figure 5.1).

A second major challenge relates to the present-day economic realities of trying to obtain an increasingly costly college education while working at part-time or full-time jobs that do not pay well. The result is an unprecedented reliance on high-interest loans that leave students with heavy indebtedness after graduation. Even after college, the jobs that recent graduates get often do not provide enough to pay off the loans and the credit card debt (Figure 5.2).

This economic burden placed on today's youth may be associated with certain changes in lifestyle. Consider, for example, this headline: "The gap between adolescence and adulthood gets longer" (Jayson, 2004). The reference

Figure 5.1. College is a time of socializing and of decision making that may have lasting consequences. Photo by Rupert van Wormer.

is to the claim that today's youth or "twenty-somethings" are going to school longer, delaying marriage and children, and often moving back home in unprecedented numbers. The facts give some credence to the claim that, for those aged 25, only 40 percent are married, and increasing numbers are living at home (Boonstra, 2009). Between 2000 and 2005 there was a continuing increase in single young adults aged 20 to 29 living at home (Rosenfeld, 2009). Still, if we go back to 1950, we would find that 89 percent were living at home, around twice as many as in 2005. One would expect more recent data forthcoming from the 2010 Census that, reflecting the 2008 to 2009 recession, would show an increased doubling up of families for savings on rent and house payments. According to the National Low Income Housing Coalition (2009), recent housing survey data confirm that related to the economic crash, rising unemployment rates, and number of foreclosed houses, many families indeed are sharing their living space.

For economic reasons, single young adults and families are often moving into their parents' homes, and older parents are sometimes moving in with their grown children.

There is some indication that the incurable optimism for which Americans are well noted, is on the decline. Described graphically by Ehrenreich (2009) in her bestseller *Brightsided: How the Relentless Promotion of Positive Thinking Has Undermined America*, this characteristic is shown to be problematic. It was such inveterate optimism, as Ehrenreich indicates, that caused much of the banking crisis in the first place. The subsequent economic crash related to mass indebtedness that followed is taking a special toll on young people ready to start their careers as well as on middle aged people who are being laid off. *Business Week* writer Peter Coy (2009), refers to today's young people as "the lost generation." The damage to them of failure to get on the first rung of the career ladder may be deep and long lasting. The statistics are not promising: In the United States

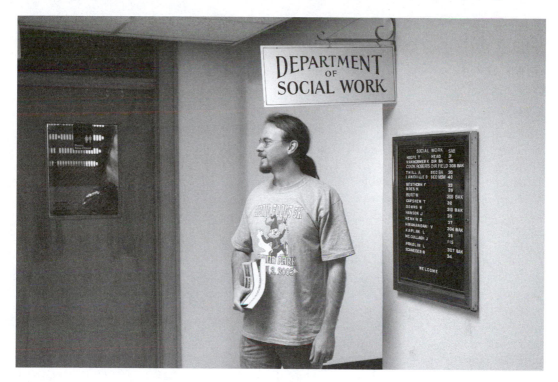

Figure 5.2. The choice of a college major or graduate program is an important step on the pathway to the future. Photo by Rupert van Wormer.

in 2009, the unemployment rate for 16- to 24-year-olds looking for work climbed to more than 18 percent. Summer jobs are now scarce. Because in a recession, companies fear taking risks and opening up new jobs, and settled employees are unable to move (or afford to retire), high school and college graduates, much less dropouts, find little opportunity. In Japan, where talk of a lost generation has been around for years, the young people themselves are often blamed for not working or job hopping. In Spain, youth unemployment has reached 39 percent; in France, 24 percent; and in Britain, 19 percent. One possible model that other countries might adopt is, as Coy suggests, Germany's apprenticeship program, which guides students from school into skilled industrial jobs. A society that does not find a way to move young people into the workforce is a society headed for serious problems ahead.

Developmental psychologists, such as Arnett (2004) and others who were writing before the economic crash, were already suggesting that a prolonged transition stage between adolescence and adulthood had become the norm. Robbins and Wilner (2001), for example, popularized the phrase "quarterlife crisis" to refer to what they saw as a prolonged period of exploration and uncertainty in young adulthood. More recently, Michael Kimmel (2008) referred to the expanded period of adolescent irresponsibility in *Guyland: The Perilous World Where Boys Become Men*. The members of this younger generation, according to these writers, are delaying the traditional rites of passage into adulthood, a trend that involves exploring relationship options before making a commitment, extensive travel, and hopping from job to job. The job hopping is in part a reflection of the sense of changing labor relations in today's global economy, an age of increasing mobility, higher standards of worker productivity, dependence on technology rather than people, and a breakdown in the sense of loyalty between employer and employee. The mostly white middle-class guys interviewed by Kimmel are depicted as subscribing to the Guy Code, where sexual conquests, locker-room jock behavior, and compulsive playing of video games define a newly extended adolescence of these 16- to 26-year-olds.

In their book on sex and love, Firestone, Firestone, and Catlett (2008) take a look at the reluctance by many young adults to make a commitment to one person. Fear of intimacy, according to the authors, often stems from voices that people carry around in their minds that stem from hurtful childhood experiences. This accounts, argue Firestone et al., for the high rate of sexual dissatisfaction that they have found to exist in many American marriages. As well, given the high divorce rate (around 44 percent of first marriages) and as young people see the wreckage from failed marriages all around them, young people become reluctant to enter into a committed relationship. Yet this fear of intimacy is probably nothing new. Erikson reported something similar in his day, the phenomenon of "fear of ego loss" in entering an intimate relationship.

Intimacy is the key defining element in Erikson's sixth of the eight "stages of man." Emerging from the search for identity of the teen years, the youth who is 20–25 years old "is eager and willing to infuse his identity with that of others" (1950/1963, p. 263). Sharing and sacrifice are integral to the completion of this task. These qualities figure prominently in the development of close family affiliations, sexual unions, and close friendships. The avoidance of such closeness may lead to a deep sense of isolation and consequent self-absorption.

Gilligan (1982, 2003) pondered the differences in the challenges facing young women at this stage and those facing young men. The threat to their identities and lifestyle is considerably less because girls and women probably have already learned to accomplish the fusion of identity and intimacy in the context of previous relationships.

Let us depart from the theoretical formulations to see what empirically based research has to say about the habits of intimacy. From the biological standpoint, the work of evolutionary psychologist David Buss (2008) is insightful. Based on his study of 10,000 people in 37 different cultures around the world, Buss concluded that, in mating behavior, the role of genetics is pronounced. Men tend to select mates based on characteristics that relate to fertility, a fact that Buss attributes to evolutionary programming—the survival of the fittest and most fertile. Both men and women, in fact, can be seen to enhance those qualities that are evolutionarily attractive in order to be chosen as mates. Men tend to exhibit behavior, for instance, that conveys strength and prowess and to display symbols of success. Women, in contrast, draw attention to their youth and health. A popular article bears out Buss's observations on love. According to the article, men have been drawn to certain-size hips and waists for more than 20,000 years—a curvaceous figure associated with childbearing—while women seem drawn to tall men (Thornhill & Palmer, 2001). Within these standards of attraction, of course, there is tremendous variation.

Mating rituals, such as flirting, for example, follow patterns that cross cultures and countries, based on gestures that seem anchored deep within our evolutionary history (Thornhill & Palmer, 2001). In *Love Signals: A Practical Field Guide to the Body Language of Courtship*, anthropologist David Givens (2005) documents courting rituals that he observed during hundreds of hours spent in bars, at parties, in elevators, on subways, and in the workplace. Givens's work is instructive. In courtship, the percentage of emotional communication that is nonverbal exceeds 99 percent. And since this language is universal, some people fall in love and marry without being able to speak one another's language.

In evolutionary terms, love's silent language predates speech by millions of years. For example, a palm-up gesture is friendly, whereas palm-down cues are not. Givens decodes the body to reveal silent messages given by facial expressions, shoulders, neck, arms, waist, calves, ankles, feet, and toes. According to him, courtship moves slowly through five distinct phases: attracting attention, recognition phase, conversation phase, touching phase, and making love. The first nonverbal message is "Notice me." A second message in this early stage is "I am harmless."

The gestures and postures that humans use to establish trust are shared with other mammals, particularly primates. For humans, being playful and childish are ways that potential lovers communicate harmlessness. Courtship gestures are regulated by the primitive part of the brain and not the prefrontal cortex. From the evolutionary perspective, in short, courtship is less about romance than about genetic fitness. For a man, what matters is sexual access to a wide variety of women, while for a woman, it is having a man who will be a good provider, not abandon her, and devote resources to his family (Buss, 2008).

Gender roles are bound to shift along with the changes in the global and U.S. economy. I am speaking here of the increasing numbers of women in the workforce. As women become less economically dependent on men, the median age of first marriage, for one thing, has risen from 21 in 1972 to 26 today. For another, births to unmarried mothers have increased from 12 percent in 1972 to 39 percent today. Ford and Van Dyk (2009) have provided a digest of statistics from official government reports to show the advance of women over time. Women now make 80 cents on the dollar for one dollar that men earn; the comparable figure in 1972 was 58 cents. Also we learn that over three times as many women are physicians today, and over ten times as many women are lawyers since the impact of the feminist movement was just beginning to make real inroads in the society in 1972.

Economists Stevenson and Wolfers (2009) similarly document women's advances but also with regard to their reported level of life satisfaction. Their results are made clear in the article's title—"The Paradox of Declining Female Happiness." Based on an analysis of data from recent surveys on happiness worldwide, the authors found that overall, women's subjective sense of well-being, or their level of happiness, has declined over the past three decades while men's has increased. For African American women, however, the pattern has reversed. The best interpretation of these findings from the survey data is that white women's expectations have increased more than the opportunities, whereas, perhaps African American women

had lower expectations in recent years and have been pleasantly surprised by the opportunities. Black men, significantly, showed a decline in their level of happiness over the period that was studied. This fact parallels the gap in educational attainment between African American females and males, which strongly favors the females.

For information on Latino gender issues relevant to work and education, we turn to date from the Pew Hispanic Center presented by Fry (2009). Young Latino adults in the United States are more likely to be in school or the workforce now than their counterparts were in previous generations. The increase in their attachment to school or the work world (which includes employment by the military) has been driven mainly by the changes in the endeavors of young Hispanic females. In 1970, only one-third of young female Hispanics were enrolled in school or college; by 2007, nearly half of young female Hispanics were pursuing schooling. The high birth rate in this age group accounts for part of the fact that so many are still neglecting their education; other reasons are not clear. We can speculate that the high rates of poverty in Latino families and the strong family ties mean that many of the young women are working or caring for relatives' children to help the family out. In the absence of employment activities, drug and alcohol involvement are other possibilities for school dropout.

The experience of love may best be viewed as a biological drive that comprises lust, romantic love, and attachment (Fisher, 2006). Romantic love has the function of narrowing our focus and energy to just one person. The neurochemical dopamine provides romantic love's intoxicating properties; dopamine levels surge when a person is confronted with the unknown. In the initial phase of romantic love, Fisher states, we may become so exhilarated that we lose the desire to eat or sleep. Such exhilaration does not last, however. The novelty wears off. This is where the drive of attachment comes in to sustain a relationship. Doing exciting things together can help keep the juices flowing. A key element in a couple's compatibility is the degree to which the two nervous systems are aligned in pursuing novel experiences. The level of sensation seeking is an important factor in relationships: the high-sensation seekers and the lows have different brain responses to activity. High-sensation seekers, due to reduced dopamine levels, get bored easily and feel impelled to explore unknown territory. Differences here clearly can drive a wedge between partners.

Biology alone does not determine sexual attraction. Pines (2000), an Israeli psychologist, has studied romantic codes cross-culturally. What she found was that early experiences are powerful. In her surveys of American and Israeli couples, for example, women described their partners as being similar to their fathers; men described their partners as similar to their mothers. In all likelihood, conditioning based on personal experience is a factor in sexual attraction as well.

Attachment is fueled by three things: proximity, stress, and sex. Hazan, Campa, and Gur-Yaish (2006) share their insights into the role of each of these key ingredients. The presence of people day after day promotes the release of oxytocin, a hormone that stimulates a desire for continued close contact. Hence, the familiar scenario that takes place at the office, where people spend so much time together. Pines (2000), in her book on falling in love, similarly emphasizes the role of proximity in attachment.

Less obviously but just as saliently is the reality that attachment sometimes emerges out of stress. Cindy Hazan (interviewed by Flora, 2004) provides the example of the original "Stockholm syndrome," when Swedish women who were held for six days in a bank vault became enamored of their captors. (I would add to this the phenomenon of "abstinence romance," in which men and women in treatment for substance abuse and at Alcoholics Anonymous meetings fall in love with each other—with disastrous consequences.) Hazan explains this as the tendency to seek comfort in times of stress. (Another example might be the temptation for widows, widowers, and newly divorced people to seek love on the rebound, even from unlikely sources. The politician John Edwards got into trouble for having a reckless affair [see Elizabeth Edwards, 2009, *Resilience*],

a behavior that may have been related to his wife's diagnosis with life-threatening cancer.)

The third and perhaps best facilitator of attachment is repeated sexual contact. The success of arranged marriages such as in India demonstrates this phenomenon. Inspired by input from students who discussed these sources of attachment, I have come up with another catalyst for bonding—the sharing of bad or addictive habits. Smoking together outside of workplaces and the university reportedly leads to a sense of bonding, even though the behavior that brings them together is rarely discussed. One student shared that when she quit smoking, the friendships dissolved and she had no interest in the smokers anymore; another said all her friends were those she smoked with, and they were very close knit. Students who did not smoke said they often feel left out; one young woman stated that she started smoking in order to have some close friendships. A fourth category for attachment can therefore be bad or addictive habits; this would include heavy drinking as well as taking the smoke breaks.

Personality Factors Related to Intimacy

Let's first take a closer look at personality factors that have been shown to relate to intimacy and which also have a strong bearing on human behavior at the young adult stage of life. Although most of the studies on personal happiness in relationships look at married couples, we can probably assume that the personality traits—ability to share, good humor, and so on—that make for compatibility allow for enduring friendships and family bonds as well. The most relevant research that I have found pertains to similarities in personality styles and values, complementary qualities, and general, all-round happiness.

Do we select romantic partners who are similar or opposite in personality traits? And does partner similarity lead to happiness? Although different studies disagree on some of the details, all of the studies I consulted seem to agree that, in a relationship, personality is important. Moreover, in a long-term relationship, as people get to really know each other,

Figure 5.3. The marriage ceremony marks a rite of passage in a tradition that goes back thousands of years. Photo by Rupert van Wormer.

there are surprises. Given the complexities of the human mind and heterogeneity in cultural expression in everything from love to table manners, the wonder is that so many pairs of human beings can work out their differences, at all. (see Figure 5.3 for a classic wedding scene.)

In her study on the shaping of personality, Ackerman (2004) explains our one-of-a-kind personalities in evolutionary terms. As the human brain grew larger and the human pelvis became smaller so that people could walk upright, women had to give birth to infants with an unfinished brain. Thus, although family genes play a considerable role, humans evolve different personalities because the brain does so much of its growing outside the womb. Family and experience are different for every child. The infant and mother or other caretakers mutually reinforce each other's behaviors. At the same time, life's unique experiences, including joys and traumas, alter brain development and personality in various ways. Flexibility was and still is our genius, says Ackerman. Some of us court danger, crave it, and thrive on it, whereas others fare well in calm, even dull, surroundings.

A mismatch between people in the degree of sensation seeking, as we have seen, is associated with conflict in a relationship because they have different brain responses to activity. Zuckerman and Kuhlman (2000) have specialized in studying sensation seeking. Smoking, drinking, sex, and drugs, they suggest, work in tandem with each other. So, unfortunately, may drinking and reckless driving, they point out. We are not talking about a behavior; we are talking about personality, they contend. Sensation seeking has been shown to be highly genetic in identical twin studies, but the greatest risk takers are young males, a fact reflected in their high rates of binge drinking, car accidents, and attraction to the military. Too much risk taking leads to an early death and too little to stagnation.

Luo and Klohnen (2005) examined personality characteristics of 291 newlyweds who participated in the Iowa Marital Assessment Project; the focus was on mate selection. The results showed that couples were highly similar with regard to attitudes and values but not on personality traits such as extroversion. Yet when marital quality was assessed, the key factor in happiness as a couple was personality similarity rather than attitudes.

The most popular form for personality (self-insight psychological) testing is the Myers-Briggs Type Indicator. A visit to http://www.google.com or other search engines reveals hundreds of thousands of listings on the use of this instrument. The theory that informs the Myers-Briggs Type Indicator derives from Jung's typology of extroverts and introverts subdivided into thinking versus feeling and sensing versus intuition (McIntire & Miller, 2007).

So what does the personality test consist of? The Myers-Briggs inventory uses four different subscales, each of which purports to measure different personality tendencies. The extroversion-introversion (E-I) subscale distinguishes between people who are sociable and outgoing and those who are more inward-looking. Sensing-intuition (S-N) refers to ways of perceiving reality and sorts people according to their attention to practical realities as opposed to relying on their imagination. Thinking-feeling (T-F) shows the difference between relying on logic versus intuition when making decisions. Finally, judging-perceiving (J-P) refers to one's tendency to analyze and categorize one's experiences, as opposed to responding spontaneously. Sixteen different types emerge from the combination of these four pairs of traits. All of those categories, except for the latter (J-P), were devised from Jung's typology of basic personality types. Myers and Briggs added this final dichotomy to assess the way in which the individual deals with the outer world (Goldenberg & Goldenberg, 2002). Extensive research on the instrument supports its reliability and validity (Moore, Dettlaff, & Dietz, 2004).

A typical score is ISFJ, which stands for introverted (versus extroverted), sensing (versus intuitive), feeling (versus thinking), and judging (versus perceiving). A social worker might be of this type. Sensing types focus on realities and may often neglect possibilities and ideas. In a social work department (or any office), different types are needed—some to attend to details and keep others on track,

others to use their imagination to develop new programming and find ways for clients to perhaps circumvent overly restrictive rules. Judging versus perceiving refers to those who seek structure in contrast to those who are more flexible. Personality differences here, although invaluable in providing diversity to a team or couple, do invite conflict.

The Myers-Briggs inventory is advertised in the form of a questionnaire taken by at least a million people per year. It is widely used in business and government as a basis of employee selection; career counselors also use it to help select careers that match applicants' interests and personality (McIntire & Miller, 2007). One would suspect that firms seeking technologically gifted types would choose ESTPs and that companies looking for salespeople would prefer ESFPs.

Moore et al. (2004) make the case for social work education to use the Myers-Briggs categories to help students select field placements suitable to their personality types. Extroverts can be expected to be more comfortable working in groups. Intuitively oriented people prefer to focus on the big picture to the neglect of details. Sensing students tend to be conventional and may need help in learning to think "outside the box" when working with clients.

Not surprisingly, in today's efficiency-conscious world, this personality indicator is widely used in matching couples on the basis of their score compatibility. It is easy to imagine the discomfort a recently married introvert might experience with extroverted in-laws who speak loudly and perhaps carry on simultaneous conversations or an extrovert coming into a quiet, introverted family whose members politely wait for others to speak (example provided by Goldenberg & Goldenberg, 2002). Introverted families often seem rather dull and even cold to more demonstrative types. Conversely, the latter families might seem loud and rude to more reserved people.

Online compatibility assessments provide testing of couples for compatibility. For a fee a recommendation is made. According to MatchIndex, for example, couples should agree on 62 percent or more of the personal characteristics for a favorable prognosis for a long-term relationship. Lange, Renfrow, and Bruckner (2004) criticize the claims that online matching enterprises (for example, www. perfectmatch.com) make that they can successfully match people for compatibility. Such online dating services match people on the basis of similarity. Yet we know, as the authors suggest, that individuals are often happy when their partner's personality characteristics complement their own. Missing from the popular Internet claims is the recognition that people with somewhat different traits can help balance each other. Two dreamers may have difficulties making realistic or prompt decisions, for instance, and concrete thinkers might receive enlightenment from people of a more intuitive or abstract mind. Besides, it might be better to have a little conflict in a relationship than for the mother and father to be carbon copies when it comes to raising children. One parent may be stronger on the feeling side, and the other on the take-no-nonsense side, and it may all balance out for the children.

One rather worrisome situation arises in people with personality disorders. Here, psychologist Florence Kaslow (interviewed by Murray, 2004) has a significant observation to share. In her 30-plus years of practice, what Kaslow saw over and over again was astonishing: couples in treatment whose personality disorders were direct opposites. "They seem to have a fatal attraction for each other," says Kaslow, "in that their personality patterns are complementary and reciprocal—which is one reason why, if they get divorced, they are likely to be attracted over and over to someone similar to their former partner." Most often these attractions are between people diagnosed with antisocial, borderline, or narcissistic diagnoses and those labeled with dependent or obsessive-compulsive personality disorders. Couples treatment is indicated so that the partners can stop feeding into each other's pathologies.

Self-doubt and low self-esteem are qualities in a relationship that can lead to the illusion of rejection and therefore be devastating. If people think negatively about themselves, they are inclined to assume their partner thinks negatively about them, too. The personality trait of being positive, even to the extent of having

positive illusions about another person, draws people together, whereas the opposite tendency (even if more realistic) causes people to distance themselves from each other. This insight comes from research on marital communication conducted by Murray, Holmes, and Griffin (2003). The recommendation here is for someone with low self-esteem to choose a person with a lot of self-confidence as a partner; this may help the insecure person to develop a better self-image.

In contemplating intimacy and relationships, it is worthwhile to consider that we are all a little bit crazy. Instead of the widespread use of personality disorder classifications, Paul (2004) recommends a more organic sense of the way individuals fit into their world. Central to this perspective, which represents, according to Paul, a paradigm shift, is a distinction between personality styles and personality disorders. The style may be quirky but not sufficiently extreme to be a full-blown diagnosable disorder. A personality disorder is dysfunctional, often resulting in the loss of relationships and jobs. Context is everything; behavior that creates havoc in one situation may be celebrated in another, so it is crucial to find the right partner or niche. Unfortunately, some negative patterns may reward the individual at a cost to society. Consider how often those with antisocial personality traits excel in business or politics. Consider also how the very trait of obsessiveness, which may create difficulties in the family, can be an advantage to a secretary or a copy editor, who must be attentive to every little detail. Think about how the trait of hyperactivity enables a person to work long hours, take risks, and do great things (as well as occasional foolish things). That personality disorders once had their uses may explain why they are so prevalent today (Paul, 2004).

A nationwide survey by the National Institutes of Health (2004) puts the number of people with a personality disorder at 15 percent, or about one in six. At 8 percent, obsessive-compulsive disorder is the most common; paranoid personality disorder occurs in 4.4 percent; and antisocial disorder, 3.6 percent. A mere 0.5 percent were diagnosed with dependent personality disorder (in which people seem to be unable to function on their own or to look out for their own interests). Risk factors for personality disorders included being Native American or African American, being a young adult, having low socioeconomic status, and being divorced, separated, widowed, never married, or male (for antisocial personality disorder).

Sexuality: Heterosexuality

Sex is one of the great mysteries of life; it defies our many attempts to explain the hold it has on people and their imaginations. Sexual fantasy alone can overwhelm one's feelings, occupy one's thoughts, and sometimes lead to behavioral compulsions. In sexual fantasies and real encounters, society and culture, biology, family, peers, the past, and identity all come calling (Saleebey, 2001). Scientific research on human sexuality has tended to focus on sexual behaviors and not the link to evolutionary biology. Alfred Kinsey, recently celebrated in the Hollywood film *Kinsey* (starring Liam Neeson), revolutionized our thinking about sex when he probed the sexual behavior of the human species. His methodology skewed his findings, however; data were derived from exhaustive interviews with 18,000 volunteers, many from nonrepresentative groups such as prostitutes and prisoners (Kinsey, Pomeroy, & Martin, 1948; Kinsey and the staff of the Institute for Sexual Research, 1953), vividly described aspects of human sexual behavior—heterosexual and homosexual—that were little known at the time.

Today Kinsey's legacy lives on in the work of scientists who study the most intimate acts of human beings, only now the studies are done in the laboratory using instruments to measure brain activation and sexual arousal. At Emory University, for example, Hamann, Herman, Nolan, and Waller (2004) found that the amygdala, the part of the brain that processes emotion, is more strongly activated in men than in women in response to erotic photographs.

Sexual activity, as was discussed in the previous chapter, begins younger than teens have the maturity to deal with the psychological and biological consequences. While rates of sexual activity among U.S. teens are fairly comparable to those in Western Europe, the incidence of adolescent pregnancy, childbearing, and contraction of venereal disease far exceeds that found in most other industrialized nations (Eckholm, 2009). Variables associated with having earlier sexual intercourse include alcohol use, high stress levels, having mothers who were sexually active at an early age, poverty, and a low grade point average (Zastrow & Kirst-Ashman, 2010). The fact that after a long decline in the numbers of very young mothers giving birth, the teenage pregnancy rate has risen significantly brings the abstinence-only sex education public school programming into question (Lewin, 2010).

Guidelines from the American Psychological Association (2007) for psychological practice with women and girls summarize some of the pressures that young women face in our society, namely, the presentation of women and girls as sexual objects, which begins in childhood and extends through adulthood, is promulgated by the media and emphasizes the role of appearance and beauty. At the same time, the internalization of stereotypes about their abilities and social roles has been shown to deflate their self-confidence and curb their aspirations for success. An earlier study by the American Association of University Women Educational Foundation (1999) has revealed that, besides the obvious issues with school and grades, girls most often struggle with social concerns such as knowing how to say yes to a relationship without having to assent to sex. Sex was rated as the most important issue confronting high school girls.

Sex education in the United States is extremely limited compared to countries in Western Europe. This fact is associated with a high rate of unplanned teen births and also with abortion. The abortion rate in the United States is nearly seven times that in the Netherlands, three times that in France, and nearly eight times the rate in Germany (Feijoo, 2001). According to the Centers for Disease Control and Prevention (CDC) (2008) report on abortion surveillance, the rate of abortions for women in the United States has stayed about the same in recent years. Most abortions are performed during the first few months of pregnancy and on women in their early 20s. In France over 80 percent of abortions are non-surgical through use of the drug mifepristine, while in the United States this drug is only used in about one-fifth of very early abortions (Guttmacher Institute, 2009).

The relatively high rate of abortion by U.S. youths is indicative of a lack of sex education (apart from abstinence-only promotions), lack of easy access to family planning services, and negative attitudes toward teenage sexuality. In connection with the total abstinence movement, many girls throughout the United States have been taking virginity pledges. In a report on research conducted at the Johns Hopkins School of Public Health, Rosenbaum (2009) found that 82 percent of those who had taken a pledge had retracted their promises, and there was no significant difference in the proportion of conservative students who had taken the pledge and those who had not done so in terms of sexual activity, including oral sex and vaginal intercourse, the age at which they first had sex, or the number of sexual partners. One difference was that students who took the pledge were less likely than others to use contraceptives. An earlier study of students' sexual behavior similarly revealed that the rate of contraction of sexually transmitted diseases in students who previously took an abstinence pledge is fairly high (Connolly, 2005). The reason appears to be lack of condom use in girls who had negative attitudes about premarital sex compared to practices by more sexually sophisticated girls who did not plan to remain virgins.

At all ages, women are more likely than men to contract genital herpes, chlamydia, or gonorrhea (Guttmacher Institute, 2002). Adolescents and youths in their 20s are the most susceptible, however. The racial/ethnic breakdown for the contraction of HIV/AIDS is 51 percent African American, 18 percent Hispanic American, 29 percent white, and one percent Asian. For black women, the most common means of contraction of the AIDS virus was through sexual contact and intravenous drug use; for black men, it was homosexual contact and intravenous drug use. The CDC (2008) suggests that, to successfully combat the spread of sexually transmitted diseases, educators, health care professionals, and policy makers need to refocus their efforts to recruit leaders from minority communities and bolster prevention services so that they are widely available to all.

An ABC News (2004) nationwide survey that was conducted by professional pollsters has revealed some fascinating information about men and women. The random-sample telephone poll of 1,501 adults paints a portrait of sex that is decidedly more frank and personal than the results of other polls. For example:

- Women report an average of 6 sex partners in their life histories, compared to 20 for men.
- Of the men polled, 70 percent think about sex every day, compared to 34 percent of women.
- Of the men polled, 35 percent approve of casual sex without a relationship, compared to 15 percent of women.
- Of the women polled, 51 percent prefer to have sex with the lights off, compared to 27 percent of men.
- Women are about half as likely as men to say they have had sex in a threesome, unexpectedly with someone new, or at work.
- Men are more than three times as likely as women to have looked at a sexually explicit website.

A fairly recent trend that Shirley Glass (Glass & Staeheli, 2004) refers to in *Not "Just Friends"* as the "shrinking double standard" relates to a reduction in casual sex by males. Increasingly, writes Glass, men as well as women are forming deep emotional attachments before their relationship becomes sexual rather than afterward. The work relationship often involves people at their best, unencumbered by the problems of everyday life. The new liaisons are threatening to marriage in that they involve the whole person, not just part of a person.

Sexuality: Gay and Lesbian

The pioneering studies of Kinsey and the Institute for Sex Research were among the first to call attention to the frequency of homosexual activity in American society. Kinsey's contribution was in showing that sexuality occurs on a continuum, with total heterosexual or homosexual conduct at each end and a wide range of bisexual conduct in between. In his interviews, around 5 percent of men and women said they were exclusively homosexual throughout their adult lives (Kinsey, 1948, 1953). Basically, gays and lesbians are sexually aroused by members of their own sex but not by members of the opposite sex, and bisexuals feel an attraction to both, not necessarily simultaneously, though.

Many people wonder what gay and lesbian people do sexually, given the seeming anatomical complications. As Zastrow and Kirst-Ashman (2010) indicate, the physiological responses of gays and lesbians are the same as those of heterosexuals. Their sexual activities consist of hugging, kissing, touching, fondling of the genitals, oral sex, and anal sex in men. Two differences between heterosexuality and homosexuality are that gays and lesbians tend to be more open to new techniques, and they are less goal oriented. Lesbians spend a lot of time kissing, holding, and caressing each other before any genital touching occurs. Most gays and lesbians, like heterosexuals, seek stability in relationships, and the emotional aspects of sexual bonding are strong (see Figure 5.4).

Healthy Love Relationships

As the young adult develops the ability to be intimate with others, love emerges as a by-product. Often one person in the relationship feels more emotional contentment, even dependency, than the other. The other person may lack the ability to bond or may be putting that emotional energy elsewhere—into a relationship with a person or an activity such as drinking or gambling. Generally speaking, in a couple relationship, the one who loves less has the power and can dominate the other person. This is not as simple as it seems, however. In an abusive relationship, the abuser is often the one who is emotionally out of control and may resent the emotional dependency and strike out.

Healthy love is nonobsessive, defined eloquently in the Bible as kind and nonenvious.

It "is not easily provoked, thinketh no evil, rejoiceth not in iniquity" (1 Corinthians 13:4–6). Healthy love is above all reciprocal; it is about both giving and receiving. The deepest love between partners depends on shared emotional resonance in the features of life they both consider the most significant. These partners often find common ground in their shared experiences of life. Carol Gilligan (2003), in her book on love, *The Birth of Pleasure*, says it best: "Maybe love is like rain. Sometimes gentle, sometimes torrential, flooding, eroding, quiet, steady, filling the earth, collecting in hidden springs. When it rains, when we love, new life grows" (p. 3).

What does it take to make love work? Researchers on happiness and compatibility of married and cohabiting couples devised a battery of questions that were administered to more than 20,000 couples nationwide to help provide an answer (Olson et al., 2009). Their Enrich Couple Inventory revealed key ingredients that make for a happy relationship even long after the initial chemistry has faded. The following qualities emerged as strongly associated with relationship contentment: Each partner is a good listener and is understanding of the other's feelings; the couple strikes a balance in leisure time spent together and apart; each partner is easy to talk to and is creative and agreeable in handling differences, including finances; and they are sexually compatible.

"Thus," writes Gilligan (2003), "a relationship fired by erotic passion leads in the end to a relationship between a man and a woman that uproots its history in patriarchy, becoming no longer uneven" (p. 233). The laws of relationships that Gilligan came up with in her work with couples in crisis are these: "I will never lie to you, I will never leave you, I will never try to possess you" (p. 233). Wouldn't such a pledge define any close relationship—mother and daughter, lesbian and gay, best friends?

Obsessive Love

Irrational love is celebrated in our culture; it is a theme that has inspired literature since time

Figure 5.4. Gay and lesbian couples lining up in Portland, Oregon to exchange marriage vows, a right granted to them only briefly by public officials in 2004. Photo by Rupert van Wormer.

immemorial and of course in modern times has provided the story line for many a tear-jerking movie. The mature person can enjoy the romanticism in our culture, cry at the opera, and disregard the implications of the message at the same time. Thus, romantic fantasy can be an exciting and healthy escape from the drudgery and monotony of everyday life.

A positive concept of love is offered in Erich Fromm's classic *Art of Loving* (1956). True love is realized only when each person is a whole and secure person. Mature love welcomes growth in the partner.

The immature, compulsive life of love is described by Leonard (1990) in her portrait of the great Russian novelist Feodor Dostoyevsky, who writes about his own private hell. In *The Gambler*, the leading character, Alexi, goes beyond all limits. An addict in love as in gambling, he pledges to risk his life for his love—he will dive headfirst from a cliff if she gives the word. According to Leonard, "Alexi is an extremist; he plays the game of all or nothing" (p. 39).

Hartman and Laird (1983) contrast the differentiated (independent) person from the one who is fused in a relationship that knows no boundaries:

The well-differentiated person is provident, flexible, thoughtful, and autonomous in the face of considerable stress, while the less differentiated, more fused person is often trapped in a world of feeling, buffeted about by emotionality, disinclined to providence, inclined to rigidity, and susceptible to dysfunction when confronted with stress. . . . The differentiated person, interestingly, is the one who can risk genuine emotional closeness without undue anxiety. (p. 78)

Leonard (1990) likens romanticism to alcoholism; both are attempts at escape and a longing to forget. While the alcoholic is hooked on a chemical, according to Leonard, the romantic is hooked on a fantasy of love that is projected on some person: "The archetypal figure of the Romantic, the one who wants absolute merger with the loved one, is present when the addict seeks to escape the stresses of the everyday practical world through a drink, a love fantasy, or whatever helps to give the absolute feeling of being at one with the universe" (p. 67). Based on her neurological research on the brains of people in love, who had recently been rejected by their lovers, Helen Fisher (2006) found that the part of the brain that was activated when the rejected partner viewed a photo of the loved one is the same lower area of the brain that is activated by addicts in addiction research.

In my work with alcoholic families (Family Week in an inpatient setting), I found it helpful to include a session on love relationships. I found that, as clients and their family members prepared to resume their relationships with their loved ones, they were often on a disaster course because their expectations of the relationship were too high. In my mind's eye is a picture of two cartoon characters—lovers in a boat—about to enter the Tunnel of Love. Ahead, out of the lovers' view, is a steep waterfall. This is my image of the posttreatment alcoholic couple blindly heading down life's course. Whether addicted to alcohol or to a newfound relationship, they are equally at risk for destructiveness. Many a recovering client has abruptly returned to the treatment center after a "slip" or relapse precipitated by a disastrous, all-consuming love affair, often with a fellow recovering alcoholic client.

Irrational thought patterns that are culturally ingrained but that most mature people would not take literally are as follows:

> ❥ I cannot live without you.
> ❥ You are the only person for me.
> ❥ I'm never going to get involved with anyone else again.
> ❥ We must agree on everything.
> ❥ We should be happy in each other's exclusive company.
> ❥ Everything that is yours is mine, and everything that is mine is yours.
> ❥ (And among alcoholics) You keep me sober.

The extreme element inherent in this kind of logic corresponds to a certain frantic quality underlying any addiction. The love partner, like the source of any addiction, is used to satisfy a deep, aching need for some sort of escapism. And although the initial euphoria may be long departed, the dependency prevails. According to psychologist Brenda Schaeffer (2009), signs of romance addiction are obsession, intense jealousy, possessiveness, depression and melancholy, and dependence on intoxicating feelings. While a certain amount of jealousy may accompany a normal relationship, addictive love can escalate to verbal and physical abuse as a punishment for imagined wavering. The addictive foundations of an unhealthy, dependency relationship come to the fore when a breakup is threatened. Emotions at this point can easily get out of hand.

As we learned in Chapter 3, research shows that, while some abusive men are cold and unfeeling, others, who are dangerous in another way, are out of control with their emotions. Their obsessions, if unrequited, can lead to stalking and in extreme cases homicide. Two famous examples are the case of O. J. Simpson and Jean Harris. Simpson, the football legend, was acquitted of the murder of ex-wife Nicole, whom he had battered for years, but he was later found responsible in a civil case. In 1981 Jean Harris was convicted of the murder of her former lover, Scarsdale diet doctor Herman Tarnower, who had started going out with someone else. (Harris served her prison term and has worked for prison reform.)

Judging by newspaper accounts, a rash of murder-suicides has swept the nation. This is a topic that speaks volumes about how far out of hand love obsession can get. Love, hate, and a loaded gun can bring grief to many.

Suicide-Murder

The nightmare of volunteers and staff at women's shelters is that a battering, love-struck spouse or boyfriend will seek revenge and kill her and even himself if the woman makes a successful break. According to a report by the Violence Policy Center (VPC, 2008), at least 554 people died in murder-suicides over the 6-month period of the study. Because the perpetrators often killed more than one victim, this amounted to 320 homicides and 234 suicides. Of the 234 suicides (done by the perpetrators), 218 were male; 45 of the homicide victims were children. The average is between one and two murder-suicide deaths each day. Florida and Texas had the most at 24 each. In Florida, many of the acts were committed by elderly caregivers, most of whom were men who were overwhelmed by their inability to care for their disabled wives. The elderly suicide-murders are different from the ones we are concerned with here. Yet, like the acts committed by their younger counterparts, they are acts driven by suicide first and foremost.

Suicide-murder is the term I use to refer to the phenomenon whereby estranged partners kill the focus of their obsessive passion in which suicide appears to be the predominant motive. Psychologically, these suicidal murderers have little regard for the lives of other people. Characteristically, suicidal murderers are antisocial and have a history of family violence. The term *suicide-murder* was originally coined to refer to the 20 case histories I documented of murderers, many of whom had landed on death row, all of whom had killed people for the sole purpose of getting themselves executed (van Wormer & Roberts, 2009).

Suicide bombers such as Arab terrorists, in contrast, are clearly of the murder-suicide variety. Here the impetus to kill and destroy takes precedence over the suicidal impulse. In his examination of the mind of the terrorist, Jerrod Post (2002), a psychiatry professor, presented the results of his 35 interviews with incarcerated terrorists in Israeli prisons. These people were suicide bombers whose missions failed because of unforeseen circumstances. In their interviews they consistently spoke of the need to defend "the land of their honor," their willingness to become martyrs to a sacrificial act, and the fact that these were not acts of suicide but actions performed in service to Allah.

Are these men sick or weak emotionally? "No, such men are fortified by religion," suggests Post. As a result of ruthless indoctrination, these men have subordinated their own individuality to the group. Individuals who are emotionally disturbed are expelled from these quasi-military units as a security risk. Unlike solitary terrorists in the United States, the members of these terrorist cells tend to have close relationships with their families, who support them in their efforts to kill Zionist or American enemies.

Common to murder-suicide and suicide-murder is the sense of male rage and the passion of youth. Access to weapons is another commonality. The VPC stresses comprehensive health and safety regulation of the gun industry so that firearms are not brought into the home. Access to a gun allows a perpetrator to quickly kill a great number of victims, as in school shootings and other cases involving multiple deaths. Gun retailers who knowingly provide firearms to domestic abusers should risk loss of their licenses to sell weapons (VPC, 2008).

Perhaps related to the economic crisis, a rash of murder-suicides has swept the nation since 2008, the most shocking of which have been whole family murder-suicides. The majority of the perpetrators have been men, and a certain pattern has emerged. My survey of the media reports on these familicides reveals that these incidents tend to occur in clusters; and the fathers tended to be in a grave economic or legal crisis. Some of the fathers evidently, in a twisted sense of concern about their families and severely depressed, decided to wipe them all out. Others facing a breakup of the marriage were seeking total destruction and revenge (see Brown, 2009). This type of situation is usually preceded by a history of domestic abuse. Let us now take a closer look at statistics on intimate partner violence.

The Bureau of Justice Statistics (BJS, 2009) has gathered statistical data from a variety of governmental sources, including the FBI's Uniform Crime Reports and Supplementary Homicide Reports. Excerpts from the report "Female Victims of Violence" are presented below in Table 5.1.

To provide a human touch to these data, read the following personal narrative that was produced as part of a consciousness-raising exercise that uses "feeling words" to describe a situation of oppression that was eye-opening in some way.

Table 5.1   Female Victims of Violence

Nonfatal Intimate Partner Violence

❯ Intimate partner violence includes victimization committed by spouses or ex-spouses, boyfriends or girlfriends, and ex-boyfriends or ex-girlfriends.

❯ In 2008 females age 12 or older experienced about 552,000 nonfatal violent victimizations (rape/sexual assault, robbery, or aggravated or simple assault) by an intimate partner (a current or former spouse, boyfriend, or girlfriend).

❯ In the same year, men experienced 101,000 nonfatal violent victimizations by an intimate partner.

❯ The rate of intimate partner victimizations for females was 4.3 victimizations per 1,000 females age 12 or older. The equivalent rate of intimate partner violence against males was 0.8 victimizations per 1,000 males age 12 or older.

❯ Females age 18 or older experienced higher rates of intimate partner violence than females age 12 to 17 (4.5 per 1,000 compared to 1.7 per 1,000, respectively).

❯ Black females historically have experienced intimate partner violence at rates higher than white females.

❯ In 2008, Hispanic and non-Hispanic females experienced intimate partner violence at about the same rates (4.1 per 1,000 females age 12 or older versus 4.3 per 1,000, respectively).

❯ In 2008, 72 percent of the intimate partner violence against males and 49 percent of the intimate partner violence against females was reported to police.

❯ About 99 percent of the intimate partner violence against females in 2008 was committed by male offenders. About 83 percent of the intimate partner violence against males was committed by female offenders in 2008.

Trends in Nonfatal Intimate Partner Violence

❯ Intimate partner violence against both males and females declined at a similar rate between 1993 and 2008.

❯ The rate of intimate partner violence against females declined 53 percent between 1993 and 2008. Against males, the rate declined 54 percent.

Fatal Intimate Partner Violence

❯ In 2007 intimate partners committed 14 percent of all homicides in the United States. The total estimated number of intimate partner homicide victims in 2007 was 2,340, including 1,640 females and 700 males.

❯ Females made up 70 percent of victims killed by an intimate partner in 2007, a proportion that has changed very little since 1993.

❯ Females were killed by intimate partners at twice the rate of males.

❯ In 2007 black female victims of intimate partner homicide were twice as likely as white female homicide victims to be killed by a spouse.

❯ Black females were four times more likely than white females to be murdered by a boyfriend or girlfriend.

Trends in Fatal Intimate Partner Violence

❯ Homicide victims killed by an intimate partner declined from an estimated 3,300 in 1993 to an estimated 2,340 in 2007.

❯ Between 1993 and 2007, female victims killed by an intimate partner declined from 2,200 to 1,640 victims, and male intimate partner homicide victims declined from 1,100 to 700 victims.

❯ The rate of intimate partner homicides of males decreased.

❯ The number of black female homicide victims killed by intimate partners fell 39 percent between 1993 and 2007. The number of white female homicide victims killed by intimate partners fell 21 percent.

Source: Bureau of Justice Statistics (2009, September). *Female Victims of Violence*. Washington, DC: U.S. Department of Justice. Retrieved from http://www.ojp.usdoj.gov/bjs/pub/pdf/fvv.pdf

Consciousness-Raising Exercise: Spousal Abuse

I *heard* him cussing at me and the thud of my body against the cement, over and over.

I *saw* craziness in his eyes, red and wide with anger.

I *smelled* beer on his breath mixed with exhaust from the car.

I *tasted* salt from my tears mixed with blood from my lips.

I *felt* fear and pain as he kept throwing me down on the cement. Each time I got up he would throw me down again.

This to me was abuse and oppression. Having my own voice and my own opinions and thoughts would enrage him. The more I stood up for myself, the more he would abuse me. I realized how badly he wanted to control every part of my being, and, if I allowed it, I would cease to exist.

I determined to stop the cycle to protect myself and my son.

(Printed with the permission of Chérilyn Glann, MSW.)

The most consistently observed predictors for the commission of intimate partner violence as revealed in the literature include violence in the family of origin; behavioral deficits; certain and multiple psychiatric diagnoses; personality disorders; substance abuse; anger; and low self-esteem (van Wormer & Roberts, 2009). Some of the vulnerability factors that help predict who will be victimized by such violence are substance abuse; pregnancy; economic dependency (emotional or through fear); low self-esteem; age difference between the partners; and violence in the family of origin.

Leaving an abusive relationship is problematic for a number of reasons, one of which

Figure 5.5. The Tombstone Project. Each October, which is domestic violence awareness month, the Seeds of Hope honors 50 of the victims of domestic homicide in this tombstone display at the First Presbyterian Church in Cedar Falls, Iowa. Each tombstone lists the woman's age and the date of her murder. Photo by Robert van Wormer.

is the risk of future violence and even death (see van Wormer & Roberts, 2009). (See Figure 5.5 for a memorial for women who were killed by their partners or husbands.) In her analysis of in-depth interviews with mothers in a women's shelter, Moe (2009) described the struggles that women faced—financially, emotionally, and socially (family pressures) in getting away. Finding housing, employment, and child care were other barriers that emerged in the interviews. Protection of their children was often a deciding factor in a woman's decision to break off from the relationship.

Rape

A factor that poses a risk to intimacy, both in destroying an ongoing relationship (for example, in marital rape) and, through trauma, in inhibiting one's ability to trust and bond sexually due to the legacy of the past, is the experience of the ultimate form of sexual abuse—rape. There are many different kinds of rape—rape as an instrument of war, as a ritual of male group bonding (gang rape), as a part of drunken debauchery, and as an act of rage and a means of exerting dominance. Rape, according to the dictionary definition, is "(a) the act of forcing a woman or girl to have sexual intercourse against her will; (b) sexual sodomy" (*Oxford Modern English Dictionary*, 1996). There are "small rapes" everywhere—the verbal sexual violations that afflict young women, acts that generally go under the heading "sexual harassment" or, in Norwegian, "sexpress." The following anonymously contributed consciousness-raising narrative captures the essence of such violation in a nutshell.

Consciousness Raising Against Oppression: Sexism

I heard: Their voices saying things to me, calling me honey and baby and why don't you stop and talk to us and aren't you a pretty thing.

I saw: The group of men standing on the sidewalk. Of course, there had been many groups of men and they all seemed to blend into each other. They seemed confident and happy, not angry at all. The believed they had the right to treat me or any

other woman who passed by them this way. They felt there was nothing wrong with it, it was harmless fun.

I smelled: The car exhaust from passing automobiles, the garbage in the nearby can, and the mix of food coming from the restaurants.

I tasted: My own fear in my mouth though it became difficult to swallow.

I felt: The tension in my body caused by my anger and fear, my heart beating faster, and my temperature rising. The need to put on a good face and ignore them. I wondered should I cross the street or pass by them, which would call more attention to me. Whatever I did, I had to pretend it did not matter and never show my feelings. I had to look impassive.

This to me was: The commonplace, everyday experience of so many women living in cities. It was oppression built into routine because it happened so often. I just snapped into the mode of how I had to appear, as if I did not care at all, as if they were not getting to me. Of course, this did not make them stop but I had to look as if the power was on my side and not on their side.

This to me was: Part of what drove me to become a feminist, to believe in other women, to feel we could make a difference, to try and change our world for the better.

(Anonymous, printed with permission.)

From the Centers for Disease Control and Prevention (CDC, 2004b) sexual violence fact sheet we learn that, since only 16 percent of women who are raped report the crime to the police, we must rely on survey data for results. According to victim surveys, one in six women over the age of 33 in the United States has experienced attempted or completed rape; between one in four and one in five college women have had this experience. Stranger rape is rare, constituting only 22 percent of the total. More than half of all sexual violations of females occur before the girls are 12 years of age. Another finding of interest in these data is the fact that approximately one-third of all rape victims have psychological symptoms that continue for 3 months or more.

Gang rape, fraternity rape, prison homosexual assault, some aspects of date and marital rape, and the sexual brutality that is inevitable in slavery and war all involve the targeting of women (or women substitutes) as fair game. All are violations that carry a certain legitimacy within the larger society or within various subgroups in the society. All are violations that say more about domination and control than about sex.

Reports from the military hotline in Kuwait indicate that in a 6-month period 83 sexual assault incidents were reported from women serving in Iraq and Kuwait (Douglas & Gibbs, 2004). Many took place on unlighted walks to latrines. Between 2002 and 2004, there were 2,100 reported sexual assaults in the U.S. military. These reports are interesting in that the reason often given for keeping women out of combat is their vulnerability to rape by the enemy, yet they are similarly victimized by their fellow soldiers. In *The Lonely Soldier: The Private War of Women Serving in Iraq*, based on 40 in-depth interviews with women who served, female veterans recount their stories of sexual harassment and assault by their male counterparts. The author, Helen Benedict (2009), estimates that at least one-third of women who served in Iraq have been sexually assaulted. The book's title refers to the isolation women feel when in combat and subject to victimization by their fellow soldiers. If they report the harassment, they are more isolated still.

Using the college scene as one example, sociologists Schwartz and DeKeseredy (1997) proved what they termed the "hypererotic subculture," in which all-male alliances can reduce sexual intercourse to a violent power game. Their book *Sexual Assault on the College Campus* illuminates the pivotal role of male peer support in legitimizing the abuse of women. Frat house conformity combines with peer pressure to score and abuse alcohol ("Party till you puke" drinking by both males and females creates a climate for aggressive sex). A rape-prevention education and counselor on three different college campuses states that even after 15 years, she has seen no reduction in rape cases (Marine, 2004).

In a research study from Glasgow, Scotland, which has generated worldwide attention, one in five boys and young men thought that forcing one's wife to have sex would be acceptable. One in ten said he would rape a woman if no one would find out. One-fourth of the boys believed it is justifiable to hit a woman if

she "had slept with" someone else. One-third of all girls surveyed thought forcing a woman to have sex was acceptable in some circumstances (Blackstock, 1999).

In *The Macho Paradox*, Jackson Katz (2006) cofounder of the Mentors in Violence Prevention program reveals the connection between sports hero idolatry in suburbia and sexual violence against women. He cites one case of a degrading sexual assault of a retarded young woman by a group of popular high school athletes. When they are accused of rape, the boys become warrior heroes as the town rallies to their defense. The brain-damaged victim was blamed for her role in bringing shame to the town.

We are, as Jackson Katz indicates, a rape-supportive culture. Young men are the worst offenders, depersonalizing women by reducing them to their body parts and engaging in extreme sexist humor, such as drinking from a "boob mug." Victim blaming is a pattern that is disproportionately associated with the crime of rape. Women in one college laboratory situation who accepted the belief that "this is a just world" were shown to blame the rape victims in a date scenario they read (Murray, Spadafore, & McIntosh, 2005). Katz suggests that reasons for the victim blaming that takes place regarding college student victims of date rape stems from denial of the seriousness of these offenses, confusion about what constitutes rape, loyalty to our brothers and friends who do not meet the stereotypical profile of the rapist, and buying into sexism. In surveys around one in 12 college men admit they have engaged in coercive sex. These are the "undetected rapists" as so labeled by David Lisak (2009). When Katz lectures before skeptical audiences on rape, he generally uses statistics from official sources rather than from women's organizations to defuse criticism, and he reads out headlines from local news sources on particular cases of rape and domestic homicide to bring the statistics to life. His mentoring program, which operates on college campuses nationwide, organizes campus leaders, such as athletes, fraternity members, and members of student government, to become coaches to boys and men to teach them to resist sexism in schools and on the college campus. As Katz (2009) stated recently before a large student

Figure 5.6. Jackson Katz addressing a student audience. An enthusiastic largely male student audience who were recruited from the athletic department and other majors on campus listen attentively to Dr. Katz describe the male mentoring program. Photo by Robert van Wormer.

audience at the University of Northern Iowa, "Girls are taught risk prevention, such as, 'watch your drink' but this is not prevention (see Figure 5.6). True prevention means getting at the root cause; for that we have to look to men and boys, about how men and boys are socialized. The bystander program teaches men how to intervene, to challenge other men on sexism. We focus on women as bystanders as well, not as victims."

The most extreme form of sexual victimization is gang rape. This topic was dealt with with much sensitivity in the 1988 Hollywood movie *The Accused*. Gang rape is portrayed in graphic detail in this film. The victim, portrayed by Jodie Foster, meets her fate while drinking at a bar. The original case on which the movie was based involved a working-class Portuguese woman from New Bedford, Massachusetts, who brought criminal charges against Portuguese

onlookers who cheered as she was raped. In her heroic fight for justice, the survivor emerges as a victor, and the prosecutor learns something about courage and determination. Sadly, however, when the movie was first shown, some young men in the audience hooted and cheered at the rape scene (Faludi, 1991). And the real victim, on whom *The Accused* was based, was condemned by her community for the negative attention brought to it by the crime. She died of alcoholism several years later.

The least serious form of rape, to judge by its rate of prosecution, is the sexual assault of a woman by her husband. Marital rape, if not socially sanctioned, has been socially tolerated for a long time (Burke, 2007). Because of the equation of rape with sex in the public mind, rather than with violence, marital rape has been generally regarded as an oxymoron. The controversy that arose in Oregon over its first marital rape case was cause for a great deal of mass media coverage and public ridicule of the young woman, who demanded justice. By 1993, however, all 50 states and Canada had laws classifying marital rape as a crime.

The literature on marital rape is sparse, perhaps because of reluctance to speak out on this subject or denial of its harm. Using data from a nationally representative telephone survey, Basile (2002) examined attitudes toward wife rape on a number of dimensions. She found that older nonwhite respondents were less likely to believe that wife rape occurs or that forced sex in marriage constitutes rape. Males and the more educated respondents were less likely to believe it occurs frequently. Among women, nonvictims of forced sex were significantly less likely than victims to believe that wife rape occurs. Auster and Leone (2001) studied the impact of college sorority and fraternity membership on attitudes toward marital rape. Their findings show a striking male/female difference and indicate that fraternity men of the groups studied (college men, college women, fraternities, sororities) were the least favorable toward legislation against marital rape. The authors attribute the findings to the tight male bonding that takes place in fraternity life.

Using a college-based sample, Krebs, Linquist, Warner, Fisher, and Martin (2007) found that 13.7 percent of undergraduate women had been victims of at least one completed sexual assault since entering college—4.7 percent were victims of physically forced sexual assault, and around 9 percent were sexually assaulted when they were incapacitated after consuming drugs and/or alcohol.

In a physically abusive marriage, sexual abuse is common. The National Coalition Against Domestic Violence (2007) reports that between one-third and one-half of all battered women are raped by their partners at least once during their relationship. Any situation in which force is used to obtain participation in unwanted, unsafe, or degrading sexual activity constitutes sexual abuse. Wife-rape victims rarely report the crime to authorities; if they do, their suffering is rarely validated. Yet as long as they stay in the relationship, rape is a constant for them. Whereas a woman who is raped by a stranger has to live with the bad memory, a woman who is raped by her husband has to live with the rapist. And whom can she tell? Bergen's (1998) research on victims at a shelter revealed four basic motives for wife rape: a belief in entitlement to sex; sexual jealousy; rape as punishment; and rape as a form of control. Sometimes a wife who is being beaten will use sex as a strategy for ending the physical violence (researcher William Downs, personal communication, February 5, 2000).

Date or acquaintance rape is rarely reported as well. Because the victim is typically dating someone of her choice and likely drinking (probably encouraged to drink), she often blames herself. Later, her reactions, dulled by the alcohol and the fact that she may not have bruises or other signs of resistance, may differ from those of the typical rape victim. Howey (2001), a survivor of date rape, tells how she first laughed off the incident and refused to use the "R word" because she was not traumatized. Finally, however, she came to a realization: "Most of all, I call it *rape* because I want to make it clear that what happened to me wasn't a bad date. It was a violation by a man who committed a crime. Though it's taken me a long time to believe this, I finally have come to the conclusion that my reaction to the crime is inconsequential. It's what he did that matters" (p. 89).

Fear of sexual violence is a defining characteristic of the male prison experience in the United States (O'Donnell, 2004). Estimates range from 12,000 (in government reports) to 240,000 (by Human Rights Watch) prison rapes per year (Lehrer, 2003). Prison rape is performed by men out of lust and a desire to dominate (Burke, 2007). This description also pertains to male rape of females. The horror of prison rape is one of the ugliest facts of prison life. Young men, especially young white males who are not streetwise, are especially vulnerable to individual and gang sexual violence behind bars. While the prison rapist commands respect as masculinized by the rape, the victim who is anally attacked is "feminized." The punk is considered a female substitute and, once initiated to prison life in this fashion, is a target for further sexual abuse by the population from then on. In the age of AIDS, such prison assault often amounts to a slow-motion death sentence (Lehrer, 2003). In recognition of the gravity of the situation, Congress passed the Prison Rape Elimination Act of 2003, which former President Bush signed into law (Carrell, 2003).

Gay males and lesbians are also subjected to sexual victimization (Burke, 2007). As with males, it is sometimes a case of date rape or of youths getting involved in a high-risk situation with an older person. With lesbians it might be a violent encounter with one or more males, a hate crime "to teach her a lesson" (Rivers & D'Augelli, 2001). Many college campuses have rape crisis centers to deal with sexual assault and rape for female and male students and therapists at counseling centers who are gay and lesbian affirming and can provide needed help.

Generativity Versus Stagnation

With the passage of the baby-boom generation from adulthood into middle age, there is a need for an expanded knowledge of this often-neglected stage of life. Gail Sheehy (2004), still well known for her work *Passages*, published in the 1980s, has refined and elaborated on her insights into what she calls the "second adulthood," an opportunity for reassessment and change of course that comes in one's 40s and 50s.

Erikson (1950/1963) states that he could have made this stage of middle adulthood the central emphasis of his book had he not been focusing his attention on children. What he does say (which is brief but significant) is that not only is the younger generation dependent on the older one but also that the older generation depends on the young. Mature people need to be needed, and this is what generativity is all about. The task of middle age is to leave something behind for future generations and begin to resolve ambivalent feelings about mortality.

Freud believed that personality change past the age of 50 was virtually impossible. His reasoning was that because the libido was reduced

past this age, the will to change is no longer there (Biggs, 2005). Biggs contrasts his view on aging to that of Erikson, whose eight-stage psychosocial model maintains that change occurs throughout life. And to Sheehy middle age offers an opportunity to do what you have always wanted to do, a period of relative freedom.

My favorite take on middle age is a funny but sobering reading by Ogden Rogers that was presented at a Midwestern social work conference:

In the Middle of a Middle

In the midlife, midweek, mid-April, in Midwestern America, I found myself thinking about middles. As a student, practitioner, and teacher of social work, I've approached the old practice chestnut "beginnings, middles, and ends" what must now be thousands of times. In my life, I've paid so much attention to the outer boundaries so far. So much time and attention to the beginnings and ends. Lately, I think, the middles are what it's all about.

When I was a younger man, a student, I never really understood anything about middles. It was almost always about beginnings. The beginnings of relationships. The start of semesters. Initial interviews. The shock of the new in a world that was just unfolding for me. Much of my experience was always coming into confrontation with novelty: ideas, people, places, lovers, enemies. Life looms more vivid when things first begin. Images and smells and textures are charged with the inflorescence of anxiety. Buildings are taller. Eyes are more telling. The first views of things hold their shape in the mind's eye so much differently than when they appear in the later days of day-to-day.

When one is young much of life is spent in anticipation. So much of what seems to be reality is really the conjuring of what will be. The moments of the present are filled with the expectation of the future . . . sometimes only minutes away. Indeed, preparation is such a way of being that when things are in the swim of the moment one can get surprised: "Oh, *this* is what it was supposed to be like!"

Social work was new to me, and my youthfulness charged hope into all the new endeavors I began. Sometimes there was no loss in this. I had clients who needed the extreme of my youth, and they borrowed hope upon the morrow. But there was tragedy when there was mismatch. When I had a vision that exceeded my client's strengths, we needed to agree upon failures that could be measured as success. It is here that one gets into middles.

Likewise "ends." Despite protestations of other writers, the ends of things get more attention than denial would suspect. Death abounds in the world, and there is more than enough awareness. We crane our necks at the highway wreck. The thoughts made taboo are the most important of all. They touch us frequently like a tooth that will not be forgotten. We tongue-touch that tooth frequently, and, knowing each time it will hurt, we persist. A woman I knew well in my days in the Emergency Room died a number of times, only to be revived to the ICU. One day she came in from the back of the ambulance, and it appeared she would finally pass on through. She looked at me and looked beyond me and smiled and gave me a wise gift. With a laugh she squeezed my hand and said, "I've left some laundry in the dryer!" and squeezed no more. At the end she told me about the middles.

Beginnings are filled with anticipation and hope. Ends are filled with the acuity of pain or joy—and memory. Middles on the other hand are duller places. Calms in the ocean of stormy relationships and problems. There is a familiarity. Difference is less acute and therefore requires less agility. There is no motion on the water. What was once a stab is now the blunted ache, perhaps getting better, perhaps not. Vague silences that once provoked questions now become moments which just lack meaning and are filled with muddled confusions: Which way now? Forward or back? Fewer declarative sentences:

Middles of things are never well announced. They tend to sneak up in, well, the middle of things. You note, for instance, one day that there is a certain boredom in the room. There is a vague indifference that has entered into a glance up at the wall. These are the hallmarks of a middle. The signs that an end is in the offing.

The writers of the Functional School of social work always had a great influence on me. I think it was Ruth Smalley who made me dread middles. I had come to expect them as confusing and sullen times. I think Jessie Taft once wrote that there weren't really any middles, just the beginnings, beginnings of ends, and ends. Yet in describing the

beginning of ends she found herself in the middle. Middles have a sense . . . The client and I both bored with each other. The hope and expectations of goals that once seemed bright, yet small and far away, were now possibly quite closer but somewhat dimmed in their development, greyer and perhaps dented. Compromises are what really come to be. They are never sought in the beginnings of things. They are the bread of what really happens.

There are times now, in these days of the "end of history," that I see it seems to be difficult for people to tolerate the middle of things. It seems funny that, in the dissolution of the Cold War, when the world was divided into the two past worlds of East and West, people now seem more polar to me than ever before. So much of public discussion has become extreme to me; "fundamental" and "radical" seem unresolvable at the very outset of a discussion. It seems as if the desire to search for the middle is lost. Here is a place for the social worker. We are the people of the middles.

Social work is always about being in the middle. We are always guests in another's house. The social worker in the hospital is the one who knows most about outside of the hospital. The health care worker on the street is the person who knows most about getting into the hospital. The genius of the social worker is that she or he is always between things. The master of the art appreciates the middle of life and demands a profession that dances down a razor's edge. The worker who has "it" is the worker who knows that between me and thee is a fuzzy ball, a place where you invite "the other" to come in. To place hands upon the keys and make music. A place to cast off the cast iron of failed expectation and work in the muddle of the moment. What will emerge is anyone's guess, but at least it is not the pain of what once was.

If life were black and white we'd have no need of social work. Police and lawyers and judges and accountants could solve most of what could be called conflict. But life is really quite a grey thing, and despite the anger that wells in those who rail against grey, who want things black and white, they know they need us.

No one wants to see a child endangered. And no one wants to see a family's privacy breached. Yet, it is the privacy of the family that allows the craziness we need to stay sane in the public. But the craziness can go too far, and private matters become public concerns. We need nonjudgmental judges. We need those who can enter respectfully into the middle of our private muddles and echo the outside of our public rule. We need those who can understand the craziness that keeps us sane and yet interpret the taboos that glue us together. We need advocates of the infinite diversities individuality provokes . . . and speak it to the Leviathan and make it understand.

I'm always impressed with how many people don't know what social workers do, and therein lies our power. If others cannot define you, you can define yourself. You can be the artist of your own practice with others. You can dwell inside the interstice, you can be in the place that is in between. If you are young and you hear me now, in your future, hear this: The middle is not as dead as it appears. It is the fear of the hand that is not sure that it will strike the key correctly. It is the weary knowledge that work is hard, and yet the work will be done. It is the pain that will subside but not be lost, but will be carried. It is a glance that looks without and within in an instant. If you are old, and you hear me now, you will recognize your past and acknowledge the debt you owe to many you have learned from and celebrate the moments when you know that you were in the middle, you were "in the zone," you had moved the world in just the smallest way. In just a way that looked into you and out of you. In just a way that a hand strikes a chord upon a piano. And in that note, nothing was ever the same.

I don't know how to end this, so I'll just stop in the . . . middle.

(Printed with permission of Ogden Rogers, University of Wisconsin–River Falls, Wisconsin.)

Viewing the developmental course of middle adulthood within a life course framework, we quickly come to recognize the complexity of biological, psychological, social, and spiritual factors during this period.

Biological Aspects of Middle Age

"Not unlike the lonely flower, the midlife individual remains full of life but becomes increasingly aware of the reality of frost" (Reid & Willis, 1999, p. 275). Perhaps it is this reality that gives to this period a special resonance, a mature determination to make the most of what you have, punctuated by an intermittent desire to count your blessings. So even if you have not achieved the great expectations of youth, and even if your children have not turned out exactly the way you expected, the sense of well-being and stability helps make this somewhat curiously the happiest time of life (see Wahl & Kruse, 2005). But before we tread too far into the psychological arena, let us return to the biological processes, beginning with mental health.

Although midlife is generally a time of good health and productive activity, it is also the time of noticeable change in strength and appearance. High school and college reunions often bring about shocking revelations: The beauty queen has a weathered, wrinkled look, and the star athlete is immensely fat; the plump, shy girl is now a poised and confident woman; the freckled, red-headed class clown is now bald; and, even more surprisingly, are the one or two alumni who seem not to have changed at all. Often in observing the changes that have taken place in others, we are made painfully aware of the impact of time on ourselves. (See Figure 5.7 for a float of a high school class reunion—the 40th.)

In midlife, there are few markers of physical change as dramatic as those in childhood or even old age. Individual differences in aging abound. Genetic makeup and lifestyle factors play an important role in whether chronic health problems will emerge and when.

In a joint U.S. and Canadian poll on physical health, 56 percent of those aged 45–64 said they were in very good to excellent health, compared to around 40 percent of those over age 65 (Centers for Disease Control and Prevention, 2004a). Around 10 percent in the age group 45–64 had experienced a major depressive episode. In both countries, those in the lower-income groups were more likely to be in fair or poor health, to smoke, and to be obese.

Health risks for baby boomers include diabetes, osteoporosis, heart disease, and cancer. Many of these scourges could be prevented or postponed by exercising, eating well, and not smoking. Yet about 20 percent of the female baby boomers smoke, around half are overweight (of which one-fourth are obese), and

Figure 5.7. Fortieth high school class reunion. Several of the floats in this annual city parade celebrated class reunions. Interestingly, among the float riders in their 60s, the men's hair had mostly turned gray, while women's hair apparently had not changed color over the years. Photo by Robert van Wormer.

exercise is often sacrificed along with leisure time in the interests of keeping up with the ever-increasing productivity standards and long hours at work. Health-related behavior in youth such as binge drinking, chain smoking, sunbathing, and playing football affect midlife health just as health habits in middle age will have consequences later.

Virtually all of the recent writings on middle age agree that the present generation in this age group is different from the previous one in that they are resisting growing old. They are having children later, using more medications, coloring their hair, and collectively spending a fortune on cosmetic surgery (see Dziegielewski, Heymann, Green, & Gichia, 2002).

Both men and women experience noticeable signs of aging in their 40s and 50s. The skin begins to wrinkle and sag due to a loss of fat and collagen in the underlying tissues. There is

a tendency to gain weight and lose height, muscle strength begins to decrease strikingly by age 45, and there is a progressive loss of bone, especially in women. Gradual hearing loss begins in the 30s and continues progressively, especially for men. With age, the lenses in one's eyes become less flexible and hence causing farsightedness, so reading glasses or bifocals become necessary. What is not necessary is the kind of plastic surgery that 12 million people underwent in 2008. Although related to the recession, there has been a decline in surgical procedures, for example, breast augmentation, nose reshaping, liposuction, and eyelid enhancements, a significant increase in minimally invasive procedures, such as Botox injections, is evident. The average age for these procedures is just over 42 years of age (ScienceDaily, 2009). Television shows such as *Extreme Makeover*, in which subjects undergo as many as six surgeries at a time and seemingly emerge as beautiful people, spur the demand for these kinds of operations.

Menopause is the term most closely associated with middle age, a term traditionally equated with irrational, emotional outbursts in women and midlife crises in men. An alternative view of the female menopause highlights the sense of freedom expressed by many women, as they experience a shift from premenstrual syndrome (PMS) to postmenstrual freedom (PMF; the latter term was coined by Myers [2003]). In a similar vein, Greer's (1993) book on aging describes the new freedom from men's ogling and other unwanted attentions that she experienced while visiting in Sicily. Dressed in mourning clothes for the death of her father in the ancient Sicilian tradition, she was able to enjoy the status of not being a sex object.

Hot flashes, additional weight gain, and vaginal dryness accompany menopause in many cases; in fact, 75 percent of menopausal women experience mild facial flush and perspiration, which are popularly called "hot flashes" or "night sweats" (Dziegielewski et al., 2002). No woman, writes Green, traverses the climacteric without a vivid awareness of change. Neurosis and menopausal troubles are not related, however.

Middle-aged men experience a decrease in sexual functioning and a slowness in arousal due to a gradual decline in their testosterone level. Some men turn to a new, younger partner for stimulation. Overall, for both men and women, a partner of a similar age seems to make acceptance of one another's situations easier (Dziegielewski et al., 2002).

Psychological Aspects of Middle Age

Psychologically, the middle years are a time of contemplation and even regret, regret at tasks left undone and (forgive the rhyme) laurels never won. Sometimes at this stage, after the experience of some sort of shock (for example, a health crisis related to diet or alcoholism), a psychological turning point occurs. (We discussed the dynamics of turning points at the beginning of this book.) In middle age, the

result of the new outlook might be a commitment to a new life role or relationship or a major career change. This transitional experience may involve a change in identity as well, one that is defined by age: "I am more than the son of (daughter of, wife of); I am a person in my own right," "I am a grandmother as well as mother," "I am a mature person, a mentor to the young."

Midlife is the time, note Wahl and Kruse (2005), when one's past is long, and a considerable part of life has materialized. Knowledge about old age is increasing as the time draws closer. The middle-aged person's identity is revealed indirectly in speech patterns, by what these researchers call "linguistic temporal references." By this they mean references to their generation or to how many years they have worked and so on. These are references (for example, to pop stars, actors, films) and use of vocabulary that distinguish themselves from a younger group of listeners. Between professors and their students such reference distinctions are common.

Greg Crosby (1998), who was laid off from his job, wrote the following in the "My Turn" column in *Newsweek:* "Heading toward 50 in a few weeks, I find it very hard to believe that I could actually be thought of as old—even in our youth oriented culture. Yet I sense that, so far, my life has gone by much, much too quickly. Yesterday I was the young, dashing, enthusiastic 'kid' just starting out in the work force. Today I am graying, overweight, suddenly out of a job and coming to terms with an identity crisis." The fate that befell this individual has now become the fate of millions over the past decade, the official unemployment rate hovering around ten percent of the working age population. Nationally, among the major worker groups, the unemployment rates for adult men is 10.0 percent, for adult women, 8.0 percent, whites, 8.8 percent, Asians, 8.4 percent, blacks, 15.8 percent, Hispanics, 12.4 percent, and teenagers, 25.0 percent (U.S. Department of Labor, 2010).

A recent National Bureau of Economic Research working paper reported that job displacement in the United States has led to a 15 to 20% increase in death rates during the following 20 years (Pfeffer, 2010). Loss of a job is associated with a shortened life span because of the resulting personal and financial stress that is associated with substance abuse, domestic violence, and depression. Research shows that people who had no history of violence were six times more likely to exhibit violent behavior after a layoff than similar people who remained employed. In all these ways, company downsizing is bad for families, for individuals, and for the whole society.

Middle aged women are also impacted by economic recession; they suffer both indirectly when the men in their lives lose their jobs and directly when pressures on them to be the breadwinners increase. Women who did not work before may find the job market uninviting when they set out to embark on a career or a career change later in life. In general, however, women in midlife often discover a sense of fulfillment beyond that which they experienced earlier. Many mature women at this time form new connections to others in the community and come to define themselves in new ways that make sense of their experiences (Starks & Hughey, 2003). For women at this stage, there may be a shift in self-identity, one that is due to a sudden thrust into single status or a realization that being single offers benefits related to freedom and that immersion in a partnership may not be "all it is cracked up to be." One woman I know who reached this realization contacted a Peruvian adoption agency, took a leave from her job (in fact two leaves), and, after separate sojourns and considerable expense, adopted two children from Peru. In middle age she knew what was missing from her life and went after it; her goals were different from what they had ever been before.

However, in a social order built around couples and families, singles can feel isolated. Nancy Roberts (2004) shares a view that must be shared by many:

> They say that you get used to it, make it work. Some don't. I live in Kentucky now, and all around me are families, self-contained entire kingdoms shaped by many generations: faithful to their clan,

nice people, but not needing an extra woman around. I am astonished to find myself exiting mid life as a kind of outcast because I am no longer married and never had children of my own. I invite couples over to dinner; they seldom reciprocate—not, I trust, because I am invisible as a social entity. I don't, as they say, take it personally. It's backwash, I think, from our country's worship of self-focused achievement, headlong competition, and newly proclaimed family values. The mermaids sing, but only to each other—and even then only if they aren't too busy. (p. 203)

Subjective well-being is an important issue that relates to psychological functioning during middle age. This is the generativity that Erikson chose for his defining characteristic of this period, a goal the opposite of which is stagnation. In his autobiographical *My Life in the Middle Ages: A Survivor's Tale*, James Atlas (2006) says rather facetiously that this is the best time of one's life: "I spend money with less hesitation . . . I don't care as much what others think of me. . . . I'm just beginning to get the hang of things; how to stand up for myself in arguments; how to dress. . . . how not to lose my temper when a cab-driver takes a wrong turn. . . . above all how to be happy for the simple reason that I'm not dead" (pp. 214–216). This brings us to the study of happiness—what it is and where we can find it.

Happiness

Happiness is a trait that is a blessing in friendship. Like depression, it can be contagious, so people like to be around others who lift their spirits. A plethora of books and articles have recently been published on this personality trait, without which other gifts and attributes—money, possessions, status—are of little consequence. Before examining individual factors in the happiness quotient, let us take a global view.

Drawing on findings from the Stockholm-based World Values Survey and research from the University of Leicester in England,

Mabe (2008) concludes that consistently, Denmark has been found to have the world's happiest people. This finding is attributed to a relaxed attitude toward life and social security. In their analysis of the data from world values surveys, political scientists Inglehart, Foa et al. (2008) attributed the level of happiness in a nation to such factors as economic development of a country, democracy, social tolerance, and gender equality. A striking fact that emerged from their analysis was the stability of the aggregate levels of happiness of nations over time. European nations generally ranked high, and higher than the United States, with the exception of former Communist nations of East Europe. Denmark tops the list of surveyed nations, along with the U.S. territory of Puerto Rico and Colombia. A dozen other countries, including Ireland, Switzerland, the Netherlands, Canada and Sweden also rank above the United States, which maintains about the same relative position as it did in the world values survey of 2000 (ScienceDaily, 2008a). In my personal travels in Denmark and Ireland, I found the friendliness, easy laughter, and hospitality to be beyond all expectations. And visitors to Puerto Rico, a land of sandy beaches, warm climate, close-knit families, and regular celebrations, rave about the joy of life and racial harmony they find there. International surveys show, in fact, that the happiness levels found throughout Latin America are relatively high despite the economic and political instability (ScienceDaily, 2008a).

Now we turn to the study of human contentment at the individual level. For most of its history, psychology has concerned itself with the darker side of human nature—anxiety, depression, trauma. Today psychological and social scientists are looking into the opposite side of the spectrum—what gives us joy in life? How does laughter heal? How can we boost our sense of pleasure? Carol Gilligan's (2003) *The Birth of Pleasure* was discussed earlier. In this company are Seligman's (2004) *Authentic Happiness*; Jamison's (2004) *Exuberance: The Passion for Life*; Layard's (2005) *Happiness: Lessons From a New Science*; Diener and Biswas-Diener's (2008) *Happiness: Unlocking the Mysteries of Psychological Wealth*; and a wealth

of articles in *Psychology Today* and other popular magazines (for example, "Sad Brain, Happy Brain," Miller (2008, *Newsweek*). Begley (2008), however, predicts a backlash against all the happy talk and indicates that research shows that extremely content people are not apt to be the most productive. Nevertheless, a positive-psychology movement has taken off as Americans everywhere seek to boost their happiness quotient.

So what makes us happy? Personal happiness is largely considered to be determined by a combination of genetic predisposition and environmental factors (ScienceDaily, 2008b). Even individuals who are inclined to have a positive outlook on life can lose their sense of joy when interpersonal stress, financial problems, or chronic illness come their way. Lykken (2000), in his reviews of scientific research, concluded that each of us has a happiness set point: No matter what happens in life, we tend to return to our natural set point. This conclusion is based on an examination of studies conducted on identical twins reared apart, which revealed the genetic nature of personality and disposition, as well as the role of experience in making our lives seem worthwhile. Lykken's analysis of the data obtained in the University of Minnesota's twin studies, which compared personality traits in identical and fraternal twins, showed that about 50 percent of one's life satisfaction comes from inborn tendencies. We can affect our overall level of happiness, concludes Lykken, by avoiding giving in to emotions such as fear, anger, and shyness.

Toward the goal of obtaining happiness, Seligman (2004) puts an emphasis on memory as opposed to transient pleasures. Based on his research, Seligman found more components of happiness—pleasure, engagement in activities, and meaning. Of these three sources, the least of these is pleasure. Interestingly, Freud (quoted by Erikson, 1950/1963) did not name sexual pleasure as the key ingredient in human happiness, but as he looked back on his life, he singled out *lieben und arbeiten* (to love and to work). He meant, according to Erikson, a general work and productiveness but not a preoccupation to the exclusion of everything else.

Seligman's search for the definition of happiness prompted him to study nuns—namely, the Sisters of Notre Dame: Of the nuns who had earlier been shown to be the most cheerful, 90 percent were still alive at age 85, compared to 35 percent of the others.

Myths about happiness that are disproved in research and surveys are that happiness is brought about by money, beauty, youth, intelligence (Layard, 2005). In fact, poverty does cause stress and despair, but over the median of income in the United States, more money does not necessarily make for more happiness, as studies of people who have won the lottery consistently show. Beauty on its own does not bring joy (apart from secondary benefits such as relationships), either (Layard, 2005). The problem with youth is the anxiety and negativism that afflict young people. Even intelligence or a college education does not necessarily provide pleasure.

On the plus side, Layard (2005) lists religious faith, leisure time activities, friendship, sense of humor, self-esteem, and volunteering as behaviors that help provide a sense of well-being. Studies confirm that active people are less prone to depression and that physical exercise can work wonders by triggering the release of endorphins in the brain (Biddle, 2001). Psychologists Lyubomirsky, Sheldon, and Schkade (2005) found in their research on happiness that life satisfaction is associated with consciously counting your blessings, acts of altruism, focusing on sensory experiences, learning to forgive, and taking care of the body. Two life events that can knock people below their set point for happiness, according to the research of Diener and Biswas-Diener (2008) are loss of a spouse and loss of a job. The impact of job loss persists even after a return to the work force. Religion, which provides a sense of community and purpose in life, is mentioned throughout the happiness literature as a source of serenity and contentment.

Starks and Hughey (2003) investigated the relationship between spirituality and life satisfaction in African American women at midlife. Religiosity rather than spirituality was found to be correlated with life satisfaction in this sample of 147 respondents. Religious teaching provided strength and resilience in that it was related to socialization in their families and ancestors, especially mothers and grandmothers.

Rick Warren's best-seller *The Purpose-Driven Life* (2002) contends that contentment comes with the recognition that everyone's life, even the least among us, has meaning. The search for meaning often comes to a head during the middle and later stages of life. Before she became the hostage of an armed and dangerous criminal and was catapulted to fame (and even a small fortune), Ashley Smith had quit taking drugs and turned her life around. She had found meaning in Warren's Christian-centered book, which is attuned to the baby boomer generation (Lampman, 2005). Smith's investment in this book paid off. She had gotten to chapter 33 when a desperate, escaped criminal who had already killed three people shoved her into her apartment and took her hostage. In the time they spent together, Smith told him how her husband had been murdered and that her child would be an orphan if he killed her. Then, recognizing the humanness of her captor, a man on the run, Smith told him about the book she was reading and convinced him that his life had purpose, too, even if he had to spend it in prison. The murderer then turned himself in.

A topic related to the search for meaning is forgiveness, which can generally be defined as a letting go of grudges or, more specifically, as accepting an apology by one who has committed a wrong. To Hallowell (2004), author of *Dare to Forgive*, forgiveness is about removing the hold that anger and resentment have so that these emotions do not rule one's life. One way to prepare oneself to forgive is to feel some empathy with the wrongdoer, recognizing that this person is a human being, too. The University of Tennessee's research on the power of forgiveness reveals that, when tested in a laboratory situation, people who score high on a forgiveness measure have lower blood pressure at rest and when angry than do others. Learning to forgive requires facing one's personal pain up front, not denying the emotional response, and putting oneself in the shoes of the wrongdoers to better understand their situation and to build empathy skills (Lawler et al., 2005).

Along with compassion, forgiveness is a teaching that characterizes all of the world's major religions. The standards of religion are high. The Koran, for example, demands that we go beyond the limitations of our egotism, insecurity, and inherited prejudice (Armstrong, 2009). The Jewish tradition of atonement illustrates how important it is to rectify mistakes and wipe the slate clean. Yom Kippur, which is paralleled in Christianity by the notions of grace and forgiveness, has its roots in the story of Moses' receiving God's forgiveness for his people (Ragsdale, 2004).

Middle age is a time when many people return to a religious faith of their youth or join a new religion consistent with their present needs. Much has been written about the ways that religious beliefs reflect one's present mental state and pivotal life experiences (Gotterer, 2001). For example, a child with abusive parents may grow up having a harsh concept of God. By the same token, someone who views God as punitive may have an oppressive conscience. Sometimes, Gotterer suggests, a person's lack of ego strength sets the stage for a religious fervor bordering on fanaticism. In treatment, the social worker needs to help clients retain and build on those aspects of religion that provide solace and a sense of wholeness. The social worker also needs to help the client distinguish between what is helpful and what is harmful.

Finding purpose and meaning in a seemingly bleak situation is one component of spirituality. Human beings, theologian Karen Armstrong (1993) suggests, cannot endure emptiness and desolation; they will fill the vacuum by creating a new focus of meaning. Often the search for meaning leads them in a spiritual direction to a sense of oneness with the universe. Spiritual developments are highly personal and do not require ritualism or recitation of religious creeds. Attending religious services, in contrast, helps meet one's need for companionship and community.

Social Aspects of Middle Age

Friendship comes easily to the young, whether attending school, living in a dorm, traveling together, or dating. Parents of small children often become friends with the parents of their children's playmates. In a neighborhood, children who play outdoors are often a link among families. Sometimes the babysitter is the link. Later, along with the empty nest may come an empty social life.

Family life changes for middle-aged persons as well. A woman's responsibilities as a caretaker for her children may lessen at this stage, while she becomes more of a caretaker for an ailing older family member. This role may provide fulfillment or distress, depending on the circumstances—medical and economic—and the personalities involved. Sibling bonds are very often strengthened as more time is spent in each other's company. Middle age is a time to mend fences as brothers and sisters together face the loss of their parents. Work roles may become more significant at this time—or less so depending on competing demands, personal needs, and opportunity. Many people are at the peak of their earning potential during this period and do not welcome the thought of retirement. Others eagerly look forward to getting out of the rat race and doing the things they were too busy to do before.

Critical to an understanding of midlife development is the degree of predictability of transitions. Anticipated changes such as the departure of grown children can be handled much more easily than sudden occurrences such as divorce or early widowhood. Grandparenthood is often a welcome event, but, even here, timing is important. Becoming a grandparent in one's 30s may not be such a good thing, while parents who are still waiting in their 60s for their children to have children may grow increasingly anxious.

According to a research study of more than 2,000 University of North Carolina alumni, major midlife jolts, especially negative ones, can apparently alter personality qualities long assumed to be stable (Herbst, McCrae, Costa, Feaganes, & Siegler, 2000). Otherwise, no evidence for a midlife crisis was found in either gender. Oddly, divorce in middle age was found to be more empowering for women and harmful for men. Men who divorced in their 40s became more depressed and lowered their achievement goals. Women, however, became more outgoing and resourceful. In general, personality, as measured in personality tests and life event surveys, changed little over time except where setbacks occurred in family, social, and work lives.

Drawing on research on human sexuality, Zastrow and Kirst-Ashman (2010) provide a holistic description of the male climacteric or menopause. A turning point may occur in a middle-aged man's life as he examines who he is and evaluates his accomplishments. This is a time of high risk for divorce and extramarital affairs. Biological changes are characterized by a decrease in physical strength and energy and a reduction in testosterone, which affects sexual functioning. Psychological factors parallel the physiological changes as one fears aging and has to face the stigma of being middle aged in a culture that prizes youth. Men who are insecure are especially susceptible to personal criticism and fear of rejection at this stage of life. Women experience parallel changes regarding sense of loss of attractiveness, sometimes weight gain, and the hormonal changes that accompany menopause.

Because so much that is social about middle age was included both under the personality discussion in the earlier intimacy versus isolation section, no more need be said here. I conclude with a description from David Brooks's (2000) sociological study of the generation he calls "Bobos in paradise." He derives the word *bobo* from a combination of bourgeois and bohemian, a mixture of conventional and rebel attitudes that he relates to the new economic realities facing people who were educated in the 1960s and 1970s. After spending several years abroad, he made the following observation: The bohemian attitudes of the 1960s merged with the bourgeois attitudes of the 1980s yuppies to form a new culture, which is a synthesis of the two: "I found that if you investigated people's attitudes toward sex, morality, leisure time, and work, it was getting harder and harder to separate the antiestablishment renegade from the pro-establishment company man. . . . Defying expectations and maybe logic, people seemed to have combined

the countercultural sixties and the achieving eighties into one social ethos" (p. 10).

My own observation is that people who came of age in the 1960s had children; their children grew up in a time of conformity and consumerism (many thought popularity went with wearing brand-name clothes), so the parents changed along with culture in order to help their children fit in. Somewhere along the way, many lost their idealism and, with it, the anger of youth. See Chapter 6, however, to read about the many innovations and political initiatives of this older generation.

Cultural and Global Perspectives on Adult Life

Across the adult life cycle, a period that encompasses elements such as career, the formation of partnership, the start of a new family, and old age and death, cultural traditions help us cope. In some cases, however, tradition—whether religious or cultural—can hold people back from self-fulfillment and threaten rather than support life. Gender and sexuality are two areas of greatest impact. To the extent that we accept that a good society is a just and compassionate society, customs such as the genital mutilation of young females in various parts of Africa, the stonings and honor killings of women for adultery in parts of the Middle East, the punishment and social isolation of rape victims, and execution as punishment for crime in the United States and China can be considered oppressive. Except for execution, the victims of these forms of subjugation are primarily girls and women.

In many nations (e.g., Colombia, Estonia, Japan, Nigeria, Poland, South Africa, Zambia) chastity is desired, even demanded, by men in a marriage partner (Gardiner & Kosmitzki, 2005). Chastity is considered indispensable in China and crucial in India, Taiwan, and Iran. In the Netherlands, Sweden, and Norway, on the other hand, chastity is considered irrelevant or unimportant. In Norway, in fact, about half of all births are to unwed parents; in Iceland, 62 percent; in France, 41 percent; and in

Ireland and the United States, around 30 percent (Lyall, 2002).

In India, attitudes among the younger generation, especially urban youths, are changing rapidly. The popularity of the Indian Bollywood film industry both echoes and influences these attitudes. Until recently, children grew up to assume the roles defined by their parents and to participate in arranged marriages (Baldauf, 2005). Today, many young people in India pursue careers and make their own love matches.

Mate selection is a process of both cultural similarity and vast differences. In his study of male preference in 37 cultures, Buss (2008) found that men and women everywhere look for mates who are kind, understanding, and healthy. The importance of physical attraction is universal. He found that, across all cultures,

women seek mates who are industrious and have good economic prospects, while men prefer younger women who are physically attractive. (Refer to the beauty pageant in Figure 5.8.)

Laumann et al. (2006) investigated sexual well-being of men and women aged 40 to 80 in 29 countries. They found that male-centered societies emphasized the centrality of men in controlling the sexual conduct of women. The highest degree of reported sexual satisfaction was in Austria, Canada, Sweden, Italy, and the United States, while the lowest levels were found in Korea, Japan, and China, with Japanese women one of the least satisfied of all nationalities. An investigation of sexual education worldwide reveals which countries have conservative and even punitive attitudes about teen sexuality and which do not. Tiefer (2004) points out the striking differences between the

Figure 5.8. Beauty pageant, Cedar Falls, Iowa. These beauty contest winners, including the Iowa Pork Princess and the Black Hawk County Beef Queen, participate in an annual community parade. Their titles reflect the farming culture of this Midwestern state; yet the beauty pageant is a traditional means for young women to receive public recognition for their attractiveness, public speaking ability, grace, and so on. Photo by Robert van Wormer.

early and open sex education provided in Western Europe and that in the United States where the conservative right wing has favored the teaching of sexual abstinence in the schools rather than taken a pragmatic approach and encouraged the use of contraceptives. The difference in policies cross-culturally is reflected in the high rate of unplanned pregnancies among teens in the United States. Muslim nations remain the most traditional societies when it comes to determining the role of women and tolerating divorce for women and homosexuality (Norris & Inglehart, 2004). Gender equity, Norris and Inglehardt convincingly argue, not politics or belief in democratic ideals, is the great divider among nations. According to the World Values Survey, in fact, while young people in Western societies have grown progressively more tolerant, younger generations in Muslim societies, including females, are still as conservative as their elders.

Domestic violence is an issue not defined as such in most nations. For example, a battered Mexican immigrant says that, in her home country, much of what she endured was not even called abuse—it was called marriage (Basu, 2002). Now she has broken free of the relationship and devotes her spare time to helping other battered Latina women in a grant-funded organization for Latina victims of sexual and domestic violence. Latina volunteers can be of immeasurable help to others of their cultural background in speaking the language and in knowing the magnitude of the decision to separate from their husbands, which in effect is to violate the principle of *familismo* (loyalty to one's family).

In many cultures, one's sense of general happiness is not determined from within but rather from without, from positive relations with others, usually one's family. For example, in a comparison of hundreds of middle-aged Korean and American adults, Koreans exhibited vastly lower levels of well-being. According to Keyes and Ryff (1999), they appear self-effacing in their answers to Western-style interview items. However, Koreans display a high level of well-being and personal fulfillment through their family rather than through

personal accomplishments. For them, well-being is a reflection of their children's success, for example. The differences can be exaggerated, though, since Korean responses are remarkably the same, while there is much diversity of cultural values in the U.S. sample.

Implications for Practice

Stresses at the intimacy versus isolation stage of life sometimes bring young adults into counseling. The ability to establish healthy, intimate relationships can be complicated by unresolved psychological issues from the past. The old tapes played in one's head may provide a script for a pathway into a self-destructive direction, including the formation of unsuitable alliances. Decision making is a key theme of this period in that the decisions that one makes in early adulthood set the course for much of all the rest that will follow—one's career, one's spouse or partner, and often the children one will have. The phrase "I made some poor choices" sums up the risks and the consequences that generally are apparent to an individual only with time. Contemporary theorists espouse a cognitive treatment approach based upon a developmental constructivist view of therapy (Dwyer & Hunt-Jackson, 2002). This approach helps the client identify and change problematic thought processes and behaviors. Cognitive therapy basically provides feedback to help clients gain perspective and learn to rely on their common sense.

Similar to the cognitive approach in that it is concerned with thought processes is motivational therapy, commonly called motivational interviewing (MI). A change-oriented strategy based on the principles of social psychology, MI originated in addictions treatment as an effective way to reinforce health-seeking behaviors. Using this model, the practitioner first assesses the level of the client's motivation for change and never fights the client but rather rolls with the resistance. In short, the practitioner follows until the client leads; following consists of skilled paraphrasing that highlights statements that reinforce movement toward the goals that the client has set. Finding a loving and supporting partner in life might be a typical long-term treatment goal set by the young adult. Using client-centered responses and friendly questioning, the social worker who is trained in this technique strives to keep the client mindful of progress toward or movement away from this ultimate goal.

William Miller (1996) formulated motivational therapy in terms of the following general principles:

> Express empathy
> Develop the discrepancy between the client's goals and behaviors
> Avoid argumentation by reminding clients that the choice is theirs
> Roll with resistance
> Support self-efficacy

Evidence-based research supports the effectiveness of this approach in enhancing decision making by the client (Marlatt, 2000; Project MATCH Research Group, 1997; van Wormer & Davis, 2008). The concepts are consistent with the strengths and empowerment perspective.

During the midlife period, a time when many people turn to social workers due to a crisis of one sort or another, relationship problems often loom large. For these types of difficulties, the counselor can refer to the personality typology offered by the Myers-Briggs instrument. My experience in drawing on a design such as this is positive because it introduces the topic of compatibility and helps people see that it may not be their fault if conflict looms in a relationship that involves opposite personalities. Performance on such a measuring device promotes self-awareness and helps clients accept their personality styles and appreciate their own talents and inclinations.

Forgiveness and healing are key concepts with much relevance to the helping effort. The need to forgive or let go may derive from a troubled childhood, but often at this stage the issue is the breakup of a relationship. Job loss, which is increasingly common among older workers in today's global economy, may also be the cause of relentless anger. Here, the therapist can play a major role in helping people cope with life's stresses. To reduce clients'

self-blame, the therapist can combine client-centered techniques. Work in the feeling area can enhance personal empowerment and the achievement of Erikson's generativity. Generativity involves the giving of the self to others; its attainment is inextricably linked to one's frame of mind.

During the middle stage of life many are haunted by broken dreams. In his book, *Overcoming Life's Disappointments: Learning from Moses How to Cope with Frustration*, Rabbi Harold Kusher (2007) leads us to a more realistic appraisal of our accomplishments. In life, there are many disappointments and failures, among them: career plans that did not work out, financial indebtedness, a son or daughter who did not turn out as we would have wished, and love relationships that have gone sour. The higher our expectations, the greater is our sense of disappointment. But we can, as Kusher suggests, re-create our lives out of the rubble of earlier failure. In his words:

> If you have been bold enough to dream and found yourself with some dreams that came true and a lot of broken pieces of dreams that didn't, that fell to the earth and shattered, then you. . . . like Moses, can realize how full your life has been and how richly you are blessed. (p. 174)

Summary and Conclusion

From a discussion of embarking on the journey of life from early adulthood to maturity in middle age, this chapter has touched upon some pivotal moments. Erikson's typology has provided the framework, while research from psychology and social work has contributed the discussion material. Illustrations from popular news sources have supplied the rest. Intimacy and generativity are organizing themes of this chapter. Viewed as a key ingredient in intimacy and in couple compatibility, love can variously be regarded as an emotion, a personal need, or a goal. Love is interactive and builds on itself in the giving and the receiving. The expression of love has a great deal to do with personality, which is the subject of the next chapter. Although there is much speculation in the therapy literature and conversations about personality conflict and marital breakup, the real source of wonder is that so many marriages and partnerships work out, not that so many fail. Attachment seems to be the key, also a history of mutual experiences and friends, familiarity and habit, and sexual bonding. Ideally, instead of mate selection through physical attraction alone, personality testing through a device such as the Myers-Briggs Type Indicator could predict areas of conflict and agreement and even the chances that a match will work out. But most people would probably prefer to heed the words of the beautiful song in the musical *West Side Story*: "When love comes, there is no right or wrong; your love is your love."

Following a discussion of heterosexuality and gay and lesbian sexuality, the topic shifted from healthy to unhealthy love relationships, which led into the topic of violence and even rape and suicide played out in the form of murder.

The period of life known as middle age (and seen by Erikson in terms of generativity versus stagnation) forms the core of this chapter. This period (dreaded by the young but mourned for by the old) has been shown, curiously, to be, in many ways the happiest time of one's life. Finding purpose in life and having the capacity to forgive have been described in this context.

Thought Questions

1. What does the opening quote mean to you? Do people really mature as they get older? If so, do they mature progressively or in spurts with maybe some backtracking?
2. Is it true what some news media are reporting—that adolescence is getting longer?
3. What are some of the advantages and disadvantages of postponing cohabitation or marriage?
4. What is intimacy, and how can we find it?
5. What is love, and how can we find it?

6. Discuss *Love Signals*. Does it have any relevance in your own experience?
7. How would you describe Kinsey's methodology and findings?
8. How do sexual practices in the United States compare with those in Europe?
9. Which is better in a relationship—complementary or similar personality traits or some of each? Relate your answer to the Myers-Briggs instrument.
10. What are some key ingredients that make for a happy relationship?
11. How would you describe obsessive love?
12. Can obsessive love in rare cases result in suicide-murder?
13. Can you list some of the irrational thought patterns connected with romantic love?
14. How would you describe the statistics on partner violence?
15. Discuss the consciousness-raising contribution on oppression manifested as sexism. Is street-level harassment of women a common occurrence in your area?
16. How do sports hero idolatry and other forms of male bonding relate to sexual violence?
17. What did you learn about middle age from the essay by Ogden Rogers?
18. How would you describe some of the myths about happiness? How would you disprove them?
19. What kinds of things might young and middle-aged adults need to forgive?
20. How does personality relate to one's religious beliefs?
21. How would you describe the transition from hippie to yuppie?

References

Ackerman, D. (2004). *The alchemy of mind*. New York: Simon & Schuster.

American Association of University Women (AAUW) Educational Foundation. (1999). *Voices of a generation: Teenage girls' struggles with sexuality, peer pressure, and body image.* New York: Marlowe.

238 Human Behavior and the Social Environment, Micro Level

American Broadcasting Company (ABC). (2004, October 21). Primetime live poll: American sex survey. *ABC News.* Retrieved February 10, 2010, from http://abcnews.go.com/Primetime/PollVault/story?id=156921&page=1

American Psychological Association (APA). (2007). Guidelines for psychological practice with women and girls. Retrieved February 10, 2010, from http://www.apa.org/about/division/activities/girls-and-women.pdf

Armstrong, K. (1993). *A history of God: The 4,000-year quest of Judaism, Christianity, and Islam.* New York: Ballantine.

Armstrong, K. (2009). *The case for God.* New York: Random House.

Arnett, J. (2004). *Emerging adulthood: The winding road.* New York: Oxford University Press.

Astin, A. W. (2004, Spring). Why spirituality deserves a central place in liberal higher education. *Higher Education Research Institute (HERI) Spirituality Newsletter, 1*(1), 1–12.

Atlas, J. (2006). *My life in the middle ages: A survivor's tale.* New York: Harper.

Auster, C., & Leone, J. (2001). Late adolescents' perspectives on marital rape: The impact of gender and fraternity/sorority membership. *Adolescence, 36*(141), 141–152.

Baldauf, S. (2005, February 17). India love songs croon of dwindling role for parents. *Christian Science Monitor, 1,* p. 4.

Basile, K. (2002, June). Attitudes toward wife rape: Effects of social background and victim status. *Violence and Victims, 17*(3), 341–355.

Basu, R. (2002, December 3). Latinas help each other out of abusive situations. *Des Moines Register.* Retrieved from http://desmoinesregister.com

Begley, S. (2008, February 11). Happiness enough already. *Newsweek,* pp. 50–52.

Benedict, H. (2009). *The lonely soldier: The private war of women serving in Iraq.* Boston: Beacon Press.

Bergen, R. K. (1998). The reality of wife rape. In R. K. Bergen (Ed.), *Issues in intimate violence* (pp. 237–50). Thousand Oaks, CA: Sage.

Biddle, S. (2001). Exercise and depression. *British Medical Journal.* Retrieved February 10, 2010, from http://www.bmj.com/cgi/eletters/322/7289/763#13653

Blackstock, C. (1999, September 25). Many men view rape as acceptable. *Guardian/Observer,* p. 5.

Boonstra, H. (2009a, Spring). The challenge in helping young people better manage their reproductive lives. *Guttmacher Policy Review, 12*(2), 13–18.

Biggs, S. (2005). Psychodynamic approaches to the lifecourse and aging. In M. L. Johnson, V. Bengston, P. Coleman, & T. Kirkwood (Eds.), *The Cambridge handbook of age and ageing* (pp. 149–155). Cambridge, England: Cambridge University Press.

Brooks, D. (2000). *Bobos in paradise: The new upper class and how they got there.* New York: Simon & Schuster.

Brown, C. (2009). Experts: Most perpetrators feel shame, humiliation. *Gazette.net. Maryland's Community Newspapers Online.* Retrieved from http://www.gazette.net/stories/10012009/urbanew163452_32526.shtml

Bureau of Justice Statistics (BJS) (2009, October 23). *Female victims of violence.* Washington, DC: U.S. Department of Justice.

Burke, J. (2007). *Rape: Sex violence history.* Berkeley, CA: Shoemaker/Hoard.

Buss, D. M. (2008). *Evolutionary psychology: The new science of the mind* (3rd ed.). Boston: Allyn & Bacon.

Carrell, B. (2003, October 10). Bush signs prison rape elimination act of 2003. *Equity Feminism.* Retrieved October 10, 2003, from http://www.equityfeminism.com/articles/2003/bush-signs-prison-rape-elimination-act-of-2003/

Centers for Disease Control and Prevention (CDC). (2004a). *Joint Canada/United States Survey of Health, 2002–2003.* Washington, DC: Author.

Centers for Disease Control and Prevention (CDC). (2004b). *Sexual violence: Fact sheet. National Center for Injury Prevention and Control.* Retrieved from http://www.cdc.gov

Centers for Disease Control and Prevention (CDC), (2008, November 28). *Abortion surveillance—United States. Morbidity and mortality weekly report.* Retrieved from http://www.cdc.gov/mmwr/PDF/ss/ss5713.pdf

Centers for Disease Control and Prevention (CDC). (2009). *HIV/AIDS among African Americans.* Retrieved from http://www.cdc.gov/hiv/topics/aa/resources/factsheets/aa.htm

Connolly, C. (2005, March 19). Teen pledges barely cut STD rates, study says. *Washington Post,* p. A3.

Coy, P. (2009, October 19). The lost generation. *Business Week,* pp. 33–34.

Crosby, G. (1998, December 7). The secret of aging: My turn. *Newsweek,* p.18.

Diener, E., & Biswas-Diener, R. (2008). *Happiness: Unlocking the mysteries of psychological wealth.* Malden, MA: Blackwell Publishing.

Douglas, C., & Gibbs, P. (2004, November–December). Iraq: Rape of U.S. women soldiers on the rise. *Off our backs, 34*, 6.

Dwyer, D., & Hunt-Jackson, J. (2002). The life span perspective. In J. S. Wodarski & S. F. Dziegielewski (Eds.), *Human behavior and the social environment: Integrating theory and evidence-based practice* (pp. 84–109). New York: Springer.

Dziegielewski, S., Heymann, C., Green, C., & Gichia, J. (2002). Midlife changes: Utilizing a social work perspective. *Journal of Human Behavior in the Social Environment, 6*(4), 65–86.

Eckholm, E. (2009, March 18). '07 U.S. births break baby boom record. *New York Times*, p. A14.

Edwards, E. (2009). *Resilience: Reflections on the burdens and gifts of facing life's adversaries.* New York: Random House.

Ehrenreich, B. (2009). *Brightsided: How the relentless promotion of positive thinking has undermined America.* New York: Metropolitan Books.

Erikson, E. (1950/1963). *Childhood and society.* New York: Norton.

Faludi, S. (1991). *Backlash: The undeclared war on American women.* New York: Doubleday.

Feijoo, A. (2001). Adolescent pregnancy, birth, and abortion rates in Western Europe far outstrip U. S. rates. *Transitions, 14*(2), 4–5.

Firestone, R., Firestone, L., & Catlett, J. (2008). *Sex and love in intimate relationships.* Washington, DC: American Psychological Association.

Fisher, H. (2006). The drive to love. In R. Sternberg & K. Weis (Eds.), *The new psychology of love* (2nd ed., pp. 87–115). New Haven, CT: Yale University Press.

Flora, C. (2004, January–February). Interview of Cindy Hazan. In Close quarters: Why we fall in love with the one nearby. *Psychology Today*, 15–16.

Ford, A., & Van Dyk, D. (2009). Then and now: A statistical look back, from the 1970s to today. *Time* magazine, p. 27.

Fromm, E. (1956). *The art of loving.* New York: Harper & Row.

Fry, R. (2009, October 7). The changing pathways of Hispanic youths into adulthood. *Pew Hispanic Center*. Retrieved from http://pewhispanic.org/reports/report.php?ReportID=114

Gardiner, H. W., & Kosmitzki, C. (2005). *Lives across cultures: Cross-cultural human development.* Boston: Allyn & Bacon.

Gilligan, C. (1982). *In a different voice: Psychological theory and women's development.* Cambridge, MA: Harvard University Press.

Gilligan, C. (2003). *The birth of pleasure.* New York: Knopf.

Givens, D. (2005). *Love signals: A practical field guide to the body language of courtship.* New York: St. Martin's Press.

Glass, S., & Staeheli, J. C. (2004). *Not "just friends": Rebuilding trust and recovering your sanity after infidelity.* New York: Free Press.

Goldenberg, H., & Goldenberg, I. (2002). *Counseling today's families* (4th ed.). Belmont, CA: Wadsworth.

Gotterer, R. (2001). The spiritual dimension in clinical social work practice: A client perspective. *Families in Society, 82*(2), 187–193.

Greer, G. (1993). *The Change: Women, aging, and the menopause.* New York: Ballantine.

Guttmacher Institute. (2002). *Sexual and reproductive health: Women and men.* Retrieved from http://www.guttmacher.org/pubs/fb_10-02.html

Guttmacher Institute. (2009, August 21). *Expectations that abortion pill would dramatically improve abortion access have not been realized.* Retrieved from http://www.guttmacher.org/media/nr/2009/08/21/index.html

Hallowell, E. M. (2004). *Dare to forgive.* Deerfield Beach, FL: Health Communications.

Hamann, S., Herman, R. A., Nolan, C., & Waller, K. (2004). Men and women differ in amygdala response to visual sexual stimuli. *Nature Neuroscience, 7*(4), 411–16.

Hartman, A., & Laird, J. (1983). *Family-centered social work practice.* New York: Free Press.

Hazan, C., Campa, M., and Gur-Yaish, N. (2006). What is adult attachment? In M. Mikulincer & G. S. Goodman (Eds.), *Dynamics of romantic love: Attachment, caregiving, and sex* (pp. 47–70). New York: Guilford Press.

Herbst, J., McCrae, R., Costa, P., Feaganes, J., & Siegler, I. (2000). Self-perceptions of stability and change in personality at midlife: The UNC alumni heart study. *Assessment, 7*(4), 379–388.

Howey, N. (2001, February–March). By any other name. *Ms.*, pp. 87–89.

Huxley, A. (1932/1969). *Brave new world.* New York: Harper & Row.

Inglehart, R., Foa, R., Peterson, C., & Welzel, C. (2008). Development, freedom, and rising happiness. *Perspectives on Psychological Science, 3* (4), 264-285..

Jamison, K. (2004). *Exuberance: The passion for life.* New York: Knopf.

Jayson, S. (2004, September 30). The gap between adolescence and adulthood gets longer. *USA Today*, p. 1D.

Katz, J. (2006). *The macho paradox: Why some men hurt women and how all men can help.* Naperville, IL: Sourcebooks.

Katz, J. (2009, October 21). *Mentors in violence prevention, the University of Northern Iowa, and the Future of Gender Violence Prevention Education.* Public presentation at the University of Northern Iowa.

Keyes, C. L., & Ryff, C. D. (1999). Psychological well-being in midlife. In S. Willis & J. Reid (Eds.), *Life in the middle: Psychological and social development in middle age* (pp. 161–80). San Diego, CA: Academic Press.

Kimmel, M. (2008). *Guyland: The perilous world where boys become men.* New York: Harper.

Kinsey, A., Pomeroy, W., & Martin, C. (1948). *Sexual behavior in the human male.* Philadelphia: Saunders.

Kinsey, A., & staff of the Institute for Sex Research. (1953). *Sexual behavior in the human female.* Philadelphia: Saunders.

Krebs, C. P., Lindquist, C. H., Warner, T. D., Fisher, B. S., & Martin, S. L. (2007). *Campus Sexual Assault (CSA) Study. Final report submitted to the National Institute of Justice, December 2007, NCJ 221153.* Retrieved from the National Criminal Justice Reference Service website http://www.ncjrs.gov/App/Publications/abstract.aspx?ID=243011

Kusher, H. (2007). *Overcoming life's disappointments: Learning from Moses how to cope with frustration.* New York: Random House.

Lampman, J. (2005, March 21). Book that freed a hostage was already making waves. *Christian Science Monitor,* p. 11.

Lange, R., Renfrow, P., & Bruckner, K. (2004). Do online matchmaking tests work? An assessment of preliminary evidence for a publicized predictive model of marital success. *North American Journal of Psychology, 6*(3), 507–526.

Laumann, E., Paik, A., Kang, J-H., Glasser, D., Wang, T., King, R., et al. (2006). Subjective well-being in older adults: Findings from the Global Study of Sexual Attitudes and Behavior (GSSAB). *Archives of Sexual Behavior, 34,* 145–161.

Lawler, K., Younger, J., Piferi, R., Jobe, R., Edmondson, K., & Jones, W. (2005). The unique effects of forgiveness on health: An exploration of pathways. *Journal of Behavioral Medicine, 28*(2), 157–168.

Layard, R. (2005). *Happiness: Lessons from a new science.* New York: Penguin.

Lehrer, E. (2003, June 2). A blind eye, still turned: Getting serious about prison rape. *National Review, 55,* 10.

Leonard, L. (1990). *Witness to the fire: Creativity and the veil of addiction.* Boston: Shambhala.

Lewin, T. (2010, January 28). After long decline, teenage pregnancy rate rises. *New York Times,* p. A14.

Lisak, D. (2009, October 7). *The undetected rapist.* Keynote presentation for the Victim Service Institute. Cedar Falls, IA. University of Northern Iowa, Cedar Falls.

Loveland, M. (2003). Religious switching: Preference development, maintenance, and change. *Journal for the Scientific Study of Religion, 42*(1), 147–157.

Luo, S., & Klohnen, E. (2005). Assortative mating and marital quality in newlyweds: A couple-centered approach. *Journal of Personality and Social Psychology, 88*(2), 304–326.

Lyall, S. (2002). Accepted concepts of "family" expand in Europe. *Des Moines Register,* p. 6A.

Lykken, D. T. (2000). *Happiness: The nature and nurture of joy and contentment.* New York: St. Martin's Press.

Lyubomirsky, S., Sheldon, K. M., & Schkade, D. (2005). Pursuing happiness: The architecture of sustainable change. *Review of General Psychology, 9,* 111–131.

Mabe, M. (2008). Why Danes are the world's happiest people. *Spiegel International.* Retrieved from http://www.spiegel.de/international/business/0,1518,573447,00.html

Marine, S. (2004, November 26). Waking up from the nightmare of rape. *Chronicle of Higher Education, 51*(14), B5.

Marlatt, G. (2000). Harm reduction: Basic principles and strategies. *Prevention Researcher, 7*(2), 1–4.

McIntire, S. & Miller, L. A. (2007). *Foundations of psychological testing: A practical approach* (2nd ed.) Thousand Oaks, CA: Sage.

Miller, M.C. (2008, September 22). Sad brain, happy brain. *Newsweek,* pp.51–56.

Miller, S. (2003). *The story of my father.* New York: Knopf.

Miller, W. (1996). Motivational interviewing: Research, practice, and puzzles. *Addictive Behaviors, 21*(6), 835–842.

Moe, A.M. (2009). Battered women, children, and the end of abusive relationships. *Affilia, 24,* 244–255.

Moore, L., Dettlaff, A., & Dietz, T. (2004). Using the Myers-Briggs type indices in field education.

Journal of Social Work Education, 40(2), 337–349.

Murray, B. (2004). Mixing oil and water. *Monitor on Psychology, 35*(3), 52–56.

Murray, J. D., Spadafore, J. A., & McIntosh, W. D. (2005). Belief in a just world and social perception: Evidence for automatic activation. *Journal of Social Psychology, 145*(1), 35–48.

Murray, S., Holmes, J., & Griffin, D. (2003). Reflections on the self-fulfilling prophecy of positive illusions. *Psychological Inquiry, 14*, 289–296.

Myers, D. (2003). *Psychology* (7th ed.). New York: Worth.

National Coalition against Domestic Violence. (2007, July). Domestic violence facts. Retrieved from http://www.ncadv.org/files/DomesticViolenceFactSheet(National).pdf

National Institutes of Health (NIH). (2004). Landmark survey reports on the prevalence of personality disorders in the United States. *NIH News.* Washington, DC: U.S. Department of Health and Human Services.

National Low Income Housing Coalition. (2009, September 23). *New census housing data confirm number of renters facing housing problems on the rise.* Retrieved from http://nlihc.org/detail/article.cfm?article_id=6440&id=48

Norris, P., & Inglehart, R. (2004). *Sacred and secular: religion and politics worldwide.* Cambridge, UK: Cambridge University Press.

O'Donnell, I. (2004, March). Prison rape in context. *British Journal of Criminology, 44*(2), 241–256.

Olson, D., Larson, P., & Olson-Sigg, A. (2009). Couple checkup: Tuning up relationships. *Journal of Couple and Relationship Therapy, 8* (2), 129-142.

Oxford Modern English Dictionary (2nd ed.). (1996). New York: Oxford University Press.

Paul, A. M. (2004). *The cult of personality.* New York: Free Press.

Pfeffer, J. (2010, February 15). The layoffs. *Newsweek*, pp. 33-37.

Pines, A. (2000). *Falling in love: Why we choose the lovers we choose.* London: Routledge.

Post, J. M. (2002). Terrorists on trial. In H. Kusher (Ed.), *Essential readings on political terrorism* (pp. 46–61). Lincoln: University of Nebraska Press.

Project MATCH Research Group. (1997). Matching alcoholism treatments to client heterogeneity: Project MATCH post-treatment drinking out comes. *Journal of Studies on Alcohol, 58*, 7–29.

Ragsdale, S. (2004, September 28). Making amends. *Des Moines Register*, p. 24W.

Reid, J. D., & Willis, S. L. (1999). Middle age: New thoughts, new directions. In S. L. Willis & J. D. Reid (Eds.), *Life in the middle: Psychology and social development in middle age* (pp. 275–286). San Diego, CA: Academic Press.

Rivers, I., & D'Augelli, A. (2001). The victimization of lesbian, gay, and bisexual youths. In A. D'Augelli & C. Patterson (Eds.), *Lesbian, gay, and bisexual identities and youth* (pp. 199–223). New York: Oxford University Press.

Robbins, A., & Wilner, A. (2001). *Quarterlife crisis: The unique challenges of life in your twenties.* New York: Penguin Putnam.

Roberts, N. (2004). Cries from the second wave. In E. Oakes & J. Olmstead (Eds.), *Life writing by Kentucky feminists* (pp. 203–213). Bowling Green: Western Kentucky University.

Rosenbaum, J. (2009). Patient teenagers? A comparison of the sexual behavior of virginity pledges and matched nonpledges. *Pediatrics, 123* (1), 110-120.

Rosenfeld, M. (2009). *The age of independence: Intraracial unions, same-sex unions, and the changing American family.* Cambridge, MA: Harvard University Press.

Saleebey, D. (2001). Human behavior and social environments. New York: Columbia University Press.

Schaeffer, B. (2009). *Is it love or is it addiction?* Center City, MN: Hazelden.

Schwartz, M. D., & DeKeseredy, W. S. (1997). *Sexual assault on the college campus: The role of male peer support.* Thousand Oaks, CA: Sage.

ScienceDaily. (2008a, July 1). Despite frustration, Americans are pretty darned happy. Retrieved from http://www.sciencedaily.com/releases/2008/06/080630130129.htm

ScienceDaily (2008b, March 6). Genes hold the key to how happy we are, scientists say. Retrieved from http://www.sciencedaily.com/releases/2008/03/080304103308.htm

ScienceDaily. (2009, March 25). Recession cuts many, not all plastic surgery procedures. Retrieved from http://www.sciencedaily.com/releases/2009/03/090325132534.htm

Seligman, M. (2004). *Authentic happiness.* New York: Free Press.

Sheehy, G. (2004). *Passages: Predictable crises of adult life.* New York: Ballantine Books.

Starks, S., & Hughey, A. (2003). African American women at midlife: The relationship between spirituality and life satisfaction. *Affilia, 18*(2), 133–147.

Stevenson, R., & Wolfers, J. (2009). The paradox of declining female happiness. *American Economics Journal, 1*(2), 190–225.

Thornhill, R., & Palmer, C. (2001). *The natural history of rape: Biological bases of sexual coercion.* Cambridge, MA: MIT Press.

Tiefer, L. (2004). *Sex is not a natural act and other essays* (2nd ed.) Boulder, CO: Westview Press.

U.S. Department of Labor (2010, February). Economic news release. Bureau of Labor Statistics. Retrieved from http://www.bls.gov/news.release/empsit.nr0.htm

van Wormer, K., & Davis, D. R. (2008). *Addiction treatment: A strengths perspective* (2nd ed.). Belmont, CA: Brooks/Cole.

van Wormer, K., & Roberts, A. R. (2009). *Death by domestic violence: Preventing the murders and the murder-suicides.* Westport, CT: Praeger.

Violence Policy Center (VPC). (2008). *American roulette: The untold story of murder-suicide in the United States* (3rd ed.). Retrieved from http://www.vpc.org/studies/amroul2008.pdf

Wahl, H.-W., & Kruse, A. (2005). Middle age and identity in cultural and lifespan perspective. In S. L. Willis & M. Martin (Eds.), *Middle adulthood: A lifespan perspective* (pp. 319–354). Thousand Oaks, CA: Sage.

Warren, R. (2002). *The purpose-driven life: What on earth am I here for?* Grand Rapids, MI: Zondervan.

Zastrow, C. (2004). *Introduction to social work and social welfare: Empowering people* (8th ed.). Belmont, CA: Brooks/Cole.

Zastrow, C., & Kirst-Ashman, K. (2004). *Understanding human behavior and the social environment.* Belmont, CA: Brooks/Cole.

Zuckerman, M., & Kuhlman, D. M. (2000). Personality and risk-taking: Common biosocial factors. *Journal of Personality, 68*(8), 999–1029.

Late Middle Age Through the End of Life

The trouble is, old age is not interesting until one gets there. It's a foreign country with an unknown language to the young and even to the middle-aged. I wish now I had found out more about it.

—MAY SARTON, *As We Are Now*, p. 15

You can be young without money, but you can't be old without it.

—TENNESSEE WILLIAMS, *Cat on a Hot Tin Roof*, Act I

6

Continuing with the Eriksonian model of transitions across the life span, we learn more in this chapter from the time of generativity in the late middle age to that period Erikson (1950/1963) saw as the forces of ego integrity pitted against the forces of despair in the final stages of life when one's uncompleted tasks, regrets, and omissions "come home to roost." Earlier joys, by the same token, are magnified in old age. Often one's religious faith from childhood and a cherishing of the joys of the present moment provide a major source of strength, almost as compensation for losses incurred through the ravages of time.

Following an overview of aging in America and a review of demographic trends from the census data, this chapter considers biological aspects of aging with an emphasis on physiological changes later in life. A discussion of the challenges facing the "young–old" or those in the first portion of the 50–75 year-old group follows. The theme of transition characterizes this segment of the population, transitions older adults have chosen and those that have been thrust upon them by economics and health considerations. A discussion of the theme of resilience introduces the concluding section of this chapter, which explores issues and concerns of the final stage of late adulthood, a stage that encompasses the reality of impending death. The final portion of the chapter is highlighted by experts from the personal narratives of older African American women who grew up in the segregated South and who worked as domestic servants.

Introduction

You know you're getting old when a restaurant worker asks, "Do you qualify for the senior discount?" (The first time can be an awful shock.) The reality also hits home when colleagues and friends begin to ask, "Have you thought about when you'd like to retire?" and when younger people ask, "What color did your hair used to be?" The loss of one's parents can also be a defining moment when the realization strikes that "I am the older generation now." No matter what one's self-perception is, one's age is very much a function of social interaction. People come to accept their new status as an elder in terms of approaching societal benchmarks (e.g., retirement) and loss of physical agility and strength. Additionally, we age in comparison to how others see us. Given the ubiquity of ageism in the society—consider the TV ads for pharmaceutical products and news stories about the pending aging crisis—it is no wonder that people want to stave off the old-age identity.

Even Erikson's positive side of the older-age spectrum lacks the vibrancy of the other categories. Ego integrity at best seems to refer to a "hanging on" of what one has left. Erikson defines this as occurring during the final stage of life; it is a readiness "to defend the dignity of [one's] own life style against all physical and economic threats" (p. 268). More positively, "ego integrity involves acceptance in the spiritual sense of one's life and of the life cycle." In such a final consolidation, Erikson contends, "death loses its sting" (p. 268).

Despair, at the other end of the spectrum, is represented in a lack of ego integration and fear of death. According to Gail Sheehy (interviewed by Spayde [2004] 25 years after the publication of *Passages* catapulted her to fame), being 60 is sobering. People at this age often give up their vices and begin to save up for retirement in earnest. "You come to terms with regrets, reopen estrangements with friends or college buddies or even a parent or child. There's a sense of trying to begin to round out the life story in a positive way" (p. 65). And what is the clear line of demarcation between middle and old age? To Sheehy it is the first major illness, something that you feel in all your senses; at this time, the intellectual becomes real.

A recent nationwide random survey on perceptions of aging conducted by the Pew Research Center (2009) documented a widespread negative perception toward old age by younger adults, especially in regard to health, emotional health, sex life, and mental functioning. The older adults in the survey, nevertheless, were much more positive about themselves and their lives than the younger people imagined they would be—the majority said they felt younger than their actual age, and they did not see themselves encountering many of the physical and emotional problems often associated with aging.

In a youth-oriented, technologically based, and individualistic society such as exists in the United States, the status of old people tends to be relatively low. Rapid advances in technology and science have made some skills and knowledge obsolete (Zastrow & Kirst-Ashman, 2010). There are differences, of course, in attitudes toward the process of aging and elderly adults based on ethnicity, social standing, and class. But generally, our national resistance to aging is reinforced by the marketing of products to cover up the signs of weathering and evidenced in the huge profits made in the marketing of merchandise and cosmetic surgery to combat the physical signs of aging, in job discrimination against older employees, and in stereotyping in the mass media and the film industry.

In some other countries, older people are accorded special respect. In Japan and China, for example, three-generation families are common, and the wishes of the older generation are honored (Santrock, 2008). Santrock singles out five factors that predict high status for older people in a culture. They are as follows:

1. Recognition for having valuable knowledge
2. Having control of key family and community resources
3. Participation in a collectivist culture
4. Being integrated into an extended family
5. Being actively engaged in a valued function, in the community

To this list I would add a valued connection to an honored past. This implies the ability to carry on tradition through the arts and storytelling. Special respect, for example, has been accorded to old southern aristocrats, to veterans of wars—especially of wars that were venerated—to Native Americans who can provide a link to the cultural past, to civil rights activists, and to survivors of the Holocaust. Gerontologists today are conducting research on cultures that accord special status to the aged, as they are researching coping mechanisms and resilience in older adults. Before discussing their findings, let us consider the statistics on the older Americans and then let us view these demographic trends in global context.

Demographic Trends

Due to better sanitation, nutrition, and disease control, over the past century, U.S. life expectancy has gone from 49 to 78 years (U.S. Census, 2009). Refer to Table 6.1, "A Profile of Older Americans." We learn from the statistics provided in this table that today over one in every eight American men and women are aged 65 and older and that over the next two decades, this older population will continue to grow significantly. This growth will occur due to the aging baby boomers—the generation born from 1946 to 1964.

The diversity of the older population is increasing as well. As we see in Table 6.1, by 2020 at the present rate of increase, 23 percent of the elderly will be minorities. Women outnumber men increasingly with each decade of age; their median income is significantly below that of males. Major sources of income are Social Security, income from assets, pensions, and earnings. Note that for about one-third of older Americans, Social Security payments constitute 90 percent or more of their total income.

Although the Social Security system, instituted in 1935 under Franklin Roosevelt as a part of the New Deal, was only designed to be supplemental income, for many Americans, these monthly payments are what they live on. Money paid into the system by present workers and their employers is paid out to retirees and their spouses. The concern is that in the future too few workers will be paying into the system to provide for the burgeoning numbers of older citizens. In anticipation of this increasing dependency rate between the payers and recipients, Congress in 1983 raised the age to receive full Social Security benefits. For those born after 1942, the age was raised to 66, and for those born after 1960 to age 67 (for the exact time periods go to http://www.social security.gov). Another issue related to Social Security benefits is that the monthly benefits are too small to raise retirees above the poverty level unless they have other sources of income (Zastrow & Kirst-Ashman, 2010).

The situation that the United States faces regarding the expanding gap in the dependency ratio is paralleled throughout the industrialized world. Since many of these countries are already where the United States will be in 20 or 30 years, a global view can be instructive.

U.S. Aging Statistics in Global Perspective

According to a recent report from the U.S. Census Bureau (2009), entitled "An Aging World: 2008," the world's older adult population is experiencing unprecedented growth and is predicted to increase from 7 to 14 percent of the total global population by 2040. And within the next 10 years, for the first time in history, as demographers report, there will be more people aged 65 and older than children under age five.

The percentage of the population aged 65 and over ranges from 13 percent to 21 percent in 2008 in most industrialized nations. The United States is considered a relatively young nation with just over 12 percent of the population of this age, while Japan emerges as number one in having the largest proportion (21 percent) at age 65 or over, supplanting Italy as the world's oldest big country. The reason for this expansion at the higher end of the age spectrum is not so much the longevity factor as it is the low fertility rates. Russia and Japan have total fertility rates of 1.4 and 1.2 births per woman, respectively.

Life expectancies are also increasing. In Japan the life expectancy at birth is 82 years. This accomplishment is matched only by Singapore, while in western Europe, France, Sweden, and Italy all have life expectancies of more than 80 years. Japan's population aged 65 and over is projected to increase by 8 million between 2008 and 2040.

Out of 30 of the most industrially advanced nations, life expectancy in the United States ranks 21st. The U.S. life expectancy is 4.6 years

Table 6.1   A Profile of Older Americans, 2008

Highlights Pertaining to the Older Population*

> ❯ The older population (65+) numbered 37.9 million in 2007, an increase of 3.8 million or 11.2% since 1997.
> ❯ The number of Americans aged 45–64—who will reach 65 over the next two decades—increased by 38% during this decade.
> ❯ Over one in every eight, or 12.6%, of the population is an older American.
> ❯ Older women outnumber older men at 21.9 million older women to 16.0 million older men.
> ❯ In 2007, 19.3% of persons 65+ were minorities—8.3% were African Americans.** Persons of Hispanic origin (who may be of any race) represented 6.6% of the older population. About 3.2% were Asian or Pacific Islander,** and less than 1% were American Indian or Native Alaskan.** In addition, 0.6% of persons 65+ identified themselves as being of two or more races.
> ❯ Older men were much more likely to be married than older women—73% versus 42% of women. In 2007, 42% of older women were widows.
> ❯ About 30% (10.9 million) of noninstitutionalized older persons live alone (7.9 million women, 2.9 million men).
> ❯ Minority populations are projected to increase from 5.7 million in 2000 (16.3% of the elderly population) to 8.0 million in 2010 (20.1% of the elderly) and then to 12.9 million in 2020 (23.6% of the elderly).
> ❯ The median income of older persons in 2007 was $24,323 for males and $14,021 for females.
> ❯ Major sources of income for older people in 2006 were Social Security (reported by 89 % of older persons), income from assets (reported by 55%), private pensions (reported by 29%), government employee pensions (reported by 14%), and earnings (reported by 25%).
> ❯ Social Security constituted 90% or more of the income received by 32% of all Social Security beneficiaries (20% of married couples and 41 % of nonmarried beneficiaries).
> ❯ About 3.6 million elderly persons (9.7%) were below the poverty level in 2007, which is a statistically significant increase from the poverty rate in 2006 (9.4%).

*Principal sources of data for the Profile are the U.S. Bureau of the Census, the National Center on Health Statistics, and the Bureau of Labor Statistics.

**Excludes persons of Hispanic origin.

Source: U.S. Department of Health and Human Services, Administration on Aging. p.1. July 16, 2009. Highlights Specific to Advanced Aging. Retrieved from http://www.mowaa.org/Document.Doc?id=69

less than Japan, 2.1 years less than France, and 2.6 years less than Canada. The contrast in life expectancy between these rich nations of the Global North and poor ones is striking. The global report shows that a person born in the Global North can expect to outlive his or her counterpart in the rest of the world by 14 years. Zimbabwe holds the record for the lowest life expectancy, which has been cut to 40 through a combination of HIV/AIDS, other diseases, famine, tribal warfare, and corruption. Due largely to the AIDS pandemic, South Africa's population in 2040 may be 8 million people lower than in 2008. Life expectancy at birth in South Africa fell from 60 years in 1996 to less than 43 years in 2008.

The U.S. Census global report views the disproportionate numbers of elderly persons in the population as a major crisis in terms of the need for health care and general caretaking responsibilities when there are so few young to take care of the frail elderly. Challenges will be presented at every level of human services, according to the report, starting with the structure of the family, which will be transformed as people live longer.

Much of the concern in rich countries is with the tax structure if fewer people are working. To meet this challenge, a majority of the advanced welfare states have initiated policies to encourage more work and alter retirement among older workers. Already the statistics on employment rates of older workers reveal a later age of retirement.

The report can be criticized for sounding the alarm bells and failing to recognize the crisis facing countries with a high percentage of youth. When competition for jobs is high, many youths drop out of school, join gangs, and get involved in drug use and crime. In many countries, boy soldiers are in big demand to fight in wars. A nation with a more mature population might be less characterized by tribal and other forms of warfare. Finally, the threat of global overpopulation will be reduced thanks to the declining birth rate. The challenge to nations of the shifting demographics is real, however, and the social consequences, both negative and positive, will be far reaching.

Ego Integrity Versus Despair

Aldous Huxley's *Brave New World* (1932/1969) depicts a future that contains death but not aging. Through the miracle of chemistry, the old do not physically age and therefore die while still in their prime. In the real world, however, only through death can we stave off the ravages of time. Aging does bring with it, Saleebey (2001) acknowledges, "a certain amount of wear and tear" (p. 456). Four out of five people over age 65 can count on having at least one chronic condition; among the most common ailments are arthritis, hearing impairment, various forms of cardiovascular diseases, and cancer.

The Biology of Aging

Shakespeare (1594) provides a graphic description of the seventh stage of aging in his play *As You Like It*:

> . . . Last scene of all,
> That ends this strange eventful history,
> Is second childishness and mere oblivion;
> Sans teeth, sans eyes, sans taste, sans
>   everything.
>
> (Act II, scene 7)

The exact relationship between chronological age and the decrease in capabilities, however, has yet to be satisfactorily determined. Leonard Hayflick (2009), a professor of anatomy and former president of the Gerontological Society of America, provides a holistic and realistic view of the biological process of aging. The accumulation of new insights has now made it possible for the first time, he states, to understand the biological reasons for aging in humans and nonhuman animals. After members of the animal kingdom reach reproductive maturity, the complex molecules of which we are all composed break down, and their repair systems break down eventually as well. Age-associated diseases such as heart failure, cancer, and strokes are thus inevitable. Hayflick argues that a larger percentage of the budget of the National Institute on Aging should be spent on studying the fundamental biology of aging rather than specific diseases. At present over 50 percent of the budget is devoted to research on Alzheimer's disease and only 3 percent to the process of aging.

Many of the health problems elderly persons face result from a general decline in the circulatory system (Zastrow, 2007). Reduced blood supply impairs mental sharpness, and other body organs are affected as well. Adjusting to changes in external temperature becomes increasingly difficult. Bones become more brittle; sensory capacities diminish as well.

According to the Centers for Disease Control and Prevention (2009), the life expectancy for males and females reached record levels in 2007. In 2007, both male and female life expectancies increased from 2006 by 0.2 years to 75.3 years for males and 80.4 years for females. The difference between male and female life expectancy at birth has been generally decreasing since its peak of 7.8 years in 1979 to 5.1 years in 2007. Life expectancies were as follows:

➤ White males (75.8 years)
➤ Black males (70.2 years)
➤ White females (80.7 years)
➤ Black females (77.0 years)

The leading causes of death for Americans as provided by the CDC are as follows:

1. Diseases of heart
2. Malignant neoplasms—cancer
3. Cerebrovascular diseases
4. Chronic lower respiratory diseases
5. Accidents (unintentional injuries)

6. Alzheimer's disease
7. Diabetes mellitus
8. Influenza and pneumonia
9. Nephritis, nephrotic syndrome, and nephrosis
10. Septicemia
11. Intentional self-harm (suicide)
12. Chronic liver disease and cirrhosis
13. Essential hypertension and hypertensive renal disease
14. Parkinson's disease
15. Assault (homicide)

Sharon Begley (2007) states that older adults fail to stimulate their brains as much as younger people because they tend to pursue activities they are good at. At the same time systems involving biochemicals necessary for paying attention and for feeling pleasure weaken. Sensory input is received less strongly and accurately; older adults neither see, hear, feel, taste, nor smell as sharply as teenagers do. With age, the inner hair cells of the cochlea deteriorate, and people lose the ability to hear high-pitched sounds. People seem to mumble or talk too fast.

Among the characteristics of the aging process is the marked inability to hear clearly in crowded places such as restaurants and theaters or where appliances, air-conditioning, TV sets, or people talking on cell phones or radios generate background noise. Hearing aids exaggerate such extraneous noise. Much of sound (such as loud music) can become irritating in later life. Because it affects one's dealings with people, hearing impairment is crucial in its consequences. Other age-related changes—in vision, muscular strength, and reaction time—lead to a sense of vulnerability and fear in strange and unusual surroundings.

Von Hippel (2007) has studied personality change related to changes in brain function. He reports on new research that shows inappropriate social behavior such as expressions of racism and problems of impulse control such as gambling can occur as the result of atrophy in the frontal lobe of the brain. Lack of the ability to control behavior that would have been inhibited in the past may explain the unacceptable behavior.

Physical limitations, coupled with a lack of adequate transportation, limit older persons in their ability to shop, obtain legal counsel, or get needed medical care. Currently, at least 80 percent of older Americans are living with at least one chronic condition, and 50 percent have at least two (CDC, 2007). Almost 43 million Americans have arthritis and related conditions, for example. Health disparities are revealed in national health surveys that indicate that 39 percent of non-Hispanic white older adults report very good to excellent health compared to 24 percent of blacks and 29 percent of Hispanics (CDC, 2007). Among older adults 95 percent of health expenditures are for chronic diseases.

With the rapid increase in the number of people over 85, Alzheimer's disease and other forms of dementia are much more frequent occurrences than in the past. The particular tragedy of Alzheimer's disease is characterized by a creeping loss of self, beginning with short-term memory loss and ending with a vacuous human being in place of a once reflective person (Saleebey, 2001). Today an estimated 5.3 million Americans are living with Alzheimer's, a number that is expected to double over the next several decades (Alzheimer's Association, 2009). Half of all nursing home residents suffer from this disease or a related form of dementia. Because someone with Alzheimer's disease lives from 4 to 20 years beyond the onset of symptoms, the demands of care can be formidable.

"The 19th century had consumption; the 20th century had the heart attack, and the 21st century will be the age of Alzheimer's disease" (Grossman, 2003, p. 65). Medical science is frantically searching for a cure for this dreaded disease, but so far no cure has been found and perhaps none ever will. Two compelling memoirs provide disturbing yet unsentimental chronicles of life with a parent in the late stages of Alzheimer's. *The Story of My Father* by Sue Miller (2003) records the mental decline of a once quiet, spiritual man whose mind led him into the darkness of paranoia to the extent that his daughter could feel only relief when his miserable existence was over. In *Death in Slow Motion*, Eleanor Cooney (2003) similarly recalls how she became distraught at her mother's fits of rage and hallucinations. As a caregiver, she resorted to medicating herself with Valium and alcohol. "Every age," states Grossman (2003), "has its own way of dying." Also from the adult children's point of view was the 2007 film *The Savages*, starring Philip Seymour Hoffman. The brother and sister in this realistic movie wrestle with the ghosts of the past as they try to work out all the problems attached to finding care for their incapacitated and aggressively angry father.

Another important target area of medical research is of course cancer. As with Alzheimer's, gene studies are the focal point. Through studies of gene instability (one of the major hallmarks of malignancy), the secrets of how the life span operates its own clock may be uncovered. Researchers from the Washington University School of Medicine are sequencing the genomes of cancer cells and normal skin cells to identify gene mutations that play a role in the disease (National Cancer Institute, 2009). Rapid advancements are being made thanks to the new technology, so there may be some breakthroughs in the future. The quest is to discover the reason for late-life vulnerability to cancer and other age-related diseases. Such research is crucial inasmuch as, after reaching late-middle age, men face a 50 percent chance of developing cancer, and women have a 35 percent chance.

As the population ages, we can expect that the increasing medical attention to treatments for the elderly will continue. Consider the plethora of TV ads for drugs for arthritis, impotence, depression, and the like. Historically, medical care was instituted to treat the young and to deal with war wounds, industrial accidents, childbirth, and children's diseases. The typical elderly person consumes a dozen different medications each day (Saleebey, 2001). Many of the drugs are prescribed by different physicians, and these, combined with herbal remedies, can lead to severe interactive effects, especially in an older person whose body has lost the ability to metabolize the product as effectively as a younger person. Two of the most common interactive effects, Saleebey points out, are depression and anxiety. These feelings in turn

can be associated with alcohol use and alcohol-related problems.

Over a third of deaths in America can be attributed to smoking, physical inactivity, poor diet, or alcohol misuse (CDC, 2007). Eating disorders research is finding that eating disorders in elderly persons is sometimes associated with adjustment to traumatic life changes and emotional distress brought on by the death of a spouse and other serious losses (Pomeroy & Browning, 2008). Alcohol abuse also is commonly involved. Recently, a Duke University health survey of 11,000 men and women found that 22 percent of men and 9 percent of women aged 50 to 64 had engaged in binge drinking within the past month of the survey (Blazer & Wu, 2009). Over age 65, 14 percent of the men engaged in such heavy drinking. The fact that the drinking was associated with tobacco use and with use of prescription medication is a major concern. The researchers urged more extensive screening of medical patients for all substance use.

A full report on characteristics of illicit drug use among the aging baby boom population at ages 50 to 59 is available from the Substance Abuse Mental Health Services Administration (SAMHSA, 2009). Revealed in the data collected from over 50,000 respondents in the United States are significantly higher rates of illicit drug use within the same age group over the period from 2002 to 2007. Characteristics associated with the use of illicit drugs among these respondents were found to be male gender, unmarried status, early age of initiation, low education and income, unemployment due to disability, heavy use of alcohol and tobacco, depression, the desire to alleviate stress, and lack of regular religious service attendance. This substance use is high-risk behavior within this older age group because of drug interactions with prescription medications and because of the physiological vulnerabilities and decreased drug tolerance of older adults. The SAMHSA report strongly recommends expanded substance abuse treatment services to meet the needs of this new generation of older Americans.

One criticism of this report that we can make is that the focus is on one of the least dangerous drugs—marijuana—rather than on the misuse of prescription medication and the health-threatening heavy alcohol consumption (see van Wormer & Davis, 2008).

Anecdotal reports from gamblers as well as other sources of evidence reveal that older adults are flocking to gambling casinos in large numbers. As Surface (2009) reports, casinos are investing scooters, wheelchairs, oxygen, and boxes in the bathroom for diabetics to dispose of needles. Surface cites research that shows that people are likely to develop a gambling problem when coping with major changes and losses. Family members can watch for signs of problems and refer relatives with gambling problems to gamblers anonymous groups and to bereavement groups if grief and loss seem to be an issue.

Elderly alcoholics rarely seek treatment on their own, but family members may accompany them to a substance abuse treatment center for help; in my experience, older persons with alcohol and other drug problems were commonly sent to treatment as a result of an arrest for drinking and driving offenses. Sadly, most elders with drinking problems go unnoticed by family and the medical community because they spend a lot of time alone, and their symptoms (e.g., declining cognitive functioning) may be confused with signs of aging.

The Psychology of Aging

Psychological aging is related to biological aging in that the mind is very closely linked to the body. The psychological dimension refers to changes in personality or ways of processing information accompanying the aging process. Factors of health, idleness, loss of contemporaries, reduced income, and many other social variables shape the psychological reality that older adults experience. Looking back can be either joyous or painful. It is important to keep in mind the saying that Fred Rogers (of *Mr. Rogers*, the children's TV show) listed as one of his favorites: "You aren't just the age you are. You are all the ages you ever have been!" (Rogers, 2003, p. 34).

The 2002 Hollywood movie *About Schmidt* poignantly yet humorously takes us on a journey with Warren Schmidt (convincingly played by Jack Nicholson) as he attempts to find meaning in his seemingly meaningless life following his retirement party and the death of his wife.

With the vastness of the future no longer before them and the typical emptiness of the present, many elderly persons find that the past assumes an ever-increasing importance. Perhaps one of the most tragic aspects of despair is the regret one feels about opportunities not seized with regard to both career and relationships, as well as regret at not having spent enough time with one's family.

In *Another Country*, Mary Pipher (1999) skillfully encapsulates the link between older people's biological condition and their state of mind. The developmental period of old age, argues Pipher, is about major physical and social disruptions and psychological stresses. Old-old persons (those over 75) often feel ashamed of what is a natural stage of the life cycle. The greatest challenge of old age is learning to accept vulnerability and to ask for help. The old-old are less sanguine than their young-old counterparts (those in their 60s or early 70s). Pipher explains, "They lead lives filled with the loss of friends and family, of habits and pleasures, and of autonomy. One of the cruel ironies of old-old age is that often when people suffer losses, they must search for new homes" (p. 30). Moving away often makes life more difficult through loss of familiar places and lifelong routines. Wherever they live, their caregivers, as well as their elderly relatives, require a great deal of support and a social system that makes the care they provide psychologically manageable.

Despite their forgetfulness, the elderly have a storehouse of memories, and the past is often more real than the present. Some of the memories involve buried parts of the past (such as war memories) that return in later years. Like other victims of trauma, the old-old can become obsessed with deeply disturbing events of the past and be inclined to tell the same story over and over. Pipher astutely observes that this storytelling is not about communication; rather, it is about therapy.

Ken Burns, in his production of the seven-part TV documentary series, "The War," which was aired on Public Broadcasting Company in 2007, drew on the memories of people who are now mostly in the 80s and 90s from four towns across America (Winn, 2007). Through interviews with men who fought in World War II and with their family members on the home front, the film presents universal themes through a highlighting of the experiences of a relative few. This documentary also inadvertently offers a study in how people who have endured and participated in horrors early in life are often haunted by them later in life when long buried memories are apt to resurface. The personal account of decorated war hero Quentin Aanenson, who engaged in 75 combat missions and returned home on leave to vow never to kill again, is the most gripping. As was revealed in the film and later summarized in Aanenson's obituary, "Later in life, after nightmares kept him from sleep, his right hand, the one that controlled the fighter's guns, would not work well enough to hold a coffee cup" (Sullivan, 2008, p.B5).

"The War," in short, is a documentary that could not have been made earlier when the combat veterans most likely would not have been so in tune with their feelings, much less willing to disclose them. Nor could the film have been made later, as the whole generation who fought in World War II is rapidly dying off. (Learn more about this remarkable film at http://www.pbs.org/thewar).

Indeed, it is a cruel twist of fate that people who have survived unimaginable horrors earlier in life against all odds and who have refused or not needed to dwell on such memories often are driven to return to those long-ago terrors in old age. A social worker, Paula David, who has worked with more than 2,000 Holocaust survivors in Toronto since the early 1990s, is amazed at the resilience of these survivors as they cope with the pain of long-repressed memories that resurface on a regular basis (Meyer,2008). The smell of certain chemicals, standing in line, the sight of the uniforms of security personnel, arrangements to take a shower—all are triggers that can lead to reactions of hysteria in these Holocaust survivors. Researchers and treatment professionals are studying these survivors as preparation for a later influx of traumatized war veterans and victims of genocide in Rwanda and elsewhere. The flashbacks are expected to get worse as these survivors reach old age. With the onset of age-related conditions such as Alzheimer's, people can no longer separate the past from the present; short-term memories begin to disintegrate, while earlier memories may remain sharply in focus. The ability to compartmentalize such memories is lost.

The Social Side of Aging

In a fast-paced, youth-oriented, industrialized society, the process of aging begins to acquire a negative meaning as we move past early adulthood. Middle-aged and elderly people often suffer from internalized ageism, seeing themselves as failing to meet prevailing ideals of beauty and health and therefore as substandard in some way. A sense of worthlessness and depression may result, not from the aging process itself but from the perception of oneself as embarking on a downward spiral, as being "over the hill." Such a perception may set in as early as the late 20s.

The *social* side of aging refers to the cultural expectations of people at various stages of their lives. Socially constructed definitions are important because they are ultimately translated into public policies. Whether the guiding ideology is that the elderly are expected to continue making an active contribution to their families and to society or, conversely, that they should disengage from responsibility in deference to the younger generation has profound—and perhaps unsettling—implications for one's social adjustment to growing old. Some persons who are very old enjoy recreational activities such as that organized at the Western Home in Iowa (see Figure 6.2 later in the chapter).

The gender gap in later life is pronounced; more than three-quarters of women aged 85 and older are widowed compared to 35 percent of men of the same age (Gonyea, 2008). Older women are therefore about twice as likely as men to live alone. These demographic facts mean that older men often have a caretaker when they are old and feeble, whereas women most often do not have the care of a spouse during those final years. They often rely on other relatives, however. Family caregiving is increasing at an unprecedented rate; the primary caregivers are adult children, spouses, and the relatives or friends (Owens-Kane & Chadha, 2008).

Race, ethnicity, and social class status are significant determinants of an individual's experience with aging. Minorities, who were only around 16 percent of the elderly population in 2000, are projected to represent about one-fourth of the total by 2030 (U.S. Department of Health and Human Services, 2009). Members of minority groups actively assume family caretaking even when the caretakers themselves have major health problems and even when the financial burden is great (Owens-Kane & Chadha, 2008). Part of the reason is the inability to afford formal social services, but the tradition of filial responsibility also plays a major role in African American, Asian American, and Hispanic American families.

Multigenerational households are increasingly common today, in part because of the harsh economic conditions associated with people losing their jobs and their homes and in part because of the increase in immigration. Sometimes it's the older parents moving in, with the adult children; sometimes it's the children returning home to live with their parents. Families are doubling up, in short, to save expenses. A portrait of America's households drawn from an analysis of U.S. Census data, shows a 25 percent increase since 1999 in the number of generations of adults living under one roof (Fleck, 2009a).

Membership in an extended family is a primary buffer against the losses associated with advancing age. About twice as many African Americans and Latinos live in extended family situations as do non-Hispanic white Americans (Older Americans 2008, 2008). The groups with the smallest percentage of persons living alone are the Asian and Pacific Islander populations.

Extended family ties are strong among many Native American groups as well. Most tribes assign meaningful roles to elders as transmitters of traditional culture, values, and education. Among upper-class Anglos, similarly,

the elderly occupy a position of honor due to their link to an illustrious and perhaps more prosperous past. Older people with higher incomes report their health as being much better than that of those with lower incomes (Popple & Leighninger, 2008). Regardless of ethnic background or social class, nevertheless, health and loss of functioning are constant concerns, while economic factors provide hardship for most of the very old.

With regard to attitudes toward the elderly, respect for those who have reached the last stage of life is higher in Japan, China, and many other countries than in the United States. Yet there, too, modernization is bringing about change, especially as workers move from rural areas to the cities, leaving their aging relatives behind. In Arab societies, the extended family is highly valued; honor and respect for the elderly are encouraged in the Koran. Traditionally, elderly parents live with the oldest son (Gardiner & Kosmitzki, 2005). People tend to treat and care for their parents in the manner that their parents cared for theirs. Read the following personal narrative to learn about the Latino tradition of family elder care, a practice that should be an inspiration to us all.

Latino Family Ties

Not long after I moved out of my parents' house I began to plan for when my parents would move in with me. Now this was never something we discussed but rather something that was observed. Like the seasons of a year, after a while you just know that this is the way it is and always has been. My first recollection of this type of living arrangement began with my occasional trips as a 4-year-old to my *abuelita*'s [great-grandmother's] shack-like house in the barrio [neighborhood] of the west side. I remember my mother explaining that, during the part of the year, Abuelita lived with her daughter (my grandma Olivia) and that she would spend the weekends living in this little house with a close friend that was her age that she considered to be family. The other half of the year, Abuelita lived with another daughter in Virginia. I found this versatility in living arrangements to be fascinating, and I remember thinking that Abuelita was a woman of adventure, despite her frailty and being 70-plus years old. She appeared to move with the seasons and like the seasons; it appeared that she determined much of her destiny. Her dark, long black hair held up in a tight bun and the masculine cigarettes she puffed on only confirmed my suspicion. I remember thinking that the bun in her hair was for show only, as if her spunky spirit was wrapped up in between the long strands of black hair that she only let down on special occasions, of which small children like me were not allowed to partake. My mother's voice while explaining Abuelita's living arrangement was not laced with pity or shame but rather with normalcy and even a tinge of admiration. And for a long time, this is how I envisioned all elderly women living, carefree and with people who loved them and longed to share in their adventure.

Twenty-four years later, like my abuelita before her, my grandma Olivia now lives in her own house with her two daughters and one of her grandchildren. By no means is she considered "dependent" upon them or a "burden." Rather, she is the spunky head of the household who calls the shots and lets few be tricked by her grandmotherly looks. She still cooks the best meals and has the best stories, and the ring of her laughter is heard throughout the house during all of our family gatherings. To have her in your household is an honor because you know you have the spirit of adventure and wisdom to look upon and admire.

And just as Latinos and Latinas throughout the world carry on this tradition with pride and a feeling of connectedness to their ancestors before them, I know that the time will come when my mother will be an addition and blessing to my home. With her dark, long black hair she will be the spunk in our home and will give more than she could ever take. She cooks better than I ever could and will always know the best way to cure a cold. An even if the time comes when I have to take on the parent role, my caring for her could never outmatch what she has given through her decades of parenting and grandparenting. Her many years of keeping our household intact and safe and holding our hands as children as we discovered the adventurous spirit within ourselves could never be outweighed or overshadowed by any temporary

swapping of care-taking roles. In the end she will always be the guide and I just the follower. I will only aspire to be so adventurous, wise, and comforting.

And because the seasons continually change, my mother will one day no longer be on earth with her children and grandchildren, but her spirit and the honor she earned from her family and ancestors will live on. I can only hope that one day when I am worn with years and filled with stories to share that my son, Nathan, will be able to see the twinkle in my eye and admire my spunky spirit. May my laughter ring across his home and bring warm memories to his heart, and may he always see me as the adventurous woman with the dark, long black hair.

(Printed with permission of Lydia Pérez Roberts, MSW, Ethnic Minorities Cultural and Educational Center, University of Northern Iowa.)

Let us now review the social science literature on persons the social scientists refer to as the "young-old" and the time frame somewhat before and somewhat beyond.

Older Americans Aged 50 to 75

Due to significant differences in the issues they confront and in their self-concept, the young-old are generally differentiated from the old-old. I will follow this approach here. Sociologist Sara Lawrence-Lightfoot (2009) focuses on a rather lengthy and variegated period encompassing the ages of 50 to 75. She refers to this time frame as "the third chapter" or the penultimate stage of life.

Mary Pipher (1999), the author of *Another Country*, differentiates between two stages of old age on the basis of the loss of health. If they have serious chronic health problems, even if in their 60s, Pipher considers those she terms "elders" to be in the class of the old-old on the basis of the physical constraints on their lives. Still, the young-old often face significant health, social, and economic transitions (Knopf, 2008). While old stresses—to do with child rearing, career choices, and so on—may vanish, new ones arise—when to retire, whether or not to relocate, how to meet the needs of frail elderly parents. The needs of this generation of older Americans are of much interest today as the baby boom becomes an aging boom. A nationwide survey conducted by the American Association of Retired Persons (AARP) reported that 27 percent of people approaching retirement age had postponed plans to retire and that about the same percentage were looking for a new job because of uncertainty. Almost one-third thought their jobs would be eliminated in the next year (AARP, 2009).

The initial period of older adulthood is experienced differently by class, the nature of one's occupation, and gender. Affluent white collar workers generally are in a position to work for a longer period than are workers whose occupations depend on their physical strength and agility. Consider the difference in work longevity for ballet dancers and gymnasts versus musicians, or construction workers versus clerical workers, for example. Mandatory retirement at age 65 was the standard practice until 1986 when Congress banned mandatory retirement except in certain industries where it was believed conditions related to advanced age might put the public at risk.

The law had the effect of creating choice where there was no choice before for many workers. This means that some people will decide to work well into their 70s and beyond, some will choose a phase retirement program, and still others will leave the labor force when they are young enough to train for a second career.

For men and women who live at the margins, retirement may not be an option because of inadequate financial resources (Knopf, 2008). Such people may need to retain low-wage and physically demanding jobs to make ends meet. The global economic crisis of 2009 has reduced many older male workers who were once prosperous and anticipating an easy retirement to a situation of financial ruin. In contrast to the previous recessions of 1973–1975 and of 1982 when younger adult men and women were the hardest hit by layoffs (Urquhart & Hewson, 1983), older white males have also been possibly even more affected in the most recent downturn.

Older workers who are laid off are less likely to find another job than younger people, and if they do eventually become reemployed, they suffer a greater loss in hourly wages than do young workers (Johnson, 2009). We learn from media accounts of cases such as the following from Columbus, Ohio:

- Harry Jackson, 55, airline pilot and supervisor, lost his job in 2007 and has found it nearly impossible to get another job. He depleted his savings while his 401K retirement account has shrunk to nothing.
- Mark Montgomery, 53, was let go from an insulation factory and cannot afford his monthly home mortgage payment.
- Timothy Miller, 56, who made roof trusses at a Weyerhaeuser plant, had his health insurance premium cut, which created a crisis with his wife's critical health care needs (Cauchon, 2009).

These unemployed men, according to Cauchon, who personally interviewed them, are desperately seeking ways to reinvent themselves, personally and professionally. Two of them are growing healthy food in the garden; one plans to seek training as an electrician's apprentice. And yet the magnitude of the loss to such seasoned workers as these, the unanticipated thrust into premature retirement, must be profound. The consequences of such layoffs bring a toll to bear on families, the community, and the whole society. Since in Western culture, the work that we do is linked to our personal identity, the inability to find or keep one's job often leads to a diminishing of one's sense of self-worth.

Especially hard hit in the 2007–2009 recession are older Latino men. Even before the recession, Latinos were earning low wages, taking the jobs others did not want, receiving few benefits such as health care and access to paid leave to cover illness. As shown in a detailed report prepared for the Urban Institute (Johnson & Soto, 2009), aging male Latinos are especially vulnerable in a downwardly spiraling economy. Because they tend to work in physically demanding jobs such as construction, aging Latino men cannot expect to maintain their jobs indefinitely and inevitably lose out in competitive times to younger workers. In the recession, many whites are reclaiming jobs they did not look at earlier. For all these workers, forced unemployment and downward mobility exemplify a transition that is generally most unwelcome, especially to people who ordinarily would have expected to have a number of good working years ahead.

Positive Transitions and Turning Points

The literature on turning points, whether in fiction or biography is generally uplifting and centered on young lives—the juvenile delinquent whose life is turned around, the artist whose talents are discovered. Turning-point stories of older people are more rare and often negative and apt to involve a loss or perhaps an insight about life or the past rather than something accomplished or gained. Laurence-Lightfoot's (2009) best-selling book, *The Third Chapter: Passion, Risk, and Adventure in the 25 Years After 50*, which tells of how people "stuck in a rut" became daring and sought out adventures that might have seemed even a little mad, therefore comes as bit of a revelation. After all, we are a youth-oriented culture, as Lawrence-Lightfoot suggests.

Inspired by her colleagues and friends, many of them from the baby boom generation, who were contemplating turning their backs on their careers to embark on new adventures, Laurence-Lightfoot traveled across the United States to record the stories of such post midlife journeys into unknown terrain. Her quest was for understanding about transformation and decision making during a time of life that is often written off as a time of increasing disengagement by other researchers and commentators. Her quest was informed by Erik Erikson and, more specifically, by his life-span organizational scheme. Life-span theory was attractive to Lawrence-Lightfoot in viewing learning as a lifelong process. Each of Erikson's stage crises is not static, but, in Lawrence-Lightfoot's interpretation, will move forward and progress and move backward and regress. Paraphrasing fails to do justice to the writing. As magnificently expressed in *The Third Chapter*:

The journey of leaving in the Third Chapter crosses borders and covers landscapes that are rich with complexity and color. The geography is rocky and irregular, beautiful and tortured, full of hills and valleys, open vistas and blind alleys, and menaced by minefields. The path moves forward and circles back, progresses and regresses, is both constant and changing. The developmental terrain grows more layered; patience trumps speed; restraint trumps ambition; wisdom trumps IQ; "leaving a legacy" trumps "making our mark," and a bit of humor saves us all. (p. 173)

Erikson's sixth stage, which involves resolution of the generativity versus stagnation crisis was discussed in Chapter 5. It is relevant here also because the period extends from early middle age to around 60 and for the emphasis on generativity. Interestingly, and probably not coincidentally, Erikson's stage is reminiscent of Shakespeare's sixth of his Seven Ages of Man, "The sixth age shifts/ Into the lean and slipper'd pantaloon,/With spectacles on nose, and pouch on side" (*As You Like It*, Scene II, vii, 156–158). This stage to Lawrence-Lightfoot is of special relevance to the issues and concerns of persons advancing into the third season of their lives.

For her research on people who took a 180-degree turn, switching the course of their lives midstream, Lawrence-Lightfoot located 40 men and women across the United States within her own relative age group who had switched gears in some dramatic fashion. This was no random sample of the older population. Most of the people interviewed enjoyed a "privileged place" within society that allowed them to consider this option (p. 13). These people are not representative in that they actually get to do what so many of us might like to do, but they are probably representative in the sense that people in their 50s and 60s ponder such moves—to a new career, to writing a novel, running for political office, moving to an exotic country, going on the stage—before it is too late. The sense of "I want more out of life than this" is probably universal and even more pronounced in those whose work has become a drudgery. The difference between Lawrence-Lightfoot's subjects and most of the rest of us is that these people both had the nerve to "make the break" and the resources to allow them to fake a risk.

The Third Chapter traces the stories of a mechanical engineer who moved into the world of art, a lawyer who enrolled in divinity school, a teacher who became an actress, and a businessman who got involved in international relief work. Sometimes the narrators left one career to pursue another; sometimes they retired to engage in new learning. The learning that takes place in the third chapter, notes Lawrence-Lightfoot, is often different from the kind of learning that takes place early in life. We were taught to rush, compete, and to avoid failure. The new learning, in contrast, involves slowing down, risking making a fool of ourselves, and above all, learning to listen. The story of Steven Fox, a 67-year-old public health doctor from an upper-middle-class African American family encapsulates this path to self fulfillment. As Lawrence-Lightfoot tells his story:

> In a decision that "snuck up" on him, Steven decided to sign up for voice lessons at the local community music school. This was a "radical departure" from his "workaholic life," which never left him any time to play. (His mother had discouraged him from becoming an opera singer.)
>
> But a few years ago, he decided that he had denied himself long enough, and he secretly began taking voice lessons. (He is not a great singer.) The sound does not matter to Steven, however. What matters is the chance he now has to live his dream. (pp. 81–82)

Many discover, as Lawrence-Lightfoot contends, in this second to last stage of life, a time of relative freedom when the traditional norms and career pressures are less demanding. It is also a time to recover from earlier negative experiences from wounds people often do not even know they have. Embedded in these stories told by the 40 subjects of their journeys to find meaning in life are the themes of risk and resilience.

Lawrence-Lightfoot's theory on aging does not fit the classic conceptualizations. To appreciate this fact, let us take a look at *disengagement theory*, which was prominent in the 1960s. This model of aging describes later life as a time of withdrawal for older adults as they exit their former roles. Based on data collected on the Kansas City Study on Adult Life from 172 older adults, Cumming and Henry (1961) maintained that for the benefit of society, disengagement from social roles is a functional and healthy response that should be encouraged. *Activity theory* was another perspective that was derived for the same Kansas City data and developed by Havighurst, Neugarten, and Tobin (1968). These researchers stressed personality characteristics as pivotal in staying actively involved in work roles or community activities and relationships. *Continuity theory*, similarly, stresses staying active but proposes that this involvement be an extension of earlier social engagement. Lawrence-Lightfoot's perspective is a departure from these; I will call it a "self-actualization theory" in that it's about pursuing dreams that have been long suppressed. Even in a time of economic hardship, people can embark on new adventures that they had long put on hold, for example, planting an organic garden, "coming out" as gay or lesbian, or taking in a foster child. And some take to social activism. One group of activists, however, ranges in age from 65 to 81. Calling themselves "Raging Grannies," these older women protest government military policy through the use of humor (see Figure 6.1). A recent tactic was for members of the group, including one 74-year-old woman, to try to enlist in the army to go to Iraq so their grandchildren could come home (British Broadcast Company [BBC], 2005).

Age 75 and Above

Between 1900 and 2007, the percentage of Americans 65+ has tripled (from 4.1 percent in 1900 to 12.6 percent in 2007). A child born in 2006 could expect to live to over 78 years old,

Figure 6.1. "Raging grannies," a demonstration by a group of older Seattle activists who use humor to protest U.S. military policy. Photo by Rupert van Wormer.

about 30 years longer than a child born in 1900. Much of this increase occurred because of reduced death rates for children and young adults. However, the period of 1985–2005 has seen reduced death rates for persons aged 65–84 as well, especially for men aged 65–74 (U.S. Department of Health and Human Services, [DHHS] 2009). See Table 6.2 for further information from the DHHS (2009) *Profile of Older Americans*. From these statistics on advanced aging, we can grasp the anticipated increase of Americans in the category of the very old (or old-old).

All the problems associated with aging accelerate with advancing years. Memory loss, hearing problems, and joint pain are among the most noticeable afflictions in this age group. By age 85 almost one in three individuals has

at least a moderate problem with memory loss (Gonyea, 2008). Such cognitive impairments, particularly Alzheimer's disease and other forms of dementia, compromise one's level of functioning. As expressed in the book on aging by Pipher (1999), "Bodies last longer than brains, support systems or savings accounts" (p. 17).

The poverty rates that were relatively low in the 65–75-year-old age group have become considerably higher in recent years. Over one in four older African- and Latin American women live below the poverty line (Gonyea, 2008). A high proportion of their limited incomes is spent on medication, but many do without it. The more economically dependent old and vulnerable people are, the more they are susceptible to situations of exploitation and abuse.

Table 6.2   Highlights Specific to Advanced Aging

➤ Persons reaching age 65 have an average life expectancy of an additional 19.0 years (20.3 years for females and 17.4 years for males).

➤ Half of older women (49%) age 75+ live alone.

➤ About 450,000 grandparents aged 65 or more had the primary responsibility for their grandchildren who lived with them.

➤ The population 65 and over will increase from 35 million in 2000 to 40 million in 2010 (a 15% increase) and then to 55 million in 2020 (a 36% increase for that decade).

➤ The 85+ population is projected to increase from 4.2 million in 2000 to 5.7 million in 2010 (a 36% increase) and then to 6.6 million in 2020 (a 15% increase for that decade).

Note. Principal sources of data for the Profile are the U.S. Bureau of the Census, the National Center on Health Statistics, and the Bureau of Labor Statistics.

Source: Administration on Aging, U.S. Department of Health and Human Services, p. 1. Retrieved from at http://www.mowaa.org/Document.Doc?id=69

Elder Abuse

Home, however, is not always the best place for the aged. Elder or parent abuse occurs most often when the parents live with their children or are dependent on them. Tensions can mount. Under the category of elder abuse, Suppes and Wells (2008) include physical mistreatment, emotional abuse, material or financial abuse, violation of rights, and life-threatening neglect. Although exact statistics are not available due to the strong reluctance of elderly family members to report their children or spouses for abuse, estimates of prevalence range from 3.2 to 10 percent of older adults who suffer some form of abuse or neglect (Brownell & Giblin, 2009). What we know from sources such as the National Center for Elder Abuse is this: Women especially over age 80 are most likely to be abused or neglected; the alleged abuser is often a family member such as the spouse; and most mistreatment occurs in the home (Thompson, 2003).

Causes of elder abuse listed by Brownell and Giblin include caregiver stress, abuser impairment (for example, dementia), abuser criminality, and victim impairment and vulnerability. Harsh economic conditions are a factor today, in both physical abuse and financial abuse. Hundreds of elders in Michigan, for example, have fallen victim to financial crimes, and over a thousand cases were investigated in 2008 by the Department of Human Services.

Between 2000 and 2008, the number of suspected cases of maltreatment increased four-fold (Jun, 2009). In Wisconsin, despite the fact that the state that does not have an advanced reporting system, over 4,000 suspected abuse and neglect cases were reported in 2006 (Mosiman, 2008). This does not include the 500 additional reports of nursing home abuse. For help in cases of elder domestic violence, programs such as the Older Abused Women's Program in Milwaukee can provide much-needed support (Wilke & Vinton, 2003).

All states have elder abuse reporting laws designed to protect vulnerable older adults from maltreatment (Barsky, 2010). Abuse laws typically protect elders from physical, psychological, sexual, and financial abuse and intentional neglect. Elder abuse laws are far more difficult to enforce, as Barsky indicates, than child protection laws. Child protection laws are based on the premise that children lack the mental capacity to protect themselves and do not have a choice whether or not to accept protective services. In the case of older adults, it is not clear whether they lack this capacity or not so their vulnerability has to be assessed on a case-by-case basis. Barring mental incapacity, the older person has the right to refuse help and many good reasons for doing so, such as the desire not to be institutionalized. Barriers to extricating oneself from a threatening situation include lack of money, family and social pressure, loss of contact with children or animals in the household, personal values about family, and fear of retribution.

Social workers are the best equipped to address elder abuse because as professionals they work with families in so many different capacities and in a variety of agency settings. Brownell and Giblin (2009) offer a social work assessment protocol. Information obtained in this format is pertinent to the intervention strategy. For example, abuse perpetuated by a spouse in the secondary stage of Alzheimer's disease would suggest a different strategy than abuse inflicted by a substance-abusing grandchild. By remaining alert to the possibility of abuse, social workers, as Brownell and Giblin suggest, can improve the safety and well-being of the clients they serve. To help the abused or seriously neglected older family member reach a decision about leaving the situation, Barsky (2010) recommends the use of motivational strategies for decision making. Motivational strategies emphasize choice in decision making and consciousness raising to enhance client awareness of one's rights and the impact of the abuse on the individual.

How about situations in which the elderly person is or was the abuser? I am referring to a reversal of elder abuse, to the configuration in which family members are providing care for elderly persons who abused them, usually in their childhoods. Fiske (2003) addresses this rarely addressed, but not unheard of, problem. When an incest survivor faces the prospect of having to care for his or her offender, complex emotions, understandably, are aroused. Other family members, such as a stepmother, are often unaware of the survivor's state of mind. The survivor who refuses to care for the now frail victimizer is often misunderstood. Jane Smiley's (1991) Pulitzer prize-winning novel, *A Thousand Acres*, brought to the screen in 1997 with memorable performances by Michelle Pfeiffer and Jessica Lange, fictionalizes such a situation. A modernized version of Shakespeare's *King Lear*, the story is told from the neglectful daughter's standpoint. In both renditions, the elderly father is treated mercilessly by two of his daughters. But in the modern version, as we learn through flashbacks, the reason for the rejection lies in dark secrets from their past.

Signs of Contentment in Old Age

Despite all the negatives, the vast majority of the old-old report in personal interviews that they are doing better than they expected, and that they are experiencing many of the good things associated with aging (Pew Research Center, 2009). These include more time with

Figure 6.2. A great grandmother and her great grandchildren. When their great grandmother comes to visit, a happy time is had by all. Photo by Natalie Moorcroft.

the family, especially with grandchildren and great-grandchildren, and reduced stress. The happiest of the respondents to the survey had good friends, financial security, and were in good health. Compared to younger age groups in the study, people at the oldest age levels stated that religion was very important in their lives. (See Figure 6.2, which captures these children's excitement over time spent with their great grandmother.)

To learn about happiness across the life span, George Vaillant (2002), a psychiatrist and expert on human development, examined the extensive data from an earlier longitudinal study in which data were collected on three cohorts of men and women of various social classes who were born in 1910, 1920, and 1930. What Vaillant found was that the goals so prominent early in life, such as high achievement, are less prominent late in life. Successful aging, he found, was associated not with achievements but with close relationships and with generativity. "The last years of life," he writes, paraphrasing the Bible, "without hope and love become a mere sounding brass or a tinkling cymbal" (p. 257). Based on his longitudinal investigation, Vaillant concluded, "I have marshaled evidence that with aging there is a widening social radius, a greater tolerance, and a maturation of involuntary coping mechanisms" (p. 281). This brings us to a closer look at the nature of resilience, a resilience that can be found in older Americans stories.

Resilience in Older African American Women

Written by Katherine van Wormer and Charletta Sudduth

Maltreatment of a population across generations can result in what some researchers refer to as historical trauma. Historical trauma is considered, for example, to be a major factor in the high Native American mortality rates from alcohol-related conditions, including suicide and homicide (Brave Heart, 2007), and in the fatalism evidenced in some of the most impoverished regions of Appalachia (O'Brien, 2001).

Researchers who are studying resilience within a socially oppressive environment need to recognize the social and cultural context in which individual resilience is embedded (Greene, 2008). Resilience, like oppression, is both a psychological and sociological phenomenon for an individual growing up in a racially hostile environment. Ethnically and racially diverse families and communities can help children cope with discrimination by teaching them means of resisting the oppression and by helping them to avoid internalizing the message.

As part of our research project in preserving the stories of African American women who worked as maids in the Deep South and who endured conditions of economic and social oppression during the times of lynchings, Jim Crow laws, and little work other than sharecropping, we also learned a lot about resilience. The excerpts below are drawn from the personal narratives of three women who today live in Waterloo, Iowa, and are well respected in the community. All of them carry memories of another time and place.

In their stories of growing up under conditions of gross economic exploitation and disempowerment,

these women demonstrated a remarkable degree of resilience. Their later success in rearing a family and in participating in church and community life in an integrated Midwestern city further attests to their ability to prevail over their personal hardship. Several of the major themes of resilience commonly found among older African Americans were evidenced in the interviews—respect for family and elders, valuing education, strong religious faith, and a belief in the meaning of life.

Respect for One's Family and Elders

Annie Pearl Stevenson fondly recalls her father, a hard-working farmer:

> When I was little, my dad was a sharecropper. But he was a very smart man though. He would not allow us to go to the store in Taylor (Mississippi). What they would do is they would allow people to buy on credit and when the crops came in they would say you had spent all your profit, and you couldn't argue with that. We did without a lot. . . . My dad saved a little and eventually bought the land. . . . He did not want us working for white folks because of pride. He was a proud man. He believed in earning a living for his family.

Annie Johnson, similarly, has fond memories of her parents—her mother sewed clothes for her and her sisters, made quilts, and baked for her neighbors, and her father taught himself to read and read Bible stories to the children.

> My daddy could read. There's always a way for everything. My daddy had to work instead of going to school. He always said, "You don't have to be crazy; you don't have to be ignorant. If you know your ABC's you can read."

Valuing of Education

"I believe education is the most important thing you can have growing up." These words of Vinella Byrd, who has done much in recent years to promote education among the youth, sum up her philosophy. Despite, or even because of their early deprivation of an education, she like the other two women has instilled a value of education in her children and grandchildren.

As Mrs. Stevenson shares:

> I know I always wanted to go to college. Always. At that time I really wanted to enroll in Ole Miss,

which we couldn't because of the color of our skin. Only whites could go there. So I turned my mind to Jackson State. I never wanted to just do that kind of work (domestic service) all my life. I wanted a better job so I could provide for my family like the couple I worked for who were going to college to better themselves.

Resistance to Oppression

Mrs. Stevenson reminisces about her participation in the historic event in 1962, when James Meredith enrolled against Mississippi law and in defiance of the whites who rioted at the University of Mississippi:

The elderly people didn't want us to go as teenagers, and they didn't go. One of the bus drivers took us down there to stand with James Meredith when he enrolled. Rocks were thrown at the windows; glass was shattered and everything. People were calling us the N word name—"Turn this bus around. Go home!" So we went, said no. Most of the busloads didn't make it, had to turn around. But we did.

Mrs. Johnson, who grew up in the 1930s, had to be more devious. In her youth she was involved in a wild rescue of a man in the Delta who was held there against his will and in considerable danger. And later, working as a maid in Illinois, she and her sister got even with the lady of the house who refused to pay them. Revenge took place in the form of putting butter on the woman's socks and contaminating a turkey that was in the oven.

Strong Religious Faith

Mrs. Stevenson was raised a Baptist and attended Antioch Missionary Baptist Church for most of her adult life; today she is Pentecostal and attends the Church of God in Christ. Mrs. Johnson, who regularly attends the Gift of Life Church, provided the most detail on this subject. In answer to the question of whether black people learned from the whites about religion, Mrs. Johnson was emphatic:

No! The whites learned from the blacks. Blacks might have had something to do with the whites—where I come from—becoming Christian. We used to—not in churches—but there used to be a white man who came to the house all the time with his Bible, and he and my daddy would sit and read the Bible.

A Positive Attitude and Belief in the Meaning of Life

When asked what was the attitude of the white people toward black people, Mrs. Johnson said simply and rather astonishingly, "It was good." To prove the point, she gave an example of how during Prohibition, the sheriff allowed her daddy to keep making his "home brew, as long as you don't have more than 5 gallons."

Mrs. Stevenson was more reflective:

I wouldn't trade nothing for the experience. I learned how to treat people. It was a learning experience, and by the way, I don't hold any animosity. I often wonder why not. It just made me the person I am today. Like that incident with the floor (she learned to tell the truth after she falsely claimed to mop the floor and was caught). I love everyone. Some of the things we went through—if there ever was a time to have hate in your heart that was it. But we didn't. Because that was the way of life and we adapted to it.

Resilience, such as that demonstrated by the lives and philosophies of the older African Americans who participated in this study, had its roots in their upbringing in the rural South during the days of segregation. The three women whose quotes were used in this boxed reading not only endured the oppression in their early lives they prevailed over them.

References

Brave Heart, M.Y. (2007). The impact of historical trauma: The example of the Native community. In M. Bussey & J. B. Wise (Eds.), *Trauma transformed: An empowerment response* (pp. 176–193). New York: Columbia University Press.

Greene, R. (2008). Risk and resilience theory: A social work perspective. In R. Greene (Ed.), *Human behavior theory and social work practice* (3rd ed.). New Brunswick, NJ: Transaction Publishers.

O'Brien, J. (2001). *At home in the heart of Appalachia.* New York: Knopf.

(Printed with permission of Charletta Sudduth.)

Figure 6.3. Social activities at the Western Home, Cedar Falls, Iowa. Photo by Rupert van Wormer.

Long-Term Care

Only about 4.4 percent of the 65+ population live in institutional settings such as nursing homes, but the percentage increases dramatically with age, going from 4.1 percent for persons 75–84 years old to 15.1 percent for persons 85 and over (U.S. Department of Health and Human Services, 2009). Senior housing is increasingly becoming an acceptable alternative to living alone for persons who can afford it. Estimates are that approximately 2–5 percent of older Americans live in senior housing with supportive services available to them. See Figure 6.3 which shows a group of older women engaged in social activities at the progressive Western Home in Cedar Falls, Iowa, a popular place for social work students to do their field placements.

The term *long-term care* traditionally was associated only with nursing homes but today refers to a variety of services for people who need care on a long-term basis (Miller, 2008). Since most people would prefer to stay in their own homes and live independently, services such as assistance with modifying the home for safe mobility, help with securing transportation, money, and medication management are increasingly available. New technologies that are being marketed include alarm systems, sensors that measure physiological responses, easy-to-use cell phones, and a system to shut off an unused stove automatically.

One innovative housing arrangement—the continuing care retirement community (CCRC) is growing in popularity (Lesser & Pope, 2007). Such community programming provides diversified and coordinated services; some models use care managers to assess an individual's need to move from one part of the program to another when a higher level of care is required (Miller, 2008). At the minimal care level, residents typically live in apartments, often adjacent to golf courses and other recreational activities. Recreational activities such as reading and card-playing clubs are regularly scheduled. Residents generally are required to pay high entrance fees as well as monthly payments.

But given the current economic crisis, even some individuals who ordinarily would have the resources to afford such retirement home living are being hit by the housing crisis. According to a recent AARP report, more than one-quarter of people who were delinquent in their mortgages or faced home foreclosures in late 2007 were aged 50 or older (Fleck, 2009b). Florida, where many older Americans live, has been especially hard hit because people's homes have become worth far less than they paid for them. Many retirement communities are struggling accordingly.

The frail elderly who are cared for in nursing homes might pay for the care themselves until their money runs out; then the residents become eligible for Medicaid. The Centers for Medicare and Medicaid Services see that nursing homes are inspected every 12 to 15 months or when a complaint is lodged. Deficiencies are noted publicly on Nursing Home Compare. In the Inspector General's (Levinson, 2008) report on trends in nursing home deficiencies, over 90 percent of nursing homes surveyed had at least one deficiency. The for-profit homes fared the worst (about 80 percent of nursing homes are for profit). Quality of care—for example, failure to prevent and treat pressure sores and urinary tract infections—was the category with the most deficiencies. Although the report did not focus on problems in funding, the deficiencies undoubtedly are associated with inadequate federal and state reimbursement rates and with too high staff/patient ratios. One problem with nursing homes, as described in an Associated Press article, is that nursing homes have become dumping grounds for persons with mental illness (Johnson, 2009). These younger, stronger people, some of whom who have been released from jails and prison, now make up 9 percent of nursing home residents. Whether violent or not, their presence can be frightening to frail elderly residents and staff who are not trained to work with them. A number of tragic assaults and killings are described in the article.

For models of well-funded and well-run long-term facilities, we can look to the Scandinavian countries and the Netherlands, where standards are very high. There, more than 8 percent of people aged 65 and over reside in such facilities (U.S. Census, 2009). Even more impressive is the wealth of home health care services available to older residents in these welfare states.

Facing Death

Elizabeth Edwards (wife of former presidential candidate John Edwards) has written a book on coping with both her husband's infidelity and her diagnosis of terminal cancer. "When I die," she writes, "my place in the lives of others will be filled by other people. I know this. It is true for all of us. Someone else will have your job; someone else will mow your lawn; someone else will kiss the cheeks of those you love. One of the reasons that I spend time labeling baskets and organizing Christmas ornaments is that I have tried to create a world for my family that will last longer than the years I now have left" (p. 189). In her memoir *Resilience: Reflections on the Burdens and Gifts of Facing Life's Adversities*, Edwards shares with us her struggles against the forces of denial, anger, and acceptance. In the end, acceptance wins out.

Viewers of the 2009 NBC documentary *Farrah's Story* vicariously went through every uplifting and agonizing moment of Fawcett's struggle against the throes of anal cancer and its treatment (NBC, 2009). The famous sex idol who also had won accolades for her serious acting performance had crusaded for domestic violence services for battered women. Now she was crusading for the right of patients to receive alternative treatments for cancer, such as embryonic stem cell treatments as she was receiving in Germany. In her video diary, which was shot with Fawcett's own video camera, we watch as this woman receives the treatments in Germany, hears good news and then bad news, then receives conventional chemotherapy and radiation treatment in California, loses all her strength, her health, and finally, her hair. Her narration is memorable:

> This disease is a terrorist inside your body fighting a war, and it's filled with hate. . . . Of all the things I've ever hoped for in my life, finding a doctor to surgically remove

my anal cancer did not even make the top one million on my list.

Cancer is a disease that is mysterious, headstrong and makes up its own rules. And mine, to this date, is incurable. I know that everyone will die eventually, but I do not want to die of this disease.

The documentary aired on May 15, 2009. Farrah Fawcett died June 25, 2009.

Cancer survivors often report that their brush with death can amplify the joys of living; this is a phenomenon reported by Goldberg (2005), who survived prostate cancer. His article begins by quoting Peter Jennings, ABC news anchor, who disclosed that "Ten million Americans are living with cancer, and I have a lot to learn from them." Goldberg sees lessons here for everyone. There is nothing like the prospect of one's own death to give one a wake-up call about living, he claims. Possibly facing death himself, he discovered that all of his accomplishments were fleeting, that the past was irrelevant, and that the future was no longer certain. What mattered was the moment, the beauty and joy of life in the present; that was everything.

Since we live in the present and invest in the future, we commonly deny old age and death. The painful paradox of death in the midst of life is addressed with rare eloquence in Becker's classic, *The Denial of Death* (1973). This paradox is two-fold, first that humans are the only creatures whose very intelligence forces them to cope with the awareness of their own mortality. The second paradox is that it takes years for people to develop the maturity to know how to live; then they are good only for dying.

With the publication of the bestseller *On Death and Dying*, Kübler-Ross (1969), who died in 2004, revolutionized the concepts of death and dying. She not only provided a window into the minds of the terminally ill but also offered a psychological road map for the end of life and the course of grief (Szegedy-Maszak, 2004). Kübler-Ross helped people understand the emotions and cognitions surrounding our awareness of the inevitable. Her stages—denial, anger, bargaining, depression, and acceptance—are universally known. Through her writings

and teachings, Kübler-Ross helped launch the hospice-care movement.

When I was working for a brief period at a community home health care and hospice in Washington State, I pondered the remarkable resilience of the staff in dealing with death and dying every day. I began to study the various styles of coping by staff and family alike. By the time I left the hospice, I had drawn up a list of coping devices, all normal reactions to the psychological demands of work with the bereaved and the dying. From the literature on death and dying and my work, I filtered out five ideologies, all different but united by one theme: denial of the reality of death. All were escape mechanisms, but under circumstances in which escape is not necessarily an unhealthy response. Elsewhere I list these ideologies as *blaming the victim* for the illness as a way of distancing oneself from the suffering and *denial of death*, which is consistent with the American creed, which stresses youth, optimism, and progress. The remaining psychological strategies for dealing with death that I have seen are *escape through medical jargon* (used by nurses where I worked); *escape through social death* (used by some family members who seemed to have already "buried" the dying person); and *escape through redefinition*, which, as the direct opposite of denial, is an overly positive approach, almost a romanticizing of death and the dying process (van Wormer, 2006).

Mexicans and Mexican Americans have much to teach us about the recognition of death. In private correspondence to me (October 13, 2003), Pérez Roberts explained that, in Mexican culture, it is unheard of to put older family members away because they are an inconvenience. Joking about doing this, however, is common. "This is kind of how the Día de los Muertos celebration is, too," she wrote. "Mexicans have a fun celebration of the day of the dead because it is their way of honoring the dead, but at the same time laughing in the face of death. Not letting it get the best of them."

One positive development borrowed from Europe and now available all over the United States and Canada is hospice. Hospice programs have been set up to provide quality of life to terminal patients and to assist them at home or in a homelike setting. Pain relief is encouraged to keep patients as comfortable as possible (Zastrow, 2004). Hospice workers (who are often social workers) also assist families throughout the bereavement process. Knowledge and understanding of the dynamics of dealing with the loss of a patient or loved one are essential to effective social work with those who have come to the end of their lives. For close family members, the emotions attached to grief and loss intensify their feelings about the loved one. Memories come to the fore. The first line of the 1968 film *I Never Sang for My Father* (spoken by Gene Hackman) is haunting: "Death ends a life, but it does not end a relationship which strives for some resolution which it may never find." The reference, which is the theme of the movie, is to an ambivalent father–son relationship.

Assisted Suicide and Euthanasia

Physician-oriented, cure-based health care is in many ways unsuited to the needs of older people, who typically have chronic conditions with social dimensions (McDaniel & Gee, 1993). The use of advanced technologies on the aged, who may finish out their lives on a respirator in intensive care, results in unnecessary pain for the patients, guilty feelings for family members, and great expense for society. This process further creates a convenient scapegoat—the elderly themselves—for a society that is facing rising health care costs.

Increasingly, Americans and some Europeans are seeking ways to exert some measure of control over where and how they die. The topic of euthanasia is highly controversial and frightening both in society's acceptance and in its rejection. The former opens up the possibility that people might be talked into dying; the latter presents images of the horrible pain and indignity of life prolonged artificially by machines.

Euthanasia literally means "good death" from the Greek *eu* meaning well or good and *thanatos* (death). Later, the word came to mean inducing an easy death (Paterson, 2009). As of 2009, some forms of euthanasia are legal in Belgium, Luxembourg, and the Netherlands; in Switzerland the doctor leaves the lethal dose for someone else to administer (Thomasson, 2009) as is allowed in the U.S. states of Oregon and Washington. Euthanasia, unlike assisted suicide, can be involuntary, for example, when a person is brain dead and on artificial life supports (Paterson, 2009). The goal in both cases is generally understood to alleviate a person's pain and suffering when there is no hope of recovery.

Whether to permit assistance in suicide and euthanasia—this is among the most contentious moral and public policy questions in the United States today. The passionate nature of the present debate came to light recently in town hall meetings centered on health care proposals. The false, yet wholly believed rumor that Obama administration's health care proposals would create government-sponsored "death panels" and "pull the plug on grandma" became so volatile that all reference to funding for "end of life" services had to be dropped from the proposal (Rutenberg & Calmes, 2009).

According to survey data cited by the Pew Research Center (2006), 70 percent of members of the public support allowing a person to die while about half favor legalizing physician-assisted suicide in cases of incurable and debilitating disease. The U.S. Supreme Court has ruled that the decision to allow physician-assisted suicide should be decided by the states. A recent survey found that nine out of ten Americans say they would want to die at home if faced with the end stages of a terminal illness, and most Americans support the removal of life support in cases such as that of Terri Schiavo (Knickerbocker, 2005).

The Schiavo case, which involved a young woman who had lapsed into a "persistent vegetative state" and whose parents fought to maintain her state by means of a feeding tube, was blasted on the news so much that some people quit watching news programs for a week or so. This frustrating case, which pitted Schiavo's husband against her parents, brought national attention to end-of-life care and indirectly to legal policies in Oregon.

Oregon, alone among the states, has legalized physician-assisted suicide under strictly controlled conditions. Oregon's Death with Dignity Act allows doctors to prescribe (but not administer) a lethal dosage of drugs at the request of terminally ill patients with less than six months to live. The final act of human life is played out at home and not in a hospital. Critics warned that a wave of suicides would follow, including a rush of patients from other states and those pressured by relatives to end their lives out of economic circumstances. None of that appears to have happened, however. The number of people who choose this option is small—about 30 a year (Knickerbocker, 2005). The vast majority are people in the late stages of cancer under hospice care. Even in countries in which physician-assisted suicide has been legalized such as the Netherlands, the reported rate of such planned suicides is still less than eight percent of all cancer deaths (Nissim, Gagliese, & Rodin 2009). Surveys of physicians, however, show that a high percentage have assisted dying patients in hastening their deaths even when such practices are technically illegal (Nissim et al., 2009). The advantage of the voluntary euthanasia option for dying patients is that it empowers them to exert some control over the manner of their death and its timing.

Implications for Practice

The shift from late middle age to old age is one that involves changes for the individual across multiple domains—the biological, psychological, social, and spiritual. Knowledge of such changes and of the demographic realities, the health and health care challenges, and the losses over time that accompany aging can inform the process of social work. Knowledge of the principles of risk and resilience theory can enrich social work and help us better understand how some individuals falter at later stages of life while others somehow can overcome the most undesirable of pasts with a resilience that can only be admired.

A recognition of economic factors in aging and the impact of unemployment in recession on the younger group of older adults is one of the themes of this chapter that social workers will want to take into account. The classism that is evident in the upbringing and educating

of children continues across the life span. The reality is that those who are born poor are apt to die poor. The feminization of poverty is a fact of life in the late stages as well. These facts are true within the United States and cross-culturally. But some other countries do have stronger social welfare states; the deficiencies in our system impact all but the very rich in the United States. Whether they work in nursing homes or in any other social work arena, members of this profession have been at the forefront of the movement to strengthen the safety net and to provide the kind of health care options that are so clearly needed.

Ego integrity at the stage of late adulthood depends on dealing with loss and grief, maintaining good health, close ties to family and/or friends, and making active contributions to the lives of others. Central to Erikson's eighth and final developmental task is the search for meaning. The struggle of frail elderly people to maintain independence and mobility in the face of multiple challenges is both psychosocial and spiritual and calls for a social work response to address both (Kovacs, 2008). Elderly people come into counseling for the same reasons others do—for substance abuse problems, to make plans due to impending afflictions such as Alzheimer's disease or cancer, for grief counseling, to reach a decision concerning the care of a dependent mentally disabled son or daughter, or as a family member of a client. People who do best at this stage (as at any stage) are those who have a positive outlook through positive reframing to help them see that life has meaning for them and that they have contributed in ways they perhaps do not realize.

One of the most difficult tasks of old age is to learn to adjust to everyday life without the care and companionship of a significant other. This often means learning to live alone, or, if in the company of others, how to cope with the lifestyles, technologies, and choices of a younger generation. For persons in bereavement, first comes a period of preoccupation with memories and images of the deceased. Sometimes there is the expression of displaced anger toward others who "do not understand." Social workers can help most through empathic listening. Bereavement and self-help groups that are found in most communities are an excellent resource for people both in finding others in a similar situation and in providing recreational opportunities.

Social workers, using a strengths perspective, can help older clients and their families draw on their own resources in gaining access to the desired services to maintain an optimum level of self-sufficiency. Empowering social work, first and foremost, is centered on the relationship. Even after the essential services have been provided, a lot of work is yet to be done to sustain the individual in the new living circumstances. The challenge of strengths-based case management with elderly clients is to resolve or at least reduce the interpersonal conflicts within the personal support networks that inevitably arise. For isolated individuals, the practitioner can help them to reestablish their ties to the community and neighborhood. The strengths model advocates employing natural helpers and resources whenever possible.

Membership in community recreational and volunteer groups, a renewed or continuing church involvement, and participation in other activities for spiritual fulfillment can provide a sense of meaning in life and a connectedness to the community. Social workers can encourage such involvement and help arrange transportation services if needed.

Attending to the spiritual realm of human life is central to a strengths perspective. In the lives of elders, the role of both organized religious institutions and private spiritual activity can assume a role of major importance. For many, a spiritual self is a critical component in defining the meaning of one's life and one's relationship with a Higher Power.

Summary and Conclusion

A discussion of late adulthood concludes the life-span portion of the chapter and of the previous three chapters of this book. These three chapters that have taken us from infancy through old age have been informed by life-span developmental theory and constructs.

Following Erikson's developmental formulation, this chapter has covered the period of generativity versus stagnation, the crisis to be resolved in the earliest stage of late adulthood to the final season of life. Erikson viewed the crisis of this latest season in terms of a wrestling between ego integrity and despair as one comes face to face with the inevitability of death.

Recognition of the ways people of different ages handle the psychological blows—abuse and oppression in childhood, loss and disease in later life—can increase our empathy with clients. In this way, psychological theory and social work practice are joined. A familiarity with risk and resilience theory can be helpful in social work with the aged as well. Three qualities we can look for in individuals—emotional stability, ego strength, and the pursuit of self-betterment—are key attributes of resilience, resilience in the very young and in the very old. To this list, I would add cultural pride and moral values. In our resilience study of older African American women who survived the assaults of the segregation era, these traits were major sources of strength (recall the boxed text by van Wormer and Sudduth). And we have seen the love that is possible when care for aged relatives is a cultural norm as in many African American families.

Consistent with an empowerment perspective, we have considered the evidence for resilience in survivors of trauma early in life. Despite the hardships— physically, psychologically, and economically—of growing old and facing unwelcome change, the degree of resilience that is found in this age group is impressive. It is, in fact, reassuring. As we learned in interviews with older African American survivors of oppression growing up, those women who were able to overcome the obstacles had the ego integrity to manage the challenges of later life. They reveal their resilience in they way they look back on their early lives with pride rather than self-pity or anger. A key continuing source of empowerment for these women is the tradition of mutual aid that is prominent among cultural minorities and rural populations.

I would like to conclude this chapter with Erikson's (1950/1963) thoughtful linking of infancy and the first of the ego values (trust) with old age and the last of the ego values (integrity): "It seems possible," he said, "to further paraphrase the relation of adult integrity and infantile trust by saying that healthy children will not fear life if their elders have integrity enough not to fear death" (p. 269).

Thought Questions

1. How can old age be considered "a foreign country"?
2. Discuss the quote from Tennessee Williams that you cannot be old without money.
3. What are the general images of older adults as portrayed in TV ads?
4. According to Santrock, what are some of the factors that predict high status for older people? Which ones apply in the United States?
5. Recall the history of Social Security and its significance today.
6. How does life expectancy vary across the world? What are some factors that affect longevity in a society?
7. What was Shakespeare's concept of aging? How did his stages (ages of man) parallel yet differ from those of Erikson?
8. Discuss the basic senses relevant to the biological process of aging.
9. Discuss one of the fictional stories mentioned in this chapter about the ravages of old age.
10. Describe addictive problems that may afflict older adults.
11. What did Mr. Rogers mean by his statement that you are all the ages you have ever been?
12. Describe male/female differences in family life during the final years. Consider economic as well as personal issues.
13. What can we learn from other cultures about caring for the elderly? Refer to the observations on Latino family ties by Lydia Pérez Roberts.
14. Discuss the impact of the global economic crisis on various age groups.
15. Consider Lawrence-Lightfoot's revelations in her book *The Third Chapter*. How do you account for these major life changes at such a mature stage of life?
16. Tell about a surprising fact that struck you from the research presented in this chapter.
17. Describe one of the biographical accounts of death and dying.
18. Relate the literature on resilience to the personal narratives of older African American women who worked as maids in the South.
19. What are some of the ethical issues raised in end-of-life care?

References

Alzheimer's Association. (2009). *2009 Alzheimer's disease facts and figures*. Retrieved from http://www.alz.org/national/documents/report_alzfactsfigures2009.pdf

American Association of Retired Persons (AARP). (2009, May). AARP Bulletin survey on employment status of the 45+ population. Retrieved from http://assets.aarp.org/rgcenter/econ/bulletin_jobs_09.pdf

Barsky, A. (2010). *Ethics and values in social work: An integrated approach for a comprehenzsive curriculum*. New York: Oxford University Press.

Becker, E. (1973). *The denial of death*. New York: Free Press.

Begley, S. (2007). *Train your mind, change your brain*. New York: Ballentine Books.

Blazer, D., & Wu, L-T. (2009). The epidemiology of at-risk and binge drinking among middle-aged and elderly community adults: National Survey on Drug Use and Health. *American Journal of Psychiatry*, 166, 1162–1169. DOI: 10.1176/appi.ajp.2009.09010016

British Broadcasting Company (BBC) (2005, July 23). US anti-war grannies face justice. Retrieved from http://news.bbc.co.uk/2/hi/middle_east/4711121.stm

Brownell, P., & Giblin, C. (2009). Elder abuse. In A. Roberts & G. Greene (Eds.), *Social workers' desk reference* (2nd ed., pp. 1106–1111). New York: Oxford University Press.

Cauchon, D. (2009, July 29). Older white males hurt more by this recession. *USA Today*, p.1A.

Centers for Disease Control and Prevention (CDC). (2007). *The state of aging and health in America, 2007.* Retrieved from http://www.cdc.gov/aging/pdf/saha_2007.pdf

Centers for Disease Control and Prevention (CDC). (2009, August 19). National vital statistics reports: Deaths: Preliminary data for 2007. Retrieved from http://www.cdc.gov/nchs/data/nvsr/nvsr58/nvsr58_01.pdf

Cooney, E. (2003). *Death in slow motion: A memoir of a daughter, her mother, and a beast called Alzheimer's.* New York: HarperCollins.

Cumming, E., & Henry, W. E. (1961). *Growing old: The process of disengagement.* New York: Basic Books.

Edwards, E. (2009). *Resilience: Reflections on the burdens and gifts of facing life's adversities.* New York: Random House.

Erikson, E. (1950/1963). *Childhood and society.* New York: Norton.

Fiske, H. (2003, April 7). Sexual abuse survivors: Caring for aging abusers. *Social Work Today*, p. 6–9.

Fleck, C. (2009a, May 1). All under one roof. *AARP Bulletin Today.* Retrieved from http://bulletin.aarp.org/yourworld/family/articles/wo05_intergen.html

Fleck, C. (2009b, February 4). The mortgage crisis: Older Americans are feeling the pain. *AARP Bulletin Today.* Retrieved from http://bulletin.aarp.org/yourmoney/work/articles/the_mortgage_crisis_older_americans_are_feeling_the_pain.html

Gardiner, H.W., & Kosmitzki, C. (2005). *Lives across cultures: Cross-cultural human development.* Boston: Allyn & Bacon.

Goldberg, S. (2005, April 13). Cancer's life lessons: How a brush with death can amplify the joys of living. *USA Today*, p. 13A.

Gonyea, J. (2008). Life span: Oldest senior/aged-late. In National Association of Social Workers (NASW), *Encyclopedia of Social Work* (20th ed., pp. 128–133). New York: Oxford University Press.

Grossman, L. (2003, March 24). Laughter and forgetting. *Time*, p.65.

Havighurst, R. J., Neugarten, B. L., & Tobin, S. (1968). Disengagement and patterns of aging. In B. L. Neugarten (Ed.), *Middle age and aging* (pp. 161–172). Chicago: Chicago University Press.

Hayflick, L. (2009, July 5-9). Ageing is no longer an unsolved problem. Paper presented at the World Congress of Gerontology and Geriatrics. Paris, France.

Huxley, A. (1932/1969). *Brave new world.* New York: Harper and Row.

Johnson, C. K. (2009, March 22). Mentally ill a threat in nursing homes. *The Associated Press.* Retrieved from http://www.physorg.com/news156957294.html

Johnson, R. W. (2009, February, 25). *Promoting economic security at older ages through workforce development.* Written testimony to the Senate Special Committee on Aging: Boomer bust? Securing retirement in a volatile economy. Retrieved from the Urban Institute website http://www.urban.org/UploadedPDF/901239_Johnson_workforce_development.pdf

Johnson, R. W., & Soto, M. (2009, June 16). 50+ Hispanic workers: A growing segment of the U.S. workforce. Retrieved from the Urban Institute website http://www.urban.org/publications/1001281.html

Jun, C. (2009, July 27). Financial abuse of elderly rises as economy sinks. *The Detroit News.* Retrieved July 27, 2009, from http://www.detnews.com/article/20090727/METRO/907270338/1409/METRO/Financial-abuse-of-elderly-rises-as-economy-sinks

Knickerbocker, B. (2005, March 30). Why Oregon is at the forefront of change and end-of-life care. *Christian Science Monitor*, pp. 1–2.

Knopf, N. (2008). Older adulthood/seniors. In National Association of Social Workers (NASW), *Encyclopedia of Social Work* (20th ed., pp. 124–128). New York: Oxford University Press.

Kovacs, P. (2008). Very late adulthood. In E. D. Hutchinson (Ed.), *Dimensions of human behavior: The changing life course* (3rd ed., pp. 417–452). Thousand Oaks, CA: Sage.

Kübler-Ross, E. (1969). *On death and dying.* New York: Macmillan.

Lawrence-Lightfoot, S. (2009). *The third chapter: Passion, risk, and adventure in the 25 years after 50.* New York: Farrar, Straus and Giroux.

Lesser, J., & Pope, D. (2007). *Human behavior and the social environment: Theory and practice.* Boston: Allyn & Bacon.

Levinson, D. (2008, September 18). *Memorandum report: Trends in nursing home deficiencies and complaints.* Retrieved from the Health and Human Services website http://oig.hhs.gov/oei/reports/oei-02-08-00140.pdf

McDaniel, S., & Gee, E. (1993). Social policies regarding care giving to elders: Canadian contradictions. In S. Bass & R. Morris (Eds.),

International perspectives on state and family support for the elderly (pp. 57–72). Binghamton, NY: Haworth Press.

Meyer, B. (2008, August 24). Holocaust haunts aging survivors heeding care. *The Plain Dealer*-Cleveland. Retrieved from http://www.cleveland.com/nation/index.ssf/2008/08/holocaust_haunts_aging_survivo.html

Miller, C. A. (2008). *Nursing for wellness in older adults* (5th ed.). Philadelphia: Wolters Kluwer Health.

Miller, S. (2003). *The story of my father*. New York: Knopf.

Mosiman, D. (2008, January 8). Elder abuse: A silent shame. *Wisconsin State Journal*. Retrieved from http://www.madison.com/wsj/topstories/index.php?ntid=254292

National Broadcasting Company (NBC). (2009, June 25). NBC's tribute to Michael Jackson and Farrah Fawcett. Retrieved from http://www.nbc.com/news/2009/06/25/nbc-tributes-to-michael-jackson-and-farrah-fawcett/

National Cancer Institute (NCI), (2009, August 11). Second cancer patient has genome sequenced. *NCI Cancer Bulletin*. Retrieved from http://www.cancer.gov/ncicancerbulletin/081109/page3#

Nissim, R., Gagliese, L., & Rodin, G. (2009). The desire for hastened death in individuals with advanced cancer: A longitudinal qualitative study. Social Science & Medicine, 69(2), 165–171.

Older Americans 2008 (2008, March). *Key indicators of well-being*. Federal Interagency on Aging. Washington, DC: U.S. Government Printing Office.

Owens-Kane, S., & Chadha, L. (2008). Family caregiving. In National Association of Social Workers (NASW), *Encyclopedia of Social Work* (20th ed., pp. 191–197). New York: Oxford University Press.

Paterson, C. (2008). *Assisted suicide and euthanasia*. Hampshire, England: Ashgate.

Pew Research Center. (2006). Strong public support for right to die. *Pew Research Center for the People and the Press*. Retrieved from http://people-press.org/report/266/strong-public-support-for-right-to-die

Pew Research Center. (2009, June 29). Growing old in America: Expectations vs. reality. *Pew Charitable Trusts*. Retrieved from http://pewresearch.org/pubs/1269/aging-survey-expectations-versus-reality

Pipher, M. (1999). *Another country: Navigating the emotional terrain of our elders*. New York: Riverhead Books.

Pomeroy, E., & Browning, P. (2008). Eating disorders. In National Association of Social Workers (NASW), *Encyclopedia of Social Work* (20th ed., pp. 93-96). New York: Oxford University Press.

Popple, P., & Leighninger, L. (2008). *Social work, social welfare, and American society* (7th ed.). Boston: Allyn & Bacon.

Rogers, F. (2003). *The world according to Mister Rogers*. New York: Hyperion

Rutenberg, J., & Calmes, J. (2009, August 13). False "death panel" rumor has some familiar roots. *New York Times*, p. 1A.

Saleebey, D. (2001). *Human behavior and the social environments*. New York: Columbia University Press.

Santrock, J. W. (2008). *Life-span development* (12th ed.). Boston: McGraw-Hill.

Sarton, M. (1973). *As we are now: A novel*. New York: W.W. Norton.

Shakespeare, W. (1594/1952). *As you like it*. In P. Alexander (Ed.), *Shakespeare: Complete works* (pp. 254–283). New York: Random House.

Smiley, J. (1991). *A thousand acres*. New York: A Ballantine Book.

Spayde, J. (2004, July–August). The new rites of passage [Interview with Gail Sheehy.] *Utne*, 63–68.

Substance Abuse and Mental Health Services Administration (SAMHSA). (2009, August). *An examination of trends in illicit drug use in adults aged 50 to 59 in the United States*. Retrieved from http://oas.samhsa.gov/2k9/OlderAdults/OAS_data_review_OlderAdults.pdf

Sullivan, P. (2009, January 2). WWII fighter pilot Quentin Aanenson dies. *San Francisco Chronicle*, p. B5.

Suppes, M., & Wells, C. (2008). *The social work experience: An introduction to social work and social welfare* (5th ed.). Boston: Allyn & Bacon.

Surface, D. (2009, March/April). High risk recreation: Problem gambling in older adults. *Social Work Today*, 18–23.

Szegedy-Maszak, M. (2004). She taught us how to die. *U.S. News and World Report*, p.16.

Thomasson, E. (2009, August 5). *Euthanasia still a dilemma for Dutch doctors*. Retrieved from The World Federation of Right to Die Societies website http://www.worldrtd.net/node/824

Thompson, K. (2003, March 28). Abuse of elderly women on the rise. *Women's e news*. Retrieved from http://www.womensenews.org

Urquhart, M., & Hewson, M. (1983). Unemployment continued to rise in 1982 as recession deepened. Retrieved from the U.S. Bureau of Labor Statistics website http://www.bls.gov/opub/mlr/1983/02/art1full.pdf

U.S. Census. (2009, June). *An aging world 2008: International population reports*. Washington, DC: U.S. Government Printing Office.

U.S. Department of Health and Human Services. (2009, July 16). *A profile of older Americans 2008*. Administration on Aging. Retrieved from http://www.aoa.gov/AoARoot/Aging_Statistics/Profile/2008/3.aspx

Vaillant, G. (2002). *Aging well: Surprising guideposts to a happier life from the landmark Harvard Study of adult development*. Boston: Little, Brown & Co.

van Wormer, K. (2006). *Introduction to social welfare and social work: The U.S. in global perspective*. Belmont, CA: Wadsworth.

van Wormer, K. & Davis, D. R. (2008). *Addiction treatment: A strengths perspective*. Belmont, CA: Brooks/Cole.

von Hippel, W. (2007). Aging, executive functioning, and social control. *Current Directions in Psychological Science, 16*(5), 240–244.

Wilke, D., & Vinton, L. (2003, Spring/Summer). Domestic violence and aging: Teaching about their intersection. *Journal of Social Work Education, 39*(2), 225–235.

Williams, T. (1954). *Cat on a hot tin roof.* Sewanee, TN: University of the South.

Winn, S. (2007, September 19). Burns' series honors his father's war. *San Francisco Chronicle*, p. E1.

Zastrow, C. (2007). *Introduction to social work and social welfare* (9th ed.). Belmont, CA: Brooks Cole.

Zastrow, C., & Kirst-Ashman, K. (2010). *Understanding human behavior and the social environment* (8th ed.). Belmont, CA: Brooks/Cole.

The Individual in the Family

They are the we of me.

—CARSON MCCULLERS

Member of the Wedding

7

The 1999 movie *The Straight Story* takes us on a journey with an elderly man, Mr. Straight, who drove his lawnmower from Iowa to Wisconsin to see his dying brother. Along the way he gets into a conversation with a teenage runaway who has fled from her family in anger. Straight tells her the allegory of sticks—how he would give some sticks to his children and say, "Break them." Of course they could. "Then I would tie them together and say break them, and they couldn't. That's family." The family is a place of safety, solace, protection against the everyday cruelties, the place where one receives unconditional love. The family is also the place of much grief and heartache.

"You can't go home again." So said Thomas Wolfe (1940/1998) in the title of his auto-biographical novel. You can't *not* go home again, either. Home, as famously described by Robert Frost (1914), is "the place where, when you go there they have to take you in" (p. 53). And home is where your family is. But your family does not have to be your biological family or even your family of origin. Some women in U.S. prisons, for example, relate to one another as "sisters" or as "mother and daughter" in a re-creation of the family bonds they have known outside. These surrogate families provide support and nurturance in an otherwise forbidding environment. And sometimes members of close-knit religious communities assume caretaking roles in the way of the family. From the beginning of time, through slave days and beyond, people have organized themselves into family forms and have taken outsiders into the family unit. There are the families we are born into (families of origin), the ones we marry into (families of procreation), and the families we choose, such as out of close friendship.

In this chapter we study the inner workings of family life. After a discussion of the question "What is a family?" we explore the family as a social system comprised of statuses, roles, and the boundaries between them. The family function of socialization is the next topic, followed by a close look at the nature of family relationships—father–son, father–daughter, and so on. The middle section of the chapter explores the inner dynamics of each of these special relationship patterns. Changes in family composition (through breakup, for instance) is the final discussion topic before we consider the practice implications of much of what has gone before.

The family plays a mediating role between individuals and society (Dominelli, 2004). In the traditional definition, a family is characterized by two first-time married parents with two or three children; the purpose of the family is to have and bring up children and to meet the social and sexual needs of the parents (Zastrow & Kirst-Ashman, 2010). Whether or not this definition ever actually applied is questionable, given the historically high death rate of mothers in childbirth and of fathers in war and the customary presence of extended family members in the household. The classical nuclear family, in fact, is a historical aberration, Saleebey (2001) suggests. Today, in the United States, well under one-fourth of all households include a married couple with their own children (U.S. Census Bureau, 2009). Between 1970 and 2007, the average number of households that were family households declined from 81 percent to 68 percent. Stay-at-home mothers were highly likely to be Hispanic and foreign born. Many families are now culturally diverse and multicultural in composition, and these demographic changes have an impact on family structure. An increase in longevity, a decline in the birth rate, and an increase in the numbers of women in the workforce are some of the obvious changes affecting family life today. According to U.S. Census (2009) data, as many as 1.3 million children in the United States are being raised by grandparents, a significant increase since 1990. While one percent of white non-Hispanic children lived with their grandparents with no parent present, this was true for 5 percent of black children (U.S. Census, 2008). The reduction in social services associated with welfare reform has had an effect on child care arrangements.

Recent data analysis from the Pew Research Center (2010) reveals a significant change in family composition from the early 1980s, when only 12 percent of people lived in multigenerational homes until today. As of 2008, a record 49 million Americans, or 16.percent of the total U.S. population, lived in a family household that contained at least two adult generations or a grandparent and at least one other generation. The ethnic/racial breakdown is that 22 percent of Latinos, 23 percent of African Americans, 25 percent of Asians, and 13 percent of whites live in a multi-generational family household. The reasons cited for the national shift in living arrangements are: the trend toward older median age for first marriage; immigration of Latin Americans and Asians, the economic recession affecting all racial/ethnic groups, and high unemployment rates among young people. Among younger age groups, the trend is more common among single men, while at the older age levels, women are more often found living with their grown children than are men, many of whom died while living with their somewhat younger wives.

One fact that emerges from these statistics is that family bonds are strong, and that family members come through in a crisis. To define family only in terms of the nuclear family is a misrepresentation of reality. Zastrow and Kirst-Ashman (2010, p. 153) define family members as people who are members of a primary group in constant and intimate interaction; are mutually obligated to each other; and usually occupy a common residence. My preference is for an even more flexible concept such as that provided by the National Association of Social Workers (NASW, 2009): "Family is defined in its broadest sense to include two or more people who consider themselves 'family' and who assume obligations and responsibilities that are generally essential to family life" (p. 135). Contemporary families, according to NASW, are an amalgam of many different lifestyles and structures. Such constellations include married couples with or without biological or adopted children; divorced, separated, or unmarried couples with children and stepchildren; intergenerational arrangements for child or elder care; gay and lesbian partners with or without children; and foster families.

How often it is said of the modern family that, in the modern industrial society, the nuclear family has lost all of its functions, that the day care center, school, health care system, and nursing home, for example, have taken over the socialization and caretaking. The mass media's portrait of the solitary nuclear family devoid of important links to extended kin is not true to reality. In fact, the family system as a whole is rarely made up of such isolated units.

Today, some of the functions that were once farmed out to outside agencies are being reclaimed. Hospital rooming-in facilities, for example, now engage family members in the childbirth process; hospice home health care and other home care initiatives keep people out of the hospital; and home schooling continues to grow in popularity. In addition, as we saw in the previous chapter, for economic reasons more single young adults and young families are moving back into the family home. Having more adults in one household might reduce reliance on outside agencies, for example, by providing care for vulnerable family members. By the same token, more women, including mothers of small children, and even grandmothers, are in the workforce today, with the result that a higher percentage of children are in day care. For mothers who receive welfare benefits, the work requirements of Temporary Assistance to Needy Families (TANF) mean that some arrangements for child care of small children have to be found.

Other modern developments affecting families in the United States include changes in eating habits and the many hours spent on the Internet or watching TV. A Gallup poll found that the number of families with children who were eating together at home every night has fallen from 37 percent in 1997 to 28 percent (Gallup Poll, 2004).

Although institutional supports for the family have eroded over the past decade, there is a great deal of political lip service to "family values," which is often a code term that entails opposition to alternative family forms, which are seen as threats to heterosexual marriage and male authority. Part of the furor no doubt stems from the strong emotions connected with our upbringing and our sense of the sanctity of the family. It is perhaps harder to accept changes in family structure and role taking than changes in other social institutions such as

work or school. Concerns about the nature of motherhood, sexual morality, and the preservation of childhood innocence are at the heart of these debates surrounding family life. Moreover, there is no sign that the intensity of the debates will diminish anytime soon.

Families as Systems

Recall from Chapter 1 that general systems theory and ecosystems theory tell us that the family is a system within itself as well as a system in interaction with other social systems. Consistent with the focus of this book on human behavior at the micro level, our concern here is with the internal workings of the family and with the person-in-the-environment, the person in constant interaction with other members (Figure 7.1) in this greater whole (the family). The second book in this set, *Human Behavior and the Social Environment, Macro Level*, focuses more on external processes, including socioeconomic forces and diverse family forms. Keep in mind that this separation between micro and macro is only an artificial construction for the sake of topic division. Clearly, forces in the wider social environment (e.g., poverty and discrimination) have a direct impact on the internal workings of the family unit, as does any external source of stress. So, although we cannot and will not disregard these factors, the emphasis here, however, is on the smallest common denominator—the family and its members.

The systems and ecological perspectives have been among the most widespread theoretical frameworks in social work that provide designs for conceiving of person and environment transactions (Saleebey, 2001). Because general systems theory is drawn from cybernetics and lacks a treatment applicability, I look to Bowen's family systems theory for insights into family membership.

Murray Bowen's formulation had a revolutionary impact on the fields of counseling and social work. The usefulness of his theory is in its description of the emotional forces that regulate the way we relate to other people

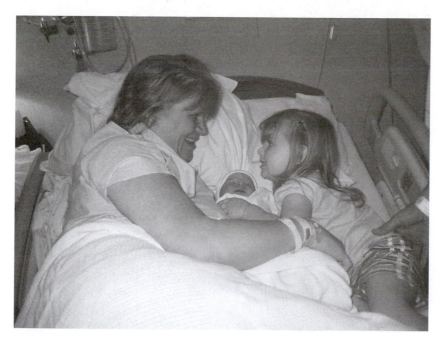

Figure 7.1. This mother, who has recently given birth, thoughtfully introduces her newborn baby to her 2½-year-old daughter. Photo by Flora Stuart.

(Nichols, 2001). Moreover, in his teaching that we carry our families with us wherever we go, Bowen helped show how much of our personal behavior and identity has its roots in the family circle.

Trained as a psychoanalyst, Bowen began his work on families at the Menninger Clinic in the 1940s. Families with a schizophrenic member became his primary focus. Bowen's study of mother–child symbiotic relationships in these families led to the formation of his concept of the importance of *differentiation of self* (Bowen, 1978; Green, 2003). In the 1950s Bowen moved to the National Institute of Mental Health, where he hospitalized entire families to study their patterns of communication. What he found was that the intense emotional tie between mothers and their mentally ill children affected every member of the family. This insight led to the concept of *triangulation*, or diverting conflict between two people by involving a third. If the parents were arguing, for example, they might reduce their anxiety by focusing on a third party such as a child.

When Bowen moved to Georgetown Medical School in Washington, D.C., he decided that the processes he had earlier observed in diseased families were present in all families (Green, 2003). Seeing himself as a researcher rather than a therapist, Bowen believed he could be more objective in his observations than clinicians could because he could avoid taking sides and therefore contribute more effectively to the resolution of family issues (Papero, 2009). Still, he was not averse to having clinicians engage in family therapy as long as they maintained emotional neutrality, and, in fact, in the psychoanalytical tradition of self-analysis, Bowen (1978) recommended that clinicians be trained through work on their own degree of differentiation of self from their families. The goal of such analysis was to train oneself to control one's emotions—to think before reacting. When Bowen used his own family of origin story to define the uniqueness of family systems theory and presented his genealogical work at a major conference, a new trend was started: It included extended family concepts in the understanding of any family (Green, 2003).

We can contrast Bowen's family systems theory with general systems concepts that grew

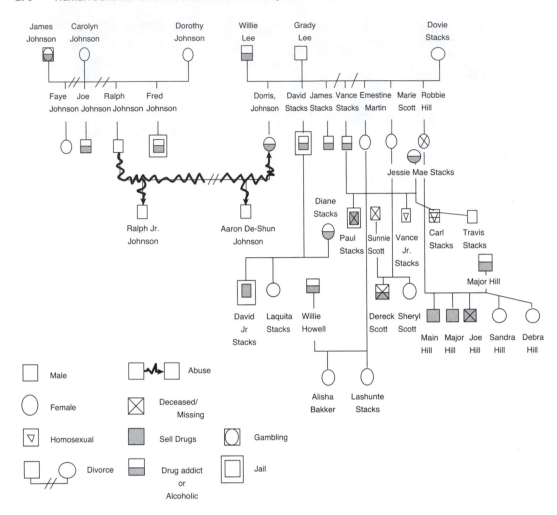

Figure 7.2. Genogram of the Johnson family.

out of the assumption that similar mathematical expressions and models could be applied to the human domain. General systems concepts were "influenced by manmade systems such as the simple domestic thermostat," whereas Bowenian family systems theory drew on metaphors from the natural environment and was based on observation (Kerr & Bowen, 1988, p. 24).

One of Bowen's major contributions was his graphic construct for representing key themes that carry over from generation to generation. Substance abuse problems, for example, can be represented through a *genogram*, or family tree. The genogram is a useful tool that helps family therapists and others reveal behavioral patterns and diseases that tend to

repeat themselves. Figure 7.2 illustrates the use of the genogram to trace addiction patterns across three generations. The positive element here is that the person who drew the genogram, Aaron Johnson, is highly resilient himself, a remarkable phenomenon given his upbringing in a family wracked by substance abuse, drug dealing, time served in jail, gambling, violence, and divorce. Johnson is the first and only one of all his relatives to attend college, which he does on a football scholarship. The one solid role model was his paternal grandmother, who always believed in him. Although the model is used almost exclusively to display problematic characteristics, a more positive approach to families in treatment would be a strengths-based genogram to indicate how strengths and survival skills are passed down from generation to generation.

In Figure 7.2, the standard symbols used are squares for males, circles for females, horizontal lines for marriage, dotted lines for partners, age in square or circle, X in square or circle for deceased with age of death, and child by line downward from center of line between parents. Divorce is indicated by a double slash on the horizontal line. For use with families a genogram template is available at Genogram Analytics: http://www.genogramanalytics.com.

What kinds of information should the genogram provide? McGoldrick (2009) mentions some useful guidelines. Family data can be scanned for repeated symptoms such as triangles and patterns of conflict across generations; coincidences of dates (e.g., death of one member and underfunctioning or depression in another); and changes in relationships related to family life events or trauma. Awareness of possible patterns, McGoldrick further notes, sensitizes the clinician to information that is missing about key family members or events and discrepancies. Such irregularities often reflect charged emotional issues. The genogram helps us to pinpoint the idiosyncrasies in the family system and to appreciate how a lack in one part of family functioning may be complemented by a higher level of responsibility in another part.

This sort of analysis can also reveal imbalances in power relationships. One possible genogram focus might be decision making and/or work and child care responsibilities. Possible patterns that may emerge are patriarchal, matriarchal, and grandmother centered. Other themes that could be graphically depicted are cultural traits and religious affiliations. A physical representation of intergenerational patterns is a powerful means of opening up dialogue on family strengths and areas for discussion.

Bowen's influence was profound. His concepts of fusion, enmeshment, and triangulation and his notion of multigenerational family patterns have become so ingrained in social work and family therapy that we tend to forget their origin. Nevertheless, Bowen has been widely criticized on a number of grounds. Despite his claim to be a researcher, his theory was not only not evidence based, but it was sometimes built on clearly faulty assumptions. The fallacy in the following assertion, written well after antipsychotic medication was having tangible success, is obvious: "Family systems [theory] does not view these signs and symptoms (of schizophrenia) as caused by a 'disease' contained within that individual. The individual's 'disease' is considered to be a *symptom* of a relationship process that extends beyond the boundaries of the individual 'patient'" (Kerr & Bowen, 1988, p. 24).

The Bowenian approach has been criticized for its Anglo American emphasis on individualism versus collectivism (Vosler, 2008). This emphasis pathologizes the value of connectedness that prevails in many cultures, as Vosler further suggests. Bowen was widely criticized for the mother blaming inherent in his theory; his conceptualization of emotional fusion was often the relationship between mother and child. This concept was the forerunner of the widely accepted location of the cause of anorexia in the mother–daughter relationship and the location of the cause of autism in the lack of nurturance by "the refrigerator mother," notions that led to guilt feelings on the part of mothers in those families.

Again, from a feminist perspective, Bowen's ideal of the differentiated self fails to take into account women's ways of relating and their focus on closeness while swallowing resentments (Vosler, 2008). Similarly, criticism is directed at the neglect of power dynamics both in theory and in practice. Bringing together all of the members of a household, for example, and having them resolve their conflicts openly can be counterproductive in the presence of power differentials (Nichols, 2008). In abusive situations such openness can lead to posttherapy session violence.

Family systems theory provides a lens for understanding interactions among a number of variables at once; as such it has expanded the social work profession's person-in-environment concept considerably and provided fuel for our imaginations as we explore the gender roles and family rules that are unique to each family. As Leo Tolstoy once wrote, "All happy families are alike, but every unhappy family is unhappy in its own way" (*Anna Karenina*, 1876/1917, p. 1). Individuals within the same family likewise adapt differently to the same stress.

Family therapists pay close attention to the boundaries among members of the family system and between the family and other systems and people—neighbors and schools, for example. Open systems exchange energy with their environment and draw sustenance from the community. Relatively open boundaries also permit families to export energy as ideas and resources (Greene, 2009). Closed systems tend to be shut off from the social environment. Boundaries may also delineate subsystems within the system or, in other words, between one family member and another. Between mother and infant the boundaries are typically fused. It is not always clear where one leaves off and the other begins. Infants have no self-concept of "I," but as they grow, they strive for independence, often before they have the mental or physical capability to be independent.

What are the characteristics of a functional family? Open communication, respect for individual differences and boundaries, stable routines and rituals, and having fun and a sense of humor are among the qualities generally elicited (from the grouping of family members). Figure 7.3 depicts various family styles related to degrees of closeness that can be shared with the group of family members. Participants often volunteer to diagram their families of origin and current families in this manner. A discussion of healthy boundaries often ensues.

Psychiatrist Ernest Hartmann (2009) devised the Boundary Questionnaire to measure what he sees as a basic dimension of personality—the tendency toward thickness or thinness in boundaries. His research was based on an analysis of questionnaire responses from over 2,000 people. The questionnaire consists of 18 straightforward questions that are rated on a five-point scale of agreement. Major differences were found in the permeability of the respondents' boundaries in their relationships with others. The first three statements were generally chosen by persons with thin boundaries,

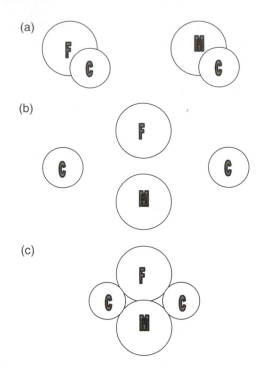

Figure 7.3. Family forms. F = father, M = mother, c = child. (a) The enmeshed family: spouses are estranged; one child is enmeshed with the father, one with the mother. (b) The isolated family: lack of cohesion and social support. Each member is protected by a wall of defenses. (c) The healthy family: All of the members are touching, but their boundaries do not overlap.

and the last three by those who were highly independent:

> I am very close to my childhood feelings.
> When I get involved with someone, we sometimes get too close.
> A good parent has to be a bit of a child, too.
> I like stories that have a definite beginning, middle, and end.
> I keep my desk and work table neat and well organized.
> A good organization is one in which all lines of responsibility are precise and clearly established.

Those who score as "thin" on the test are likely to be unusually sensitive to loud noises and bright lights and feel unsure of who they are at times. Their dreams are especially vivid and apt to be remembered; sometimes they are not sure whether something really happened or they dreamed it. Respondents at the extreme poles of the boundaries often have problems. Those with weak boundaries, according to Hartmann, are at risk of dependent relationships; persons with very thick boundaries are incapable of deep relationships and are lacking in imagination.

When boundaries are clearly defined between individuals, one's thoughts and feelings are respected. This means that differences—in interests, politics, and so on—are accepted in a family because each family member has a unique personality. In *enmeshed* families, a narrow range of acceptable behavior is tolerated. Worden (2003) describes the boundaries as enmeshed when in each of the following situations:

1. Family members speak for one another.
2. A parent tells the children what they really think and feel or what they should think and feel.
3. Guilt is used as a means of controlling others.
4. There are hints that parents have not separated psychologically from their own parents. (p. 21)

Disengaged families, according to Worden, sacrifice belonging for autonomy. Privacy is taken to the extreme. Within the family unit, subgroups may exist: Mother and son may be enmeshed, and husband and wife may be disengaged.

Virginia Satir, another of the premiere pioneers of family therapy, developed her understanding of family influences in her first career as a schoolteacher. What impressed her was the degree to which children's behavior reflects what is going on at home. Her fascination with this insight led her to pursue a master's degree in social work and to develop a clinical practice that treated families. Through her warmth, genuineness, and ability to move large audiences with her demonstration workshops, Satir became family therapy's most celebrated figure (Nichols, 2008). She traveled across the United States engaging audience members in lively family role plays (of "the rescuer" and "the scapegoat") and thus teaching family systems concepts until her death in 1988. In her clinical work she expressed her belief in the healing power of love. Satir agreed with Bowen that the troubled person is often the symptom bearer for the entire family. Also like Bowen and influenced by his research, she believed that emotional problems and mental illness derive from forces in the family structure, not in the inner dynamics of the individual.

Before I became a social worker, I had occasion to attend one of Satir's public sessions. The audience seemed mesmerized, and Satir's easy, humorous, and jargon-free style enhanced her appeal. She told us about her work and how she taught medical students to view their patients' problems within the context of the whole. Then she engaged the audience and prepared us for her technique of family sculptor, in which people stood in certain positions to represent their family roles. Members of the audience eagerly joined her on the stage to act out the roles of parents and children. After eliciting feeling words from the volunteers in their role, Satir explained her theory to the audience (e.g., "Little Billy's acting out reflects what was going on between mom and dad"). Then she explained how she taught doctors in her workshops and that they had to view the client's problems within the context of the whole.

Whether placing people to reflect their family positions and roles or presenting her observations, Satir used a great deal of touching, and her observations were straightforward and easy to understand. In her popular writings, similarly, Satir did not use words the layperson could not understand, nor did she use citations or references. Her books were all bestsellers, accordingly. In *The New Peoplemaking* (Satir, 1988), for example, she described how she tuned in to her own feelings and body language and then recognized them in other people: "In troubled families, people's bodies and faces tell their plight. Bodies are either stiff and tight, or slouchy. Faces look sullen, or sad, or blank like masks. Eyes look down and past people. Ears obviously don't hear. Voices are either harsh and strident, or barely audible" (p. 11).

Satir contrasted this troubled family with a nurturant one: "One can actually see and hear the vitality in such a family. The bodies are graceful, the facial expressions relaxed. People look at one another, not through one another or at the floor; and they speak in rich, clear voices. A flow and harmony permeates their relations with one another. The children, even as infants, seem open and friendly, and the rest of the family treats them very much as persons" (p. 13).

Although her theoretical explanations were often unidimensional and deterministic (the biological basis of mental disorders was over-looked), Satir helped make practitioners more aware of the intricacies of family communication. When one family member is experiencing emotional pain, this distress is communicated to the others and felt by them in some way. Therapists learned from Satir to recognize how people communicate through body language (e.g., facial gestures, posture), tone of voice, and choice of words. Many such messages, Satir (1983) claimed, are "validate me" messages. Satir's overall goal was to help people connect with each other and communicate their needs. Her approach anticipated the strengths and empowerment perspectives in her belief that each individual is geared to survival and growth and that people are limited only by their lack of understanding.

Recent health statistics give credence to systems theory in showing the impact on the whole family of the poor health of one of its members. According to research from the Harvard Medical School (Christakis & Iwashyha, 2003), we are all more prone to illness and death when our family members are in trouble. Surviving spouses die at twice the normal rate during the first year of bereavement, and the risk of suicide increases 22-fold for people whose spouses take their own lives. The loss of a child doubles the odds of a woman's being hospitalized for depression even years later. The strain on a marriage in having a chronically ill child can be overwhelming, while

siblings often suffer from feelings of neglect that are long lasting. The health of one affects the health of all, in other words.

Socialization

Family communication has a lot to do with socialization; through feedback, the child learns how to behave both in the family and in the world outside. Children are taught in various ways: through modeling, mentoring, and observing how others perform the roles (such as gender roles) that will be a part of their life (Saleebey, 2001). Then there is socialization into the peer group. Even though many young people swear they will never be controlling and certainly not snobbish about their children's choice of friends, when they have children, they often find themselves doing exactly what their parents did to them. The reason is their recognition of the power of the peer group to mold the child's behavior—from manners to attitudes to speech patterns. Peers then, like parents, are powerful agents of socialization. Older brothers and sisters, of course, have a significant impact as well.

The essence of parenting is caring for and contributing to the life of the next generation (Cox, 2009). A *latent*, or hidden, function of the family includes socialization into the norms of society. This generally means that prejudicial attitudes, some of which the parents are not even aware, are not so much taught as absorbed. These include reactions to people whose skin is a different color and to those who speak in different accents, as well as discomfort in the presence of persons with disabilities. Judgmental attitudes toward people of different social classes are often imparted, along with cautionary tales about the cruel fate that befalls those who do not work hard or who violate the norms of society through slovenly living standards. Family members may even be taught that "we are better than the Joneses," while religious values are often inculcated in conjunction with a message that other religions are less holy and less true. Other groups' religious rituals may be described as bizarre.

Gender role socialization starts early and is pervasive (see Chapter 4). Both at home and in peer groups, boys are socialized to act like boys and girls like girls. Although there is much more sex role flexibility today than formerly, in most modern industrialized societies, sexual oppression is still alive and well in many families. In contrast to racism, classism, and ethnocentrism (which relates to groups outside the family circle), sexism and heterosexism are often first experienced at home. About this bell hooks (1984) says:

> It is this form of the family where most children first learn the meaning and practice of hierarchical, authoritarian rule. Here is where they learn to accept group oppression against themselves as non-adults, and where they learn to accept male supremacy and the group oppression of women. Here is where they learn that it is the male's role to work in the community and control the economic life of the family and to mete out the physical and financial punishments and rewards, and the female's role to provide the emotional warmth associated with motherhood while under the economic rule of the male. Here is where the relationship of superordination to subordination, of superior-inferior, or master-slave is first learned and accepted as "natural." (p. 36)

In violent families, dominance of the weak by the strong—of children by adults, smaller children by larger, male by female—is the rule. In this way families are often the setting for much suffering and pain. And sadly, as Allport (1954/1981) taught us, citing Adorno's study of fascism, the lessons of dominance and brutality acquired in the authoritarian home are commonly redirected toward weaker out-groups by children raised in such settings. The aggression that one could not express toward one's abusive parents is sometimes displaced onto minority groups.

Socialization, therefore, is a double-edged sword. Whereas each generation has the potential to rise beyond the narrowness and biases of the succeeding one, many of the beliefs and

allegiances from the old order are passed on. Because these beliefs and allegiances are associated with the love and nurturance of family life, they possess a salience that cannot be overestimated.

The paradox of the family is that, although so many are flawed and so many of their teachings are unsound, family affection serves as a glue that holds lives together. In viewing the family as a social institution, we need to be cognizant of Palmer's (1998) "warning against putting ourselves or others in either-or boxes" and his recommendation that "we think things together" (p. 66). "Paradoxical thinking," Palmer informs us, "requires that we embrace a view of the world in which opposites are joined, so that we can see the world clearly and see it whole. Such a view is characterized . . . by a creative synthesis of the two" (p. 66). Relevant to the family are the following paradoxes. The family is at once:

➤ A buffer against the pain of society and a source of pain in itself
➤ A teacher of brotherly and sisterly love and of ethnic hate
➤ A booster of children's potential and a force that holds them back
➤ The embodiment of our warmest memories and our greatest despair
➤ The source of pride in each other's achievements and of shame in their ignorance and failures

In any case, children do better in families than in any other social arrangement (the one exception is the traditional Israeli kibbutz, which combines community and family life). We are programmed, Saleebey suggests, to grow best and prosper most within "a constant and steadfast intergenerational network of human connections" (2001, p. 263). Families, whether biological or chosen, are what give most people's lives their shape (Pipher, 1996).

Family Relationships

Relationships, according to Virginia Satir, are the living links that join family members.

By exploring the many aspects of these relationships, social workers can come to an understanding of the system in which their clients (and they themselves) are intertwined.

Perhaps there is no change in the family system as dramatic as the introduction of a new member. When individuals in a family become parents, the arrival of the child often transforms the unit; a whole new generation is added. Not only do the roles of those in the immediate household change but so do those of extended family members. The young couple often bond much more closely with their own parents and in-laws as everyone shares in the care of the growing child. Through the pressures of parenting, moreover, members of the younger generation may reach a greater understanding of what their parents went through in their day.

Parent–child relationships are among the most common social roles played over the life course and among the most enduring in terms of social ties. We begin our examination of family relationships with parent–child links (father–son, father–daughter, mother–son, mother–daughter), then proceed to a look at sibling ties, and finally to the important roles of grandparents and aunts and uncles.

Father and Son

The concept of fatherhood has shifted dramatically over the years (Rohner & Veneziano, 2001). The ideal image of the European American father in the seventeenth century was the stern patriarch. From 1830 to 1900, the distant breadwinner was the predominant image. For most of the twentieth century, the designated role for the father was that of general playmate and role model. Today, due to the women's movement and the need for two incomes, a coparenting role is the preferred model. (We will consider the African American experience later.) There is evidence that the nature of the father–son relationship is changing as well. In their study of 138 father–son pairs, Morman and Floyd (2002) found that the fathers displayed much more affection toward their own sons than their fathers did with them. Still, as formerly, sports is often emphasized, especially team sports (Figure 7.4).

One of the most fascinating relationships in history and legend is that of father and son. While the father often seeks in his son the acclaim he failed to achieve himself, the son aspires to live up to his father's image or even surpass him. For the son of a prominent hero, this task may be daunting. Huffington (2004) mentions Shakespeare's Henry V, who led an English army into France as a way of following in his powerful father's footsteps and overcoming his youthful reputation for bawdy drunkenness. Huffington likens King Henry's motivation to that of George W. Bush. British historian Niall Ferguson (2004) has drawn a similar parallel between the two famous pairs of fathers and sons. Ascending the throne, Henry is suddenly transformed, justifying an invasion with obscure claims, waging war with a tyrant's zeal, and bankrupting his country. Similarly, by chasing Saddam Hussein from his palace in Baghdad, the son had finished a job his father had left undone. Carrying his father's name and following in his footsteps—from Andover, Yale, military flying, and into the oil business—the son had faltered at each turn. Only by being a "war president" could the younger Bush prove his worth. Several books on the market pursue the ambivalent father–son relationship theme (Frank, 2004; Schweizer & Schweizer, 2004; Wead, 2005).

Two biographies of interest to the father–son research literature are those of Barack Obama, who described his identity crisis in growing up as a black in a white family and with a father in Kenya who played no role in his life, and that of John McCain, the candidate who opposed Obama in the 2008 presidential election. Obama did get his dreams from his father, however, and he followed in his father's footsteps in going to Harvard for law school. The title of his autobiography, *Dreams from My Father: A Story of Race and Inheritance* (Obama, 1995), shows the significance of the father–son relationship even when the father is absent. Today, even as President of the United States, Obama works hard to be a good father to his children, in contrast to his father who abandoned that role altogether (Meacham, 2009).

John McCain's story has more in common with that of George W. Bush. The title of McCain's

Figure 7.4. Father roots for their sons at a Little League baseball game. Photo by Rupert van Wormer.

(1999) autobiography, *Faith of My Fathers*, tells of his life in a few words. McCain, like Bush, grew up in the shadow of ancestors who played prominent roles in American history and who had been recognized as war heroes. Both his father and grandfather graduated from Anapolis and became Admirals in the Navy. McCain's father was away a lot, his memory kept constantly alive by McCain's mother. Although John McCain III was in constant trouble at Anapolis and graduated near the bottom of his class, his political ambitions no doubt stemmed from his early failures in combination with his family legacy. He sought the White House for over a decade.

Research on fathering consists of two basic varieties—research on the impact on children of the father's absence and studies of the father's roles in the home. Popular literature and research by neoconservative social scientists have replaced the earlier exclusive focus on mothers with attention to the role of fathers (through their absence) in a wide range of social problems. Especially for boys who are seen as needing a male role model, the literature stresses the unique and essential role that

fathers have to play in their child's development (Sigelman & Rider, 2006; see Figure 7.5).

Fathers' love of their sons and frequency of contact have been found to be correlated with academic achievement (Jones, 2004). Fathers of small boys generally respond to them through engagement in rough-and-tumble play. The presence and frequency of such play was shown in a survey of parents to be linked to social competence in small boys but not in girls (Mellen, 2002). In their extensive review of the empirical literature on father–child relationships, Rohner and Veneziano (2001) found that the influence of father love on children's and young adults' social and emotional development is as great as the influence of mother love. Father nurturance was shown to have differential outcomes for sons and daughters and to be more important in determining how well sons (but not daughters) performed on an IQ test, for example. Viewed as a whole, the literature on father–child relationships shows that paternal acceptance or rejection is heavily implicated in sons' well-being and also in problems of aggression, drug use, and delinquency.

Figure 7.5. Father and son on a ferry boat share a learning moment. Photo by Rupert van Wormer.

Over one-third of children grow up without a father's presence in the home. In the best-selling book *The Conversation: How Black Men and Women Can Build Loving, Trusting Relationships*, Hill Harper (2009) analyzes the lack of relationship commitment among black males, including his own 20-year reluctance to "tie the knot." Harper is concerned with the harm caused to children growing up in a world in which they bond with their mothers' boyfriends, only later to feel abandoned as the relationships break up. The impact of father absence was summarized in an extensive review of the literature by DeBell (2008). The consensus in the literature reviewed indicated that children in father-absent homes compared to children who live with both parents experience reduced well-being: worse health, lower academic achievement, worse educational experiences, and less parental involvement in school activities. When socioeconomic factors are controlled, however, the deficits of well-being are far less. De Bell concludes, therefore, that the conventional wisdom may exaggerate the harmful effects of father absence on the child. Paschall, Ringwalt, and Flewelling (2003), in their review of the literature found that the presence of fathers in the home is associated

with reduced aggressive behaviors in boys. Their own research on delinquency rates confirmed the impact of father absence in combination with low socioeconomic status on the male child. The presence of healthy adult male role models evidently attenuates the effect of cultural messages valuing hypermasculinity in men.

In African American families, the patriarchal family style within two-parent households, which endured for most of the twentieth century, has been largely overlooked in the literature. "In the world I grew up in," notes bell hooks (2001), "adult black males were present in most homes; like my dad, they were providers and protectors" (p. 130). On learning from her sociology classes in the 1970s of the black matriarchy, which had emasculated black men, hooks was astonished because the information did not match the reality she had known. Relevant to the classic father–son relationship is hooks' description of her brother and his relationship with his father:

While he liked sports as a boy, he was just not that interested in being a major sports figure. Our father had been a soldier and gone to war. We had pictures of him playing basketball, of him in the boxing ring, pictures of him with his all-black infantry unit. My brother was bad at sports. He was a disappointment to our dad, and as punishment Dad withheld from him affection and affirmation. (p. 130)

In their unique collection of essays, *Between Fathers and Sons*, Pellegrini and Sarbin (2002) explore themes of silence, independence, and identity. Among the situations they describe is that of a Korean immigrant who faces the difference between his concept of fatherhood and his son's American view. They also relate the case of a boy who seeks guidance from stories about his late father as he wrestles with his stepfather's betrayal.

The research on father–son relationships generally takes a positive stance in terms of the way the women's movement has freed both women and men from gender role restrictions. Men are now encouraged to express feelings in addition to anger, to increase their sensitivity to others' feelings, and to assume active caregiving roles when at home. The number of children who are raised by a primary care father, for example, is now more than 2 million, while one in five with fathers with employed wives as the primary caregiver for the family's preschool children (U.S. Census Bureau, 2005). On the negative side, feminist scholars such as Faludi (2000) point to pressures from the global economy that have altered men's social utility, coupled with men's history of lack of paternal nurturance during childhood. Shortage of time due to long commutes to work and ever-increasing productivity demands at the workplace limit the amount of casual interaction that can take place between father and son even when fathers want a close, bonding relationship.

Fatherloss is the title of a book by Chethik (2001) that describes how men cope with the death of their fathers. Many of the men interviewed had their lives shattered by their fathers' premature death; virtually all of them experienced father loss as a transformation for which they were unprepared. Chethik's personal profiles of father–son relationships draw on a survey of 300 men and interviews with 70 others. The title could also refer to the separation of fathers and sons through incarceration. It is estimated that more than 1.5 million young people nationwide have had a mother or father—or both—behind bars (DeAngelis, 2001). Many of these children continue to be emotionally, economically, and socially scarred as a result (Mazza, 2002). The majority of men in prison in the United States are fathers of dependent children for whom they had some responsibility prior to incarceration. Studies of fathers in prison have shown that visits with their children are infrequent and that most fathers express concern for their children, worry about them, and are anxious about being replaced in their children's lives by someone else (Hairston, 2001). Due to racist practices in drug sentencing laws, African American children are disproportionately fatherless due to the imprisonment explosion. Rigid child welfare policies and punitive prison regulations (not to mention sentencing practices) are keeping many fathers from playing a role in their children's lives.

As described in Chapter 6, death does not always end a relationship. Such is the theme of the powerful 1970 movie *I Never Sang for My Father*, based on the Robert Anderson (1968/1980) play of the same title. In the drama, Gene Hackman plays a son who wrestles with his ambivalent feelings for his authoritarian father, who now suffers from Alzheimer's. "I can't tell you what it does to me as a man . . . to see someone like that . . . a man who was distinguished, remarkable . . . just become a nuisance" (p. 94). The father, in turn, always had an ache in his heart because his son, as a child, would never sing for him. The autobiographical *I Never Sang for My Father* tells us graphically what empirical research cannot—the emotional depth of feeling between fathers and their sons, feelings that often are not expressed.

Father and Daughter

If there is little research on the father–son dyad, there is an absolute paucity of systematic attention to the dynamics that characterize the father–daughter relationship. Such literature as there is focuses on abuse and the legacy of abuse (Perkins, 2001). Freud (1933/1964) viewed this relationship as problematic—the daughter's attachment to her father created competition with her mother during the phallic stage. Freud termed this situation the *Electra complex.* The theory also includes another component, that girls become hostile to their mothers, whom they blame for not giving them a penis like their brothers. This masculinist notion dominated Western thought, especially that of mental health professionals, until challenged by proponents of the women's movement.

From the daughter's perspective, *Memoirs of a Dutiful Daughter*, written by Simone de Beauvoir (1959), elicited world acclaim and anticipated the second wave of feminism. In one notable passage, de Beauvoir describes the shift from mother to father affection: "I was jealous of the place she (my mother) held in my father's affections because my own passion for him continued to grow. . . . I was dazzled by my father's superior character. . . . As long as he approved of me, I could be sure of myself. For years he had done nothing but heap praises on my head. But when I reached the awkward age, he was disappointed in me" (p. 114).

The importance to a girl of her father's pride in her personal attributes and potential is revealed in de Beauvoir's passage. Most women, simply by growing up, experience a transition in the form their father's love takes. Sophie Freud (1988), granddaughter of Sigmund Freud, explored in some depth the pain a young woman experiences when she can no longer be her father's "little princess."

To Virginia Satir (1988), who spent most of her life engaged in family therapy, the early father–daughter relationship was instrumental in preparing girls for life. A girl who grows up without a father, Satir suggested, might "be handicapped by having a skewed picture of what males are like" and what male–female relationships are like (p. 159). But a girl who grows up with a close relationship with her father is blessed in many ways (Figure 7.6).

Perkins (2001) studied the self-perception and assertiveness of 96 young college women

Figure 7.6. The father–daughter relationship is special in many ways. Photo by Flora Stuart.

in relation to the type of relationship they experienced with their fathers. Her hypothesis was that childhood father–daughter relationships have the potential to shape adult interaction patterns as evidenced in the women's descriptions of their personal experiences. The six categories addressed by a questionnaire were a doting father; a distant father; a demanding/supportive father; a domineering father; an absent father; and a seductive father.

Findings indicated that a daughter of a doting father strongly identified with him but may not have felt psychologically free to be herself. In contrast, daughters of demanding/supportive fathers appeared to have the strength to assert behaviors unlike those of their fathers. Daughters of distant fathers often engaged in a silent alliance with them; this unhealthy relationship had implications for their future partnerships. Daughters of domineering fathers often felt disconnected emotionally in a relationship based on fear; identification with the father was weak. Results showed that daughters of absent fathers were highly assertive but felt separated from and misunderstood by their fathers. Women with seductive fathers also felt separated but, in addition, stressed that they had been violated.

The bulk of the literature on the father–daughter relationship, as any search engine check will show, is concerned with sexual abuse. One academic study of note (in that it used a rare longitudinal design) examined the impact of three forms of childhood victimization on self-reported delinquency and aggression in adolescent girls. This study by Herrera and McCloskey (2003) analyzed reports of 141 mother–daughter pairs from the time the children were in school. The girls were followed up in later adolescence and reinterviewed. The three kinds of violence studied were children exposed to marital violence; escalated physical abuse against the child; and child sexual abuse. Results in adolescent self-reports indicated that, of the three forms of victimization, child sexual abuse was the strongest predictor of girls' violent and nonviolent criminal behavior. Girls with a history of physical abuse were most likely to assault their parents. Witnessing marital violence did not seem to contribute further to delinquency.

Another study examined data on the long-term effects of parental marital quality and divorce on their children (Orbuch, Thornton, & Cancio, 2000). In the 867 marital relationships studied, the authors found that divorce actually seemed to improve mother–daughter relations, while hurting father–daughter relations more than father–son relations. The only long-term effect (apart from decline in economic standard of living) was that children of divorce considered divorce a viable alternative to marital conflict. Parental divorce in literature surveyed by Sigelman and Rider (2006) did not seem to affect later attachment styles, but children who grew up in troubled homes were more likely to have negative romantic experiences as young adults. Since father absence in itself is associated with long-term relationship problems for girls (see East, Jackson, & O'Brien, 2006), one could speculate that parental divorce would also be associated with such problems. In white families, after parental separation, fathers were likely to see their children infrequently, compared to the situation in African American homes.

How does the quality of the father–daughter relationship affect later intimate relations? In their review of the literature on intergenerational learning, Gadsden and Hall (1996) found some indication from a Hawaiian study that men marry women who resemble their mothers and women marry men who resemble their fathers, consistent with psychoanalytic theory. This theory received empirical support in a more recent study from Hungary by Bereczkei, Hegedus, and Hajnal (2008). The research design involved the mapping of the faces of 67 young, long-term couples at their university, as well as each parent, measuring facial proportions such as the ratios of face length to width, nose length to face height, and mouth width to height. Based on their observations, Bereczkei's team found that, overall, the face of a woman's boyfriend more closely resembles her father's than the faces of other males in the study. The correlation was most striking for measurements of the center of the face, such as the ratios between nose length to face height and eye width to face height. Men also dated women whose faces more closely resembled their mothers than other women in the study. But here, men seemed to focus on the lower part of the face. The ratios between jaw and face width and lip fullness (height) and width of their mothers and girlfriends tended to match. These findings, according to the authors, hint at a process well documented in nonhuman animals—and only beginning to emerge from studies of humans—called sexual imprinting.

Regarding communication and intimacy, recent research shows that fathers play a key role in their daughters' sex-role development. Surveys conducted on over 3,000 high school students found that girls in homes where fathers were highly involved tend to delay sexual encounters and pregnancy as compared to homes where fathers are less actively involved in family life (Coley, Votruba-Drzal, & Schindler, 2009). In her sample of over 100 African American girls, Cooper (2009) found the quality of the father–daughter relationship to be closely related to girls' academic achievement. The key determining factor that emerged in the study was the girls' self-esteem.

Apparently father–daughter relationships are drawing closer, at least regarding encouragement of girls to pursue more challenging careers. In a comparison of women who were born at the beginning of the past century when 6 percent of women pursued their father's career, today 18 percent work in the same general field as their father (reported by Lloyd, 2009).

Girls often feel a sense of protection in having a father in the home. With the father's death, that sense of protectiveness is gone. In *Fatherless Women: How We Change After We Lose Our Dads*, Simon (2002) writes of the challenges daughters face after the death of the father. Most of the stories included in this book involve the loss of the father in childhood. The author's personal story, which is the major theme of the book, involved a dysfunctional relationship, a factor that makes the consequences of premature loss even more compelling and realistic in that no family relationship is perfect.

Mother and Son

"The mother: We suffer in their coming and their going." I had always pondered the meaning of these haunting lines that I remembered reading in a poetry book years ago. Recently, I consulted a popular listserv and learned their history. These lines were written by Irish patriot and poet Patrick Pearse and given to his mother in anticipation, most likely, of his untimely death. He and his brother were executed after the Easter Rising of 1916. The poem he wrote was from the point of view of his grieving mother, and it was indicative of a close bond.

Historically, every mother must have feared the loss of her sons to war (and the loss of daughters to childbirth). Sometimes the resistance to such tragic loss has been palpable. With reference to her son who was killed in the war in Iraq, for example, Cindy Sheehan (2005) declared the following: "When I nursed him, I promised him that I would never let him go to war. I broke that promise to him. I can't bear for another mother to go through the pain that I'm going through. And that is the only reason I'm doing what I'm doing [protesting]" (p. 4).

The mother–son bond is often the strongest and least conflicted in the family. From a man's point of view, the mother–son relationship defines the man a son will become and serves as a reservoir from which he may later draw memories and affection that will guide him as a husband and father (Lang, 2004). Tisdale (2001 has graphically described the mother's perspective on this emotionally close and deeply perplexing relationship:

> Four years ago he was born and everything changed. . . . We are strangely entangled. When I wake from a bad dream without a sound, he wakes in the next room and cries for me. Between us there is no shame, no holding back. I take risks with him I wouldn't dare take with anyone else. . . . We fight and then make up with a tentative, weary kiss. I demand so much: loyalty, obedience, faith. And he gives me all I demand and more—he thinks me beautiful; he wants to grow up to be just like me. And I am bound to fail him, and bound to lose him. Strangers' hands will stroke where I stroke now, and already I'm jealous of this secret future apart from me. (p. 17)

Tisdale's narrative is one of the 18 in Stevens' (2001) anthology of women's experiences in raising their sons. In these disarmingly honest accounts, the reader can appreciate the tensions that sometimes ensue in later mother-in-law/daughter-in-law relationships. A common thread running through the stories of this ethnically diverse group is that growing boys will too soon retreat from the intense intimacy that occurs between mothers and their young sons.

Freud (1933/1964), of course, had a lot to say about the love between mother and son. His perspective was the child's unconscious desire for the parent of the opposite sex. In small male children the conflict is termed the *Oedipus complex*, named for the Greek king in the play *Oedipus Rex*. Oedipus killed a man who turned out to be his father and married a woman who was actually his mother. He suffered greatly when he realized he had violated one of the greatest of the universal taboos. From the Freudian viewpoint, a boy's fantasies about his mother and the sense of rivalry with his father lead to secret guilt feelings that must be resolved at a later stage. Typically, he does this by repressing his feelings, burying them in the unconscious mind.

As the sons reach adolescence, mothers find it hard to truly understand them, especially if they conform to gender role expectations, seeking adventure and tinkering with mechanical equipment, especially cars. Erikson (1950/1963) describes the American youths in this manner: "The boy has a delinquent streak, as had his grandfather in the days when laws were absent or not enforced. This may express itself in surprising acts of dangerous driving or careless destruction and waste" (p. 318). The connection between father and son Erikson describes as a "joking relationship," in which the son may hope "to get away with something—i.e., elude the mother's watchful eye" (p. 313). The implication here seems to be that father and son are in collusion against the mother's high, somewhat rigid, standards.

There is no doubt that the mother–son relationship differs in many ways from the father–son and the mother–daughter relationship. To test this hypothesis and further define family ways of interacting, Thompson and Zuroff (1999) set up experimental situations in which mothers were instructed to coach their sons and daughters on computer problem-solving puzzles. The situations were manipulated so that the sons were believed to be doing only average in one scenario and above average in another. Results indicated that mothers who scored high on dependency needs on a questionnaire reacted positively to sons described as high in competence and encouraged their autonomy in choosing a discussion partner. However, these same mothers related to less competent sons by thwarting their attempts at autonomy. A previous study found that mothers reacted in a critical, controlling fashion with their daughters regardless of whether their performance was described as highly competent. Perhaps this is why there is often more friction in mother–daughter than in mother–son relationships; the mothers are self-critical and project their own lack of confidence on their daughters.

We can learn much about the complexity and power of the African American mother–son bond from Keith Brown's (1998) tribute to motherhood, *Sacred Bond: Black Men and Their Mothers*. Drawing on 36 interviews and accompanying photographs, Brown examines the mother–son relationship in terms of the instinctive drive most mothers feel to protect their children from harm, especially within tough environments such as inner-city neighborhoods. Because all of the men interviewed have become successful in a variety of ways, these personal histories are stories of triumph over adversity, in every case due to the mother's love and indomitable courage. The first story, told by a narcotics officer, for example, describes how his uneducated mother said over his seriously wounded body, "God spared you for a reason" (p. 1). Later the same mother rescued her other son by practically dragging him away from a group of gang members who were initiating him into their group.

Collectively, the mothers described in *Sacred Bond* believed that their sons could make something of themselves and stressed education as the way out of poverty. Among the stories is that of a choreographer who tells about the day his mother, a strict evangelist, tore into him about his homosexuality. Years later, however, when his lover was dying of AIDS, along came his mother, leading a group of prayer warriors marching and singing into the sick room.

Benjamin Carson, a famous neurosurgeon, relates how his mother, who worked as a maid, assigned her two sons weekly book reports that they dared not fail to turn in, even though they realized she was unable to read them (Brown, 1998). Although the impact of race and racism are constants in the life stories, these recollections have a message about the power of maternal love and caring.

Mother and Daughter

Folk wisdom teaches us that "a son's a son 'til he takes him a wife; a daughter's a daughter for the rest of her life." Christiane Northrup (2005), an obstetrician and gynecologist, brings us insight of another kind in her best-selling

Mother-Daughter Wisdom: Creating a Legacy of Physical and Emotional Health. Her concern is with the relationship in the family that is certainly the most passionate of the parent–child dyads: the relationship between mother and daughter.

The mother–daughter relationship, according to Northrup, who has become a regular guest on television programs, has more clout biologically, emotionally, and psychologically than any other relationship in a woman's life. Northrup is referring primarily to health issues; her point is that the way our body was cared for by our mother determines how we care for ourselves. Our mothers, she says, are our most potent role models. The core beliefs and behaviors that most profoundly affect a woman's health are passed from mother to daughter. This is the intergenerational legacy of information that is unconsciously passed on in the form of advice and attitude. If the mother regards her menstrual cycle as a curse and aging as the pits, the daughter may develop symptoms that are psychosomatic. As a physician dealing with women's gynecological problems, Northrup found she had to go upstream to the headwaters of health to explore the legacy of attitudes about the female body passed down from mother to daughter.

Northrup has devised a map of female development in the form of a house with many rooms of passage toward the roof of life hereafter. Each woman can access her own blueprint for health in terms of the "five facets of feminine power," which range from the basics of physical self-care to the discovery of passion and purpose in life. To break the "chain of pain" passed down the generations, a woman must be resourceful—find a surrogate mother, perhaps, and change her thoughts about her body. The medicine called forgiveness can be a powerful antidote to anger—anger because something painful happened to her when she didn't have the emotional capacity to deal with it.

Consistent with her training in obstetrics, Northrup emphasizes the force of the biological links between a mother and the child she carried in her body for 9 months. Yet there is no indication that ties between mother and adoptive children are any less strong. Sometimes adopted children, on reaching maturity, search for their birth parents. But occasionally this is a disaster, as dramatized in the 1996 British movie *Secrets and Lies.* An already complex interracial situation (the mother is white and the daughter black) is further complicated in the movie by an ugly event early in the mother's life.

When the mother–daughter relationship is problematic, the results for the girl can be dire. This may be especially so in Latino families, where the role of the mother tends to be exalted. Yet culture clash between first and second generations regarding the sex-role behavior of girls can make such conflict likely. Crean (2008) found in an extensive survey of Latino sixth and seventh graders that if boys had a conflict with their mothers, a solid relationship with the father could help compensate, but that for Latina girls, highly conflictive mother–daughter relationships were associated with serious behavior problems and lowered self-esteem. Crean's research findings are consistent with recent media reports of a high number of suicide attempts among Latina girls following conflict with their mothers. Media accounts drew on results from the Centers for Disease Control and Prevention's (CDC, 2008) *Morbidity and Mortality Report* that showed the rate of suicide attempts for Latina girls was almost twice the white rate and much more than the black female suicide attempt rate. The media accounts explored the mother–daughter conflicts; the suicide attempts are generally made by the girls' ingestion of pills and slitting their wrists.

The award-winning documentary *Daughter From Danang* (produced in 2000 by Gail Dolgin and Vicente Franco) records the excited preparation for a reunion between a young woman, Heidi, and her Vietnamese mother, who had sent her away to the United States during the panic of the U.S. retreat from Vietnam in 1975. The mother had given up her child to Operation Babylift because of her fear that the child, who was fathered by a U.S. soldier, would be persecuted as half-caste, or *bui doi* (the lust for life.) Twenty-two years later they were destined to meet again. The cultural clash, as brought out in the film, is jolting. Despite the intense closeness that develops between Heidi and her biological siblings and mother, the reunion is tainted by stark financial realities. The family anticipates that Heidi will provide financial help for the Vietnamese mother, but Heidi recoils from her unwanted kin obligations and heads home. The almost overwhelming love that the birth mother feels for her given-away daughter is not reciprocated by the one who has no memory of her birth mother and no understanding of (or respect for) the culture.

For a critical look at twenty-first-century demands on middle-class American mothers of small children, Judith Warner's (2005) *Perfect Madness* comes to mind. In contrast to Northrup, who focused on the daughter's perspective, and the *Daughter From Danang*, which was also basically the daughter's tale, Warner's research centers on interviews with mothers, mostly of small children. Warner found they were incredibly stressed by the new taxing standards of motherhood and that some appeared to have lost nearly all sense of themselves as adult women. The women were highly self-critical, blaming themselves for not being a perfect mother and judging other mothers equally harshly. Many of them were facing dismal choices of pursuing professional dreams at the cost of abandoning the children to long hours of inadequate child care or facing social isolation at home. Many other women, Warner acknowledges, must work full time in a society where the average work week is the longest in the industrialized world, just to put food on the table. Motherhood, concludes Warner, can stop being the awful burden it has become and the joy it should be only with proper societal supports and family subsidies. Above all, mothers need affordable, flexible child care, combined with tax subsidies, for an expression of true family values.

Similarly, Anna Quindlen (2004) maintains that "motherhood changed from a role into a calling" and that it has thus become professionalized. Quindlen's focus is on life after the children have grown up, the emotional sense of loss that comes with hearing, as Quindlen once did from her daughter, "We don't have that family anymore." As a mother's children grow up, her identity changes; the result is an empty nest without a role inasmuch as all of those sacrifices become "the warp and woof of our lives." "It's not simply the loss of these particular people, living here day in, day out," Quindlen writes, "the bickering, the inside jokes, the cereal bowls in the sink and the towels in the hamper—all right, on the floor. It was who I was to them. . . . Mom is my real name. It is, it is" (all of these quotes are from p. 64).

Another kind of mother–daughter passage occurs in the ties between caregiving daughters and their dependent, advanced-age mothers. Relationships between elderly parents and adult children in general appear to be strongest for mothers and daughters (Gadsden & Hall, 1996). In the African American community, the adult mother–daughter relationship is especially close and supportive. African American women are more likely than their European American counterparts to live in the same household, which is often three generational (Strauss & Falkin, 2001).

A description of how aging white mothers and their caregiving daughters negotiate issues of connection and autonomy is provided by McGraw and Walker (2004) in their study of videotaped interactions between 31 white mother–daughter pairs. The healthiest patterns occurred when each member of the pair was attentive to the other's needs, a fairly predictable finding. Although most of the pairs minimized open conflict and most of the participants were thoughtful of each other, subtle behavioral cues also exposed underlying emotional tension in some of the relationships. Mother–daughter relationships are much more complex when more than one child is involved.

Sibling Relationships

In my hospital visitation work in Washington State and in my supervision of the Family Week program at a Norwegian alcoholism treatment center, I witnessed many intense relationships among brothers and sisters, mostly between sisters, as brothers less often attended the family sessions. Among the most memorable of the situations I dealt with were these: (in the hospital ward) an attempted suicide case of a young woman who was raped by her brother-in-law and not believed by her sister until that very day as a result of the near suicide; three middle-aged, red-headed sisters, all of whom had attended the Family Week to confront their father for his incest with all three; and a teen-age brother and sister pair who, in the family circle, told their father that, as small children, they had heard their mother's screams as he was beating her.

A Thousand Acres, a 1997 movie starring Jessica Lange, Michelle Pfeiffer, and Jason Robards, tells the story of three sisters in crisis over their father's decision to turn his land over to them. Based on the Pulitzer Prize-winning novel of the same title by Jane Smiley (1991), this is a retelling of the tragedy of *King Lear*. The interrelationships of the three sisters, the elder two of whom have withheld dark secrets from the younger, are powerfully played out to the bitter end in this drama.

Relationships between brothers and sisters are distinctive, often precious, and the longest family relationship in one's life. However, Saleebey (2001) states, they are often conten-tious: Siblings compete for a scarce resource—the attention, affection, physical resources, and care of their parent or parents. The Bible is replete with stories of rivalry between brothers, most notably Cain and Abel (Genesis 4:2–12) and Joseph and his brothers (Genesis 37:3–4). God's favoritism of Abel—whose gift was accepted whereas Cain's was not, and of Joseph, whose father gave him a "coat of many colors"—is a theme that most children readily can understand: jealousy and retribution. Chil-dren can readily grasp the concept because it hits close to home. Child abuse reports rarely take sibling abuse into account, maybe because it is so commonplace. Yet research shows that around one-third of children are assaulted by a sibling each year, and this is true across all races and ethnicities (Finkelhor, Turner, & Ormrod, 2006). A minority were attacked on a regular basis, and over four percent were seri-ously injured. The impact of such abuse can be lasting.

Studies have shown that of the three types of sibling pairs, sister/sister pairs (Figure 7.7) are the closest and brother/brother pairs are the most rivalrous (Thomas, 2000). Identical male twins tend to be the most competitive since adults often force them to compete. Except for twins, siblings are unequal by nature because the older ones have more power, knowledge, and privileges than the younger ones; at the same time, the younger ones are generally considered cuter and can get away with more since parents generally soften up with subsequent children. And, of course, some are better looking and brighter or have better dispositions than others. One of the best descriptions of sibling relationships in the lit-erature is provided by Simone de Beauvoir (1959) in her *Memoirs of a Dutiful Daughter*:

> I was sorry for children who had no brother or sister; solitary amusements seemed insipid to me: no better than a means of killing time. But when there were two, hopscotch or a game of ball were adventurous undertakings, and rolling hoops an exciting competition.
>
> Relegated to a secondary position, the "little one" felt almost superfluous. I was a new experience for my parents: my sister found it much more difficult to surprise and astonish them; I had never been compared with anyone: she was always compared with me. (p. 46)

First-borns often become the family heroes; a good deal of pressure is often put on them to pursue dreams unfulfilled by their parents (van Wormer & Davis, 2008). Since the best place in the family system is already taken, the second born is at risk of playing a more mischievous, even scapegoat, role, thus establishing a unique identity while avoiding competing with the high achievements of child number one. By means of illustration, consider the British royal family, the forever proper Queen Elizabeth, whom commentators regularly compared to her rebellious sister, Princess Margaret.

Whether birth order has a long-lasting effect on personality is debatable. Saleebey (2001) believes that there is actually not much of a relationship between the ordinal role a child plays in the family and how that child behaves outside the family. In reviewing the literature on birth order, Harris (2009) states that no

Figure 7.7. Sisters often grow very close despite some early annoyances. Photo by Robert van Wormer.

significant differences between the first- and second-born emerge consistently in the personality testing conducted. The only significant difference is that the last-born male in families of three or more scored lower on masculinity than did other males in the family. Harris contends that children in a family have distinctly different inborn traits and that parents relate to them accordingly. Sigelman and Rider (2006) concur. First-borns may be bossy with younger siblings, they suggest, but outside of the family context, there may not necessarily be any carryover. Family theorists such as Bowen (1978) and Satir (1988) firmly believed that ordinal rank in childhood was related to roles that were played in both the family of origin and the family of procreation. Substance abuse counseling draws heavily on these theories in their family programming by encouraging family members to identify themselves as hero, scapegoat, last child, or mascot (van Wormer & Davis, 2008).

Leman (2009) studied the impact of birth order by examining data from the biographies of key historical personalities. First-borns, he argues, have a tendency to identify with power and authority. Around two-thirds of U.S. Presi-

dents were first-borns, or in effect first-borns. Later-borns, in contrast, tend to be more liberal, innovative, inclined to identify with underdogs, and question the status quo. Scientists Darwin and Copernicus did such questioning and revolutionized our view of biology and the universe, respectively. Obviously more systematic research is needed on the impact of birth order on personality characteristics.

Much attention is given in the recent literature to the distress caused to brothers and sisters growing up with a sibling who has a mental or a physical disability. The effects are both negative (in depriving the other children of attention they might need) and positive (in teaching compassion and tolerance). Cuskelly, Gunn, Schonell, and Schonell (2003) interviewed 54 siblings of children with Down syndrome and their parents and a matched comparison sample. There were no group differences in parental reports, but siblings of children with Down syndrome displayed differences. They reported higher levels of empathy and more caregiving activities than were found in the comparison group. Rossiter and Sharpe (2001), however, in their study of siblings of people with mental retardation, found some evidence of depression and anxiety in these siblings due to the amount of attention the parents had to give the disabled child. Lynn Jones (2009) notes that siblings of children with developmental disabilities receive less attention than their brothers or sisters but that the attention they receive is more of a positive nature. Sometimes they become overly invested in being the good child, trying to help their parents feel better. Children with siblings with disabilities often express concern about the future for these children. The reason, as Jones suggests, may be that these children may realize at some point that they will be responsible for their sibling with a disability.

Findings in the research literature concerning the long-term impact of growing up in a home with an autistic brother or sister are contradictory (Kaminisky & Dewey, 2002). Because of the demands on time, energy, and emotions of parents and their family members, who must be constantly vigilant and infinitely patient in teaching even simple skills and acceptable behaviors, the siblings of autistic children inhabit a family environment that is very different from that of other children. They may hesitate to bring friends home, and they may suffer from lack of companionship from the brother or sister who is so often in a different world. On the other hand, the research of Kaminisky and Dewey (2002) shows that siblings of autistic children, especially younger ones, have developed entirely satisfactory levels of social and academic competence.

The important role that siblings play in providing support systems for each other is rarely explored in the research literature apart from attention paid to family supports in general. Three books, however, provide moving accounts of sibling relations. In *No Friend Like a Sister*, Neale (2004) emphasizes their lifelong bonding and communication. Interviews with 48 women of all ages who have sisters encompass both the highs and lows of the often-emotional intensity of sisterhood. Issues with the most impact on the sisters ranged from facing the repercussions of early childhood abuse to expecting reciprocity to coping with the death of a parent.

Sister relationships, according to Deborah Tannen (2009), are among the most passionate of our lives. In her intimate look at female sibling relationships, *You Were Always Mom's Favorite*, Tannen drew on anecdotes from more than 100 women. These family ties, she says, are almost like marriages. In her growing up, she shared a room with her next older sister who had access to all her belongings; this led to territorial disputes. Her oldest sister was more distant due to the age difference and played a motherlike but not nurturant role. The impact of birth order looms through the interviews with younger sisters who reported that their older sisters were bossy and judgmental. "There is the bond of 'a close bond—close connection,'" notes Tannen. "But there is also the bond of 'bondage'—being tied up, lashed to a post or a person" (p. 45). From the big sister's point of view, she often feels like she needs to be protective of the younger one; the sense of protectiveness is especially strong if one sister is disabled.

Millman (2004), author of *The Perfect Sister*, similarly based her study on personal interviews, but she included as subjects two or more sisters from the same family. How sisters who grew up together may have completely different perceptions of the family is among the topics she discusses. Another is the way in which sisterly relations are entwined with relations with mothers, fathers, and so on. Divided into three sections, the book focuses on sisters who nurture each other, those with troubled relationships, and those who have reconciled their differences late in life.

In a somewhat different vein, Hawthorne (2003), a clinical social worker and educator, provides a self-help guide titled *Sisters and Brothers All These Years* to foster closer relationships among adult siblings. In old age, Hawthorne points out, siblings are the last remaining members of our family of origin. Our brothers and sisters not only offer us the opportunity to reminisce about our little-known unique histories but can also be a source of much-needed emotional support.

The way that parents treat their children may affect how children treat each other when the parent is gone. Favoritism of one child over the other may never be forgiven, and the resentment may be taken out on the favored sibling.

Inheritance differences may leave wounds that never heal; these differences may involve the grandchildren—one sibling's child favored over the other. The siblings are then torn between preserving their relationship and advocating on behalf of a child. Inheritance battles can create situations where siblings are forever split apart (Tannen, 2009). The children of Martin Luther King have been involved in lawsuits against each other over control of the "legacy" of their father (Wheaton, 2009).

Marriage research shows that sibling relationships change drastically following the marriage of one or more of the grown children (Thomas, 2000). Marriage frequently creates a wedge in an otherwise bonded relationship, especially when the spouse does not "fit in" with the family and pulls the sibling away from the family circle. In his book on sibling rivalry, Thomas discusses the most devastating event that can occur between siblings—brother/sister incest. Such victimization divides families forever—brother from sister and parents from child, depending on whose side they take and whether they even know. In the case of incest, reconciliation is usually out of the question.

Politics and religion in later life can likewise cause irreparable damage. As I was writing this section for the original edition, I received the following e-mail from an unknown woman seeking advice:

> I am a liberal. I have a sister who is born again, and she is absolutely off her rocker. She thinks Armageddon is just around the corner. I can't seem to reach her. She attends a small "Baptist" church out in the country with a preacher who is a former drug addict. And my niece is in cahoots with her. I wish I knew how to get my sister back. I miss her. My sister told me yesterday that our mother is still burning in hell because she wasn't "saved." That makes me want to sever ties. My mother was a fine person, loving and giving. (personal communication, March 15, 2005)

Aunts and Uncles

This book, you will note, was dedicated to my aunts. When I was 8 years old, one of my life's tragedies was when my favorite aunt married and moved away. Then she had children of her own and was out of my life for many years. Today I am an aunt myself; there are photos of my niece and my great nieces in this chapter and elsewhere in this book. When families were large and geographical mobility not such an issue, practically all children grew up surrounded by their parents' brothers and sisters. Maiden aunts or aunts without children often doted on their nieces and nephews. In a book of one of my ancestors is the following description (Talmage, 1902) of Aunt Phoebe who turned down proposals in order to care "for her invalid father until the bloom of her life had somewhat faded" (p. 21):

> The patron saint of almost every family circle is some unmarried woman, and among all the families of cousins she moves around, and her coming in each house is the morning and her going away is the night. . . . Was there a sickness in any of the households, she was there ready to sit up and count out the drops of medicine. Was there a marriage, she helped deck the bride for the alter. . . .
> If you would know how her presence would soothe an anxiety or lift a burden or cheer a sorrow or leave a blessing on every room in the house, ask any of the Talmages. (p. 21)

Fictional accounts abound in children's literature or literature about children in which the orphaned child is brought up by an aunt. The characters, Aunt Betsey Trotwood in *David Copperfield*, Aunt Polly in *Tom Sawyer*, and Aunt Polly in *Pollyanna*, and Auntie Mame in the novel of the same name. Uncles do not seem quite as lovable in the literature, the most prominent of which is, of course, Uncle Scrooge of *A Christmas Carol*.

Today, fewer children have aunts and uncles in abundance, but they may grow close to the ones they do have. A major challenge today, however, is for extended families to be close for the duration of a lifetime given the mobility of today's society. Generally speaking, if family rituals are celebrated regularly the relatives will be able to maintain their close ties over time.

When the siblings are very close, there is a better chance that cousins will grow up together, sometimes more like brothers and sisters than like cousins. And the aunt/uncle/niece/nephew relationships will be close as well.

From the perspective of the children, aunts and uncles can come in all ages. If your mother, for example, had a much younger sister or brother, your aunt or uncle could be perhaps only 5–10 years older than you. And there are great aunts and uncles who are much older. In her book on aging, Mary Pipher (1999) describes where some of the stories interwoven in *Another Country* came from:

> In the houses of all five of my aunts,
> I listened to family stories, looked at
> pictures, and ate their home-cooked meals.
> In the faces and gestures I saw the faces
> and gestures of my children. As I talked to
> them, I better understood my own parents
> and I learned about myself. I understood
> more of our country's history and
> I received lessons in how to age. (p. 320)

Except for children's books, books on aunts and uncles are rare. To my knowledge there are only one on each. *Aunts: A Celebration of Those Special Women in Our Lives* by Annette Cunningham (1997) provides a witty, affectionate, descriptive account. And Russell Wild (1999) did pretty much the same thing in his *Uncles: A Tribute to the Coolest Guys in the World*. From England a landmark contribution to family scholarship is the recently published *The Forgotten Kin: Aunts and Uncles* by Robert Milardo (2009). Drawing on over 100 interviews of aunts, uncles, nieces, and nephews, Milardo analyzes the reciprocal benefits of kinship ties that are so often overlooked by family researchers and the media. The relationships between aunts and nieces are shown to be strikingly different from those of uncles and nephews; while the former is more relationship based, the latter is oriented more toward shared activities. But both aunts and uncles commonly assume mentoring roles toward their younger relatives and can be a major influence in a family crisis. Often the nieces and nephews will listen to these siblings of their parents and go to them for advice when they would be reluctant to go to their parents.

When Senator Edward Kennedy died recently, the memorial service and funeral were nationally televised events, the likes of which had not been seen since the deaths of his brothers and of Martin Luther King. Of the eulogies provided, none was more powerful than those offered by Ted Kennedy's nieces and nephews. Joe Kennedy (2009), the son of the late Attorney General and presidential candidate Robert F. Kennedy, addressed mourners at the memorial service in Boston with these words:

> Every single one of my brothers and sisters
> needed a father, and we gained one
> through Teddy. For so many of us, we just
> needed someone to hang onto, and Teddy
> was always there. I'm here today because
> I loved my uncle so very much, so very
> much. He did so much for me and for my
> brothers and sisters and my mother when
> we needed a hand.

And the daughter of President John F. Kennedy echoed her cousin's words in her eulogy at the memorial service. The previous year, almost to the day, Caroline Kennedy Schlossberg (2008) gave this tribute to her uncle at the Democratic National Convention:

> In our family, he's never missed a first
> communion, a graduation, or a chance to
> walk one of his nieces down the aisle. He
> has a special relationship with all his nieces
> and nephews, and his 60 great nieces and
> nephews all know that the best cookies
> and the best laughs are always found at
> Uncle Teddy's. Whether he's teaching us
> about sailing, about the Senate, or about
> life, he has shown how to chart the course,
> take the helm and sail against the wind.

When siblings are close, they play active roles as aunts and uncles; then when they have children close in age, there are cousins who are sometimes like brothers and sisters to each other (see Figure 7.8).

Grandparents

The two-generation gap notwithstanding, the relations between grandparents and grandchildren yield satisfactions that the parent–child

Figure 7.8. Cousins. Cousins who grow up together are often bonded for life. Photo by Marcy Capell.

relationship often does not afford. Grandparents play a role in passing down the cultural heritage and family traditions, but unless they live in the household with the children, they do not generally provide the discipline, gladly leaving that task to the parents. Thus, they are free to spoil the grandchildren in a way they could not or dared not do with their own children.

Grandmothers tend to outlive their husbands and play a more active role in caring for their grandchildren than do grandfathers. The maternal grandmother tends to be more involved in the child rearing than the paternal grandmother (Findler, 2000). Norwegians make a linguistic distinction between the *mormor* (mother's mother) and the *farmor* (the father's mother). In cases of divorce in Norway as elsewhere, the grandparents on the father's side are sometimes deprived of contact with the grandchildren.

Ordinarily, grandparenting brings the generations together in new and wonderful ways as everyone shares in the joy that babies and children bring, and the novice parents may greatly appreciate the grandparents' expertise in infant care. With the birth of additional children, grandparents often help with child care, and, if the young children do not get along and need to be separated, the grandparents may be lifesavers in keeping one child for an extended period of time. Grandfathers often loosen up, compared to how they were with their own children, and express their love and pride in their grandchildren freely. Pipher (1999) describes her conversation with a former professor as he pulled out his photos of his grandkids:

> Whatever you have heard and expected about being a grandparent, it is better than that. . . . When I had my own kids I was always exhausted, overworked, worried about money and stupid things like tenure. I had papers to grade. . . . This time I am present. (p. 278)

If they are in a position to help the growing family financially, grandparents often do so by paying for extras such as piano lessons and summer camp, as well as contributing in major ways to house payments and medical expenses. Regarding their roles as extended family members, grandparents vary in their degree of closeness. If they are geographically distant, their role may be emotionally distant as well. If they are old and frail as the grandchildren are growing up, their health problems may hinder them in playing an active part in these children's lives. At the other end of the spectrum, grandparents may assume the role of surrogate parents or coparents.

With the birth of a child in the family, it is not clear what exact role the grandmother is supposed to play, how much advice to offer, how much caretaking is expected or even allowed. For the father's mother, the expected role is probably more distant than for the mother's mother. In *Eye of My Heart*, Graham (2009) offers an anthology of 27 grandmothers who record their diverse experiences. Although many of the stories are sentimental, some are gripping, such as the writer who lashes out at her daughter-in-law for depriving her of closeness with her grandchild, and another who has to continually rescue her irresponsible son who keeps having children that he cannot afford to care for.

In the absence of a father figure in the family, the child's grandfather often assumes the role. This happened to comedian and social commentator Bill Cosby (2009) who states in an interview with the *Washington Post* that he learned storytelling not from his father who was away most of the time but from his father's father. Cosby considers his grandfather, who lived to be 95, a savior in his life, a surrogate father. But even when a child has a father in the home, he or she can really enjoy spending time with a grandfather who may be less pressed for time. As high school teacher Aaron Benscoter (in private correspondence with van Wormer on September 5, 2009) writes:

> I lost my grandfather when I was 15. I spent six weeks living with him every summer for about eight years in Mesa, Arizona. When I was 15 he was diagnosed with pancreatic cancer. I was largely his caretaker during the two months he lived following the diagnosis. I was very close to him. He had taught me a number of things my parents were too busy to teach. He was one of the reasons I went to and graduated from

college (the only person in my family to have gone to college). To watch him suffer was very difficult.

And we hear from MSW student Ryan Rasmussen (in a class assignment on turning points shared with van Wormer of August 31, 2009):

> I was very close to my grandfather, staying overnight at his house as often as I could. He would spoil me like most grandfathers do. He lived his life with fun and energy, always putting his family and friends before himself. He was a leader and a mentor in my eyes. There was not a day that went by when he wasn't sharing his knowledge or making someone laugh; he was quit the kidder.
>
> I am not completely sure if this an example of a turning point, but through his passing, I became a better man. I wanted to make my grandfather proud and I felt I could do this by or through my decisions in life.

U.S. Census 2000 was the first time questions on grandparents' caregiving were asked (U.S. Census, 2003). Census results showed that 3.6 percent of families had coresident grandparents, and, of these, 42 percent of grandparents were residing with a grandchild under the age of 18 and were solely responsible for the parenting role. This number no doubt represents a significant increase due to incarceration of parents related to illicit drug use.

A second factor concerns the revision of child welfare policies to acknowledge the importance and convenience of kinship care when child placement is necessary. The overwhelming majority of grandparents who are primary caregivers for their grandchildren, however, provide this care through informal kinship care arrangements. Jane Addams College of Social Work in Chicago conducted an in-depth investigation of kinship care arrangements in a sample of over 200 mostly African American relative caregivers of children (Gleeson et al., 2008). In the interviews, the caregivers described many reasons for taking care of their relatives' children. Just under one-third mentioned parental substance abuse as a reason the birth parents were unable to care for the children. Other contributing factors mentioned were parental neglect, abandonment or abuse, incarceration, young and inexperienced parents, the parents' unstable home life/homelessness, lack of resources, and problems related to health and mental health. Other findings in the study were that the caregivers were highly committed to providing the needed care for the children; birth parents were frequently in and out of the household; and lack of economic resources was a major cause of stress. Some of the children had emotional problems and mental disorders.

When parents give birth to a child with a physical disability, the role of the support system is essential to the family's ability to cope. Findler (2000) interviewed 47 mothers of children with cerebral palsy and compared their responses to those of 43 mothers of healthy children. This study, which was conducted in Israel, found that the mothers of the children with the handicap received far more professional help than the other mothers and that the maternal grandparents were highly involved in both situations. Interestingly, the mothers turned to their mothers anytime the need arose but felt they would receive a cold response from their in-laws.

When Parents Break Up

Family breakups occur frequently in our modern, industrialized society. Forces that previously held families together—extended family ties, an economically dependent wife, large families, strict religious beliefs about the sanctity of marriage—have diminished with rapid social change. Divorce, moreover, is no longer stigmatized as it once was. So when the joy has gone out of marriage and when the partners find they have grown apart, the chances are great they will begin to look elsewhere. Newman and Newman (2006) single out four variables that are associated with the likelihood of divorce. These are age of marriage

(under age 20), socioeconomic instability, differences in level of maturity, and the family's history of divorce.

Given the extent of divorce (in the United States around 40 percent of all first marriages end in divorce) (Hurley, 2005), the family forms that result—single parents raising kids, joint custody arrangements, blended families with stepchildren—can hardly be viewed as strange or deviant. According to the U.S. Census (2008), blended families include those that contain stepchildren and their stepparents, half-siblings, or stepsiblings. Overall, 17 percent (12.2 million) of all children lived in blended families. The fact that divorce is so common does not mean, however, that a failed marriage (like any failed long-term relationship) does not bring much suffering and even bitterness in its wake. Moreover, midlife courtship and remarriage can bring about complications beyond anyone's expectations. And what happens to the children after a breakup?

At the turn of this century, numerous media accounts (including editorial columns) warned about the long-term consequences to children of parental splits. Reference was usually to *The Unexpected Legacy of Divorce* by Wallerstein, Lewis, and Blakeslee (2000). What was this legacy? Wallerstein et al. tracked 93 children of divorce since the 1970s and showed that the effects on them were negative and permanent. Harris (2009) had harsh words for Wallerstein's earlier studies on the same population of children of divorce: "Her books sold a lot of copies but as science they are useless: all the families she studied had sought counseling and all were getting divorced. There was no control group of children who grew up in intact families" (p. 288). Hereditary factors, Harris argues, would have to be controlled as well.

Wallerstein, Lewis, and Blakeslee (2000) interviewed the children from the original sample 25 years later. Their marriage rate was low—40 percent had never married, and most had no children. One clear difficulty with these findings was that the sample consisted of divorced families that were initially referred to her clinic. The sample was therefore biased in a negative direction from the start. This is not to say that there are not consequences to growing up in a home in which parents do not get along. I believe the problem is the tension and hostility (psychological if not physical abuse) that precedes the separation that can have damaging long-term effects. Hetherington and Kelly (2002), drawing on a careful sampling of divorced families and comparison families, concluded that about one-fourth of the children of divorce still had psychological problems in young adulthood. Most parents and children, however, rebound from their crisis period and sometimes have a growth experience or draw closer together as a smaller, more peaceful family unit after weathering the storm of divorce.

Lisa Strohschein (2005) examined Canadian government data from a large cohort of almost 17,000 children who are interviewed every two years. She was able to determine the level of anxiety and depression in children before and after divorce took place. She found that troubled families were at risk regardless of whether they broke up. She determined that, following the parents' divorce, the levels of child anxiety and depression increase. However, in some highly dysfunctional families, the level of the child's antisocial behavior dropped off. Allen Li (2007) studied a large sample of over 6,000 children over time from ages 4 to 15. Using a longitudinal approach, he was able to discover how children's behavior changed following parental divorce. He found only a slight increase in problematic behavior following family breakup.

Ginther and Pollak (2004) obtained results that were widely reported on U.S. news wire sources and which on the surface seemed to indicate that nontraditional family forms were harmful to children. This research involved the examination of achievement test results and levels of educational attainment of 11,064 children tracked up to 15 years in two national studies. Results showed that stepchildren and their half-siblings (who are the biological product of the new marriage) and children who spent their childhoods in single-parented families achieved at virtually similar levels and well below children from traditional nuclear families. When the researchers took into account family income and the mother's education,

however, the results were no longer so significant, especially for single-parent homes. Ginther and Pollak discuss the results and speculate on the reasons the children within this reconstituted family show as poor progress at school as the stepchildren. Their explanation is that there is stress in the blended family and that the children thus receive inadequate attention. We could add to this the speculation that parents who start a second family after one or more failed attempts have personality characteristics that are somewhat different from those of parents in intact families. Personality factors associated with neuroticism and poor communication styles have been linked with the risk of divorce (Scheewind & Gerhard, 2002).

A *stepfamily* can be defined as a household that contains a child who is the biological or adopted offspring of only one of the parents. The report, *Living Arrangements of Children: 2004* (U.S. Census Bureau, 2008), which recorded the numbers of households with stepchildren under age 18, found that roughly 1 in 10 children living with two parents lived with a stepparent or adoptive parent. In 2004, 5.7 million children lived with one biological parent and either a stepparent or adoptive parent (11 percent of all those living with two parents). This percentage was statistically unchanged from 11 percent of children living with two parents in 2001. This is a clear underestimate because many of the stepchildren, the father's biological offspring, do not reside in the father's home, yet they may spend a good deal of time there. Five percent of all children under 18 lived with a cohabiting parent. The percentage of all children who lived with a cohabiting parent ranged from 2 percent for Asian children to 7 percent for Hispanic children. The number of parents children lived with varied by race and Hispanic origin—87 percent of Asian children lived with two parents, as did 38 percent of black children.

Women generally experience more stress in marriage than men do. According to a news report, medical research conducted on 422 middle-aged women shows that, over a period of 12 years, unhappily married women were more than twice as likely to have heart attacks and strokes after menopause than were women who were happily married (Troxel, Matthews, Gallo, & Kuller, 2005). The explanation is that stress drives up blood pressure, causes sleep disturbances, and triggers stress hormones. Staying single or being happily married is better for a woman than being in a stressful marriage. Divorce, however, can create great stress for both parties, especially for the person who does not initiate it (Newman & Newman, 2006). And if the partner lacks a stable means of support, the economic stress can be considerable.

Blood ties alone do not make a family. The love that a mother's or father's mate and/or their children bring to a family broken by death or divorce can be a godsend. Abraham Lincoln, for example, gave his stepmother credit for the love that he received and his thirst for education. Television host Tony Brown (2003) describes in *What Mama Taught Me: The Seven Core Values of Life* how a strong but uneducated woman rescued him as a baby from his biological mother, who suffered from a depression too deep to care for him. Years later, in gratitude to "Mama" for the wisdom she taught him and the character she instilled, Brown authored this tribute in her honor.

Implications for Practice

Kinship care, which is care offered by members of the extended family, is what families are all about. Yet for years social workers outside of the South and in minority communities have equated the term *family* with the nuclear family. Fortunately, today state child welfare policy is changing in recognition of kin—grandparents, aunts, and uncles as a great resource in a family crisis. Social workers today seek foster care placements with the child's own kin because the advantages are considerable. Children know their relatives, and their relatives often share in the love for the children's parents. The community and the church will most likely be the same. The continuity provided with kinship care cannot be equated in any other type of foster care. Much more needs to be done policy-wise, however, to provide for health care needs and

adequate income for the entire family. Much of what has been learned, lessons that can be extended to all racial groups, has been learned from African American grandmothers.

In open-ended interviews with 12 African American caregivers providing kinship care, Gibson (2002) captured the essence of cultural values that made such generous care natural. Gibson recruited women from Denver Head Start and the Center for Developmental Disability programs. Unlike traditional kinship care, which was temporary until the young parents could get on their feet financially, many of these grandparents are assuming parenting roles on a permanent basis due to social problems, many drug related. In either case, the grandmother is typically viewed as a second mother. Of Gibson's sample, nine of the grandparents assumed the responsibility through informal arrangements, and around half had begun to receive governmental assistance to supplement their incomes. The tradition of kin keeping as a typical rationale for assuming the parenting role is well expressed by one of the grandmothers in the survey:

> Because I came from a bonded family, a really bonded family. we always pitched in and took care of each other. My mother, my grandmother took care of me. Let me see. There was my nannie, my nina, my mother, my uncle and aunt. We all lived together. And she would always take in. she took in—like her family. She would just take them in and help them. I came from a family like that and so—I feel comfortable doing it [caring for the grandchild]. (Gibson, 2002, p. 38)

There are always global lessons to be learned from other nations, as well as from diverse cultures, lessons about policies that first and foremost guarantee that everyone gets adequate health care, including subsidies for prescription medication. Kinship care, elder care, child care, and care of pregnant women and U.S. workers would all benefit from a social welfare system that truly honors family values. Social workers long have advocated such systemic supports and no doubt will continue to do so.

Social workers, family therapists, and substance abuse counselors can all expect to be relating to clients as members of diverse family forms. The nuclear family of two parents and their biological offspring still exists but is no longer the norm. From my experience in family counseling, my advice would be to do the following:

1. Be prepared for the unexpected in family forms and for unique solutions.
2. Provide guidelines to all clients in communication skills and teach them through role plays how to make a request of another family member in order to get their needs met.
3. Never lose sight of the legacy of the past, cultural (including patterns of child rearing) or personal, and help the family members understand this legacy.
4. Be aware that couples therapy can be conducted with one partner alone, even though the focus is on a relationship.
5. Strive to strengthen father roles in the care of children where they are weak, and where they are strong, reinforce them.
6. Impart lessons learned from one family's solution (for example, relying on kinship care or attending a PFLAG or Al-Anon group) to other families.
7. Help people who are estranged from family members to find surrogate family members.
8. Seek resilience in people, and you will find it.

In sum, social workers who are engaged in family work will find it necessary to draw on every ounce of their imaginations. Social workers need to be intermediaries and to open up the world to another person, even as they gain a new or altered perspective from the same source. The energy of mutual discovery feeds on and recharges itself. An active imagination is essential to the multifocal vision essential to family-centered social work practice. Imagination makes it possible to perceive the congruities in the incongruities in family life and to experience the beauty of social work in the face of the bureaucratic assaults that often impede treatment of the whole family.

Summary and Conclusion

Families and individual family members affect each other in strange and mysterious ways. Saleebey (2001) says that families "are the site of oppression and liberation, of meaning-making, of the development of capacities. of the intersection of body, mind, and environment. They can be wonderful or terrible or both . . . but they are us" (p. 290).

This chapter has approached the study of the family first from a theoretical standpoint, drawing insights from systems theorists Bowen and Satir. From this perspective, the family systems paradigm teaches us that each family has a pattern, a rhythm that is more than the sum of its parts. From generation to generation, this rhythm persists. Central to systems theory is the concept of boundaries between individual family members and between the family and larger systems in the community, boundaries that can be either impenetrable or porous. Role playing is another systems concept that shows how a gap in one aspect of family functioning may be compensated for by a heavier contribution somewhere else. Family members play various roles according to their personalities and the family's needs. The genogram, a Bowenian concept, helps the clinician illustrate in a tangible way the various themes and patterns of families across the generations.

Moving from the abstract to the more tangible and from research by family therapists to research that is more psychological in nature, we have ventured into the heart of family life, into intimate relationships. First came the most problematic—father and son. Next came one of the most enjoyable, especially prepuberty—father and daughter. Then we looked at probably the closest relationship initially—mother and son. Finally, we discussed the most passionately expressive—mother and daughter. Because I have found that the psychological research fails to capture the drama of these relationships, I supplemented the research findings with personal narratives drawn from biographical and autobiographical sources. Next the microscope was placed on sibling relationships, probably the most complex and certainly the most long-lasting of any in the family. That section ended with a positive discussion of the contribution of grandparents. An analysis of the impact of family breakup on the individual members concluded this chapter.

Thought Questions

1. What does Robert Frost's definition of home mean to you?
2. Do you think it is true that "You can't go home again"? Explain your answer.
3. Is the story of the family at the micro or macro level of discourse or both?
4. How does a familiarity with systems theory help us understand the family?
5. What are Bowen's contributions?
6. Where did Bowen go wrong in his theory, and what are the implications of his theoretical overzealousness?
7. If you constructed a genogram of your own family, what sorts of patterns would it reveal?
8. What was Virginia Satir's contribution?
9. How is gender role socialization especially apparent?
10. What are the hidden functions of the family?
11. Pick one of the family dyad arrangements. What are its strengths and pitfalls?
12. Choose another dyad. Can you analyze it in terms of where the relationship can go wrong or right?
13. How would you evaluate the claim that the father–son relationship is the most inherently conflict-ridden of dual relationships within the family?
14. Why can mother–daughter relationships be considered the most passionate, if not compassionate, of relationships?
15. Discuss competition among siblings. How can too much competition be avoided or overcome?
16. How would you compare brotherly love to sisterly love?
17. From your own experience discuss the possible important roles that aunts and uncles can play in the family.
18. How would you explain the importance of kinship care to child welfare?
19. To what extent does the society support family values?
20. How do stepfamilies make a contribution to family members and the society?
21. How would you compare various research studies on the long-term consequences on children of divorce? What do the findings say about the importance of how the sample is selected?

References

Allport, G. (1954/1981). *The nature of prejudice.* Reading, MA: Addison-Wesley.

Anderson, R. (1968/1980). I never sang for my father. In R. Lyell (Ed.), *Middle age, old age: Short stories, poems, plays, and essays on aging* (pp. 55–110). New York: Harcourt Brace Jovanovich.

Bereczkei, T., Hegedus,G., & Hajnal, G. (2009). Facialmetric similarities mediate mate choice: Sexual imprinting on opposite-sex parents. *Proceedings of the Royal Society, 276,* 91-98.

Bowen, M. (1978). *Family therapy in clinical practice.* New York: Jason Aronson.

Brown, K. (1998). *Sacred bond: Black men and their mothers.* New York: Little Brown.

Brown, T. (2003). *What Mama taught me: The seven core values of life.* New York: William Morrow.

Centers for Disease Control and Prevention (CDC). (2008, June 6). *Morbidity and mortality weekly report. Youth risk behavior surveillance.* Retrieved from http://www.cdc.gov/mmwr/preview/mmwrhtml/ss5704a1.htm

Chethik, N. (2001). *Fatherloss: How sons of all ages come to terms with the deaths of their dads.* New York: Hyperion.

Christakis, N. A., & Iwashyna, T. (2003). The health impact on families. *Social Science and Medicine, 57,* 465–475.

Coley, R. L., Votruba-Drzal, E., & Schindler, H. (2009). Fathers' and mothers' parenting predicting and responding to adolescent sexual risk behaviors. *Child Development, 80,* 808–827.

Cooper, S. M. (2009). Associations between father-daughter relationship quality and the academic engagement of African American adolescent girls: Self-esteem as a mediator? *Journal of Black Psychology, 35*(4), 495–516.

Cosby, B. (2009, October 26). Bill Cosby's gift of gab: In his genes via a sock. *Washington Post.* Retrieved from http://www.washingtonpost.com/wp-dyn/content/article/2009/10/25/AR2009102502245.html?hpid=topnews

Cox, F. (2009). *Human intimacy: Marriage, the family and its meaning, research update.* Belmont, CA: Wadsworth.

Crean, H. (2008). Conflict in the Latino parent-youth dyad: The role of emotional support from the opposite parent. *Journal of Family Psychology, 22*(3), 484–493.

Cunningham, A. (1997). *Aunts: A celebration of those special women in our lives.* Chicago: Contemporary Books.

Cuskelly, M., Gunn, P., Schonell, F., & Schonell, E. (2003). Sibling relationships of children with Down syndrome: Perspectives of mothers, fathers and siblings. *American Journal of Mental Retardation, 108*(4), 234–244.

de Beauvoir, S. (1959). *Memoirs of a dutiful daughter.* Cleveland: World Publishing.

DeAngelis, T. (2001). Punishment of innocents: Children of parents behind bars. *Monitor on Psychology, 32*(5), 56. Retrieved from http://www.apa.org/monitor/may01/punish.aspx

DeBell, M. (2008). Children living without their fathers: Population estimates and indicators of educational well-being. *Social Indicators Research, 87* (3), 427-443.

Dominelli, L. (2004). *Social work: Theory and practice for a changing profession.* Cambridge, England: Polity Press.

East, L, Jackson, D., & O'Brien, L. (2006). Father absence and adolescent development: A review of the literature. *Journal of Child Health Care, 10* (4), 283-295.

Erikson, E. (1950/1963). *Childhood and society* (2nd ed.). New York: Norton.

Faludi, S. (2000). *Stiffed: The betrayal of American men.* New York: Perennial.

Ferguson, N. (2004, September). The monarchy of George II. *Vanity Fair,* 382–414.

Findler, L. (2000). The role of grandparents in the social support system of mothers of children with a physical disability. *Families in Society, 81*(4), 370–381.

Finkelhor, D., Turner, H. A., & Ormrod, R. K. (2006). Kid's stuff: The nature and impact of peer and sibling violence. *Child Abuse & Neglect, 30*(12), 1401–1421.

Frank, J. (2004). *Bush on the couch.* New York: Regan Books.

Freud, Sigmund. (1933/1963). New introductory lectures in psychoanalysis. In J. Strachey (Ed.), *The standard edition of the complete psychological works of Sigmund Freud* (Vol. 22). London: Hogarth Press.

Freud, Sophie. (1988). *My three mothers and other passions.* New York: New York University Press.

Frost, R. (1914). The death of the hired man. In *The complete poems of Robert Frost* (p. 53). New York: Henry Holt.

Gadsden, V., & Hall, M. (1996). *Intergenerational learning: A review of the literature.* National Center on Fathers and Families. Annie E. Casey Foundation. Baltimore, MD: Ford Foundation.

Gallup Poll. (2004, January 20). Empty seats: Fewer families eat together. Retrieved from http://www.gallup.com/poll/10336/Empty-Seats-Fewer-Families-Eat-Together.aspx

Gibson, P. (2002). African American grandmothers as caregivers: Answering the call to help their grandchildren. *Families in Society: Journal of Contemporary Human Services, 83*(1), 35–43.

Ginther, D., & Pollak, R. (2004). Family structure and children's educational outcomes: Blended families, stylized facts, and descriptive regressions. *Demography, 41*(4), 671–696.

Gleeson, H., Hsieh, C-M., Anderson, N., Seryak, C., Wesley, J., Choi, E., et al. (2008, February 26). *Individual and social protective factors for children in informal kin care: Executive summary.* Grant Number HHS 90-CA-1683. Retrieved from http://www.uic.edu/jaddams/college/kincare/research/ExecutiveSummary-2-26-08.pdf

Graham, B. (2009). *Eye of my heart: 27 writers reveal the hidden pleasures and perils of being a grandmother.* New York: Harper Collins.

Green, J. B. (2003). *Family theory and therapy: Exploring an evolving field.* Belmont, CA: Brooks/Cole.

Greene, R. (2009). General systems theory. In R. Greene (Ed.), *Human behavior theory and social work practice* (3rd ed., pp. 165–197). New York: Norton.

Hairston, C. (2001). The forgotten parent: Understanding the forces that influence incarcerated fathers' relationships with their children. In C. Seymour & C. Hairston (Eds.), *Children with parents in prison* (pp. 149–71). New Brunswick, NJ: Transaction Publishers.

Harper, H. (2009). *The conversation: How black men and women can build loving, trusting relationships.* New York: Gotham Books.

Harris, J. (2009).). *The nurture assumption: Why children turn out the way they do, revised and updated.* New York: Free Press.

Hartmann, E. (2009). *Dreams and nightmares: The origin and meaning of dreams.* New York: Basic Books.

Hawthorne, L. (2003). *Sisters and brothers all these years: Taking another look at the longest relationship in your life.* Acton, MA: VanderWyk & Burnham.

Herrera, V., & McCloskey, L. (2003, June). Sexual abuse, family violence, and female delinquency: Findings from a longitudinal study. *Violence and Victims, 18*(3), 319–335.

Hetherington, E., & Kelly, J. (2002). *For better or for worse: Divorce reconsidered.* New York: Norton.

hooks, b. (1984). *Feminist theory: From margin to center.* Boston: South End Press.

hooks, b. (2001). *Salvation: Black people and love.* New York: William Morrow.

Huffington, A. (2004, June 3). Shakespeare turns a spotlight on Bush and Iraq. *Common Dreams News Center.* Retrieved from http://www.commondreams.org/views04/0603-12.htm

Hurley, D. (2005, April 19). Divorce rate: It's not as high as you think. *New York Times,* p. F7.

Jones, K. (2004). Assessing psychological separation and academic performance in nonresident-father and resident-father adolescent boys. *Child and Adolescent Social Work Journal, 21*(14), 333–354.

Jones, L. K. (2009, July/August). Siblings of children with developmental disabilities. *Social Work Today, 9*(4), 6–7.

Kaminsky, L., & Dewey, D. (2002). Psychosocial adjustment in siblings of children with autism. *Journal of Child Psychology and Psychiatry, 43*(2), 225–232.

Kennedy, J. (2009, August 28). *The celebration of life. Eulogy* presented at the memorial service for Senator Edward Kennedy, Boston, Massachusetts.

Kerr, M. E., & Bowen, M. (1988). *Family evaluation: An approach based on Bowen theory.* New York: Norton.

Lang, G. (2004). *Why a son needs a mom: 100 reasons.* Nashville: Cumberland House.

Leman, K. (2009). The birth order book: Why you are the way you are. Grand Rapids, MI: Revell

Li, A. (2007). *The kids are OK: Divorce and children's behavior problems.* Santa Monica, CA: RAND Corporation.

Lloyd, R. (2009, March 16). Trend: Daughters follow Dads' footsteps. *Live Science.* Retrieved from http://www.livescience.com/culture/090316-dads-career.html

Mazza, C. (2002, September–December). And then the world fell apart: The children of incarcerated fathers. *Families in Society: Journal of Contemporary Human Services, 9,* 521.

Meacham, J. (2008, September 1). On his own. *Newsweek,* pp. 27–36.

McCain, J. (1999). *Faith of my fathers: A family memoir.* New York: Harper.

McCullers, C. (1951/1985). *Member of the wedding.* New York: Bantam.

McGoldrick, M. (2009).). Using genogram to map family patterns. In A. R. Roberts (Ed.), *Social workers' desk reference* (2nd ed., pp. 409–423). New York: Oxford University Press.

McGraw, L., & Walker, A. (2004). Negotiating care: Ties between aging mothers and their care-giving daughters. *Journals of Gerontology, Series B, 59*(6), 324–332.

Mellen, H. (2002). Rough-and-tumble between parents and children's social competence. *Dissertation abstracts international, Section B, 63*(3–B), 1588.

Millman, M. (2004). *The perfect sister: What draws us together, what drives us apart.* San Diego, CA: Harcourt.

Milardo, R. (2009). *The forgotten kin: Aunts and uncles.* Cambridge, England: University of Cambridge Press.

Morman, M., & Floyd, K. (2002). A "changing culture of fatherhood": Effects on affectionate communications, closeness, and satisfaction in men's relationships with their fathers and their sons. *Western Journal of Communication, 66*(4), 395–411.

National Association of Social Workers (NASW). (2009). Family policy. In *Social work speaks: National Association of Social Workers policy statements 2009–2012* (7th ed., pp. 134–139). Washington, DC: Author.

Neale, J. (2004). *No friend like a sister: Exploring the relationships between sisters.* Victoria, Australia: Victoria University Press.

Newman, B., & Newman, P. (2006). *Development through life: A psychological approach* (9th ed.). Belmont, CA: Wadsworth.

Nichols, M. P. (2008)). *The essentials of family therapy* (4th ed.). Boston: Allyn & Bacon.

Northrup, C. (2005). *Mother-daughter wisdom: Creating a legacy of physical and emotional health.* New York: Bantam.

Obama, B. (1995). *Dreams from my father: A story of race and inheritance.* New York: Crown.

Orbuch, T., Thornton, A., & Cancio, J. (2000). The impact of marital quality, divorce, and remarriage on the relationships between parents and their children. *Marriage and Family Review, 29*(4), 221–246.

Palmer, P. J. (1998). *The courage to teach.* San Francisco: Jossey-Bass.

Papero, D. (2009). Bowen family systems theory. In A. R. Roberts (Ed.), *Social workers' desk reference* (2nd ed) (pp. 447–452). New York: Oxford University Press.

Paschall, M., Ringwalt, C., & Flewelling, R. (2003). Effects of parenting, father absence, and affiliation with delinquent peers on delinquent behavior among African-American male adolescents. *Adolescence, 38,* 15–34.

Pearse, P. (1916). The mother. Irish culture and customs. Retrieved from http://www.irishcultureandcustoms.com/Poetry/PadraicPearse.html

Pelligrini, R., & Sarbin, T. (Eds.). (2003). *Between fathers and sons: Critical incident narratives in the development of men's lives.* New York: Haworth Press.

Perkins, R. (2001). The father-daughter relationship: Familial interactions that impact a daughter's style of life. *College Student Journal, 35,* 616–627.

Pew Research Center (2010, March 18). The return of the multi-generational household. Social and economic trends. Retrieved from http://pewsocialtrends.org/pubs/752/the-return-of-the-multi-generational-family-household

Pipher, N. (1996). *The shelter of each other: Rebuilding our families.* New York: Ballantine.

Pipher, N. (1999). *Another country: Navigating the emotional terrain of our elders.* New York: Riverhead Books.

Quindlen, A. (2004, January 12). Flown away, left behind. *Newsweek,* p. 64.

Rohner, R., & Veneziano, R. (2001). The importance of father love: History and contemporary evidence. *Review of General Psychology, 5*(4), 382–405.

Rossiter, L., & Sharpe, D. (2001). The siblings of individuals with mental retardation: A quantitative integration of the literature. *Journal of Child and Family Studies, 10*(1), 65–85.

Saleebey, D. (2001). *Human behavior and social environments: A biopsychosocial approach.* New York: Columbia University Press.

Satir, V. (1983). *Conjoint family therapy* (3rd ed.). Palo Alto, CA: Science & Behavior Books.

Satir, V. (1988). *The new peoplemaking.* Mountain View, CA: Science & Behavior Books.

Scheewind, K., & Gerhard, A-K. (2002). Relationship personality, conflict resolution, and marital satisfaction in the first five years of marriage. *Family Relations, 51,* 63–71.

Schlossberg, C. K. (2008, August 25). *Introduction of Senator Edward Kennedy.* Speech given at the Democratic National Convention, Denver, Colorado.

Schweizer, P., & Schweizer, R. (2004). *The Bushes: Portrait of a dynasty.* New York: Doubleday.

Sheehan, C. (2005, November–December). Interview by Nina Utne in Crawford, Texas, August 24, 2005. Quoted in: It starts with mothers: Let a spirit of compassion and nurturing guide us. *Utne,* 4.

Sigelman, C., & Rider, E. (2006). *Life-span human development.* Belmont, CA: Wadsworth.

Simon, C. (2002). *Fatherless women: How we change after we lose our dads.* New York: Wiley.

Smiley, J. (1991). *A thousand acres.* New York: Knopf.

Stevens, P. (2001). *Between mothers and sons: Women writers talk about having sons and raising men.* New York: Scribner Touchstone.

Strauss, S., & Falkin, G. (2001). Social support systems of women offenders who use drugs: A focus on the mother–daughter relationship. *American Journal of Drug and Alcohol Abuse, 27,* 65–89.

Strohschein, L. (2005). Parental divorce and child mental health trajectories. *Journal of Marriage and Family, 61,* 1286–1300.

Talmage, T. D. (1902). *T. DeWitt Talmage: His life and work.* Philadelphia: Winston.

Tannen, D. (2009). *You were always Mom's favorite: Sisters in conversations throughout their lives.* New York: Random House.

Thomas, P. (2000). *My brother, my sister, and me: A first look at sibling rivalry.* New York: Barrow's Educational Series.

Thompson, R., & Zuroff, D. (1999). Dependency, self-criticism, and mothers' response to adolescent sons' autonomy and competence. *Journal of Youth and Adolescence, 28*(3), 365–384.

Tisdale, S. (2001). Scars: In four parts. In P. Stevens (Ed.), *Between mothers and sons: Women writers talk about having sons and raising them* (pp. 17–23). New York: Scribner Touchstone.

Tolstoy, L. (1876/1917). *Anna Karenina*. New York: Collier & Son.

Troxel, W., Matthews, K., Gallo, L., & Kuller, L. (2005). Marital quality and occurrence of the metabolic syndrome in women. *Archives of Internal Medicine, 165*, 1022–1027.

U.S. Census Bureau. (2003). *U.S. Census 2000: Grandparents living with grandchildren*. Retrieved from http://www.census.gov/prod/2003pubs/c2kbr-31.pdf

U.S. Census Bureau (2005). *Who's minding the kids?* Retrieved from http://www.census.gov/prod/2005pubs/p70-101.pdf

U.S. Census Bureau. (2008). *Living arrangements of children*. Retrieved from http://www.census.gov/prod/2008pubs/p70-114.pdf

U.S. Census Bureau (2009). *America's families and living arrangements*. Retrieved from http://www.census.gov/population/www/socdemo/hh-fam/p20-561.pdf

van Wormer, K., & Davis, D. R. (2008). *Addiction treatment: A strengths perspective* (2nd ed.). Belmont, CA: Brooks/Cole.

Vosler, N. (2008). Families. In E. Hutchison, *Dimensions of human behavior: Persons and environment* (3rd ed.) (pp.347-374). Thousand Oaks, CA: Sage.

Wallerstein, J., Lewis, J., & Blakeslee, S. (2000). *The unexpected legacy of divorce: The 25-year landmark study*. New York: Hyperion.

Warner, J. (2005). *Perfect madness: Motherhood in the age of anxiety*. New York: Riverhead.

Wead, D. (2005). *The raising of a president: The mothers and fathers of our nation's leaders*. New York: Atria.

Wheaton, S. (2009, October 13). King siblings settle estate lawsuit. *New York Times*. Retrieved from http://www.nytimes.com/2009/10/14/us/14king.html

Wild, R. (1999). *Uncles: A tribute to the coolest guys in the world*. New York: McGraw-Hill.

Wolfe, T. (1940/1998). *You can't go home again*. New York: Perennial Classics.

Worden, M. (2003). *Family therapy basics* (3rd ed.). Belmont, CA: Brooks/Cole.

Zastrow, C. H., & Kirst-Ashman, K. (2010).). *Understanding human behavior and the social environment* (8th ed.). Belmont, CA: Brooks/Cole.

Epilogue

An Ending That Is a Beginning

Human beings are social animals. It is therefore fitting to end this book on human behavior with a view of the person not as a lone figure in the universe but as one linked through the family to others in unique and meaningful ways. Our longing for connection cuts across the biopsychosocial and, above all, spiritual realms of life. This longing (for soul and soul mate) can never be completely satisfied. One consequence of our yearning for connection—to be merged in a sense of "we" rather than standing alone as merely "I"—is that we live in a constant state of tension between the desire to meet our own needs and the drive to conform to group norms. Much of human behavior can be studied and understood within this social context: Without a consideration of the context, in fact, individual behavior often makes little or no sense. A major focus of this book, therefore, is on behavior in context—that of a child in a family, a boy in a schoolroom, a woman living in a violent household.

In other words, human behavior is interactive and complex. Many of the individuals and families that social workers see are estranged from healthy relationships, oppressed in one way or another, or enmeshed in relationships that are conflict ridden. An understanding of the person-in-the-environment configuration is thus essential for effective social work intervention.

The domain of human behavior is vast, even when we narrow down the content (as reflected in the title of this book) to an individual—or a micro—level. Each chapter could easily have been expanded into a book in itself, and each section heading could have been developed into a whole chapter. My response to the enormity of the task was to introduce the theoretical notion of learning from the microcosm—learning from one aspect of human behavior in one setting about the psychology of human behavior in general.

So much of human behavior is unpredictable and paradoxical that there can be no one complete body of knowledge about how people behave in all circumstances. And just as such a comprehensive body of knowledge is lacking, so there can be no grand theory to account for all of the conundrums of human behavior—why people do the things they do. Psychologists and sociologists have been searching for a broad, explanatory model for years, but, in my opinion, only literary artists such as playwrights and poets have come close. The secret of the success of artists has arguably been their uncanny ability to do more with less, to see the whole in the part, and, above all, to handle paradoxes or opposites, and, in Palmer's words, to "think things together" (1998, p. 66).

In order to deal with the challenge of addressing life in its infinite complexity, I needed a suitable metaphor. From art I chose a line from William Blake's (1863/1988) poem "Auguries of Innocence": "to see a world in a grain of sand," and from science, the metaphor of the holon. The image of the holon teaches us to conceive of each part as both a whole and a portion of a larger whole. We can think of the family in this context, at once a whole and a part of another whole. Relevant to human behavior, the holon directs our attention to patterns of behavior (in either an individual or a cultural sense). Consistent with the representation of the holon is the paradox that in every ending is a new beginning. We saw this contradiction in the turning-point narratives that highlight Chapter 1, in personal struggles that were the starting point of something else—most often, a new direction in one's life.

The related notions of viewing events microcosmically and of grasping larger truths from smaller ones are consistent with the micro-level focus of this volume, one that also reflects Blake's insight. Thus, we can learn about human behavior in the study of one violent family and about eldercare from a three-generational Latino family. The former teaches us about power and control, and the latter about the cultural tradition of care and nurturance. The single event is key to the wider cultural pattern or system.

These insights bring us to another truth about human nature, the way in which micro- and macro-phenomena merge. We can look at an individual and at the social or physical environment, but when it comes to understanding human behavior, we cannot comprehend the one without the other. This is why, as a guiding theoretical framework, ecosystems theory, with its holistic grasp of human interaction, is, in my opinion, the most useful conceptualization for the study of human behavior, especially when combined with an empowerment and strengths perspective for social work practice.

The journey of this book, for purposes of organization, has been from the micro-micro level in which the human organism is viewed biologically as an amalgam of cells and as a complex psychological being—and at the micro-macro level with attention to the social, interactive side of human nature. We have traveled past the theoretical landscape across the inner worlds of body and mind, and we have surveyed some inner biopsychosocial forces that both connect us with and distance us from other people. Along the way we have heard stories of despair, triumph, and, above all, resilience.

The journey for some readers may end here, in which case you will want (as they say on airplanes) to disembark now, not forgetting to take with you what is yours (new insights and metaphors, perhaps). For those who continue on, the next journey is into wider and more open spaces—the realm of the collectivity, the community of being and doing, the spiritual and natural world, and the culture of beliefs and norms—*Human Behavior and the Social Environment, Macro Level.*

References

Blake, W. (1863/1988). Auguries of innocence. In D. Erdman (Ed.), *The complete poetry and prose of William Blake* (p. 489). New York: Doubleday Anchor.

Palmer, P. J. (1998). *The courage to teach.* San Francisco: Jossey-Bass.

Appendix

Relevant Internet Sites

Professional Links

Social Work Gateway: www.pantucek.com/
  swlinks_gb.html
Council on Social Work Education: www.
  cswe.org
International Association of Schools of Social
  Work: www.iassw-aiets.org/
International Federation of Social Workers:
  www.ifsw.org/
Heatherbank Museum of Social Work,
  Glasgow: www.gcal.ac.uk/heatherbank/
  index.html
National Association of Social Workers:
  www.naswdc.org
World Wide Web Resources for Social
  Workers: http://blogs.nyu.edu/social
  work/ip/
University of South Carolina, multiple links:
  http://cosw.sc.edu/swan/organizations.html
Hull House Museum: www.uic.edu/jaddams/
  college
United Nations Development Programme:
  www.undp.org

Links Related to Family Practice

Autism Spectrum Disorders:
  www.cdc.gov/ncbddd/autism/index.html
Children's Defense Fund:
  http://childrensdefense.org
Connection the Disability Community to
  Information and Opportunities:
  http://disability.gov
Family Violence Prevention Fund:
  http://endabuse.org
Forum on Child and Family Statistics:
  www.childstats.gov
Genogram Analytics: www.genogram
  analytics.com
Information for Practice: http://blogs.nyu.edu/
  socialwork/ip
Latino Social Workers Organization:
  www.lswo.org
National Center on Fathers and Families:
  www.healthfinder.gov/orgs/hr2906.htm

National Sexual Violence Resource Center:
www.nsvrc.org

National Suicide Prevention Lifeline:
http://suicidepreventionlifeline.org

Substance Abuse Resource: Join Together:
www.jointogether.org

Video Clips that relate to this text:
http://delicious.com/vanwormer

Government Resources

Canadian Government main site:
canada.gc.ca

Centers for Disease Control and Prevention:
www.cdc.gov

U.S. Bureau of the Census:
www.census.gov

National Institute of Drug Abuse:
www.nida.nih.gov

National Institute of Mental Health:
www.nimh.nih.gov

Substance Abuse and Mental Health Services
Adminstration: www.samhsa.gov

U.S. Bureau of Justice Statistics:
www.ojp.usdoj. gov/bjs

U.S. Department of Health and Human
Services: www.os.dhhs.gov

Social Policy

American Association of Retired Persons:
www. aarp.org

Center for Restorative Justice Peacemaking:
www.cehd.umn.edu/ssw/rjp

Child Welfare League: www.cwla.org

National Coalition against Domestic Violence:
www.ncadv.org

National Sexual Violence Resource Center:
www.nsvrc.org

Population Reference Bureau, family
information: www.prb.org

Rape, Abuse, and Incest National Network:
www.rainn.org

Restorative Justice Resources, articles:
www.restorativejustice.org

Restorative Justice Consortium:
www.restorativejustice.org/uk

Influencing State Policy: www.state
policy.org

Signs of Homelessness.org:
www.signsofhomelessness.org

Violence Policy Center: www.vpc.org

War Resisters League: www.warresisters.org

World Health Organization: www.who.int/en/

Social Action

Addiction Treatment Forum:
www.atforum.com

Amnesty International: www.amnesty.org

Children's Defense Fund:
www.childrensdefense.org

Data Lounge: Lesbian/gay:
www.datalounge.com

Disability information: www.disabilityinfo.gov

Drug Policy Alliance Action Center:
www.drugpolicy.org

FatherWork: http://fatherwork.byu.edu

Gay, Lesbian, and Straight Education Network:
www.glsen.org

Harm Reduction Coalition:
www.harmreduction.org

Human Rights Watch: www.hrw.org

Mental Health Matters:
www.mental-health-matters.com/

Minority Rights Group International:
www.minorityrights.org

Minnesota Center against Violence and Abuse:
www.mincava.umn.edu/vaw.asp

National Alliance for the Mentally Ill:
www.nami.org

National Gay and Lesbian Internet Task Force:
www.ngltf.org

Parents, Families, and Friends of Lesbians and
Gays: www.pflag.org

Social Welfare Action Alliance (SWAA):
www.socialwelfareactionalliance.org

Transsexuality: http://transsexual.org

Index

abortion, 111, 158

Adams, H.E., 120

Adams, R., 40, 41, 42

Addiction, 71–73, 75, 98
   and the brain, 76, 59–68
   and genetic factors, 57–59

adolescence and youth, 176–190
   and brain development, 59, 69–70, 177
   and dating violence, 179–180, 181
   and drug use, 59, 115, 178–179
   and identity, 180
   and religious faith, 112, 192–193
   and risk taking, 175
   See also rituals for coming of age
   See also growing up rituals

adolescent girls, 120

adoption, 290–291

African Americans
   and child rearing, 172
   and family life, 117, 260, 291
   and identity, 116–118
   and kinship care, 298–299
   and religious faith, 124, 261
   See also oppression

ageism, 251

aging. *See* old age

aggression
   and biology, 71–74
   cross-culturally, 164

AIDS, 86, 80, 106, 213, 224
   in Africa, 246

alcohol, 66
   and the brain, 62
   and health, 62. *See also* alcoholism,
     substance abuse.

Alcoholics Anonymous (AA), 13, 59, 61, 193
   See also 12-Steps

alcoholism, 28, 58, 90
   and research, 31, 64, 69, 179
   treatment of, 23, 31, 69, 124, 291
   See also addiction

all-or-nothing thinking, 126–127

Alvarez, L., 120

Alzheimer's disease, 248–249
   biological basis, 53, 93–94

American culture, 71, 108, 243, 246
   and religion, 113, 123
   and independence, 113

Andreasen, N., 79, 87

Angelou, M., 153, 174–175

anger, 126
  management, 127–129
  myths about, 129
anorexia, 46, 92–93
anti-oppressive approach, 39–41
antisocial behavior, 72, 74
Appalachia, 118, 260
Appleby, G.A., 117, 118
Armstrong, K., 15, 112, 232
Aronson, E. 174
Asians, 189. *See also* separate countries
assessment, 10
assisted suicide for terminally ill,
  265–266
attachment. *See also* Bowlby
  attachment theory, 153, 154–155
  in adulthood, 208, 214
attention deficit hyperactivity disorder
  (ADHD), 70–71, 172
aunts, v, 295–296, 301
Australia, 54–55
autism, 38, 168, 169
  models of, 23

Barker, R., 18, 34
Barsky, A., 107, 258, 259
Basham, K., 27, 174, 187
battering
  impact of, 132–134
  by men, 130–132
Beck, A., 30, 31
Becker, G., 14
Begley, S.
  on adolescence, 59
  on the brain, 248
  on cognitive approach, 32
  on obsessive compulsive disorder, 92
  on orphan studies, 93
  on personality, 55–56
Besthorn, F., 36
  on spirituality, 37
Bettelheim, B., 123
  on Freud, 123
biological components in human behavior,
  50–98
  and aggression, 71–74
  and depression, 90
  and gender, 75, 76–79, 82
  and personality, 76, 85–86
  and sexual orientation, 79–82

biopsychosocial/spiritual model, 109, 130,
  173, 307
  and study of human behavior, 5, 6, 11,
  307, 309
bipolar disorders, 90–92
birth order, 81
Black, D., 75
Blake, W., 9, 11, 309
blindness, 58–59
Bosnia, 140
Bowen, M., 35, 36, 38, 274, 275
  and genogram, 276, 302
  criticism of, 277, 279
  on child rank, 293
Bowlby, J., 26, 27, 154–155, 157, 158
boys,
  and male identity, 111, 180
  and sex role socialization, 281, 284–285
  in the classroom, 170, 171
  media attention to problems of, 171–172
brain. *See also* neurotransmitters
  and addictive behavior, 59–71
  and ADHD, 70–71
  and adolescence, 59–68, 69–70
  and aging, 249
  and music, 94–95
  and schizophrenia, 59
  damage, 74
  research, 58–71
brainwashing, 134
Brandell, J., 157, 159
Bricker-Jenkins, M., 22, 42, 45
  personal narrative of, 184
British theoretical approach, 40
Brizendine, L., 79
Brownmiller, S., 140
Brownell, P., 258–259
bulimia, 92, 180
bullying in school, 183–184
Bush, G.W., 282
Buss, D.M., 206, 207
Buttell, F., 131

Canada, 156, 158, 223, 230, 234
  and hospice, 264
  and life expectancy, 246
  children of, 160, 163
Canda, E., 24, 45, 110
Carroll, M., 112
child abuse, 172–175

physical punishment as abuse, 172–173
    sexual abuse, 175
    statistics on, 164
child neglect, 157, 163
child rearing and culture, 157–159
    in Japan, 164
    Latino, 119
children,
    and development, 111. *See also* Erikson,
        Piaget
    and living arrangements, 165
    and resilience, 152
    and schizophrenia, 87–88
    and trauma, 173–175
    demographics on, 165
    developmentally disabled, 166–167
    gifted, 168
    *See also Canada, Fetal Alcohol Syndrome,
        religion*
China, 158, 233
    and values, 21
    and treatment of older adults, 244
class impact of, 118–119. *See also* social
    class
Cloninger, C.R., 58
cocaine, 64
    and the brain, 59, 66
code of ethics, 28, 46, 47
cognitive approaches, 29–33, 46
    and practice, 125, 216
Cole, B., 82–85
college life, 204–205
    and binge drinking, 203
    and religious faith, 203
    See also youth
Colon, E., 119
conflict theory, 20, 26
Conroy, P., 13
Council on Social Work Education (CSWE),
    4–5, 6, 10
    and curriculum, 52
criminal behavior and biology, 74–76
critical thinking, 21–24

Dabbs, J.M., 72, 75
Dalrymple, J, 39, 40
Davis, D.R., 23, 31, 32, 33
    on addiction, 61, 64, 68, 70
    on gambling, 58
    on harm reduction, 97

on strengths, 42
on thinking, 126, 129
on trauma, 174
Deaf culture, 123
death and dying, 263–265
    and forms of denial, 264–265
deep ecology, 37
defense mechanisms, 24–25, 26, 106,
    132–133
dementia, 93–94
Denmark, 170, 230
depression, biological aspects of, 90,
    125–126
developmental theories, 107–108
*Diagnostic and Statistical Manual of
    Mental Disorders* (DSM), 27, 70, 74
    and PTSD, 138
    on autism, 168, 169
Dickens, C., 11, 153
disability, 41, 166, 167–170, 293–294
    and identity, 121–123
disengagement theory, 256
divorce, 299
domestic violence, 130–133, 219, 220
    among gays and lesbians, 133
    and rape, 223
    statistics on, 218
    See also battering
Dominelli, L., 40, 44
    and identity, 122, 123, 177, 178
    on the family, 273
Dostoyevsky, F., 215
Down syndrome, 11, 166, 293
Downs, W., 223
dreams, 25, 26, 27
DuBois, B., 42
Dulmus, C., 31, 32
Dunn, P., 144
Dwyer, D., 235
dyslexia, 167
Dziegielewski, S., 34, 227, 228

ecofeminism, 37, 39
economic difficulties related to recession,
    187, 190, 203–205
ecosystems approach, xii, 6, 7, 23, 33–39
    and biology, 52
Edwards, E., 208, 262
Ehrenreich, B., 204
Elder abuse, 258–159

Ellis, A., 30, 32
empowerment approaches, 39–47
  black empowerment, 46
English literature, 3, 6, 9, 11, 16–17
epidemiological paradox, 158
Erikson, E., 26, 28
  on adolescent stage, 177, 183
  on adult life, 244
  and the eight developmental stages, 106,
    108–109, 115, 166
ethics and health, 95. *See also* code of ethics
evidence-based research and practice, 5, 23,
    35, 38, 44, 56
  and cognitive approach, 31–32
  and empowerment theories, 44
  and psychoanalytical theory, 26
  and systems model, 35–36
  practice, 194

Faludi, S., 182, 285
families,
  alcoholic, 276, 291
  and divorce, 299
  and living arrangements, 273
  and socialization by, 280–281, 284–285
  at middle age, 232
  as systems, 274–280
  blended, 299, 300
  boundaries of, 278–279
  disengaged, 279
  enmeshed, 279
  functions of, 280
  Latino, 252–253, 273
  nuclear, 273
  statistics on, 273
  See also mothers, fathers, aunts, uncles,
    siblings, grandparents
family systems theory, 23, 274–279
family therapy, 279–280
Farley, O., 6, 34
Farmer, R., 52, 68, 69, 74
Farwell, N., 140
father absence or loss, 284, 285
father–daughter relationship, 248, 259, 283,
    285–288
father–son relationship, 282–285
Faulkner, W., 3, 145
Fawcett, F., 263
feelings, 100–104
  and healing work, 127

feminism
  and empowerment, 45
  and therapy, 22, 38
  backlash against, 171–172
  types of, 43
feminist perspective, 22, 38, 42–45,
    277, 285
fetal alcohol syndrome, 55, 155, 166
Finland, 165
Fiske, H.,259
forgiveness, 231–232, 236
Foucault, M., 43
Fowler, J., 107, 112–114, 144, 192
France, 164, 212, 233
Freire, P. 21–22, 41
Freud, Sigmund, 24–28, 29
  and dreams, 25, 26, 27
  on jealousy, 129
  on middle age, 224
  on spirituality, 28, 123
  on trauma, 24, 55
Freud, Sophie, 286
Fromm, E., 26, 29
Frost, R., 17, 272
functionalism, 20

Gage, J., 121
Gambrill, E., 22, 23
gay bashing
  See bullying, homophobia
Gay Lesbian Straight Education Network
    (GLSEN), 184
gay/lesbian identity issues, 183–187
gay males. *See also* homosexuality; sexual
    orientation, identity, and domestic
    violence
gender
  and brain development, 157
  and sex roles, 212, 280–281
  biology of, 75, 76–79, 82
  and identity, 119–120, 182, 206
  differences in learning, 170
generalist practice, 5, 11, 17, 18, 22
generativity, 203, 224
genetic factors in human behavior, 53–58,
    65, 97
  and gender, 81, 157, 209
  and homosexuality, 80–82
  and personality, 85–86
genogram, 276

genome, 53, 54, 56, 57, 65
  definition of, 53
genome project, 53
Germain, C., 34, 37, 201
Germany, 137, 158, 212, 263
Gibran, K., 152
Gibson, P., 301
Gilligan, C., 5–6
  and girls' identity, 182, 206
  and moral development, 45
  on love, 214
Ginsberg, L.
  on genes, 53, 55, 56–57, 81
  on mental disorders, 87, 91
girls,
  and body image, 180
  and gender identity, 182–183. *See also*
    Gilligan
  and need for gender-specific approach,
    170, 172
  as victims, 163, 164. *See also* rape, child
    abuse, trafficking
  in the classroom, 170, 171
  Latina, 290
  socialized by society, 119–120
  treatment globally, 158, 164
Gladwell, M., 118
global perspectives. *See* child care, old age,
    separate countries
Goffman, E., 121
Gonyea, J. 257
Goodwin, D., 58
Gotterer, R., 232
Grandin, T., 169
grandparents, 252–253, 296–299, 301
Greene, R.
  on Erikson, 109
  on Freudian theory, 25, 26
  on resilience, 260
  on systems theory, 26, 34,
    38, 278
growing up rituals
  among Jews, 190
  for Latina girls, 190
Gutiérrez, L., 39, 42, 43

Haight, W., 36
Hairston, C., 285
happiness, 208–209, 229–232
  and marriage, 209

Harlow, H., 154, 155
harm reduction, 97, 193–194
Harris, J.R., 56, 155, 166
  on adolescence, 177, 178
Hartman, A., 21, 215
Hartmann, T., 71
Head Start, 193–194
Hearn, G., 12
hierarchy of needs, 107, 108
Hilarski, C., 34
Hill, R., 117
historical trauma, 175
HIV/AIDS,
  research on, 86
Holocaust, 137, 162, 244, 251
holon, 12, 309
homicide, 218
homophobia, 120–121, 122, 183–184
homosexuality,
  and biology, 79–82
  and religion, 185, 187
hooks, b., 22
  on class, 118
  on family roles, 281, 284–285
  on harsh child rearing, 173
  on oppression, 143
  on patriarchy, 182
  on rage and soul murder, 175
hospice, 264–265
human behavior curriculum, 7, 46, 47,
    10–11, 22, 50
    at Smith College, 26
Hurricane Katrina, 14
Hutchison, E., 23, 27
Huxley, A., 247

identity, 115–116
  and disability, 121–123
  class, 118–119
  formation in adolescence, 115–116
  gay, 120–121
  gender, 119–120
  multicultural, 188–190
  racial, 116–118
incarceration, 15
India, 158
infancy
  and brain development, 155
  and signing, 156
infant mortality, 158

infants,
  intersexed, 76, 156
intimacy, 206, 208–212
Iraq War, 137–138, 221
Ireland,
  Northern, 175
Israel, 281
Islam, 185, 232, 235

Jacobson, N.S., 130
Jamison, K.R., 90–91
Japan, 164, 190, 233
  and treatment of older adults, 244
jealousy, 129–130
Johnson, E., 35, 36
Johnson, H. 55–56
  on addiction, 65, 66
  on brain studies, 96
  on fear, 124
  and mental health,
  on orphans, 93
  on Parkinson's, 64
  and stress, 86
Jones, K., 283
Jones, L., 294
Jung, K., 26, 28, 123–124, 210

kangaroo care, 194
Katz, J., 181, 221, 222
kidnap victims, 134–136
Kimmel, M., 205–206
Kinsey, A., 212, 213–214
kinship care, 298, 301, 302
Kirst-Ashman, K.
  on aging, 244, 245
  on critical thinking, 23
  on child development, 155, 168, 177,
    212, 273
  on developmental models, 106, 110,
    111, 112
  on ecology, 34
  on families, 273
  on generalist practice, 11
  on Kohlberg, 110
  on learning disabilities, 168
  on menopause, 233
  on sexual orientation, 79, 81, 214
  on sexuality, 233
  on stress, 212
  on theory, 34

Kohlberg, L., 110–111
Kondrat, M. E., 38
Korea
  North, 156
  South, 156, 190, 235
Kwanzaa, 117
Kübler-Ross, E., 264

Laird, J., 215
Latino culture,
  attitudes toward death, 253, 264
  and gender roles, 120, 207, 218
  and low infant mortality, 158
  and machismo, 119
  and the family, 252–253
Latinos
  and economic recession, 207
  and education, 110, 207
  older, 254–255
Lawrence-Lightfoot, S., 253, 256
learning disabilities, 167–170
Lee, J., 41
Leighninger, L., 252
Lein, J., 174
lesbians, 16, 92
  and domestic violence, 133
  and identity, 120
  See also gay/lesbian
Lesser, J., 262
Levay, S., 80
Levinson, D., 109–110
life model, 37
life span theories, 108–110
Ligon, J., 42
long-term care, 262–263
love
  and biology, 208
  obsessive, 214–216
  relationships, 208
  romantic, 206, 214

Malcolm X, 153
male
  body image, 180
  brain, 77, 79
  honor code, 119
  identity, 180–182
  See also boys, gender, schools
marriage, 209, 295. See also domestic violence
  and stress in, 300–301

Marlatt, G.A., 97, 236
Martin, E.P., 124
Martinez, D.G., 185
Mary, N., xi, 37, 38, 39
masculinity, 111. *See also* Katz, Kimmel
Marx, K., 26, 28
Maslow, A., 107, 108, 144
Maté, G. 155, 156
Mazza, C., 285
McCain, J., 282–283
McGoldrick, M., 277
McMillen, D., 37
McMillen, J., 14
medication
    for addiction, 69
    for mental disorders, 69
memories, false, 174
men
    across the lifespan, 110
    African American, 207
    and aging, 227
    and domestic violence, 130–132
    and gender studies, 156
    in middle age, 232
    and sex, 228
    and the brain, 156
    as older Latino, 254–255
    See also gender, intimacy, males
mental disorders, 86–90, *See also* bipolar
    disorders; schizophrenia
mental retardation, 166–167, 293–294
methamphetamine, 61, 64
Mexicans and Mexican Americans, 165
    See also Latino culture
Michilin, P.M., 121
Microcosm, 11–12, 47, 308
middle age
    and happiness, 229–232
    and midlife crisis, 232
    and spirituality, 232
    biological aspects of, 226–228
    psychological aspects of, 228–229
    social aspects of, 203, 224, 232
Miehls, D., 127, 174, 187
Miley, K., 42
Miller, W.R., 30, 31, 32
Moe, A.M., 220
Monti, P., 128
Moorcroft, N.S., vii, 259
moral development theories, 110–114

mother–daughter relationship, 91, 92, 136,
    275, 277
    role analyzed, 289–291
mother–son relationship, 288–289
motivational interviewing, 30–32, 236
multicultural identity, 189
Mullaly, B., 38, 45, 46
murder-suicide, 216–217
music and the brain, 94–95
Myers-Briggs inventory, 210, 228,
    236, 237

National Alliance on Mental Illness
    (NAMI), 96
National Association of Social Workers
    (NASW), 28–29
    and code of ethics, 28
    policy on physical punishment, 173
National Institute on Alcohol Abuse and
    Alcoholism (NIAAA), 63, 64
National Institute on Drug Abuse (NIDA),
    60, 61
Native Americans, 28, 108, 158, 244
    and culture, 244
    and youth, 187
nature vs. nurture, 55–57
Netherlands, 266
neuroplasticity, 59
neurotransmitters, 60–61
Newsom, E., 4
Norway, 233, 297
    and Sami people, 157
    and spirituality, 124
nursing home care, 258, 262, 263, 266

Obama, B., 15, 116, 117, 189–190, 282
obsessive compulsive disorder, 92–93.
    See also love, obsessive
old age
    and family ties, 252
    and the brain, 249
    and medications, 249
    biology of, 247–250
    facing death, 263–266
    in global context, 245–246
    persons aged 50–75, 253–256
    persons aged 75 and above, 256–257
    psychological and social aspects, 245,
        247, 250–253
    statistics on, 258

the old-old, 250, 262
older adults
  and contentment, 259–260
  and employment of, 254
  and gambling problems, 250
  narratives of, 17
oppression, 143
  racial, 118, 261
  sexist, 220–224, 281
Owens-Kane, S., 252

Padilla, Y., 158
Palmer, P., 11, 12, 13, 14, 47, 281, 309
Papero, D., 275
paradox, 12–14, 281, 309
Parents, Families and Friends of Lesbians
    and Gays (PFLAG), 194, 302
Pate, A.P., 64–65
Payne, M., 20, 29, 33
  on anti-oppressive approach, 40
  on cognitive approaches, 33
  on social work, 31
personality,
  and biology, 79, 85–86
  development, 232–233
  and genes, 56
  and intimate relationships, 208–212
  and shyness, 85
  See also genetic factors
physical punishment, 172–173
Piaget, J., 153, 159, 166
  on adolescence, 176
Pipher, M., 120, 170, 250, 253
  on family ties, 281, 296
Pomeroy, E., 249
Popple, P., 252
posttraumatic stress disorder (PTSD),
    138–140. *See also* trauma
postmodernism, 42
primates, 7, 69, 72, 73, 74, 78, 207
Praglin, L., 124
prescription drugs, 65, 69, 71, 91, 172
Prochaska, J., 24, 25, 27
  on research, 32, 38
  on stages of change, 114
Project MATCH, 31
psychoanalytical theory, 24–26
psychodynamic perspective, 20, 24–29
psychological factors in human behavior,
    105–145

Puerto Ricans, 188
  race, impact of, 116–118

racial and ethnic identity, 187–190
racism, 117, 143. *See also* oppression, racial
Raging Grannies, 256, 257
rape, 220
  and biology, 73
  in war, 140
  gang, 222
  male-on-male, 223–224
  marital, 222–223
  of children, 175
  supportive culture, 221
Rapp, C., 41, 42, 44
rational emotive behavior therapy (REBT),
    30–31
religious affiliation, 203
religious beliefs, 15, 33, 86, 112–114
  and homosexuality, 185, 187
  and rituals, 190
  as divisive, 175, 184–185, 187
  of children and youth, 112, 192–193
research,
  on addiction, 57, 59–68, 75, 76, 98
  on aggression, 71–73
  medical, 156, 158, 174, 185, 191
  on temperament, 55, 85, 191
  See also the brain, evidence-based
resilience
  among African Americans, 5, 14
  and theory, 28, 33, 37–38
  definition of, 191
  in childhood, 190–193
  in old age, 260–261
Reynolds, B., 25
Ridley, M., 54–55, 65
right brain/left brain, 78–79
Riley, J., 52, 53
Rindel, S., 157, 159
Robbins, S., 24
  on developmental models, 110,
    113, 114
  on empowerment, 39, 44, 45
  on Foucault, M., 43
  on Freud, 24, 25–26, 29
  on postmodernism, 43
  on systems, 35
  on transpersonal theory, 114
Roberts, N., 229

Roberts, Pérez, L., 252–253, 264
Rogers, F., 250
Romanian orphans, 93, 176
Rothery, M., 36, 39

Sacks, O., 94–95
Saleebey, D., 15, 42
    on adolescence, 177, 178
    on aging, 247, 248
    on biology, 43, 44, 45, 60, 64, 152
    on empowerment, 42
    on families, 273, 280, 281, 292, 302
    on gender, 78, 79, 119, 180, 181, 182
    on identity, 115, 152 177, 178
    on labels, 42
    on medications, 64, 107, 249
    on oppression, 38
    on schizophrenia, 87
    on sexuality, 212
    on spirituality, 123
    on strengths perspective, 15, 34, 41,
        42, 44, 45
    on systems theory, 37–38, 274
    on the arts, 5
Samantrai, K., 154
Samenow, S., 31
Satir, V., 279, 280, 281, 293
schizophrenia, 87–90
    and the brain, 59
school shootings, 185–186
schools,
    and boys, 170, 167
    and bullying, 183–184
    and gender differences, 170
    small, arguments for, 171
Schriver, J., 43
Schucket, M., 58
Schwartz, J., 59, 92
Schwartz, M.D., 221
Scotland, 221
Seeds of Hope, 219
serotonin, 72, 73, 85
    and addiction, 59, 65, 68, 92, 98
    and depression, 69, 91, 130, 191
sexism, 143, 220–224
sexual orientation. *See* gay and lesbian
sexuality, 212–214
    statistics on, 213
    global expression of,
Shakespeare, W., 106, 154, 247

Sheridan, M.J., 113–114, 121
shyness, 85
sibling relationships, 232
    and birth order, 81, 292
Smiley, J., 259, 292
Simon, B., 39
social class, 116, 117, 133, 143, 171
    and abuse, 173
    and aging, 252, 254
    and occupation, 119
social security, 245
social work
    and theory, 33, 39
    as a profession, 10
    values, 33, 46
    See also NASW, social work practice
social work imagination, 23
social work practice
    and empowerment, 46–47
    and genetic counseling, 96–97
    and spirituality, 45, 124
    for healing, 143–145, 144
    in health care, 62, 69, 96
    to shape policy, 96–97
    with youth, 193–194
social work theory. *See individual*
    theories
social system. *See* ecosystems framework,
    families
Solomon, B., 39
Sommers, C., 171
South Africa, 233, 246
spanking as abuse, 172–173
spirituality, 123–124
    and ecosystems approach, 37
    and social work, 28, 45, 110, 124
    and the self, 123–124
    developing in youth, 112, 192–193
    in later life, 259, 261, 280
    See also Canda, Fowler, religion,
        Wilber
Spitz, R., 154–155
stages of change, 114
Starks, S., 229, 231
Stockholm syndrome, 133
strengths perspective, 46
    See also Rapp, Saleebey
stress
    and health, 86
    management, 125

Stuart, F., vii, 275
substance abuse, 57–58, 293. *See also*
    addiction, alcoholism, youth,
    prescription drugs
Sudduth, C., 260–261, 267
suicide-murder, 216–217
Suppes, M., 258
Surface, D., 250
sustainability, xiii, 37, 38, 39
    and the environment, xi, 39
    and spirituality, 37
Sweden, 58, 80, 135, 165
systems theory. *See also* ecosystems;
    families

Talmage, E., 13–14, in photo, 259
Talmage, J.V., 295
Tavris, C., 129
teen dating violence
        warning signs, 181
testosterone, 72, 75, 81
theory, 17–21, 38
    definition of, 18
Thomas, F., 119
Thornhill, R., 73
Tolstoy, L., 277–278
trafficking, sexual, 141–143, 176
transgenderism, 81, 82–85, 157
transpersonal theory, 113
trauma, 27
    and children,
    and Iraq war, 138–140
    and the brain, 191
    from all wars, 136–138, 174
traumatic bonding, 134–136
treatment for addiction, 62, 69
    for health-related disorders, 96
    for trauma, 143–145
    See also cognitive approach, feeling work,
        social work practice
Turner, F., 42
turning points, 14–17
    later in life, 256
12-Step approach, 30, 31, 32
twin studies, 56, 76, 80–81, 209

unconscious mind, 25
uncles, 295–296, 301

United Kingdom, 108, 119, 163, 167, 185
United States. *See also* child rearing and
    culture

Vaillant, G., 259–260
Van Voorhis, R.M., 45, 111
van Wormer, K.
    on addiction, 61, 68, 69, 70
    on domestic violence, 73, 180
    on harm reduction, 97
    on death and dying,
    on stages of change, 114
    on thinking, 126, 129
    on trauma, 174
van Wormer, R., vii
    photography by, 12, 18, 122, 167, 193,
        205, 215, 283
victims of abuse, 132–136. *See also*
    domestic violence.
Vietnam
    and babylift, 290
    veterans, 138
Volkow, N., 66, 70
Vonk, E., 31, 125
Vosler, N., 277
Vourlekis, B., 29, 30, 32

Wallerstein, J., 299–300
war, 250–251. *See also* specific war
Wells, C., 258
white privilege, 116
whites, 189, 203, 261
    and work, 255, 228
    attitudes toward race in, 72, 116, 117, 187
Wilber, K., 33, 113, 192
Wilde, O., 16–17
Wilke, D., 258
Williams, T., 243
Wodarski, J., 34
Wolfe, T., 272
women
    African American, 207, 143
    biracial, 189
    and blaming, 38
    and brain research, 77, 79
    and health, 17, 120, 228
    and spirituality, 231
    and trafficking, 141–143, 176

globally, 233–235
impact of battering on, 73, 132–134.
  See also traumatic bonding
in middle age, 232
offenders, 75, 76
to Freud, 25, 29
See also domestic violence, gender,
  Gilligan, rape, sexism, sexuality,
  lesbians
women's movement, 41, 77, 285
Wordsworth, W., 124
World War II, 137, 250–251
Wrangham, R., 72, 73

youth
  and sex, 212, 213
  dating, 206, 207
  gender roles, 205–206, 207
  living at home, 204

unemployment among, 205
See also adolescents and youth

Zastrow, C., 11, 34
  on aging, 244, 245
  on child development, 155, 168, 177,
    212, 273
  on Erikson, 106
  on families, 273
  on generalist practice, 11
  on learning disabilities, 168
  on homosexuality, 79, 81, 214
  on moral development models, 106, 110,
    111, 112
  on menopause, 233
  on older adults, 247, 265
  on stress, 212
Zimbabwe, 246
Zittel, K., 107